# Management for Professionals

The Springer series *Management for Professionals* comprises high-level business and management books for executives. The authors are experienced business professionals and renowned professors who combine scientific background, best practice, and entrepreneurial vision to provide powerful insights into how to achieve business excellence.

More information about this series at http://www.springer.com/series/10101

Ganesh Sankaran · Federico Sasso ·
Robert Kepczynski · Alessandro Chiaraviglio

# Improving Forecasts with Integrated Business Planning

From Short-Term to Long-Term
Demand Planning Enabled by SAP IBP

 Springer

Ganesh Sankaran
Ingolstadt, Germany

Robert Kepczynski
Rothrist, Switzerland

Federico Sasso
Deloitte Consulting AG
Zurich, Switzerland

Alessandro Chiaraviglio
Polytechnic University of Turin
Turin, Italy

ISSN 2192-8096        ISSN 2192-810X   (electronic)
Management for Professionals
ISBN 978-3-030-05380-2      ISBN 978-3-030-05381-9   (eBook)
https://doi.org/10.1007/978-3-030-05381-9

Library of Congress Control Number: 2018964048

This Springer imprint is published by the registered company Springer Nature Switzerland AG
The registered company address is: Gewerbestrasse 11, 6330 Cham, Switzerland

*It gives me great pleasure to acknowledge the contributions of some special people in my life who have made this moment, of me enjoying this opportunity to write a dedication for my book, possible. My wife, Meena, who has been a pillar of strength, who has helped me stay focused through thick and thin, who has kept me sane through all the deadlines missed and weekends and nights spent catching up, and who has in no small measure helped me emotionally and literally complete this project. My parents for their boundless love, endless desire and innumerable sacrifices in pursuit of my happiness and success. My sister, Meera, for gifting me my first PC. She had to wade through customs with great difficulty as a PC was still an object of curiosity back in the day. Thank you for kindling my passion in computers—I wouldn't be here if not for that act of sisterly love.*

*Finally, thanks to my coauthors for their patience. Special thanks to Robert for inviting me onboard and for his stewardship. Thanks Federico for keeping it all together!*

—Ganesh Sankaran

# Preface

The idea of this book came to light as an extension of Integrated Business Planning, especially a need on how to leverage statistical forecasting, demand sensing, how to set up competencies and demand planning organization, how to leverage technology to improve forecasting. My colleagues **Robert Kepczynski** and **Ganesh Sankaran** have encouraged me to shape this book and to manage the overall "project." As part of this book, we elaborate on standard and custom methods to deal with forecasting, outlier detection and correction, product seasonality, product intermittent. We exemplify technology part of the solution with SAP IBP cloud software enabled on HANA. We did it that way to make it tangible, meaning we talk about organization, skills, processes as well as about what you can do in SAP IBP to make it happen.

Thanks to Robert and Ganesh's proven experience in supply chain processes and technology, we were able to define what this book should focus on, how to structure it and how to link it to previous Springer publications about Integrated Business Planning. We can say that for S&OP process step called "demand review" this publication is an extension of (Kepczynski et al., 2018) "**Implementing Integrated Business Planning**" by Springer 2018.

Since day one, this project has been supported and pushed to birth by the entire initial team, with a special contribution provided by **Alessandro Chiaraviglio**. He envisioned a new practice toward intermittent demand forecasting, and during the early stages of the project we discussed and managed to on board his competence and ideas to enhance and enlarge the coverage of the book.

From that moment on, the full team has exchanged ideas and opinions about SAP IBP enhancements and SAP IBP out-of-the-box solutions to make the book useful in hands of demand planning, statistical forecasting and demand sensing practitioners.

In addition, the final book would not have reached the finish line without our colleague who provided a great support: **Alexei Koifman.**

"Integrated Business Planning improves forecasting" brings to you how to:

- Connect short-term with mid- and long-term forecasting
- Prepare organizational structure and capabilities to leverage advanced techniques
- Understand the value of SAP IBP statistical forecasting
- Leverage IBP functionalities to configure custom methods for intermittent demand forecasting
- Leverage IBP functionalities to configure custom methods for detecting and correcting outliers for seasonal products
- Understand the value and algorithms of SAP IBP demand sensing
- Define forecasting value-added measurements and how to improve forecasting with the use of Six Sigma methodology proven on real projects.

Enjoy reading

Zurich, Switzerland                                                         Federico Sasso
Rothrist, Switzerland                                                Robert Kepczynski

## Reference

Kepczynski, R., Jandhyala, R., Sankaran, G., & Dimofte, A. (2018). *Integrated business planning—How to integrate planning processes, organizational structures and capabilities, and leverage sap IBP technology*. Switzerland: Springer.

# Contents

# About the Authors

**Ganesh Sankaran** has been consulting large multi-national companies for over 11 years on their supply chain processes and IT solutions and helping them solve business problems and generate value from their investments. He possesses a skill set that combines theoretical insights into SCM and implementation experience in SAP solutions further supplemented by around 7 years of software development experience. He is passionate about teaching and research and continues to engage closely with his alma mater to pursue these interests.

**Federico Sasso** is Junior Consultant with a solid background on logistics and supply chain management. He got specialized in SAP Integrated Business Planning focusing on demand planning and developing new algorithms and processes for the detection and correction of seasonal outliers. He disposes an interdisciplinary expertise in engineering and economics, a proven experience in risk and crisis management, and he is ISCEA Certified Demand Driven Planner (CDDP), leveraging the concepts of the demand-driven methodology (DDMRP—DDI).

**Robert Kepczynski** has more than 20 years of experience in supply chain management. He did manage demand planning function and introduced differentiated forecasting enabling step change in effectiveness and efficiency of the process. He is specialized in supply chain planning processes and technology. He took business roles from production planning in the plant and supply chain and S&OP solution lead in the regional or global process owner. He contributed to the second in the world SAP IBP implementation, which has started in 2013 and proven that he has heart, head and hands for Integrated Business Planning.

**Alessandro Chiaraviglio** has obtained his M.Sc. degree in Aeronautical Engineering at the Polytechnic of Turin. Since 1998, he is Lecturer in the field of industrial plant and safety, and he has taught the course of basics of the engineering economics. He provides consultancy for technology innovation in the industrial production sector for several Swiss companies. He consults and trains Lean Manufacturing and Total Productive Maintenance.

# Introduction

## 1.1 The What and Why of Forecasting

This book is part of our Integrated Business Planning series with a special focus on how to make short, medium and long-term forecasting processes more effective and efficient through the use of rigorous analytical tools and techniques. We explain how we can walk away from the "one-size-fits-all" thinking to more tailored approaches for forecasting enabled by SAP IBP for demand. Let's start by taking a step back and defining what forecasting is and why it is such a crucial process for any company.

The organizational structures and capabilities that the companies can build to successfully navigate in uncertainty play a pivotal role in its success on the market. Such capabilities are particularly relevant when it comes to the demand planning and forecasting process. As uncertainty continues to grow in its fame with rapid change becoming the new normal, practitioners need effective tools to navigate the choppy waters of uncertainty. Forecasting is one such tool. Forecasting done well can serve as a steadying force—it can be seen as a stand-in or a proxy for reality. The better the forecast, the more ready is a practitioner when planning meets reality.

Forecasting is the art and science of making predictions about the future. Science, because of the quantitative rigor involved in making extrapolations on the basis of relevant historical data. It is said that history doesn't just repeat, it rhymes. The ability to see patterns and tell signal and noise apart calls for more than just science. This is one among several aspects of forecasting that justifies the expression "the art of forecasting." Sometimes, it is better to not forecast and instead bide one's time until more information becomes available. Daniel Kahneman in his influential book "Thinking, fast and slow" quotes comedian Danny Kays as having said of someone "...her favorite sport is jumping to conclusions" (Kahneman, 2011).

To expand on this, one could say if it were an Olympic sport, it would probably be the one most fiercely fought. To avoid the trap of jumping to conclusions with not enough data is also something of an art form. It is also essential to, as Paulo

G. Sankaran et al., *Improving Forecasts with Integrated Business Planning*,
Management for Professionals, https://doi.org/10.1007/978-3-030-05381-9_1

Saffo puts it, be open to the full range of possibilities instead of a "limited range of illusory certainties" (Saffo, 2007). In this sense, the forecaster needs to not lose sight of the impact of her or his acts of commission and omission on decisions that will be made on the basis of the forecast. A keen understanding of the tools in the forecasting toolbox is therefore important in order of the key people involved in the process to not just be "trusting bystanders," but active participants (Saffo, 2007).

Let's question the need for forecasting. If only customer order lead times can be negotiated to be at least as long as the total replenishment lead time (see Figs. 1.1 and 1.2.), most tactical and operational decisions can be made on the basis of *real* demands and the analog world of statistical forecasting would have limited use. Unfortunately (for companies and fortunately for customers), in this hypercompetitive, on-demand world, decisions have to be hedged on forecast. Therefore, the quality of forecast will directly or indirectly determine the quality of decisions and, consequently, the achievement of business goals. It is altogether fitting that demand forecast accuracy has pride of place in Gartner's metrics hierarchy and sits atop the pyramid (more on this in the chapter on performance management)

It is therefore absolutely essential to establish a sound basis for decision making. "Sound basis for decision making" just about summarizes the role of statistical forecasting. It is an extremely crucial cog in the wheel of demand management. It is perhaps the only unbiased input into the demand management process. Why? Machines don't show biases, at least not today. With AI developing as fast as it is, who knows? Levity aside, statistical forecasting lends itself well as the first input, and an objective one, to the overall demand management process, which can then be enriched with other inputs based on more forward-looking factors and actions.

In cognitive psychology, the concept of "anchoring" is well known and researched. It is the idea that, when faced with decision making, we humans tend to stick onto the first piece of information and start making adjustments anchored to

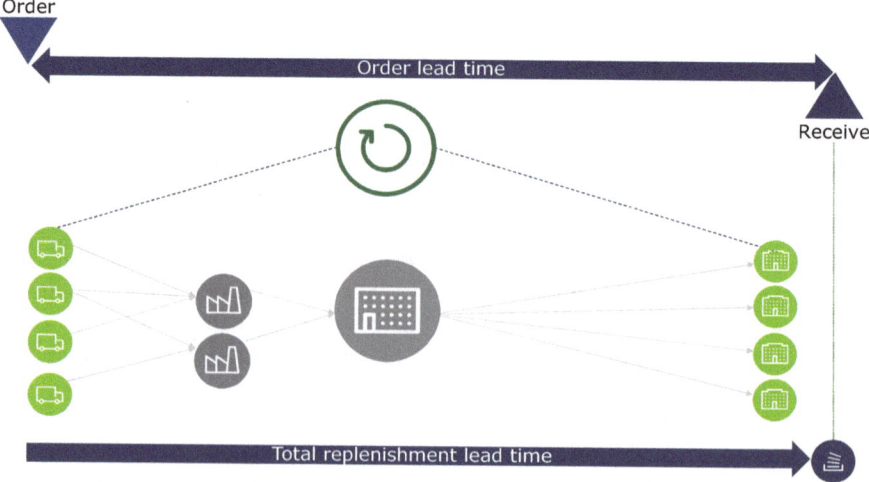

**Fig. 1.1** Order lead time versus total replenishment lead time

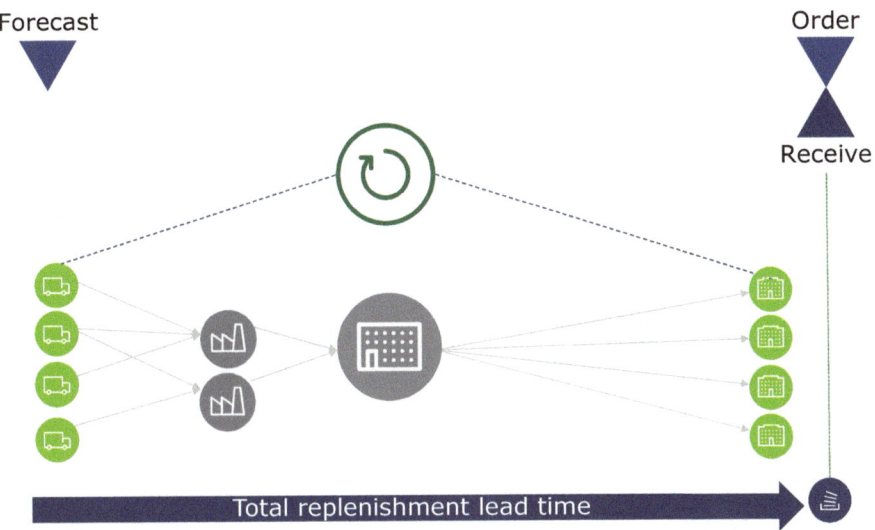

**Fig. 1.2** Reality for most companies

this piece of information. Statistical forecasts are that anchor. If done poorly, it can adversely impact all of the activities that follow. In other words, first impressions matter.

There are essentially two basic types of forecasting: qualitative (reliance on judgmental factors) and quantitative (consisting of time series and causal methods). Quantitative methods are (and should be) steeped in science, whereas there is a heavy dose of art involved in qualitative methods. In this chapter, our focus will be primarily on quantitative methods—we will use the term "statistical forecasting" to refer to these.

When it comes to forecasting models, one could take one of two approaches: Try to understand causal factors and interdependencies between relevant control variables that impact what is being estimated or simply focus on the estimate alone. The former requires answering the question why, but the latter is simply about what. One can intuitively recognize that answering why requires far more sophistication (and has far higher data requirements) than answering what. Models that concern themselves with "why" are called explanatory models—causal algorithms belong in this category. Time series models on the other hand are only concerned with "what" (see Fig. 1.3). We will discuss a conceptual framework for selecting an appropriate algorithm later in the book.

Regardless of the type of algorithm, forecasting has its basis on the assumption of continuity. It relies on algorithms to interpret historical time series data and extrapolate it into the future. Sometimes, additional forward-looking inputs such as weather data or economic indicators are used, but in its simplest form the assumption is that history will repeat itself in some shape or form and that historical data are a good representation of how things will play out in the future.

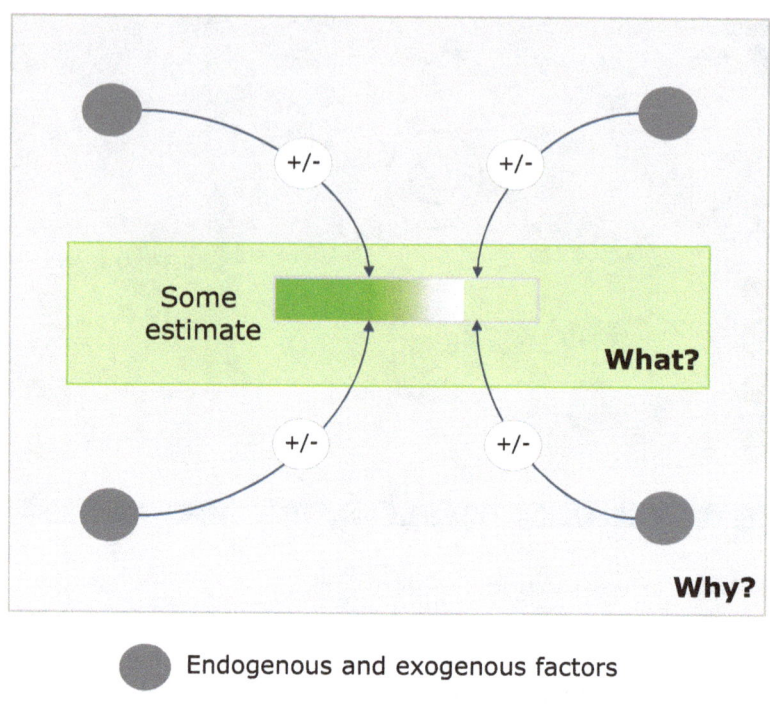

**Fig. 1.3**  Why and what of forecasting

## 1.2  Planning Types

Having looked at what forecasting is and why it is needed, let's delve into the planning types and their relationship to the overall forecasting process. There are three planning types, namely operational, tactical and long-term planning (Fig. 1.4). In operational planning, the forecasting horizon is very short and it is granularity very high; this is the reason why demand sensing, which emphasizes the use of automation thereby limiting manual enrichment, plays a vital role in predicting short-term future. Tactical planning should be supported by statistical forecasting and cover horizons typically up to 3 years. Finally, in long-term planning, the activity of predicting the future happens on highly aggregated levels and often in monetary terms. As one can see, each of the planning types imposes certain requirements and challenges on the forecasting process. Let's explore these further in the following paragraphs.

Demand sensing as part of operational planning will need to deal with data with high granularity, often scattered, often from multiple sources (for example, in the case of point of sales data). A use case on how to integrate point of sales data with a

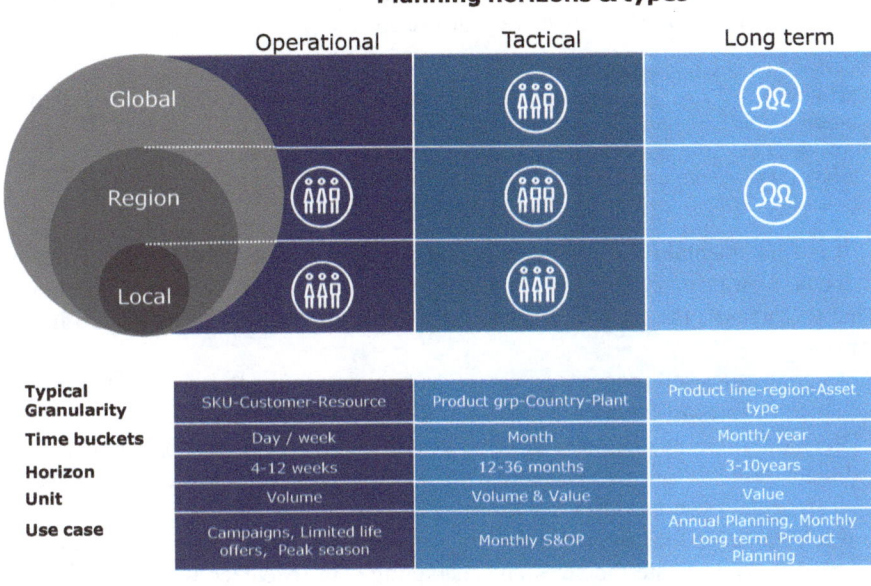

**Planning horizons & types**

| | Operational | Tactical | Long term |
|---|---|---|---|
| Global | | | |
| Region | | | |
| Local | | | |

| | Operational | Tactical | Long term |
|---|---|---|---|
| **Typical Granularity** | SKU-Customer-Resource | Product grp-Country-Plant | Product line-region-Asset type |
| **Time buckets** | Day / week | Month | Month/ year |
| **Horizon** | 4-12 weeks | 12-36 months | 3-10years |
| **Unit** | Volume | Volume & Value | Value |
| **Use case** | Campaigns, Limited life offers,  Peak season | Monthly S&OP | Annual Planning, Monthly Long term  Product Planning |

Key planning meeting

**Fig. 1.4**  Planning types and its characteristics

special SAP solution into SAP IBP called SAP DSiM is provided in another book in our SAP IBP series—"Implementing Integrated Business Planning" (Kepczynski et al., 2018).

Within tactical S&OP, a demand planning process strongly supported by statistical forecasting is most commonly leveraged to make predictions. They deal with products that may have stable but at the same time also high seasonal or intermittent demand patterns. It is not simple to forecast products that are highly seasonal, e.g., sold few months in a year or intermittent. We will shed light on how to address this challenge in the course of the book.

Long-term planning covers in some industries up to 10-year horizon. Demand predictions are often based on qualitative inputs provided by marketing, business planning and finance. Long-term macroeconomic situations, researches and development pipelines, appetite and funds for mergers and acquisitions and plans to extend manufacturing footprints play a key role in this process. Predicting what will happen in the markets on a global scale relies on data that is typically coarse-grained leading to plans that are on a high level of aggregation.

Let us summarize different types of planning and forecasting and provide the definition below for IBP which we will use for the purposes of this book:

INTEGRATED BUSINESS PLANNING IS A BUSINESS MANAGEMENT PROCESS WHICH AIMS
AT CONNECTING LONG TERM, TACTICAL AND OPERATIONAL PLANNING, ON LOCAL (MARKETS, SITES),
REGIONAL (INCL. PRODUCTION SITES) AND GLOBAL LEVEL,
TO ASSESS RISK AND OPPORTUNITIES, VERIFY ASSUMPTIONS
AND GENERATE WITH CROSS FUNCTIONAL COLLABORATION
A FEASIBLE INTEGRATED BUSINESS PLAN IN VOLUME AND VALUE.

It is fundamental for the efficiency and effectiveness of the demand predictions to focus, as a primary step, on predicting volumetric sales. As to the question of what to forecast, the answer is quite easy—you should forecast what the market demands.

As companies sell products and services (and not money!), it is essential that the sequence of forecasting reflects this fact: That is, volume precedes value.

Very often, companies mix sales forecasts (market demand), operational plans and sales targets. Sales forecast is a demand projection, provided with a set of environmental assumptions. Operational plan is a set of operational actions required to reach the sales forecast regardless of the outcome. Sales targets are sales goals established to motivate the sales and marketing staff (Mentzer Jr & Moon, 2004).

## 1.3  Scope of This Book

The primary focus of this book will be on the demand-driven and volumetric side of the forecasting processes covering short-, medium- and long-term horizons.

As to tools and techniques, algorithmic support (statistical forecasting and sensing algorithms) will be our particular focus throughout this book.

Statistical forecasting techniques for long-term planning often rely on models that are based on selected variables to determine the impact on long-term volumetric predictions; e.g., the change of gross income per capita will increase the buying power of people in a specific region or country.

In tactical S&OP, the demand review process is a crucial step. We have learned that statistical forecasting can be performed in different ways depending on the demand patterns. We want to share how to design statistical forecasting processes and how to leverage the out-of-the-box features and the instruments of SAP IBP to build your own customized features. In Fig. 1.5, we can observe that the demand review process is composed of the qualitative inputs from sales, marketing and demand planning, the quantitative inputs and of the right amount and quality of demand planning and data scientist capabilities. However, not all the components of the tactical S&OP process steps will be investigated in this book, but only those highlighted in Fig. 1.5. You may have noticed that between the process steps, there is cross/multiplication sign; the reason for such a choice relies on the fact that we strongly believe that the ultimate performance and efficiency of the demand review process depend on all the elements, acting as a whole and not as standalone ones.

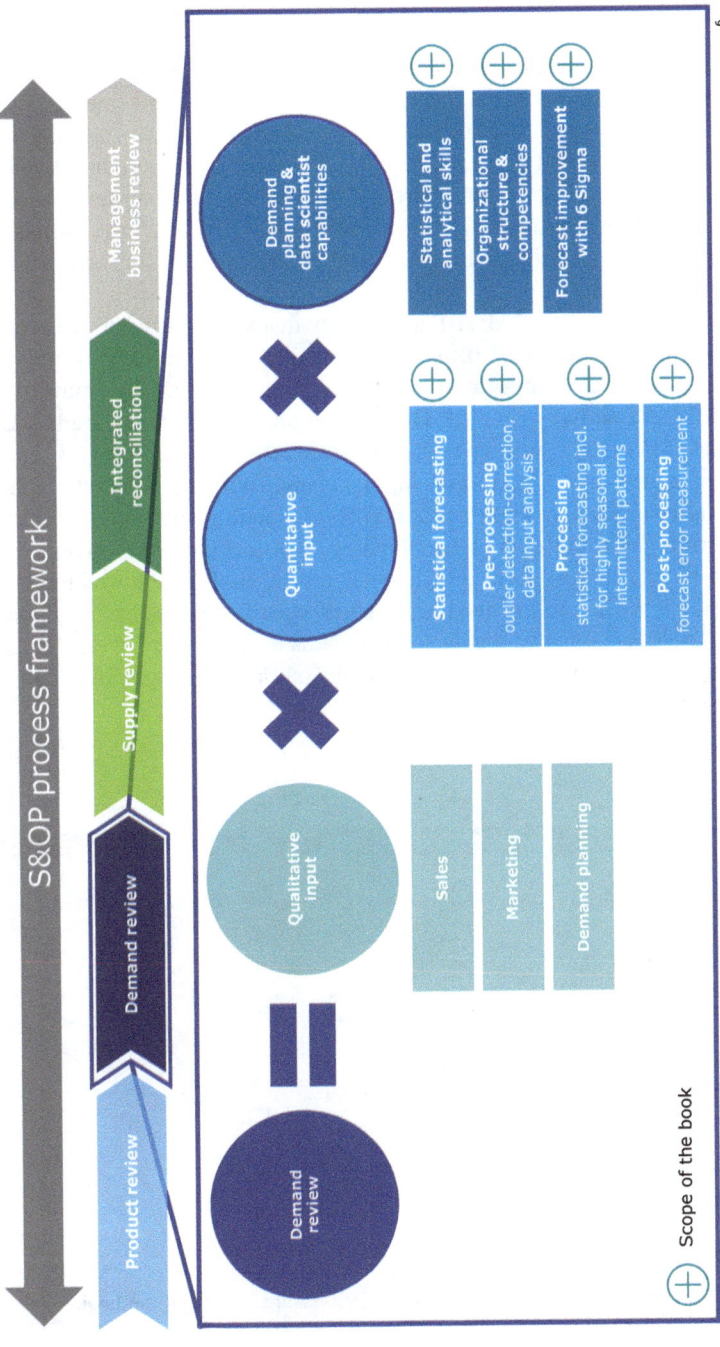

**Fig. 1.5**  Forecasting in tactical S&OP, scope of the book

Along with the traditional mid to long-term forecasting processes, which are part of the tactical S&OP and the long-term planning process, many companies leverage the demand sensing techniques. Operational planning uses demand sensing to detect signals from the market to make changes, within the short-term horizon, in the deployment/distribution plans, late customization plans and sometimes to even tackle production. Demand sensing may be perceived as an optimization technique for the consensus forecast that acts within the short-term horizon. Eventually, combining the outputs of short-term forecasting with mid- to long-term forecasting can give you several improvements in responsiveness and can help to make your supply chain more agile. Figure 1.6 illustrates the demand sensing topics that will be discussed in this book.

Let us briefly explain the SAP IBP technology that supports the above processes. In SAP IBP, **SAP Integrated Business planning** is a real-time supply chain planning solution built to profitably meet the future demand by optimizing the supply chain. Built natively on SAP HANA and deployed on the cloud, SAP IBP provides the flexibility, agility and performance to meet complex planning requirements of the next-generation supply chain. With an integrated planning covering long-term, tactical and operational-level planning and a unified integrated model covering sales and operations planning, demand planning, inventory optimization, response and supply, and control tower, SAP IBP provides a single platform for all the planning needs. Together with robust planning algorithms, real-time simulations, what-if analysis, dashboards and analytics, alerts, embedded social collaboration and data integration with external sources, SAP IBP is the state-of-the-art planning solution (Fig. 1.7).

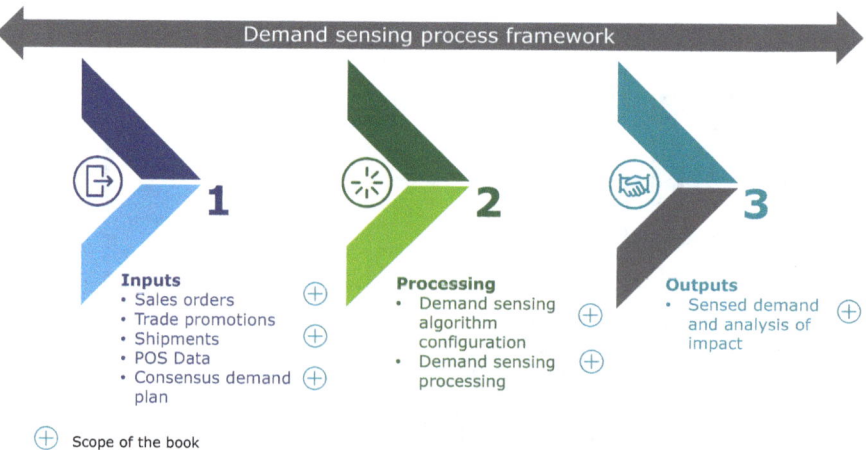

**Fig. 1.6** Forecasting in operational planning, demand sensing—scope of the book

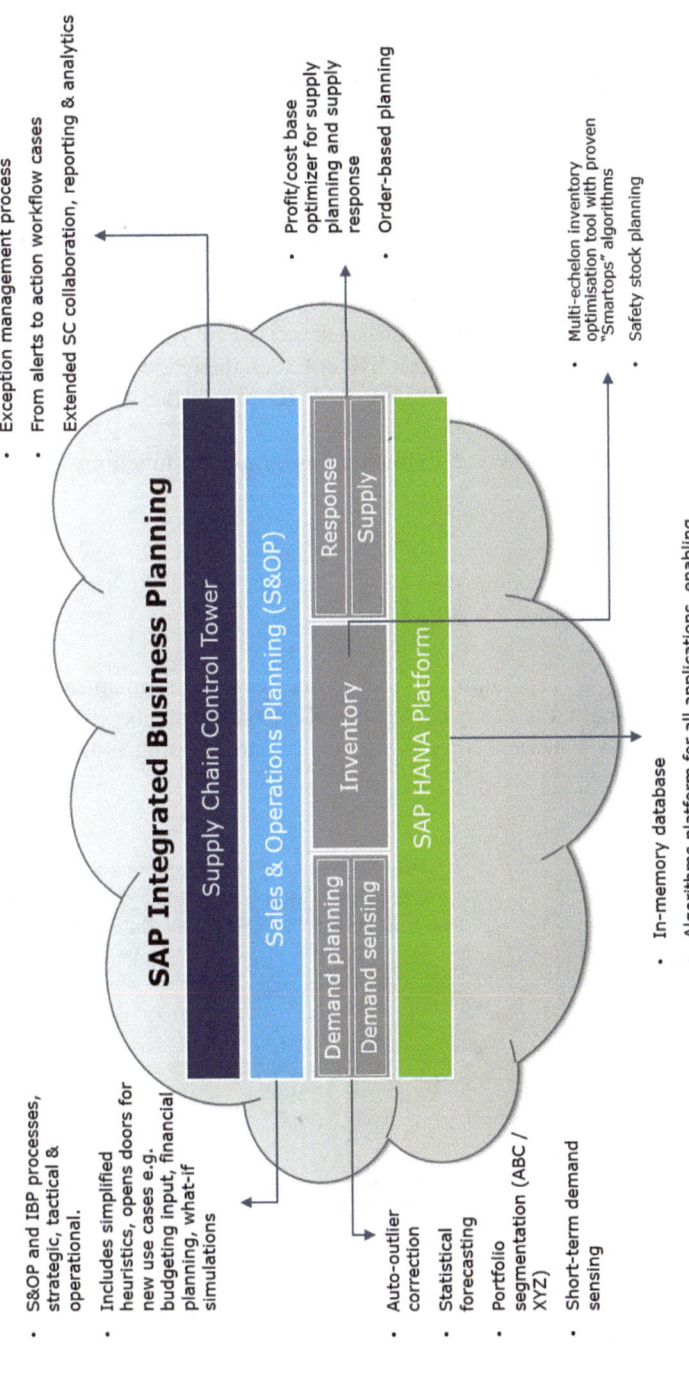

**Fig. 1.7** SAP IBP applications overview

SAP IBP for demand will provide a key logic for forecasting in the long-term, tactical and operational horizons. IBP for demand in large and complex organizations with comprehensive processes could be supported with improved visibility and exception management embedded in SAP IBP for Supply Chain Control Tower. In addition, another element which improves the end result is a functionality which facilitates collaboration; this is done via SAP JAM.

In this book, we present how to leverage out-of-the-box functionalities for the processes we will be covering. Besides, we will describe some special configurations that were built making use of the standard mechanisms available in SAP IBP, e.g., the possibility to add stored key figures, calculated key figures, definition of custom rules to manage copy and default rules, definition of custom disaggregation and aggregation, of alerts and visualizations in Excel UI or Web UI. Last but not least, since the main user interface of SAP IBP is Excel, the reader could also learn how to combine the strengths of Excel with SAP HANA in the various planning templates.

In SAP for demand, there are the following key groups of functionalities:

- Statistical forecasting
- Segmentation
- Demand sensing
- Forecast error measurement (see Fig. 1.8).

We explained how we can improve "focus" and leverage segmentation in the book Integrated Business Planning use cases (Kepczynski et al., 2018). In this book, we will focus on statistical forecasting and demand sensing functionalities.

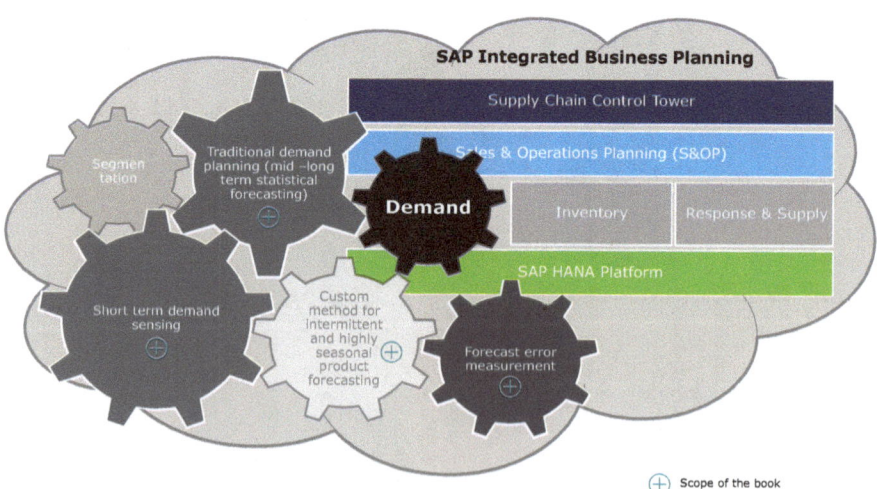

**Fig. 1.8** SAP IBP demand application scope of the book

## 1.4   Statistical Forecasting Process Framework

Doing statistical forecasting right requires forethought and preparation and calls for a formal process framework. One such framework is presented in Fig. 1.9. We will use this framework as our reference model. The first step "define purpose" will be discussed in this chapter, and the remaining steps will be addressed in Chap. 3.

## 1.5   Purpose

Purpose definition involves getting clarity on various aspects such as: Who or what is most impacted by the forecast? What is the time frame of validity for decisions taken on the basis of forecasts? This is connected to the decision phase (long term/tactical/operational) the decisions belong to. One also needs to articulate the consequences of inaccuracy. This requires considering the nature of decisions that will be made based on the forecast as it will help determine the desired level of accuracy. For example, cost of item-level inaccuracy tends to be lower compared to inaccuracy on a higher level of aggregation (say, product group). Similarly, inaccuracies in the short term are also less dire when compared to mid-/long-term inaccuracies as these decisions are revisited more frequently.

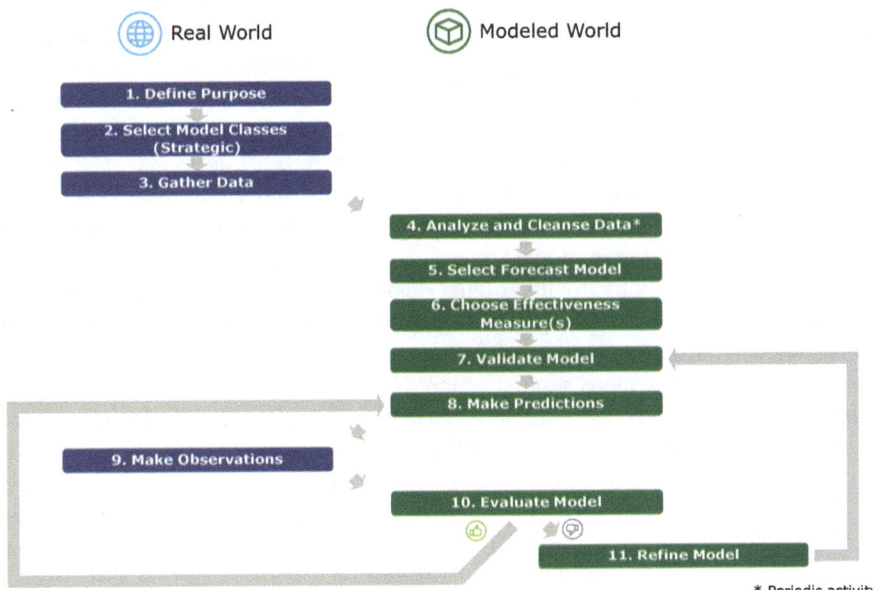

**Fig. 1.9**  Statistical forecasting process model

It also needed to be careful to not fall into the trap of forecasting for its own sake. It helps to have an appreciation for factors of uncertainty impacting the subject that is being forecasted while being mindful of the diminishing marginal utility of investing additional time and resources to unmask uncertainty in an effort to improve accuracy. When Donald Rumsfeld famously spoke about "known unknowns" and "unknown unknowns" at one of his press briefings during the height of the Iraq war, he must have been talking about "epistemic" and "aleatory" uncertainty (Rumsfeld, 2002). Epistemic uncertainty refers to things that are knowable, but aleatory refers to things that fall into the category of impossible to know for certain. When forecasting, it is important to acknowledge that sometimes it is impossible to predict certain things and a better approach in such instances would be to assess the risk exposure and hedge against such uncertainty, for example, by using time, capacity or inventory buffers.

Span of control is also an important aspect to consider early in the forecasting process. This determines what gets classified as external, therefore the object of forecasting, and what gets classified as internal (controllable) and therefore is the scope of planning and decision making based on predictions of external factors (say, sales). In relation to this, it is worth mentioning that one should avoid forecasting requirements that can be "derived," that is dependent requirements. It is the independent requirement (external demands) that needs to be the focus of forecasting, but it does not mean companies do not predict dependent requirements, e.g., for their highly important raw materials (steel for white goods manufacturers, active ingredient for chemical companies, varieties for agriculture industry). Levels in a bill of material are like the nodes of a supply chain and are similarly susceptible to the bullwhip effect if individual levels are forecasted in isolation.

There are essentially two types of forecasts—market-oriented and production-oriented (Silver, Edward, Pyke, David, & Peterson, 1998). A clear understanding of purpose and scope determines the type of methods that are appropriate. Market-oriented methods are more qualitative in nature and when quantitative tend to be more sophisticated and expensive—higher forecasting costs. They drive decisions regarding resource requirements (long-term scope). Production-oriented methods on the other hand drive decisions regarding acquiring and scheduling of resources (tactical and operational scope).

As long-term decisions involve higher degrees of freedom (see Fig. 1.10) or, in other words, offer a broader scope for decision making involving alternate scenarios and as such requiring a number of factors to be considered (external as well as internal), they call for more sophistication. Since decisions on this level have the power to change the givens (e.g., new markets and new locations), the assumption of continuity (past is a good indicator of the future) falls apart sometimes, which in turn calls for more qualitative or causal methods for forecasting. As one gets closer to execution, there is a pressure of the decision space and simpler time series methods start to become a lot more useful for decisions involving higher granularities and increased frequencies.

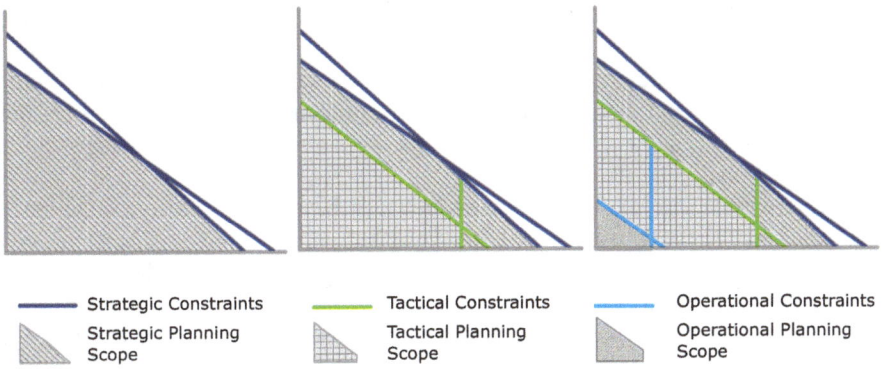

**Fig. 1.10**  Decision making, forecasting and planning scope

With a better appreciation for how purpose shapes the focus of forecasting, let's turn our attention in the next section to some key challenges in forecasting related to both technical and human aspects.

## 1.6  Key Challenges of Forecasting

### 1.6.1  Seasonality

Uncertainty, complexity and volatility in supply chains are here to stay. A well-established process for detecting and correcting seasonal outlying events represents one of the first steps toward supporting the companies in the improvement of forecast accuracy and customer service levels and reducing process variances and working capital tied to inventory.

In addition, companies deal with the increased number of SKUs in their portfolios, strong seasonal sales cycles, exceptional events and intermittent or erratic sales patterns. Activities such as data cleansing, outlier detection and correction and forecasting are not currently properly supported by viable and agile processes and would require a specialized set of skills/capabilities and right system functionalities. Outlier detection, correction and forecasting are often addressed with too much human subjective guessing; in addition, the lack of data analysis for supporting decisions does not help for a more effective management. Those challenges and symptoms are even more exposed if we look on products that are highly seasonal or offer limited life, often not repeatable. It all results in high forecast errors, high supply chain and operating costs, loss of sales and not optimized inventory levels. Obviously, the overall result is frequently the following: During the season in which a company is supposed to account for most of its revenues, it is actually reporting for most of its lost compared to the realistic potential!

The demand or the sales of a given product exhibit seasonality when the underlying time series undergo a predictable cyclic variation depending on a specific time within the year. More commonly, seasonality refers to regular periodic fluctuations that recur every year with about the same timing and intensity. For example, some consumer habits, like festivals, days off, and celebration days, could bring to seasonal patterns.

Furthermore, there are some patterns that can be addressed as quasi-seasonal. They constantly reveal themselves every year, but with a different cadence or with discrepancies among countries or even within the years as the mother day which varies from country to country or Eastern which changes from year to year.

Almost all businesses have some form of seasonality since factors such as weather, holidays, special events, specific time of the year, fiscal end-year and back-to-school day can all contribute to some short-term or long-term spikes in demand (Metersky, 2003).

It is known that seasonality can be caused by internal and external factors, and it can create enormous inefficiencies. The seasonal cycle, which is the smallest time period for the repetitive cycle, has a huge impact on supply chains and operations; furthermore, the seasonal cycle influences and disturbs the variance of the ordering quantity, the forecasting process, the variance of the lead time and the normal ordering processes (Cho & Lee, 2012).

Seasonality is uncertain and inevitable. It can happen at any time of the year, and it creates often managerial headaches and dramatic consequences if it is not addressed with the right attention (Amy & Partridge, 2017). It requires effective decision making and fast response and reactiveness.

As a consequence, understanding, identifying and reacting to seasonality are subjects of interest for almost all the businesses. Improvement toward this topic can lead to a substantial benefit in the bottom line profits as well as to a competitive advantage toward other companies or to an added value to be exploited. Seasonality is also one of the most frequently used statistical patterns to improve the accuracy of demand forecasts.

Among the influencers of seasonality, a brief mention should be addressed to the rogue seasonality, also called unintended cyclic variability. It is an endogenous disturbance generated by a company internal processes such as inventory, production and forecasting control systems ((Shukla, Naim, & Thornhill, 2012). Unintended seasonality can propagate all along the supply chain causing instability and higher cost propagation. It is often present in all supply chains with different degrees of intensity, and it commonly manifests itself in the ordering process. The unintended cyclic variations are present only for make-to-stock businesses, and it affects more the FMCG and technology businesses. The consequences of an unintended seasonality on a business are the same as the ones mentioned before, with the particularity that a root cause analysis is much more difficult to be assessed as all the departments contribute to the propagation of the disturbances and errors.

When seasonality is unmanaged, the usual objective of getting the right amount, at the right place, at the right moment may become even trickier (Amy & Partridge, 2017). Seasonal stress is felt all along the supply chains and distributions networks:

manufacturers, retailers, third parties, transportation carries and infrastructure out-posts. It happens that everyone peaks at the same time and often, to make things worse, the 40/50% of the revenue of the year is earned in that very short lapse of time. Real-life examples suggest us problems such as lack of truckload capacity, congestions, nervousness and inaccurate demand planning (Amy & Partridge, 2017).

Dealing with seasonality is money consuming, visibility gets poor, expenses are run at the last minute, sales are often missed, and organization stress reaches the same high peaks of the demand (Amy & Partridge, 2017).

The common outputs of seasonality are lost revenues, inaccurate demand fore-casting, missed production schedule, ineffective transportation and excessive inventory management (Cho & Lee, 2013) resulting in sky roofing operating costs. The phenomenon can also potentially cause a mismatch between supply and demand, and it frequently increases the costs of inventory and stock-out (Cho & Lee, 2013).

Seasonality is not only related to the customer side, but also to the supply side; fluctuations may concern raw materials and labor availabilities hitting also the long-term corporate strategies. As a consequence, whether seasonality comes from supply or demand, the variability creates always significant challenges for all the actors involved.

The forecasting processes often suffer from seasonal products as they are difficult to predict; their demands are unstable and always changing in quantities. Estimating the seasonality implies several complications as the following (Seasonality Definition, 2017):

- Time series are short. The life span of most consumer goods does not exceed 3 or 4 years. As a result, for a given product, sales history offers on average very few points in the past to estimate each seasonal cycle.
- Time series are noisy. Random market fluctuations impact the sales and make the seasonality more difficult to isolate.
- Multiple seasonality is involved. When looking at sales at the store level, the seasonality of the product itself is typically entangled with the seasonality of the store.
- Other patterns such as trend or product life cycle also impact time series, introducing various sorts of bias in the estimation.

In addition, seasonal forecasting is complicated also because it requires a cross-functional collaboration and a rich information sharing. Often, information sharing is identified as the solution to enhance the company understanding of business seasonality. Moreover, the use of an established collaboration and shared inputs can lead the analysis to a further step of comprehending the root causes of each season. It is considered that a 360 degree approach will deliver the right benefits; for example, analyzing the historical peaks of the past year may require an understanding of the marketing activity, the contingency of that period, the pro-motions launched over the past years, the competitors' activities during that period and many other influencers. Collecting information requires the right technology and the right skill set of people, because not all the data are useful and only few of them are the drivers toward the solution. Advanced mathematical analysis like the failure mode, effects and criticality analysis (FMECA) and the fault tree analysis (FTA) can enhance capabilities to understand seasonality and its impact.

Sometimes, seasonality can appear easy to understand and predict: For example, if a company sells an anti-pollen pill, it is expected to see a peak during the spring; however, understanding and giving a weight to the influencers of the peak of that particular year are a much more difficult exercises that demands internal communication, external collaboration and a huge data system.

However, most of the companies look for short-term solutions, the easy way, failing to consider the whole picture, all the causes, repercussions, consequences, but at the same time also the benefits that could be generated on a large organizational scale (Metersky, 2003).

Besides, an outlier is an observation that appears to deviate significantly from other observations in the sample (NIST, 2012). They are data points that have extreme values relative to other observations observed under the same condition (Gunst, Mason, & Hess, 2003). Outliers are often named as aberrant, discordant, anomalous, straggler and wilds.

SAP defines an outlier as an observation that lies outside the overall pattern of a distribution (Sap & Planning, 1999). Others name an outlier as an entry in a data set that is anomalous with respect to the behavior seen in the majority of the other entries in the data set (Watson, Tight, Clark, & Redfern, 1991).

Outliers are very important in the area of data analysis; they have been studied in various disciplines within which supply chain processes, pharmaceutical researches, weather predictions, financial applications, marketing and customer segmentations (Cherednichenko, 2005). For an introductive purpose, outlier is exceptional values that need to be found in order to reduce their impacts (Sharma & Singh, 2013).

The today new normal dares imply the need for data collection, and more data with a high level of granularity have to be constantly available and maintained; data analysis and its comprehension are on the raise, and its new challenges must also consider all the spectrum of outliers detection techniques as a form toward better management and control.

Outliers are a real pain for the majority of the companies of the entire business panorama. Most of them are facing difficulties in identifying those strange points, others in correcting, some of them in both. As it will be described in the next chapters, the outlier analysis covers a specific step of the forecasting process, however, standard, tested and reliable methods are often missing in that respect, leading to a mismanagement of these controversial outlying points.

The objective in this regard is to investigate and look for the "exception" in order to let the organizations better benefit for a further comprehension of their data. Nevertheless, best practices are shadowed. The reason for such a thing is thought to be due to both bad management and to the difficulty of the subject.

In recent years, this subject has attracted more and more attention, and consequently, this study positions itself in this growing trend of interest. The aim of this section will be to introduce the matter and define some common techniques and methods that can be adopted to better manage the outliers all along a supply chain.

The detection and location of all types of outliers in logistic networks, supply chains and internal corporate processes have also attracted much attention recently, because such outliers tend to affect also unit root inference among other things. Most of the procedures developed in regard to outliers were related for non-seasonal products, while most of the firms of the world deal with seasonality and have to tackle it.

Besides, the presence of seasonality in the form of seasonally varying means and variances affects the properties of outlier detection procedures, and hence, appropriate adjustments of existing methods are needed for seasonal data (Haldrup, Montañes, & Sansó, 2011).

Outlier methodologies are generally applied to all kind of data, but it is often forgotten to consider specific business characteristics as well as the differences of the data itself. Let's have a deeper look at how outliers are classified.

## 1.6.2  Outliers

Identifying, detecting and correcting outliers are important for the following reasons (NIST, 2012; Gunst et al., 2003):

- An outlier may indicate a bad data. The data may have been coded incorrectly, or an experiment may not have been run correctly. If it can be determined that an outlying point is in fact erroneous, then the outlying value should be deleted from the analysis or corrected.
- In some cases, it may not be possible to determine if an outlying point is a bad data. Outliers may be due to random variation or may indicate something scientifically interesting. In any event, we typically do not want to simply delete the outlying observation. However, if the data contains significant outliers, we may need to consider the use of robust statistical techniques.
- The presence of outliers in a data set may obscure some characteristics about the phenomena being studied.
- Outliers may contain important information that if not noted and considered may go lost.
- Outliers may identify errors in data or faulty measurements. Other sources of error are manual human errors and finger touches with the data (Watson et al., 1991). The consequences of not detecting an outlier have a superior cost than the effort for detecting the outlier itself.
- An outlier can represent an error: It is an anomaly, discordant observation, exception, fault or defect. They may occur because of human errors, mechanical faults, or change in the environment (Sharma & Singh, 2013).
- An outlier can represent an event: They may be generated by a different mechanism indicating that this type of outliers belonging to an unexpected pattern that does not conform to the normal behavior and may include useful and interesting information about rarely occurring events within numerous applications (Sharma & Singh, 2013).

- The outliers are the instances of errors or indications of the events. Outlier detection allows to improve the analysis of data and further discovering unseals events in different domains (Sharma & Singh, 2013).

## Company strategies toward outliers

In supply chain contexts, outliers are investigated and inquired in order to get a more stable and predictable management of the internal processes employed to generate profit. Outlier detection in supply chain processes can be explained with regard to localization, tracking, logistics, shipments, transportation, sales, reverse logistics and procurement. The objective is often identified in filtering out any erroneous data due to human errors or inaccurate management from the collection of raw data to calibrate efficiently the target. Sometimes, data that look strange and bizarre are not wrong at all, and they have to be kept and not being incorrectly eliminated.

Let's bear in mind that companies' nightmare is both not to respond to customer demand and, at the same time, not being capable of predicting changes in customers' behaviors (Cherednichenko, 2005). In this respect, companies are looking for automation, greater visibility, smarter use of the data, efficient tracking for faster and more dynamic decision making (Sharma & Singh, 2013). One of the tools heavily implemented in the previous year has been the RFID, an innovative tracking tool for supply chain management systems. Almost all the retailers will use RFID to track their shipments of products from suppliers to the warehouses, while tracking customer demand. Those data are capable of providing useful information about trend, seasonality and outliers' analysis (Sharma & Singh, 2013).

Companies normally react in four different ways in front of a possible outlier situation (Budzier & Flyvbjerg, 2013):

1. Rejection: It is the most common method to deal with outliers, consisting in rejecting and forgetting the existence of an anomalous point. Outliers do not need to be thrown out of the window because they result unusual, but rather they need to be included and considered as they can provide useful and not previously noted information about the data set.
2. Accommodation: It means that the inferences are made by adjusting the method with which the data have been analyzed and investigated.
3. Incorporation: It consists of revising some assumptions in order to let the extraordinary point come back into its normal expected range. This bad practice is often run in operations management.
4. Identification: It implies the action of clustering and then recognizing those points that interfere with the normal data set.

It is also frequently experienced the tendency of considering and labeling an outlier as a perfect storm or a black swan. This labeling is criticized for implying that the event in question is uncontrollable and unforeseeable resulting in "nothing can be done about it," "nothing can be done to prevent it," and "nothing can be done to manage it" (Budzier & Flyvbjerg, 2013).

Furthermore, it has to be reminded that also the subject of whether or not to consider an event as black swan needs to undergo a more rational inspection compared to what common practices normally propose. By applying a rigorous and systematic approach, we want to avoid retracting the topic of outlier detection and correction as what the risk and crisis management experts at Riskope & Associates calls "Black Swan Mania", a sort of viral epidemic that culminates in labeling everything as an unpredictable event whose consequences cannot be mitigated in advance as a black swan (Riskope Blog, 2011).

As a conclusion, it has to be reminded that wrong practices about outlier detection do exist and persist and one-fits-for-all solutions and rules do not exist at all. Methods, techniques and algorithms vary depending on the organization's perspectives and processes followed; as a result, a fully efficient unified method is still a mirage (Sap & Planning, 1999).

The main field of application of outlier detection and identification is the one related to the sales demand history of a particular time bucket, within the demand forecasting process. The planners usually do not manage to explain differences and discrepancies in the data or the root causes of the exceptions. Correcting is a tricky task, often subjective and little objective that influences the accuracies of predictions.

In the following pages, we will see how to improve those practices.

**Outliers Classifications**

A school of thought has classified the outliers in three different categories: the system, the event and the process-centric; each category differs in the understanding and assumption about the nature and causes of uncertainty (Budzier & Flyvbjerg, 2013).

The system-centric theory defines an outlier as a normal accident. This theory considers the complexity of systems as the root causes for anomalies and failures.

The event-centric view considers organizational failures as the result of the occurrence of an external event followed by an insufficient response (Budzier & Flyvbjerg, 2013).

The process-centric view estimates that organizational failures are the gradual sum up of smaller errors over time. The amplification of small errors leads to a large disaster allowing to the risk acceptance to slowly enlarge with time passing. When dealing with organizational outliers, it must be defined as the causes and effects of the trigger, for example, if the outlier has been caused internally or externally and its degree of controllability.

As a conclusion of this first classification, a brief digression needs to be addressed to the internal causes of outliers; it has been mentioned before how unintended organizational seasonality can lead to variations and internal variances. A unintended seasonality index can be assessed using the Fourier transform, and it can be of help stopping the propagation of outliers all along a supply chain by concentrating on managerial actions and routines (Shukla et al., 2012).

The communality among these theories is that the outlier or the unexpected event stays undiscovered until when the fact happens. Besides, once again, the future does not go according to plans and unattended consequences arise and create problems. All theories still wonder if outliers are common and stable phenomena or the opposite. The former assumption implies that outliers are not isolated; the latter suggests that an outlier happens, because of random chance events.

The analogous of this debate can be transposed into the statistic field, asking whether outliers are part or not of the same population. Outliers can also be classified as (Watson et al., 1991):

- Single abnormal flow measurement
- Multiple abnormal flow measurement
- Same abnormal repeated flow values
- Flow values at zero
- Abnormal flow values as a result of events.

According to such a theory, an outlier is a data that lie sufficiently far from their immediate neighbors after having considered all factors affecting the sales/demand of the item in question. The outliers can be also classified as additive outliers, innovative outliers, level shift and transitory change. An additive outlier represents an isolated spike, a level shift is a step function, a transitory change is a spike that takes a few periods to disappear, and an innovative outlier is a shock in the innovations of the model (Kaiser & Maravall, 1999).

The objective for this section is also to list the main broad outlier methods classifications usually employed for statistical forecasting purposes. It must be said that the list is not comprehensive of all the techniques present in the overall panorama and not all will be investigated; only those relevant for improving and enhancing the practices toward the statistical outlier correction and detection will be considered (see Fig. 1.11).

Some techniques can be used to check for a single outlier, others for multiple and others for both; sometimes, the specific number of outliers that wants to be detected has to be declared before the test, and sometimes, this is not the case.

It results that some models can be global and others local; some methods are considered labeling methods and others scoring ones. Others methods are also based on modeling properties such as rational and sample features; among those, there are other subdivisions as proximity-based and angle-based approaches (Kriegel & Kroger, 2010).

Despite the numerous approaches, the phenomena of masking and swamping can occur and make the tests fail. Masking is said when one outlier masks a second outlier that could have been considered a single standing outlier by itself, if the previous was not present at all. To be clearer, if the first outlier had been deleted, the second would have resulted as an outlier (Seo & Marsh, 2006). Swamping is said when one outlier swamps a second observation, resulting in both observation outliers because of the presence of the first one. If the first point is deleted, the second observation does not result in a standing alone outlier (Seo & Marsh, 2006).

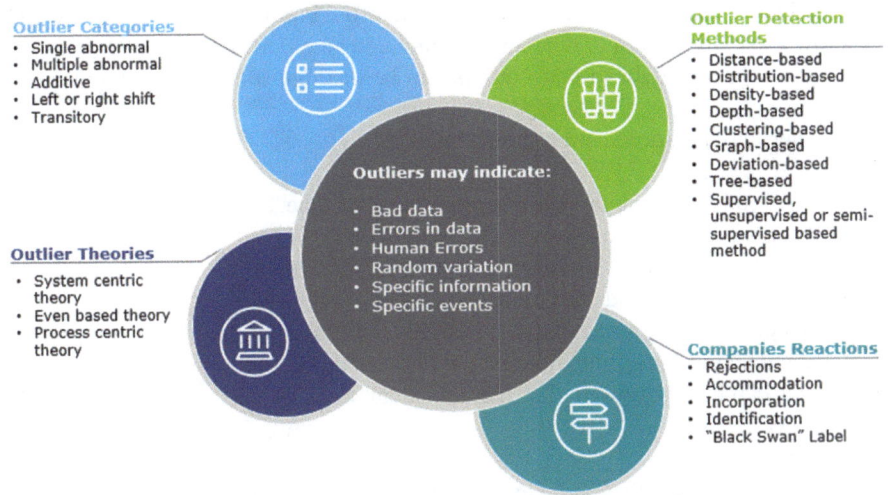

**Fig. 1.11** Overview on outlier classifications, methods, theories and strategies

These are the reasons why graphical techniques, also called labeling methods, are often recommended, and their complementary use is advised by experts.

Outliers' detection techniques can be divided into these main categories (Cherednichenko, 2005; Kriegel & Kroger, 2010; Sharma & Singh, 2013):

1. Distance-based method which distinguishes potential outliers from others based on the number of objects in the neighborhoods.
2. Distribution-based approach which deals with statistical methods that are based on probabilistic data models.
3. Density-based approach which detects local outliers based on the local density of an object's neighborhoods.
4. Depth-based approach which searches for outliers at the border of the data space. An outlier will be an object on outer layers.
5. Deviation-based approach which detects outliers as points that do not fit the general characteristics of the set. An outlier is the outermost point of the data set.
6. High-dimensional approach where the concept of neighborhoods becomes meaningless and detects outliers in projections of the original feature space.
7. Graph-based approach which detects outliers on images generated by powerful tools and maps.
8. Clustering-based approach that identifies an outlier as a point that does not belong to a cluster of data set. Clustering-based outliers' detection algorithms are about finding cluster and outliers which are often considered as noise that should be removed in order to make more reliable clusters. Some points may be far out from the data mean others can be closer and further out they are, greater is the probability of exclusion.

9. Tree-based approach which detects outliers by building specific trees which allow a decomposition of the data structure and an efficient measure of similarity for the sequence data so that outliers can be distinguished from non-outliers.

Another classification can be the following:

- Supervised learning approach where outliers are detected on the basis of fit in a model.
- Unsupervised learning approach detects outliers without the use of pre-labeled data, and these methods are more general.
- Semisupervised learning approach requires some training on pre-labeled normal data, and an outlier is thought to be the one that does not fit the normality model.
- Models can be also clustered as mathematical, numeric and non-numeric/logical ones (Watson et al., 1991).

All of these approaches include many and various techniques that can provide different outputs in relation to the outliers' detection topic. The objective would not be to go through all the viable tests, but rather screening and applying those that will create organizational benefits in terms of better supply chain management.

## 1.6.3  Intermittent Demand

Intermittent demand appears at random, with many time periods having no demand. The most significant factor that turns a normal demand into an intermittent demand is the presence of sequences of zero values in a demand series. Moreover, the non-zero demand is often also "lumpy," which defines the case in which there is great variability among the non-zero values.

Intermittent demand is often experienced in industries such as aviation, automotive, defense and manufacturing; it also typically occurs with products nearing the end of their life cycle. Items with intermittent demand include service spare parts and high-priced capital goods, such as heavy machinery.

Some companies operating in these areas observe intermittent or lumpy demand for over half the products in their inventories. In such situations, there is a clear financial incentive to inventory control and retaining proper stock levels and therefore to forecasting demand for these items. The difficulty in assessing good planning strategies for these items is in their specific nature.

Forecasting lumpy and intermittent demand is challenging because it is not only affected by the variability of the demand size, but also by the variability of the time between the arrival of a non-zero demand and the following one.

Intermittent demand creates significant problems in the manufacturing and supply environment as far as forecasting and inventory control are concerned.

Given that inventory management and stock control is based on demand forecasting, it is obvious that intermittent demand nature could create significant problems in the manufacturing and supply environment since demand forecasting strongly influences aspects such as overproduction, under- or overstocking.

In the competitive environment where the majority of the businesses operate, managing intermittent and lumpy demand patterns represents an increasingly frequent and complex issue.

The complexity of dealing with these kinds of demand patterns lies in finding the best trade-off between negative effects related to high storage levels, such as high amount of space and resources for keeping large warehouse areas, high holding costs, as well as high risks and cost due to items obsolescence, and negative effects related to low storage levels, such as lost demand and customers.

Usually, inventory management and demand forecasting are traditionally treated as independent problems.

Most inventory methods ignore forecasting altogether and simply assume that the distribution of demand and all its parameters is known, while most forecasting techniques do not evaluate the stock control consequences.

This can lead to under- or overstocked inventories, the former of which can increase lead times, while the latter equates to excess spending better used elsewhere in the supply chain. Supply imbalances in any direction can disrupt production and inhibit lean manufacturing efforts.

The interactions between forecasting and stock control must be analyzed for items with intermittent demand, and the forecasting method is an important determinant of the customer service that can be obtained from a given level of inventory investment.

The positive effects of an integrated approach are:

- Increasing customer satisfaction
- Reducing inventory stock-outs
- Scheduling production more effectively
- Lowering safety stock requirement
- Reducing product obsolescence costs
- Doing more with less - In accordance with the lean manufacturing paradigm.

Therefore, when treating irregular and sporadic demand patterns, two relevant issues must be considered:

1. Demand forecasting in the future periods
2. Utilization of demand forecasting obtained for managing stocks

Hence, issues related to when and how much it costs to create stocks for satisfying the forecasted customers' orders are faced at the same time.

### 1.6.4   Human Judgment

A forecasting process requires differentiated treatments in process, people capabilities and system solutions. This amalgam improves the way in which a business problem will be addressed. We see that an important element for the problem-solving success is associated with how we leverage data scientists' capabilities and how we will combine it with the typical/standard demand planning skill set. The demand review process steps, which are part of the S&OP process, are the most suitable placeholders for improved outlier detection for seasonal products.

The outlier detection for seasonal products process highly focuses on statistical techniques; however, it recognizes the crucial role played by the qualitative market inputs such as marketing, promotions and competitors to complement the solution.

At the same time, the use of specific metrics and assigning the ownership to the new steps of the processes will help in tracking the benefits and guaranteeing a mindset toward the continuous improvement (see Fig. 1.12).

It is worthwhile to have a particular digression on the role of the people involved in the process, their attitudes toward statistics and the influence of what is normally called the "human touch."

It has been proven that there is a natural human tendency to trust one's feelings more rather than trusting computer-generated statistical data (Bobenstab, 2017). According to a research on a pool of 100 people, 8 used statistical baseline and 92 made manual overrides, which in most of the cases meant adding 92 chances of being wrong (Chase, 2009).

Makridakis, Wheelwright and Hyndman (1998) stated that "While we accept the deficiency of our memory, we rarely do anything to remedy the deficiency of our judgment."

**Fig. 1.12** Operating model for forecasting process

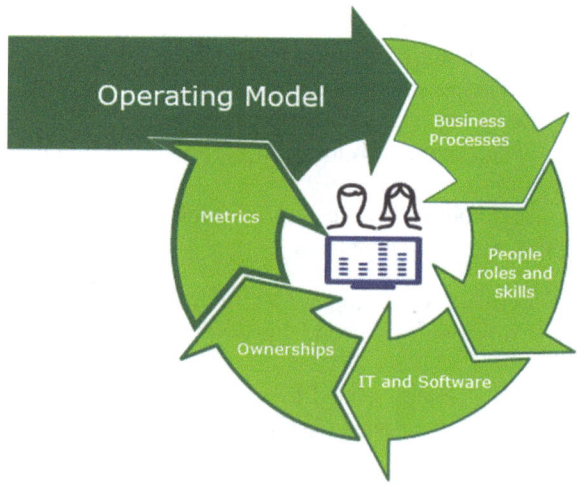

If a group of people are asked to predict the demand of an item according to same historical information, their outputs will be often very different depending on the level and degree of education of the person, to the amount of external information coming from the market and to the internal information coming from the product itself (a mature one or a new one).

A common erroneous trend seems to be that people believe that past represents the future. Inconsistency is one of the major problems causing fluctuations and variations among periods, often because people are unwilling to apply the same rules or because they are influenced by their mood of the day. Building expert teams can help to solve the problem of inconsistency and process adherence.

It should be noted that group thinking is risky, because of people's personalities to follow more or less the superior's lead and that recency is a well-defined common bias that consists of on remembering short-term facts easily and giving less importance to older ones.

Other errors may still be conservatism, availability, anchoring, illusory correlations, search for supportive evidence, regression effects, attribution of success and failure, optimism and pessimism, selective perception.

Conventional wisdom lets us believe that sometimes more information is better, but it can happen that more information just makes us feel more confident about the decisions we take. Often information is redundant or time consuming, be it "good" or "bad."

Since forever, people have always dreamt of predicting the future in order to diminish their fear against the unknown and the uncertain. Mathematical tools are needed in forecasting to predict the future, but they are not a substitute for prophecy. Forecasting errors will always be present, and no statistical method will match exactly the future reality.

However, forecasting is needed to launch production, supply, scheduling, production and replenishment, and as a result, the best and most rational approach toward forecasting will create benefits for an entire organization.

Concluding, it is not said that qualitative inputs must be eliminated or banned; however, they need to be used cautiously and prudently. Combining qualitative with quantitative is possible as Daniel Kahneman's book "Thinking, fast and slow" proposes:

- Identifying a baseline forecast using statistics and relying on the computer generated statistical data, being aware that there is no one-fit-for-all solution for forecasting technique
- Intuitive estimation addition where some casual actors were not included in the baseline
- Identifying the spectrum of factors utilized in your intuitive suggestion
- Adjusting the baseline by the percentage of factors that your intuitive suggestion took into consideration.

It allows a sort of compromised solution between data and self-intuition reliance, mitigating the human error and at the same time helping to trust the data system.

People can see that is possible to combine data generated solution with their own thoughts. In this way, people are less reluctant to trust and follow technology (Bobenstab, 2017).

The final point to be assessed in that regard is to verify the amount of improvement generated by the manual adjustments. Enhancement and benefits should not be verified only in respect of pure accuracy and bias, but rather based on the final bottom line improvement and cost savings. The stakes of the game must be worth the cost of the candle light by which it is played; the efforts spent to raise a percentage of a forecast error must be worth the payoff (Singh, Raman, & Wilson, 2015). That is also one of the reasons why there is a growing tendency toward segmenting the supply chains and its activities pointing how a one-size-fits-all solution does not exist and mostly does not deliver expected results (Davis, 2011).

In conclusion, the direction for the future of forecasting processes, which has been already underpinned by some companies, is to build a center of forecasting excellence composed by people with high statistical skills (demand analytics) and people who work closely to market businesses (demand planners) (Chase, 2016).

### 1.6.5   Effectiveness and Efficiency

Many of us have experienced that forecasting and demand planning are:

- Workload-intensive especially for qualitative inputs
- Not addressed with enough time by sales and marketing team
- Have an overrated basic statistical forecasting
- Characterized by large portfolio of the products
- Run by few business models
- Problematic since not enough focus was introduced
- Performing below expectations.

Besides, many have faced challenges on how to:

- Distinguish promotions signal from baseline demand, and product mix shifts in volume
- Find the right balance between statistical forecasting and collaborative bottom-up inputs from demand organization
- Make stakeholders more accountable for forecast accuracy (Steutermann, Scott, & Tohamy, 2012).

How to turn it around, how to become more efficient and effective in your forecasting and demand planning process? To increase the process efficiency and effectiveness, you should walk away from "one-size-fits-all" forecasting and build "differentiated forecasting and demand planning" which is really about introducing tailored ways of working for different product segments. For some products, the process should be more labor-intensive or methods should be more sophisticated.

Differentiated forecasting consists of the elements as shown in Fig. 1.13:

- Qualitative inputs provided by various functions: sales, marketing and demand planning. Furthermore, sometimes business development should provide forecast inputs aligned to the best insights
- Statistical forecasting: functional system capabilities of basic and advanced statistical forecasting supported by demand planners or data scientists
- Product segmentation: instruments that will help you to introduce the focus on right materials, in a way to be aligned to your long-term objectives (e.g., revenue or profitable growth)
- Process measurement: measurement of all forecasting inputs (qualitative, quantitative), consensus unconstrained forecast with the agreed parameters aligned to the S&OP characteristics
- Demand planning capabilities: analytical and communication skills for a full set of capabilities and skills refer to the next chapter of the book.

The segmentation of a product portfolio by criteria such as "volume, predictability, channel/customer, promotional and seasonal items" with forecasting types assigned accordingly seems to be very important. The combination of a collaborative approach and statistical forecasting is "the" key (Steutermann et al., 2012).

What is the rationale behind differentiated forecasting and tailored ways of working?

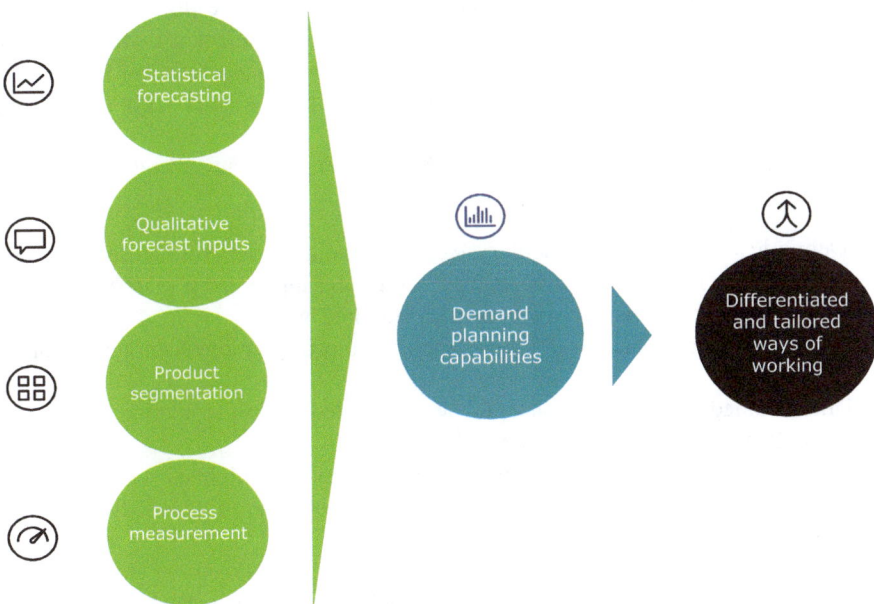

**Fig. 1.13** Differentiated forecasting building blocks

- Balance which function you ask for what type of input. Does is not sound like a waste of time to ask marketing and sales to provide inputs for extremely easy-to-forecast stable portfolio that has minor impact on revenue or profitable growth? Can demand planning be responsible for forecasting low-value contribution/high predictability product segments? They should be leading such a task while sales and marketing should only review on aggregated level their efforts, providing the right guidance.
- A sales team does not need to provide inputs for all SKUs/customers. Why not to leave in their forecasting portfolio those forecasting combinations which are critical to the business?
- Sales or marketing should own sales forecasts; however, the process design and process improvements should be done by demand planning. Sales and marketing could focus on their core activities and gain time for selling.
- Time being gained from transformation to "differentiated forecasting" can be leveraged for selling, analytical support, development of business risks and opportunities, in other words in more value-adding activities. Demand planning plays a crucial role in optimizing the time being spent on forecasting. Demand planning, considered as a function, must make those changes happening.
- Once you have most of the building blocks in place, it is most probably inevitable to consider the introduction of target settings. Target settings should be also done based on segments or at least groups of segments, the so-called blended targets.

The ABC/XYZ visualization matrix is a foundation of the differentiated forecasting and can make an impact on how a company organizes a demand review process, e.g., bottom-up, top-down qualitative forecast inputs, statistical forecasting and demand review preparation. Furthermore, there may be other ways to segment and sub-segment the demand; refer to Chap. 4.

Figure 1.14 illustrates an example on how a company can leverage the differentiated forecasting concept:

1. Define leading and supplementary techniques, e.g., input from sales and marketing (S&M), statistical forecasting (STAT) and inputs from marketing (M).
2. Set forecast performance targets in more tailored ways.
3. Share responsibility across different functions to provide more accurate forecasts.

Differentiated forecasting concept was elaborated in Implementing Integrated Business Planning (Kepczynski et al., 2018).

The definition of leading forecasting techniques should result in a list of qualitative or quantitative methods agreed as being the leading ones or the only ones. The segment BX and CX may be forecasted only with the use of statistical forecast, but they should be reviewed maybe even on an aggregated level during the demand review.

The definition of shared responsibility should result in a better balance of the workload for the inputs, reviews and the analysis of the forecast among sales, marketing and demand planning. It would make sense to allocate forecasting of a

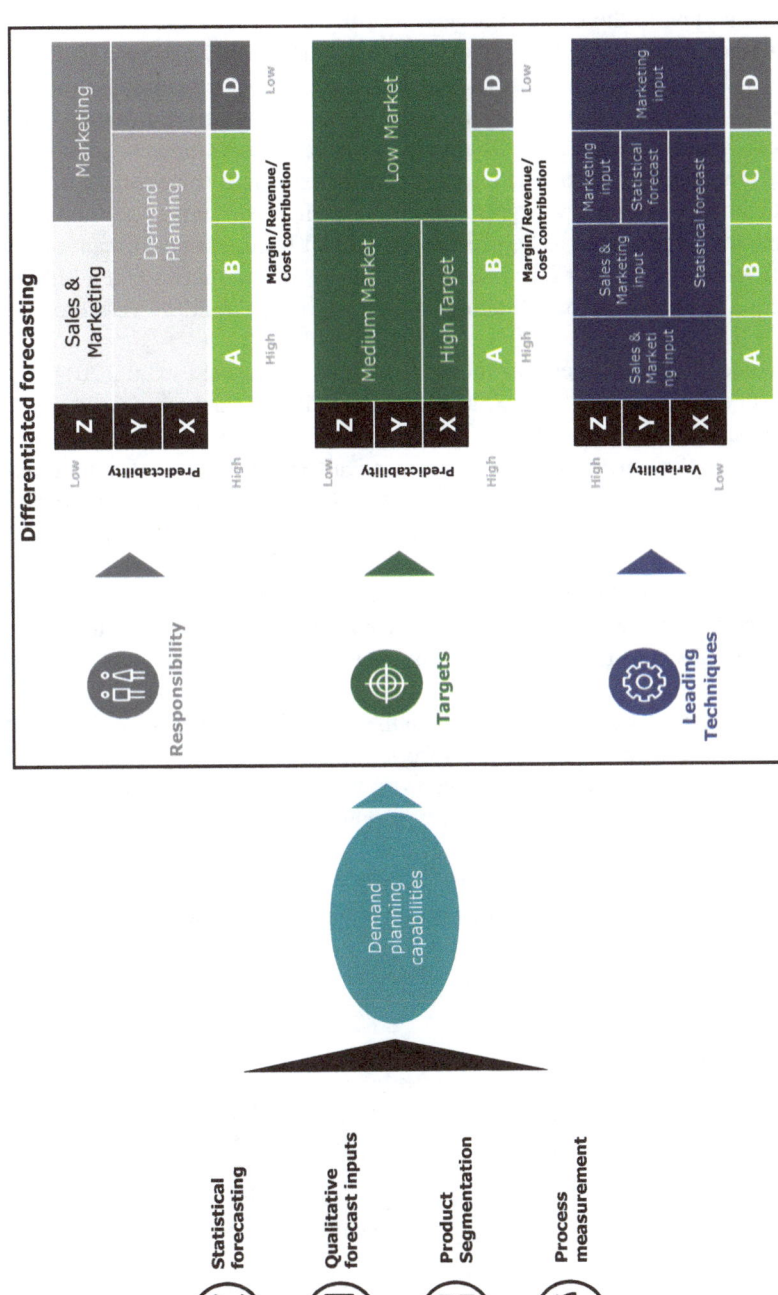

**Fig. 1.14** Differentiated forecasting—shared responsibilities, weighted targets, leading methods

certain group of products to the demand planning while still keeping those segments under review in the demand review meeting.

Last but not least is the topic of forecasting performance targets. Targets in differentiated forecasting should be established with a lot of sensitivities, and they should be shared among stakeholder group of sales, marketing and demand planning. Targets should be challenging but realistic. Therefore, a company should start the targets preparation with the data analysis of its past performances.

Do not start from visionary targets without knowing your current performances.

Performance targets need to be prepared based on historical performances with the identification of ABC/XYZ segments; an analysis of time series and a full year view is required. In addition, differentiated error targets should be set across the portfolio.

In Implementing Integrated Business Planning (Kepczynski et al., 2018), we have introduced this concept and explained in detail how a company could run the products, customers and services segmentation. It is possible to have few segmentations, e.g., for operational planning, tactical S&OP or even for long-term planning. With the use of segmentation, we will define different ways of working balancing the workload efforts, product importance and demand patterns.

In this book, we explain even further how to differentiate statistical forecasting methods depending on the underlying data patterns; refer to Chap. 3 about the "out-of-the-box" statistical forecasting models available in SAP IBP and to Chap. 4 for some custom ways of forecasting seasonal and intermittent products.

Once all of the differentiated forecasting building blocks are in place, a company will be able to map the whole concept against the ABC/XYZ matrix as per Fig. 1.15.

In Fig. 1.15, we share some examples from a chemical company's differentiated forecasting framework. On the left-hand side, the ABC/XYZ shows the leading techniques where the S&M is sales and marketing input and Stat is statistical forecasting. Then, in the visualization of the middle, the targets that vary per segment are shown, and finally, on the right-hand side, we assign the responsibility; e.g., S&M—sales and marketing provides key inputs, DP—demand planning takes a lead, M—marketing takes a lead.

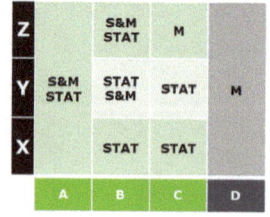 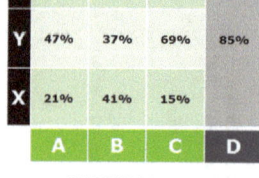 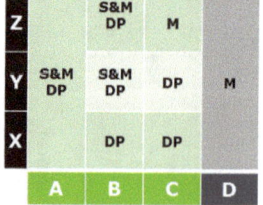

Leading and supplementary technique          wMAPE [%] targets          Shared responsibility

**Fig. 1.15**  Differentiated forecasting leading techniques, targets, shared responsibility

Now, you are ready to define the effective forecasting strategies:

In this use case, we will generate the consensus forecast based on forecasting strategies. Besides, below we share an example on how to leverage SAP IBP. The forecasting strategy will be defined as a characteristic (attribute) of the product/country and will be maintained against the ABC/XYZ segmentation, as per Fig. 1.16.

So far, we have defined the following strategies (see Fig. 1.17):

- "A"—automatic—consensus forecast defaulted from Statistical Fcst Qty. For "CX" products with small volatility and low profit contribution, the consensus forecast will be defaulted from statistical forecast.
- "AM"—automatic and manual—consensus forecast is calculated based on Statistical Fcst Qty and the manual input (s). In our example, we combine statistical forecast with demand planner input; however, it is possible to combine statistical forecast with many inputs (sales, marketing, demand planning) and use the weighted combined forecast concept to combined methods. For "XY" products due to its importance, we decided to combine the quantitative and qualitative inputs.
- "M"—manual—consensus forecast in our example will be defaulted to demand planner inputs, but it can be also defined with other combinations of inputs.

As a conclusion, it is important to understand that statistical forecasting may be done in further differentiated ways. We share the opinion that the more advanced techniques should be applied only where it makes sense.

For example, the seasonal and intermittent products are the ones for which you should use more analytical and statistical knowledge to run your predictions.

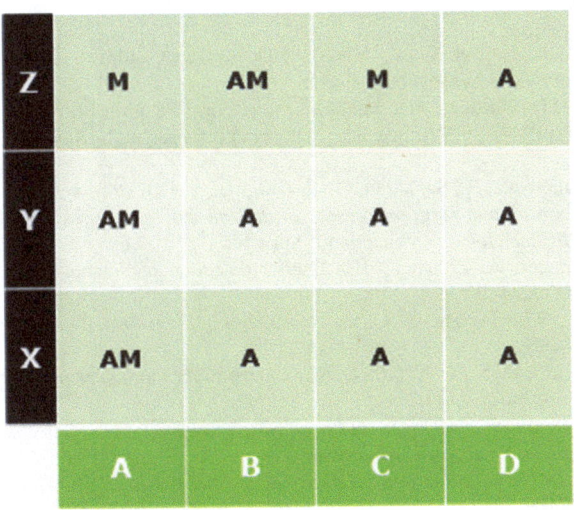

**Fig. 1.16** Forecasting strategies matrix visualization

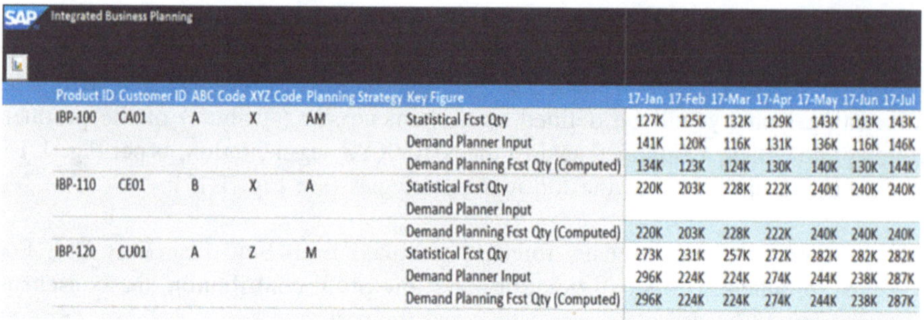

| Product ID | Customer ID | ABC Code | XYZ Code | Planning Strategy | Key Figure | 17-Jan | 17-Feb | 17-Mar | 17-Apr | 17-May | 17-Jun | 17-Jul |
|---|---|---|---|---|---|---|---|---|---|---|---|---|
| IBP-100 | CA01 | A | X | AM | Statistical Fcst Qty | 127K | 125K | 132K | 129K | 143K | 143K | 143K |
|  |  |  |  |  | Demand Planner Input | 141K | 120K | 116K | 131K | 136K | 116K | 146K |
|  |  |  |  |  | Demand Planning Fcst Qty (Computed) | 134K | 123K | 124K | 130K | 140K | 130K | 144K |
| IBP-110 | CE01 | B | X | A | Statistical Fcst Qty | 220K | 203K | 228K | 222K | 240K | 240K | 240K |
|  |  |  |  |  | Demand Planner Input |  |  |  |  |  |  |  |
|  |  |  |  |  | Demand Planning Fcst Qty (Computed) | 220K | 203K | 228K | 222K | 240K | 240K | 240K |
| IBP-120 | CU01 | A | Z | M | Statistical Fcst Qty | 273K | 231K | 257K | 272K | 282K | 282K | 282K |
|  |  |  |  |  | Demand Planner Input | 296K | 224K | 224K | 274K | 244K | 238K | 287K |
|  |  |  |  |  | Demand Planning Fcst Qty (Computed) | 296K | 224K | 224K | 274K | 244K | 238K | 287K |

**SAP** Integrated Business Planning

**Fig. 1.17** SAP IBP—forecasting strategies in differentiated forecasting concept

# References

Amy, B., & Partridge, R. (2017). *Unwrapping seasonality challenges*. Inbound Logistics.

Bobenstab, J. (2017). *A Nobel Prize-winning economist's four steps to minimize forecast bias*. ToolGroup.

Budzier, A., & Flyvbjerg, B. (2013) Making sense of the impact and importance of outliers in project management through the use of power laws. In *IRNOP Conference* (pp. 1–28).

Chase, C. W. (2009). *Demand-driven forecasting: A structured approach to forecasting*. Wiley.

Chase, C. W. (2016). *Next generation demand management: People, process, analytics, and technology*. Wiley.

Cherednichenko, S. (2005). *Outlier detection in clustering* (p. 57). University of Joensuu.

Cho, D. W., & Lee, Y. H. (2012). Bullwhip effect measure in a seasonal supply chain. *Journal of Intelligent Manufacturing, 23,* 2295–2305.

Cho, D. W. & Lee, Y. H. (2013) The value of information sharing in a supply chain with a seasonal demand process. *Computers & Industrial Engineering*, Elsevier Ltd.

Davis, M. (2011). *Customer value analytics for supply chain segmentation*. Gartner.

Gunst, R. F., Mason, R. L., & Hess, J. L. (2003). *Statistical design and analysis of experiment* (2nd ed.). Wiley.

Haldrup, N., Montañes, A., & Sansó, A. (2011) Detection of additive outliers in seasonal time series. *Journal of Time Series Econometrics*.

Kahneman, D. (2011). *Thinking, fast and slow*. New York: Penguin Books.

Kaiser, R., & Maravall, A. (1999). Seasonal outliers in time series. In *Banco de Espana Working Papers 9915*.

Kepczynski, R., Jandhyala, R., Sankaran, G., & Dimofte, A. (2018). *Integrated business planning —How to integrate planning processes, organizational structures and capabilities, and leverage sap IBP technology*. Switzerland: Springer.

Kriegel, H. P., Kroger, P., Zi, A. (2010). Outlier detection technique. In *SIAM International Conference on Data Mining*.

Makridakis, S. G., Wheelwright, S. C., & Hyndman, R. J. (1998). *Forecasting, methods and applications*. Wiley.

Mentzer, J. T., Jr., & Moon, M. A. (2004). *Sales forecasting management*. Thousand Oaks, CA: Sage Publications.

Metersky, J. (2003). *Weathering highs and lows*. Food Logistics.

NIST. (2012). *Engineering statistical handbook*.

Rumsfeld, D. (2002). *Donald Rumsfeld unknown unknowns!* Retrieved from https://www.youtube.com/watch?v=GiPe1OiKQuk.

Riskope Blog. (2011). *Black swan mania: using buzzwords can be a dangerous habit.* Retrieved from https://www.riskope.com/2011/06/14/black-swan-mania-using-buzzwords-can-be-a-dangerous-habit/.

Saffo, P. (2007). *Six rules for effective forecasting.* HBR.

Sap, A., & Planning, I. B. (1999). *SAP integrated business planning—outlier detection and correction* (pp. 1–9).

Seasonality Definition. (2017). *Lokad quantitative supply chain.*

Sharma, M., & Singh, M. (2013) Outlier detection in RFID datasets in supply chain process: A review. *CiteSeerX.*

Shukla, V., Naim, M. M., & Thornhill, N. F. (2012) Rogue seasonality detection in supply chains. *International Journal of Production Economics,* Elsevier.

Silver, E. A., Pyke, D. F., & Peterson, R. (1998). *Inventory management and production planning and scheduling.* New York: Wiley.

Seo, S., & Gary M. Marsh, P. D. (2006) A review and comparison of methods for detecting outliers in univariate data sets. *Department of Biostatistics, Graduate School of Public Health.*

Singh, H., Raman, S., & Wilson, E. (2015) *Practical considerations in forecast value added (FVA) analysis.* FORESIGHT.

Steutermann, S., Scott, F., & Tohamy, N. (2012). *Building an effective demand-planning process.* Gartner.

Watson, S. M., et al. (1991). *Detection of outliers in time series.* Leeds: Institute of Transport Studies, University of Leeds.

# Building Demand Planning Organization and Competencies

The demand planning organization along with the finance controller plays a vital role in Integrated Business Planning. They integrate and hold the whole IBP together. We see a huge value of connecting the demand management and the planning organization with finance under the Integrated Business Planning framework.

Demand planning is about developing an unconstrained forecast that needs the S&OP finalization. If this process reaches mature levels, it evolves into the sophisticated modeling of segmented channels. Very often this is combined with demand sensing which requires advanced techniques. When enhanced further to VMI, demand is made transparent and visible through the use of collaboration (Steutermann, Salley, & Lord, 2012).

Demand planners should drive the development of unconstrained forecasts, connect product planning and product review inputs, qualitative inputs from various functions and quantitative inputs from statistical forecasting. Demand planners should ensure that the development of the forecast starts from volume and it is followed by monetization. In no case should the forecast start from a value forecast—in simple terms, sales forecast should reflect what you predict to sell. The development of the forecast should aim to be efficient and focused. The development of the unconstrained forecast should aim to deliver realistic predictions with documented assumptions.

The demand plan should be based on a combination of statistical forecasts and inputs from sales, marketing and product management, and it should be backed by assumptions. Demand planners should update the related assumptions at least monthly (Crum & Palmatier, 2003).

Demand managers should drive the development of allocation plans based on supply signals. The demand manager, along with finance controllers, should lead development of the integrated business plan in volume and value and coordinate proper monetization of forecasts and plans. Demand managers should lead organizational integration between different types of planning (operational, tactical and long-term). Last but not least, their focus should be to maximize business returns

© Springer Nature Switzerland AG 2019
G. Sankaran et al., *Improving Forecasts with Integrated Business Planning*,
Management for Professionals, https://doi.org/10.1007/978-3-030-05381-9_2

and facilitate processes to find trade-offs and capture them in the integrated business plan.

Demand managers should be responsible for demand shaping, which is specific to industry and business strategy (consumer products, commodity products and medical device products). Demand shaping requires synchronization with the decision-making processes and agility throughout the internal processes (Steutermann et al., 2012).

Demand planning and demand management role(s) should be full-time roles (FTE role(s)) and not ad hoc activities. They should have the power to communicate agreed forecasts and plans, coordinate changes and become main go-to person for sales and marketing and supply and finance topics (Crum & Palmatier, 2003).

Let us visualize the key focus areas of the demand planner, demand manager, finance controller in the Integrated Business Planning framework (see Fig. 2.1).

As we see the demand planner and the demand manager roles have different focuses.

In the demand review process, product management, marketing, sales and demand planning excellence should provide an active contribution. Demand planner should ensure the right connection to those functions.

Sales and marketing should take the lead and should be accountable for forecasting. Sales and marketing should also be in charge of allowing a timely (two-sided) communication between the company and the customers. It means that they should not only sell a product, but as well get the needed information from the customers. As the demand planner and manager, it is important to avoid the vicious circle generated where the demand plan is unreliable due to the lack of time to provide inputs, while loads of time is spent chasing supply on one hand and apologizing to customers on the other hand (Crum & Palmatier, 2010).

## 2.1  Organizational Structures, Placement

### 2.1.1  Some Insights on Organizational Structures and Roles

There are several organizational models for demand planning and demand management. We highlight one organizational model applicable in two types of organizations. An organizational structure could be visualized as follows (Fig. 2.2). The proposed structure is composed of demand planning, demand management and demanding planning excellence including data scientist. We see in the combination of those functions into one unified organizational unit as the leading practice. The rationale to consolidate and assign integration tasks are the following:

- They are connected to sales and marketing.
- They are connected to supply and finance.
- They have experts to managerial roles.
- They lead development of forecasts and plans in volume, value.

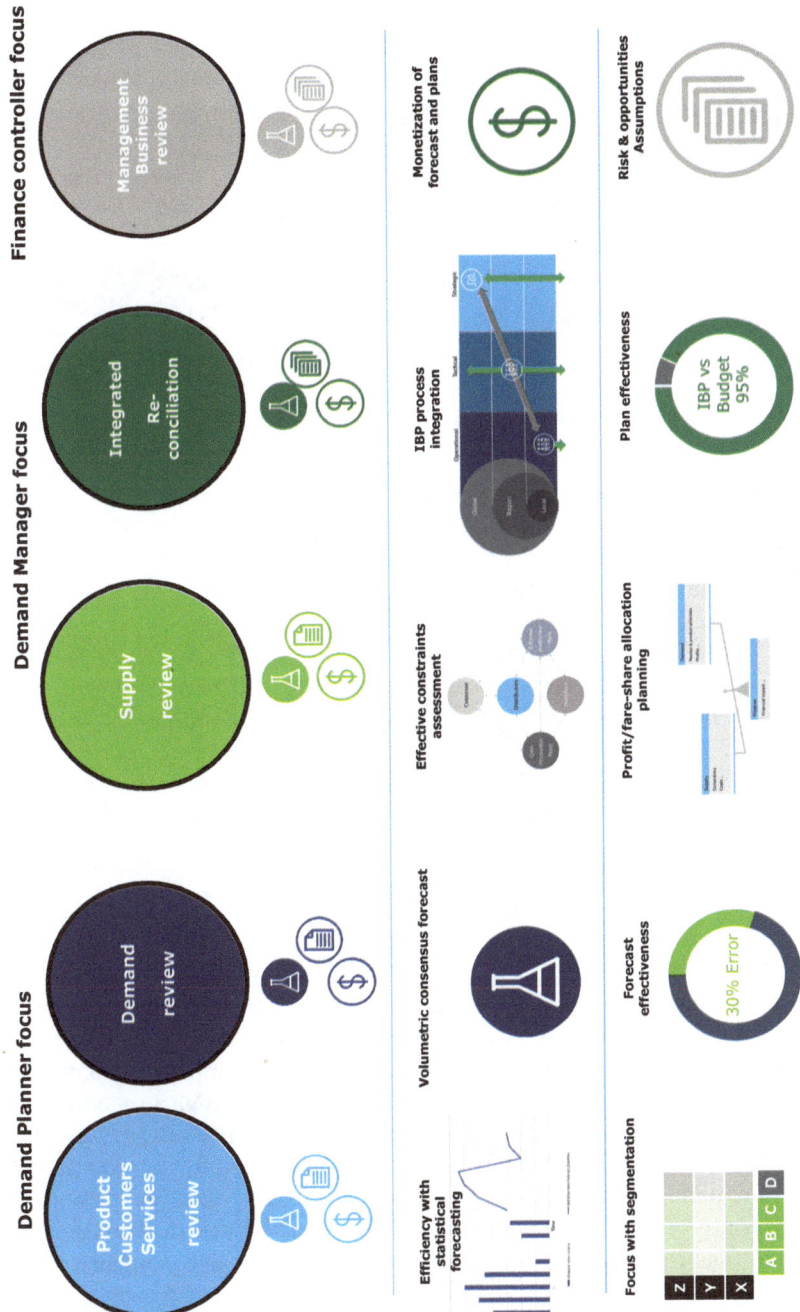

**Fig. 2.1** Demand planner, demand manager, finance controller focus in IBP

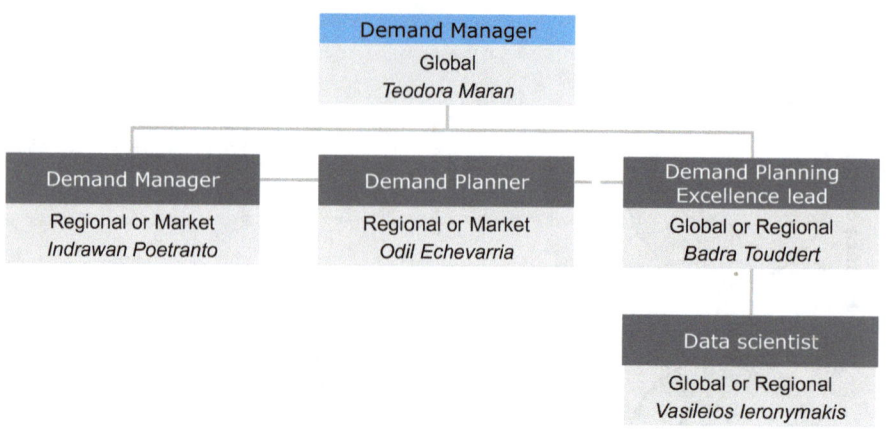

**Fig. 2.2** Demand planning and demand management org. structure model

– They capture and communicate assumptions.
– They oversee data management and system integration.
– They are experts in IBP system and can connect to IT.
– They are familiar with statistics.
– They monitor, improve, align process with leading practices.

The organizational structures of demand planning and demand management should enable the organizational integration required by IBP. Organizational integration should ensure the functional connection required between planning processes (operational, tactical, long-term), the operational connection between levels (local, regional and global), volume and value, risk and opportunities. There might be some differences in organization structures mainly because of

– Market-driven organizational inclination.
– Product-driven organizational inclination.

A mix of market and product-driven organizational model works in many companies. A mixed model is very often in place where specific business lines are more centralized around product management and locally around customers and channels. We have seen that in many companies that grow through an acquisition or mergers. We have observed that in the mixed model market strategy, P&L accountability is still in the country, but manufacturing footprint is shared; therefore, it still requires the product view on demand. We have seen one product line organized in a product-driven mode with distinctive sales and marketing, supply chains and finance teams, but the rest of the product lines organized in a market-driven mode with shared sales and marketing, finance and supply chain.

Here are few characteristics of the mixed model:

- Sales and marketing are organized by portfolio in the market.
- P&L accountability is typically above the market, normally on regional level for product line/brand/business line.
- Manufacturing footprint may be shared cross-countries.
- S&OP process is executed on market/brand/product line level.
- Demand planners are close to the demand signal in the market often organized by product line/brand.

Let us visualize the market- and product-driven organizational implications (see Fig. 2.3)

A **market-driven demand planning** organization may be described by the following characteristics:

- Sales and marketing are organized by market (countries).
- Customer base is organized by customer type/groups.
- Markets typically have profit and loss accountability.
- Big markets have in certain extend dedicated E2E supply chain/portfolio.
- Manufacturing footprint is not fully and commonly shared globally.
- The S&OP process is also executed on market level.
- Demand planners are close to the demand signals generated in the market.

The organizational model visualization for market-driven demand planning is shown in Fig. 2.4.

A **product-driven demand planning** organization may be described by the following characteristics:

- Sales and marketing are organized by portfolio (products).
- Customer base is organized by country; typically there is more than 1 sales rep per customer.
- P&L accountability is typically above the market, normally on a regional level for product line or brand or business line.
- Manufacturing assets are often commonly shared.
- Demand planners are aligned to sales structure, placed often the market sometimes per product line/brand. Demand planners can be per market if the brand is local.

The organizational model visualization for product-driven demand planning is shown in Fig. 2.5.

There are quite some different views on organizational models in demand planning. Gartner (Tohamy & Stiffler, 2012) reports that there are four qualitatively different models in demand planning organizations:

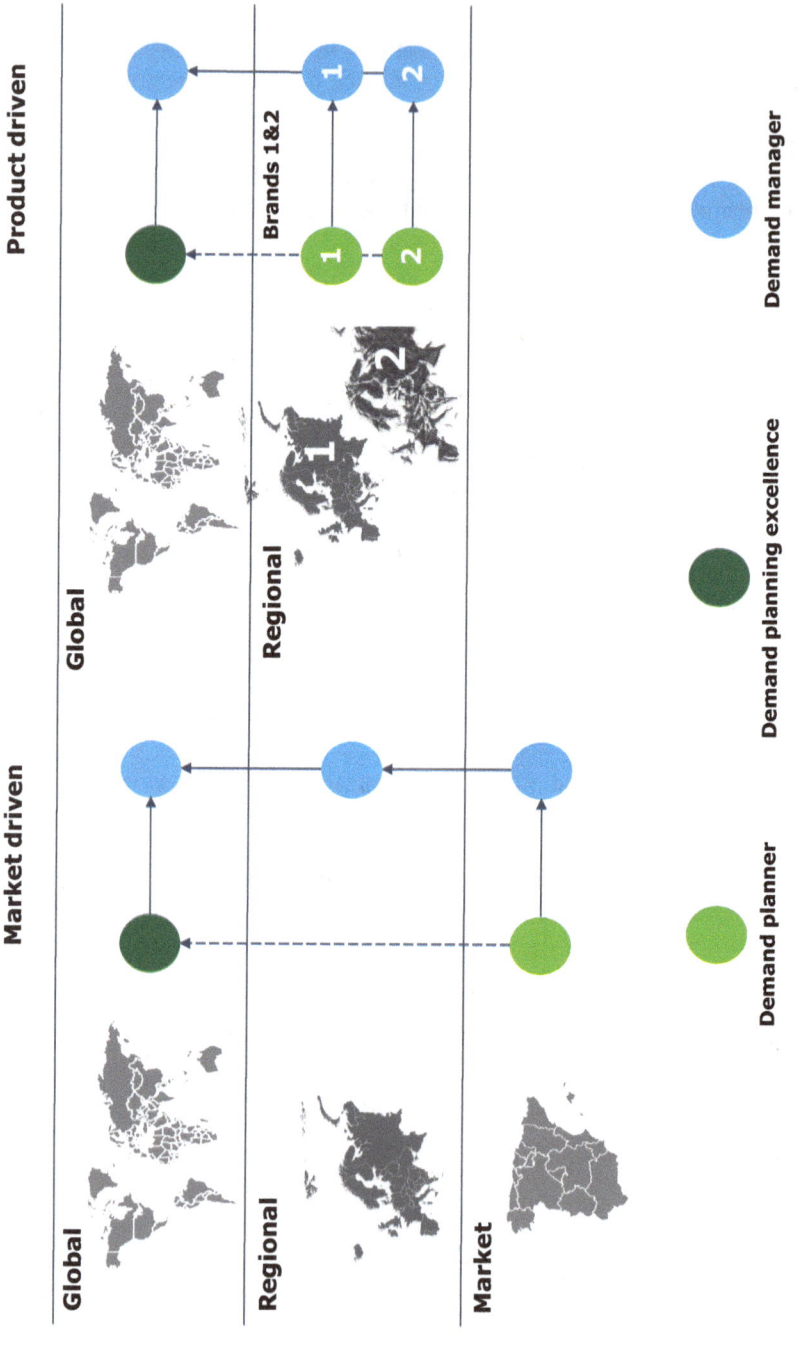

**Fig. 2.3** Market versus product-driven organization implications

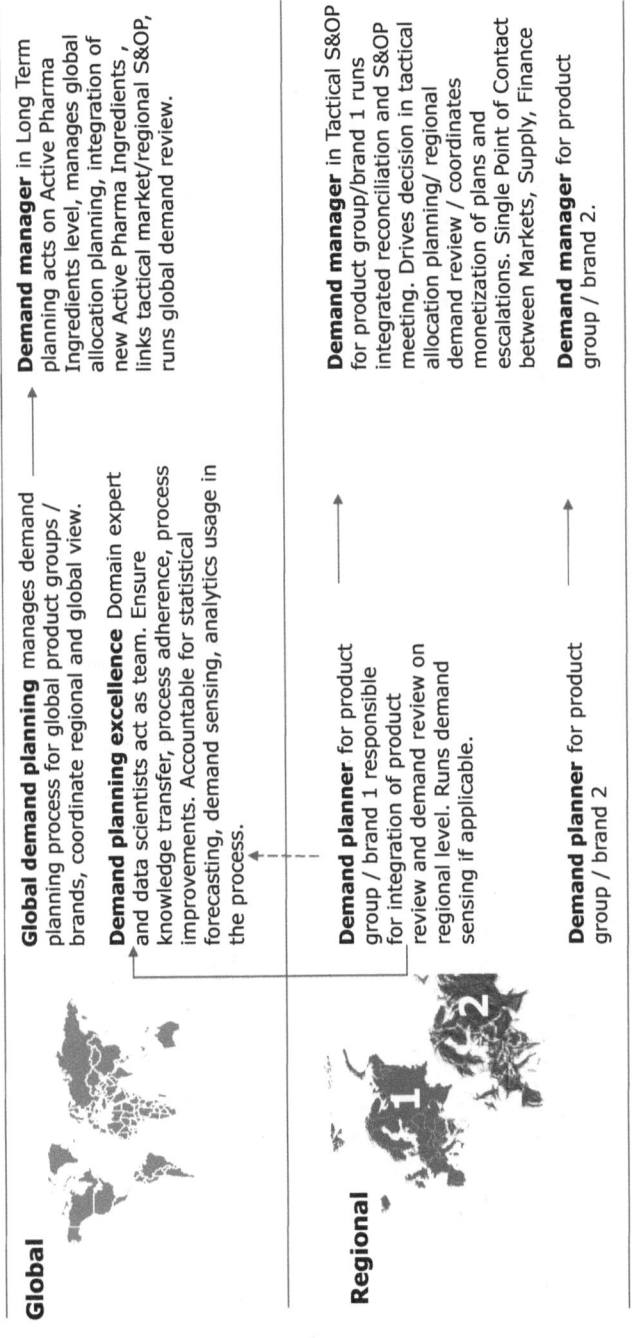

**Global**

**Global demand planning** manages demand planning process for global product groups / brands, coordinate regional and global view.

**Demand planning excellence** Domain expert and data scientists act as team. Ensure knowledge transfer, process adherence, process improvements. Accountable for statistical forecasting, demand sensing, analytics usage in the process.

**Demand manager** in Long Term planning acts on Active Pharma Ingredients level, manages global allocation planning, integration of new Active Pharma Ingredients , links tactical market/regional S&OP, runs global demand review.

**Regional**

**Demand planner** for product group / brand 1 responsible for integration of product review and demand review on regional level. Runs demand sensing if applicable.

**Demand planner** for product group / brand 2

**Demand manager** in Tactical S&OP for product group/brand 1 runs integrated reconciliation and S&OP meeting. Drives decision in tactical allocation planning/ regional demand review / coordinates monetization of plans and escalations. Single Point of Contact between Markets, Supply, Finance

**Demand manager** for product group / brand 2.

**Fig. 2.4** Market-driven demand planning organization

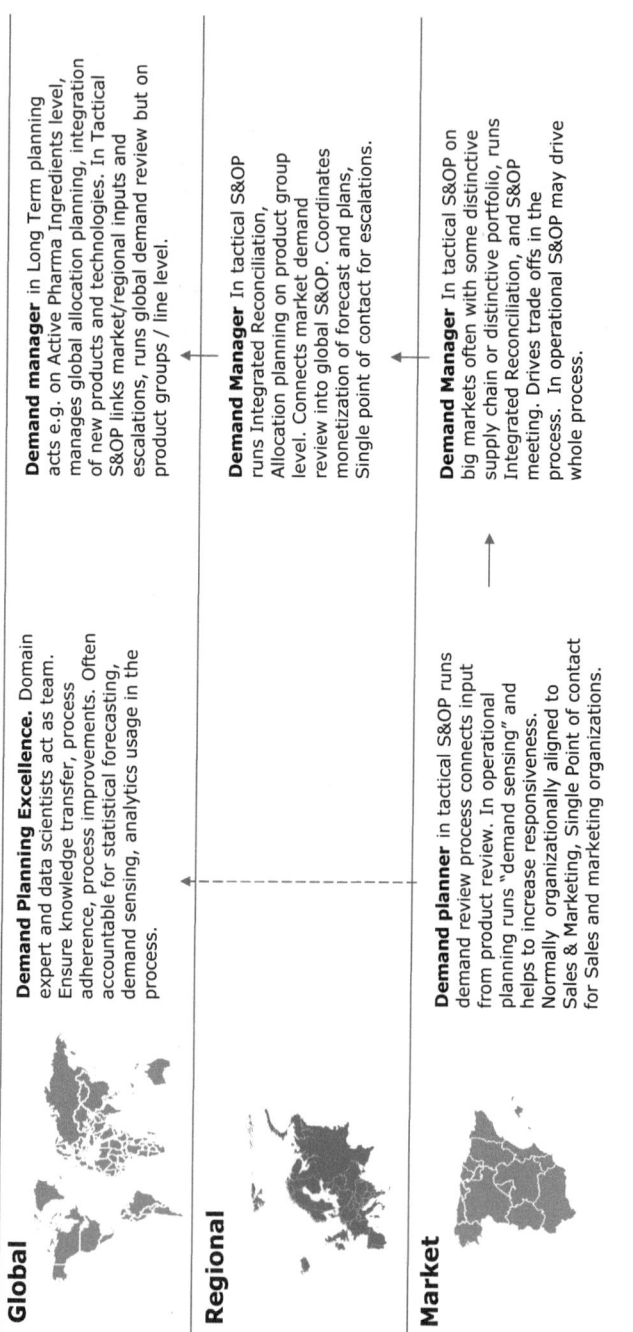

**Global**

**Demand Planning Excellence.** Domain expert and data scientists act as team. Ensure knowledge transfer, process adherence, process improvements. Often accountable for statistical forecasting, demand sensing, analytics usage in the process.

**Demand manager** in Long Term planning acts e.g. on Active Pharma Ingredients level, manages global allocation planning, integration of new products and technologies. In Tactical S&OP links market/regional inputs and escalations, runs global demand review but on product groups / line level.

**Regional**

**Demand Manager** In tactical S&OP runs Integrated Reconciliation, Allocation planning on product group level. Connects market demand review into global S&OP. Coordinates monetization of forecast and plans, Single point of contact for escalations.

**Market**

**Demand planner** in tactical S&OP runs demand review process connects input from product review. In operational planning runs "demand sensing" and helps to increase responsiveness. Normally organizationally aligned to Sales & Marketing, Single Point of contact for Sales and marketing organizations.

**Demand Manager** In tactical S&OP on big markets often with some distinctive supply chain or distinctive portfolio, runs Integrated Reconciliation, and S&OP meeting. Drives trade offs in the process. In operational S&OP may drive whole process.

**Fig. 2.5** Product-driven demand planning organization

- DP is decentralized and regionally dominated (11%).
- DP is decentralized and brand dominated (14%).
- DP is decentralized and market dominated (35%).
- DP is centralized as a corporate function for all brands and markets (40%). In this model, the process relies on the inputs from individual local markets and brand managers. The main advantage is the use of scale effects by exploiting the unified pool of planning talents and by common tech solutions.

Some other observations from Gartner studies (Salley & Griswold, 2015):

- **Younger companies** tend to have a decentralized demand planning (DP) embedded to the commercial and merchandising unit.
- **When the company becomes more mature,** the DP transforms to the centralized function led by a supply chain organization, which invests in initiatives to improve collaboration with trading partners. It also co-owns metrics with partners having thus an easier way to analyze the forecast error.
- **The most mature companies** are sharing DP services across the entire organization through the centralized delivery model. This approach allows tracking down the customer level with the corresponding financial influence analyzed. Also, it allows what-if scenarios with risk assessment. The DP team takes a part in the demand shaping.

You should consider that demand planning and demand management organizational structure has to be aligned to the processes (long-term, tactical and operational) and to the levels (local, regional, global) at which they operate. Misalignment will cause major problems in operating globally and across many brands.

Let us briefly discuss the role of demand planning organization in operational planning, tactical S&OP and long-term planning.

**Demand Planning organization in Operational planning**: for market or product-driven organizations it is required to make decisions that affect cost to serve, availability, profits, and that need to be aligned with the tactical S&OP plan (in volume and value). Decisions should not be left either to logistics and operations department or to sales only. Demand planners and managers should ensure that trade-offs will be discussed and agreed and that short-term objectives will be put on scale with mid-term objectives.

More often demand managers and not demand planners ensure:

- An organizational link between operational and tactical S&OP process
- X-functional but operational collaboration
- A decision that takes trade-offs into consideration.

This process could be about predicting and evaluating the impact of the performance of a campaign, a promotion on the consensus forecast. Often, predictions in operational planning are optimized with the use of demand sensing.

**Demand planning organization in Tactical S&OP**: this process requires the involvement of both roles to develop and agree on market unconstrained forecasts and to integrate the non-standard revenue and cost drivers into the Integrated Business Plan.

Demand planners and demand managers should ensure:

- Timely execution of the process, development and agreement of unconstrained forecast
- Coordination of financial elements required in the monetization of the forecasts and plans
- Follow-up on actions escalated in the operational S&OP
- Organizational link between tactical S&OP and long-term S&OP process
- X-functional, cross the levels, but tactical collaboration
- Coordination of management or business risks and opportunities
- Agreement in volumetric and monetized Integrated Business Plan.

This process is supported by qualitative and quantitative methods. It is critical that the demand manager with the demand planning team drives the definition of the differentiated forecasting framework.

**Demand planning organization in *MONTHLY LONG-TERM PRODUCT PLANNING***: this process requires the involvement of both functions from development of statistical unbiased forecast to balancing supply with demand and consensus, expressed in the volumetric and monetized Integrated Business Plan.

Demand planners and demand managers should ensure:

- Timely execution of the process, development and agreement of long-term product long-term unconstrained forecast
- Coordination of financial elements required in monetization of the forecasts and plans
- Follow-up on actions escalated in tactical S&OP
- Organizational link between tactical S&OP and long-term S&OP process
- X-functional, cross the levels, but long-term collaboration
- Coordination of management or business risks and opportunities
- Agreement in volumetric and monetized Integrated Business Plan.

This process could be about predicting dependent and independent demand for long-term forms of the product, e.g., active ingredient in the chemical industry.

**Demand planning organization in *LONG-TERM ANNUAL PLANNING***: this process requires a very strong business acumen and a well-rounded individual who can help the senior management concluding on their long-term visions and making them tangible.

Senior demand managers could support marketing to ensure that:

- Inputs from various functions are prepared and assessed in timely manner.
- Long-term initiatives impacts are expressed in a tangible way and that the assumptions are captured and clear.
- Business risks and opportunities are coordinated and managed.
- Organizational links between long-term S&OP, tactical S&OP, budgeting are done once per year.
- X-functional, cross the levels, but long-term collaboration.

This process often is about predicting long-term business plans prepared on aggregated levels, considering changes in the market, portfolio of services, etc.

For further explanation and examples about planning types, e.g., operational, tactical and long-term, refer to Implementing Integrated Business Planning (Kepczynski et al., 2018b).

This table (Fig. 2.6) should help you to understand where specific demand managers and demand planners linked to financial controller's roles could be organizationally and functionally placed.

The demand planner, demand manager and finance controller should have their "integrator role" aligned to planning type and experience needed (see Fig. 2.6).

## 2.1.2   Some Insights on Organizational Placement

A commonly asked question is: Where should demand planning and demand management organizationally belong to? This question is very important since the organizational placement decides on the key performance indicators assigned to the functions and drives behaviors as well as typical bias.

We have seen two main types of organizational placements of demand planning organization in supply chain and operations or sales and marketing.

Each of the organizational placements brings some challenges and opportunities, but what should it really be? On one hand, demand planning and demand management should be placed in the organization as close as possible responsible for sales/demand. On the other hand, they should help the organization to find the right balance between short- and long-term objectives. Most probably marketing would be the most desired place for demand planning organization.

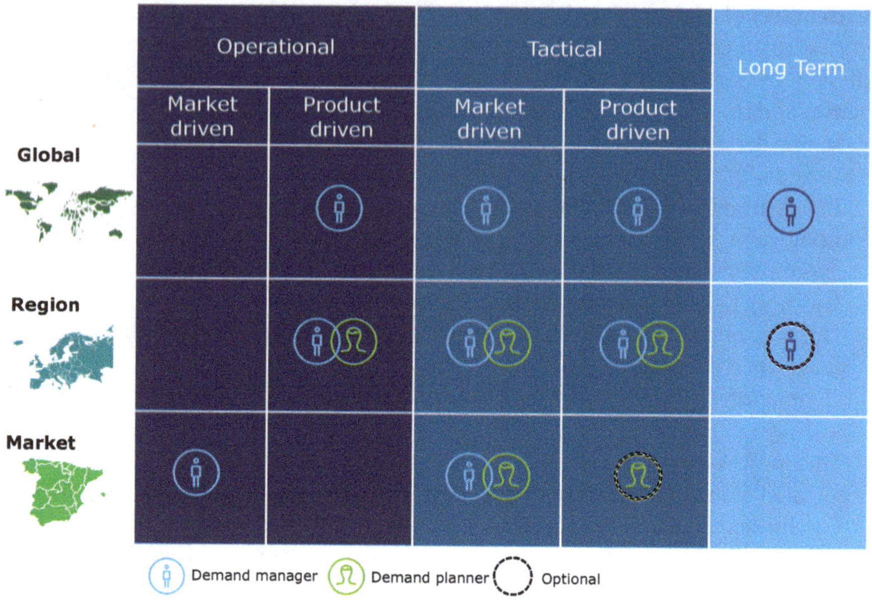

| | Operational | | Tactical | | Long Term |
|---|---|---|---|---|---|
| | Market driven | Product driven | Market driven | Product driven | |
| **Global** | | 👤 | 👤 | 👤 | 👤 |
| **Region** | | 👤👥 | 👤👥 | 👤👥 | 👤 |
| **Market** | 👤 | | 👤👥 | 👥 | |

👤 Demand manager   👥 Demand planner   ⭕ Optional

**Fig. 2.6** Minimum representation of roles to connect planning processes and levels

Mark Moon says that in an ideal world the forecasting group should be directly reporting to the COO without any organizational bias from demand, supply or finance. Nevertheless, in the real world it is good when forecasting reports somewhere to demand units, e.g., in manufacturing companies to sales and marketing and in retail to merchandising (Moon, 2013).

Let us share some considerations when deciding on organizational placement of demand planning organization:

– Which functions have the biggest chance to balance short-term and long-term objectives?
– Which functions have the biggest chance to integrate various groups of stakeholders in the market to a global level?
– Which functions have the biggest chance to integrate functionally sales and marketing, supply chain and operations (incl. manufacturing), finance and business development?
– Which functions have the biggest chance to establish x-functional Center of Expertise and drive transformation supported by experts and led by senior management?

Where is the demand planning organization built typically? (Tohamy et al., 2012),

- The survey shows that more than half of the respondents have the demand planning organization within sales/marketing and this often results in positively biased forecasts.
- About a third of the respondents indicated that the demand planning belongs to supply chain.

In contrast, the organizations that moved the demand planning ownership to the supply chain cited several reasons for the move:

- Objectivity—Buyers and merchants tend to show a bias toward overforecasting.
- End-to-end perspective—Visibility to all the three levels of demand gives the supply chain the complete end-to-end picture of the expected demand.
- Skill set alignment—Buyers and merchants typically focus more on qualitative skill sets. Demand planning requires a more quantitative focus (Griswold, 2015).

Demand planning and demand management normally should be as close as possible to the organizations that own sales; therefore, it is recommended to position demand management within sales org (market proximity and sales accountability) until the process is stabilized (Crum & Palmatier, 2003). Furthermore, the key role of demand manager should be a full-time position, and it should sit within the demand organization at least while the process is being defined/transformed (Crum & Palmatier, 2010).

A Gartner research done by Steutermann shows that there might be a correlation between centralized demand planning functions and more accurate forecasts. Centralized organizations might provide:

- Better training or career opportunities for demand planners.
- More statistical modeling, reducing forecast bias introduced by an overreliance on collaborative forecasting methods.
- Benefits from proximity to other centralized functions.

There seems not to be any correlation between the numbers of SKUs managed and forecast accuracy (Steutermann, 2016).

## 2.2  Responsibilities, Interactions, Size of a Team

Demand planning, demand management and demand planning excellence have their focus areas of responsibilities and key collaboration functions as per visualized in Fig. 2.7.

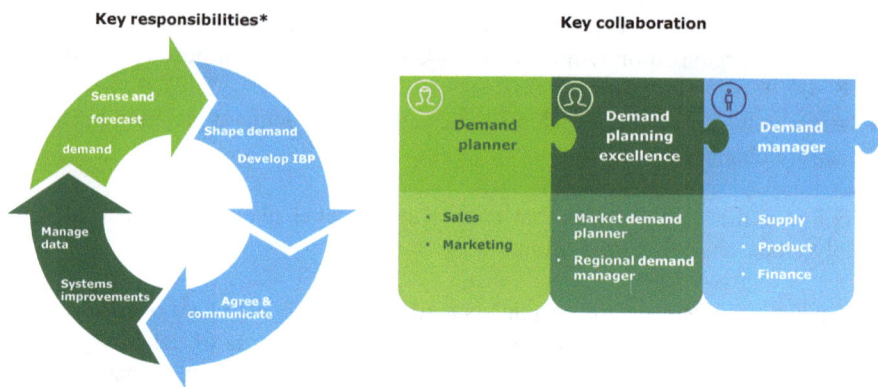

**Fig. 2.7** Demand planning organization and their responsibilities, collaboration. *Source* Revised based on own experience and Crum, Palmatier—Oliver Wight and APICS (2003)

The key to understand the needed responsibilities of demand planners, demand planning excellence and demand managers is the knowledge about with whom they should interact.

Demand planners should interact mainly with sales and marketing and finance in the assessment of the forecast inputs and the development of the consensus market forecast in volume and value. This role is very operational, as it has to ensure that the team does perform the activities on time.

Besides, the demand managers' interactions may change depending on the planning types and horizons in which a particular role acts. In the tactical S&OP, the demand manager should focus on the interactions with finance, supply and less with product marketing organization. Demand managers in the operational planning should focus on the interactions on sales leaders, customer service and operations (Logistic) functions. Demand managers in long-term planning work with marketing, business planning and development, manufacturing, research and development.

Demand management and planning can be considered as the bridge between product development, brand management, marketing and sales and operations. Bridging with product development and brand management allows, from a lean perspective, to keep only the product features considered valuable for the clients, while meeting customers' needs with the right price and within the right time. Furthermore, it helps considering demand planning as a part of the IBP. Bridging marketing means allowing communication and working across internal boundaries to manage market risks and opportunities. Bridging sales means defining and conforming priorities with the people who are mostly in contact with the clients. Bridging operations allows internal highly specialized operations people not to consider sales and marketing as an enemy (APICS—module 1.G—Demand Planning, 2015).

The demand planning excellence focus should be on the stakeholders who provide inputs to the IBP planning framework, e.g. sales and marketing, in or above the market, to the market demand planners. It is critical that demand planning excellence has a right combination of business process domain and scientific (data scientist) knowledge and skills. Only both set of skills (process and data) can provide the appropriate approach to change management and improvement.

As you see from the illustrated overview, demand planning and demand management are like two sides of the same medal. One is focusing on sales and marketing and the other is focusing on supply, product and finance organizations. Both roles together should help the organization to achieve horizontal and vertical integration between planning types and horizons.

The definition of roles, competencies and interactions is critical for the whole team.

As an example, many chemical companies have struggled with a proper definition of the roles that affect, drive and lead demand planning and demand management. They have been overlapping roles and titles like asset manager, product manager, commodity manager and inventory manager. These different roles sometimes conflict with the need to manage cross-functional processes that enable balanced demand management optimization across the value chain. Consequently, it is recommended to define the demand management roles that will provide the leadership and the influence skills necessary to propose and pursue an improved demand planning (Lord, 2013).

## 2.2.1 Responsibilities (Incl. Job Profiles) and Impact

Below you will find a detail explanation of demand manager, demand planner, demand planning excellence responsibilities and the impacts of those roles, aligned to the following categories (see Fig. 2.7):

– Forecast and sense demand
– Shape Demand and Develop Integrated Business Plan.

# Demand Manager

──────── Role Definition ────────

Coordinates monetization of forecasts and plans, ensures that business risk and opportunities are captured and understood. Leads development of integrated business plan.

Responsibilities

**Forecast & sense demand**

- Ensures Finance & Pricing process involvement to monetize volumetric forecasts
- Coordinates price, cost and margin information required for standard and scenario planning flows
- Ensures proper connection of forecasting and planning at both the detail and aggregated level
- Aligns and integrates out of cycle forecast adjustments in sync with tactical S&OP calendar of activities
- Supports product range review
- Ensures product customer segmentation measures are aligned to company objectives e.g. profitable growth, top line growth

**Shape Demand & Develop Integrated Business Plan**

- Ensures Finance & Pricing process involvement to monetize volumetric plans and scenario planning
- Ensures preparation for scenario planning of business risks & opportunities are prepared. Enables the consensus and decision making process
- "Ensures business risk & opportunities are captured & evaluated in product, demand, supply and reconciliation in volume and value.
- Reviews and analyses unconstrained forecasts and integrated business plan results in relation to the business direction
- Ensures assumptions for scenario planning are captured and agreed
- Drives cross-functional collaborations and consensus approach to influence the market demand and maximize business returns
- Harmonizes promotional plans, price changes, new/discontinued products with demand forecasts and manage implications on supply planning
- Reviews and assesses risk to supply and demand variability and identifies opportunities to manage and mitigate risk (gap exposure and gap closure)
- Point of contact for demand and supply planning in order to manage supply and demand imbalance to achieve fit desired customer service levels, inventory targets and safety stock levels

- Confers with stakeholders regarding price optimization opportunities and establishes an alignment on how to manage supply / operations upsides e.g., excess stock/capacity, etc.
- Develops the rules and methods for demand management based on business priority
- Ensures alignment and consistency by coordinating substitutions and replacements in the operational and tactical processes
- Ensures that profitable allocation planning decisions are taken timely and are integrated with the order to cash process
- Helps to resolve availability and allocation issues
- Aligns with supply and marketing Phase in/phase out activities
- Ensures IBP stakeholders understand supply response constraints
- Drives demand management of substitutions, shortages and constraints to maximize business return
- Ensures that profitable allocation is linked to O2C

|  |  |
|---|---|
| **Agree & Communicate**  | <ul><li>Ensures the forecast error impact on the business performance is analyzed, understood and improvements actions are agreed</li><li>Helps to expose gap to budget and manage gap closure</li><li>Timely communicates integrated business plan information to all stakeholders</li><li>Manages the decision making and communication for Integrated Reconciliation and SOP meetings and preparations</li><li>Builds consensus among the stakeholders on the integrated business plan in volume and value, assumptions and risk & opportunities</li><li>Reviews and challenges the unconstrained market forecast based on data and performance metrics. Equips sales and marketing management with inputs to be used in demand consensus review meetings</li><li>Ensures organizational integration between operational and tactical S&OP</li><li>Ensures organizational integration between tactical and Long Term Planning</li><li>Day to day contact person for operations and finance</li><li>Supports Finance and Management with gap exposure to budget and monitoring of actions to close the gaps.</li><li>Ensures the Integrated business plans are timely agreed and integrated with supply, finance and BI systems</li><li>Supports Sales, Marketing, Finance in the budgeting process</li></ul> |

- Helps the organization to make IBP decisions aligned to business goals by maximizing the business return
- Ensures that bottom up and top down views are reconciled in volume and value
- Provides the finance IBP with full year outlook vs annual budgets
- Drives that all non-standard cost and revenue drivers are incorporated in IBP process / data waterfall. Drives that IBP becomes the business management process
- Drives that financial planning is incorporated into IBP to strengthen it as business management process

**Manage Data, Systems & Improvements**

- Champions the data driven process improvements
- Champions the efficient usage of analytics in IBP
- Champions the efficient usage of the IBP system
- Coordinates data integrity and data quality activities
- Makes recommendations to enhance business processes and helps identify opportunities to improve operational efficiencies by consulting with functional teams such as sales and marketing, operations and finance on integration with e.g. Budgeting
- Champions the transformation towards demand not invoice driven forecasting
- Ensures that IBP data models enables translation to supply/capacity and financial planning

# Demand Manager

**Role Impact**

Maximizes business return, ensures the most profitable decisions, and helps organization to achieve balance between short term and mid to long term goals, lead development of tradeoffs.

| | Business Impact | Skills & Competences |
|---|---|---|
| **Forecast & sense demand**  | ▪ Supports agreement on consensus unconstrained forecast | ▪ Analytical and problem solving skills<br>▪ Statics forecasting awareness<br>▪ Understanding of product lifecycle management<br>▪ Focused on meeting deadlines and achieving goals. Ability to lead team and build team competencies<br>▪ Project management<br>▪ Practical knowledge of Sales & Marketing and Customer Service activities<br>▪ Mandatory strong business acumen, company policies and strategies knowledge, industry and competitor knowledge |
| **Shape Demand & Develop Integrated Business Plan**  | ▪ Develops the Integrated business plan covering a holistic company business model in volume and value | ▪ Able to translate company goals and Long Term plans into tactical and operational requirements.<br>▪ Persistent and goal oriented to drive results towards the Long Term objectives of the organization. Ability to make decisions aligned to Long Term goals<br>▪ Supply chain and finance processes awareness<br>▪ Understanding of forecast and plan monetization<br>▪ Proven leadership of S&OP Sales or Marketing functions<br>▪ Ability to coordinate demand shaping |
| **Agree & Communicate** | ▪ Leads stakeholder to timely achieved agreement on assumptions, risks, opportunities scenarios and integrated business plans | ▪ Ability to communicate in concise manner with managers and senior managers. Collaboration skills |

- Provides clear and concise recommendations to senior management about risk, opportunities, assumptions, volumetric & monetized plans and gap to budget
- High levels of personal integrity when dealing with sensitive and confidential data
- Ability to influence IBP stakeholders
- Ability to manage relationships & network
- Influential and charismatic business believer
- Able to find consensus and negotiate actions, ownership

| **Manage Data, Systems & Improvements** | - Champions usage of data, analytics and the IBP system. Sets directions for process improvements | - Integrated Business Planning expert<br>- IBP system and analytical tools awareness<br>- Ability to motivate, encourage to generate & build on new ideas<br>- Able to identifying conflicting interests from sales, marketing, finance and supply functions |

# Demand Planner — Role Definition —

Develops in coordination with other functions unconstrained forecast in volume and value. Captures assumptions linked to demand review. Maintains and continuously improve the forecasting processes and systems.

Responsibilities

**Forecast & sense demand**

- Support sales and marketing in timely development of unconstrained forecast inputs
- Assist sales and marketing in usage of forecast error metrics when developing / assessing forecast
- Facilitate development of forecast with qualitative inputs linked to best insights e.g. provided at multiple levels of aggregation (bottom up, top down) across multiple time horizons
- Support development and approval of portfolio/customer segmentation. Coordinate lifecycle status management.
- Support marketing / portfolio managers in maintaining phase -in and phase out

- Support marketing in sample & free of charge items forecasting
- Help to assess data inputs used in integrated business planning (shipments, orders, POS, pricing, margins, stocks, supply plans)
- Act as data manager for IBP
- Sense-check quantitative (statistical forecast) & qualitative inputs to highlight any unexpected trends.
- Detect and correct outliers on data set being used as input for statistical forecasting
- Develop proposal of consensus unconstrained market forecast. Lead team to achieve consensus on unconstrained market forecast and associated assumptions. Documents assumptions, tasks from Demand review
- Introduce usage of weighted combined forecast as one of the methods to prepare consensus demand market forecast
- Review regularly the parameters that are incorporated in statistical forecast models (time series) to achieve greater accuracy.
- Develop and maintain statistical forecast models, gather, analyse and validate all data that will be used in statistical forecasts
- Ensure that assumptions are captured
- Ensure that Product and Demand risk & opportunities are being discussed, captured in the system and approved
- Ensures measurement and communication of analysed process metrics and KPIs (effectiveness, efficiency, process adherence)
- Continuously reviews and challenges the drivers and assumptions supporting the unconstrained market forecast
- Analyses and informs significant forecast changes and trends-levels-seasonality changes

- Ensures demand drivers are known and documented (e.g. tender orders, price changes, PI/PO cannibalization, sales and marketing campaigns)
- Analyses actual/forecast linked to different material/commercial dimensions
- Understands demand signals and drivers and converts them into forecast inputs
- Ensures market insights are captured in qualitative forecast
- Ensures that all Demand review meetings deliverables are achieved

**Shape Demand & Develop Integrated Business Plan**

- Ensure usage of forecast/demand variability in safety stock planning
- Supports portfolio managers/product marketing in defining substitutions and replacements rules
- Co-refines regression forecast model variables to ensure scenario planning for key business risk & opportunities
- Helps to Align forecast adjustments between Phase In & Phase outs. Interacts with stakeholders to achieve suitable supply responses
- Supports demand managed in development profitable allocation planning and management
- Reviews levels and rules in exception management process on a regular basis and recommends appropriate revisions
- Focus stakeholders on business critical products/customers and uses exception management
- incorporates demand sensing algorithms in the operational S&OP forecast review, monitoring of tactical S&OP performance between the cycle changes

**Agree & Communicate**

- Interacts with Sales & Marketing to understand and to align on demand forecast drivers and assumptions
- Utilizes a collaborative and consensus approach to ensure that current and accurate information is incorporated in unconstrained market demand forecasts
- Facilitates demand forecast review meetings, prepares all required information, data, actions, visualizations, and assumptions
- Implements controlled processes to introduce between the cycles forecast and response changes
- Coordinates that financial elements are provided on time and at the desired level to ensure revenue, profit projections and gap exposure to budget
- Ensures regular refreshes of information, knowledge about the process, system in sales, marketing and finance stakeholder group
- Drives preparation for operational S&OP meeting
- Highlights changes and exceptions in the demand review process
- Ensures that detail forecasts on product level are verified in the demand review preparation
- Day to day system and data expert, contacts person for sales and marketing

- Collaborates with marketing and sales to understand market drivers
- Drives forecasting process stakeholders to consensus on demand review meetings
- Ensures that unconstrained forecast is timely agreed and integrated within the supply organization
- Ensures awareness and transparency in the demand review process
- Helps sales and marketing to validate how market trends and demand drivers are captured in the forecast
- Is the technical owner and introduces forecast changes in the consensus unconstrained forecast
- Communicates performance of PI/PO
- Leads preparation of Pre-SOP and SOP meetings
- Leads Pre-SOP meeting

| | |
|---|---|
| **Manage Data, Systems & Improvements**  | - Leads the organization to introduce differentiated ways of working to increase process effectiveness and efficiency<br>- Leads the organization to incorporate tailored forecast error incentives for forecast input stakeholders<br>- Helps the organization to move towards demand driven, and not invoice driven, forecasting<br>- Identifies and leads the data driven improvements. Embeds the usage of analytics in the decision making process<br>- Leverages, where possible, CPFR concepts and/or integrates customer data<br>- Ensures data models enable connections of aggregates and details and that forecasting can be aligned to best insights<br>- Introduces the Forecast Value-add Analysis<br>- Collaborates with Demand Planning excellence in the development of regression and more advanced models<br>- Manage the data used in demand forecasting/planning and function as system manager for IBP stakeholders<br>- Aligns best practices across stakeholder groups and ensures the process alignment and consistency by organizing regular refresher trainings on tools, processes, systems, rules and KPIs<br>- Ensures that the whole documentation for demand forecasting processes and systems is up-to-date and complies with company/global standards<br>- Organizes and coordinates the necessary system trainings<br>- Supports tactical S&OP stakeholders with data analysis<br>- Continuously reviews data, identifies unusual occurrences, searches for explanations and develops corrective actions to prevent such occurrences<br>- Coordinates quality assurance of the IBP system master data<br>- Drives the process and IBP data modelling |

Below you will find a detail explanation of the demand planner role, its business impact and the competencies to help achieving the desired outcome.

# Demand   Planner    ———  **Role Impact**  ———

Ensures agreement and drives timely execution of demand review, keeps knowledge of the stakeholder group up to date. Keeps process adherence under control. Initiates process improvements.

|  | Business Impact | Skills & Competences |
|---|---|---|
| **Forecast & sense demand**  | ▪ Drives development of consensus unconstrained forecast in volume and value prepared based on current and accurate market information and assumptions. | ▪ Analytical, data-processing and problem solving skills<br>▪ Solid practical experience in using of statistical forecasting fundamentals<br>▪ Ability to gather and process data, execute quantitative and qualitative data analysis<br>▪ Understanding of product lifecycle management<br>▪ Focused on meeting deadlines and achieving goals. Ability to work with limited or without supervision<br>▪ Able to organize own and others work<br>▪ Awareness of Sales & Marketing Activities |
| **Shape Demand & Develop Integrated Business Plan**  | ▪ Embeds exception management driven process and entry methods aligned to best insights | ▪ Persistent and goal oriented to drive results toward tactical and operational objectives of the organization<br>▪ Understanding of forecast monetization<br>▪ Proven understanding of S&OP and Integrated Business Planning<br>▪ Very often industry knowledge is important but not always mandatory<br>▪ High attention to details |

| | | |
|---|---|---|
| **Agree & Communicate**  | ▪ Improves communication and relationships among planners, sales, marketing and finance, which will allow effective knowledge sharing and an optimal consensus forecast | ▪ Ability to communicate in concise manner with experts and managers. Collaboration skills<br>▪ Ability to provide clear and concise recommendations to sales, marketing, finance regarding demand review proposed decisions and assumptions<br>▪ Ability to leverage information<br>▪ Ability to influence sales and marketing stakeholders<br>▪ Ability to manage relationships & network |
| **Manage Data, Systems & Improvements**  | ▪ Drives continuous improvement of the forecasts. Acts as an IBP data manager and becomes an IBP system expert | ▪ Expertise in the demand-planning process formulation and improvement<br>▪ Data management and IBP System and Analytical tools proficiency<br>▪ Strong computer skills with knowledge of Microsoft applications, particularly Excel and Access<br>▪ Awareness or practical knowledge of data driven process improvement methodology e.g. 6 Sigma<br>▪ Generating & building on new ideas |

Below you will find a detailed explanation of the demand excellence responsibilities aligned to the following categories (see Fig. 2.7):

– Forecast and sense demand
– Shape demand and develop Integrated Business Plan
– Agree and communicate
– Manage data, systems and improvements.

# Demand Planning Excellence

—————————— **Role Definition** ——————————

Maintain and continuously improve the forecasting processes and systems through using demand drivers and assumptions, historical analysis, market trends, statistical models and by utilizing collaboration and consensus across various stakeholders

Responsibilities

**Forecast & sense demand**

- Utilizes advanced analytics in capturing and analysing demand signals and transforming them into forecast input for forecasting models
- Reviews and assesses regularly Time Series and Simple Regression Statistical Forecasts
- Develops with Demand Planners and stakeholders Multiple Regression models
- Develops instruments and tools that monitors and assess accuracy of statistical and qualitative forecasting models
- Ensures the ways to incorporate the accurate and current market intelligence into statistical forecasting
- Provides coaching and training to demand planners in identifying, monitoring and mitigating problems as well as in identifying and executing basic process improvements
- Co-defines rules of forecast sales/demand based on sales orders (forward, backward)
- Defines weekly split rules reflecting market patterns

**Shape Demand & Develop Integrated Business Plan**

- Drives and promotes the use of demand shaping by utilizing what-if scenario analysis technique in forecasting
- Embed a management-by-exception approach to forecasting and planning as a way of improving the utilization of resources within the organization
- Ensures all non-standard cost and revenue drivers are incorporated in IBP process / data waterfall

**Agree & Communicate**

- Reaches consensus on how to measure forecast performance and how to link it to integrated business plans and objectives
- Establishes and monitors one integrated set of KPIs from demand side to supply side and at every level of forecast aggregation
- Set ups instruments to measure effectiveness, efficiency and process adherence
- Drives organization to introduce differentiated forecasting, walking away from "one size fit all"
- Ensures process improvements are communicated

**Manage Data,
Systems &
Improvements**

- Identifies and monitors the strengths and weakness of different statistical models used in demand forecasting
- Coordinates with demand planners root cause analysis and corrective action planning to understand demand forecast accuracy and bias performance
- Provides scientific detailed analysis of forecast errors, trends, root causes for local, regional and global stakeholders
- Searches for any potential use of ARIMAx and any advanced other statistical forecasting models
- Monitors forecasting best practices and usage of technology
- Actively promotes and transforms organization towards demand driven forecasting
- Coordinates the IBP system improvements
- Continuously searches and identifies areas of opportunity for improvements in processes by questioning data, challenging assumptions and highlighting exceptions by utilising 6 Sigma principles
- Leads development and knowledge sharing. Runs internal wiki, discussion boards, and regular on boarding, trainings.
- Drives organization to integrate with sell-in and sell through partners
- Drives organization toward digitalization of forecasting process
- Acts as DP & DM process owner
- Regularly prepares personalized forecast performance analysis as input for forecasting error target setting
- Escalates to management big deviations in performance, process adherence and data quality
- Exploits ex-post forecasting techniques to improve forecasting algorithms
- Utilizes data mining techniques to produce insights
- Keeps system and process documentation up to date
- Drives toward demand driven and use of Nielsen or other syndicated consumer data if applicable
- Drives DP& DM towards differentiated ways of working
- Drives process and data consistency across the business
- Drive process and IBP data modelling. Coordinates the definition of authorization concept
- Drives to use advanced analytics for end to end IBP segmentation

Below you will find a detail explanation of the demand excellence role, its business impact and the competencies to help achieving the desired outcome.

# Demand Planning Excellence Excellence

—————————  **Role Impact**  —————————

Leads and delivers tangible process improvements, balances efforts with the results/outputs. Keeps

| | Business Impact | Skills & Competences |
|---|---|---|
| **Forecast & sense demand**  | • Develops advanced statistical algorithms | • Analytical, data-processing and problem solving skills<br>• Solid practical experience in the use of basic and advanced statistical forecasting algorithms<br>• Ability to gather and process data, execute quantitative and qualitative data analysis<br>• Awareness of product lifecycle management<br>• Focused on meeting deadlines and achieving goals. Ability to work with limited or without supervision<br>• Able to organize own and others work |
| **Shape Demand & Develop Integrated Business Plan**  | • Develops algorithms to improve demand sharing and scenario planning | • Persistent and goal oriented to drive results toward tactical and operational objectives of the organization<br>• Awareness of forecast and plans monetization<br>• High attention to details<br>• Ability to coach and train<br>• Project management and ability to build business case<br>• Ability to challenge process stakeholders |
| **Agree & Communicate**  | • Agrees improvements plans. Agrees learning and development plans | • Ability to communicate in concise manner with experts and managers. Collaboration skills<br>• Ability to provide clear and concise recommendations to process improvement stakeholders<br>• Ability to leverage information<br>• Ability to influence sales and marketing stakeholders<br>• Ability to manage relationships & network |

| Manage Data, Systems & Improvements  | <ul><li>Coaches, trains and drives knowledge sharing and extensions. Ensures process adherence globally</li></ul> | <ul><li>Expertise in demand-planning process formulation and improvement</li><li>Data management, IBP System and Analytical tools proficiency</li><li>Strong computer skills with knowledge of Microsoft applications, particularly Excel and Access</li><li>Practical knowledge of data driven process improvement methodology e.g. 6 Sigma</li><li>Generating & building on new ideas</li></ul> |

## 2.2.2  Insights on Role Comparison and Size of the Team

### 2.2.2.1  Insights on Role Comparison

As we see from Fig. 2.8, the roles have a different focus and that should be reflected in their competencies and development plans. The most important aspect is that they should be complementing each other.

In the last few years, the perception on key competencies has changed quite substantially.

- Creativity and critical thinking have become more and more important (automatization can do repetitive tasks, but cannot be creative).
- Negotiation and flexibility will decrease in importance as almost all decisions will be based on data and artificial intelligence.
- Active listening will go down and emotional intelligence will go up in importance (Gray, 2016).

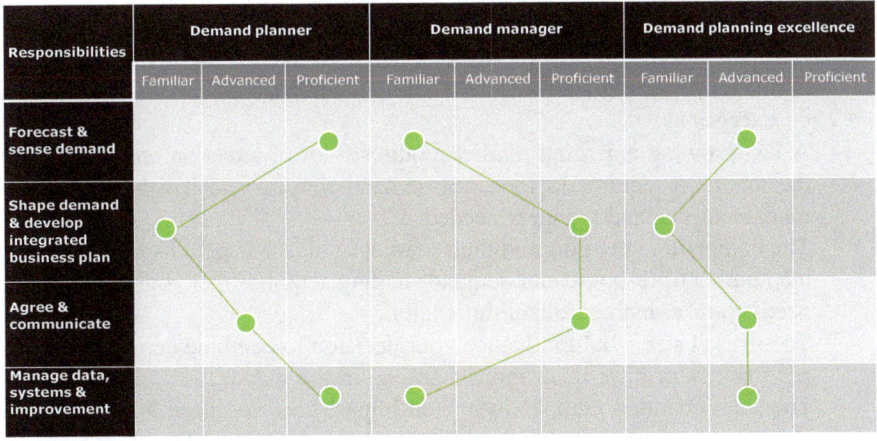

**Fig. 2.8**  Demand planning organization roles comparison

We face a growing importance in the professional environment of the so-called soft skills or non-cognitive skills combined with an excellent educational background (Gray, 2017). Alex Gray assesses that the soft skills are so important, because the jobs itself have changed and require new skill sets. The majority of the rewards are dedicated for people embedding non-cognitive skills. They guarantee a successful long-term full-time employment and they allow to keep up with changes.

In addition, we stress the attention on another perspective to be considered when building demand planning organization: have you thought about the fact that since SAP IBP is a cloud system with effective collaboration instruments, some team members may want to switch more to home office? Maybe we should think to find the right place for each task of your job! Measuring productivity and counting working hours is a concept that is experiencing its wading away:

- It makes no sense measuring time in our seats.
- It requires additional and useless effort to track the productivity of people who get their job done.
- Most of the people are knowledge workers who can work from everywhere (Ross, 2014).

### 2.2.2.2 Insights on Size of the Team

How to evaluate the size of the team needed? What should be considered?

This is not an easy exercise and a "one-size-fits-all" will not work for every company. There will be always considerations like budget for head count and the ability to "make or buy" required skills. On the other hand, there are some insights you may consider as helpful in your evaluation and planning.

The size of the demand planning and demand management team may depend on many factors, but the main ones are the following:

- Business characteristics

  - A stable and mature market does not need to have many demand planners but rather several instruments that help to automatize the processes and focus on exceptions.
  - A fast-growing emerging market requires a lot of attention and analysis of the inputs; it requires to focus on demand sensing and it would affect the number of demand planners needed.
  - The competitor strengths and their market influence capability would impact the number of response and demand shaping activities that your organization needs to take and coordinate internally.
  - The market size would influence your decision to combine demand planners per markets or have them more than one in the market.
  - The sales channels complexity would impact how you need to organize the inputs, reviews and analytics and if the demand signals should be isolated.

- Portfolio complexity and changes

  - The size of the so-called long tale of SKUs may increase substantially how you need to structure the processes and reviews.
  - The high rate of changes in the portfolio (phase in/phase out) makes the predictability of the inputs more challenging and makes the reviews and preparations efforts to cannibalization due to the fact that the replacements will consume much more time.

- Process design

  - A wrong process design may affect the workload substantially, e.g., you need to carefully define on which base level you will do forecasting, how many inputs are needed and if the qualitative methods are balanced off with quantitative methods.

- System functionality

  - in large-scale operations, the same system functionality that can support you with the introduction of differentiated ways of working, will help you in balancing the effort with the outcome; in addition a robust process exception management will help you to manage the required headcount.

Note that a larger number of demand planners will not ensure better process outputs!

Our personal experience says that a demand planner in a well-designed process, with the right supporting system functionality and data, can manage up to 2000 SKUs in his portfolio.

Studies show that:

- Top demand planning workload measurement is the number of forecasting combinations at a region product and region ship to level.
- The number of forecasting combinations per demand planner varies, but is on average from 1500 to 15,000 product/ship to combinations at distribution center level.
- Companies rate whether they have good or average demand planning capabilities, but on the other hand, the results are only ranked on average.
- Companies report rather low turnover within demand planning (52%).
- In 39.2% of the cases, the demand planning reports to supply chain planning organization.
- In most companies (52%), demand planning is a starting point toward other roles within supply chain or finance. Unfortunately, those roles do not have their own career path (Demand Planner Benchmark survey, 2013).

This brings us to the topic of how to find and retain talents in demand planning and demand management on which we touched base in our Integrated Business Planning book (Kepczynski, Jandhyala, Sankaran, & Dimofte, 2018a).

## 2.3 Concluding Remarks

- The demand planning and demand management organizations and competencies should be designed in the context of the integration needed in IBP.
- The demand planning and management organizational design should not be done in isolation and only focused on forecasting; these functions, jointly with the Finance controller, should hold IBP together and, as suggested, should be part of x-functional IBP Center of Expertise [see (Kepczynski et al., 2018b)].
- Demand planning and management have different org. structures, especially if we place them into product or market inclined organization.
- Demand planning, demand management and demand planning excellence should be in one organizational unit. Demand planning excellence should combine process and data knowledge.
- Demand planning and management: sense and forecast demand, shape demand and develop integrated business plan, agree and communicate forecasts and plans, manage data and lead IBP system improvements.
- Demand planning and demand excellence should have their roles and impacts clearly defined and aligned to the levels and planning process types (operational, tactical and long-term) in which they act.
- The size of the demand planning organization should depend on the business characteristics, portfolio complexity, process design and system functional support.

## References

APICS—module 1.G—Demand Planning. (2015). *APICS—module 1.G—Demand Planning*. APICS.

Crum, C., & Palmatier, G. E. (2003). *Demand management best practices: Process, principles, and collaboration*. Oliver Wight, APICS.

Crum, C., & Palmatier, G. E. (2010). *Demand management: Lessons learned*. Oliver Wight.

Demand Planner Benchmark survey. (2013). *Supply chain digest*.

Gray, A. (2016). *The 10 skills you need to thrive in the Fourth Industrial Revolution*. World Economic Forum.

Gray, A. (2017). *Goodbye, maths and English. Hello, teamwork and communication?*. World Economic Forum.

Griswold, M. (2015). *Learning from leaders—Three best practices in retail demand planning*. Stamford: Gartner.

Kepczynski, R., Jandhyala, R., Sankaran, G., & Dimofte, A. (2018a). *Integrated business planning —How to integrate planning processes, organizational structures & capabilities, and leverage sap IBP technology*. Berlin: Springer.

Kepczynski, R., Dimofte, A., Jandhyala, R., Sankaran, G., & Boyle, A. (2018b). *A guide exemplified with process context and SAP IBP use cases*. Switzerland: Springer.

Lord, P. (2013). *Demand management brings balance to chemical supply and product networks*. Stamford: Gartner.

Moon, M. A. (2013). *Demand and supply integration: The key to world-class demand forecasting*. FT Press.

Ross, P. (2014). *Scrap your work from home policy*. LinkedIn. Available at https://www.linkedin. com/pulse/20141204164621-12715656-scrap-your-work-from-home-policy.

Salley, A., & Griswold, M. (2015). *Focus on three key elements when building a forward-thinking demand-planning process*. Stamford: Gartner.

Steutermann, S. (2016). *Defining demand-planning excellence in consumer products: Structure, talent and technology*. Stamford: Gartner.

Steutermann, S., Salley, A., & Lord, P. (2012). *Demand management elevates value network performance*. Stamford: Gartner.

Tohamy, N., & Stiffler, D. (2012). *How to structure the demand-planning organization*. Stamford: Gartner.

Tohamy, N., Scott, F., & Steutermann, S. (2012). *How to build an effective demand planning organization*. Stamford: Gartner.

# Efficient and Effective Usage of Out-of-the-Box Statistical Forecasting

In the first chapter, we set the foundation to statistical forecasting framework and briefly visited the differentiated forecasting concept. We will now continue to expand on the framework as depicted in Fig. 1.11 and explain the value of the statistical forecasting process as outlined in Fig. 3.1.

## 3.1 Model Class Selection

Once the purpose of forecasting is defined, a strategic choice needs to be made regarding classes of models that will be authorized for use. A conceptual framework that visualizes the trade-off between cost of inaccuracy and cost of sophistication (forecasting costs) is useful (see Fig. 3.2). At one end of the spectrum, we have advanced models that impose high forecasting costs, but incur low inaccuracy costs. At the other end, there are models that are fairly simplistic and therefore are inexpensive to use (easier to set up and maintain) but incur higher inaccuracy costs. A key cost driver when it comes to model choice is the data requirements. For example, causal models require data for independent variables or causal factors that influence the dependent variable or that which is being estimated. The right choice involves optimizing total relevant costs—a choice that should land us in the region circled in Fig. 3.2. The first rule of forecasting, which is often repeated, is that forecast is always in error. It is important to remember this concept and to not be dazzled by sophistication and also to not confuse sophistication with automation. The focus should be "acceptable accuracy" (Mulllick Satinder, 1971).

In creating a portfolio of algorithms that will be considered for model selection, planning characteristics of products should be an important decision variable.

For instance, one important consideration is product life cycle. The type of method should also be guided by the lifecycle stage of the product. Generally speaking, time series methods are more suitable for products that are in their steady

© Springer Nature Switzerland AG 2019
G. Sankaran et al., *Improving Forecasts with Integrated Business Planning*,
Management for Professionals, https://doi.org/10.1007/978-3-030-05381-9_3

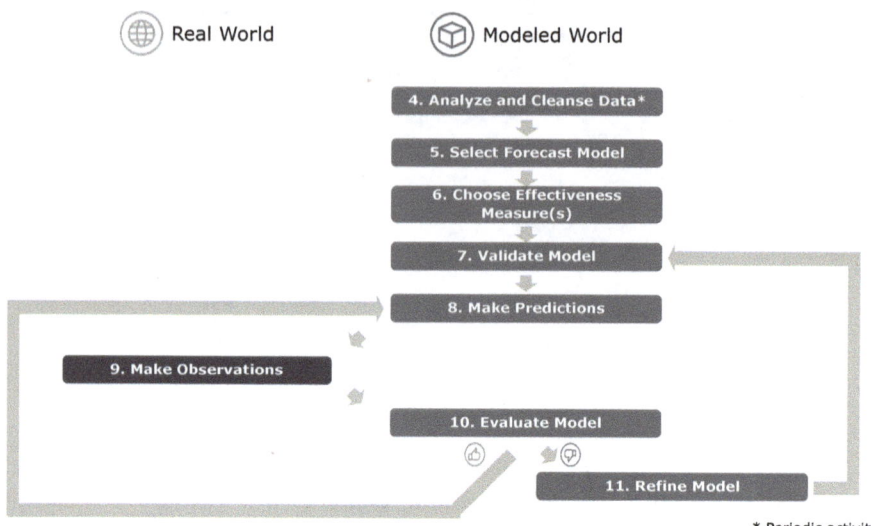

**Fig. 3.1** Develop a statistical forecasting model that works for your data

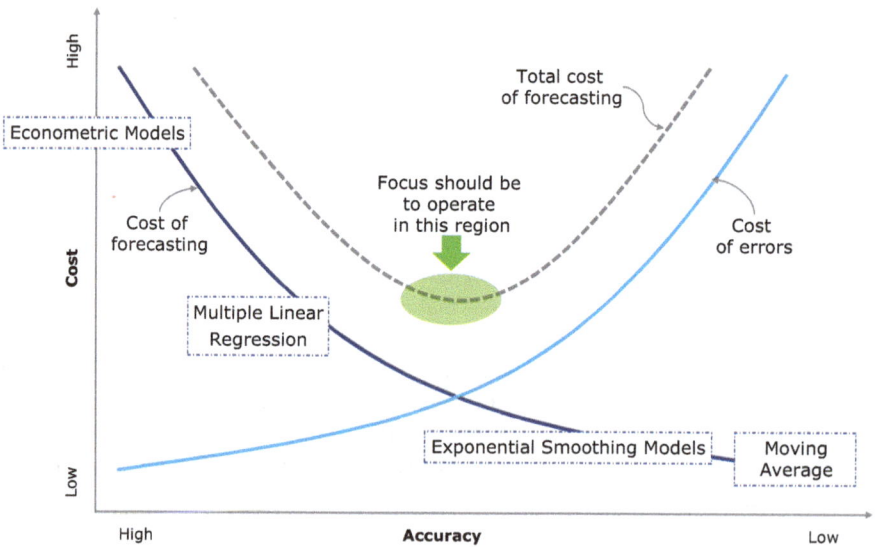

**Fig. 3.2** Select an appropriate forecast model

state and qualitative/causal methods are more suitable for products in their launch/testing, growth and decline stages (see Fig. 3.3).

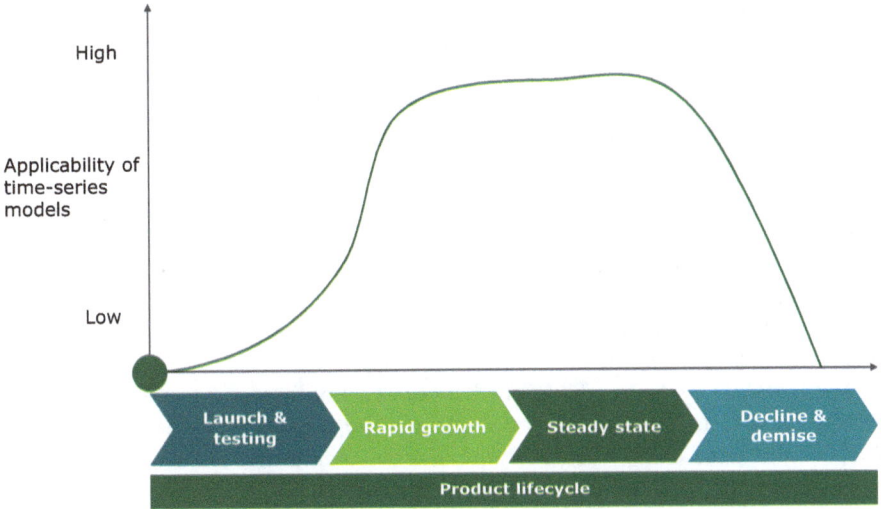

**Fig. 3.3** Relationship between model choice and product lifecycle stage

In relation to product life cycle, it would pay to be aware of the cognitive bias of overestimation in the short term and underestimation in the long term. That is, one tends to overestimate how soon rapid growth will start, but once it happens, underestimate how explosive it will be. This is particularly relevant when dealing with products that have relatively short life cycles (case of innovative products, limited life products). Therefore, it is important to have a mechanism to aid practitioners to be on the lookout for inflection points. One such mechanism (tracking signal) is discussed later in this chapter.

A decision on classes of models to be used can also benefit from a broader discussion around whether constraints for products under consideration are external (market) or internal (supply). Causal methods or, more generally, costlier methods are likely to bring more value in case of external constraints than in the case of internal constraints. If supply is the limiting factor, additional investments in estimating true demand will not pay dividends as the firm's current supply falls short of what the market is willing to take.

Another characteristic that can be used for good effect is the fact that cost of errors on an aggregate level (structurally as well as on the basis of time) is higher than on a lower level. Therefore, more sophistication could be justified, depending on the complexity of forecasting on aggregated planning levels (e.g., product family) compared to lower levels (e.g., product item) where simpler time series models might do the job. The rationale behind this assertion is that aggregate forecasts are used in decisions that are of a more tactical or long-term nature and are revisited less frequently (and therefore offer less scope for course correction) compared to forecasts used for operational decisions. This approach of connecting planning level to forecast model sophistication and time and resource invested for selection was used in one of the projects the authors had worked on. In the project, we realized that statistical forecasting was not used before and it was perceived in an apprehensive way in terms of workload by the planners. In order to not overwhelm the planners, an approach was taken whereby model and parameter assignments would be carried out, after a careful analysis of time series patterns, on a family level. However, on a product level, the automatic model selection of statistical forecasts was used to rationalize the effort. The disaggregation proportions from statistical forecast on a product level were determined to split statistical forecast carried out on family levels.

The steps of this approach are described in Fig. 3.4. More details on this example can be found here: (see SAP use case: statistical forecasting on aggregated and product level).

Lastly, while evaluating trade-offs between cost of forecasting and inaccuracy, it would be wise to recognize that uncertainty and opportunity are oftentimes two sides of the same coin. With heavy investments being made in big data and analytics, there are opportunities opening up for companies to deploy insights gained from data to reduce uncertainty and improve accuracy. In this era where a tweet by a celebrity can cause precipitous changes to demand, trade-offs need to be assessed/re-assessed in light of risks posed by not fully utilizing existing investments in big data and digital technologies.

In Fig. 3.5, the correlation between analytical sophistication, as it relates to forecasting, and improvements to service level and reduction in inventory levels is visualized. In the project referenced in the illustration, the transformation was focused on making forecasting market-driven through the use of statistical forecasting and analytics (Desmet & Sterckx, 2012).

As you see from the illustrated representation, adding sophistication to your forecasting methods and building new capabilities and skills pay off. It means that the selection of the models and the application of the right one to the right data may involve more effort and higher costs, but provide an opportunity to be more profitable. Our key observation is that one method does not fit all data sets and we share the same observations made by Desmet and Sterckx that by investing time and effort into advanced methods, analytics and data management generate value and return on investment. The key to success here is differentiating the methods applied.

## 3.2   Gathering, Analyzing and Cleansing Data

**Data Selection**

The data gathering requirements are determined based on the outcome of the model selection. For time series methods, we only need historical data of the factor(s) to be estimated. You may select different data inputs though. In the following example,

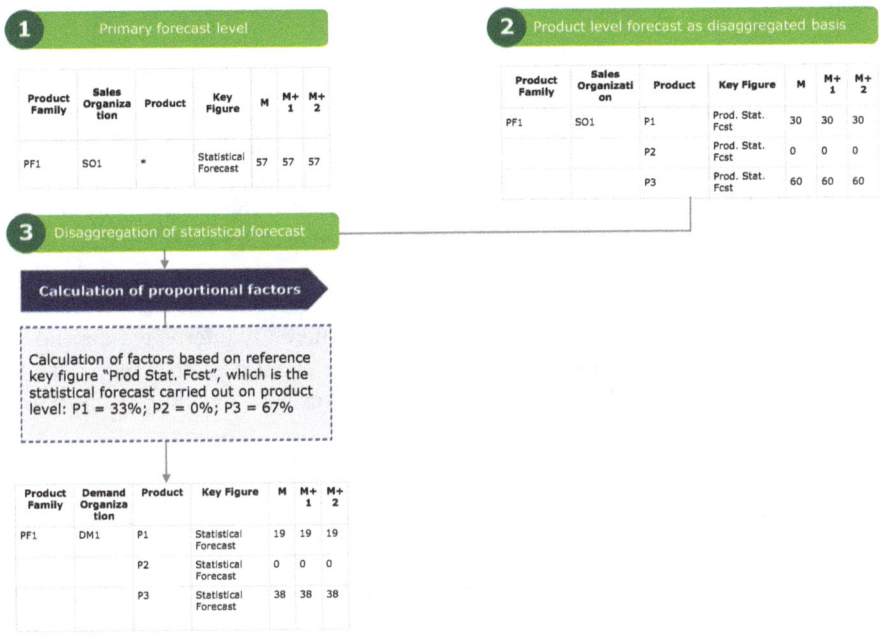

**Fig. 3.4** Forecasting on aggregated and product level

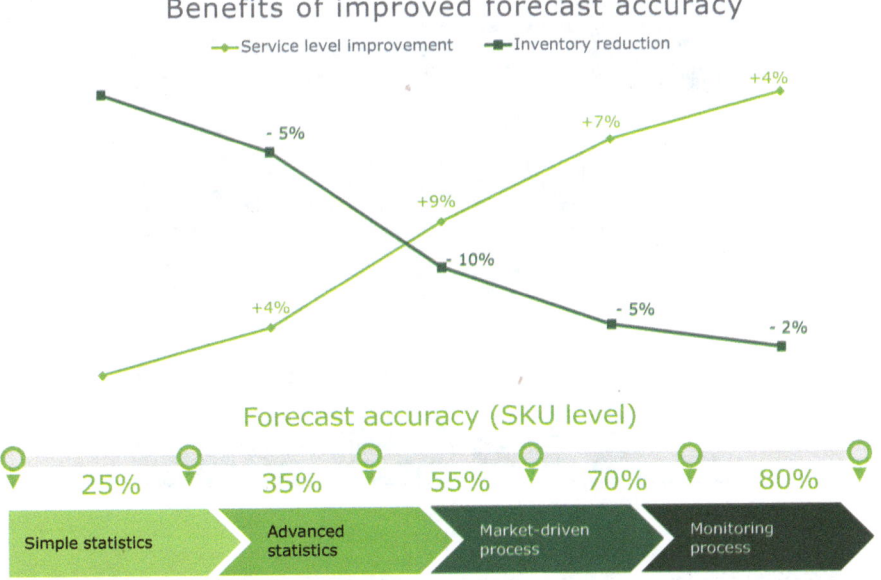

**Fig. 3.5** Service level versus inventory reduction versus forecasting techniques (Desmet & Sterckx, 2012)

we illustrate how selection of primary data input will influence the process outcome.

In Fig. 3.6, we see data inputs distributed layer after layer, going from invoiced quantity netted with return quantity (credit notes) to demand quantity at the bottom. On the left, we see periods and quantities provided by specific data input type. If you select invoice netted with returns, you forecast 80 for next March, assuming the same level of sales. But comparing it to demand quantity which says 10 in January and 120 in February makes a huge difference. It happens very often that the use of invoice and shipment data is misunderstood as being demand-driven or as the right demand signal for forecasting under the IBP framework. You can clearly see from Fig. 3.6 that the quantities that are needed can be differently interpreted depending on the primary data inputs used in the process. More about what to forecast can be found in our publication Implementing Integrated Business Planning (Kepczynski et al., 2018).

Data gathering for causal models is more involved as the data for all of the identified external factors need to be collected. Variables which may be correlated and have an influence on demand can be many and are often related to the industry and the market. In the consumer goods industry, the per capita income may influence the buying power and therefore the demand for the products and services, whereas in the food and beverages industry, weather may influence the demand.

**Fig. 3.6** What you forecast if you select wrong data input

One needs to bear in mind the basic underlying assumption when it comes to time series models: Past is a good indicator of the future which should be used to guide the decisions concerning the length of the historical planning horizon.

**Data Analysis Using Segmentation**

In one of our past projects, a decision was made to identify representative SKUs and perform an analysis of the demand variability using the coefficient of variance as the measure (see Fig. 3.7) for 6, 12, 24 and 36 months of history. A change in the classification between the period groupings under analysis was considered as a cause for closer inspection. This reasoning facilitated the discussion on whether there were significant changes in demands in the recent history that would call for restricting the scope of the data collection, thereby also rationalizing the overall effort. In summary, it would be beneficial to use some means to look for tipping points (significant shifts in demand pattern) that should inform decisions around historical planning horizon to be used for forecasting. In the case of seasonal models, one should aim to at least have 3–4 full seasons. For example, if 12 months constitute one complete season, at least 3–4 years of demands should be made available.

One way to analyze the data is to segment it. You can segment your potential data inputs for forecasting with the use of coefficient of variation. This is a very simple measure that can help you to understand the variability in the data. The more variable the data, the harder it is to predict the future.

The coefficient of variance (CoV) can be used to provide some guidance in identifying the SKUs that have high demand variability—an indication of the presence of one-off events (promotions or results of internal actions) that ought to be cleansed out. This technique is discussed in detail along with graphical depictions in the section for outlier detection for seasonal products later in the book.

Figure 3.8 captures the essence of what data input and data output segmentations aim to achieve. For further advice on segmenting data inputs and data outputs, refer to the chapter on data segmentation in the Integrated Business Planning book in the IBP series (Kepczynski et al., 2018).

**Data Analysis Using Time Series Elements**

Another way to analyze data for representative sets of SKUs is to test out the components of a time series. There are potentially five components (see Fig. 3.9).

| Co-efficient of Variance (CoV) = $\left(\frac{\sigma}{\mu}\right)$ | Classification |
|---|---|
| CoV > 0.75 | Low |
| 0.75 >= CoV < 1.33 | Medium |
| CoV >= 1.33 | High |

**Fig. 3.7**  CoV classification of variability

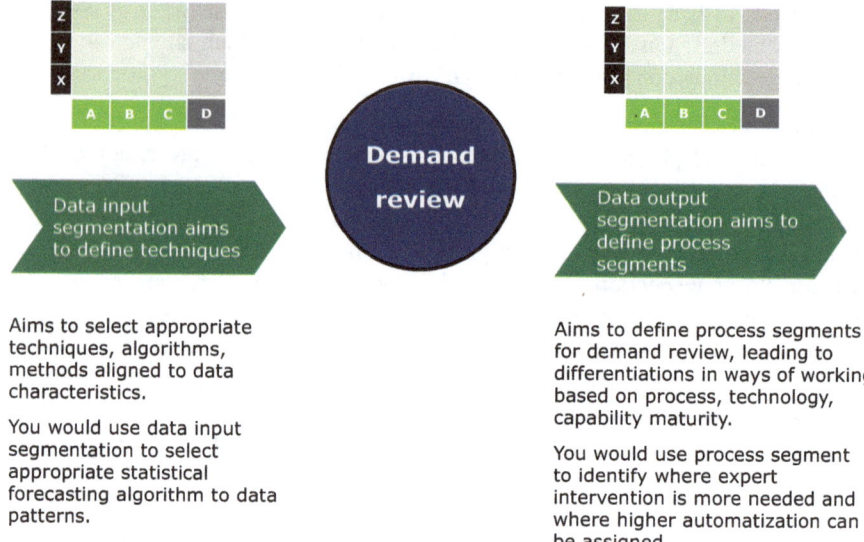

Data input segmentation aims to define techniques

Aims to select appropriate techniques, algorithms, methods aligned to data characteristics.

You would use data input segmentation to select appropriate statistical forecasting algorithm to data patterns.

Data output segmentation aims to define process segments

Aims to define process segments for demand review, leading to differentiations in ways of working based on process, technology, capability maturity.

You would use process segment to identify where expert intervention is more needed and where higher automatization can be assigned.

**Fig. 3.8**  Data input or data output segmentation

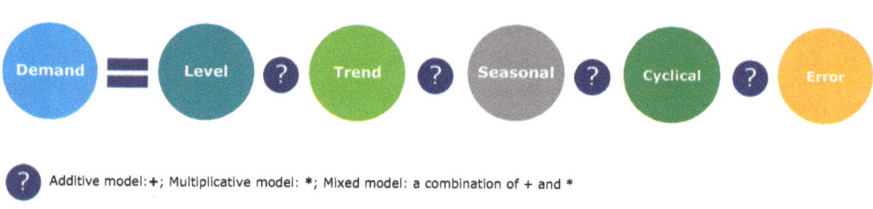

Additive model: +; Multiplicative model: *; Mixed model: a combination of + and *

**Fig. 3.9**  Five components of a time series

Such an analysis serves to provide insights into historical data patterns and helps gauge the need for data cleansing and usefulness of incorporating additional inputs (say, explanatory variables for use in causal models).

The demand components may be classified as follows (APICS—module 1. G—Demand Planning, 2015; Levenbach, 2017):

- Demand average: the average value of the series
- Trend: the long-term variation of the average value. A trend is not always a straight line. A trend is seen as the tendency for the same pattern to be predominantly upward or downward over time
- Seasonality: average value variations which repeat themselves several times within a well-defined cycle

- Cycle: average value variations due to unexpected exogenous factors. A cycle in demand forecasting is a tricky component as the duration and the amplitude of the cycle are not constant. The quantification of a cycle is one of the most elusive tasks in the times series analysis
- Randomness: random unexpected influencers, "the noise"
- Autocorrelation: it indicates that an even persists and, in every point, the expected value is strictly correlated with its past values.

Understanding the time series components will help in revealing the features of the times series and to be able to extrapolate it into the future. Below, it is shown how the four components, trend (T), cycle (C), seasonality (S) and the residuals (R), are combined for the purposes of prediction in time series forecasting:

Time series are mostly used as additive models, and this book will particularly focus on them:

$$y(t) = T(t) + C(t) + S(t) + R(t)$$

In addition, there are also the multiplicative models:

$$y(t) = T(t) * C(t) * S(t) * R(t)$$

which can be easily transformed into additive ones using logarithms:

$$\log y(t) = \log T(t) + \log C(t) + \log S(t) + \log R(t)$$

As previously indicated, the use of representative SKUs is a reasonable approach. Product segmentation analysis could be utilized to ensure that the data set chosen is truly representative. Time series decomposition is a useful technique to perform such an analysis. This involves breaking down a time series to its constituent components as in the example scenarios below:

1. The presence of large residuals (errors) can point toward the presence of promotional demands. As promotions are a result of internal actions, they need to be cleansed out and should not be part of the baseline demand that is used for statistical forecasting. The presence of a pattern in residuals (see MLR discussion later in the book) could reveal that not all of the regular components have been explained and broken down—perhaps, there is seasonality and only trend–cycle component has been teased out.
2. There could be residuals (errors) also due to one-off actions like large direct shipments from a central warehouse to customers. As it is a good practice to forecast "demand" (not sales)—that is, if unimpeded by internal constraints, what would have been sold? From where? And how much?—it might be required to cleanse out the effects of such one-off actions.
3. Are there any significant shifts in level? What could be causing those? If there are such shifts, this could lead to a deeper investigation to ascertain whether the assumption of continuity still holds true (future like the past). It could be that for

certain product segments, a smaller time horizon needs to be used for forecasting. It could also be that the recent shift is only temporary, a cleansing activity is required and/or appropriate smoothing constants (see section on exponential smoothing later) need to be chosen to assign relatively lower weights to most recent periods.

4. It is important to make a distinction between induced seasonality and inherent seasonality. Induced seasonality is a result of human actions and is more prone to getting shunted backward or forward. A time series analysis can reveal the need for corrections.

5. In certain situations, applying a mathematical transformation might lead to more easily interpretable patterns for forecasting purposes (Makridakis, Wheelwright, & Hyndman, 1998; Hyndman & Athanasopoulos, 2014):

- Square root function: With the application of this mathematical transformation, each observation has to be square rooted. The reason behind this transformation lies in the fact that the variations of data will be reduced at the end of the permutation, guaranteeing an easier baseline for the forecast process.
- Logarithm: Applying the logarithmic transformation means also leveraging the additive property of the logarithmic function. As a consequence, the output data of the permutation may be easier to be interpreted and predicted for the future.
- Power transformation: Such a permutation enables the stabilization of the variance of the data making them more normal distributed-like. As a result, the forecasting process may be easier when dealing with those types of transformed data.

**Data Adjustments**

However, the interest is in predicting original data and not the transformed ones. Therefore, a back-transforming process has to be performed. Back-transforming is applied also to prediction intervals, which are the estimates of an interval where a future data observation may range. It should be remembered that mathematical transformation performs best when variations are high.

- Inflation adjustment: To remove additional sources of variation, it is advised to use an equivalent value to make data comparable between past and present.
- Population adjustment: Per capita analysis is advisable.
- Calendar day adjustment is one of the more common corrections that may be required (a preprocessing step in SAP IBP). For example, variations may be caused by the varying number of days in a month. If these variations are not removed, a seasonal pattern may be wrongly detected. Similarly, trading day adjustments are needed when different months have not the same amount of working days. This adjustment normalizes demand for a given period as depicted below:

$$\text{Adjusted Demand}\,(t) = \text{Actual Demand}\,(t) * \frac{\text{Average days in a month}\left(\frac{360,25}{12}\right)}{\text{Days in month}\,(t)}$$

### Data Cleansing

Demand history cleansing is crucial as it eliminates inaccuracies and noise factors in order to normalize a more smoothed baseline, to make it more predictable and more accurate for the future. Current forecasting methods such as exponential smoothing, which are used by 90% of the companies, cannot detect outliers or noises and as a result make data cleansing vital. The same concept is applied to seasonality which has to be detected in the time series in order to apply the right models and foster a better comprehension of the types of demand and its components (Chase, 2016).

We touched briefly on outliers in the first chapter, and Fig. 3.10 is a quick reference to the ways in which outliers can be detected. The mathematical solutions and techniques toward data cleansing and more specifically outlier detection and correction will be discussed later in the chapter.

Once outliers are identified and validated, data should be corrected so that it can be used for statistical forecasting. On a regular basis, the original historical data inputs for forecasting (can be historical orders, shipments, invoices) should be copied into data sets which can then be adjusted and cleansed. It is good practice to not correct the original data captured from source systems, but instead work with a duplicate that is transferred to another key figure or key figures. The key reason is that outlier correction may itself be flawed and preserving original data provides an opportunity to understand reasons when this happens and learn from it.

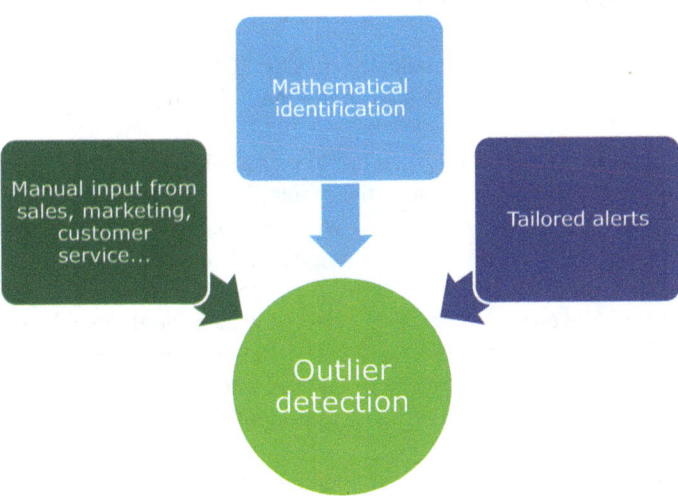

**Fig. 3.10** Outlier detection methods

**Data Analysis and Cleansing Overview**

The activities discussed so far were aimed at devising an overall strategy and preparing the data for forecasting and are visualized in Fig. 3.11. The outcomes thus far, depicted in the illustration, are leveraged for the next set of activities that are about running statistical forecasting on cleansed and transformed data inputs. The heart of this process is data analysis, and there are some leading practices you may consider taking into account for that:

- Cleansing data manually may lead to bad results.
- The need for data cleansing is considered crucial to extrapolate a historical baseline and tackling shortages, outliers, promotions, etc.
- One of the most difficult tasks is to remove the right amount of outliers or abnormal drivers.
- Data cleansing eliminates inaccuracies and noise factors in order to normalize a more smoothed baseline and makes it more predictable and more accurate for the future.
- New analytical methods such as ARIMA and ARIMAX can take into account unpredictable events making the cleansing process less needed (Chase, 2016).

On the other hand, manual input from sales, marketing and customer service can be useful to understand what we may call as uncommon behaviors of the customers, which are anomalous conducts mostly driven and influenced by the competitors' plays. This information would need to be validated against main data inputs used in forecasting, for example, if some orders/shipments show abnormal peaks or huge decrease.

## 3.2.1  SAP Use Case: Outlier Detection Variance Method

Outliers can be detected mathematically in SAP IBP. The system would run and analyze deviations from normal behavior and mark data points deviating outside of tolerances.

Alerts may help you to identify abnormal peaks during your forecasting period; e.g., you normally sell by 3rd week of the month 75% of monthly volumes, but this month it is only 30%. This type of alert will rather support demand sensing as an optimization technique for demand planning/statistical forecasting.

Turning to automatic outlier detection, it is used in case extreme values in the time series should be corrected and the corrected values should then be the basis for forecasting. This is not meant to replace the human component in the periodic cleansing activity but is merely meant to be used in conjunction. Exceptionally, for certain planning clusters of relatively low importance, this method can also be used in isolation.

Outlier detection works by first establishing lower and upper threshold limits (LTL, UTL) around a value, most commonly around the mean. The values outside

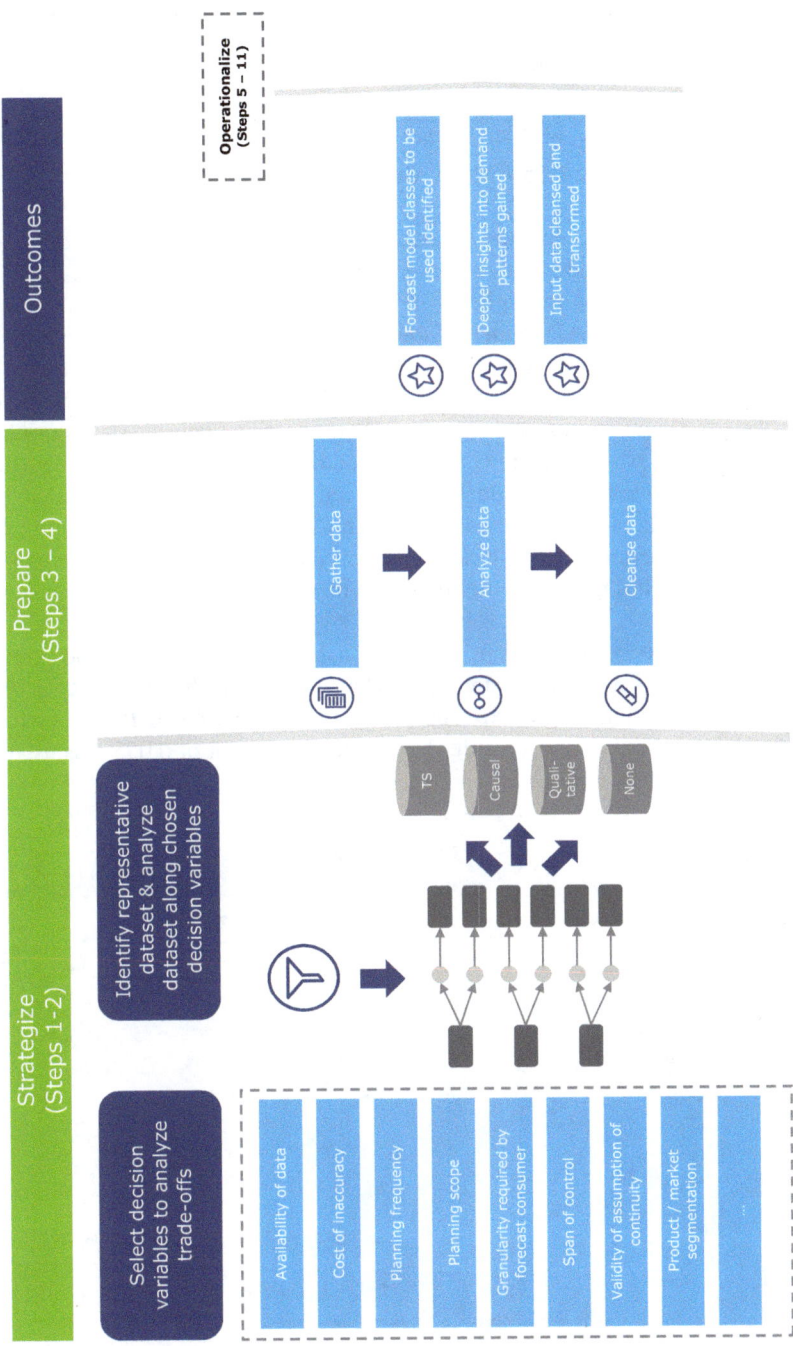

**Fig. 3.11** Process framework grouped into strategize, prepare and operationalize

the established limits are treated as outliers and are corrected to, say, the mean value. In the typical approach, mean squared error (MSE) or mean absolute deviation (MAD) is used to set the limits. Both these measures have a useful property in that they relate to σ (sigma, the standard deviation) as follows:

$$\sigma \approx \sqrt{\text{Mean Square Error}}$$
$$\sigma \approx 1.25 * \text{Mean Absolute Deviation}$$

This can be used to calculate the bandwidth by using a certain multiplier on the approximation for one standard deviation. For example, if one wants to set the LTL and LTL to [−2σ, 2σ], the multiplier if the error measure is MAD should be 2.5.

An example of using MAD to identify outliers in Excel is illustrated in Fig. 3.12. This is a sample data set of newsprint production (source: Australian Bureau of Statistics). A multiplier of 3 has been used, and the gray band signifies the space between the lower and the upper thresholds. Here, the mean value (102) is used as the midpoint around which the limits are calculated. The data points that lie outside (either below or above the LTL and UTL, respectively) are shown as outliers.

The detected outliers are corrected to the mean value. The result of running the forecast based on the corrected historical values is shown in Fig. 3.13. As it can be seen, the bandwidth has narrowed slightly as the mean has shifted down post-outlier correction.

This behavior can be modeled in SAP IBP using the variance method, which should be included as a preprocessing step. The settings are shown in Fig. 3.14.

The result of running single exponential smoothing in SAP IBP is shown in Fig. 3.15. This mirrors the Excel result. A smoothing constant of 0.053 was used—

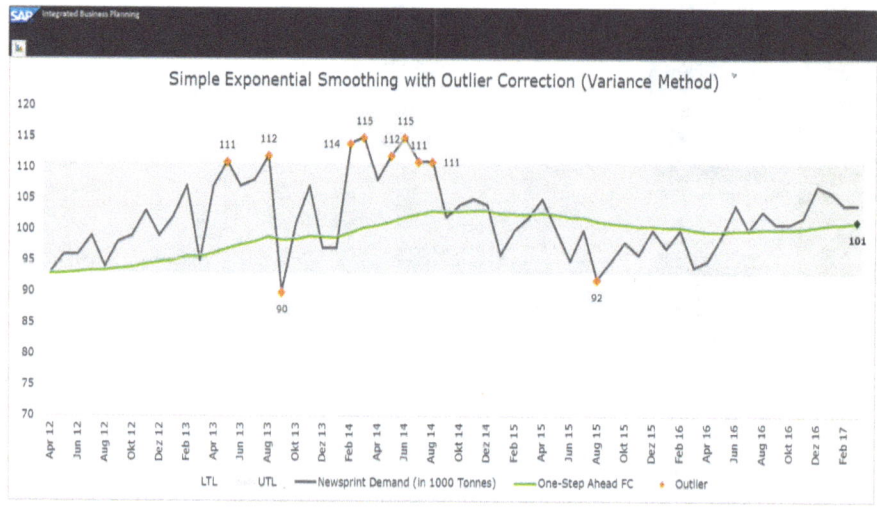

**Fig. 3.12** Outlier correction using variance method in Excel

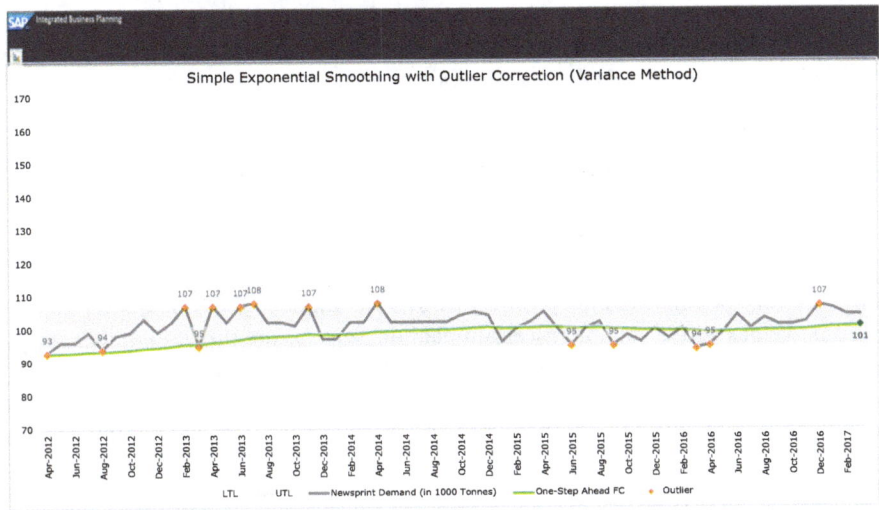

**Fig. 3.13** Outliers corrected to mean and forecast rerun using variance method

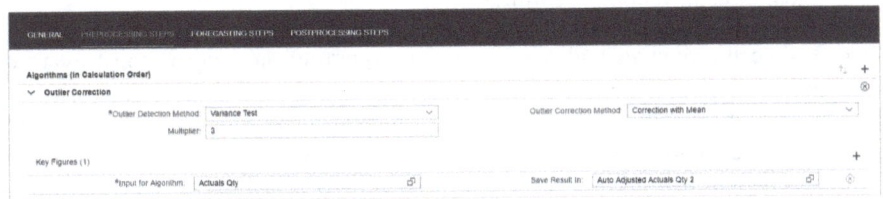

**Fig. 3.14** Settings for outlier correction using variance method in IBP

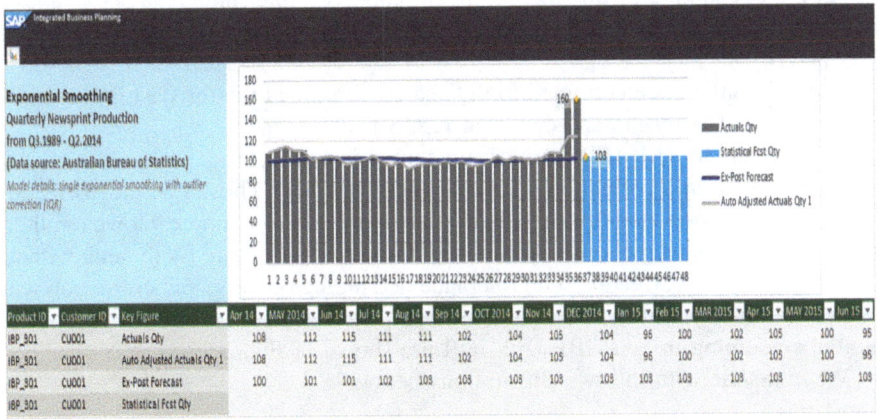

**Fig. 3.15** SES using the variance outlier correction method

this was determined by minimizing MSE using Excel's Solver. As it will be explained in the coming pages, this is a reasonable approach to identify typical smoothing constants by analyzing representative data sets.

## 3.2.2   SAP Use Case: Outlier Detection Interquartile Range

Another method that can be used to detect outliers and is available in SAP IBP uses the interquartile range (IQR). This is based on a rule of thumb called Tukey fences, which is very popular. A nice property of this technique is that it is quite robust to extreme values and is suitable if certain planning groups are prone to quite extreme values and where manual cleansing is not worth the effort investment.

However, it must be remarked that the interquartile test is highly prone to detect as outliers the majority of the points of the high season, with results much influenced by the nature of the seasonal data. This consequently makes IQR not highly suitable for identifying seasonal outliers.

IQR is the difference between the 95th and the 25th percentile values. This difference is multiplied with a factor, typically around 3, which is then used to establish the lower and upper "fences."

The method can be built as follows:

1. Calculate the median and the lower (first quartile) and upper (third quartile) quartiles.
2. Calculate the standard deviation.
3. Calculate the interquartile range (the difference between the upper and the lower quartiles) and call it IQ.
4. Calculate the upper limit for outliers as the third quartile plus 0.5 times the interquartile range.
5. The outlying points are those that overcome the set threshold.

An Excel example of this method being applied to the same data set as above, but with two simulated outliers in the last two periods (160 TO), is shown in Fig. 3.16.

The two outliers are corrected to the nearest limit, and the forecast is calculated on this basis. The results are shown in Fig. 3.17.

The settings in SAP IBP for IQR are shown in Fig. 3.18.

As can be seen, "correction with tolerance" has been chosen as the correction method, which corresponds to what was done in the Excel example. However, there are other methods to choose from like: correction to mean (with and without outliers included), correction with tolerance (excluding outliers) and correction with median (with and without outliers included). The results of running single exponential smoothing in SAP IBP with IQR are shown in Fig. 3.19.

We conclude with the two illustrations below.

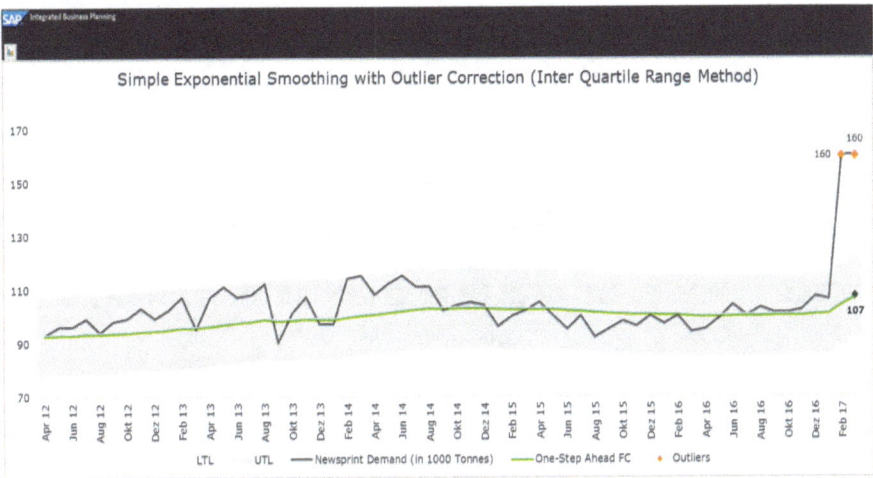

**Fig. 3.16**   Outlier correction using IQR method in Excel

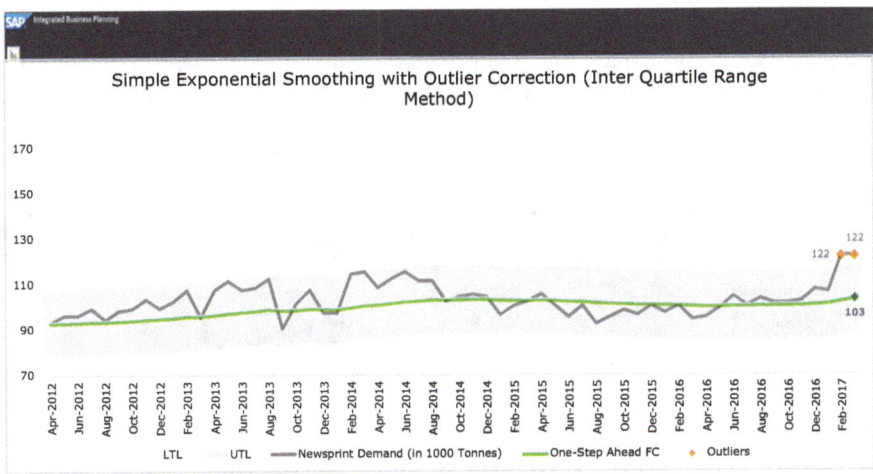

**Fig. 3.17**   Forecast based on corrected outliers using IQR method

**Fig. 3.18**   Preprocessing settings for IQR method in IBP

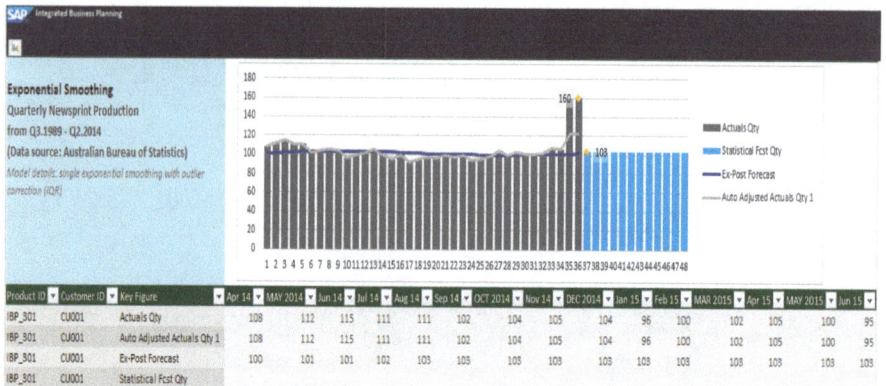

**Fig. 3.19**  Results of SES with IQR in IBP

Figure 3.20 provides an overview of the SAP IBP outlier detection techniques along with the settings to be used, the scenarios they are most recommended for and insights to bear in mind when using them.

Figure 3.21 illustrates the list of the outlier correction methods in SAP IBP, their main correction principles and their recommended usage mapped against the demand components (trend, cycle, season, intermittency and random stable fluctuations).

| | Substitute missing values | Variance Test | Interquartile Range test (IQR) | Promotion sales lift elimination |
|---|---|---|---|---|
| **Upper bound** | Not Detected | Detected | Detected | Detected |
| **Lower bound** | Not Detected | Detected | Detected | Not Detected |
| **Degree of qualitative inputs** | Extreme | Low | Medium | Medium |
| **Dependence on normality assumption** | Low | High | Medium | Low |
| **Recommended usage** | • Reduced usage | • Only for normally distributed data | • Not recommended as a stand alone test • In conjunction with more quantitative tests | • Recommended: if the promotion was occasional and will not repeat itself in the future • No: if every year promotions happen |
| **Comments** | • The most prone method to human errors • Without a proper understanding of the data set the substitution will be a simple guessing | • A reliable test for outlier detection if the sales history is stable and not variable | • Poor results for seasonal and highly variable products • It is not among the most reliable tests | • The less manipulated the data, the better • It requires a tight collaboration with marketing & sales • Promotions elimination removes insights from the data |

**Fig. 3.20**  SAP IBP outlier detection technique overview settings

| Outlier correction methods | Outlier corrected value | Stable demand | Intermittent demand | Seasonality | Trend | Cycle |
|---|---|---|---|---|---|---|
| Correction with mean | Average of all data values | Recommended (case sensitive: no pre-defined decision making process) | Not recommended | Not recommended | Recommended | Not recommended |
| Correction with mean excluding outliers | Average of all data values excluding all outliers | Recommended (case sensitive: no pre-defined decision making process) | Not recommended | Recommended | Not recommended | Recommended |
| Correction with tolerance | Upper threshold or Lower threshold | Recommended | Not recommended | Not recommended | Recommended | Not recommended |
| Correction with tolerance excluding outliers | Newly evaluated value of Upper threshold or Lower threshold | Recommended | Not recommended | Not recommended | Not recommended | Not recommended |
| Correction with median | Median of all data values | Recommended | Not recommended | Not recommended | Recommended | Not recommended |
| Correction with median excluding outliers | Median of all data values excluding all outliers | Recommended | Not recommended | Not recommended | Not recommended | Not recommended |

**Fig. 3.21** SAP IBP outlier detection mapping

## 3.3  Forecast Model Selection

The operationalization of forecasting concepts starts with translating the forecasting levels, historical, forecast horizons and data correction (preprocessing) activities to the desired outcomes. Let us start with discussing the key elements in the forecast model selection.

**Forecasting Level** The goal here is to derive the selection criteria that were used to assign model classes to homogeneous planning clusters to create a list of planning levels.

The planning level can be classified into three types on the basis of the level on which the consumer of the forecast requires it—let's call this the publish level, for example, for procurement or production.

*Disjoint*: forecast is calculated on a more aggregate level vis-à-vis the level users work with it. Disaggregation is proportional or based on proportions determined by another time-series, say, historical actual orders. This approach might be useful for product clusters where cost of forecasting on publish level outweighs benefits. This decision could also be due to the fact that the demand patterns on the lower level are very irregular but are more easily interpretable on the given higher level of aggregation. This assessment needs to be based on the earlier trade-off analysis and data analysis done for representative SKUs.

*Congruent*: forecast is calculated on the level users work with it. This is done where additional effort is likely to bring proportional benefits. For example, this approach is suitable for products with fairly involved time-series that include several components (trend, seasonal, business cycles). This is also the case, for example, where causal methods should be used since explanatory variables have been identified that when modeled will result in better accuracy (a positive trade-off).

*Hybrid*: The hybrid approach was described under "Model class". This approach makes sense if one seeks to strike the right balance between time investment and accuracy by focusing more management attention on an aggregate level and resorting to a more autonomous process on the detailed level. Autonomy can be achieved by say, use of automatic model selection procedure that selects the method that returns the lowest error for the chosen measure.

**Forecasting Time Horizons** Insights into data analysis on representative SKUs related to tipping points (shifts in level, growth curves), seasonal patterns, validity of the assumption of continuity, outliers, etc., inform decisions concerning planning horizons. If for certain clusters the recent history is far more representative than the older history, a decision might be taken to restrict the historical planning horizon accordingly. If, on the other hand, the recent historical data are affected by temporary effects, cleansing or appropriate smoothing constants (see discussion on alpha parameter later) can be used to temper impact on forecasts.

**Data Preprocessing** Cleansing and transformation need to be identified during the data analysis phase and must be performed on an ongoing basis to help identifying the needed preprocessing steps to be carried out before the forecasting run.

**Algorithms and Parameters** Model classes (quantitative to be specific) need to be broken down into specific algorithms that can then be assigned to planning clusters. Also, this decision is informed by the results of the data analysis phase. For example, if there are planning clusters that exhibit a dampened trend, a smoothing algorithm that has trend dampening enabled needs to be included in the toolbox (in SAP IBP, this would be double exponential smoothing with trend dampening set to enabled). As to parameters, some insights regarding the relative importance of historical periods are, for example, used to determine smoothing constants.

Among the forecasting algorithms, the single exponential smoothing (SES) is the workhorse. It is probably the most widely used.

Chase (2009) says that:

- Moving average is easy to implement, but it detects only trend and cycle.
- Simple exponential smoothing does not handle seasonality well, and alpha needs to be calculated with an optimum research.
- Holt's two parameters are easy to implement, but it detects only trend and cycle.
- Winters' three parameters are the one that predicts seasonality, but difficult to find optimal weights.
- Regression models require more data, but it can handle trend, cycle and seasonality—it is really accurate.
- ARIMA model is known to be the most accurate model.
- UCS requires more data, but it can handle trend, cycle and seasonality.

### 3.3.1  Averages

Let us briefly discuss the algorithms and the SAP IBP aspects of the forecasting models.

Forecasting models which are available in SAP IBP along with a qualitative estimation of forecasting costs involved are listed in Fig. 3.22.

**Simple Average**
The standard average method is considered as a method linked to low forecasting cost and quite easy to grasp conceptually. It fits demand patterns that are neither in a steep increasing trend nor in a strong descending trend. Capturing the future sales/demand of a product or of an item with a stable and regular sales/demand throughout the years can easily be done with the simple average method. However, even in such simplistic and easy-to-forecast case, there is already a data insight that the simple average method cannot capture: random or casual fluctuations in stable sales/demand patterns.

**Moving Average**
In order to neutralize the effects of such sudden fluctuations, the simple moving average comes in help. The moving average is based on a limited number of periods "$k$", and it runs in a way that every time that the new most recent data appear in the historical data set, the oldest one exits from the data set. This is the principle of "moving" of the data, as for each new period of sales/demand the newest data cause the elimination of the oldest one.

According to the below formula, the demand forecast for the successive period $t + 1$ is calculated as follows:

$$P_{t+1} = \frac{\sum_{i=1}^{k} X_{t-k+i}}{K}$$

| IBP Algorithm | Algorithm Type | Forecasting Cost |
|---|---|---|
| Simple Average | Time-Series / Constant | Low |
| Simple Moving Average | Time-Series / Constant | Low |
| Weighted Average | Time-Series / Constant | Low |
| Weighted Moving Average | Time-Series / Constant | Low |
| Single Exponential Smoothing | Time-Series / Constant | Low |
| Adaptive-Response-Rate Single Exponential Smoothing | Time-Series / Constant / Adaptive | Low |
| Double Exponential Smoothing | Time-Series / Trend | Medium |
| Triple Exponential Smoothing | Time-Series / Seasonal | Medium |
| Automated Exponential Smoothing | Time-Series / Automatic Detection / Adaptive | Medium |
| Croston Method | Time-Series / Intermittent | Medium |
| Multiple Linear Regression | Causal | High |

**Fig. 3.22** Algorithms in SAP IBP (1711)

where $X_i$ is the sales/demand during the period $i$.

The most important decision point for running the moving average method corresponds to the assessment of the number of periods "$k$" to be considered in the projection. It is advised to choose the number of periods "$k$" of the moving average that minimize the value of the standard deviation associated with it.

$$S_k = \sqrt{\frac{\sum_{j=k+1}^{t}(P_j - X_j)^{\wedge}2}{t - (k+1)}}$$

where $P_j$ is the forecast for the period $j$ and $X_j$ is the effective sales/demand of the period $j$.

The procedure to calculate the forecasted demand is as follows:

1. Calculate all the standard deviations associated with the different "$k$ periods" chosen.
2. Choose the "$k$ periods" value which minimize Sk.
3. Define the forecasted demand only for the "$k$ periods" defined at point number 2.
4. Determine the confidence interval with the formula that follows:

$$P_{t+1} \pm t_{\frac{alpha}{2}, t-(k+1)} S_k$$

Figure 3.23 represents an example of the table of critical values for Student's $t$ distribution value. To calculate a statistic, as for the interval of confidence, it is necessary to make use of the observations acquired from the sample as well as some parameters from the population. When some of the population parameters are not known, we need to estimate them through the sample itself; this is the work we need to accomplish to be capable of detecting the confidence interval.

The degree of freedom is the number of observations within the sample minus the "$k$" parameters that require an estimation from the sample, while the $t$ value is said "critical value" or "coefficient of confidence" as it depends on the degree of confidence chosen and on the amplitude of the sample.

Consequently, it is possible to assign the right value of "$t$" depending on the degree of freedom and on the alpha chosen; the degree of freedom row that matches the alpha column chosen will indicate the correct value of "$t$". For example, if we dispose of seven degrees of freedom (column d.f) and an alpha value of 0.05, the $t$ value corresponds to 1.895.

Figure 3.24 illustrates a practical way to organize the calculations for the determination of the optimal "$k$" value (number of periods) which minimizes the standard deviation of the forecasted error.

The alpha value indicates the degree of confidence of the test, while the "$t$" index has previously been calculated (in Fig. 3.23). On the left is the monthly

| TABLE of CRITICAL VALUES for STUDENT'S $t$ DISTRIBUTIONS |
|---|

| Column headings denote probabilities ($\alpha$) *above* tabulated values. |
|---|

| d.f. | 0.40 | 0.25 | 0.10 | 0.05 | 0.04 | 0.025 | 0.02 | 0.01 | 0.005 | 0.0025 | 0.001 | 0.0005 |
|---|---|---|---|---|---|---|---|---|---|---|---|---|
| 1 | 0.325 | 1.000 | 3.078 | 6.314 | 7.916 | 12.706 | 15.894 | 31.821 | 63.656 | 127.321 | 318.289 | 636.578 |
| 2 | 0.289 | 0.816 | 1.886 | 2.920 | 3.320 | 4.303 | 4.849 | 6.965 | 9.925 | 14.089 | 22.328 | 31.600 |
| 3 | 0.277 | 0.765 | 1.638 | 2.353 | 2.605 | 3.182 | 3.482 | 4.541 | 5.841 | 7.453 | 10.214 | 12.924 |
| 4 | 0.271 | 0.741 | 1.533 | 2.132 | 2.333 | 2.776 | 2.999 | 3.747 | 4.604 | 5.598 | 7.173 | 8.610 |
| 5 | 0.267 | 0.727 | 1.476 | 2.015 | 2.191 | 2.571 | 2.757 | 3.365 | 4.032 | 4.773 | 5.894 | 6.869 |
| 6 | 0.265 | 0.718 | 1.440 | 1.943 | 2.104 | 2.447 | 2.612 | 3.143 | 3.707 | 4.317 | 5.208 | 5.959 |
| 7 | 0.263 | 0.711 | 1.415 | 1.895 | 2.046 | 2.365 | 2.517 | 2.998 | 3.499 | 4.029 | 4.785 | 5.408 |
| 8 | 0.262 | 0.706 | 1.397 | 1.860 | 2.004 | 2.306 | 2.449 | 2.896 | 3.355 | 3.833 | 4.501 | 5.041 |
| 9 | 0.261 | 0.703 | 1.383 | 1.833 | 1.973 | 2.262 | 2.398 | 2.821 | 3.250 | 3.690 | 4.297 | 4.781 |
| 10 | 0.260 | 0.700 | 1.372 | 1.812 | 1.948 | 2.228 | 2.359 | 2.764 | 3.169 | 3.581 | 4.144 | 4.587 |

**Fig. 3.23** Table of critical values for Student's $t$ distribution (Kim, 2010)

| alfa | 5% |
|---|---|
| t | 2.36 |

| | | K= | 2 | K= | 3 | K= | 4 |
|---|---|---|---|---|---|---|---|
| | Xj | Pj | (Xj-Pj)^2 | Pj | (Xj-Pj)^2 | Pj | (Xj-Pj)^2 |
| Okt 15 | 200 | | | | | | |
| Nov 15 | 216 | | | | | | |
| Dez 15 | 194 | 208.00 | 196.00 | | | | |
| Jan 16 | 240 | 205.00 | 1225.00 | 203.33 | 1344.44 | | |
| Feb 16 | 250 | 217.00 | 1089.00 | 216.67 | 1111.11 | 212.50 | 1406.25 |
| Mär 16 | 235 | 245.00 | 100.00 | 228.00 | 49.00 | 225.00 | 100.00 |
| Apr 16 | 220 | 242.50 | 506.25 | 241.67 | 469.44 | 229.75 | 95.06 |
| Mai 16 | 248 | 227.50 | 420.25 | 235.00 | 169.00 | 236.25 | 138.06 |
| Jun 16 | 212 | 234.00 | 484.00 | 234.33 | 498.78 | 238.25 | 689.06 |
| Jul 16 | 222 | 230.00 | 64.00 | 226.67 | 21.78 | 228.75 | 45.56 |
| Aug 16 | 230 | 217.00 | 169.00 | 227.33 | 7.11 | 225.50 | 20.25 |
| Sep 16 | 240 | 226.00 | 196.00 | 221.33 | 348.44 | 228.00 | 144.00 |
| t = | 12 | | 4449.50 | | 4019.11 | | 2638.25 | SUM((Xj-Pj)^2) |
| | | | 9 | | 8 | | 7 | dof |
| | | | 22.23 | | 22.41 | | 19.41 | oK |
| P October | | | | | | | 226.00 | |

| Confidence of interval | | 226.00 | ± | 45.8163994 |
|---|---|---|---|---|
| LIM INF | | 180.18 | | |
| LIM SUP | | 271.82 | | |

**Fig. 3.24** Example for the determination of "$k$" number of periods

sales/demand of an item, while on the right there are three different sections that illustrate the calculation for the different values of the "$k$ periods": $k = 2$, $k = 3$ and $k = 4$. For each "$k$" indicator, the moving average method is run as described above, resulting in the standard deviation of the forecast error ($\sigma k$). In this example, $K = 4$ is the optimum value, as it minimizes the standard deviation to a value of 19.41. The forecasted quantity for the next period is only calculated for this "$k$", and it accounts for 226 units.

In Fig. 3.24, the concept of the confidence interval is introduced. The inferior limit of the forecasted value is 181 units (LIM INF), while the upper bound is set to 272 units (LIM SUP).

The advantage of the moving average method is mostly due to the simplicity of its application and to its capacity to reduce the cyclical effects of data. On the other hand, it is a method that does not take into consideration trend and seasonal effects.

**Weighted Average**

An enhancement of the moving average method is the weighted average method. It allows to attribute a different weight to different data of the same data set. The formula for the weighted average is as follows:

$$P_{t+1} = \sum_{i=1}^{k} X_{t-k+i} * W_i$$

$$\sum_{1}^{k} W_i = 1$$

where $W_i$ is the associated weight for the effective sales/demand within the period $i$.

The complexity of this method lies in the necessity to properly identify both the number of "$k$" (periods that minimize the standard deviation of the forecast error) and the periodic value that has to be assigned as a weight of the past data ($W_i$). A general rule that is commonly applied is that the most recent data are the most reliable indicator of the future; consequently, it is assigned the greatest weight.

Figure 3.25 provides an example of the principle behind this forecasting method. The weights constantly decrease as time passes, giving always more relevance to the most recent data. Automatically, when new data is added to the data set, the weights associated with each period shift to the left by one period and the last data of the set are excluded from the calculations.

The advantages of the weighted moving average method are mostly due to the possibility of switching and changing the weights assigned to the past data. It allows adaptability and flexibility from a user standpoint. On the other hand, it is a method that requires a scrupulous assessment of the "$k$" values and "$w$" weights.

Furthermore, it is more time consuming and less accurate than the single exponential smoothing.

As for the other average methods, it is not a suitable solution for the more complex data set with trend, seasonality or higher variability.

### 3.3.2  SAP Use Case: Moving Average, Moving Weighted Average

In Fig. 3.26, general time settings are shown. Historical periods and forecast periods will commonly be shared among simple time series forecasting models. Among the mandatory fields, it is fundamental to set the periodicity of the

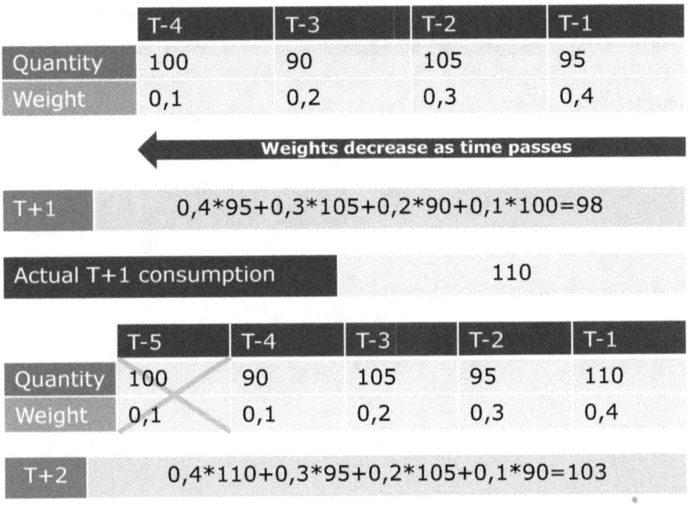

| | T-4 | T-3 | T-2 | T-1 |
|---|---|---|---|---|
| Quantity | 100 | 90 | 105 | 95 |
| Weight | 0,1 | 0,2 | 0,3 | 0,4 |

Weights decrease as time passes

| T+1 | 0,4*95+0,3*105+0,2*90+0,1*100=98 |
|---|---|

| Actual T+1 consumption | 110 |
|---|---|

| | T-5 | T-4 | T-3 | T-2 | T-1 |
|---|---|---|---|---|---|
| Quantity | 100 | 90 | 105 | 95 | 110 |
| Weight | 0,1 | 0,1 | 0,2 | 0,3 | 0,4 |

| T+2 | 0,4*110+0,3*95+0,2*105+0,1*90=103 |
|---|---|

**Fig. 3.25** Example of weighted moving average

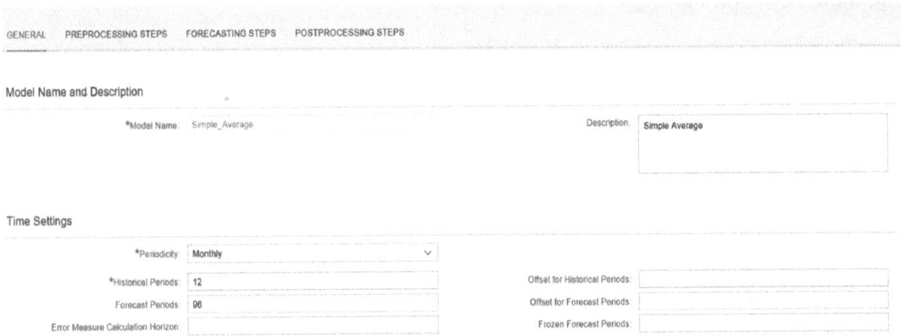

**Fig. 3.26** SAP IBP general settings for the average methods

calculations (monthly in the example), the historical periods to be considered (12 in the example) and the forecast periods in the future (96 in the example).

In Fig. 3.27, we see the outcome of the calculation with the simple average forecast model. Besides, we are able to notice the calculation outcome for a specific product, its adjusted actual quantity that corresponds to the sales history already preprocessed and the statistical forecasting quantity that relates to the average of the adjusted actual quantity. As a result, the light blue bars in the graph below indicate the monthly forecast.

In addition, the statistical forecast MAPE row indicates the forecasting error in relation to each month; it is displayed, as a conclusion, that the MAPE, mean average percentage error, of 2017 accounts for only 6%.

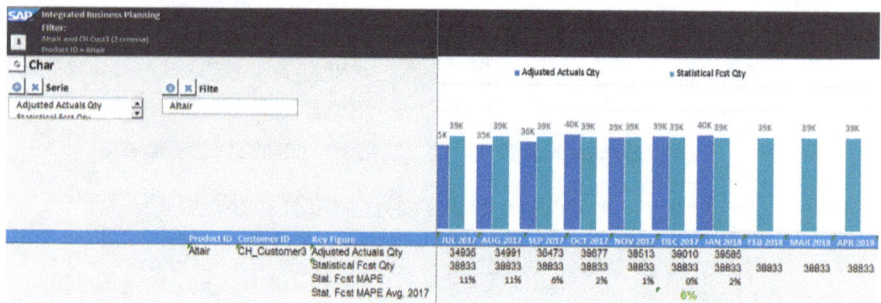

**Fig. 3.27** SAP IBP simple average

**Fig. 3.28** SAP IBP moving average specific settings

While for the simple average there are no additional critical configuration parameters, for the moving average, the number of periods, which corresponds to the "$k$" value described above, has to be inserted in the forecasting step settings. Figure 3.28 illustrates the specific configuration.

Ideally, after having set the optimal "$k$" value for your specific product, group of products, family or for the type of cluster chosen, it has to be entered in the "number of periods" field to guarantee a more effective and accurate forecasting solution.

Figure 3.29 represents the same analysis as in Fig. 3.27 (SAP IBP simple average); however, the simple moving average is used. Its evident that, the forecasted quantity differs from the simple average calculated before. It is interesting to notice that the forecasted volume provided with this model, which has been running with an optimal "$k$" value equal to 3, accounts for 39,036 units. At the same time, in Fig. 3.30, the same model has been running, but the periods "$k$" taken into consideration changed from three to five. The expected sales/demand changed, deviating approximately 500 units.

In terms of forecast accuracy, it is displayed how an optimized assessment of the "$k$" periods leads to a reduced forecast error: in this case a forecast error of only 5%. As explained, there is no better assessment for the number of periods to be considered in the analysis than the linear optimization algorithm for the standard deviation of the forecasting error. Consequently, it is highly recommended to identify a priori the most suitable value of "$k$" and successively configure the forecasting model with the value of "$k$" provided by the optimization run.

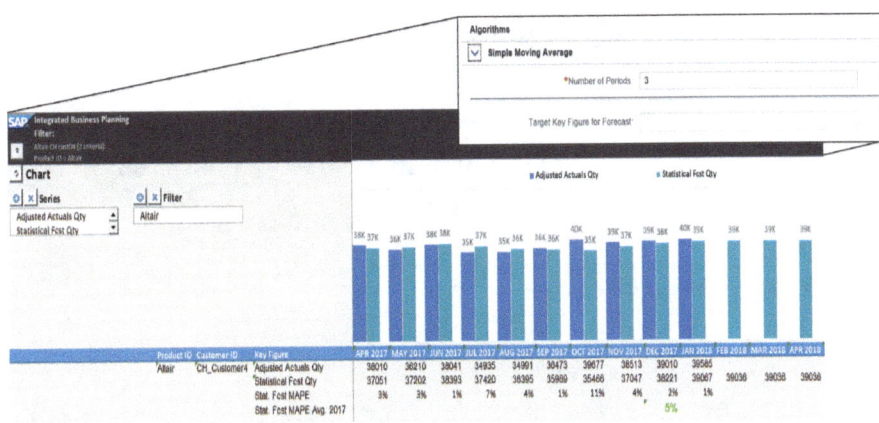

**Fig. 3.29** SAP IBP simple moving average with $K = 3$

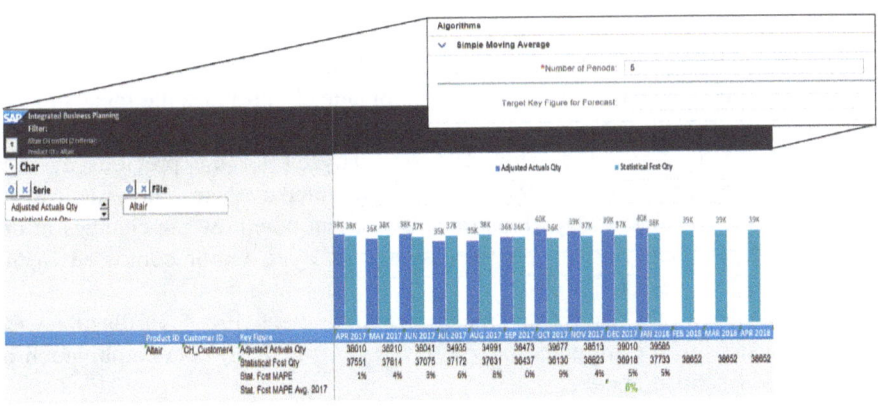

**Fig. 3.30** SAP IBP simple moving average with $K = 5$

The simple weighted averages were configured as it is shown in Fig. 3.31. The source of the weights has to be specified, and its assessment comes from the data provided as an input for the forecast model calculation.

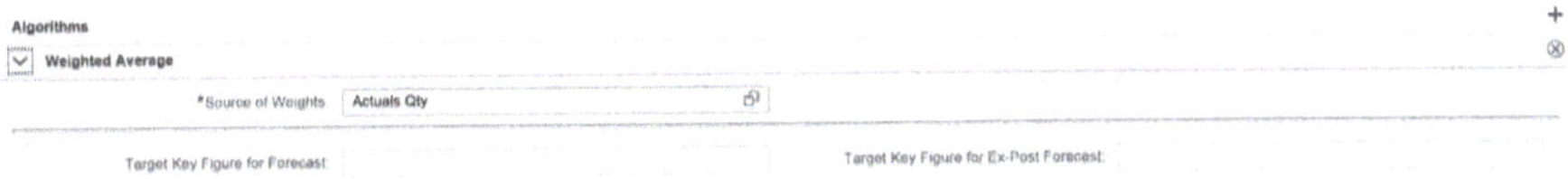

**Fig. 3.31** SAP IBP weighted average specific settings

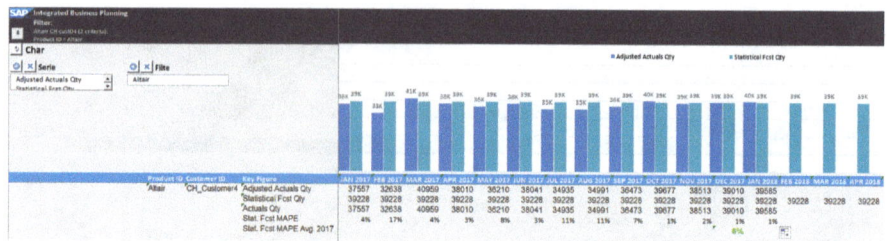

**Fig. 3.32** SAP IBP weighted average

**Fig. 3.33** SAP IBP weighted moving average specific settings

The determination of the weights is a crucial step to guarantee a positive forecasting outcome for this model. SAP IBP automatically provides the most suitable weights from the data provided.

Figure 3.32 illustrates the same data set analyzed for the previous average forecast models, but it has been applied to the weighted average. The visualization structure is the same as the previous models; we can note how the changes in the foreseen sales/demand and in the forecast accuracy are minor compared to the previous methods depicted above.

As a conclusion, for the average method configurations, Fig. 3.33 illustrates the forecasting steps of the weighted moving average. It is the simple combination of the settings described above:

- Calculation of the number of time periods, "$k$" value
- Estimation of the weights of the time series.

Figure 3.34 illustrates the weighted moving forecasting mechanism with the usual visualization. The forecasted amount is displayed with the light blue bars, while the adjusted actual quantity with the dark blue bars. The overall forecast error in 2017 accounts for 5%, resulting in one of the most accurate methods for the data set analyzed.

In Fig. 3.35, we see the simple average (statistical forecasting quantity 1), the simple moving average (statistical forecasting quantity 2) and the weighted moving average (statistical forecasting quantity 3). The most accurate forecasting model, based on the MAPE, out of those three models is then selected for the statistical forecasting quantity. The forecasting error of the selected method that in this case is the simple moving average accounts for only 5%. The visualization allows to

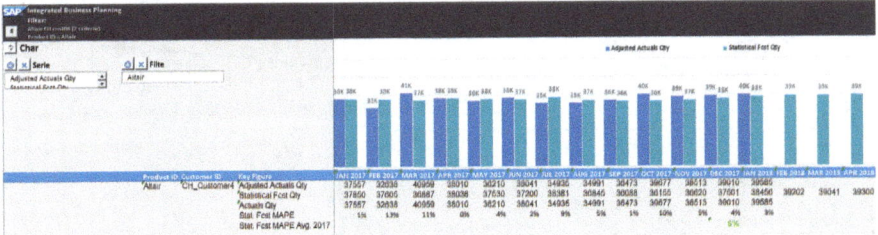

**Fig. 3.34** SAP IBP weighted moving average

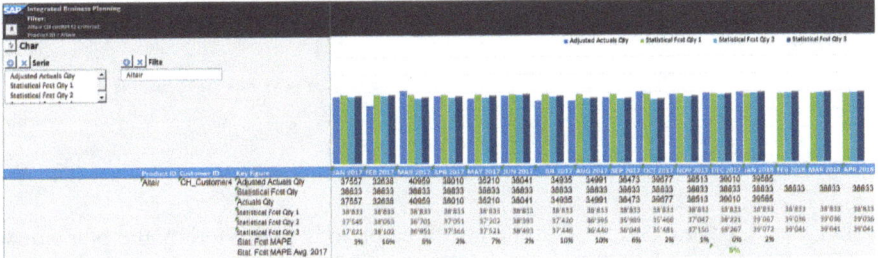

**Fig. 3.35** SAP IBP average algorithm comparison

compare the amount of the adjusted actual versus the foreseen sales/demands proposed by the three different methods.

### 3.3.3   Single Exponential Smoothing (SES)

Single exponential smoothing (SES) is a technique in which the historical periods are weighted progressively higher, in the calculation of the forecast, from older to more recent periods. The relative weights depend on the smoothing constant used—called $\alpha$, alpha. More formally (at the end of $t + 1$):

$$\text{Forecast}_{t+1} = \text{Forecast}_t + \alpha^*(\text{Demand Observation}_{t+1} - \text{Forecast}_t)$$

The smoothing constant $\alpha$ takes a value between 0 and 1. The formula translated means the new forecast (at the end of period $t + 1$) equals a certain percentage ($\alpha$) of the forecast error plus the previous forecast. So, the higher the value of $\alpha$, the higher will be the weights assigned to the more recent periods. This is graphically depicted in Fig. 3.36.

The illustration (see Fig. 3.36) provides cumulative weights for three typical $\alpha$ values (0.1, 0.3 and 0.5). The dark cumulative line is assigned to $\alpha = 0.1$, the light green to $\alpha = 0.5$ and the blue one to $\alpha = 0.3$.

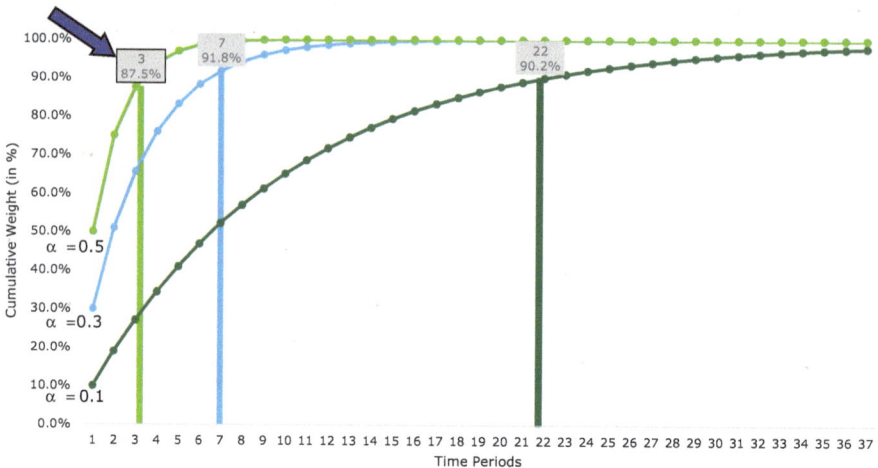

**Fig. 3.36** Impact of smoothing constant α

For α = 0.5, for example, just the last three periods (indicated by the blue arrow in the graph) give a cumulative weight of around 90%. This means the new forecast is purely made up of the weighted sum of the previous three periods. This should sound a cautionary note on the selection of α. The index selection is additionally explored in the coming sections.

The exponential smoothing has the advantage of detecting the inner cyclical component of the demand; however, it does not catch the trend and the seasonal component. It might be used for quite stable and low random data. If a data set shows high variability in sales/demand and a high inner variability, this method will not be the most ideal.

For the best definition of the alpha parameter, it is possible to apply the same reasoning applied to the optimal assessment of the "$k$ periods" value of the moving average. In this case, the most ideal α, alpha, value will be the one that minimizes the standard deviation of the forecast error.

Figure 3.37 indicates how it is possible to set the optimal alpha value and how to establish the tiniest confidence interval for the forecasted sales/demand. The 0.441843 value of alpha is the one chosen in the example below and established by the optimization algorithm, while the forecasted quantity accounts for 233 units. The structure and the principle behind the model are the same as the one described for the moving average method.

The Excel Solver plug-in is set in a way that minimizes the cell G56 which corresponds to the formula of the standard deviation. The changing cell relates to the parameter α of the single exponential smoothing itself, and the constraints are equivalent to those explained before: α value cannot be higher than 1 and inferior to 0. The confidence interval accounts for only 47 units, which is a small and reliable interval considering the amount of the forecasted demand.

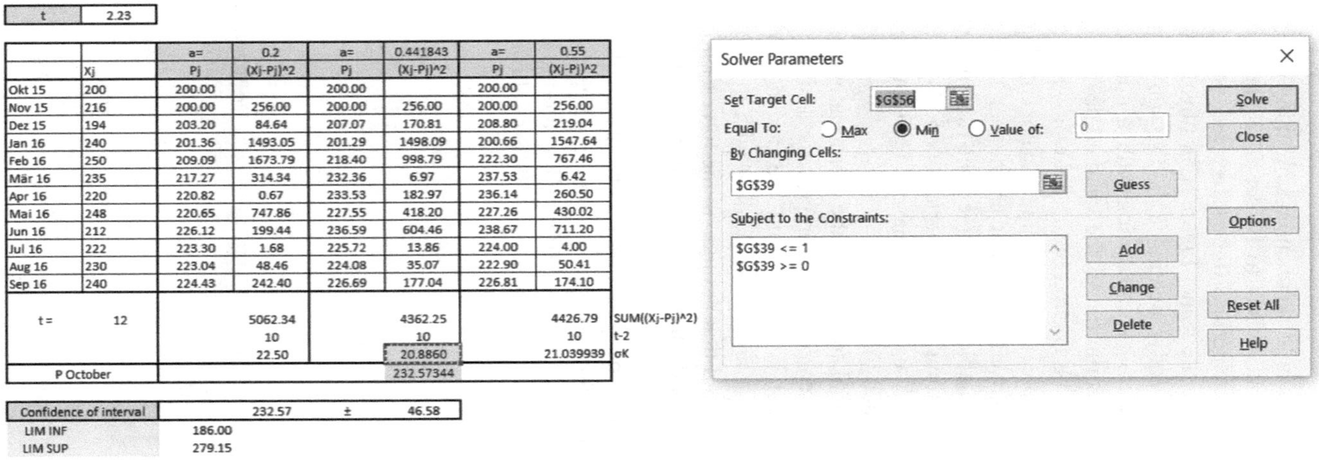

t = 2.23

| | Xj | a= 0.2 Pj | (Xj-Pj)^2 | a= 0.441843 Pj | (Xj-Pj)^2 | a= 0.55 Pj | (Xi-Pj)^2 |
|---|---|---|---|---|---|---|---|
| Okt 15 | 200 | 200.00 | | 200.00 | | 200.00 | |
| Nov 15 | 216 | 200.00 | 256.00 | 200.00 | 256.00 | 200.00 | 256.00 |
| Dez 15 | 194 | 203.20 | 84.64 | 207.07 | 170.81 | 208.80 | 219.04 |
| Jan 16 | 240 | 201.36 | 1493.05 | 201.29 | 1498.09 | 200.66 | 1547.64 |
| Feb 16 | 250 | 209.09 | 1673.79 | 218.40 | 998.79 | 222.30 | 767.46 |
| Mär 16 | 235 | 217.27 | 314.34 | 232.36 | 6.97 | 237.53 | 6.42 |
| Apr 16 | 220 | 220.82 | 0.67 | 233.53 | 182.97 | 236.14 | 260.50 |
| Mai 16 | 248 | 220.65 | 747.86 | 227.55 | 418.20 | 227.26 | 430.02 |
| Jun 16 | 212 | 226.12 | 199.44 | 236.59 | 604.46 | 238.67 | 711.20 |
| Jul 16 | 222 | 223.30 | 1.68 | 225.72 | 13.86 | 224.00 | 4.00 |
| Aug 16 | 230 | 223.04 | 48.46 | 224.08 | 35.07 | 222.90 | 50.41 |
| Sep 16 | 240 | 224.43 | 242.40 | 226.69 | 177.04 | 226.81 | 174.10 |
| t = 12 | | 5062.34 | | 4362.25 | | 4426.79 | SUM((Xi-Pj)^2) |
| | | 10 | | 10 | | 10 | t-2 |
| | | 22.50 | | 20.8860 | | 21.039939 | oK |
| | | | | 232.57344 | | | |

P October   232.57   ±   46.58

Confidence of interval
LIM INF   186.00
LIM SUP   279.15

**Solver Parameters**

Set Target Cell: $G$56

Equal To: ○ Max  ● Min  ○ Value of: 0

By Changing Cells: $G$39

Subject to the Constraints:
$G$39 <= 1
$G$39 >= 0

Solve   Close   Guess   Options   Add   Change   Delete   Reset All   Help

**Fig. 3.37** SES Excel Solver results

### 3.3.4  SAP Use Case: SES

The configuration settings of the single exponential smoothing differ in the moment in which the specific alpha parameter has to be set. The general settings of the forecasting models such as the time periods to be forecasted, periods of history and periodicity of the calculations are the same. Figure 3.38 illustrates the alpha field. According to what has been already mentioned in the sub-chapter above, this parameter is to be recommended by a calculation with a nonlinear optimization algorithm; once the coefficient that minimizes the standard deviation of the forecast error has been identified, it must be entered in the field shown below.

Figure 3.39 indicates an example of how the single exponential smoothing is run in SAP IBP. The data taken into consideration are neither seasonal nor trendy; consequently, they represent a suitable sample to test the running and the goodness of the single exponential smoothing. The historical periods considered for the calculations are 48. Normally, it is suggested to have at least four years of history to be capable of forecasting accurately the future.

For the below single exponential smoothing, the alpha parameter has been set to 0.4; the adjusted actual quantity represents the preprocessed history we dispose of. The result of the forecast model is shown until the period April 2018, and it accounts for 354,433 units. As we are simply dealing with the single exponential smoothing, it is important to remind that through all the forecast horizon sets in the configuration setting, the forecasted quantity delivered by the SES algorithm will always account for 354,433.

The row actual quantity shows the actual from February 2014 to January 2018, while the row MAPE accounts for the "mean average percentage error" of the algorithm considered. A MAPE that accounts for 11% is a quite positive result as it means that the forecast quantity is accurate for 89% of the cases or that the forecasting error is only 11%.

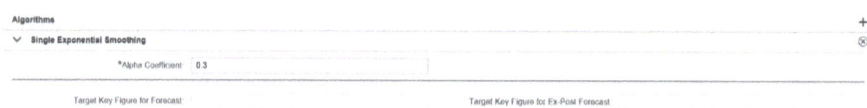

**Fig. 3.38** SAP IBP SES settings

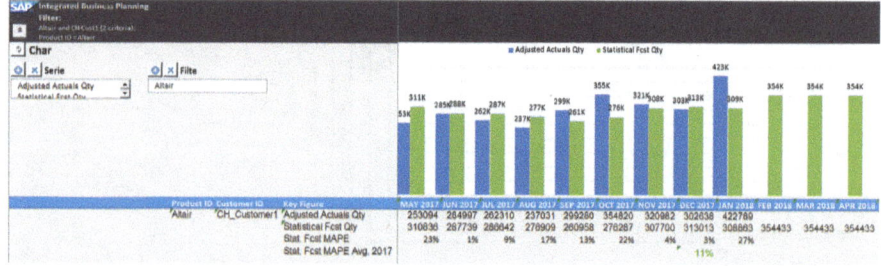

**Fig. 3.39** SAP IBP SES with alpha manually assigned (0.3)

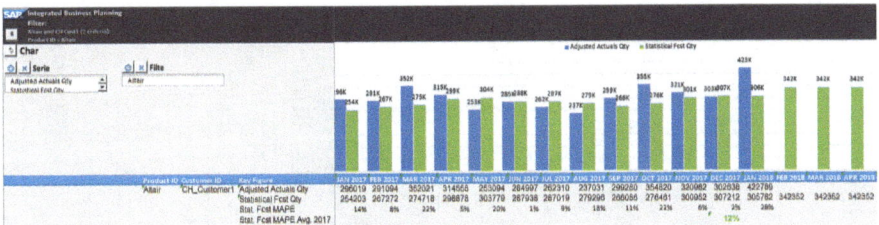

**Fig. 3.40** SES run with parameters assigned by the Solver

In the below visualization, the green bars identify the forecasted quantity, while the blue ones, the adjusted actual quantity.

It is notable how the outcome of the algorithm changed from the 354,433 units forecasted before (Fig. 3.39) with alpha = 0.3 to the 342,352 units displayed in Fig. 3.40. The reason for such a change lies in the running of the Excel Solver plug-in optimization algorithm that determined the alpha value that minimizes the standard deviation of the forecast error. The benefit out of this practice is to better focus and center the forecasted value within a thinner confidence interval.

### 3.3.5  Double Exponential Smoothing (DES)

The double exponential smoothing relies on the same smoothing principle described before, but it introduces a new smoothing variable "beta" that has the functionality of capturing the trend pattern within a data set. It helps also to diminish the impact of the error between the forecasted quantity and the actual one.

The formula for the double exponential smoothing is as follows:
Additive:

$$P_{t,t+\tau} = S_t + \tau G_t$$

$S_t$    estimates the time series level at the time $t$
$G_t$    estimates the time series trend at the time $t$

The choice for the parameters alpha and beta can be run in two different ways:

- "Brute force" algorithm that consists of running and exploring all the possible combinations of alpha and beta and eventually picking the combination that minimizes the standard deviation of the forecast error
- Algorithm of nonlinear optimization.

Figure 3.41 shows a comparison between a "brute force algorithm" on the left and the "nonlinear optimization" algorithm on the right. The degree of confidence is set to 95%, and the values of alpha and beta are automatically set to 0.35. Once

| Degree of confidence | 95% |
|---|---|
| alpha | 5% |
| t | 2.36 |

**Brute force attempt**

| | Smoothing | Trend |
|---|---|---|
| a | 0.35 | |
| b | 0.35 | |

| Week | [kg] Xi | St | Gt | Pt | (Xi-Pi)^2 |
|---|---|---|---|---|---|
| 1 | 2'800 | 2'800 | 170 | | - |
| 2 | 2'970 | 2'970 | 170 | 2'970 | |
| 3 | 2'920 | 3'063 | 143 | 3'140 | 48'400 |
| 4 | 2'810 | 3'067 | 95 | 3'206 | 156'856 |
| 5 | 3'070 | 3'130 | 83 | 3'162 | 8'458 |
| 6 | 3'020 | 3'145 | 60 | 3'213 | 37'267 |
| 7 | 3'050 | 3'151 | 41 | 3'205 | 24'056 |
| 8 | 3'300 | 3'229 | 54 | 3'191 | 11'786 |
| 9 | 3'190 | 3'251 | 42 | 3'283 | 8'715 |
| 10 | 3'330 | 3'306 | 47 | 3'293 | 1'357 |
| P(11) | | | | 3'353 | |

| | | ∑(Xi-Pj)^2 | 296'894 |
|---|---|---|---|
| | | t-1-2 | 7 |
| | | oK | 206 |

| | | t | 486 |
|---|---|---|---|
| | | dev standard | |

**Confidence of interval** | 3'353 | ± | 486

**Non-linear optimization algorithm**

| | Smoothing | Trend |
|---|---|---|
| a | 0.6195 | |
| b | 0.4037 | |

| St | Gt | Pt | (Xi-Pj)^2 |
|---|---|---|---|
| 2'800 | 170 | | |
| 2'970 | 170 | 2'970 | 0 |
| 3'004 | 115 | 3'140 | 48'400 |
| 2'927 | 38 | 3'119 | 95'287 |
| 3'030 | 64 | 2'965 | 10'977 |
| 3'048 | 45 | 3'094 | 5'494 |
| 3'067 | 35 | 3'094 | 1'905 |
| 3'224 | 84 | 3'101 | 39'546 |
| 3'235 | 55 | 3'309 | 14'066 |
| 3'315 | 65 | 3'290 | 1'622 |
| | | 3'379 | |

| | | ∑(Xi-Pj)^2 | 217'297 |
|---|---|---|---|
| | | t-1-2 | 7 |
| | | oK | 176 |

| | | t | 416 |
|---|---|---|---|
| | | dev standard | |

**Confidence of interval** | 3'379 | ± | 416

**Fig. 3.41** Comparison of DES parameter setup

again, the explicative structure of the table and its components is the same as the ones experienced for the previous forecasting models.

The forecasted value on the left accounts for 3,353,052 units with a standard deviation of 205,945; on the contrary, adopting the mathematical algorithm, as it is shown on the right, the standard deviation gets reduced to a value of 176,189. As a result, the power of the nonlinear algorithm lies on the opportunity to better center the forecasted value and reduce the margin of errors.

However, as a conclusion, the DES is not yet capable of detecting the effects of seasonality and the phenomena behind it. The triple exponential smoothing comes to assistance for that purpose.

### 3.3.6  SAP Use Case: DES

The same reasoning as for SES is applicable to the double exponential smoothing. The parameters calculated out of the nonlinear optimization algorithm have to be set in the specific fields displayed in Fig. 3.42: alpha coefficient and beta coefficient.

Figure 3.43 depicts an example of the double exponential smoothing in SAP IBP. The blue bars indicate the amount of the history and the green bars the amount of the forecasted quantity.

Using an alpha parameter equal to 0.3 and a beta parameter equal to 0.3, the forecasted amount for the beginning of 2018 is expressed by the green bars and by the statistical forecasting quantity. We can assess from Fig. 3.43 that the double exponential smoothing detects the trend of the historical data sales; as a matter of

**Fig. 3.42**  SAP IBP DES settings

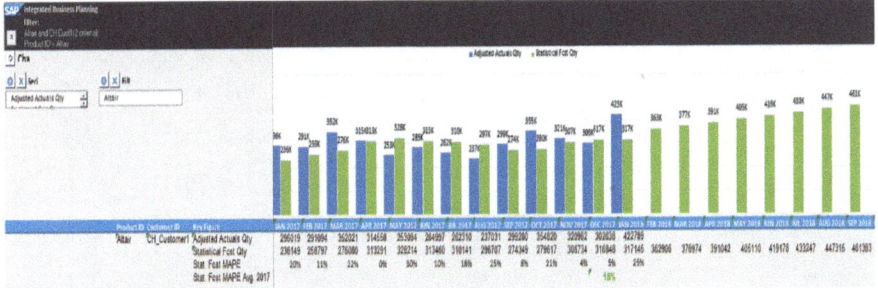

**Fig. 3.43**  SAP IBP DES with alpha 0.3 and beta 0.3

**Fig. 3.44** SAP IBP DES with parameters assigned by the Solver

fact, in the visualization, it is possible to see how the green bars tend to indicate an increase in sales/demand and the underlying positive trend. Furthermore, the data set applied to the DES is the same that one used for the previous example of the SES: The accuracy for the past forecasted values stays approximately the same (15% of error), while it differs for the expected future trendy sales/demand.

The same algorithm is shown in Fig. 3.44; however, the setting of the Excel Solver plug-in parameters has been optimized. Once the configuration of alpha and beta had been changed in SAP IBP, we could rerun the double exponential smoothing with the following result: a forecast error of only 12%. The improvement of the error has to be attributed to the nonlinear optimization algorithm as a better definition of the parameters of the time series.

### 3.3.7 Triple Exponential Smoothing (TES)

The triple exponential smoothing is one of the most suitable techniques for forecasting seasonal data. As the previous ones described above, this method is also a procedure for continually revising a forecast in light of more recent experiences. It assigns exponentially decreasing weights as the observations get older. In other words, recent observations are given relatively more weight in forecasting than the older observations (Kalekar, 2004).

This method is used to detect seasonality, and it can be additive or multiplicative.

Additive

$$P_{t,t+\tau} = S_t + \tau G_t + C_{t-s+\tau}$$

Multiplicative

$$P_{t,t+\tau} = (S_t + \tau G_t)C_{t-s+\tau}$$

$S_t$        estimates the time series level at the time $t$

$G_t$        estimates the time series trend at the time $t$

$C_{t-s} + \tau$    estimates the time series seasonal component dependent on the season length $S$ previously defined

One of the core aspects of the triple exponential smoothing is the establishment of the smoothing indexes. The three indexes are as follows:

- Alpha, it detects the inner cyclical variances of the demand. As seen above, if the alpha index is used as a stand-alone factor, the exponential smoothing is said to be "simple" and it is called the Brown model. Unfortunately, the alpha factor is not capable of detecting the trend and the seasonal components of the demand; hence, consequently an enhancement of the model is necessary.
- Beta, once the exponential smoothing is run with both the indexes alpha and beta, is said "double", and it is also called the Holt model. The beta factor is capable of capturing the trend factor, and it reduces the error which arises between the actual data and the previsions. Unfortunately, this model still does not detect the seasonal component of the demand.
- Gamma, the exponential smoothing that uses the three mentioned indexes, is said "triple" and is also called Winters' model. The gamma factor is eventually able to detect the seasonal component and coupled with the other indexes captures the trend, the inner variances and it reduces the errors between what is experienced in reality and the suggested forecasts for the future.

For TES, it is common to assign the same values of the indexes to a group of products or to a company portfolio. However, this generalization of the values of the parameters does not lead to an optimal result out of the statistical forecasting technique: the generated forecasted value.

The most convenient and result-driven solution toward this decision is also in this case to apply the already mentioned algorithm of optimization to define the indexes of the triple exponential smoothing. The approach for the TES is the following:

Set the values of alpha, beta and gamma in order to reduce the standard deviation of the forecast error. This solution can be easily built with the Excel Solver, and it looks as below.

The only constraints that need to be set are that the indexes range from 0 to 1, while the target value is the minimization of the STDEV of the forecast error. The illustration exhibits also the values of the indexes set by the Excel Solver plug-in for a random data set employed for the example in question (Fig. 3.45).

The importance of properly setting those indexes is essential for the output error. The common practice of randomly setting those indexes for the entire set of the data that require a statistical forecasting is misleading, and it has the effect of distancing the forecast from the actual value.

If we try to stick to some of the suggested values provided by the literature, the results from a forecast accuracy perspective could be often inferior or much more

| Alpha | 0,21 |
|---|---|
| Beta | 0,11 |
| Gamma | 0,001 |

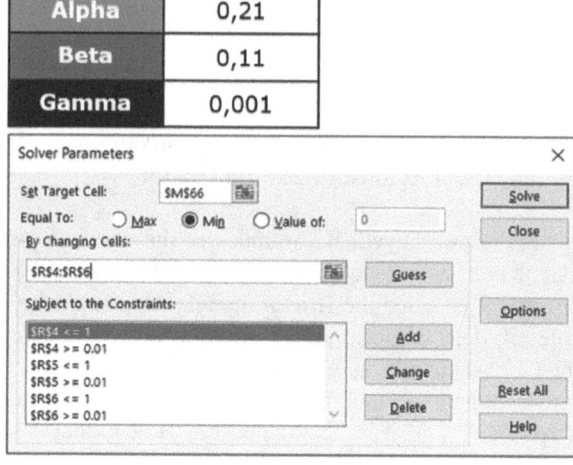

**Fig. 3.45**  Alpha, beta, gamma in Excel Solver

| Class | Alpha | Alpha (Seasonal) | Beta (Seasonal) | Gamma (Seasonal) |
|---|---|---|---|---|
| High | 0.3 | 0.51 | 0.176 | 0.5 |
| Med | 0.1 | 0.19 | 0.053 | 0.1 |
| Low | 0.01 | 0.02 | 0.005 | 0.05 |

**Fig. 3.46**  Tabulated values for Winters' model indexes per seasonal classes

dispersed in terms of confidence interval from the forecasted value to the one equipped by the Excel Solver plug-in (see Fig. 3.46).

Figure 3.46 indicates some tabulated values for the indexes, depending on the degree of variability of the seasonal component of the demand. Before testing how a typical seasonal SKU reacts in terms of forecasting accuracy changing among the suggested indexes, it must be specified that a possible drawback of this type of preselected classification lies in the fact that there is not a common definition of what is a low or medium type of seasonality.

As a result, it is recommended to cluster the SKUs based on the behavior of the data and their demand components. Once some SKUs are identified as similar to distribution and the data behavior, the same or similar indexes can then be set.

The forecast accuracy metric used for this exercise is the mean average percentage error; it will be largely explained in all of its facets in successive sections of the book. For now, it is sufficient to bear in mind that lower the value of the percentage error, better the accuracy and as a consequence the goodness of the

**Fig. 3.47**  Seasonal data set

| Scenario Summary | | | | |
|---|---|---|---|---|
| | Solver | Low | Medium | High |
| **Changing Cells:** | | | | |
| alpha | 0.014 | 0.010 | 0.190 | 0.510 |
| beta | 1.000 | 0.005 | 0.053 | 0.176 |
| gamma | 0.010 | 0.050 | 0.100 | 0.500 |
| **Result Cells:** | | | | |
| Statistical Forecast quantity January | 6322 | 9058 | 6460 | 7107 |
| Actuals quantity January | 6436 | 6436 | 6436 | 6436 |
| MAPE January | 1.8% | 28.9% | 0.4% | 9.4% |
| Statistical Forecast quantity February | 4919 | 7836 | 5289 | 6811 |
| Actuals quantity February | 3332 | 3332 | 3332 | 3332 |
| MAPE February | 32.3% | 57.5% | 37.0% | 51.1% |
| Statistical Forecast quantity March | 2963 | 5973 | 3373 | 5195 |
| Actuals quantity March | 2249 | 2249 | 2249 | 2249 |
| MAPE March | 24.1% | 62.3% | 33.3% | 56.7% |
| **Avg.MAPE** | 19.4% | 49.6% | 23.6% | 39.1% |

**Fig. 3.48**  TES parameter impact on forecast accuracy

indexes set. We take as an example a seasonal data set (see Fig. 3.47), and we try to run several times the TES algorithm changing the model parameters at every run. Then, for each run we calculate the forecast error.

The scenario summary displayed in Fig. 3.48 indicates the comprehensive overview of the effects of the different settings for the smoothing parameters on the forecasted quantity and consequently on the overall accuracy of the model. For each of the seasonality classes, low, medium, high and the Excel Solver plug-in, the values of the parameters are displayed. We can see as well the related actual, MAPE and at the very bottom of each column the average of the MAPE for the three months considered in the example.

Going into further detail, for the seasonality low class, the overall forecast error accounts for 49.6%; it is the worst forecasting solution among the ones proposed. On the other hand, applying the highest seasonal class values to the smoothing parameters does not lead to exceptional results: 39.1% for the forecast error.

The medium seasonality class is the best solution among the ones proposed by the given table. The average MAPE decreases to 23.6%.

Eventually, it is the Excel Solver plug-in and its smoothing parameters that account for the best forecasting accuracy and consequently for the least average forecasting error: 19.4%.

The former comment pivots around the fact that not only the Excel Solver plug-in solution allows for the best accurate forecasting model, but it is also the most reliable one as it builds the tiniest of confidence interval for the forecasted sales. For example, if the forecasted value for the month of January accounts for $6322 \pm 800$, the reliability of the interval of confidence is extremely poor, especially considering that it includes negative values in the interval! The smaller the standard deviation of the forecast error, the more centered is the forecasted quantity.

The latter comment justifies itself in the fact that analyzing the scatter plot of the data set (see Fig. 3.47) shows that the data pattern is extremely seasonal; however, Fig. 3.48 shows how the medium class values allow to account for the most accurate forecasting solution among those proposed by the table from the literature.

Eventually, in the process for outlier detection for seasonal products we will see how the highest accuracy peak will be reached once the correction of the outliers will be applied and the new forecasted value is automatically generated.

### 3.3.8  SAP Use Case: TES with Solver Parameters

Figure 3.49 shows the additional settings specific to the triple exponential smoothing. The gamma coefficient has to be inserted as well, implying the same optimization logic of the other parameters. In addition, the periods in a season have to be established in advance specifying the type of seasonality: multiplicative or additive.

The periods within a season, similarly as the estimation of the parameters of the TES, cannot be stated in advance without having run a proper analysis of the time series. Usually, a season of six periods is expected; however, each data series and each sales/demand type are different, resulting in multiple types of seasonality and a different number of periods within a season.

In Fig. 3.50, the outcome of the triple exponential smoothing is illustrated. As for the other methods, the history of the data accounts for 48 periods and the data set considered is still the same one analyzed for the SES and the DES. We might

**Fig. 3.49** SAP IBP TES settings

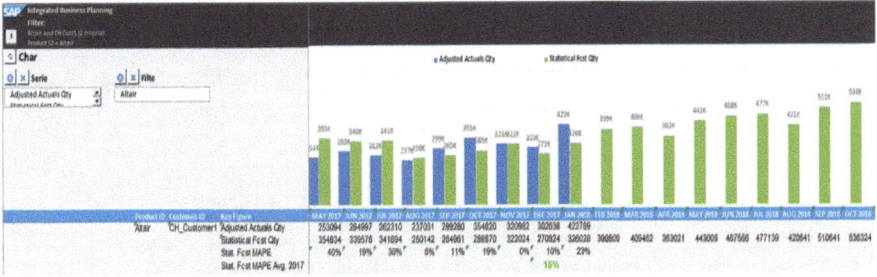

**Fig. 3.50** SAP IBP TES with parameters randomly assigned

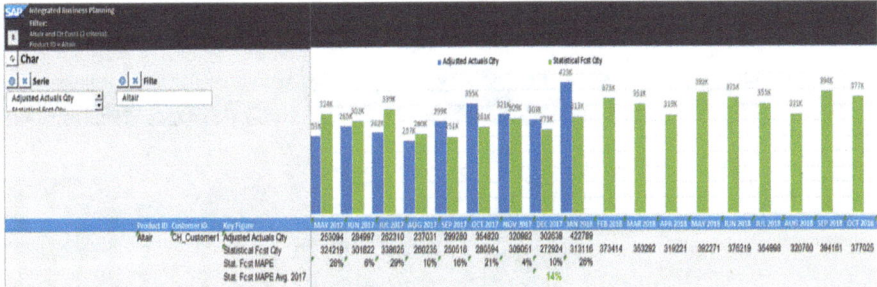

**Fig. 3.51** SAP IBP TES with parameters assigned by the Solver

say that the inner variability of the data is not excessively high and the presence of a seasonal component is quite low.

The visualization of the results is still the same as the other smoothing algorithms. The parameters set for this algorithm assign 0.3 for alpha, beta and gamma. The periods in a season are set randomly to 6. The forecast error accounts for 15%. It is possible to see in the visualization below how the triple exponential smoothing detects differently the inner variations of the data and it projects for the future a variable sales/demand depending on the months of the year.

In order to increase the accuracy of the forecast, we run the Excel Solver plug-in optimization algorithm to try to identify the best indexes that approximate the data set to be forecasted. Still keeping a season period equal to 6, we reduce the forecast error by only 1–14%. See Fig. 3.51.

Furthermore, we decided to graphically identify the exact number of periods within a season; the aim is to check if the prediction could be improved by utilizing the outcomes of this analysis. Figure 3.52 illustrates a scatter plot of the sample of the data set considered for testing the triple exponential smoothing. For this particular data set, however, the presence of a seasonal pattern is not clear from the scatter plot and it is not easy at the same time, to assess the length of a potential season.

**Fig. 3.52** Determination of periods in a season

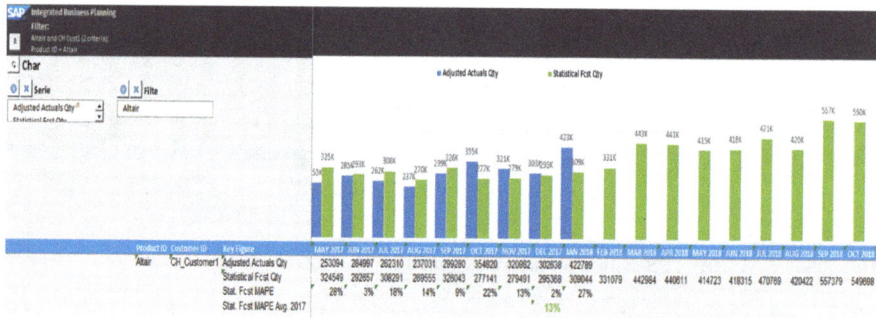

**Fig. 3.53** SAP IBP TES with parameters randomly assigned

Consequently, the decision taken has been to randomly switch the parameter of the seasonal period from 6 to 12 and detect the major changes, considering that the SKU analyzed does not present any specific or marked seasonal component.

Figure 3.53 displays the new forecasted quantities with a seasonal period of 12 and alpha, beta and gamma set to 0.3; the forecasted accuracy slightly improved; nevertheless, no major changes in the forecast errors are experienced. However, we can see that the expected forecast quantity changes.

Figure 3.54 illustrates the same SKU, but the TES parameters are optimized with the Solver. The forecast accuracy does not vary, but the forecasted sales/demand changes for each month. It is noticeable as well how the impact on the degree of the forecasted season, trend and cycle varies among all the TES runs. For example, in Fig. 3.53 the expected amount of quantity for October 2018 is 550 K, while in Fig. 3.54, October 2018 accounts for 380 K. The green bars are a good indicator for detecting how the sales/demand is expected to fluctuate.

As a conclusion, we tested all the types of smoothing algorithms so far and we concluded that for a quite stable SKU, with limited variability and without a clear

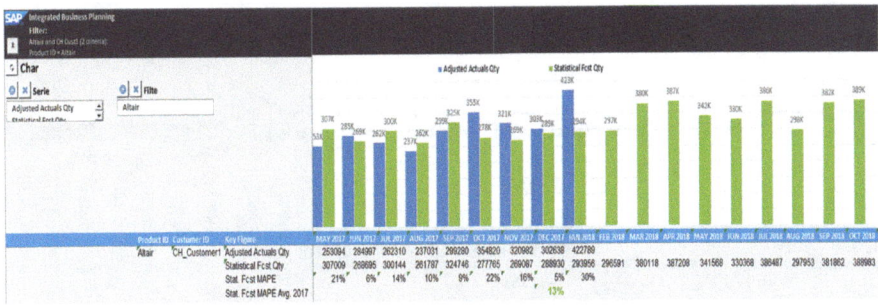

**Fig. 3.54** SAP IBP TES with parameters assigned by the Solver

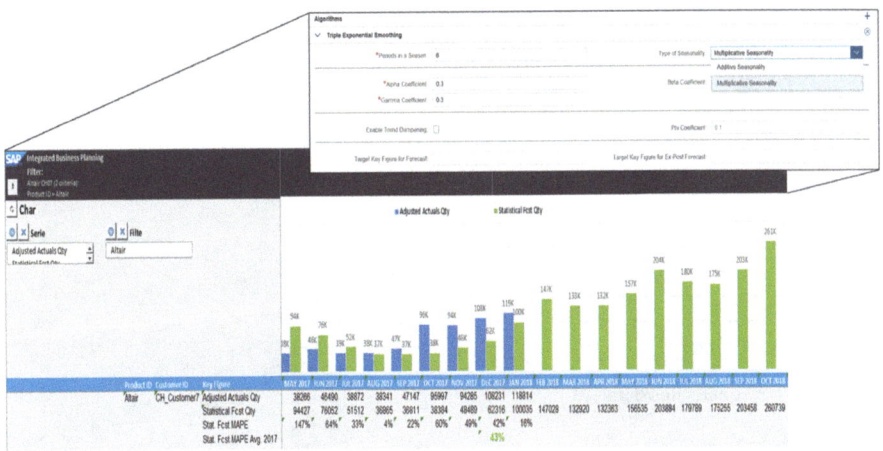

**Fig. 3.55** SAP IBP TES multiplicative seasonality

presence of a seasonal component, the three different types of smoothing models almost give the same result in terms of forecast accuracy, but they differ in the way in which the future is predicted. In addition, applying the Excel Solver plug-in was a good choice for most of the methods except for TES where it did not bring substantial added value.

To enhance the TES testing, we have selected a highly variable SKU and run a second set of examinations. Being sure of the presence of a seasonal pattern, we decided to test the impact of an additive seasonality compared to a multiplicative seasonality in the settings of SAP IBP. In Figs. 3.55 and 3.56, the results are illustrated.

The multiplicative seasonality is represented with the green bars, while the additive seasonality with the light blue bars. We can notice how the forecast error almost does not change; however, the perception of the seasonal component forecasted for the future changes hugely—for example, the expected sales/demand

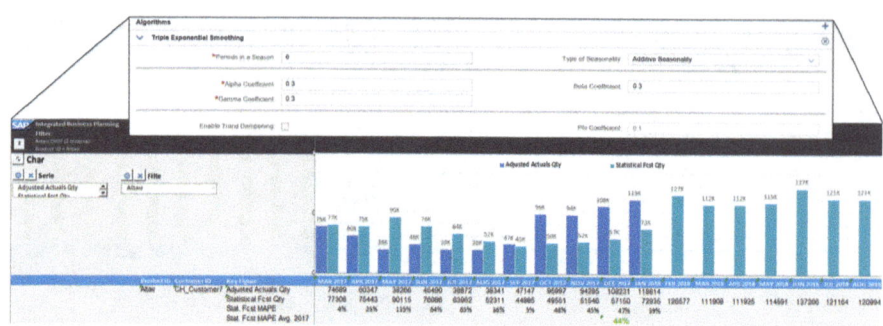

**Fig. 3.56**  SAP IBP TES additive seasonality

**Fig. 3.57**  Seasonal sales/demand

for June 2018 is 20 K for a multiplicative seasonality and 13 K for an additive seasonality.

For such a highly variable SKU, we tried to run the Solver to optimize the parameters, to better understand the seasonal length of the data set and adjust the configuration accordingly; nevertheless, we did not manage to drastically reduce the forecast error. We will see in the custom method chapter how the detection and correction of the outliers will allow to experience improvement of the forecast accuracy.

Figure 3.57 illustrates the monthly sales/demand along the time periods of the considered SKU. The seasonal length appears accounting for six periods, and the peaks are always experienced during the winter periods.

Consequently, in Fig. 3.58 we tried to run the TES with a seasonal length wrongly set to 12 and check how the algorithm reacted in case when a parameter mismatches the actual behavior of the data. As expected, the forecast error increased and the sales/demand for the future, its trend and seasonal pattern varied accordingly.

As a conclusion for this part, it is fundamental to re-iterate how randomly assigning the parameters of the forecasted models can lead to less accurate results

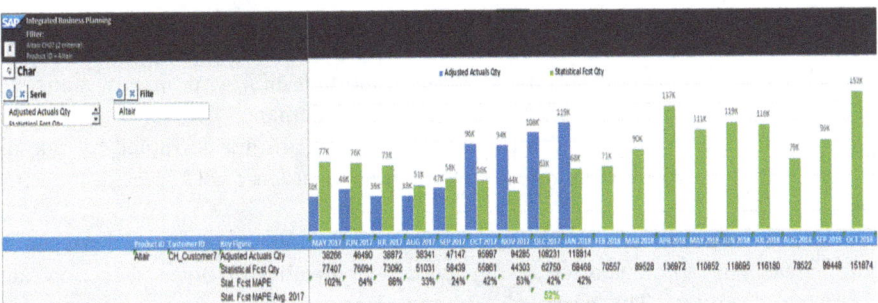

**Fig. 3.58** SAP IBP TES with a wrongly set seasonal period

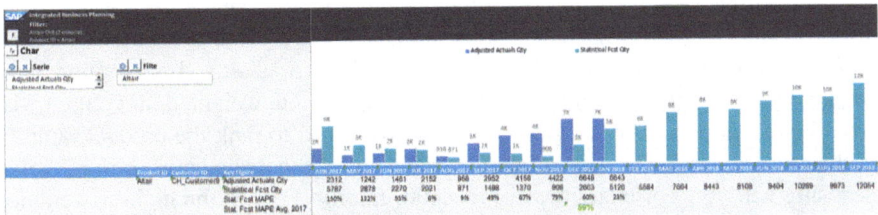

**Fig. 3.59** SAP IBP TES with settings randomly assigned

even if the forecast model chosen for predicting the sales/demand of an SKU is the right one. Figure 3.59 illustrates how the forecast error can reach even higher levels when an accurate analysis of the behavior of the data set is not performed, i.e., when modeled with wrong seasonal period and wrong alpha, beta and gamma parameters.

### 3.3.9 SAP Use Case: Statistical Forecasting on Aggregated and Product Level

In this use case, we describe how you can forecast on an aggregate level and leverage the output to improve the forecast on an SKU level.

These are the steps involved in forecasting on a family and product level:

1. Assessment of cleansing needs on a product family level
2. Exception-driven cleansing on a product level
3. Forecast model selection and assignment on a product family level
4. Automatic statistical forecast model selection on a product level
5. Calculation of proportional factors based on a product-level statistical forecast and calculation of the final product-level statistical forecast
6. Review of the forecast on a product level with the help of insightful visualizations.

Step 1: Assessment of cleansing needs on a product family level:

The cleansing of historical demand is an important first step in any statistical forecasting process. The purpose is to ensure that demands that form an input to statistical forecasting are valid for extrapolation and are not corrupted by one-off events—are not a result of non-repeating actions or at least not repeat in the same fashion.

There are several ways by which cleansing can be done and some of them can be automated. An automated cleansing process typically involves detection and cleansing of outliers. This approach, although less demanding on planner's time, is error prone. What might be seen as an outlier from a purely statistical standpoint could well be a valid data point that should play a role in the calculation of the future forecast. It is advisable to limit the influence of automatic outlier correction (e.g., by setting very high thresholds) and incorporate a manual cleansing step to ensure a sound basis for statistical forecasting.

The approach adopted in this use case involved assessing the variation on a product family level of the most recent historical demand, weighted on volume, vis-à-vis the recent past. The weighted variation was used to rank the product families in the descending order of variation. This helped the planner prioritize his/her cleansing activity. For example, in Fig. 3.60, family 023 has the highest weighted variation—i.e., the demand in the previous month compared to the previous three-month average weighted by volume is the highest among all product families. Weighted variation value is color-coded in the tabular display. Visual control played an important role in this solution; therefore, only top product families are plotted on the charts.

The weighted variation was calculated using a local member (see Fig. 3.61) in the Excel UI front end. Once ranked, illustrative graphs were used to visualize the top N families ranked by weighted variation.

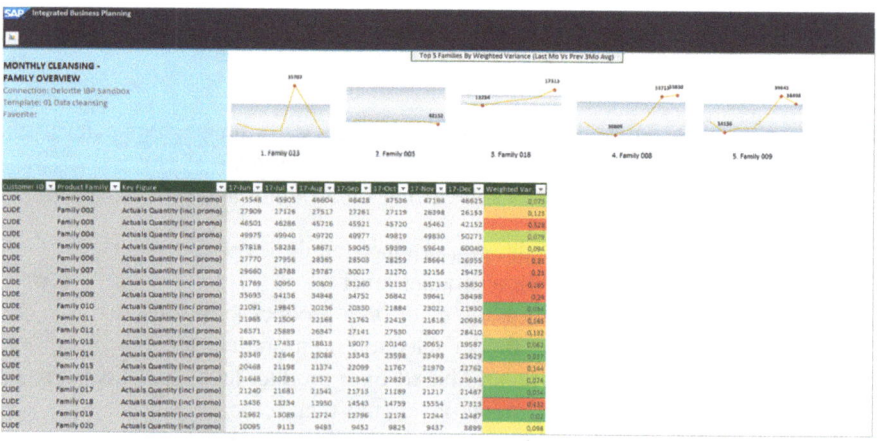

**Fig. 3.60** SAP IBP product family cleansing view

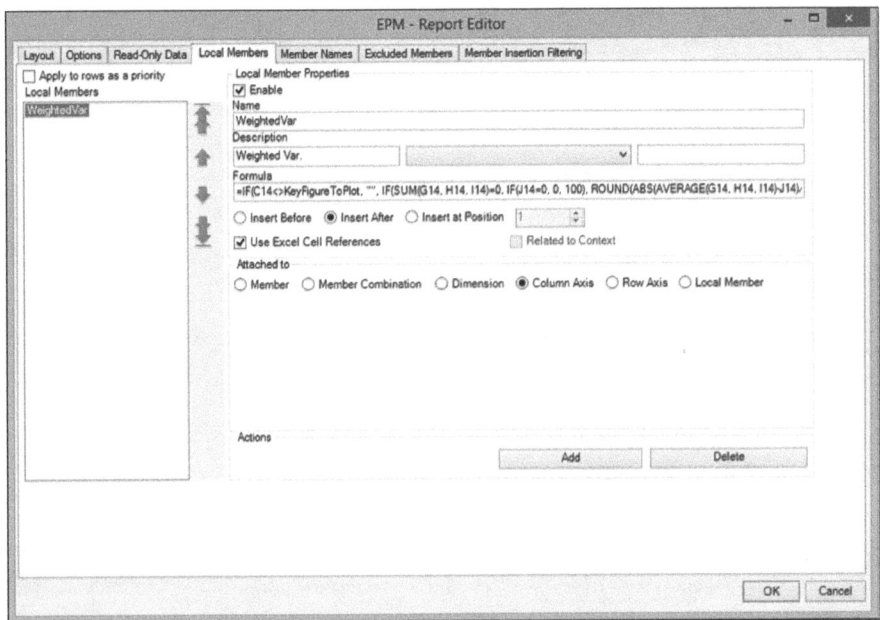

**Fig. 3.61** SAP IBP local member for calculation of weighted variation in actual demand

The analysis of variation in demand with respect to short-term trend could drive deeper analysis on a product level and subsequent cleansing of demand.

Step 2: Exception-driven cleansing on a product level:

The product family view was only provided to identify candidates for cleansing. Adjustments to historical demand were only done on a product level. A product-level cleansing view was provided to facilitate a deeper analysis and the subsequent cleansing activity. An alert was also configured with the aim of comparing the previous month's demand with the historical average to support prioritization on a product level. Adjustments to historical demand were carried out on the cleansed demand key figure, which is different from the actual demand key figure. The actual demand key figure is left intact to serve as reference as it represents what was imported from the source system (see Fig. 3.62).

Step 3: Forecast model selection and assignment on a product family level

It was much easier and more efficient for planners to monitor and control the product family forecast. They verified that levels, trend, seasonality and the changes of packaging or shipment locations did not bring any noise. Product family was supposed to be used as a basis for the disaggregation; therefore, more attention on statistical forecast model assignment was carried out on this level. Demand planners

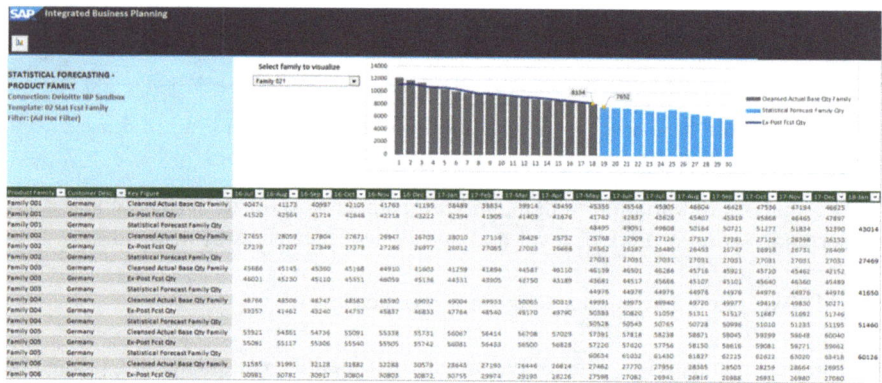

**Fig. 3.62**  SAP IBP product-level data cleansing

**Fig. 3.63**  SAP IBP product family statistical forecast model assignment

analyzed the data and the current forecast assignment and were obliged to assign
better models if needed. In this routine, the system was calculating ex-post forecast
for them. The planners, with the use of the comparison between ex-post forecast
and cleansed actual, were also able to assess the goodness of the statistical forecast
family model assignment (see Fig. 3.63).

Display of ex-post forecast plotted over cleansed actual bars on the chart helped
a lot to increase the process efficiency.

Step 4: Automatic statistical forecast model selection on a product level

The demand planner assessed the model assignment using the so-called spider web
charts, where the results were plotted for constant or seasonal models. These charts
show the assignment of products to specific forecasting profiles. This helped

visualize the assignments and assess the spread. For example, "pick best" is the default assignment which represents "best fit" method (automatic model selection). If on the primary forecasting level planners would see a majority of products assigned to the best fit model, it would be an indication that not too much market knowledge was incorporated into the model assignment. It also shows an overuse of a certain algorithm/profile (see Fig. 3.64).

Nonetheless, the SAP IBP configuration of the models to be included in the "best fit" required the parameterization of alpha, beta and gamma. This was quite a straightforward task since, for the purposes of data analysis, each model is permitted to have a target key figure different than the "best fit." The best fit model was established based on the measures selected by the planner which in this specific case was the Mean Absolute Percentage Error (see Fig. 3.65).

The analysis of the forecast error was performed as part of the model assignment. The performance analysis was done with the use of mean absolute scaled error (MASE). The MASE is a ratio between the accuracy of the current algorithm

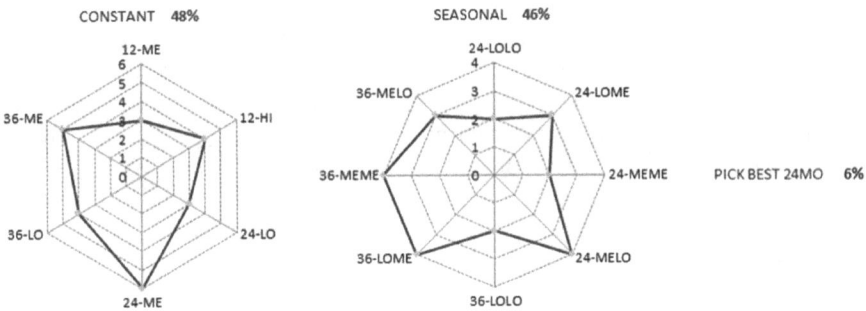

**Fig. 3.64**  SAP IBP product forecast model assignment spider web chart

**Fig. 3.65**  SAP IBP statistical model configuration

and the naïve method (that is, new forecast = previous period demand) as encapsulated in the MASE formula:

$$MASE = \frac{\frac{\sum_{t=1}^{n}|F_t - Y_t|}{n}}{\frac{\sum_{t=2}^{n}|Y_t - Y_{t-1}|}{n-1}}$$

The closer the MASE is to 1, the smaller is the difference of using a naïve method. It means, at the end, that the "naïve" way of forecasting is better if the MASE is above 1. The naïve method assumes that the forecast equals the sales from the past period; therefore, if the MASE is above 1, it could also mean that the model does not perform appropriately, not better than even simple "naïve."

A validation of the model assignment was done on the aggregated level, e.g., ABC/XYZ with MASE as a measure (Fig. 3.66).

Step 5: Calculation of proportional factors based on a product-level statistical forecast and calculation of the final product-level statistical forecast

Once the product family and product-level statistical forecast were calculated, a special calculation was introduced. As mentioned before, the product family statistical forecast was easier to control; therefore, it served as a basis for the disaggregation of the total with the use of the proportions for a specific product statistical forecast. This method may be viewed as disaggregation of aggregated statistical forecast with detailed statistical forecast and is visualized in Fig. 3.67.

| ABC Code | XYZ Code | Mean Absolute Scal... |
|----------|----------|-----------------------|
| A | X | 0.843304 |
| A | Z | 0.856869 |
| B | X | 0.540363 |
| C | X | 0.270619 |

**Fig. 3.66** SAP IBP ABC/XYZ matrix with model assignment measurement

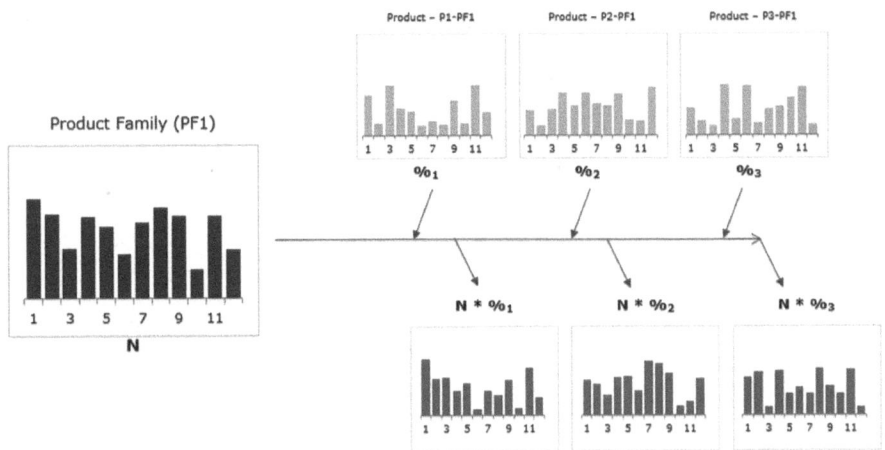

**Fig. 3.67** Product family statistical forecast disaggregation with product statistical forecast

The calculation of the ratios revealed itself fundamental, and it was used in the disaggregation of the family forecast into the product level. Eventually, family and product-level forecasts were stored on two different key figures.

Step 6: Review of forecast on a product level with the help of insightful visualizations.

The demand planner analyzed the product-level statistical forecast with the use of nanocharts positioned in tabular displays as part of the Excel add-on of SAP IBP. The nanochart shows in red the highest peaks, in green the lowest data points, in gray all the other data points in history and in yellow the statistical forecast (Fig. 3.68). It took very little time to visually review the forecast and was much easier to spot the obvious mistakes. The final product-level statistical forecast was then used in the demand review meeting preparation.

### 3.3.10 SAP Use Case: Automated Exponential Smoothing Within SES

In SAP IBP, the automated exponential smoothing is a forecasting model that allows to automatically detect and select the best smoothing algorithm or to optimize the parameters within a preselected smoothing algorithm. The criteria for the choice of the best smoothing algorithm are often depending on the measure of the forecast accuracy chosen. In the coming section, we will delve into the technicalities and functionalities of those automated models.

The automated methods available are the following:

– Automated exponential smoothing within SES
– Automated exponential smoothing within DES

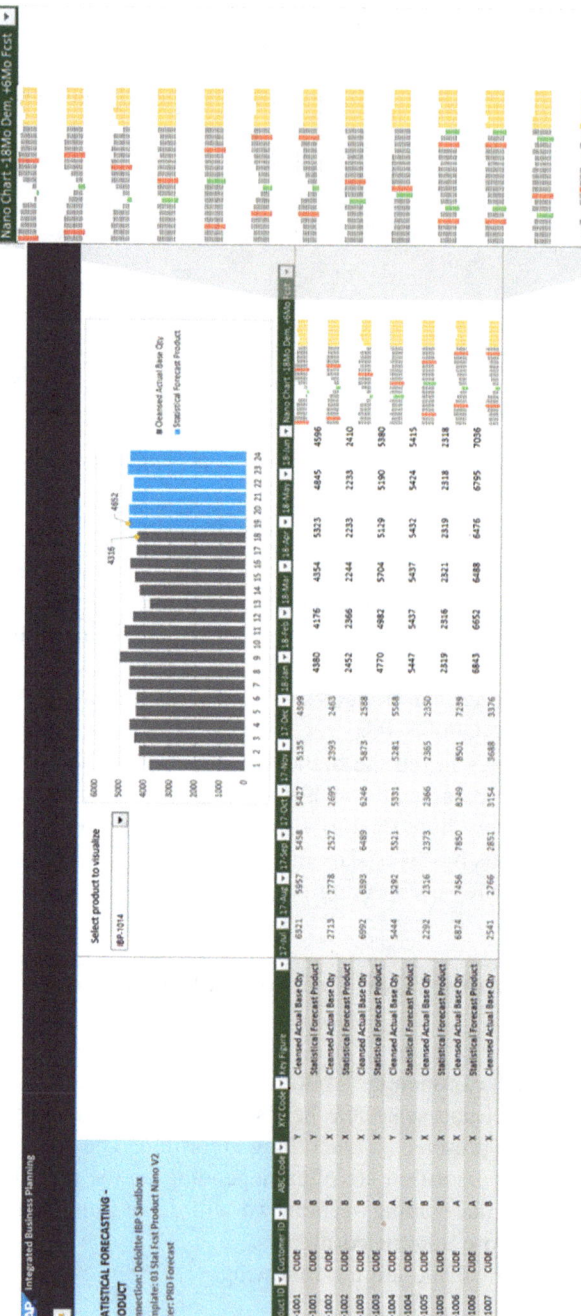

**Fig. 3.68** SAP IBP product statistical forecast visual controls with nanocharts

– Automated exponential smoothing within TES
– Automated exponential smoothing with best results.

Figure 3.69 illustrates the main configuration of the automated exponential smoothing within the single exponential smoothing. This method optimizes the parameters of the SES automatically. The complete scope of the optimization spreads over all the possible optimizations of the selected smoothing algorithms.

The measure used for the optimization is the mean squared error, but also the mean average percentage error can be employed. As we are dealing with the SES, the fields for the type of seasonality and periods of the season are grayed out and for the first time an upper and a lower bound for the parameters concerned by the smoothing model are introduced. In our case, we set the typical constraint of the alpha value: lower than 1 and greater than 0.

Figure 3.70 shows how we used the same data set employed for all the previous tests of the SES. If we compare the accuracy of the automatically optimized parameter settings for SES with the one provided with the Excel Solver plug-in, we can come to the conclusion that the differences in terms of forecast error and the changes to sales/demand are negligible.

The advantage of this method is that there is no need for the end user to manually set the parameter of the smoothing algorithm as the system automatically assesses the alpha value. However, we can see from the results that the alpha value set by the system does not align with the parameter set by the Excel Solver plug-in and consequently the type of optimization is not identical.

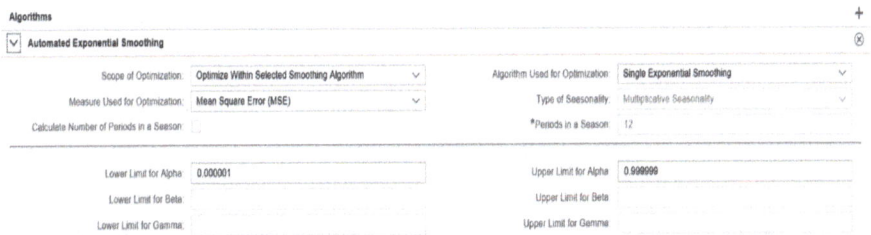

**Fig. 3.69** SAP IBP automated exponential smoothing within SES settings

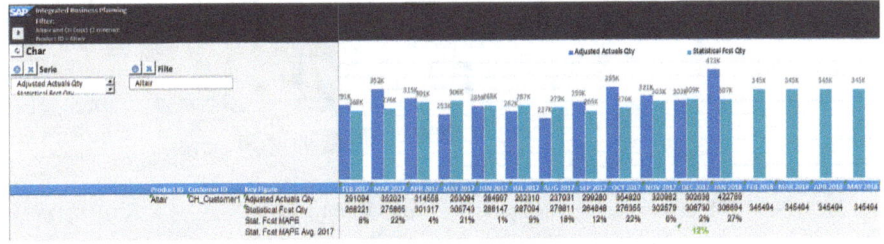

**Fig. 3.70** SAP IBP automated exponential smoothing within SES

## 3.3.11   SAP Use Case: Automated Exponential Smoothing Within DES

The optimization principle of the double exponential smoothing is the same as the one experienced in the SES. However, some additional configurations have to be done (Fig. 3.71):

- Upper limit for beta
- Lower limit for beta.

From Fig. 3.72, it is interesting to notice how, for this specific case, the optimization run is equivalent to the nonlinear optimization run with the Excel Solver plug-in. The results of this visualization are exactly the same from the ones displayed in Fig. 3.44.

This is good news since the end user may now choose to use the Solver just on an occasional basis to verify the model performances and spare the greater effort involved in configuring the model manually.

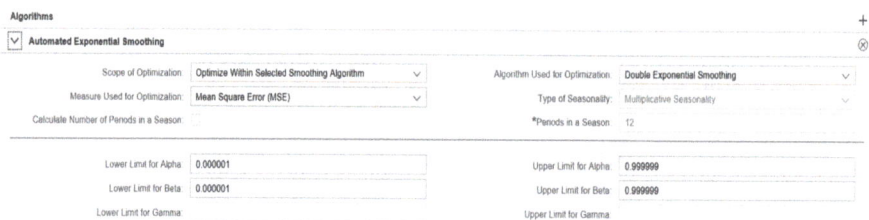

**Fig. 3.71**  SAP IBP automated exponential smoothing within DES settings

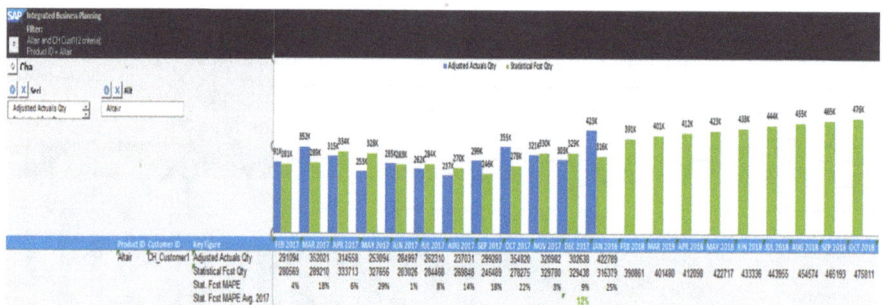

**Fig. 3.72**  SAP IBP automated exponential smoothing within DES

### 3.3.12 SAP Use Case: Automated Exponential Smoothing Within TES

As mentioned above, also for the triple exponential smoothing some additional configurations are needed, as it is shown in Fig. 3.73:

- Lower limit for gamma
- Upper limit for gamma
- Type of seasonality
- Periods in a season.

Applying the optimization within the triple exponential smoothing and analyzing the same data set for this forecasting model, it allowed to experience the smallest forecast error: only 8% as displayed in Fig. 3.74.

Here again, the automated exponential smoothing within each specific smoothing model has the advantage of avoiding the manual parameter setting required for the Excel Solver plug-in while guaranteeing a more than acceptable forecast accuracy.

**Fig. 3.73** Automated exponential smoothing within TES settings

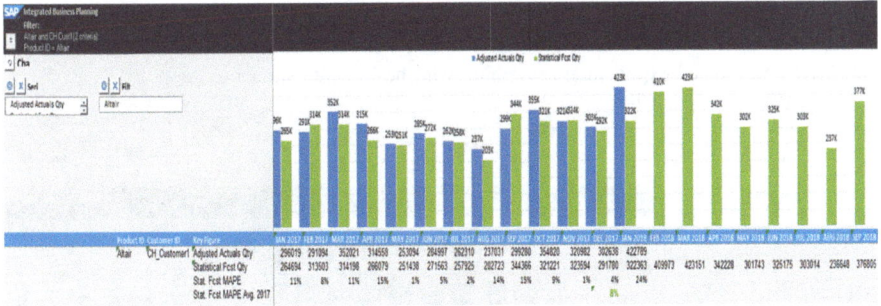

**Fig. 3.74** SAP IBP automated exponential smoothing within TES

### 3.3.13    SAP Use Case: Automated Exponential Smoothing with Best Results

Figure 3.75 illustrates the type of settings for the best result solution. As it is possible to see in the figure, the scope of the optimization has now changed to the selection of the best smoothing algorithm with best results and the choice of the algorithm to be optimized is consequently grayed out, as the system itself will evaluate the more accurate model among the three smoothing algorithms, based on the MAPE. The type of seasonality is grayed out since it is automatically done by the system; however, the number of periods in the season has to be configured.

All the lower and upper bounds of the parameters have to be pre-filled as well, and the reason for this is quite obvious—to ensure that all the parameters are correctly chosen based on the smoothing algorithm picked.

Figure 3.76 displays the results out of the best result optimization. The light blue bars indicate the forecast quantity until September 2018. The fact that the forecasted quantity is neither stable nor steadily trendy is possible to conclude that TES algorithm has been selected here. The accuracy of the forecasting solution is very high, accounting for a forecast error of only 8%.

If we compare those results with the automated exponential smoothing within the TES, we can notice how the general forecast error stays the same; however, the predicted sales/demand slightly changed by approximately 400 units per period. The changes might be due to the type of seasonality preselected and optimized by the system or by a different optimization algorithm employed for the parameters.

We can conclude that the automated exponential smoothing is a good place to start to get insights into the forecasted volumes of the time series analyzed. It allows

**Fig. 3.75** Automated exponential smoothing with best result settings

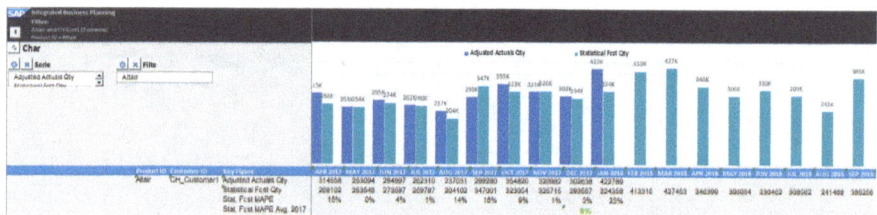

**Fig. 3.76** SAP IBP automated exponential smoothing with best results

a few manual interventions in the settings and at the same time guarantees good accuracy from the first statistical forecasting run. However, it still requires meticulous analysis during the forecasting review and cannot always represent the best solution matching the practitioners' needs.

In Fig. 3.77, it displayed the same data set used for the analysis conducted in Fig. 3.59. Previously, by randomly running the TES, the forecast error accounted for 59%. In the visualization below, running the automated smoothing and implying a seasonal period of 6, the forecast error decreased to 35% depicting TES as the algorithm yielding the best results.

However, if we analyze the behavior of the data set, as it is displayed in Fig. 3.78, the commonly shared length of the season among the year is closer to 12 rather than 6.

Consequently, by replacing the periods in a season input, from 6 to 12, the forecast error result decreased further from 35% to 21% (see Fig. 3.79). This

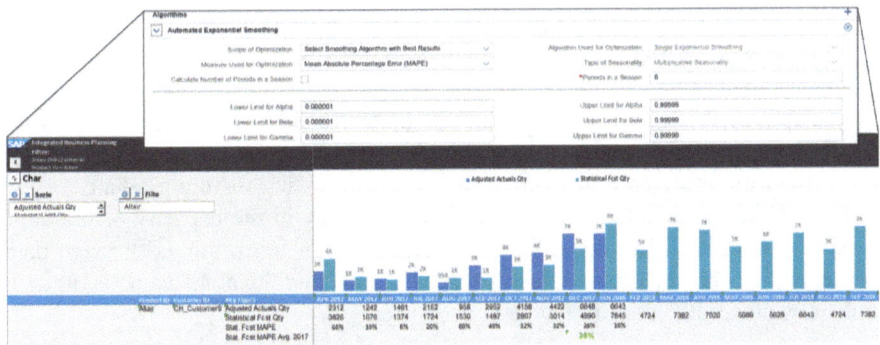

**Fig. 3.77** SAP IBP AES with best result and manual periods of season inputs (6)

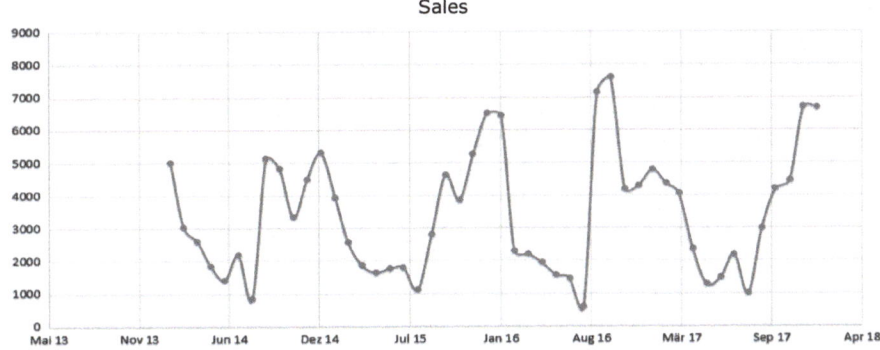

**Fig. 3.78** Seasonal length in a data set

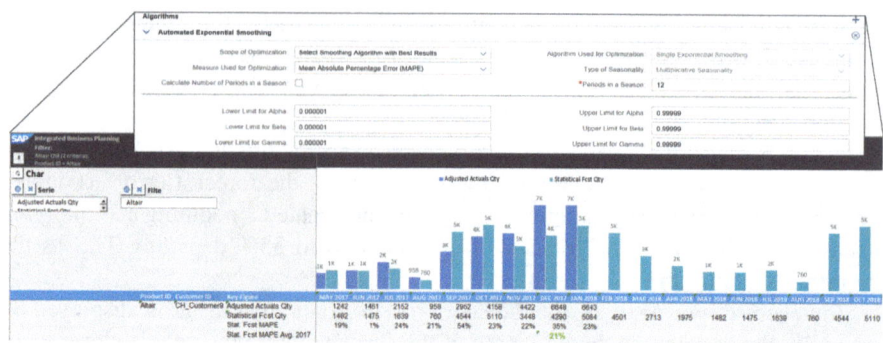

**Fig. 3.79** AES with best result and manual periods of season inputs (12)

highlights the importance of revising the forecast model settings assigned to the different SKUs based on the behavior of the data set.

### 3.3.14  Adaptive Response Rate Single Exponential Smoothing

The adaptive response rate algorithm is quite similar to a principle working standpoint to the single exponential smoothing. It is mostly used for stable and with low variability products fulfilling the needs of forecasting mature products.

The added value of the adaptive response rate lies in the capacity of the algorithm to constantly adapt the value of the alpha parameter to the most recent data. Consequently, the smoothing effect is more accurate and the alpha value is more up to date as new data come in the set.

### 3.3.15  SAP Use Case: Adaptive Response Rate Single Exponential Smoothing

From a configuration point of view, the settings are quite straightforward. The only field needed is the first alpha coefficient value of the data set that has to be set. See Fig. 3.80.

Figure 3.81 illustrates the results from the above-mentioned algorithm. The data set is still the same as the one in the previous single exponential smoothing testing, and the overall forecast error for the year 2017 remains at 12%. However, with the other automated variations, the forecasted amount for the entire 2018 changes slightly from the previous single smoothing models discussed.

**Fig. 3.80** Adaptive response rate settings

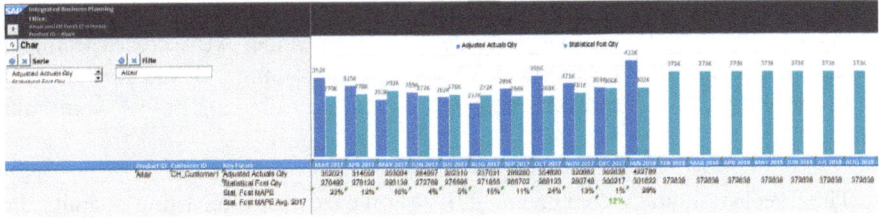

**Fig. 3.81** SAP IBP adaptive response rate single exponential smoothing

### 3.3.16 Brown's Linear Exponential Smoothing

Brown's linear exponential smoothing has been thought with the aim of forecasting a time series with a trendy component, but without any type of seasonality. The linear component of the exponential smoothing lets us think it may be comparable with the single exponential smoothing; however, its capacity of dampening and detecting the trend suggests a similar functional aspect as of the double exponential smoothing. We will see in the examples explained below how the forecasting algorithm behaves according to the time series proposed.

Brown's algorithm comes in two versions: adaptive and non-adaptive. The non-adaptive algorithm uses only one smoothing coefficient—alpha—whereas the adaptive one also uses a delta coefficient which has to be set equal to alpha.

We will delve into the smoothing differences, but we will analyze the consequences in the forecasting run, accuracy and type of forecasted outputs.

### 3.3.17 SAP Use Case: Brown's Linear Single Exponential Smoothing

Figure 3.82 explains the fields to be populated in Brown's setting. As you can see, the alpha coefficient has to be filled in, while there is an optional check box for the adaptive method that automatically populates the delta coefficient to 0.2. It is important to remember that one of the core assumptions of the adaptive method is to set the value of alpha exactly the same as the value of delta.

As shown in Fig. 3.82, the current setting displays an alpha value equal to 0.3 and we tried to run Brown's model with the same data employed for Fig. 3.39, where an alpha value of 0.3 resulted in a MAPE value of 11% and a forecasted

---

Algorithms

∨ Brown's Linear Exponential Smoothing

| | | |
|---|---|---|
| Alpha Coefficient: | 0.3 | Adaptive Method: ☐ |
| Delta Coefficient: | 0.2 | |

Target Key Figure for Forecast:                    Target Key Figure for Ex-Post Forecast:

**Fig. 3.82** SAP IBP Brown's linear exponential smoothing settings

quantity of 354,433 units. Figure 3.83 shows the results of Brown's model with the setting described above. As we only set the alpha value, we were expecting a similar forecasting behavior to Fig. 3.39 since the smoothing index is the same and set to the same value. However, the results w.r.t. the following points were quite different:

- The forecast accuracy changed slightly, but the ex-post forecasting quantity did not differ too much.
- The biggest difference appeared in the future sales/demand pattern. The month of February 2018 is aligned with the SES prediction; however, from March onward the forecasted quantity constantly decreases with a clear pattern.

The results indicate that Brown's solution, even if set with the only alpha value, cannot be compared with the functionalities of the SES as its inner capability of detecting the trend seems to have a high impact on the outcome of the method. Consequently, we believe that the trend dampening solution makes this model more similar to the double exponential smoothing even if only the alpha parameter is set.

Triggered by the curiosity to compare, we selected a specific data set that clearly displays a decreasing trend throughout the years taken in analysis (see Fig. 3.84). This specific data set is suitable for both a DES and Brown's algorithm due to the presence of the trend component and the absence of the seasonal one.

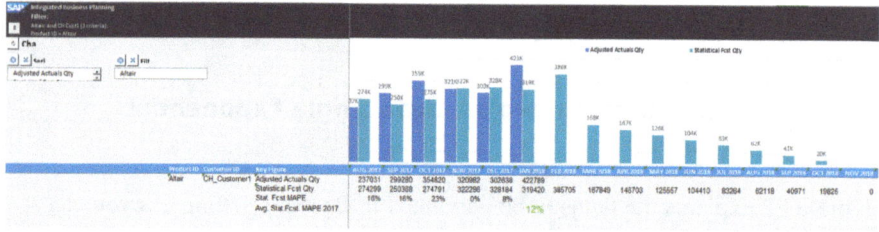

**Fig. 3.83**  SAP IBP Brown's linear exponential smoothing

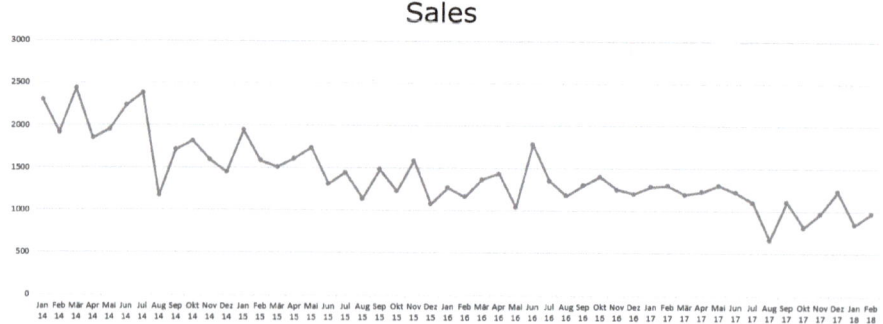

**Fig. 3.84**  Trendy sales/demand

We then performed the following tests:

1. For DES with alpha and beta configured (see Fig. 3.85), we experience a forecast error of 14% and a clear decreasing trend in the foreseen sales/demand for 2018.
2. For DES with alpha, beta and trend dampening configured (see Fig. 3.86), we experience slightly higher forecast error of 15% with a constant forecast quantity for the entire 2018. The difference in the forecasted sales/demand depicted by the light blue histograms is due to the enabled trend dampening that did not allow for forecasting a decreasing trend in 2018.
3. For Brown's linear exponential smoothing with alpha coefficient configured (see Fig. 3.87), we experience a forecast error of 15%, similar to the DES with only alpha and beta. It also displays the usual diminishing trend for the coming year. As expected, only by setting the alpha value within Brown's model, the outcomes are really similar to the DES. The trend in the sales/demand shown in Fig. 3.84 is perfectly detected and projected.

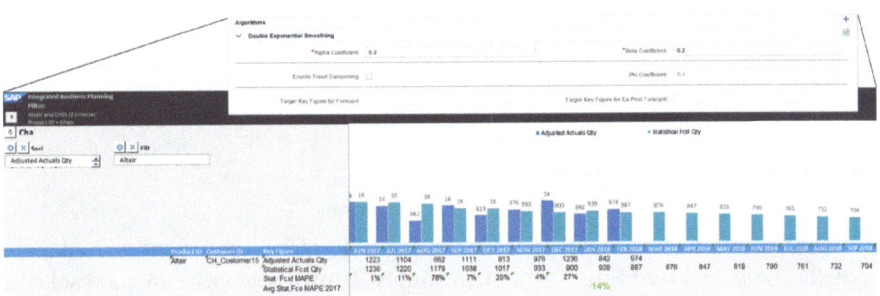

**Fig. 3.85** SAP IBP DES (alpha and beta)

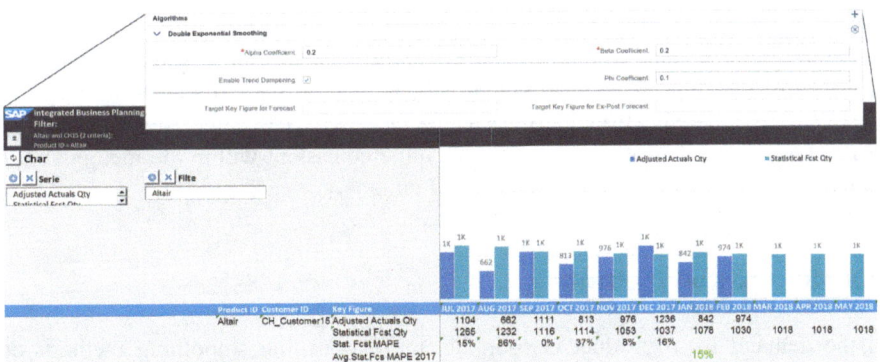

**Fig. 3.86** SAP IBP DES (alpha, beta and trend dampening)

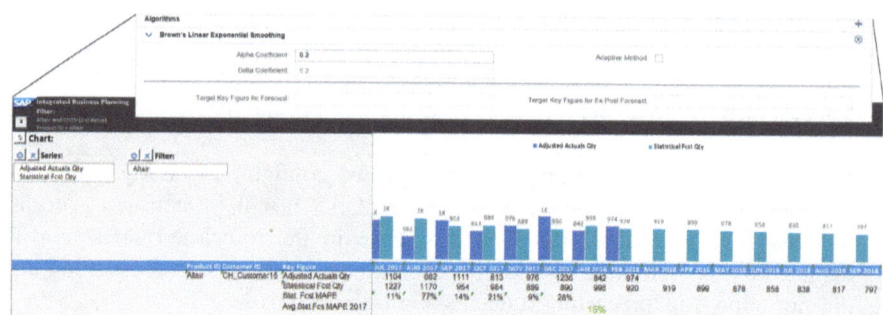

**Fig. 3.87** SAP IBP Brown's model (alpha)

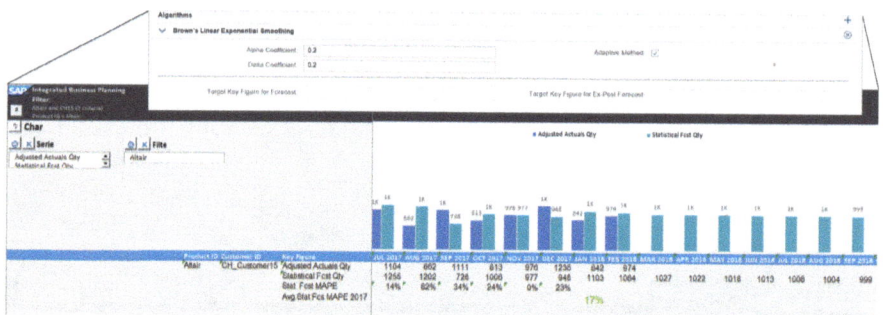

**Fig. 3.88** SAP IBP adaptive method

4. For Brown's linear exponential smoothing with alpha coefficient and adaptive
   delta coefficient (see Fig. 3.88), interestingly, Brown's adaptive method set with
   the parameters equal to 0.2 gives a result worse than the DES with alpha and
   beta equal to 0.2 and with the trend dampening enabled and automatically set to
   0.1.

As a conclusion, for the example displayed above, the DES without trend
enabling gives the best forecast accuracy. Brown's algorithm and the DES mostly
differ in the threshold from where the trend dampening starts: the DES from a value
of 887 units whereas Brown from a value close to 1050 units. Nevertheless, the
percentage of the dampening itself seems quite consistent within the methods: The
month-to-month difference is less than 30 units.

### 3.3.18   Croston Method

If the demand for a product is sporadic, the exponential smoothing methods do
perform quite poorly. In single exponential smoothing (SES) procedure, the
resulting demand forecast behaves according to the sawtooth pattern.

The forecast is strongly influenced by the value of alpha parameter (the smoothing constant), and its variability is directly proportional to the value of the parameter (Fig. 3.89).

Using low values of alpha (standard choice in SES method), the forecast will be close to the average of the period, while with higher values it will be close to the "naïve" forecast.

Besides, the use of low values of alpha implies that even in case of long zero demand sequences the forecast will have non-zero values. This means that when the real demands are zeros, the forecast is most likely non-zero, which may not be desirable.

Considering the effects just described, Croston highlighted that single exponential smoothing produces very large forecasting errors. Thus, he proposed a forecasting method in which the updates of the demand estimations are performed only after a non-zero demand occurs. At the same time, the estimation of the interdemand intervals has to be performed separately, corresponding to the first differences of the time periods in which a non-zero demand has occurred (Fig. 3.90).

Croston's method is considering non-overlapping temporal aggregations using time buckets, the length of which varies over time, so that only one non-zero demand occurs at the end of each time bucket and in this way intermittent demand is removed.

The two estimates could be considered to generate a sporadic forecast or divided to produce an estimation of the average demand per time period.

Using the same principle as that of the SES, each of the two series, the non-zero demand and the interdemand intervals, is estimated individually.

If $X_t \neq 0$, then:

$$Z_{t+1} = \alpha X_t + (1 - \alpha)Z_t$$
$$V_{t+1} = \beta Q_t + (1 - \alpha)V_t$$

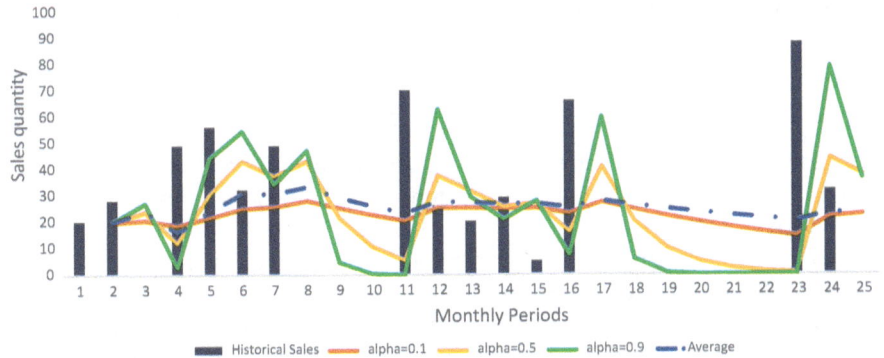

**Fig. 3.89** Single exponential smoothing versus sporadic demand

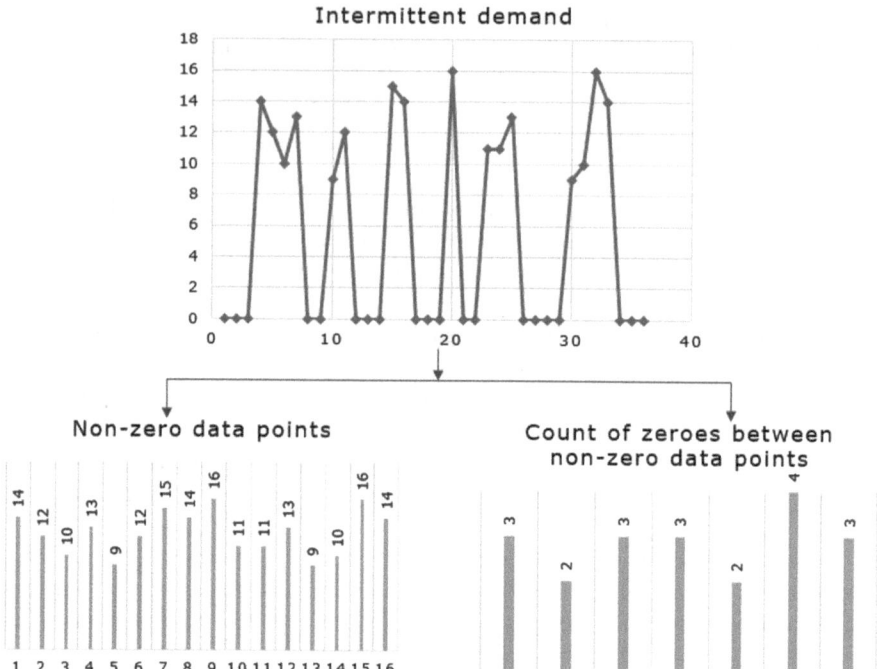

**Fig. 3.90** Croston two components: zero occurrence and transaction size

If $X_t = 0$, then:

$$Z_{t+1} = Z_t$$
$$V_{t+1} = V_t$$

where $\alpha$ and $\beta$ are, respectively, the smoothing parameters for the non-zero demands and the intervals, respectively.

The final output of Croston's method is simply the division of these estimates:

$$Y_{t+1} = \frac{Z_{t+1}}{V_{t+1}}$$

The combined output is not an estimate of the actual demand but a demand rate which, if accumulated, should be the estimate of the non-zero demand occurring every $V_{t+1}$.

Intuitively, Croston's procedure is more likely to get the timing right if the variance of the count of zeroes between non-zero demands is very low. If the variance is high, it might be a better idea to not generate an intermittent forecast, but an average of the estimated size across the estimate of the number of intermittent zeroes—that is, $F_t = S_t/n_t$.

Both options are available in SAP IBP Croston procedure.

### 3.3.19 SAP Use Case: Croston Method

The configuration settings of Croston's method are really similar to the single exponential smoothing, since it applies the same algorithm to the series of non-zero demand and for the interval size between non-zero demands (Fig. 3.91).

As for the single exponential smoothing, a specific alpha parameter has to be set and it is used in the procedure to smooth both the non-zero demand and the interval size between the non-zero demands. The general settings of the forecasting models such as the time periods to be forecasted, periods of history and periodicity of the calculations are the same.

The system also requires choosing between two alternatives of forecasting procedure:

- "Create Sporadic Forecast"
- Not creating a sporadic forecast.

In case this option is not selected, the result will be the calculation of a constant demand rate that is applied to all the periods in the forecast horizon (the system does not infer anything about the timing). If the option "Create Sporadic Forecast" has been selected, the system will calculate timing and a value for the demand.

For the below Croston's example (Fig. 3.92), the option "Create Sporadic Forecast" has been selected and the alpha parameter has been set to 0.1; the adjusted actual quantity represents the preprocessed history. The result of the forecast model is shown until the period December 2018, and it consists in a recurring sequence in which a first zero demand period is followed by two positive demand periods, each one of them accounting for 142 units. As we are simply dealing with the single exponential smoothing of non-zero demand and of an

**Fig. 3.91** Croston method alpha parameter setting

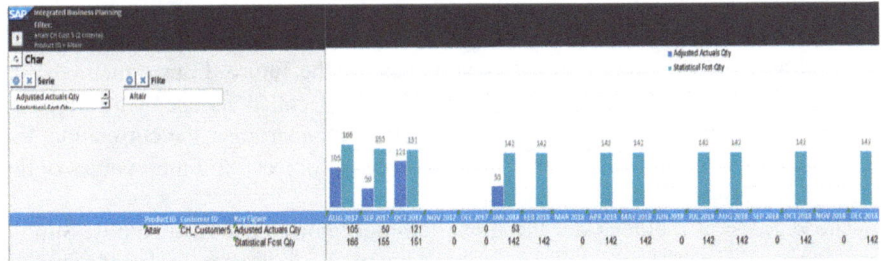

**Fig. 3.92** SAP IBP Croston method

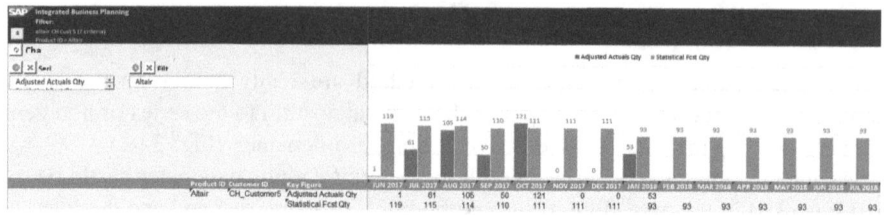

**Fig. 3.93** SAP IPB Croston method without "sporadic forecast"

interval size between non-zero demands, it is important to remind that for the complete forecast horizon set in the configuration setting, the forecasted quantity and timing delivered by Croston's algorithm will remain constant.

In the below visualization, the light blue bars identify the forecasted quantity, while the blue ones the adjusted actual quantity. As already mentioned in Sect. 3.3.2 about SES, it is recommended that the alpha value is set based on a calculation using a nonlinear optimization algorithm. Once the coefficient that minimizes the standard deviation of the forecast error has been identified, it must be entered in the same field as shown above.

Figure 3.93 unveils the result if the option "Create Sporadic Forecast" is not selected, and the same product is considered.

The result of the forecast model is shown until December 2018, and it consists of a constant demand rate equal to 93 units per month. This value could be calculated considering the results of the "sporadic forecast" in which the forecast for a month with zero demand followed by two months with a demand of 142 units results in a demand of 284 units over three months with a demand rate of 94 units per month.

The comparison of the two forecast methods (sporadic or non-sporadic) highlights that in the sporadic ex-post forecasts, the smoothing algorithm is applied to the quantity and not to the interval between non-zero demands, implicitly assuming that the forecasted timing equals the actual one, while in the non-sporadic ex-post forecast, when the actual demand is zero, the forecasted value is equal to the one that has been calculated for the last non-zero demand period.

### 3.3.20 Multiple Linear Regression Model

The time series methods make use of historical values as estimated variables for the past and aim at extrapolating them as variables for the future. Causal methods, on the other hand, use additional explanatory variables called independent variables that correlate with the forecast variable. Intuitively, the stronger the correlation, the better suited would the independent variable(s) be in forecasting future values of the forecast object also called the dependent variable.

The regression methods are the most common among causal methods. Simple regression, which is a special class of regression methods, uses a single independent variable. The relation between the dependent and the independent variables in the case of simple regression can be expressed as follows:

$$Y_i = a + b * X_i + e$$

where $Y_i$ and $X_i$ are paired dependent and independent variables, respectively, and e is the error term (also known as residual). The explanatory variable $X$ can also represent the time: referred to as the time series regression.

An example is provided in Fig. 3.94. As we can see, the two variables seem to be highly correlated. Our intuition is confirmed statistically as the coefficient of determination ($R^2$), which is a measure of correlation, is calculated at 82%. This can be interpreted by the fact that the 82% of variation in $Y$, the dependent variable, can be explained by the independent variable $X$.

Explanatory variables can also be justifiably termed as predictors as they have a predictive quality to them. In the above example, knowing the value of $X$, it is possible to plug this into the equation (which consists of an intercept—01.4341— and a slope—0.6945) and predict the dependent variable $Y$.

Given this, Foreman (2013) does not exaggerate when he says "IF YOU'VE EVER SHOVED A TREND-LINE THROUGH A CLOUD OF POINTS ON A SCATTER PLOT, YOU'VE BUILT AN AI MODEL."

However, when it comes to highly variable SKUs, the simple approach of the linear regression is no longer sufficient to predict the correlations of the variables and some additional explanatory variables are needed in the regression model.

Figure 3.95 reports an example of a seasonal SKU which clearly states how the correlation index is not capable of detecting a sufficient and acceptable correlation

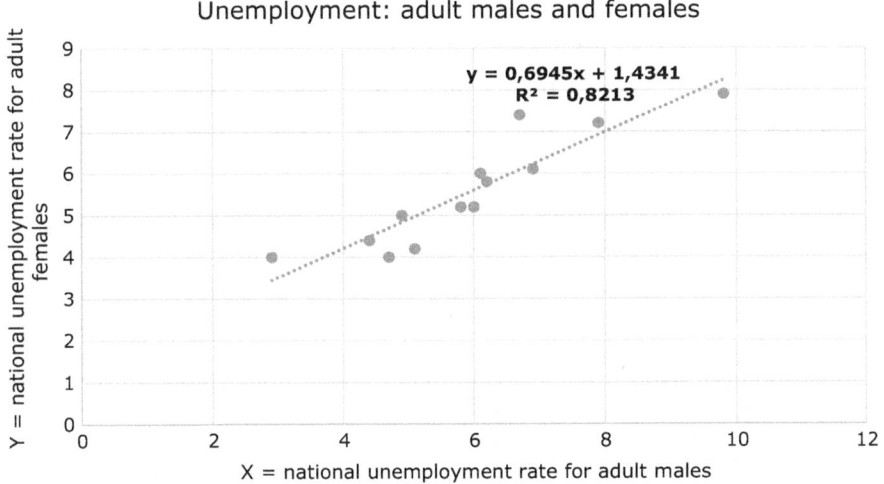

**Fig. 3.94** Simple regression example (*Data Source* Statistical abstract of the United States)

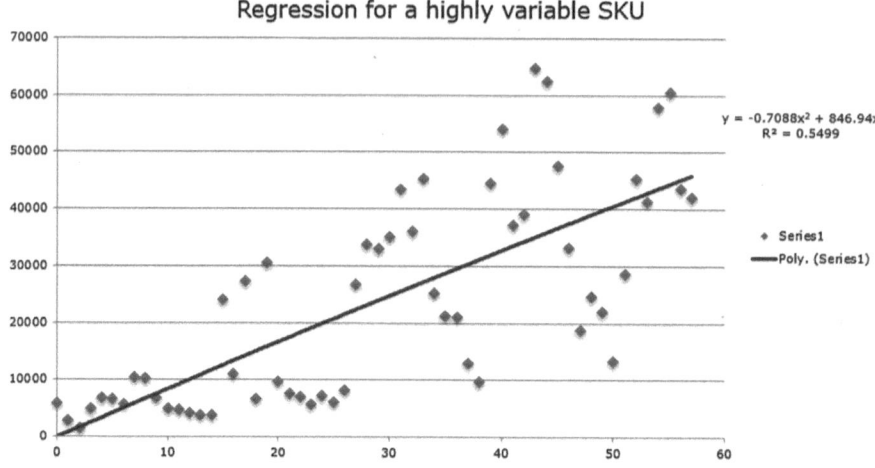

**Fig. 3.95** Linear regression analysis for a highly variable SKU

between the variables due to a high level of variability in the sales/demand pattern. A higher degree of the regression analysis becomes necessary at this point.

Regression starts to become quite ingenious when we start incorporating additional explanatory variables (more than one)—this is known as multiple regression or multiple linear regression (MLR) if the form of the model is linear. We will restrict our discussion to MLR, which is the feature that SAP IBP provides. In the following paragraphs, we will build a simple MLR model in Excel, plug the data into SAP IBP and compare the results. This should serve to:

1. Demystify model sophistication.
2. Clarify conceptual finer points when it comes to causal models, in particular, and quantitative forecasting in general.

For our model, we will use data for beer production sourced (and moved forward in time) from Australian Bureau of Statistics. The plot of the data is presented in Fig. 3.96.

By looking at the quarterly plot of production quantities of beer, we are able to see that there is a certain seasonality and that the production quantities among the different quarters in a given year seem to be correlated. There is also a noticeable downward trend. To be able to forecast the production quantities using MLR, we need to model the quarterly and trend effects (independent variables) on beer production (dependent variable).

Let's start with a simple regression model by considering only the trend effect on production quantities (see Fig. 3.97). As it can be seen, a linear trend can be modeled by including an indicator that takes the period value. In the example, we use a running serial number starting with one for the earliest historical period.

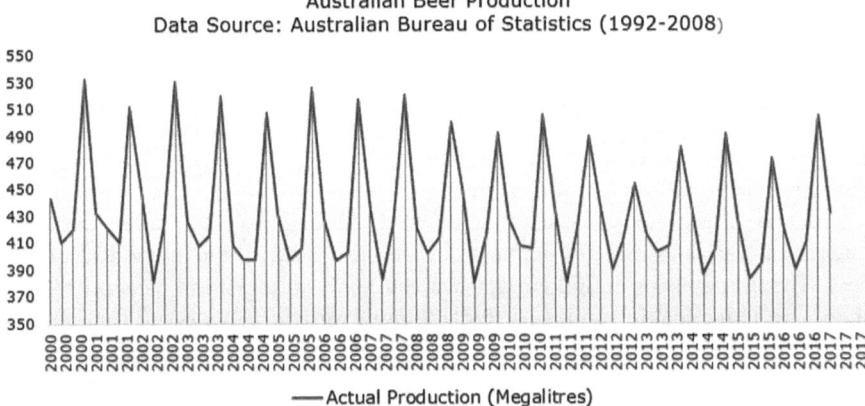

**Fig. 3.96** Plot of data set to be used for MLR model

| Month-Year | Year | Actual Production (Mega litres) | Trend (t) |
|:---:|:---:|:---:|:---:|
| 03-2012 | 2012 | 435 | 49 |
| 06-2012 | 2012 | 390 | 50 |
| 09-2012 | 2012 | 412 | 51 |
| 12-2012 | 2012 | 454 | 52 |
| 03-2013 | 2013 | 416 | 53 |
| 06-2013 | 2013 | 403 | 54 |
| 09-2013 | 2013 | 408 | 55 |
| 12-2013 | 2013 | 482 | 56 |
| 03-2014 | 2014 | 438 | 57 |
| 06-2014 | 2014 | 386 | 58 |
| 09-2014 | 2014 | 405 | 59 |
| 12-2014 | 2014 | 491 | 60 |
| 03-2015 | 2015 | 427 | 61 |
| 06-2015 | 2015 | 383 | 62 |
| 09-2015 | 2015 | 394 | 63 |
| 12-2015 | 2015 | 473 | 64 |
| 03-2016 | 2016 | 420 | 65 |
| 06-2016 | 2016 | 390 | 66 |
| 09-2016 | 2016 | 410 | 67 |
| 12-2016 | 2016 | 493 | 68 |
| 03-2017 | 2017 | 418 | 69 |

**Fig. 3.97** Snippet of data used to model trend effects only

Using the regression method from Excel's analysis toolset, we are able to get the results of applying simple regression and they look less than spectacular.

In the summary sheet, Excel reports that the coefficient of determination ($R^2$) is measly 2%, which means the trend indicator can only explain 2% of the variation in the dependent variable (production quantities).

By plotting the errors or residuals (see Fig. 3.98), we clearly see that we have missed out modeling the effect of seasonality (series of negative errors followed by a series of positive errors). The residual plot is a good tool to be used when assessing the completeness of a model.

But how do we model the seasonal effects? The quarters are what are known as categorical variables and are unlike what we have used so far (numerical quantities). There is a useful technique that we can apply to transform categorical variables into numerical quantities—use of dummy variables. We could use Boolean indicators to denote each of the quarters. We need to be careful not to over specify by modeling four variables, because we only need three (a {0,0,0} means the corresponding historical quantity represents the effect of the quarter that has been omitted). This is not just for cosmetics because if we have a perfect correlation between the variables—individual variables or subsets—the regression method will fail as it relies on minimizing errors (using least squares) and it cannot generate a solution in the presence of collinearity. In other words, we need to model one less than the number of values that the category we want to model can take (also known as degrees of freedom in stats-speak).

In our example, we can model the indicators for Q2, Q3 and Q4 as they relate to Q1 (see Fig. 3.99). A one in Q2 means we would like to see the impact of Q2 on the production quantity in comparison with Q1's impact (the missing indicator).

By selecting a range of independent variables, we are able to use the Excel regression method applying the MLR logic. The results after having modeled both

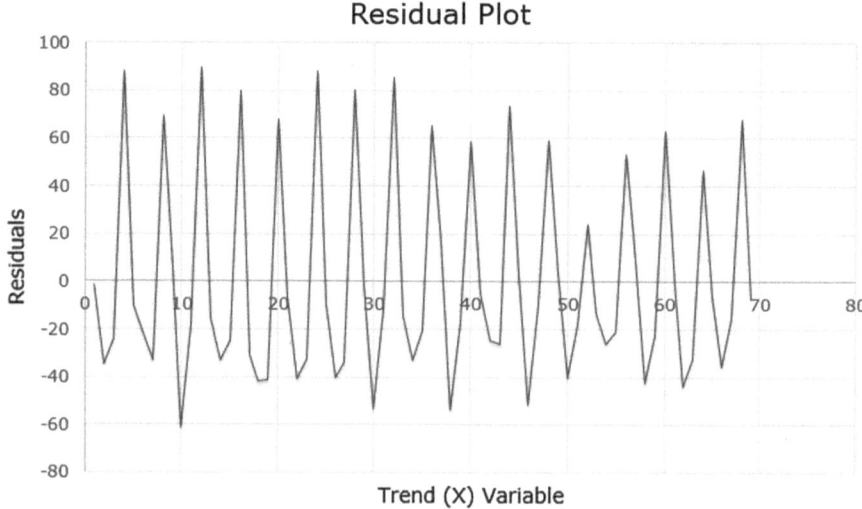

**Fig. 3.98** Residuals using simple regression method

| Month-Year | Year | Actual Production (Mega litres) | Trend (t) | Q2 | Q3 | Q4 |
|---|---|---|---|---|---|---|
| 03-2012 | 2012 | 435 | 49 | 0 | 0 | 0 |
| 06-2012 | 2012 | 390 | 50 | 1 | 0 | 0 |
| 09-2012 | 2012 | 412 | 51 | 0 | 1 | 0 |
| 12-2012 | 2012 | 454 | 52 | 0 | 0 | 1 |
| 03-2013 | 2013 | 416 | 53 | 0 | 0 | 0 |
| 06-2013 | 2013 | 403 | 54 | 1 | 0 | 0 |
| 09-2013 | 2013 | 408 | 55 | 0 | 1 | 0 |
| 12-2013 | 2013 | 482 | 56 | 0 | 0 | 1 |
| 03-2014 | 2014 | 438 | 57 | 0 | 0 | 0 |
| 06-2014 | 2014 | 386 | 58 | 1 | 0 | 0 |
| 09-2014 | 2014 | 405 | 59 | 0 | 1 | 0 |
| 12-2014 | 2014 | 491 | 60 | 0 | 0 | 1 |
| 03-2015 | 2015 | 427 | 61 | 0 | 0 | 0 |
| 06-2015 | 2015 | 383 | 62 | 1 | 0 | 0 |
| 09-2015 | 2015 | 394 | 63 | 0 | 1 | 0 |
| 12-2015 | 2015 | 473 | 64 | 0 | 0 | 1 |
| 03-2016 | 2016 | 420 | 65 | 0 | 0 | 0 |
| 06-2016 | 2016 | 390 | 66 | 1 | 0 | 0 |
| 09-2016 | 2016 | 410 | 67 | 0 | 1 | 0 |
| 12-2016 | 2016 | 505 | 68 | 0 | 0 | 1 |
| 03-2017 | 2017 | 432 | 69 | 0 | 0 | 0 |

**Fig. 3.99** Incorporating independent variables to model seasonal effects

trend and seasonality look significantly better (see Fig. 3.100). The residual plot is zigzagging, indicating a lack of systematic bias.

The improvement is seen in the forecast fit prediction of Fig. 3.101.

The $R^2$ value of 92.3% (in the summary sheet) indicates that most of the variation can be explained by the four independent variables we have modeled. We can then use the intercept and the coefficients of the independent variables determined by the model to forecast the future values by using the following formula.

$$F_t = \text{Slope} + \text{Trend}_t * C_1 + Q2_t * C_2 + Q3_t * C_3 + Q4_t * C_4$$

where:

- $F_t$ is the forecast for time period $t$.
- $\text{Trend}_t$, $Q2_t$, $Q3_t$ and $Q4_t$ are the independent variables.
- $C_1$, $C_2$, $C_3$ and $C_4$ are the corresponding coefficients of the independent variables calculated by the MLR algorithm.

The results are shown in Fig. 3.102.

The standard error (included in the summary sheet) is 12.75 (was at 43.4 earlier). The standard error is the standard deviation of the errors—a measure of forecast variability (and consequently the quality of the forecast). The standard error can be used to calculate the prediction interval for a given probability by multiplying it

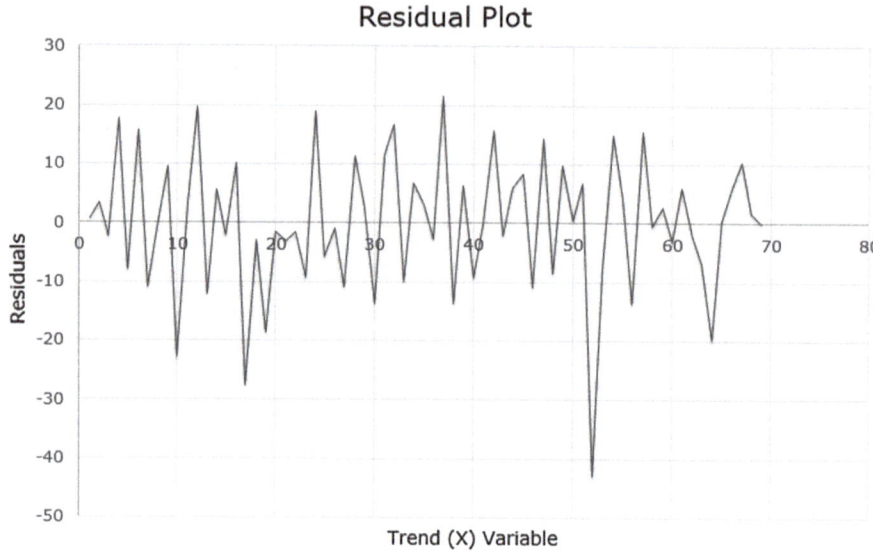

**Fig. 3.100** Residuals using multiple linear regression

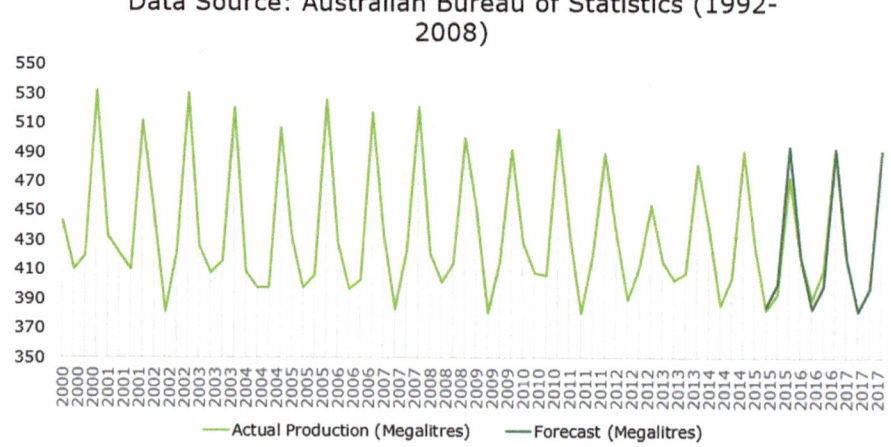

**Fig. 3.101** Forecast results visualized

with the "$z$" (read from the standard normal distribution table or using Excel's NORM.S.INV function).

For example, for a 95% probability, the estimated forecast error is 1.65 * 12.75 = 20.9. So, for the month of June 2017, the corresponding prediction interval is [382 − 20.9, 382 + 20.9] = [361.1, 402.9]. This is a very useful information as it

| Month-Year | Year | Actual Production (Mega litres) | Trend (t) | Q2 | Q3 | Q4 | Forecast (Mega litres) |
|---|---|---|---|---|---|---|---|
| 03-2012 | 2012 | 435 | 49 | 0 | 0 | 0 | |
| 06-2012 | 2012 | 390 | 50 | 1 | 0 | 0 | |
| 09-2012 | 2012 | 412 | 51 | 0 | 1 | 0 | |
| 12-2012 | 2012 | 454 | 52 | 0 | 0 | 1 | |
| 03-2013 | 2013 | 416 | 53 | 0 | 0 | 0 | |
| 06-2013 | 2013 | 403 | 54 | 1 | 0 | 0 | |
| 09-2013 | 2013 | 408 | 55 | 0 | 1 | 0 | |
| 12-2013 | 2013 | 482 | 56 | 0 | 0 | 1 | |
| 03-2014 | 2014 | 438 | 57 | 0 | 0 | 0 | |
| 06-2014 | 2014 | 386 | 58 | 1 | 0 | 0 | |
| 09-2014 | 2014 | 405 | 59 | 0 | 1 | 0 | |
| 12-2014 | 2014 | 491 | 60 | 0 | 0 | 1 | |
| 03-2015 | 2015 | 427 | 61 | 0 | 0 | 0 | |
| 06-2015 | 2015 | 383 | 62 | 1 | 0 | 0 | |
| 09-2015 | 2015 | 394 | 63 | 0 | 1 | 0 | |
| 12-2015 | 2015 | 473 | 64 | 0 | 0 | 1 | |
| 03-2016 | 2016 | 420 | 65 | 0 | 0 | 0 | |
| 06-2016 | 2016 | 390 | 66 | 1 | 0 | 0 | |
| 09-2016 | 2016 | 410 | 67 | 0 | 1 | 0 | |
| 12-2016 | 2016 | 505 | 68 | 0 | 0 | 1 | |
| 03-2017 | 2017 | 432 | 69 | 0 | 0 | 0 | |
| 06-2017 | 2017 | | 70 | 1 | 0 | 0 | 382 |
| 09-2017 | 2017 | | 71 | 0 | 1 | 0 | 398 |
| 12-2017 | 2017 | | 72 | 0 | 0 | 1 | 491 |

**Fig. 3.102** Forecasted values based on MLR model

allows to communicate clearly the limits of the forecast at a certain confidence level.

Let's now proceed to review how the example described so far has been modeled in SAP IBP.

## 3.3.21  SAP Use Case: Multiple Linear Regression

The multiple linear regression (MLR) algorithm was selected in SAP IBP, and the trend and seasonality indicators were modeled as independent variables (see Fig. 3.103).

The indicators were configured as additional key figures and values populated according to the logic described earlier. The result of the forecast calculation is shown in Fig. 3.104.

As it can be seen, the results line up nicely with what we got using the Excel's analysis toolset. In stats-speak, a good fit at a model level is expressed using something called "$F$-statistic." The $F$-statistic is calculated as the product of the ratio of explained to unexplained squared error and the ratio of degrees of freedom (number of data observations minus the number of model coefficients) to dependent variables. From the $F$-statistic, the p-value can be determined. This is simply the probability that the model is as good a fit as it is by sheer luck. In our example,

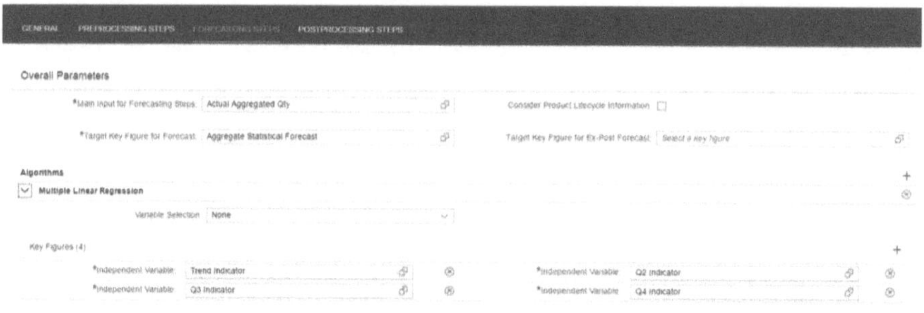

**Fig. 3.103** Forecast parameters in IBP for MLR

the p-value is very, very close to 0—this means that it is nearly impossible that we would be able to achieve this level of fit through chance.

Similar to $F$-statistic, which expresses overall model fit, $t$-statistic expresses significance of individual coefficients. Stepwise regression is an approach that helps to identify significant explanatory variables from a candidate list.

There are two methods that are particularly relevant as they are supported in SAP IBP: forward and backward. In forward, the algorithm starts by picking the explanatory variable that has the highest correlation with the dependent variable. The resulting residuals are then the basis for picking the next explanatory variable —this is the one that has the highest correlation with the residuals. The algorithm proceeds in this fashion until it is left with no more explanatory variables with a significant correlation with the residuals. The backward method on the other hand uses elimination—it starts by including all explanatory variables but starts the elimination process by removing the one that is least significant. This process is repeated iteratively, and at each step the solution is recalculated. The process stops when all remaining variables are significantly correlated with the dependent variable.

The sophistication in a model such as MLR comes at additional costs in terms of data collection, cleansing, model setup and maintenance to name a few. How can a practitioner make an objective assessment of the implicit promise of reduced forecast variability that comes along with a more advanced model?

One way is the use of mean absolute scaled error. It is akin to Theil's $U$-statistic. The MASE metric, like the $U$-statistic, is the ratio of forecast error (using the present model) to forecast error if one were to use naïve forecast (NF1) where the forecast for the subsequent period equals the observed demand for the current period.

Both formulas (Theil's $U$-statistic and MASE) are provided for reference below.

$$U = \sqrt{\frac{\sum_{t=2}^{n}\left(\frac{F_t - Y_t}{Y_{t-1}}\right)^2}{\sum_{t=2}^{n}\left(\frac{Y_t - Y_{t-1}}{Y_{t-1}}\right)^2}}$$

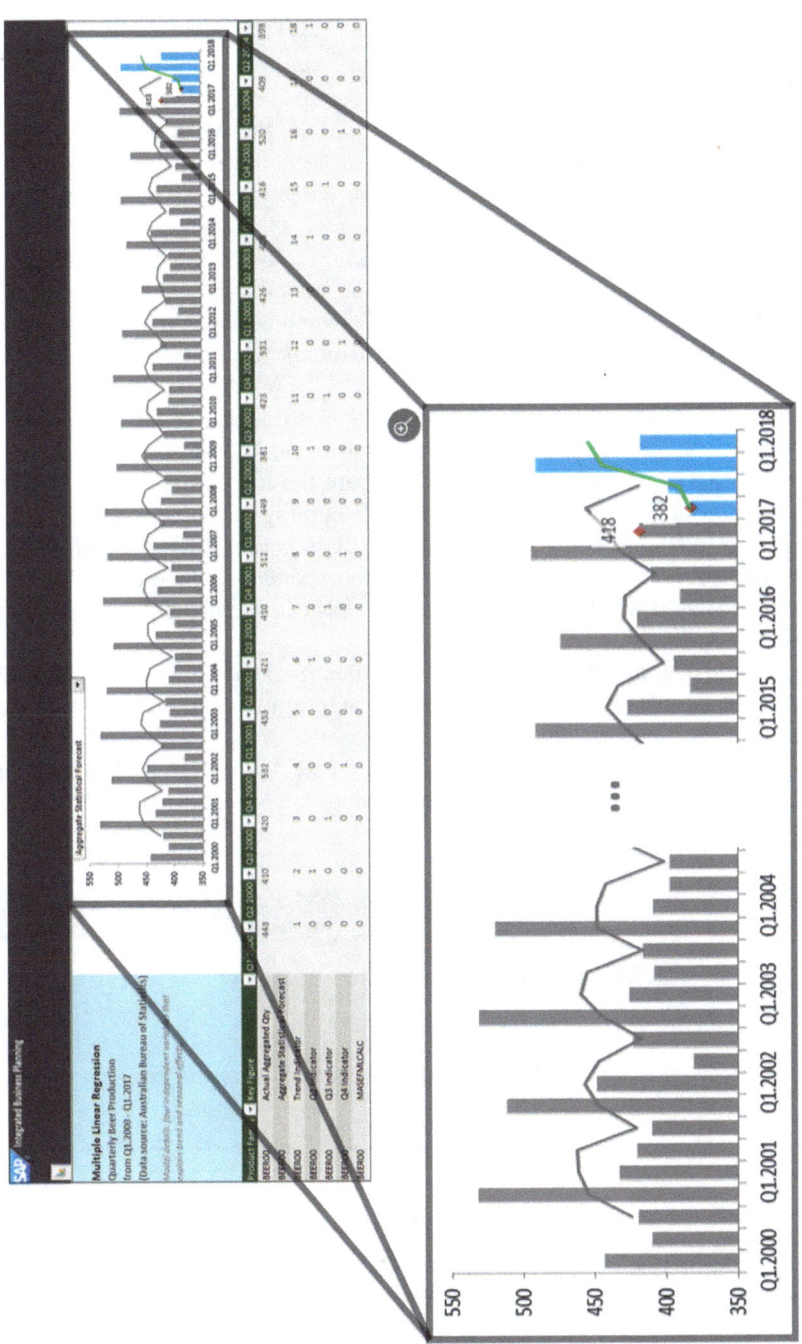

**Fig. 3.104** Results of MLR run in SAP IBP

$$\text{MASE} = \frac{\frac{\sum_{t=1}^{n}|F_t - Y_t|}{n}}{\frac{\sum_{t=2}^{n}|Y_t - Y_{t-1}|}{n-1}}$$

For the example discussed (beer production) in the MLR section, a simple exponential smoothing model was applied to make an objective assessment of the added value of a more sophisticated treatment, namely the use of a causal model such as MLR.

As can be seen in Fig. 3.105, the forecast into the future is constant (blue bars) as one can expect from a simple exponential smoothing model. What is quite revealing is the MASE metric. The value is 0.7, which is quite close to 1. A value of 1 indicates that the forecast accuracy is the same as what one would achieve by using NF1 (naïve method).

Figure 3.106 shows how the calculations are carried out (refer to the formula provided earlier). As one can see, the Theil metric and MASE are nearly the same.

This in itself is not conclusive. Let's compare the forecast results for the same data set, but with the more sophisticated MLR coming in place.

The MLR method results in a MASE of 0.1 (see Fig. 3.107), which is a significant improvement over 0.7 (result of single exponential smoothing). This goes to show that if used wisely, more advanced models can significantly reduce forecast variability.

On the flip side, they may be a lost cause when it comes to demand patterns that are either too simple (where even a simplistic algorithm would result in acceptable accuracy) or too unpredictable.

The table below (see Fig. 3.108) shows the calculations for MASE and Theil U-statistic. Here again, one can see that the values are very close to each other and

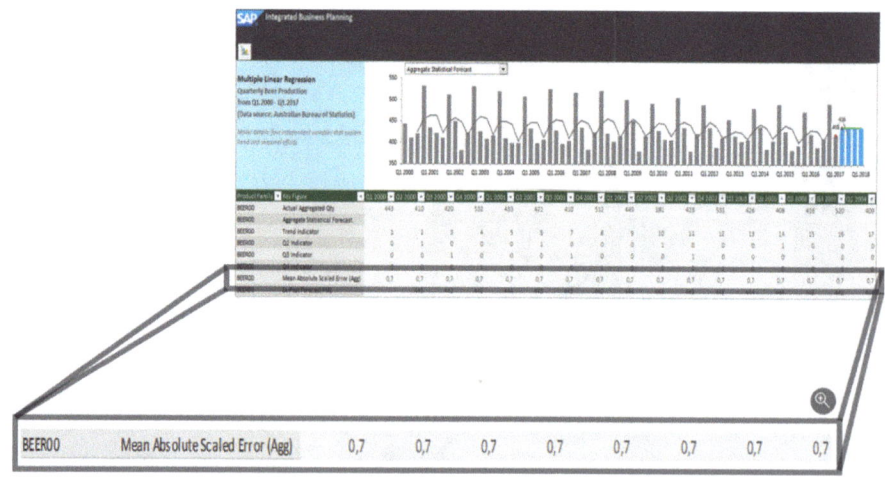

**Fig. 3.105** Choosing a simplistic model for a fairly complex demand pattern

| Ex-Post | Actual | Relative Actual Change (MASE) | Relative FC Change (MASE) | Relative Actual Change (Theil-U) | Relative FC Change (Theil-U) |
|---|---|---|---|---|---|
| 441 | 414 | 12 | 27 | 0.0009 | 0.0045 |
| 441 | 500 | 86 | 59 | 0.0432 | 0.0206 |
| 442 | 451 | 49 | 9 | 0.0096 | 0.0003 |
| 442 | 380 | 71 | 62 | 0.0248 | 0.0188 |
| 441 | 416 | 36 | 25 | 0.0090 | 0.0042 |
| 440 | 492 | 76 | 52 | 0.0334 | 0.0154 |
| 441 | 428 | 64 | 13 | 0.0169 | 0.0007 |
| 441 | 408 | 20 | 33 | 0.0022 | 0.0059 |
| 440 | 406 | 2 | 34 | 0.0000 | 0.0071 |
| 440 | 506 | 100 | 66 | 0.0607 | 0.0266 |
| 441 | 435 | 71 | 6 | 0.0197 | 0.0001 |
| 441 | 380 | 55 | 61 | 0.0160 | 0.0196 |
| 440 | 421 | 41 | 19 | 0.0116 | 0.0024 |
| 439 | 490 | 69 | 51 | 0.0269 | 0.0144 |
| 440 | 435 | 55 | 5 | 0.0126 | 0.0001 |
| 440 | 390 | 45 | 50 | 0.0107 | 0.0133 |
| 439 | 412 | 22 | 27 | 0.0032 | 0.0049 |
| 439 | 454 | 42 | 15 | 0.0104 | 0.0013 |
| 439 | 416 | 38 | 23 | 0.0070 | 0.0026 |
| 439 | 403 | 13 | 36 | 0.0010 | 0.0074 |
| 438 | 408 | 5 | 30 | 0.0002 | 0.0056 |
| 438 | 482 | 74 | 44 | 0.0329 | 0.0119 |
| 438 | 438 | 44 | 0 | 0.0083 | 0.0000 |
| 438 | 386 | 52 | 52 | 0.0141 | 0.0143 |
| 437 | 405 | 19 | 32 | 0.0024 | 0.0070 |
| 437 | 491 | 86 | 54 | 0.0451 | 0.0179 |
| 438 | 427 | 64 | 11 | 0.0170 | 0.0005 |
| 438 | 383 | 44 | 55 | 0.0106 | 0.0163 |
| 437 | 394 | 11 | 43 | 0.0008 | 0.0124 |
| 436 | 473 | 79 | 37 | 0.0402 | 0.0089 |
| 437 | 420 | 53 | 17 | 0.0126 | 0.0012 |
| 436 | 390 | 30 | 46 | 0.0051 | 0.0121 |
| 435 | 410 | 20 | 25 | 0.0026 | 0.0042 |
| 435 | 493 | 83 | 58 | 0.0410 | 0.0201 |
| 436 | 418 | 75 | 18 | 0.0231 | 0.0013 |
| | | 54.87 | 37.98 | 1.46 | 0.75 |

**MASE**    0.69

**Theil's U-Statistic**    0.71

**Fig. 3.106** MASE versus Theil's U for MLR for exponential smoothing

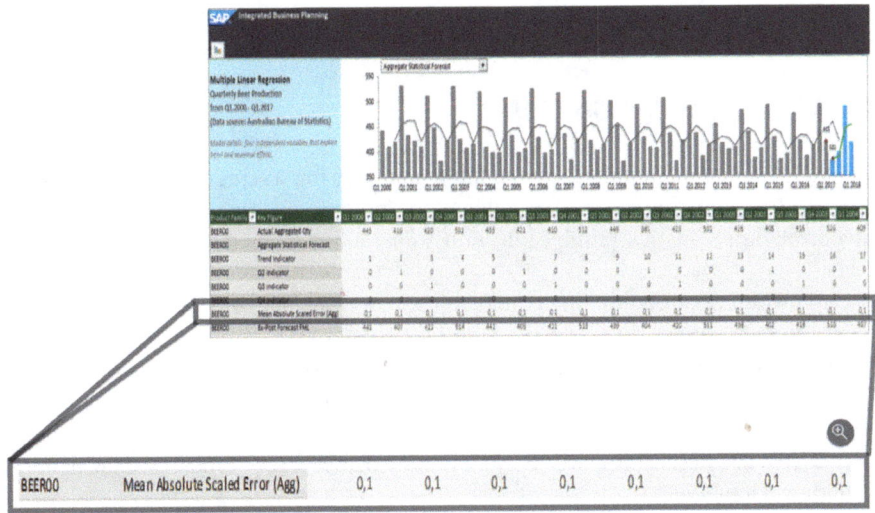

**Fig. 3.107** MASE when using MLR

| Ex-Post | Actual | Relative Actual Change (MASE) | Relative FC Change (MASE) | Relative Actual Change (Theil-U) | Relative FC Change (Theil-U) |
|---|---|---|---|---|---|
| 395 | 402 | 19 | 7 | 0.0020 | 0.0003 |
| 411 | 414 | 12 | 3 | 0.0009 | 0.0001 |
| 503 | 500 | 86 | 3 | 0.0432 | 0.0000 |
| 430 | 451 | 49 | 21 | 0.0096 | 0.0018 |
| 394 | 380 | 71 | 14 | 0.0248 | 0.0009 |
| 410 | 416 | 36 | 6 | 0.0090 | 0.0003 |
| 501 | 492 | 76 | 9 | 0.0334 | 0.0005 |
| 428 | 428 | 64 | 0 | 0.0169 | 0.0000 |
| 392 | 408 | 20 | 16 | 0.0022 | 0.0013 |
| 408 | 406 | 2 | 2 | 0.0000 | 0.0000 |
| 500 | 506 | 100 | 6 | 0.0607 | 0.0002 |
| 427 | 435 | 71 | 8 | 0.0197 | 0.0003 |
| 391 | 380 | 55 | 11 | 0.0160 | 0.0006 |
| 407 | 421 | 41 | 14 | 0.0116 | 0.0014 |
| 498 | 490 | 69 | 8 | 0.0269 | 0.0004 |
| 425 | 435 | 55 | 10 | 0.0126 | 0.0004 |
| 389 | 390 | 45 | 1 | 0.0107 | 0.0000 |
| 405 | 412 | 22 | 7 | 0.0032 | 0.0003 |
| 497 | 454 | 42 | 43 | 0.0104 | 0.0109 |
| 424 | 416 | 38 | 8 | 0.0070 | 0.0003 |
| 388 | 403 | 13 | 15 | 0.0010 | 0.0013 |
| 404 | 408 | 5 | 4 | 0.0002 | 0.0001 |
| 496 | 482 | 74 | 14 | 0.0329 | 0.0011 |
| 422 | 438 | 44 | 16 | 0.0083 | 0.0011 |
| 387 | 386 | 52 | 1 | 0.0141 | 0.0000 |
| 402 | 405 | 19 | 3 | 0.0024 | 0.0000 |
| 494 | 491 | 86 | 3 | 0.0451 | 0.0001 |
| 421 | 427 | 64 | 6 | 0.0170 | 0.0002 |
| 385 | 383 | 44 | 2 | 0.0106 | 0.0000 |
| 401 | 394 | 11 | 7 | 0.0008 | 0.0003 |
| 493 | 473 | 79 | 20 | 0.0402 | 0.0025 |
| 420 | 420 | 53 | 0 | 0.0126 | 0.0000 |
| 384 | 390 | 30 | 6 | 0.0051 | 0.0002 |
| 400 | 410 | 20 | 10 | 0.0026 | 0.0007 |
| 491 | 493 | 83 | 2 | 0.0410 | 0.0000 |
| 418 | 418 | 75 | 0 | 0.0231 | 0.0000 |
| | | 54.54 | 9.09 | 1.47 | 0.05 |
| **MASE** | | | 0.17 | | |
| **Theil's U-statistic** | | | | | 0.19 |

**Fig. 3.108**  MASE versus Theil's U for MLR

MASE can be effectively used in a similar fashion to U-statistic to evaluate the value of a certain model in relation to NF1.

### 3.3.22   Auto-ARIMA/SARIMA

The ARIMA method, autoregressive integrated moving average, and the SARIMA method, seasonal autoregressive integrated moving average, make part of the autocorrelation statistics family, but with some enhancements:

– Capture autocorrelation in a more elaborate way and are performed directly on the data series.
– Are more suitable than autocorrelation for forecasting purposes.
– Have a strong underlying mathematical concept and theory, implying heavy use of statistics.
– Are very flexible, allowing to capture and detect many types of data patterns within data series.

These methods, as it may be already clear, are very technical and require a deep mathematical expertise not only to fully comprehend the facets of the models, but also to interpret and set them correctly to perform forecasting with better results. As a result, for ARIMA and SARIMA methods, some ground rules needed to understand when to use the models and how to set them will be explained with statistical details.

Additionally, ARIMA and SARIMA still lack popularity at the management levels and hence a bird's eye view of the methods should suffice.

The key concepts behind the ARIMA models are:

- The "order," "*p*": It includes predictors that are lag versions of the series. It refers to the concept of autoregression, hence the name AR. The value of "*p*" indicates the number of time lags. Figure 3.109 shows the complementary purpose of making the understanding of the "*p*" order a bit clearer. From the data set, it is possible to see how the data lags by 1 in a sort of cascade mode.
- The "differencing," "*d*": It includes as new predictors the lag versions of the forecast error that are called the moving average component of the model, hence the name ARIMA. The value "*d*" indicates the number of times the data had the past values deducted.

As a consequence, the ARIMA model captures all the forms of autocorrelation by including the lags of the time series and of the forecast errors. We rely on the assumption that the time series is stationary, which means it has no trend or seasonality and has a constant level of variance of autocorrelations. Basically, it simply tries to predict the future based on the similarity with the past.

The last key concept is:

- Integration concept, called differencing operator "*q*", hence ARIMA. The value of "*q*" indicates the order of the moving average model.

Lag = "p" = 1

| Data set | (Data-Average) | | | | | | | | | | |
|---|---|---|---|---|---|---|---|---|---|---|---|
| 4741 | -1089.982759 | | | | | | | | | | |
| 5382 | -448.9827586 | -1089.9828 | | | | | | | | | |
| 2802 | -3028.982759 | -448.98276 | -1089.9828 | | | | | | | | |
| 6288 | 457.0172414 | -3028.9828 | -448.98276 | -1089.9828 | | | | | | | |
| 12797 | 6966.017241 | 457.017241 | -3028.9828 | -448.98276 | -1089.9828 | | | | | | |
| 11910 | 6079.017241 | 6966.01724 | 457.017241 | -3028.9828 | -448.98276 | -1089.9828 | | | | | |
| 15832 | 10001.01724 | 6079.01724 | 6966.01724 | 457.017241 | -3028.9828 | -448.98276 | -1089.9828 | | | | |
| 13499 | 7668.017241 | 10001.0172 | 6079.01724 | 6966.01724 | 457.017241 | -3028.9828 | -448.98276 | -1089.9828 | | | |
| 14158 | 8327.017241 | 7668.01724 | 10001.0172 | 6079.01724 | 6966.01724 | 457.017241 | -3028.9828 | -448.98276 | -1089.9828 | | |
| 6849 | 1018.017241 | 8327.01724 | 7668.01724 | 10001.0172 | 6079.01724 | 6966.01724 | 457.017241 | -3028.9828 | -448.98276 | -1089.9828 | |
| 6582 | 751.0172414 | 1018.01724 | 8327.01724 | 7668.01724 | 10001.0172 | 6079.01724 | 6966.01724 | 457.017241 | -3028.9828 | -448.98276 | -1089.9828 |
| 4798 | -1032.982759 | 751.017241 | 1018.01724 | 8327.01724 | 7668.01724 | 10001.0172 | 6079.01724 | 6966.01724 | 457.017241 | -3028.9828 | -448.98276 |
| 5453 | -377.9827586 | -1032.9828 | 751.017241 | 1018.01724 | 8327.01724 | 7668.01724 | 10001.0172 | 6079.01724 | 6966.01724 | 457.017241 | -3028.9828 |
| 5731 | -99.98275862 | -377.98276 | -1032.9828 | 751.017241 | 1018.01724 | 8327.01724 | 7668.01724 | 10001.0172 | 6079.01724 | 6966.01724 | 457.017241 |
| 2909 | -2921.982759 | -99.982759 | -377.98276 | -1032.9828 | 751.017241 | 1018.01724 | 8327.01724 | 7668.01724 | 10001.0172 | 6079.01724 | 6966.01724 |
| 5557 | -273.9827586 | -2921.9828 | -99.982759 | -377.98276 | -1032.9828 | 751.017241 | 1018.01724 | 8327.01724 | 7668.01724 | 10001.0172 | 6079.01724 |
| 11664 | 5833.017241 | -273.98276 | -2921.9828 | -99.982759 | -377.98276 | -1032.9828 | 751.017241 | 1018.01724 | 8327.01724 | 7668.01724 | 10001.0172 |
| 9614 | 3783.017241 | 5833.01724 | -273.98276 | -2921.9828 | -99.982759 | -377.98276 | -1032.9828 | 751.017241 | 1018.01724 | 8327.01724 | 7668.01724 |

**Fig. 3.109** Example of the concept of lag = 1

The lag 1 differencing, "$d$", is used to remove the trend, and it answers the following question: How many times do we need to perform the lag 1 differencing?

- $d = 0$ means there is no trend.
- $d = 1$ means the differencing has to be performed once, implying a linear trend.
- $d = 2$ means a double differencing has to be performed.

From a business perspective, the reasoning can be immediately simplified. If we believe the data set has a trendy component, the "$d$" order should be set to 1; otherwise, it should be set to 0.

At the same time, if we are dealing with a seasonal data set, additional parameters are needed in the model:

- $P$: predictors that are seasonal lag versions of the time series.
- $D$: It denotes whether or not to perform seasonal differencing. If $D = 0$, we aim at not performing a seasonal differencing, while if $D = 1$ we aim at running the seasonal differencing.
- $Q$: seasonal differencing predictors based on the moving average.

At the very end, to properly configure a SARIMA model, six parameters have to be indicated ($p, d, q, P, D$ and $Q$). This is not at all a simple choice, and it requires experience and expertise to properly and correctly set the parameters of the tests. The most common method is to use visual inspection of the series or to make use of the autocorrelation chart. To simplify the approach, we propose the following rule of thumb:

- Use differencing to remove trend and seasonality.
- Keep the model as simple as possible.
- Set $d = 0$ or 1.
- Set $D = 0$ or 1.
- Use small values of $p$ and $q$.
- Set $P = 0$ or 1.
- Set $Q = 0$ or 1.
- Be careful with overdifferencing.
- In most cases, either p is 0 or $q$ is 0.
- $p + q$ is less than or equal to 3.

SAP IBP provides two different strategies that are helpful to choose the best parameters of the method:

- Stepwise strategy: This strategy is very efficient as it reiterates the calculations of the parameters until the method does not find those that guarantee the best improvements. Only when the model cannot find any better solution, the reiteration will end. To take a practical example, we suppose that we would like to consider the autoregression for the past month ($p = 1$), for the past two months

($p = 2$) and for the past three months ($p = 3$). We do not know what is the best value of p that will yield the best results, and consequently we tell the system to apply a stepwise strategy to run each case scenario and select the "$p$"-value with the best autoregression.

– Exhaustive strategy: It calculates all the possible combinations of "$p$" and "$q$", and it selects the combination that gives as an output the lowest information criterion. This concept will be explained in the coming lines. To give a practical example, if we choose as the maximum order of "$p$" the value 1 and the maximum order of "$q$" the value 1, the system will consider the following combinations: (0, 0), (0, 1), (1, 0) and (1, 1). The same logic is applied when the seasonal component comes into play: The matrix that will have to be considered will be ($p$, $q$, $P$, $Q$).

As a conclusion, the stepwise strategy is more time efficient, but the exhaustive strategy is meant to provide more accurate results in terms of forecast accuracy.

As mentioned above, an information criterion is a measure for the quality of a statistical model. We could simplify the reasoning by stating that lower the criterion higher the accuracy will be. The useful criterion normally used to select the orders of the models is the following:

– Akaike information criterion: It approximates to the current data set.
– Corrected Akaike information criterion: It must be used for small sample sizes.
– Bayesian information criterion: It chooses the data set that is the best fit with the reality.

The objective is to minimize those models for a forecasting model with a good fit.

The forthcoming use cases show how these statistical methods could be applied to make the practitioners' lives easier, in their efforts to improve forecast accuracy.

### 3.3.23  SAP Use Case: ARIMA/SARIMA

First of all, we introduce the basic ARIMA and SARIMA settings, highlighting the key fields where a manual intervention is required. In Fig. 3.110, we can see that top portion of the configuration is dedicated to the ARIMA settings and the bottom portion to the SARIMA settings.

Let's start with ARIMA. The user has to decide for the search strategy. The two options available are, as described above:

– Exhaustive strategy
– Stepwise strategy.

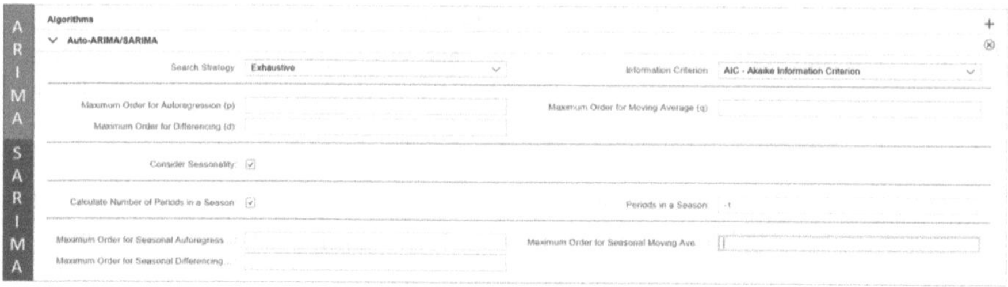

**Fig. 3.110** SAP IBP ARIMA/SARIMA settings

By setting this choice, the practitioner identifies the search strategy of all the parameters that need to be optimized by the system. It is a rather simplistic choice. In addition, the information criterion has to be defined:

- AIC: Akaike information criterion
- Corrected AIC
- BIC: Bayesian information criterion.

By setting this field, the practitioner identifies the information criterion whose minimization will guarantee the optimization of the model itself. The information criterion is a complex formula that we will not shed light on; however, it is useful to understand that the system will minimize the result of the information criterion formula and by doing so we are guaranteed to have found the best parameters to have an accurate forecast.

Besides, the maximum orders for the three parameters of ARIMA have to be set:

- Autoregression order, "$p$". By setting "$p$" equal to 2, we impose the system to try to identify, based on the search strategy and information criterion chosen, the best value for the order "$p$". By setting "$p$" maximum to 2, the system will investigate only the lag = 0, lag = 1 and lag = 2. The concept of the lag is explained in Fig. 3.109.
- Differencing order "$d$": To keep it simple, it is advisable to set the index to 1 as it will allow the system to detect the presence of a trend. In case of trend presence, the "$d$" order will set automatically by the system to 1, otherwise to 0.
- Moving average order "$q$": As explained in the moving average algorithm, this index indicates the number of past months that will be considered for generating the forecasted amount.

The configuration of ARIMA is now completed. To apply SARIMA, some further steps need to be added from the previous fields. Basically, by clicking on the "consider seasonality" field we apply the SARIMA method and the news entries of the configuration become available.

The first thing to be decided is to manually calculate the number of periods within a season or to tick the check box that automatically lets the system to identify the length of the season. It highly recommended to use the second option.

Then, like in ARIMA, the maximum orders for the three parameters of SARIMA have to be set:

– Seasonal autoregression order, "$P$"
– Seasonal differencing order "$D$"
– Seasonal moving average order "$Q$".

The purpose of those parameters is the same for the parameters of the ARIMA; however, the focus is on the seasonality side and not on the trend. For example, in this case, the "$D$" order if set to 1 implies the presence of seasonality, while if set to 0 implies that no seasonality pattern has been automatically detected by the optimization run.

Only at this point, we will be able to save the configuration as the SARIMA ($p$, $d$, $q$, $P$, $D$, $Q$).

We need to remember that the most suitable data patterns for ARIMA can be with or without a trend, with high or low variability, with high or low cyclicity: The crucial point is to provide the algorithm a meaningful data set, where there are no 0 points and at least 48 periods of history. Due to the inherent mathematical algorithms of the ARIMA model, it has been proven that bigger the sales history provided, larger will be the data set to be analyzed and the more it will exploit the statistic performance of the test.

The benefits of having as big a historical data set as possible are displayed in Fig. 3.111. The data used are quite variable in sales/demand. There might be a trend detected depending on the confidence level for this assessment. However, the crucial point to let the algorithm reach such a low forecast error is the fact of having used 58 months as historical data set.

The same process also shows positive results for one of the most variable and seasonal SKUs we selected from a product portfolio. Using 58 months of history, and by letting the system automatically optimize the SARIMA parameters, without any type of preprocessing and data cleansing, we managed at a first run to be 80% accurate (see Fig. 3.112).

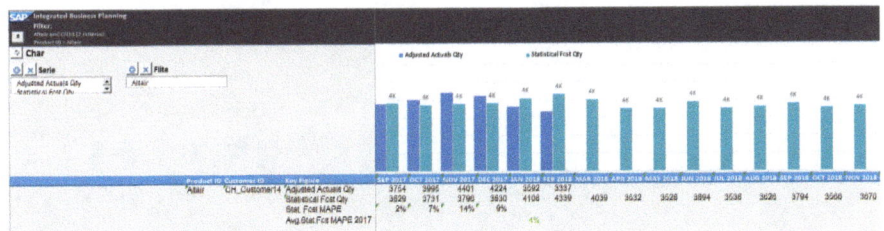

**Fig. 3.111** SAP IBP ARIMA

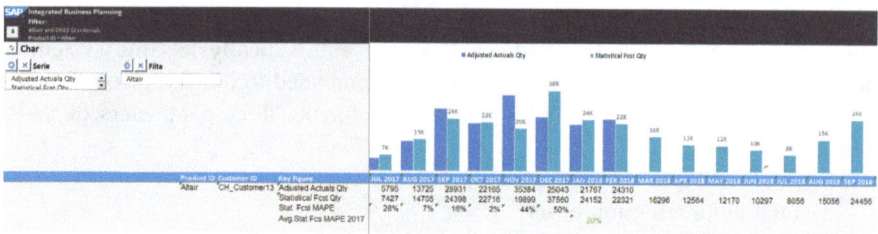

**Fig. 3.112** SAP IBP SARIMA

Furthermore, we then run some different forecasting tests by changing the configuration variables of ARIMA and SARIMA in order to understand and compare the differences within the configurations available. For the ARIMA tests, the data set we displayed in Fig. 3.84 is employed.

According to the previous run of DES and Brown's linear exponential smoothing, the best value of forecast error is accounted for 14%. In the following figures, we show and interpret the results out of some different ARIMA runs:

1. ARIMA stepwise optimized by the Akaike information criterion. Figure 3.113 displays the results out of this first ARIMA run. Normally, it is advisable to let the maximum orders to a value of 3 for "$p$", 1 for "$d$" and 3 for "$q$". The average forecast error for 2017 accounts for 14%, while for 2017 a slight decreasing trend is foreseen.

2. ARIMA stepwise optimized by the Bayesian information criterion. Figure 3.114 displays ARIMA that has been optimized differently. The average forecast error worsens 1%, while the decreasing trend stays approximately the same.

3. ARIMA exhaustive optimized by the Akaike information criterion. Figure 3.115 shows the attempt. The threshold of forecast error and expected sales/demand are similar to the previous one and quite identical to the following test as well.

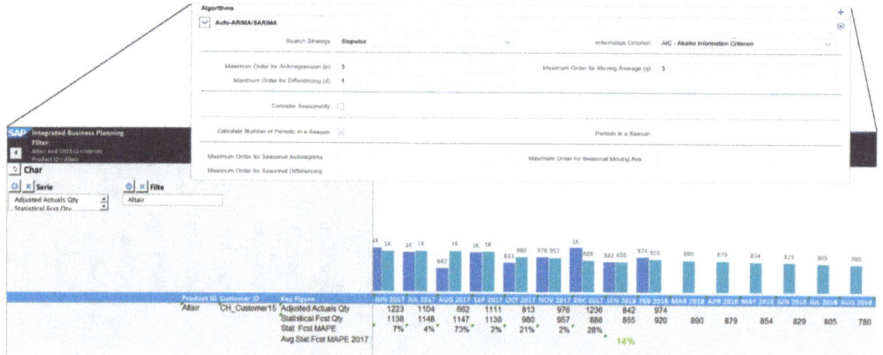

**Fig. 3.113** SAP IBP ARIMA stepwise (Akaike)

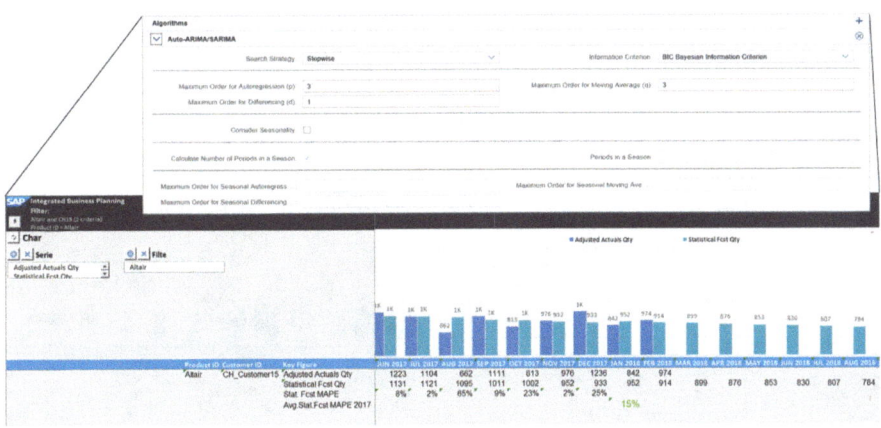

**Fig. 3.114**   SAP IBP ARIMA stepwise (Bayesian)

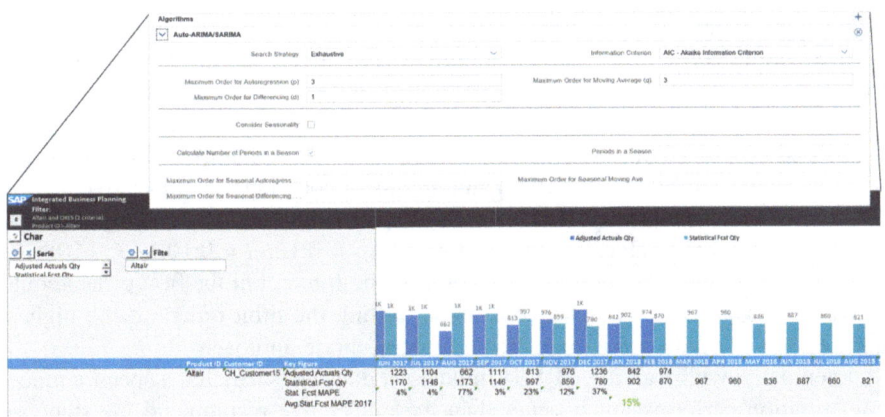

**Fig. 3.115**   SAP IBP ARIMA exhaustive (Akaike)

4. ARIMA exhaustive optimized by the Bayesian information criterion. Figure 3.116 represents the best optimization available and also the most time consuming in terms of software running time. Once again, the results are very similar to the previous one. It is interesting to notice how, within the exhaustive method, it only changes the ex-post forecasting while the foreseen sales/demand for 2018 stays the same.

As a conclusion, we highlight why the corrected Akaike information criterion has not been employed: If we select a large data history, using the C-AIC to forecast the future will not provide better results as it must be used only for small data sample. It is interesting to see how for all the tests conducted, a diminishing trend is displayed for the future (2018) sales/demand. This factor indicates how the

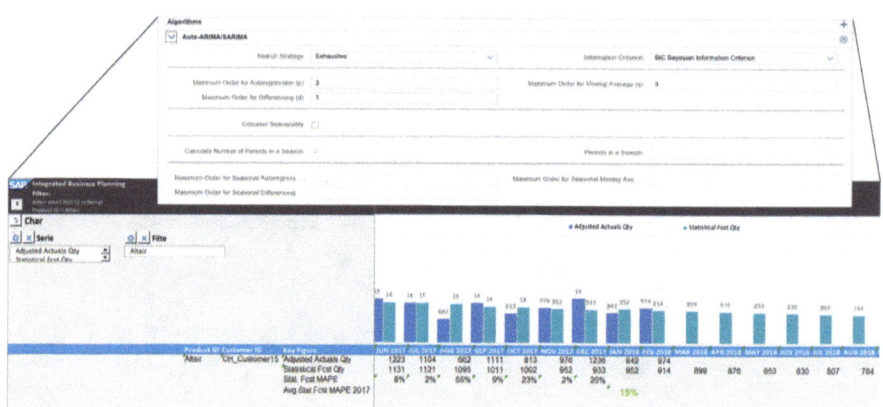

**Fig. 3.116** SAP IBP ARIMA exhaustive (Bayesian)

automatic optimization of ARIMA selected 1 as the value of "$p$", which is the trend differencing order, was the correct one as there is a trend present in the data set.

In addition, considering that a maximum threshold for the three parameters has to be set, we may think that such a decision is quite essential for the final results; however, for those types of tests, the values of those entries are less relevant as an automated optimization is anyway performed. The only thing that could change is the time consumed by the system for running the model, but it is not said at all that if we set the maximum orders to 10 we may expect better results. The only certainty is that with the limit values set to 10 (ARIMA ($p$ = 0:10, $d$ = 0:10, $q$ = 0:10)) the forecast model will take more time to forecast the future, but the best orders could still be ARIMA (0, 2, 1). As a conclusion, setting the limit orders to the highest allowed threshold does not guarantee a more accurate approach.

Eventually, within all the ARIMA models, it does not seem that a specific model configuration performs much better than the others. We recommend the stepwise approach as it is less time consuming; however, we could also expect a DES or Brown's algorithm or even the automated exponential smoothing solution to give similar results in terms of forecast accuracy.

A similar approach has been used to test the SARIMA optimization option. Considering that a seasonal component has to be present to check the goodness of this forecast model, the data set employed corresponds to the one used for the seasonal triple exponential smoothing in Fig. 3.57. The most accurate forecasting model related to this profile was the automated smoothing algorithm with best results, where with a seasonal period of 12 months, the forecast error got reduced to 15%. Let's see how the SARIMA performs in relation to this seasonal profile:

1. SARIMA stepwise optimized by Akaike. Figure 3.117 displays the SARIMA enabled settings by ticking the consideration of seasonality. The average MAPE for 2017 accounts for 16%, and we see for 2018 how the seasonal behavior is

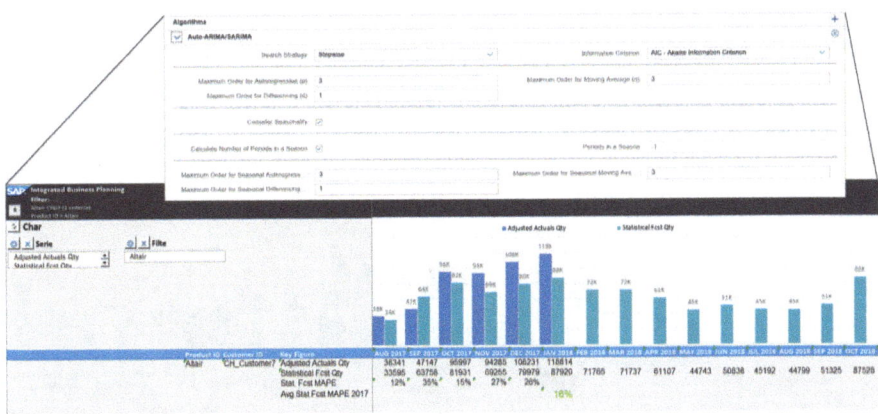

**Fig. 3.117**  SAP IBP SARIMA stepwise (Akaike)

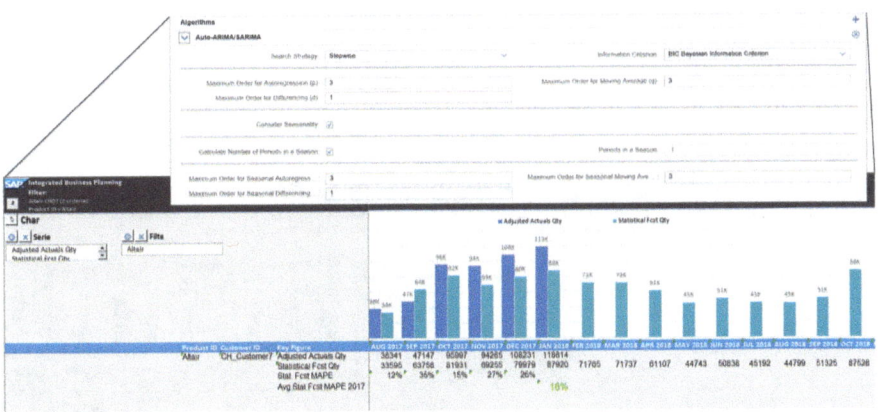

**Fig. 3.118**  SAP IBP SARIMA stepwise (Bayesian)

reflected for the entire year. This suggests us how the "*D*" differencing seasonal order has been, correctly, optimized to 1 as the data set contains a seasonal pattern.

2. SARIMA stepwise optimized by Bayesian. Figure 3.118 illustrates the same result as the previous one even if the optimization run is based on a different method.

3. SARIMA exhaustive optimized by Akaike. Figure 3.119 is the only test that actually performs differently from the others. The accuracy stays approximately on the same level, but the foreseen seasonal pattern does not match with the previous ones. If in the other tests the peaks of the season happen in winter, this method forecasts an early decreasing trend in the winter season of 2017, while it detects an increase in sales/demand in the early stage of 2018 summer and again starting from November 2018.

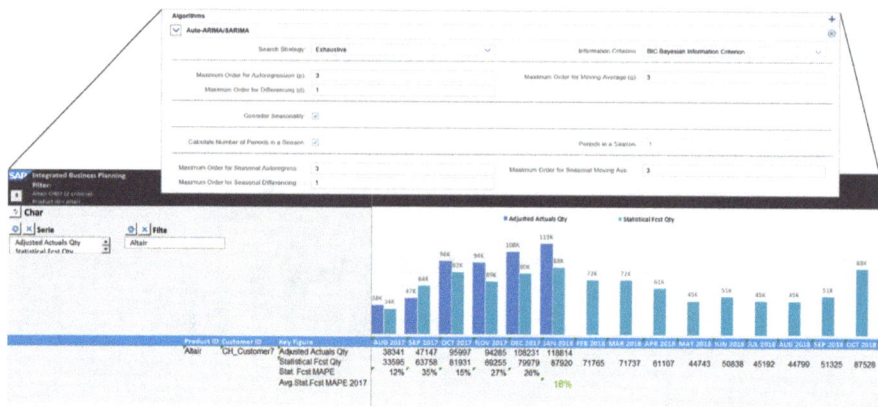

**Fig. 3.119** SAP IBP SARIMA exhaustive (Akaike)

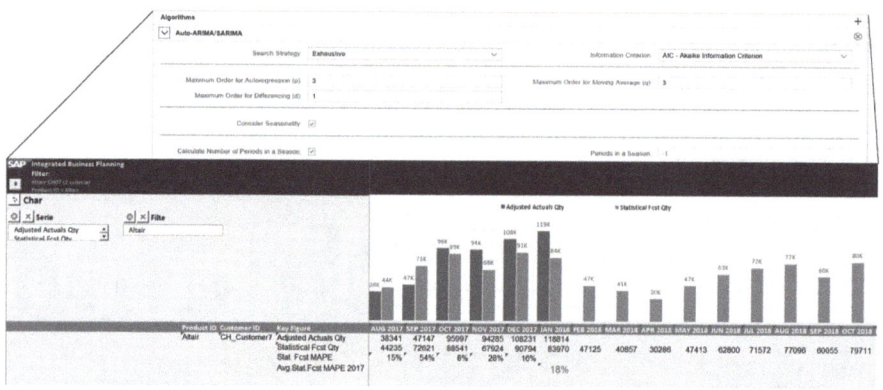

**Fig. 3.120** SAP IBP SARIMA exhaustive (Bayesian)

4. SARIMA exhaustive optimized by Bayesian. Figure 3.120 illustrates the same result as the previous one even if the optimization run and the method itself are based on a different method.

Results indicate that all the methods detect the seasonal component and perform accurately enough from a forecast error standpoint. The same generic consideration mentioned for the ARIMA method is also valid for the SARIMA methods.

We conclude by highlighting that applying an fully SARIMA test on an SKU that displays a marked seasonality allows the practitioners to already reach an acceptable forecasting accuracy. In addition, the longer the historical data set, the higher the chances are to get a more accurate forecast, since we are letting the algorithm perform at the best of its capabilities.

### 3.3.24  Automatic Model Selection

The automatic model selection is a forecasting model that in SAP IBP allows the user to automatically select the best or the most accurate forecasting model out of a selected number of pre-defined forecasting algorithms. It may be used for all types of data sets and data behavior; however, it has to be used in a functional and prudent manner.

The possibility of executing several forecasting models and letting the system choose the best one for your data is a great functionality that may reduce the time and the effort toward the forecasting exercise for the practitioners. Nonetheless, the choice of the preselected forecasting models needs to be rational and reasonable; otherwise, the automatic model selection out of incomparable forecasting models will give meaningless insights. We will delve into more detail in the next section regarding the model selection criteria.

Besides, the automatic selection can be run not only based on the best forecast solution, but also based on the calculated weighted average forecast. These two criteria for the automatic selection will be explained in more detail in the coming sub-sections.

### 3.3.25  SAP Use Case: Best Fit

Figure 3.121 represents an example of a non-rational best fit model whose outputs are expected to be quite useless, due to the poor selection of algorithms. The preselection of the methods for the best fit is paramount if we want to optimize our forecasting model based on the right criterion—usually the way the data behave, for example the average demand and inner variability detected. For more detail regarding the right criterion, we recommend the reading of Chap. 5.

The data set used is still the same employed for all the single exponential smoothing tests: not highly variable and stable sales/demand. Consequently,

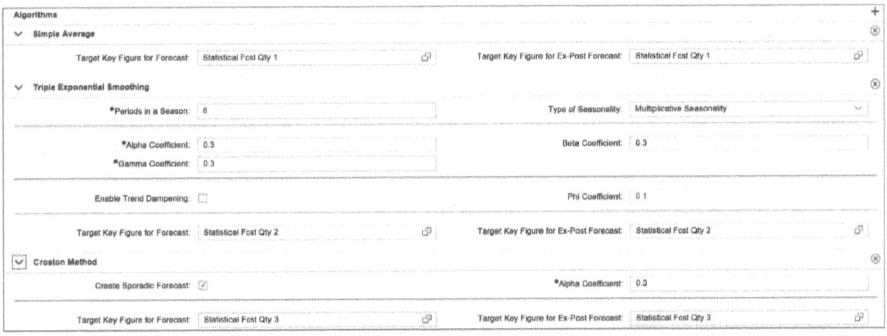

**Fig. 3.121**  Best fit settings

inserting the Croston method as a possible forecast model could be already avoided considering the type of data. The triple exponential smoothing with randomly assigned parameters and settings can also be expected to fail in terms of forecast accuracy due to the data type.

Nevertheless, the visualization depicts how it is allowed to select between the three different algorithms:

- Simple average
- Triple exponential smoothing
- Croston method.

For each of them, the same settings are selected as before.

Figure 3.122 illustrates the method criteria. In this case, we opt for the best forecast solution based on the mean percentage error (MPE).

In Fig. 3.123, the results out of the best fit model are shown. The statistical forecast quantity 1 contains the results of the simple average forecast model, the statistical forecast quantity 2 the outcomes of the triple exponential smoothing and the statistical forecast quantity 3 the ones of Croston method. Based on the MAPE, the most accurate forecast model results in the simple average as it is shown in the statistical forecast quantity row and with the light blue bars. As a matter of fact, for this type of SKU, a simple average method would be more than enough to reach an accurate prediction for the future using low time and cost algorithms.

Another example of the best fit model is to compare at the same time the three different smoothing algorithms. See Fig. 3.124 for the specific settings related to

**Fig. 3.122**  Best fit method criteria

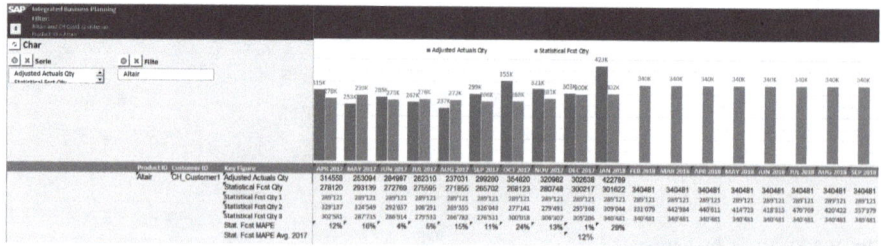

**Fig. 3.123**  Best fit algorithm

each specific forecasting model. This approach makes more sense if applied to non-intermittent data.

The data sets analyzed in the next two visualizations, Figs. 3.125 and 3.126, indicate how the results in terms of forecast error are hugely worsened compared to the results we managed to get out of the optimized smoothing algorithms and from the best result of automated smoothing. It is fundamental to notice that it is actually the double exponential smoothing selected as the most accurate smoothing algorithm. From the two visualizations below (where the statistical forecast quantity 1

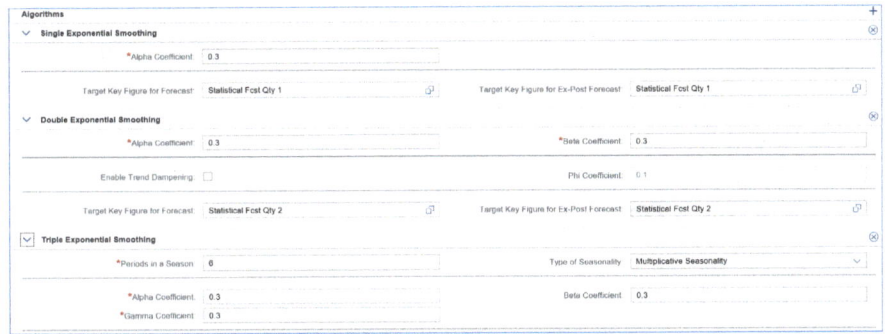

**Fig. 3.124** Best fit smoothing algorithms

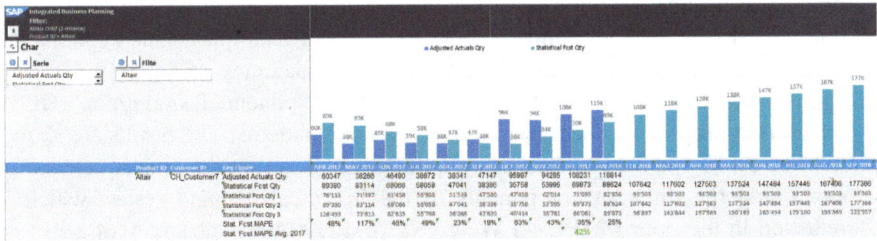

**Fig. 3.125** SAP IBP best fit smoothing algorithm (1)

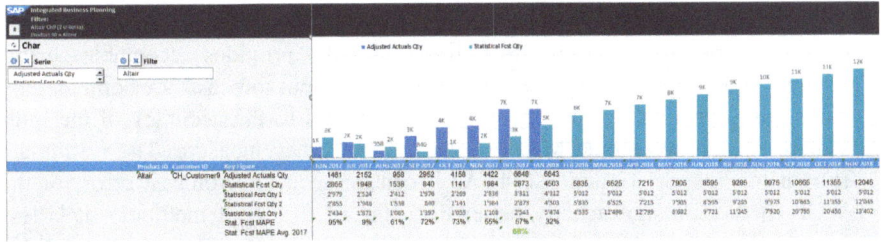

**Fig. 3.126** SAP IBP best fit smoothing algorithm (2)

contains the results of the SES, the statistical forecast quantity 2 the outcomes of DES and the statistical forecast quantity 3 the ones of TES), we can see how only the trend for 2018 is detected.

As a conclusion, we attribute the worsened forecast to the high degree of manual settings for the configuration. Higher the manual inputs, more accurate should the analysis of the data set be to actually map the right setting to the data set.

### 3.3.26   SAP Use Case: Weighted Combined Forecast from SES, DES, TES

Weighted combined forecast can be one of the methods used to extract the best of the statistical forecasts' inputs into the final statistical forecast. In the first scenario, three statistical forecast models are combined to create a weighted combined forecast. The models combined are: single exponential, double exponential and triple exponential smoothing.

The steps required are as follows:

- A single exponential smoothing (SES) forecast model profile is set up with the right parameters. For this scenario, outlier correction (preprocessing step) using the interquartile range (IQR) method was selected and is used in all three input models. In the post-processing tab, forecast error measures MAPE and Weighted MAPE (weighted on actual values) were selected.[1] The results of the SES method are shown in Figs. 3.127 and 3.128. As one can see, the historical time series seems to follow a certain pattern that has not been captured in the output that is a constant number (4986 units in our example). This explains the high forecast error—Weighted MAPE is 55.6% (accuracy of 44.4%).
- The second forecast model used is the double exponential smoothing (DES), which is appropriate for forecasting trend demand patterns. The results are shown in Figs. 3.129 and 3.130. Here as well, the model does not do an adequate job of explaining the different components of the historical demand series, which is reflected in the poor MAPE—a Weighted MAPE of 61% (accuracy of 39%).
- Finally, the third forecast model uses triple exponential smoothing. The forecast error is still high, but lower than the other two as it seems to do a better job of capturing the effects of seasonality in the historical demand series. Still, the Weighted MAPE is 50% (an accuracy of 50%). The results are shown in Figs. 3.131 and 3.132.
- Given that none of the three models individually provides acceptable performance, a combination of forecast is created. The input forecasts are combined by calculating weights that are inversely proportional to the accuracy of the individual method. Weighted MAPE is used as accuracy measure. The results are shown in Figs. 3.133 and 3.134. As it can be seen, the forecast error for the WCF method is significantly better than any of the input methods—it is less

---

[1]These are calculated automatically by the system.

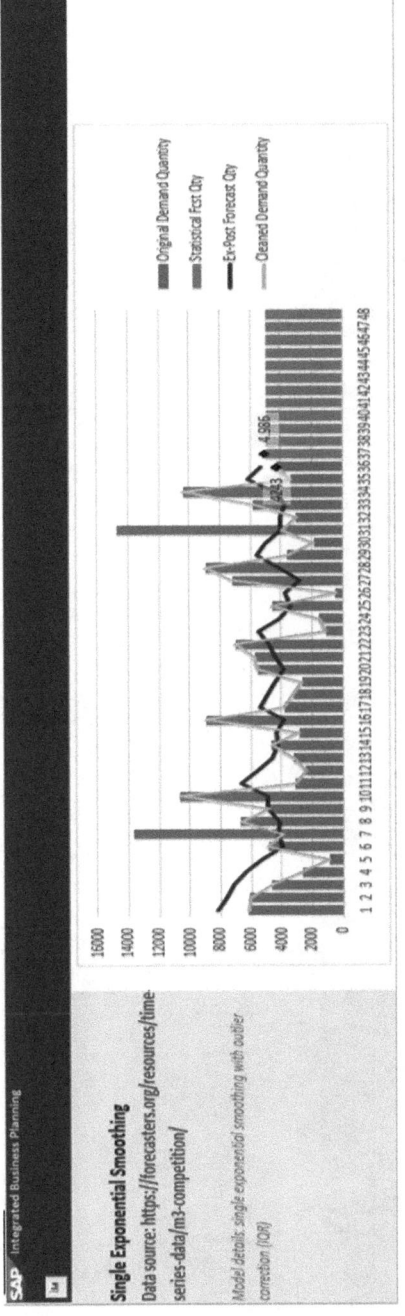

**Fig. 3.127** Result of single exponential smoothing (SES)

| Product ID | Customer ID | Key Figure | JUL 2017 | AUG 2017 | SEP 2017 | OCT 2017 | NOV 2017 | DEC 2017 | JAN 2018 | FEB 2018 | MAR 2018 | APR 2018 | MAY 2018 | JUN 2018 | JUL 2018 | AUG 2018 |
|---|---|---|---|---|---|---|---|---|---|---|---|---|---|---|---|---|
| IBP_P003 | IBP_C001 | Original Demand Quantity | 3360 | 4243 | 2542 | 5512 | 9277 | 7113 | 4367 | 16477 | 7001 | 5661 | 11635 | 8793 | 3821 | 39094 |
| IBP_P003 | IBP_C001 | Cleaned Demand Quantity | 3360 | 4243 | | | | | | | | | | | | |
| IBP_P003 | IBP_C001 | Ex-post Forecast Qty | 6138 | 5305 | | | | | | | | | | | | |
| IBP_P003 | IBP_C001 | Statistical Fcst Qty | | | 4986 | 4986 | 4986 | 4986 | 4986 | 4986 | 4986 | 4986 | 4986 | 4986 | 4986 | 4986 |
| IBP_P003 | IBP_C001 | MAPE SES | 105,39 | 105,39 | 105,39 | 105,39 | 105,39 | 105,39 | 105,39 | 105,39 | 105,39 | 105,39 | 105,39 | 105,39 | 105,39 | 105,39 |
| IBP_P003 | IBP_C001 | Weighted MAPE SES | 55,59 | 55,59 | 55,59 | 55,59 | 55,59 | 55,59 | 55,59 | 55,59 | 55,59 | 55,59 | 55,59 | 55,59 | 55,59 | 55,59 |

**Fig. 3.128** Result of SES—numerical data

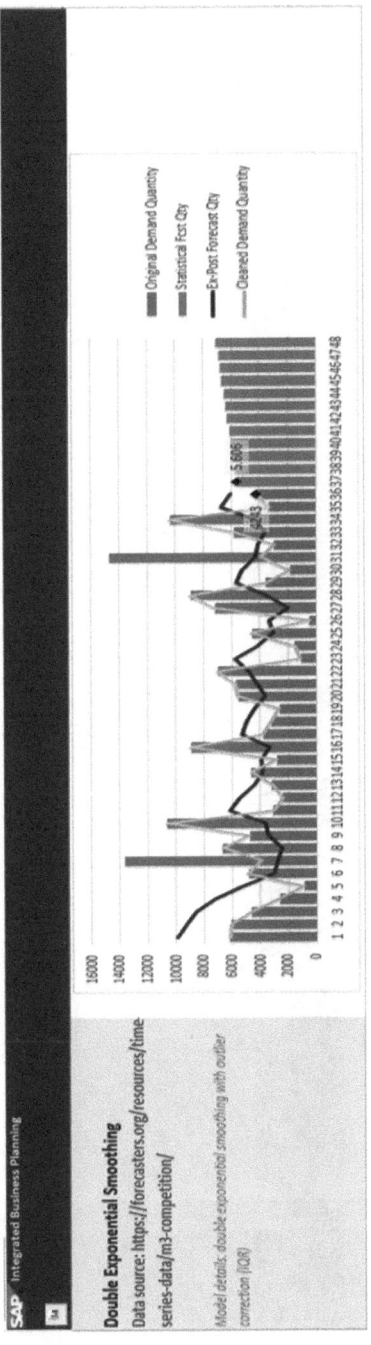

**Fig. 3.129** Result of double exponential smoothing (DES)

| Product ID | Customer ID | Key Figure | JUL 2017 | AUG 2017 | SEP 2017 | OCT 2017 | NOV 2017 | DEC 2017 | JAN 2018 | FEB 2018 | MAR 2018 | APR 2018 | MAY 2018 | JUN 2018 | JUL 2018 | AUG 2018 |
|---|---|---|---|---|---|---|---|---|---|---|---|---|---|---|---|---|
| IBP_P003 | IBP_C001 | Original Demand Quantity | 3360 | 4243 | 2542 | 5512 | 9277 | 7113 | 4367 | 16477 | 7001 | 5661 | 11635 | 8793 | 3821 | 39094 |
| IBP_P003 | IBP_C001 | Cleaned Demand Quantity | 3360 | 4243 | | | | | | | | | | | | |
| IBP_P003 | IBP_C001 | Ex-post Forecast Qty | 6730 | 6006 | | | | | | | | | | | | |
| IBP_P003 | IBP_C001 | Statistical Fcst Qty | | | 5606 | 5734 | 5863 | 5991 | 6120 | 6249 | 6377 | 6506 | 6634 | 6763 | 6891 | 7020 |
| IBP_P003 | IBP_C001 | MAPE DES | 106 | 106 | 106 | 106 | 106 | 106 | 106 | 106 | 106 | 106 | 106 | 106 | 106 | 106 |
| IBP_P003 | IBP_C001 | Weighted MAPE DES | 61 | 61 | 61 | 61 | 61 | 61 | 61 | 61 | 61 | 61 | 61 | 61 | 61 | 61 |

**Fig. 3.130** Result of DES—numerical data

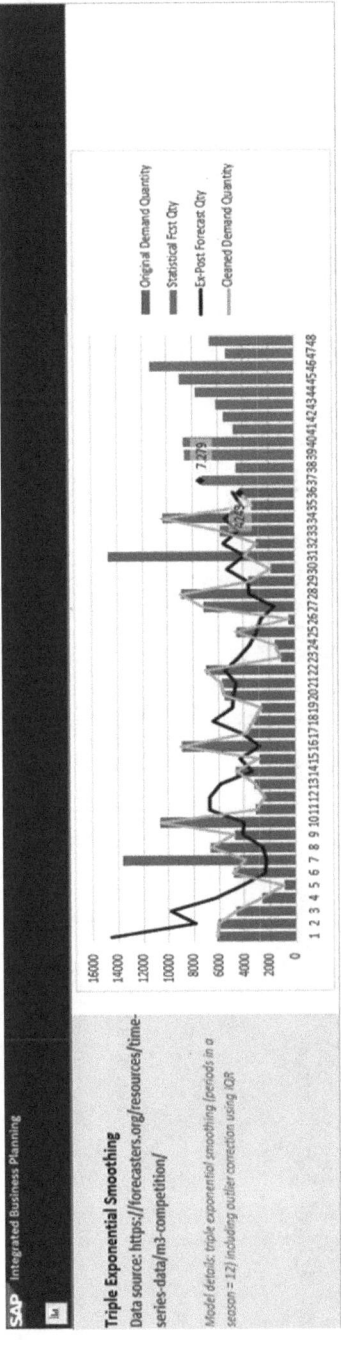

**Fig. 3.131** Result of triple exponential smoothing (TES)

| Product ID | Customer ID | Key Figure | JUL 2017 | AUG 2017 | SEP 2017 | OCT 2017 | NOV 2017 | DEC 2017 | JAN 2018 | FEB 2018 | MAR 2018 | APR 2018 | MAY 2018 | JUN 2018 | JUL 2018 | AUG 2018 |
|---|---|---|---|---|---|---|---|---|---|---|---|---|---|---|---|---|
| IBP_P003 | IBP_C001 | Original Demand Quantity | 3360 | 4243 | 2542 | 5512 | 9277 | 7113 | 4367 | 16477 | 7001 | 5661 | 11635 | 8793 | 3821 | 39094 |
| IBP_P003 | IBP_C001 | Cleaned Demand Quantity | 3360 | 4243 | | | | | | | | | | | | |
| IBP_P003 | IBP_C001 | Ex-post Forecast Qty | 4091 | 4789 | | | | | | | | | | | | |
| IBP_P003 | IBP_C001 | Statistical Fcst Qty | | | 7279 | 4550 | 8596 | 8719 | 4747 | 5538 | 6112 | 7698 | 9013 | 11319 | 5365 | 6592 |
| IBP_P003 | IBP_C001 | MAPE TES | 83 | 83 | 83 | 83 | 83 | 83 | 83 | 83 | 83 | 83 | 83 | 83 | 83 | 83 |
| IBP_P003 | IBP_C001 | Weighted MAPE TES | 50 | 50 | 50 | 50 | 50 | 50 | 50 | 50 | 50 | 50 | 50 | 50 | 50 | 50 |

**Fig. 3.132** Result of TES—numerical data

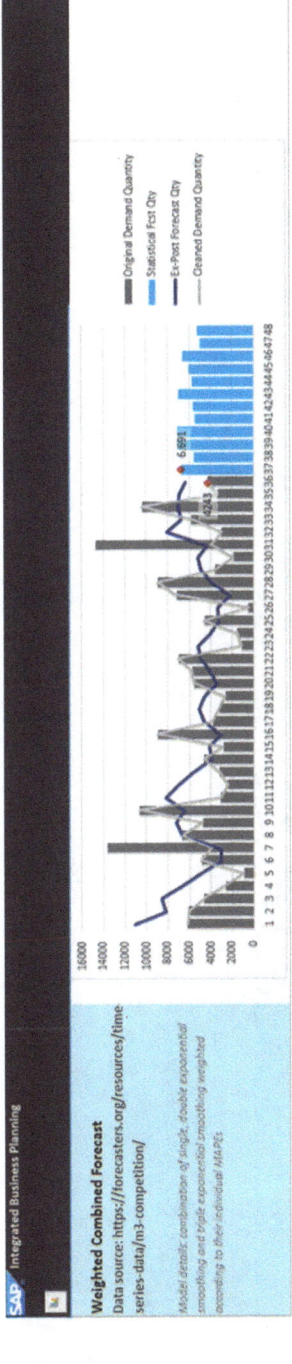

**Fig. 3.133**  Result of weighted combined forecast (WCF)

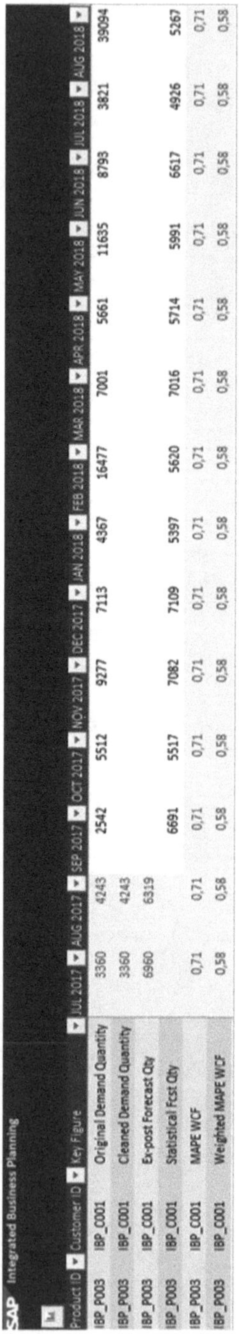

| Product ID | Customer ID | Key Figure | JUL 2017 | AUG 2017 | SEP 2017 | OCT 2017 | NOV 2017 | DEC 2017 | JAN 2018 | FEB 2018 | MAR 2018 | APR 2018 | MAY 2018 | JUN 2018 | JUL 2018 | AUG 2018 |
|---|---|---|---|---|---|---|---|---|---|---|---|---|---|---|---|---|
| IBP_P003 | IBP_C001 | Original Demand Quantity | 3360 | 4243 | 2542 | 5512 | 9277 | 7113 | 4367 | 16477 | 7001 | 5661 | 11635 | 8793 | 3821 | 39094 |
| IBP_P003 | IBP_C001 | Cleaned Demand Quantity | 3360 | 4243 | | | | | | | | | | | | |
| IBP_P003 | IBP_C001 | Ex-post Forecast Qty | 6960 | 6319 | | | | | | | | | | | | |
| IBP_P003 | IBP_C001 | Statistical Fcst Qty | | | 6691 | 5517 | 7082 | 7109 | 5397 | 5620 | 7016 | 5714 | 5991 | 6617 | 4926 | 5267 |
| IBP_P003 | IBP_C001 | MAPE WCF | 0,71 | 0,71 | 0,71 | 0,71 | 0,71 | 0,71 | 0,71 | 0,71 | 0,71 | 0,71 | 0,71 | 0,71 | 0,71 | 0,71 |
| IBP_P003 | IBP_C001 | Weighted MAPE WCF | 0,58 | 0,58 | 0,58 | 0,58 | 0,58 | 0,58 | 0,58 | 0,58 | 0,58 | 0,58 | 0,58 | 0,58 | 0,58 | 0,58 |

SAP Integrated Business Planning

**Fig. 3.134** Result of WCF—numerical data

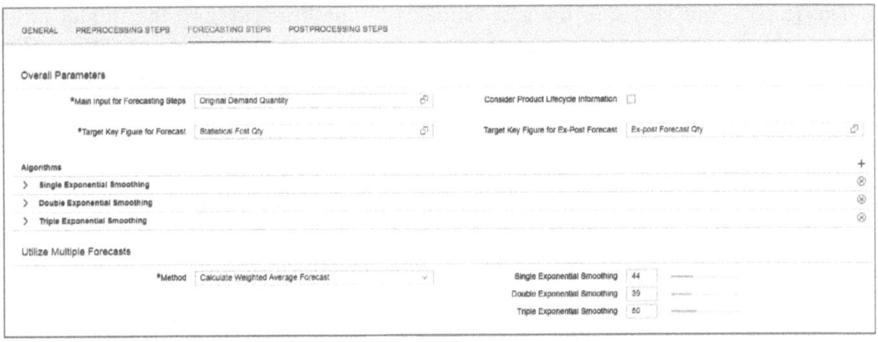

**Fig. 3.135** Forecast profile for calculating weighted average forecast

than 1%. It needs to be noted though that this says nothing about post-sample errors (performance in the real world). It is the risk mitigation aspect, above anything else that makes combination forecasts an attractive option.

- For this scenario, to calculate the final forecast, a forecast model was created that uses the "utilize multiple forecasts" option where the input methods are the three models described above (see Fig. 3.135). The input models were run individually to determine the Weighted MAPE, and the results were provided as weights (see Fig. 3.135). This approach requires one to manually enter the calibrated weights in the forecast profile, which is far from ideal. An alternative approach could configure special key figures to calculate the weights dynamically and then calculate the final forecast without requiring an additional profile to be configured. This approach is used in scenario 2 described below. If on the other hand a simple average of the input methods would suffice, a single profile that uses the "utilize multiple forecasts" options would work. It is worth to point out that the research shows simple average typically outperforms combinations calculated using weights. So, the need for (and calculation of) weights needs to be well thought through.

## 3.4 Validate Model

Once an algorithm and parameters are chosen, it pays to check how well it models the data it will base its predictions on. In this context, it translates to: Focusing on the past, you can use fitting (polynomial function of a sufficiently high degree) to make the model fit the data. It does not, however, tell you how good a job it will do in predicting future values.

The lesson here is not to try and "shoehorn" randomness into the model in an effort to minimize historical forecast errors, but instead to do a good job of forecasting repeatable components and simply estimate the random components (to help downstream processes make informed decisions).

The antidote to overfitting is the measurement of out-of-sample accuracy. This is done by partitioning the data into an initialization data set and a test data set (it is also known as the holdout data set). The initialization data set as the name suggests is used to calculate the model parameters (typically through minimization of errors of an effectiveness measure such as MSE). The model is then used to predict values in the holdout partition, and its performance is evaluated. As the holdout data set was "held out" from the initialization process, the accuracy so calculated is a fair predictor of performance in the field.

In SAP IBP, the parameter "offset for historical periods" under general time setting section of the forecast model configuration app can be used to define such a holdout period.

There are several ways to visualize the appropriateness of the model in use. In this regard, the correlogram is one of the most powerful visualizations and deserves a special mention.

A correlogram visualizes the correlation of forecast errors—that is, correlation of forecast error of a certain period to a certain other period (e.g., $e_t$ and $e_{t+2}$). The difference in time, calculated in terms of forecast update periods, between the two is called a lag (in the example, it is two). If a pair of forecast errors at a certain lag move in sync, it could mean that the basic assumption that the errors are random (uncorrelated) is being violated. One of the most common reasons for this occurring is when a certain time series component, say seasonality, is not explained by the model well enough.

The formula for autocorrelation is the following:

$$\frac{\sum_{t=k+1}^{n}(e_t - \bar{e})(e_{t-k} - \bar{e})}{\sum_{t=1}^{n}(e_t - \bar{e})^2}$$

The steps to calculate it in Excel are provided below. This logic can be implemented in the SAP IBP planning view where the ex-post forecast and actual values are used as inputs to generate data points in a preprocessing sheet, which is then used to generate a correlogram.

1. Calculate the forecast error for a given period for all periods—actual at $t$ minus forecast for period $t$ ($e_t$).
2. Calculate the average forecast error ($\bar{e}$).
3. Multiply the difference between the forecast error for a given period and the mean forecast error (one period ahead) and the difference between the forecast error at a given lag and the mean forecast error. Repeat this calculation for all of the periods, and calculate the sum (numerator in the above equation).
4. Calculate squared sum of the deviation between forecast errors and the mean forecast error (denominator in the above equation).

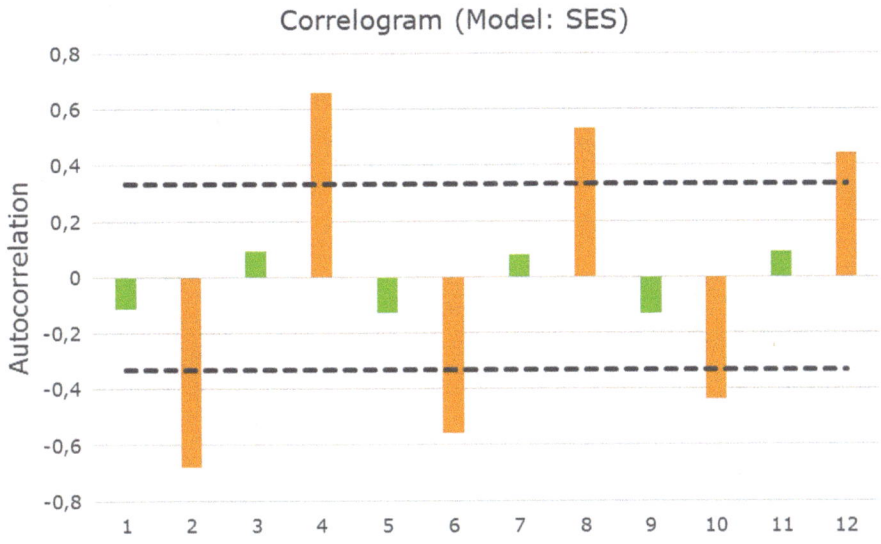

**Fig. 3.136**  Beer production data set—correlogram when SES is used

5. The ratio of the result of step three to step four is the autocorrelation.

Imagine if the beer production example we used for describing the Multi Linear Regression (MLR) procedure, a dataset which clearly exhibits seasonality and trend, were to be forecasted using Single Exponential Smoothing (SES). The correlogram for the same is shown in (Fig. 3.136). Following the theory, the bandwidths have been established by calculating $[-2/\sqrt{n}, +2/\sqrt{n}]$ where n is the number of periods. As 36 periods have been used, the limits are $[-0.33, +0.33]$. As it is evident, errors in even periods are correlated and the direction of correlation switches alternatingly. What can also be seen in the below figure is that the magnitude decreases gradually. Both of these observations suggest that the SES method does not adequately account for seasonality and trend in the time series.

When using the MLR model, the correlations do not exceed the thresholds (see Fig. 3.137). This indicates that the MLR model is able to adequately incorporate seasonal and trend effects in its predictions.

As a conclusion, we introduce a summary overview (see Fig. 3.138) of the forecasting models available on SAP IBP recommending their best usage depending on the types of demands to be forecasted.

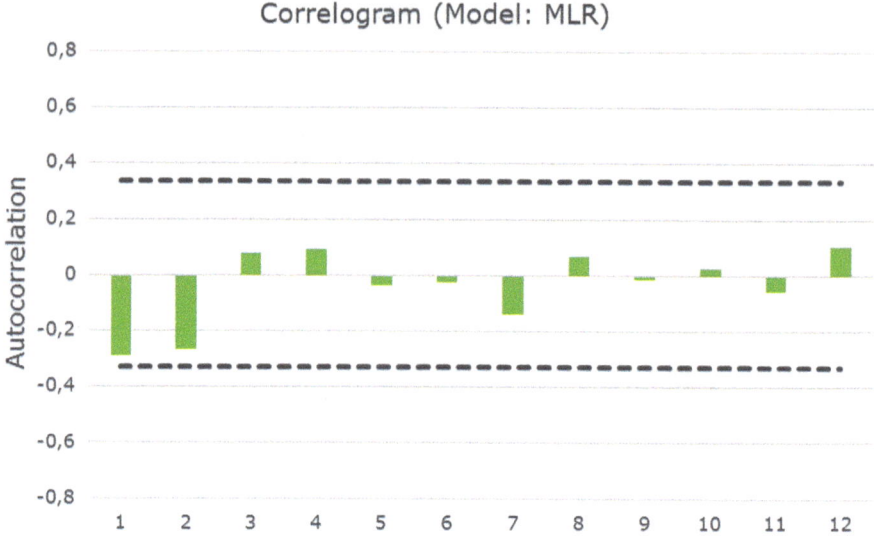

**Fig. 3.137** Beer production example—correlogram using MLR

| IBP algorithms | Forecasting cost | Stable demand | Intermittent demand | Trend | Season | Cycle |
|---|---|---|---|---|---|---|
| Simple average | Low | ✓ | ✗ | ✗ | ✗ | ✗ |
| Simple moving average | Low | ✓ | ✗ | ✓ | ✗ | ✗ |
| Weighted average | Low | ✓ | ✗ | ✗ | ✗ | ✗ |
| Weighted moving average | Low | ✓ | ✗ | ✓ | ✗ | ✗ |
| Single exponential smoothing | Low | ✓ | ✗ | ✗ | ✗ | ✓ |
| Adaptive-Response-Rate-Single Exponential smoothing | Low | ✗ | ✗ | ✓ | ✗ | ✓ |
| Double exponential smoothing | Medium | ✗ | ✗ | ✓ | ✗ | ✗ |
| Triple exponential smoothing | Medium | ✗ | ✗ | ✗ | ✓ | ✗ |
| Automated exponential smoothing | Medium | ✗ | ✗ | ✓ | ✗ | ✗ |
| Croston method | Medium | ✗ | ✓ | ✗ | ✗ | ✗ |
| Multiple linear regression | High | ✓ | ✗ | ✗ | ✗ | ✓ |
| Brown's linear smoothing algorithm | Medium | ✓ | ✗ | ✓ | ✗ | ✗ |
| ARIMA | High | ✓ | ✗ | ✓ | ✗ | ✓ |
| SARIMA | High | ✓ | ✗ | ✓ | ✓ | ✓ |

**Fig. 3.138** SAP IBP forecasting model mapping

## 3.5  Make Predictions and Observations

Statistical forecast is carried out for all of the planning clusters based on model assignments made. Typically, batch processing jobs are scheduled to run on a designated day and time that are aligned with the global S&OP calendar of activities. In a global implementation of SAP IBP, there are several numbers of statistical forecast runs. They are for specific markets, regions and form of the product, e.g., active ingredient forecast mentioned in Implementing Integrated Business Planning (Kepczynski et al., 2018). Statistical forecasts are then stored in relevant key figures.

Actual values and demand, which are typically a result of the order to cash process, are made available in SAP IBP as well. These actual observations are compared to predictions (forecasts) for the same period to assess statistical forecast performance.

In Fig. 3.139, we see a comparison between the adjusted actual quantity (after outlier detection and correction) and the predictions of sales team and statistical forecast. We can see that the statistical forecast error which is calculated may have some trends.

## 3.6  Evaluate a Model

There is a famous war idiom that goes: NO BATTLE PLAN SUCCEEDS THE CONTACT WITH THE ENEMY.

When it comes to forecasting, no plan truly survives contact with reality (it is a corollary of the first rule of forecasting, which is that forecast is always wrong). Evaluating a model is about measuring how close one has gotten to predicting reality. Some of the same measures that will be described in the coming chapters (choose effectiveness measures) can be used to evaluate the mode. However, the comparison needs to be between the forecast for a given period and the actual observation.

Additionally, depending on the purpose and the consumer of the forecast, it might be required to measure the accuracy with a certain lag. For example, if the consumer requires a forecast for a certain number of periods ahead of the actual event that is being forecasted, the number of periods in question should be the lag with which the forecast accuracy is measured. This topic is covered in greater detail in the final chapter of this book.

In addition to the effectiveness measures, the tracking signal is a metric that is quite useful when it comes to assessing if the bias (assuming there is) in the forecast is significant enough to warrant intervention.

The formula for the tracking signal is provided below.

As mentioned during the discussion on the mean absolute deviation (MAD), MAD has a special property since the formula $2/\sqrt{2}\prod$ * MAD approximates one standard deviation (or $\sigma \approx 1.25$ * MAD). This relationship can be used to set

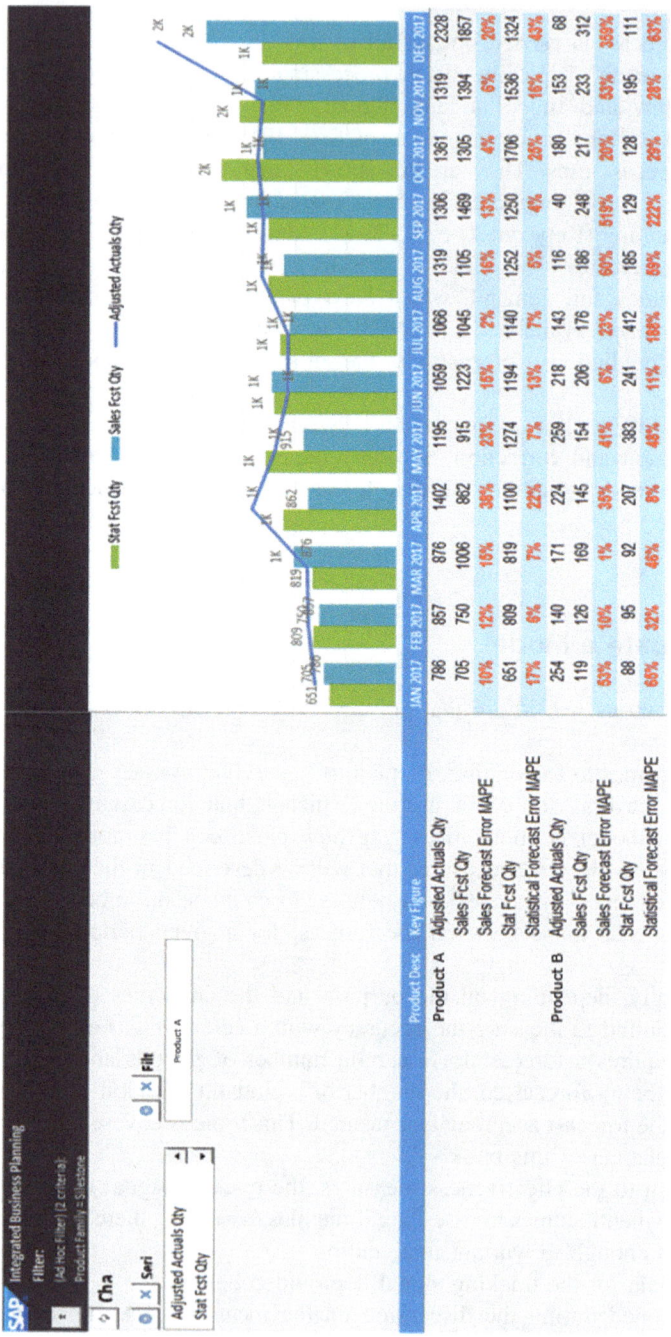

**Fig. 3.139** Comparisons of observations (actuals) and predictions (forecasts)

limits for the tracking signal in relation to σ. For example, the limits of [−3.75, +3.75] for the tracking signal translate into approximately a bandwidth that has a spread of three standard deviations.

$$\text{Smoothed Tracking Signal (TS)} = \frac{\text{Error Total}}{\text{Smoothed MAD}}$$

### 3.6.1   SAP Use Case: Tracking Signal

The tracking signal is modeled in SAP IBP as per Fig. 3.140. Here are the steps to be followed in order to create a tracking signal in SAP IBP:

1. Include the error total and MAD as effectiveness measures in the post-processing steps. Since these key figures do not include a period attribute (planning level only includes structural attributes), they need to be assigned to the key figures, created specifically for this purpose, that have one so that calculations can be performed on them.
2. Create a calculated key figure (or a local member) that calculates the cumulative error total for the historical time periods (where ex-post forecast is calculated) and divides it by MAD—this is then the tracking signal.
3. The tracking signal can be plotted, and bandwidths (lower and upper threshold limits) can be set by utilizing the relationship between the tracking signal and the standard deviation (explained above).

Another useful way to evaluate model effectiveness is by plotting demand variability against forecast variability (both calculated using coefficient of variance, which is equal to σ/μ—time series is composed of actual values in the case of demand variability and forecast errors in the case of forecast variability). An example is shown in Fig. 3.141.

The purpose of such a plot is to study and understand the reasons for outliers. In the graph, there are two clear outliers—the good kind (green) is where the demand variability is 11%, but the forecast variability is only 4%; the bad kind (orange) is where the demand variability is 9%, but the forecast variability is 23%. The former needs to be understood, because we ought to deconstruct what is going on here and try and replicate it. The latter is important because for the given demand variability, the forecast accuracy ought to be better—so, it calls for model refinement.

Forecasting is not made in a vacuum, it serves a certain purpose, and that purpose is primarily dictated by the consumer or the recipient of the forecast who relies on it to make decisions. It is therefore only relevant that one would provide the customer(s) of the forecast with a range of forecast values within which the true value is expected to lie.

The breadth of this range is a function of the standard deviation of the forecast errors and the measure of certainty (or probability) that this claim is true.

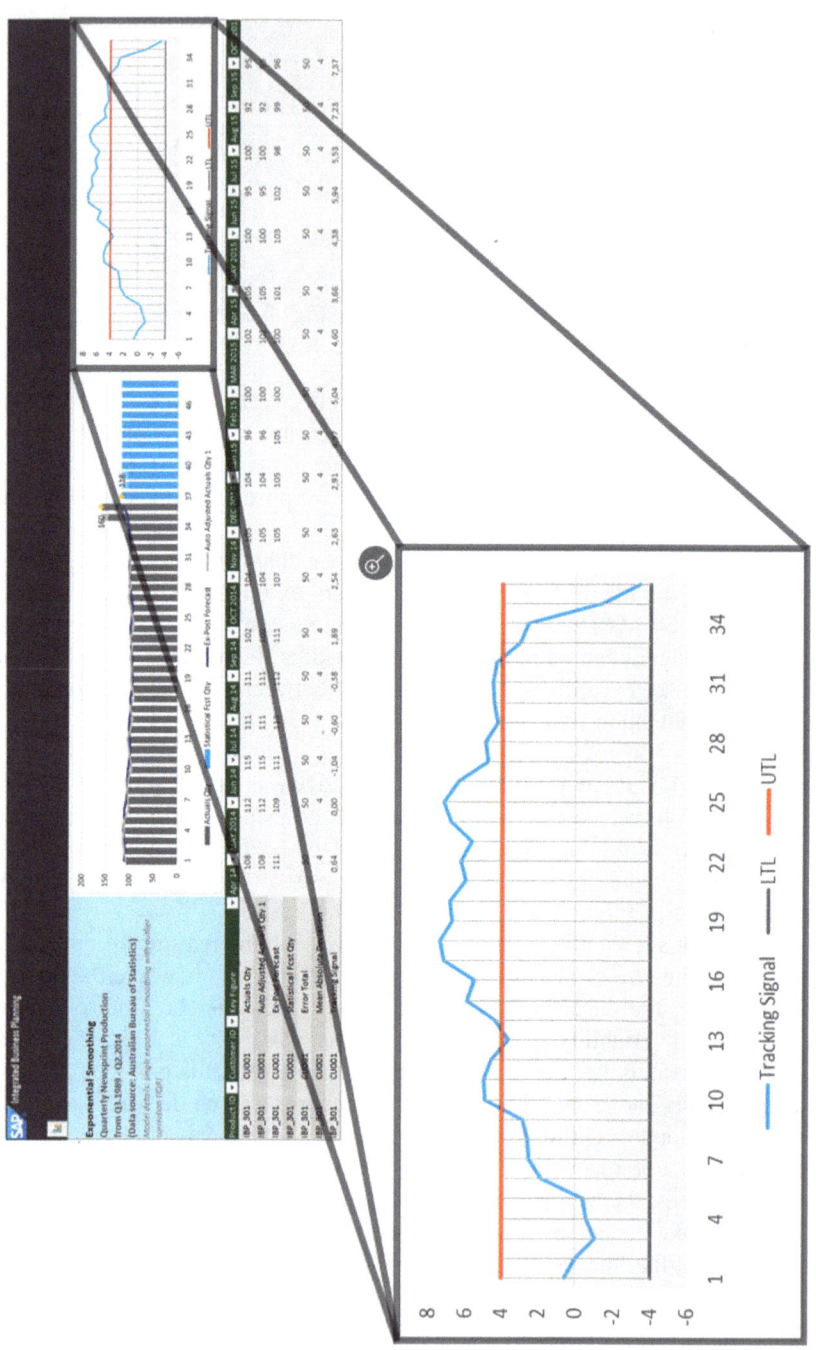

**Fig. 3.140** Example of tracking signal modeled in IBP

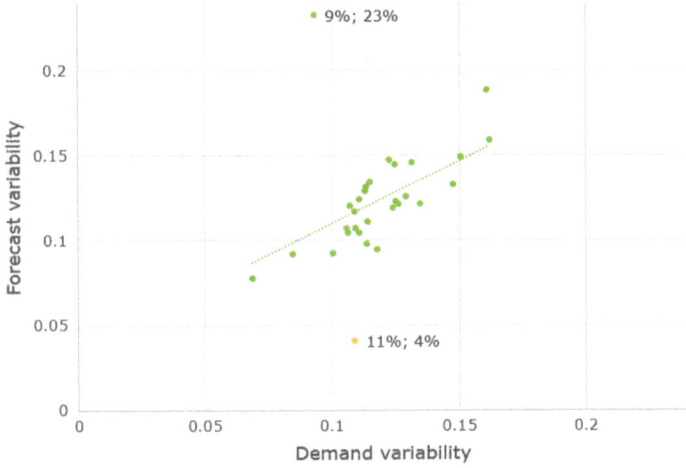

**Fig. 3.141**  Plotting inherent variability (demand variability) versus forecast variability

The standard deviation can be calculated based on MAD or MSE. With MSE, $\sigma = \sqrt{MSE}$. The estimated forecast error for a given probability can be expressed using the formula: $z * \sqrt{MSE}$ where $z$ can be looked up from the standard normal distribution table given the probability.

For example, if the desired probability is 95%, $z = 1.645$. From this, the range for period t can be calculated as:

$$[\text{Forecast}_t - (z * \sqrt{MSE}), \text{Forecast}_t + (z * \sqrt{MSE})]$$

## 3.6.2   SAP Use Case: Forecast with Prediction Interval

Generating prediction intervals in the visualization below (see Fig. 3.142) known as a fan chart was coined by the Bank of England, for its inflation reports. In SAP IBP, prediction intervals were modeled by using the MSE (selected as a post-processing measure) and using it to estimate forecast error.

In a preprocessing sheet, the forecast error is used to simulate actual demands by using the Excel formula: <Forecast> + NORM.INV(RAND();0; <SQRT(MSE)>). The RAND() function generates a random probability. The result is a simulated actual observation for a random probability value and for the given probability distribution (with mean 0 and standard deviation = $\sqrt{MSE}$). Finally, the PERCENTILE function is used to estimate forecast at different percentile values to generate prediction intervals with varying levels of confidence. These "fan out" from the central value, which is the forecast itself that represents the most likely outcome.

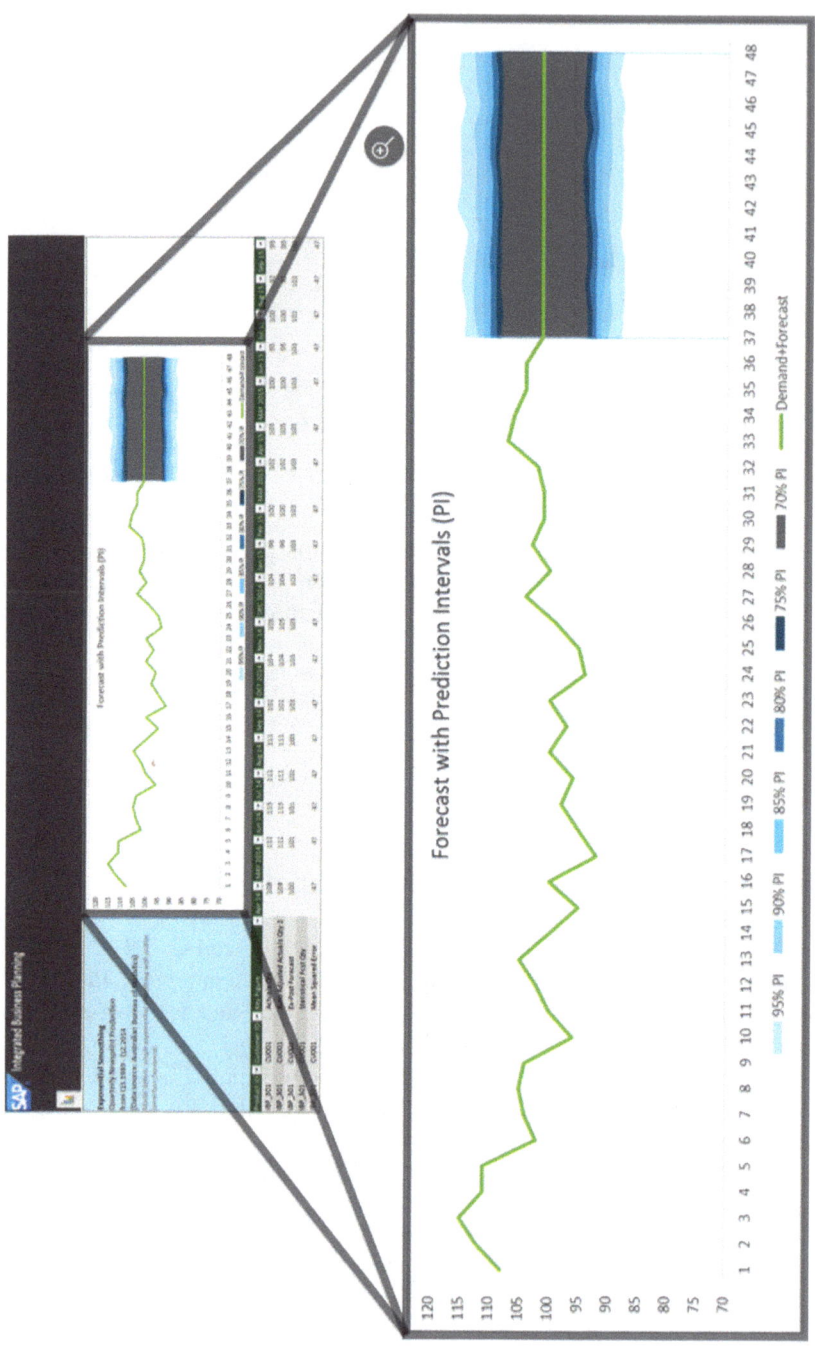

**Fig. 3.142** Visualization of prediction intervals using fan chart

## 3.7 Refine Model

If the results of model evaluation are not satisfactory—for example, one or more of the effectiveness measures are showing performance not within expected tolerance limits—model choice and parameters need to be evaluated. One needs to be careful not to overreact to what could be a random effect—perhaps, impact of promotion or a natural disaster. In such cases, a cleansing is called for rather than adjustments to the model or parameters. It is also important to be mindful of special cases such as shifts in level due to new accounts/customers or inflection points in the case of new products entering a rapid growth phase or where the predicted timing of demand for a product with intermittent demand was wrong, etc. Such instances require carefully considered responses as it is more about adjusting to a new reality, which might require a combination of cleansing/realignment of historical data and adjusting model parameters to give more weight to recent history.

There is a large body of research that provides evidence that a linear combination of models performs better than individual methods. This fact can be used for favorable effect if none of the individual procedures produce satisfactory results. As to weights and the number of procedures that should be combined, let simplicity be the guide. Research suggests that trying to find optimal weights is not worth the effort and equal weights produce good enough results and also that a combination of two models is a good place to start (Silver, Pyke, & Peterson, 1998) (Fig. 3.143).

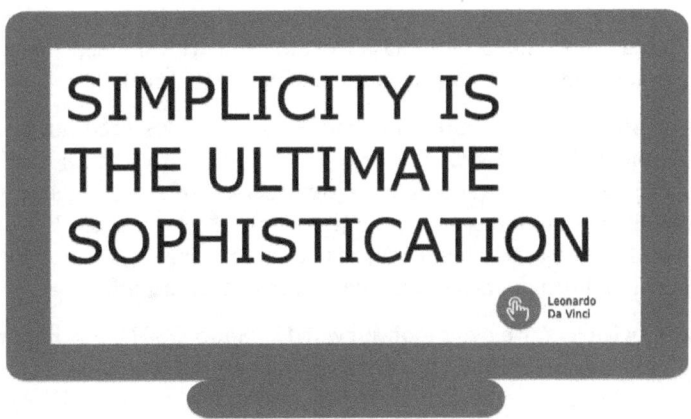

**Fig. 3.143** Simplicity is the ultimate sophistication

## 3.8  Concluding Remarks

**Fallacy of Mistaking Sophistication for Accuracy** There are a lot of researches to prove that use of complex methods does not automatically lead to better accuracy. In fact, a comprehensive research done by (Makridakis et al., 1998) involving micro- and macro-data sets concluded that use of simpler methods is better for micro-data sets—this means, for item-level forecasts, simpler methods should do. However, there is a benefit to using more sophisticated methods for aggregate data sets (both from a structural—think product group instead of product—and a time perspective). As we've pointed out that the margin for error is low for aggregate forecasting and typical decisions (e.g., estimating resource requirements and acquiring resources) made on that basis, so use of more advanced methods is justified.

**Ex-ante not Ex-post** Out-of-sample accuracy should be the go-to method for validating suitability of model, that is, ex-ante forecast, which means using a data set for testing that was not used in model fitting and finding appropriate model parameters.

**Correlation and Causality** This point has relevance if one is using the MLR procedure. There are numerous humorous examples of correlated variables that clearly do not imply causality. Although correlation does not imply causality, for forecasting using MLR, the distinction is not always important. That is, causality is not a necessary precondition for good results. Ease of data gathering and clearly understood temporal link between the (non-causal) independent variable(s) and the dependent variable could all be reasonable justifications for choosing explanatory variables that are not linked in a causal relationship with the dependent variable. However, it is important to understand the distinction and make conscious choices.

**Diversity of Measures** Selection of effectiveness measures need not be a process of selecting one to the exclusion of others. A set of carefully chosen metrics can be complimentary, each one providing a different perspective and together serving to provide insights required to perform the right type of intervention. For example, a combination of high bias and highly correlated forecast errors is a stronger evidence that the model and/or parameters may be incorrect than each measure separately.

**"Look back twice as far as you look forward"** (Saffo, 2007). It is important to be mindful of not being swayed too much by volatility in the recent past that might just be a blip in the larger scheme of things. This also reinforces the point earlier about choosing reasonable values for smoothing constants and avoids use of adaptive smoothing.

**Remember, there are Factors that are Inherently Unpredictable** The human psyche seeks coherence, and we like when things fall into neat patterns. However, there are factors that are impossible to predict (at least at a justifiable cost). One needs to acknowledge this and at times decide in favor of not forecasting—at the minimum, bide one's time until more information becomes available that makes forecasting possible.

A key strength of a demand planning tool is its ability to handle complex algorithms, both statistical and causal. Even if the planners are not using all the features now, it will leave room for future growth needs. Software as a service (SaaS) solutions need to have robust integration with the enterprise back-end systems; provide low-latency processing and analytical capabilities, and collaborative planning and forecasting processes; and must be clearly aligned with the organization's objectives for reduction in cycle time in high-mix, high-volume environments (Tarafdar & Tohamy, 2012).

Let us close concluding remarks with …. (Fig. 3.144).

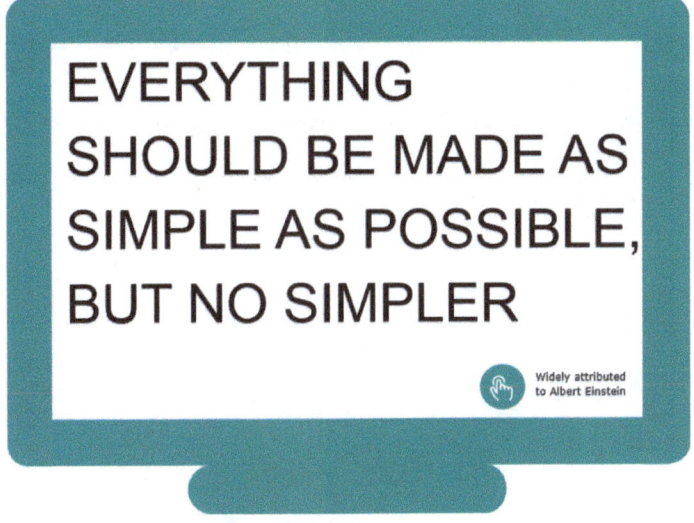

**Fig. 3.144** Everything should be made as simple as possible, no simpler

# References

APICS—module 1.G—Demand Planning. (2015). *APICS—module 1.G—Demand Planning.* APICS.

Chase, C. W. (2009). *Demand-driven forecasting: A structured approach to forecasting.* Wiley.

Chase, C. W. (2016) *Next generation demand management: People, process, analytics, and technology.* Wiley.

Desmet, B., & Sterckx, P. (2012). *Benefits of market-driven demand forecasting approach.* MÖBIUS.

Foreman, J. W. (2013). *Data smart: Using data science to transform information into insight.* Wiley.

Hyndman, R. J., & Athanasopoulos, G. (2014). *Forecasting: principles and practice.* OTexts.

Kalekar, P. (2004). 'Time series forecasting using holt-winters exponential smoothing.

Kepczynski, R., Jandhyala, R., Sankaran, G., & Dimofte, A. (2018). *Integrated business planning—How to integrate planning processes, organizational structures and capabilities, and leverage sap IBP technology.* Switzerland: Springer.

Kim, A. (2010). 'T-student'. Available at: http://albertskblog.blogspot.ch/2010/08/student-t-distribution-table.html.

Levenbach, H. (2017). *Characterizing demand variability: Seasonality trend and the uncertainty factor.* Scotts Valley: Createspace.

Makridakis, S. G., Wheelwright, S. C., & Hyndman, R. J. (1998). *Forecasting, methods and applications.* Wiley.

Mulllick Satinder, K. (1971). *How to choose the right forecasting tecnique.* Harvard Business Review.

Saffo, P. (2007). *Six rules for effective forecasting.* HBR.

Silver, E. A., Pyke, D. F. & Peterson, R. (1998). *Inventory management and production planning and scheduling.* NY Wiley.

Tarafdar, D., & Tohamy, N. (2012). *Demand-planning challenges among chinese manufacturers: Taking a closer look.* Gartner.

# Custom Method to Forecast Seasonal Products

For the explanatory purposes of this book, a specific end-to-end process toward statistical forecasting, with a marked focus on seasonal outliers detection and correction, has been developed to prove how it is possible to reach an acceptable forecast accuracy of a company's product portfolio by better understanding the data series and by applying the right techniques depending on data distributions and behaviors.

The E2E forecasting process for seasonal products is subdivided into seven sequential steps as shown in Fig. 4.1:

1. Segmenting and classifying the demand allow to prioritize the portfolio with a funnel logic, paying more attention only to a restrict set of data that shows variability, high volumes and a cyclical plotted pattern. It allows a better focus on the product portfolio, a more effective and faster decision making and a quicker response toward variability.
2. Analyzing seasonality makes use of the right techniques to confirm if a seasonal pattern is present or not in a data set; it permits avoiding loss of revenues and excessive inventories while reducing the missed production schedules and inefficient transportation.
3. Understanding data series helps comprehending how the data behave, their symmetry and dispersion. The key methods are skewness and kurtosis.
4. Checking normality assumption is a crucial decision point of the process as it allows to understand and filter the techniques available and viable for identifying seasonality and detecting outliers. Besides, it allows to eliminate wrong and meaningless insights from the tests while enhancing the accuracy of the analysis.
5. Detecting outliers focuses on the techniques and tests that can be run according to the distribution of the data.
6. Correcting the outlying points only when the indexes of the statistical forecasting method are set, we make use of a tailor-made Solver which identifies the indexes of the method by minimizing the standard deviation of the forecast error.
7. Statistical forecasting with triple exponential smoothing or SARIMA.

© Springer Nature Switzerland AG 2019
G. Sankaran et al., *Improving Forecasts with Integrated Business Planning*,
Management for Professionals, https://doi.org/10.1007/978-3-030-05381-9_4

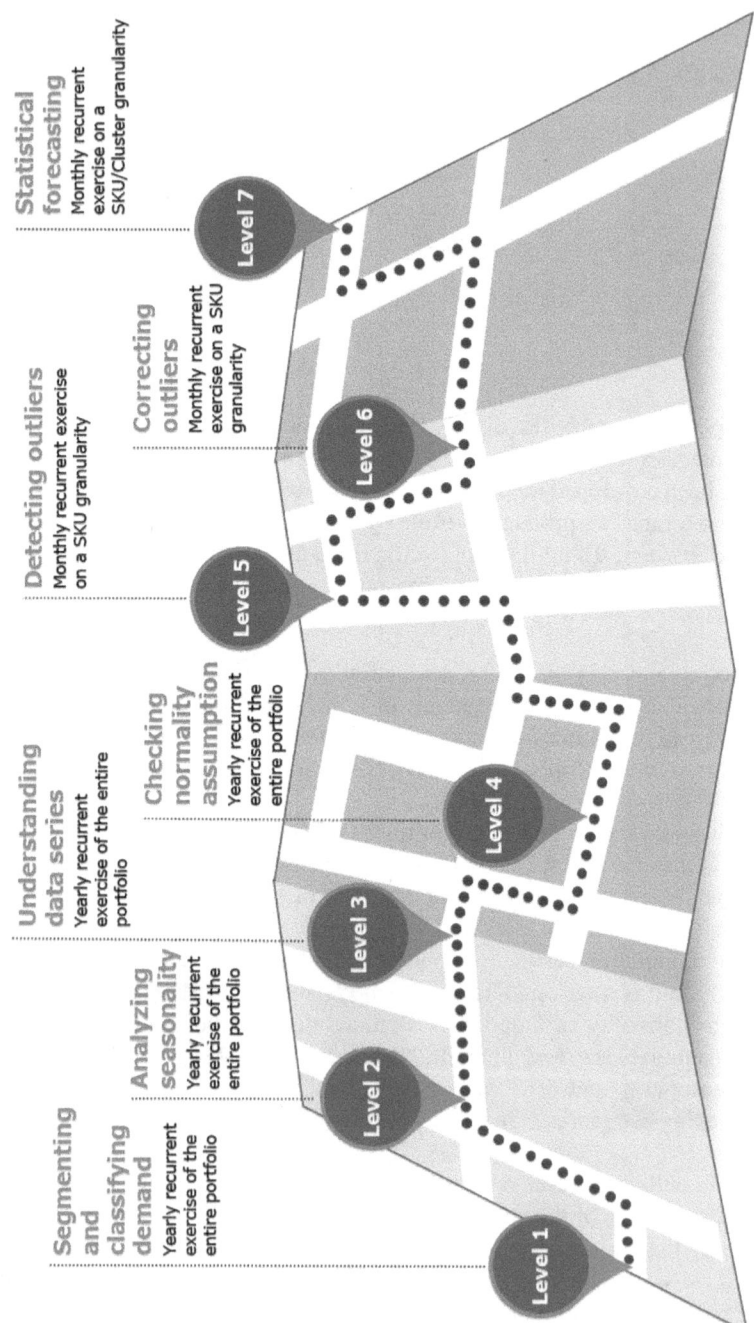

**Fig. 4.1** Custom process steps toward forecasting

The overall process (see Fig. 4.2) can easily be seen as a decision tree, where, based on outcome of certain analyses, some specific techniques and tests are applied. In the case in which a set of data does not fall into the paths identified as subjects of these analyses, those will be dropped and left to the normal common practices available.

This process will be covered in a solution that is not available as "out of the box" in SAP IBP, but it has been built making use of the standard configuration mechanisms existing in the software.

## 4.1  Segmenting and Classifying Demand

Figure 4.3 illustrates the sub-steps that will be described within the segmentation and classification part of the process. As a short summary, the key points to note are the following:

1. Collect the data.
2. Classify data based on custom criteria.
3. Analyze the portfolio based on the *ABC/XYZ* analysis.
4. Cluster the entire portfolio following a cascade logic.

All those sub-steps will be the focus of this specific sub-chapter.

Segmenting and classifying the demand correspond to a fundamental analysis that has to be conducted to understand the types of demand a company has to work with. It is often a good starting point for the analysis to determine the characteristics of the demand and its profiles in order to set the forecasting strategies and accuracy targets (Demand classification, 2017). For a more thorough description of the demand segmentation, aspects refer to "How to make IBP process happening" in the section "Focus is King and exception is a Queen" (Kepczynski et al., 2018).

First of all, the collected data set has to be validated to remove erroneous data. Furthermore, it has to be mentioned that the data set employed for the analysis was completely unknown to the users and testers, with no external information about the SKUs or contingent clusters. As a result, we think it might be interesting to provide a brief explanation and a short recommendation for the case in which a practitioner has to face an entire huge portfolio, where no preliminary filtering is applied or no briefing is provided.

For this case, it is important to distinguish from the beginning the types of products within the portfolio to establish sub-clusters based on data behaviors.

Based on the literature, four different clusters are defined for the different types of demand profiles (Demand classification, 2017):

1. Smooth demand, where the demand is very regular in time and in quantity
2. Intermittent demand, where the demand history shows very little variation in demand quantity but a high variation in the interval between two demands

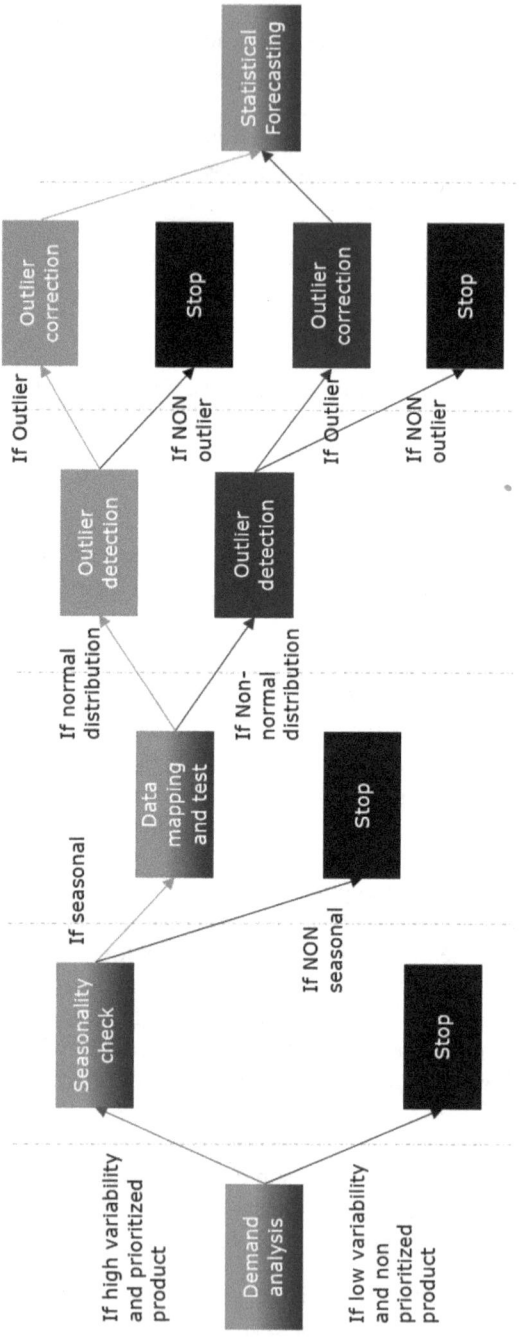

**Fig. 4.2**  Decision tree for custom method toward forecasting

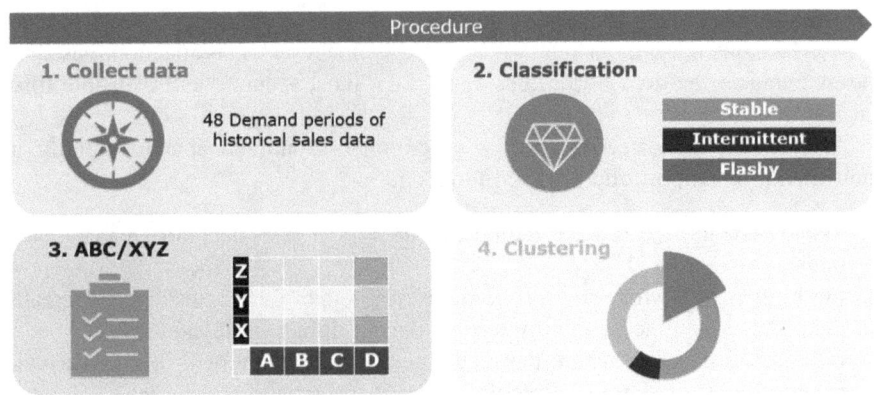

**Fig. 4.3** Segmenting and classifying demand steps

3. Erratic demand, where the demand has regular occurrences in time with high quantity variations
4. Lumpy demand, where the demand is characterized by a large variation in the quantity of demand and in the interval between two demands.

Figure 4.4 illustrates a graphical representation of the above-described data profiles.

However, from a forecasting perspective, we believe it is essential to make use of the previous demand categorization to come up with a more business related and realistic classification, bearing in mind the way in which each demand category or class could actually be forecasted. As we already discovered in the previous

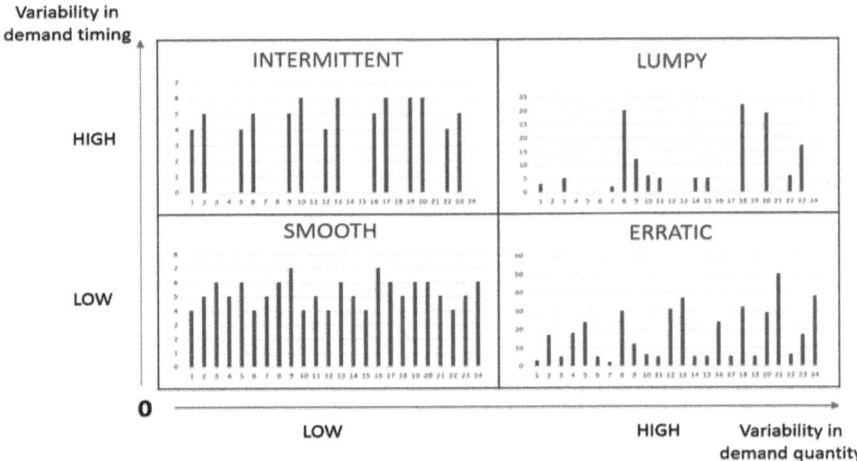

**Fig. 4.4** Demand categorization

chapter, there are many forecasting models applicable to different data and product profiles; for this reason, our intent is to try to define a new classification, based on the mapping of the demand profiles against the most accurate and plausible forecasting models.

As a result, the categories that a practitioner should be able to identify in their own product portfolio are the following:

1. Stable demand, where each month accounts for a sales/demand greater than 0 units
2. Flashy demand, where not all the months accounts for a sales/demand greater than 0 units and the variability in the demand timing is elevate
3. Intermittent demand, where the recurrence of the months with a sales/demand greater than 0 units is quite regular in terms of quantity and timing
4. Unforecastable demand, where the maximum length of zero demand sequences is greater than a specified threshold. For the purpose of this book, it has been chosen a threshold of 18 corresponding to a product in which for 18 consecutive months, the historical sales were 0.

The reasoning behind this classification justifies itself in the fact that for each category, some specific forecasting algorithms are available to forecast at best the different demand profiles:

1. Stable demand: It may contain trendy, seasonal or cyclical products; however, the typical forecasting models usually applied for those profiles will still be suitable, for example, all the average methods and smoothing models. This category requires an additional funnel procedure to map the different demand profiles within the "stable" group against the most accurate forecasting models.
2. Flashy demand: As per described in the previous chapter, this type of demand profile can be forecasted, e.g., by the Croston method.
3. Intermittent demand: As per described in the previous chapter, the revised Croston method or the revised average and smoothing methods are applicable to reach accurate forecasting levels.
4. Unforecastable demand: The historical sales' series have too little data to allow a reliable forecast.

In order to determine the characteristics of the above demand profiles, the following coefficients have to be introduced and calculated:

1. Average demand interval (ADI): It accounts how much a demand is regular in a certain period of time by analyzing the average interval between the demands.

$$ADI = \frac{\text{Summation of the intervals between non-zero demand periods}}{\text{No. of non-zero demand periods}}$$

2. Coefficient of variance (CoV): It measures the variation in demand quantities and represents the standard deviation of demand values divided by the average demand over the referenced time periods.

$$CV = \frac{\text{Standard deviation of demand}}{\text{Average value of demand}}$$

3. Length of $i$th demand sequence (LDS$_i$): It shows immediately some information about the length of non-zero sequences in a data set.

$$LDS_i = (ZDI_i - 1)$$

where ZDI$_i$ is the $i$th zero demand interval.

4. Length of $j$th zero demand sequence (LZS$_j$): It shows immediately some information about the length of zero sequences in a data set.

$$LZS_j = (DI_j - 1)$$

where DI$_j$ is the $j$th demand interval.

5. Furthermore, to categorize flashy and intermittent demands, the practitioner has also to calculate the range of positive values of LDS$_i$ and LZS$_j$.
6. Average zero demand interval (AZDI): It accounts how much a demand is regular in a certain period of time by analyzing the average interval between the zero demands.

$$AZDI = \frac{\text{Sum of the intervals between zero demand periods}}{\text{No. of zero demand periods}}$$

Let's assume we use three different products, $A$, $B$ and $C$ (see Fig. 4.5) and we would like to classify them considering the coefficients stated above.

| A | Period | 1 | 2 | 3 | 4 | 5 | 6 | 7 | 8 | 9 | 10 | 11 | 12 | 13 | 14 | 15 | 16 |
|---|---|---|---|---|---|---|---|---|---|---|---|---|---|---|---|---|---|
| | Demand quantity | 9 | 6 | 7 | 11 | 8 | 5 | 6 | 7 | 10 | 9 | 11 | 8 | 7 | 10 | 9 | 11 |

| B | Period | 1 | 2 | 3 | 4 | 5 | 6 | 7 | 8 | 9 | 10 | 11 | 12 | 13 | 14 | 15 | 16 |
|---|---|---|---|---|---|---|---|---|---|---|---|---|---|---|---|---|---|
| | Demand quantity | 14 | 1 | 0 | 0 | 7 | 0 | 2 | 0 | 10 | 0 | 0 | 0 | 0 | 22 | 5 | 0 |

| C | Period | 1 | 2 | 3 | 4 | 5 | 6 | 7 | 8 | 9 | 10 | 11 | 12 | 13 | 14 | 15 | 16 |
|---|---|---|---|---|---|---|---|---|---|---|---|---|---|---|---|---|---|
| | Demand quantity | 4 | 5 | 7 | 0 | 0 | 0 | 0 | 5 | 6 | 7 | 0 | 0 | 0 | 0 | 7 | 6 |

**Fig. 4.5** Demand categorization example

For the product $A$, the calculation for the ADI is as follows:

$$\text{ADI} = \frac{(2-1)+(3-2)+(4-3)+(5-4)+\cdots(14-13)+(15-14)+(16-15)}{15} = 1$$

For the product $B$, the calculation for the ADI is as follows:

$$\text{ADI} = \frac{(2-1)+(5-2)+(7-5)+(9-7)+(14-9)+(15-14)}{6} = 2.33$$

For the product $C$, the calculation for the ADI is as follows:

$$\text{ADI} = \frac{(2-1)+(3-2)+(8-3)+(9-8)+(10-9)+(15-10)}{6} = 2.33$$

For the product $A$, the calculation for the CV is as follows:

$$\text{CV} = 0.23$$

For the product $B$, the calculation for the CV is as follows:

$$\text{CV} = 1.64$$

For the product $C$, the calculation for the CV is as follows:

$$\text{CV} = 1.03$$

For the product $A$, the calculation for the $\text{LDS}_i$ and $\text{LZS}_j$ can be ignored since ADI = 1 that means there are no zero values in the data set.

$$\text{AZDI} = \frac{0}{0} = \text{lowest value possible}$$

For the product $B$, the calculation for the $\text{LDS}_i$ and $\text{LZS}_j$ is as follows:

$$\text{LDS}_i = [(3-1),(1-1),(2-1),(2-1),(2-1),(1-1),(1-1),(1-1)]$$
$$\text{LZS}_i = [(1-1),(3-1),(2-1),(2-1),(5-1),(1-1)]$$

And the positive values of $\text{LDS}_i$ and $\text{LZS}_j$ are (see Fig. 4.6):

$$\text{LDS}_i = [(2),(1),(1),(1)]$$
$$\text{LZS}_i = [(2),(1),(1),(4)]$$

And finally, the calculation of the range $(\text{LDS}_i)$ and range $(\text{LZS}_j)$ is as follows:

| Period | 1 | 2 | 3 | 4 | 5 | 6 | 7 | 8 | 9 | 10 | 11 | 12 | 13 | 14 | 15 | 16 |
|---|---|---|---|---|---|---|---|---|---|---|---|---|---|---|---|---|
| **B** Demand quantity | 14 | 1 | 0 | 0 | 7 | 0 | 2 | 0 | 10 | 0 | 0 | 0 | 0 | 22 | 5 | 0 |
| DI |  | 1 |  |  | 3 |  | 2 |  | 2 |  |  |  |  | 5 | 1 |  |
| LZS |  |  |  |  | 2 |  | 1 |  | 1 |  |  |  |  | 4 |  |  |
| ZDI |  | 3 | 1 |  | 2 |  | 2 |  | 2 | 1 | 1 | 1 |  |  |  | 3 |
| LDS |  | 2 |  |  | 1 |  | 1 |  | 1 | 1 |  |  |  |  |  | 2 |

**Fig. 4.6** Product $B$ LDS and LZS calculations

| Period | 1 | 2 | 3 | 4 | 5 | 6 | 7 | 8 | 9 | 10 | 11 | 12 | 13 | 14 | 15 | 16 |
|---|---|---|---|---|---|---|---|---|---|---|---|---|---|---|---|---|
| **C** Demand quantity | 4 | 5 | 7 | 0 | 0 | 0 | 0 | 5 | 6 | 7 | 0 | 0 | 0 | 0 | 7 | 6 |
| DI |  | 1 | 1 |  |  |  |  | 5 | 1 | 1 |  |  |  |  | 5 | 1 |
| LZS |  |  |  |  |  |  |  | 4 |  |  |  |  |  |  | 4 |  |
| ZDI |  |  | 4 | 1 | 1 | 1 |  |  |  |  | 4 | 1 | 1 | 1 |  |  |
| LDS |  |  | 3 |  |  |  |  |  |  |  | 3 |  |  |  |  |  |

**Fig. 4.7** Product $C$ LDS and LZS calculations

$$\text{RANGE}(\text{LDS}_i) = 2 - 1 = 1$$
$$\text{RANGE}(\text{LZS}_i) = 4 - 1 = 3$$
$$\text{AZDI} = \frac{(3 - 2) + (6 - 3) + (8 - 6)}{3} = 2$$

For the product $C$, the calculation for the $\text{LDS}_i$ and $\text{LZS}_j$ is as follows:

$$\text{LDS}_i = [(4 - 1), (1 - 1), (1 - 1), (1 - 1), (4 - 1), (1 - 1), (1 - 1), (1 - 1)]$$
$$\text{LZS}_i = [(1 - 1), (1 - 1), (5 - 1), (1 - 1), (1 - 1), (5 - 1), (1 - 1)]$$

And the positive values of $\text{LDS}_i$ and $\text{LZS}_j$ are (see Fig. 4.7):

$$\text{LDS}_i = [(3), (3)]$$
$$\text{LZS}_i = [(4), (4)]$$

And finally, the calculation of range $(\text{LDS}_i)$ and range $(\text{LZS}_j)$ is as follows:

$$\text{RANGE}(\text{LDS}_i) = 3 - 3 = 0$$
$$\text{RANGE}(\text{LZS}_i) = 4 - 4 = 0$$
$$\text{AZDI} = \frac{(4 - 3) + (7 - 4) + (8 - 7)}{3} = 1.66$$

Based on these coefficients described and calculated above, we propose the following thresholds to easily cluster a huge and variate company portfolio:

1. Stable demand (ADI < 1.32, CV < 0.49)
2. Flashy demand (ADI $\geq$ 1.32, CV > 0.49, RANGE (LDS$_i$) > 2 or RANGE (LZS$_j$) > 2)
3. Intermittent ("almost recurring") demand, (ADI $\geq$ 1.32, CV < 0.49, RANGE (LDS$_i$) $\leq$ 2 and RANGE (LZS$_j$) $\leq$ 2)
4. Unforecastable demand, MAX (LZS$_j$) $\geq$ THRESHOLD

The SAP IBP use case below illustrates how these categorization procedures can be addressed and configured in the SAP IBP system.

### 4.1.1  SAP Use Case: Classifying Demand

To build the demand classification approach mentioned above, a custom configuration was required in SAP IBP as the normal out of the box standard configuration settings do not allow yet such an option. Furthermore, for the type of calculations sketched out for this technique, we had to resort to the use of SAP IBP Excel UI local member, which allowed us to perform entirely the steps of the proposed classification method. As an example, a sequencing count of non-zero and zero intervals is crucial for getting the desired outcome: Those types of calculations have to be performed using a combination of macros and SAP IBP local members.

Figure 4.8 displays in the system the configuration outcomes. The example pivots around a specific SKU randomly selected, while the key figure rows illustrate all the manual steps necessary to reach the optimal output:

1. NZDS1—Non-Zero Demand Signal 1 counts the number of months where a sales/demand higher than 0 happens.
2. NZDS2—Non-Zero Demand Signal 2 has the same purpose, but it keeps as a record the exact counting until the new sales/demand comes in; only at that moment, the number will be increased by one.

**SAP** Integrated Business Planning
Filter:

| Product ID | Key Figure | OCT 2014 | Nov 14 | DEC 2014 | Jan 15 | Feb 15 | MAR 2015 | Apr 15 | MAY 2015 | Jun 15 | Jul 15 |
|---|---|---|---|---|---|---|---|---|---|---|---|
| IBP A | NZDS1 | 16 | | | | | 17 | | | 18 | |
| IBP A | NZDS2 | 16 | 16 | 16 | 16 | 16 | 17 | 17 | 17 | 18 | 18 |
| IBP A | NZDS | 1 | | | | | 1 | | | 1 | |
| IBP A | Historical Sales | 676 | 0 | 0 | 0 | 0 | 5427 | 0 | 0 | 4500 | 0 |
| IBP A | ZDS1 | | | | | 7 | | | 9 | | 10 |
| IBP A | ZDS2 | 3 | 3 | 3 | 3 | 7 | 7 | 7 | 9 | 9 | 10 |
| IBP A | ZDS | | | | | 4 | | | 2 | | 1 |
| IBP A | Zero Demand Sequence | | | | | 4 | | | 2 | | 1 |
| IBP A | Non-zero Demand Sequence | 1 | | | | | 1 | | | 1 | |

**Fig. 4.8** SAP IBP demand classification configuration

3. NZDS—Non-Zero Demand Signal 3 counts the number of months with a sales/demand higher than 0 between a specific interval: from the months where we experienced the last 0 sales/demand to the months where we re-experience the following 0 sales/demand.
4. The historical sales illustrate our selected history.
5. ZDS1—Zero Demand Signal 1 counts the number of months where a sales/demand equal to 0.
6. ZDS2—Zero Demand Signal 2 has the same purpose, but it keeps as a record the exact counting until the new zero sales/demand comes in; only at that moment, the number will be increased by the length of the zero sequence.
7. ZDS—Zero Demand Signal counts the number of months with a sales/demand equal to 0 between a specific interval: from the month where we experienced the last higher than 0 sales/demand to the month where we re-experience the following higher than 0 sales/demand.

Consequently, at the very bottom, we have the final two key figures where the positioning and the accounting of the zero and non-zero demand sequence are displayed.

Figure 4.9 illustrates the results out of the classification. It is possible to display in the column called SIF CODE the resulting classification:

1. F for flashy products
2. S for stable products
3. I for intermittent products.

We can also easily notice how the SKU we took as an example of the configuration fell into the flashy category. The usual and common filtering options of Excel also allow to directly filter for the specific classification the user is interested in.

Besides, it is important to mention that while operating with the normal techniques for demand classification, the use of the coefficient of variance can lead to mistakes. In fact, if the CoV is used on a large scale to filter the stable, intermittent, erratic or lumpy products, its outcomes can be misleading as the CoV gets

| Product ID | SIF CODE | Key Figure | OCT 2015 | Nov 15 | DEC 2015 | Jan 16 | Feb 16 | MAR 2016 | Apr 16 | MAY 2016 | Jun 16 |
|---|---|---|---|---|---|---|---|---|---|---|---|
| IBP A | F | Historical Sales SIF Classified | 977 | 0 | 0 | 5480 | 0 | 0 | 0 | 9470 | 0 |
| IBP B | F | Historical Sales SIF Classified | 0 | 0 | 0 | 0 | 0 | 2496 | 0 | 7484 | 0 |
| IBP C | F | Historical Sales SIF Classified | 0 | 0 | 0 | 0 | 1017 | 0 | 0 | 1062 | 0 |
| IBP D | I | Historical Sales SIF Classified | 0 | 0 | 0 | 0 | 0 | 0 | 0 | 0 | 0 |
| IBP E | I | Historical Sales SIF Classified | 0 | 0 | 0 | 0 | 0 | 0 | 0 | 0 | 0 |
| IBP F | F | Historical Sales SIF Classified | 13 | 2 | 0 | 239 | 0 | 0 | 0 | 0 | 0 |
| IBP G | F | Historical Sales SIF Classified | 0 | 939 | 0 | 0 | 0 | 0 | 1550 | 0 | 4603 |
| IBP H | F | Historical Sales SIF Classified | 0 | 0 | 0 | 0 | 0 | 0 | 960 | 1455 | 3180 |
| IBP I | F | Historical Sales SIF Classified | 0 | 11814 | 0 | 0 | 0 | 0 | 917 | 7971 | 2000 |
| IBP L | F | Historical Sales SIF Classified | 1000 | 3001 | 3000 | 3007 | 3531 | 4050 | 4095 | 4053 | 5723 |
| IBP M | F | Historical Sales SIF Classified | 0 | 0 | 0 | 0 | 0 | 0 | 0 | 0 | 0 |
| IBP N | I | Historical Sales SIF Classified | 0 | 0 | 0 | 0 | 0 | 0 | 0 | 0 | 0 |
| IBP O | I | Historical Sales SIF Classified | 797 | 0 | 216 | 91 | 19 | 4277 | 2373 | 139 | 1561 |

**Fig. 4.9** SAP IBP SIF classification

automatically inflated by the presence of "0" points. This is the reason why, for this analysis, the coefficient of variance will be considered accurate only for the stable products, while for the other types of demand classification that have been identified, the length of the zero and non-zero sequences is used as per described by our analysis.

Furthermore, as we mentioned before, the use of the CoV will be very useful in the stable portfolio where we sub-cluster the products to identify the cyclical, trendy and seasonal ones.

In SAP IBP, there are many other visual interpretations that we can attribute to our segmented portfolio. For example, as per shown in Fig. 4.10, one of the easiest and most intuitive representations is reported with the use of Analytics in Web UI. Per year we can detect the total amount of the historical sales classified in flashy, intermittent and stable. The year 2018, as we can see, has not been populated yet.

After having collected the demand, uploaded the master data in SAP IBP, having performed a first screening of the portfolio, a yearly *ABC* analysis is run to identify which SKUs should undergo a more detailed investigation and control. The *ABC* aims at pursuing the more important SKUs so that a different treatment in terms of attention and accuracy will be dedicated to certain products. The funnel logic hugely impacts the first steps of the process.

According to the data available and used to configure this process, it has been run on a volume *ABC/XYZ* analysis; however, it is recommended to go also for a value *ABC/XYZ* analysis so that the more important SKUs will result in the ones that bring more revenue, margin and volume contribution to the organization. If the *ABC* component of the analysis focuses on the rate of each SKU, in terms of volume or revenue, against the total volume of revenue of the entire portfolio, the *XYZ* component of the analysis emphasizes on the degree of inherent variability that is present within each data set.

To easily summarize the concept and to set a sufficient background to understand and proceed with the analysis, Figs. 4.11 and 4.12 help to clarify the aim of the investigation.

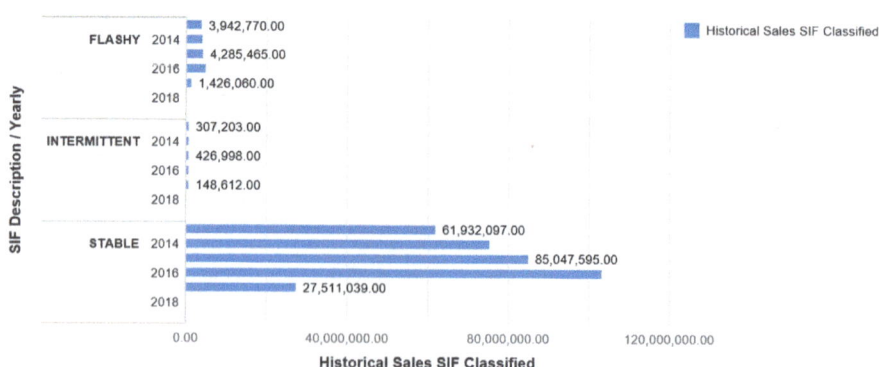

**Fig. 4.10** SAP IBP SIF classification dashboard

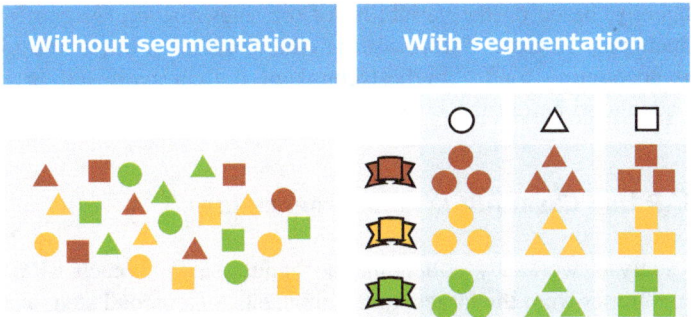

**Fig. 4.11** Why to segment

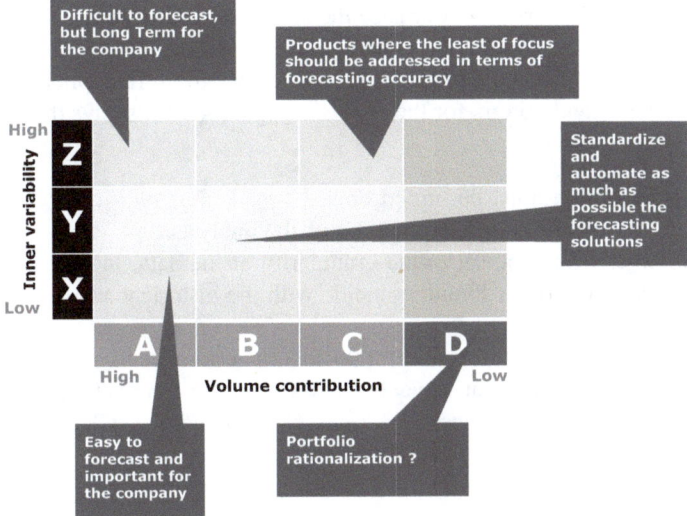

**Fig. 4.12** *ABC/XYZ* versus replenishment, demand planning strategies

As displayed in Fig. 4.11, the purpose of segmenting our stable portfolio is to create clear clusters, where the products with similar characteristics, aspects or facets are grouped together. However, it is important to properly define a priori which types of products we want to group together and for which purposes.

Figure 4.12 illustrates our segmenting purpose: We want to cluster our stable portfolio in terms of volume contribution (*ABCD*), but also in terms of inherent variability of the single SKU (*XYZ*). Defining the variability clusters allows to determine which SKUs may be more or less difficult to be forecast. It does not necessarily mean that a SKU falling into the *AZ* cluster will account for a high forecast error, but it highlights the concept that if we would like to reach a more than acceptable forecasting accuracy for that SKU, additional efforts may be needed, since randomly automating its forecasting procedure increases risk of failure.

Consequently, based on the variability of the sales history, we can foresee that the $X$ products may be easier to forecast than the $Y$ and the $Z$ ones; additionally, the $A$ products accounting for the highest chunk of the company selling in volume should be addressed before the $D$, $C$ and $B$ ones.

## 4.1.2  SAP Use Case: *ABC/XYZ* Segmentation

The *ABC* analysis works by collecting the annual sales of each SKU and then sorting the volumes from the largest to the smallest. As a second step, a cumulative function of the volume is defined and related to the percentage of the items considered for the analysis. It will result that each SKU volume is a representative indicator of importance. At the same time, the *XYZ* works by clustering the products based on a specific criterion: in our case the coefficient of variance. The CoV is the ratio of the standard deviation over the average of a data series.

In order to configure the *ABC/XYZ*, it is necessary to go in application jobs and set the parameters and criteria for the analysis. Figure 4.13 displays the key settings for the segmentation:

1. *ABC* segmentation must be turned on.
2. The *ABC* code should be the outcome of the analysis.
3. The periodicity must be set to the granularity of the data, in our case monthly.
4. The calculation horizon should coincide with the historical sales we dispose of.

The *ABC* analysis relies on the Pareto theory; consequently as it is shown in Fig. 4.14, the thresholds that have been assigned for each class, $A$, $B$ and $C$, correspond to the common ones: 80% ($A$), 15% ($B$) and 5% ($C$).

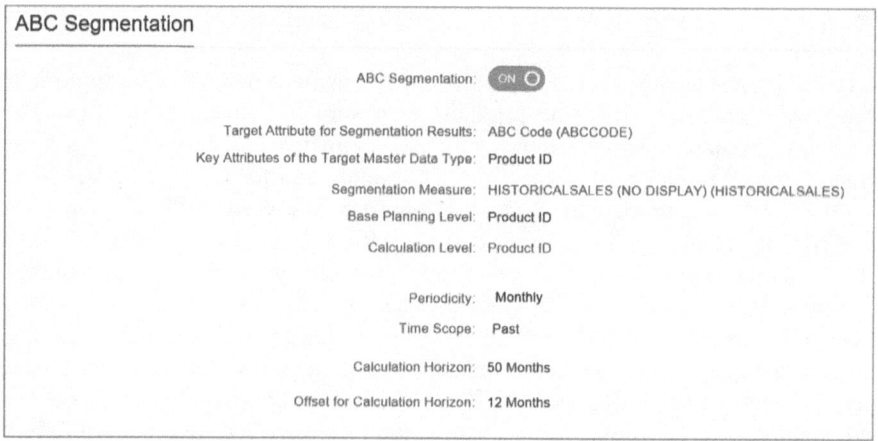

**Fig. 4.13** *ABC* segmentation settings

It is crucial also to highlight the functionality of locking; for some products, we may want to prevent manual overwriting on the *ABC* category or we would like to overwrite the code of a product. Reasons for such changes may be multiple and variate, qualitative or quantitative, or driven by external information related to a product. Consequently, for some products, we might like to change the level of priority as the standard degree of magnitude cannot be set by a classic *ABC* grouping.

At the same time, as we did for the *ABC* segmentation, the *XYZ* parameters have to be established following the same logic. See Fig. 4.15.

As we did for the *ABC* thresholds, we need to assess the *XYZ* clusters. Considering that we make use of the coefficient of variance to the power of one, Fig. 4.16 displays the parameters chosen for the analysis. They have been adopted based on client experiences and literature recommendations.

Figure 4.17 shows how, in the Excel UI, the outcomes of the *ABC/XYZ* could be displayed. Avoiding any graphical representations, as they will be discussed more in details in the coming section, the figure illustrates that for each product ID, we have the mapping of the *ABC*, in the column called *ABC* code, and the mapping of the *XYZ*, in the column called *XYZ* code.

After having run the *ABC/XYZ* analysis, it is useful to go in the Web UI and graphically monitor and investigate the results out of the run. There are many

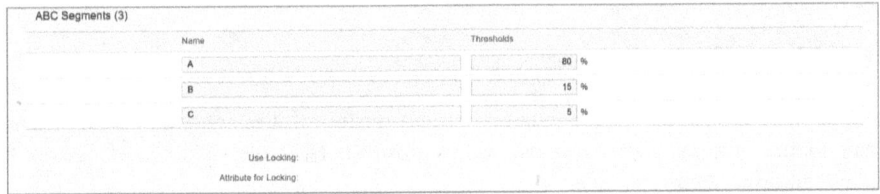

**Fig. 4.14** *ABC* segmentation Pareto criteria

## XYZ Segmentation

XYZ Segmentation: ON

| | |
|---|---|
| Target Attribute for Segmentation Results: | XYZ Code (XYZCODE) |
| Key Attributes of the Target Master Data Type: | Product ID |
| Segmentation Measure: | HISTORICALSALES (NO DISPLAY) (HISTORICALSALES) |
| Base Planning Level: | Product ID |
| Calculation Level: | Product ID |
| Periodicity: | Monthly |
| Time Scope: | Past |
| Calculation Horizon: | 50 Months |
| Offset for Calculation Horizon: | 12 Months |

**Fig. 4.15** *XYZ* segmentation settings

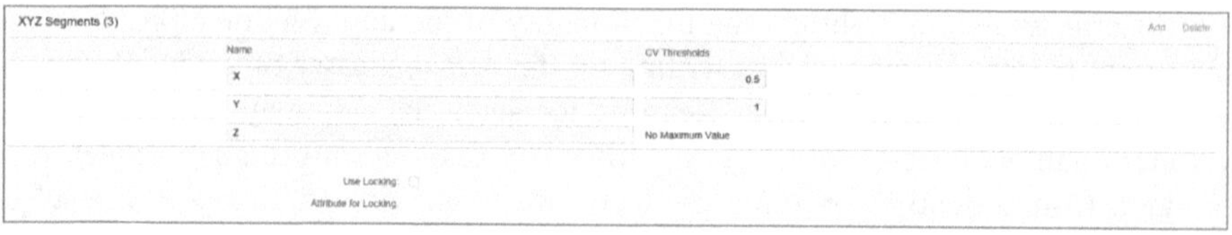


**Fig. 4.16** *XYZ* segment thresholds

SAP Integrated Business Planning
Filter:
(Ad Hoc Filter) (1 criteria):

| Product ID | ABC Code | XYZ Code | Key Figure | Apr 13 | MAY 2013 | Jun 13 | Jul 13 | Aug 13 | Sep 13 | OCT 2013 | Nov 13 |
|---|---|---|---|---|---|---|---|---|---|---|---|
| IBP A | B | Y | Historical Sales | 1200 | 1200 | 1200 | 1200 | 1200 | 1200 | 1200 | 1200 |
| IBP B | A | Y | Historical Sales | 5500 | 5500 | 5500 | 5500 | 5500 | 5500 | 5500 | 5500 |
| IBP C | A | X | Historical Sales | 17567 | 19680 | 21067 | 19768 | 14987 | 24131 | 20928 | 22428 |
| IBP D | A | X | Historical Sales | 315527 | 287265 | 296480 | 276112 | 206450 | 327188 | 297840 | 323633 |
| IBP E | B | X | Historical Sales | 5126 | 4738 | 4909 | 4675 | 3562 | 5647 | 4837 | 5322 |
| IBP F | C | Y | Historical Sales | 3108 | 2621 | 2509 | 2400 | 1779 | 3022 | 3456 | 3332 |
| IBP G | B | Y | Historical Sales | 10080 | 8391 | 6789 | 6900 | 5478 | 9427 | 9424 | 8976 |
| IBP H | A | Y | Historical Sales | 23226 | 21256 | 21979 | 19654 | 15449 | 25092 | 24990 | 27135 |
| IBP I | A | Y | Historical Sales | 19516 | 18516 | 19488 | 20640 | 15702 | 25130 | 21655 | 22788 |
| IBP L | A | X | Historical Sales | 27030 | 24379 | 25301 | 23749 | 17660 | 27316 | 24480 | 26905 |
| IBP M | A | Z | Historical Sales | 23829 | 21840 | 22799 | 20713 | 16809 | 25637 | 22093 | 24775 |
| IBP N | A | X | Historical Sales | 93675 | 98880 | 111180 | 109783 | 83880 | 134232 | 111855 | 119274 |

**Fig. 4.17** SAP IBP *ABC/XYZ* example

opportunities to play with the data and obtain meaningful insights that may be used later in the coming process steps; we propose an example of a set of figures to investigate the data.

Figure 4.18 displays on the *X*-axis the *ABC* code per year, while on the *Y*-axis the historical sales in quantity. The blue lines indicate the category *X*, the orange the *Y* one and the green the *Z* one. It is noticeable how the *Z* products, within the *A* class, are increasing in quantity throughout the years, while for the other classes the *X*, *Y* and *Z* amount of quantities stay approximately the same from 2013 to 2016.

We need to remember as well that, due to the fact that we use only a few months of the year 2017, we see from the graphical solution a steep decrease for the year 2017.

Additionally, Fig. 4.19 illustrates another graphical representation of the portfolio clusters. On the *X*-axis, the percentage of the historical sales is displayed, while on the *Y*-axis the *ABC* code per year. The color of the bars reflects the *X*, *Y* and *Z* categories. We start noticing that the *AZ* products are increasing in percentage as in the year 2013 they accounted for the 6% of the *A* class while in the year 2017 for the 31%.

Besides, the *Z* category itself is increasing in percentage, as every year the percentage of the *Z* component within each class tends to augment.

**Fig. 4.18** SAP *ABC/XYZ* dashboard 1

**Fig. 4.19** SAP *ABC/XYZ* dashboard 2

The union of these insights is really important to give a practitioner a first insight on what the portfolio deals with. He/she can understand the trend of each class and category as well as the quantity and percentage related to them. Those features are mostly qualitative, but they will be very useful in the coming steps when tailor-suited decisions will have to be made on a higher granularity.

It is the fact itself of increasing and magnifying the detail of the analysis that brings even additional insights. For example, as we already know, the *A* class is the one where we should start addressing our attention; but, how is the *A* class behaving in terms of sales/demand and cluster throughout the years we dispose of? Does it keep being stable? Or is it the *A* group accounting for more and more sales/demand?

Figure 4.20 answers the majority of our questions! On the *Y*-axis, we have the historical sales quantities, while on the *Y*-axis the *ABC* code per year. We can detect how there is a positive trend in the *A* class, while for the other two classes their accounting stays approximately the same from 2013 to 2016. Moreover, the year 2017 sales/demand looks promising as we already see that, for the *A* class, few months of the year 2017 already account for half of the 2013 *A* class sales.

Figure 4.21 complements the previous insights! Thanks to a graph where on the *X*-axis we have only the *A* class through the years considered and on the *Y*-axis the historical sales, we easily realize how the $Y$ and X cluster did not change in quantity from 2013 to 2016, but the $Z$ cluster is steadily increasing! The practioners' work, for reaching a positive forecasting accuracy for those $AZ$ products, seems increasing as well for the year 2017.

We can derive a lot of information, but the positive news is that the customization of the Web UI dashboards is very flexible and the practitioner can look for the more suitable information needed for letting him make the most accurate decision.

As a conclusion, to simplify the practitioners' life further, we can increase the granularity level of the graphics, easily reaching the SKU level. There, we can display the class of the SKU, its variability cluster and its trend of sales/demand.

Figure 4.22 illustrates an example of a $XB$ SKU that is maintaining its sales/demand in a stable way from 2013 to 2016, as it should be. The remark is not meaningless at all, because it reinforces the goodness of the approach and it builds confidence in the practitioner since he can, on his own, prove the coherence of his approach.

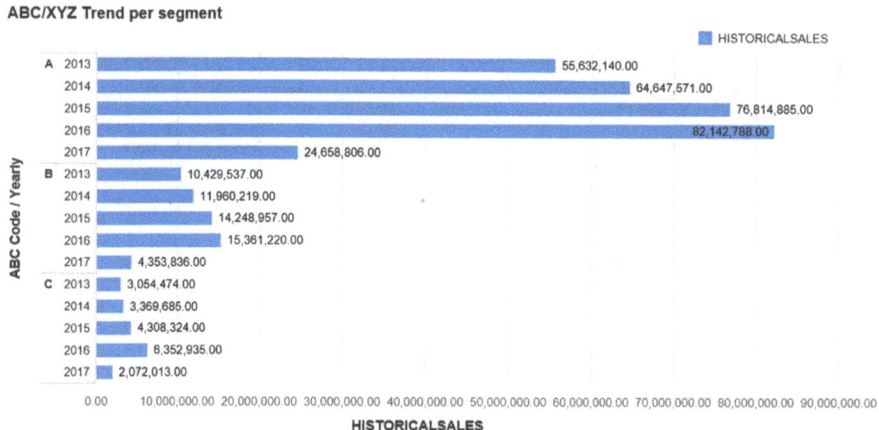

**Fig. 4.20**  SAP IBP $XYZ$ dashboard 3

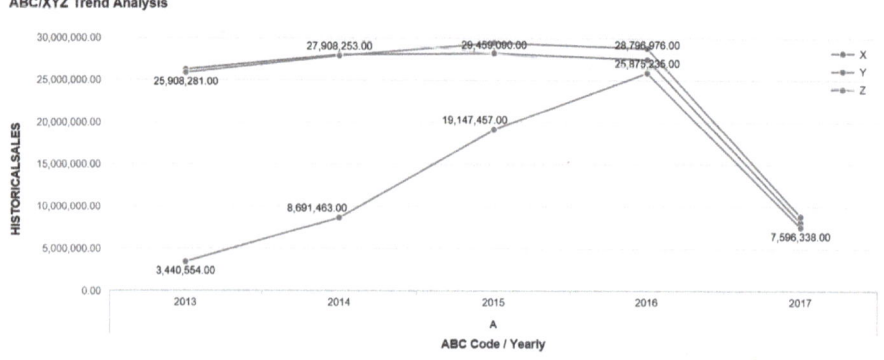

**Fig. 4.21**  SAP IBP $XYZ$ dashboard 4

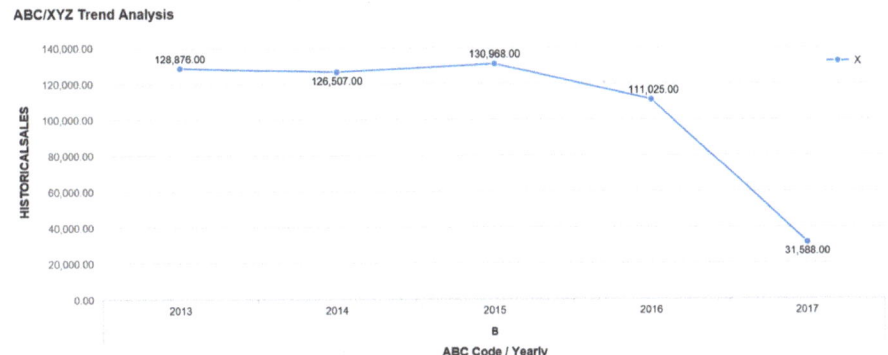

**Fig. 4.22**  SAP IBP *XYZ* dashboard 5

### 4.1.3  SAP Use Case: Use of CoV for Data Cleansing

A planning view where CoV is being used could look like the one shown in Fig. 4.23. In this view, CoV and the corresponding *XYZ* classification are displayed (last two columns). The CoV column is color-coded, and this offers finer granularity within a given classification (darker the color, higher the CoV). Such a planning view was used at one client as a pre-go-live cleansing watchlist. It also offers the added benefit of highlighting cases where lifecycle planning data are missing, for example, phased-out SKUs that should not be on the list or new SKUs with gaps in the time-series because predecessors were not mapped.

| Mar.15 | Apr.15 | May.15 | Jun.15 | Jul.15 | Aug.15 | Sep.15 | Oct.15 | Nov.15 | Dec.15 | Jan.16 | Feb.16 | CoV | XYZ |
|---|---|---|---|---|---|---|---|---|---|---|---|---|---|
| 337 | 181 | 240 | 162 | 215 | 208 | 231 | 135 | 248 | 62 | 309 | 229 | 0,33 | X |
| 0 | 0 | 0 | 0 | 0 | 0 | 0 | 0 | 0 | 0 | 0 | 0 | 0,33 | X |
| 124 | 107 | 276 | 269 | 206 | 61 | 83 | 114 | 82 | 40 | 44 | 17 | 0,70 | X |
| 124 | 107 | 276 | 269 | 206 | 61 | 83 | 114 | 82 | 40 | 44 | 17 | 0,70 | X |
| 0 | 0 | 0 | 0 | 0 | 0 | 0 | 0 | 0 | 0 | 0 | 0 | 0,70 | X |
| | | | | | | | | | | 32 | | 3,18 | Z |
| | | | | | | | | | | 32 | | 3,18 | Z |
| | | | | | | | | | | 0 | | 3,18 | Z |
| 58 | 36 | 99 | 58 | 60 | 64 | 35 | 43 | 52 | 51 | 80 | 33 | 0,33 | X |
| 58 | 36 | 99 | 58 | 60 | 64 | 35 | 43 | 52 | 51 | 80 | 33 | 0,33 | X |
| 0 | 0 | 0 | 0 | 0 | 0 | 0 | 0 | 0 | 0 | 0 | 0 | 0,33 | X |
| 506 | 242 | 320 | 592 | 276 | 551 | 141 | 122 | 471 | 142 | 88 | 186 | 0,57 | X |
| 506 | 242 | 320 | 592 | 276 | 551 | 141 | 122 | 471 | 142 | 88 | 186 | 0,57 | X |
| 0 | 0 | 0 | 0 | 0 | 0 | 0 | 0 | 0 | 0 | 0 | 0 | 0,57 | X |
| 577 | 215 | 231 | 331 | 184 | 204 | 56 | 56 | 370 | 353 | 191 | 101 | 0,60 | X |
| 577 | 215 | 231 | 331 | 184 | 204 | 56 | 56 | 370 | 353 | 191 | 101 | 0,60 | X |
| 0 | 0 | 0 | 0 | 0 | 0 | 0 | 0 | 0 | 0 | 0 | 0 | 0,60 | X |
| 2 | 0 | | | | | | | | | | | 3,19 | Z |
| 2 | 0 | | | | | | | | | | | 3,19 | Z |

**Fig. 4.23**  Demand classification example

CoV formula is as follows:

$$CoV = \frac{\text{Standard deviation}}{\text{Average}}$$

*Clustering*

Coming to the clustering phase not only means reaching the final step of the segmentation and classification step, but also signifies being able to make use of the outputs of previous steps to properly identify meaningful clusters. Clustering can be done automatically, and it indicates the moment in which the results need to be collected to move forward.

Figure 4.24 illustrates the overall procedure largely described on the above lines and the possible clustering output.

As we can see from the visualization, the clustering output is a smart automatic combination of the techniques of the procedures, oriented in a way that allows the user to establish and identify the future processes toward statistical forecasting. More in detail, the clustering solution is a matrix where for each *ABC* category and for each *XYZ* category, the total amounts of historical sales or even the total count of records are performed for each demand class:

– Stable
– Intermittent
– Flashy.

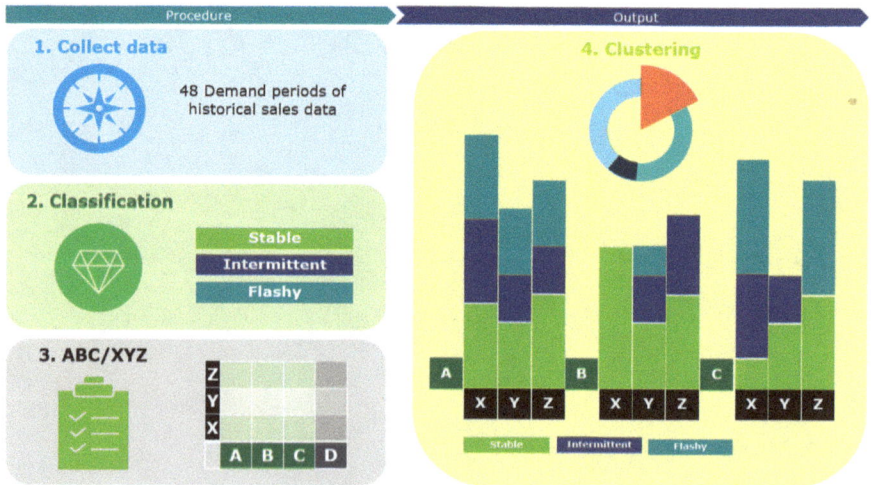

**Fig. 4.24** Segmentation and classification output: clustering

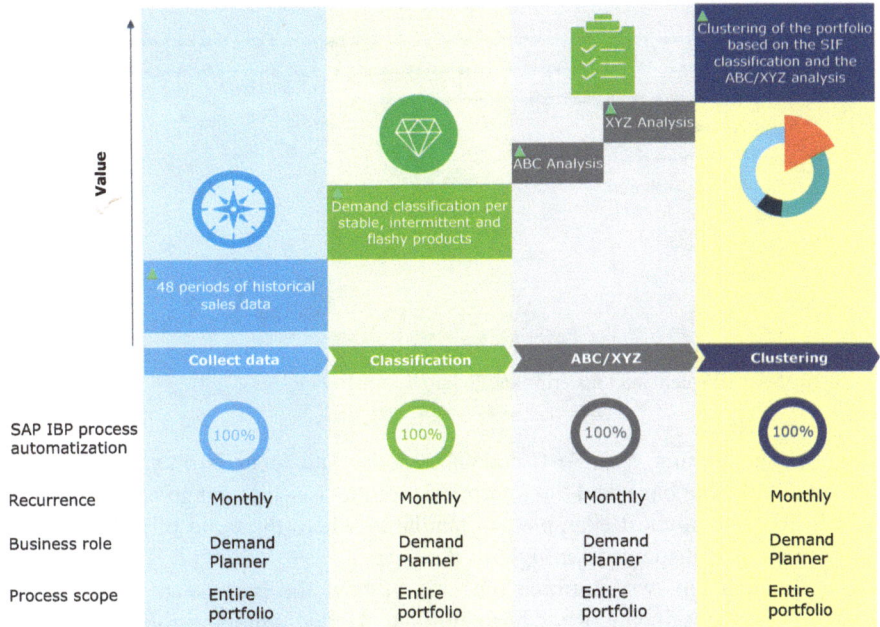

**Fig. 4.25** Segmentation waterfall

Figure 4.25 depicts the value added by each of the steps until reaching the final clustering part where the portfolio matrix can be established. In addition, some other crucial information about the process is also reported in order to set the recurrence, the ownership and the granularity of the process itself. The SAP IBP custom automation is also indicated.

The benefits are very interesting, since the practitioners use 27 different clusters, and for each of those, different specific processes can be addressed to reach the best forecast output. If at the beginning of our data collection we did not know anything about the portfolio, at this point in time, thanks to the procedure described, we can start thinking about how to proceed further based on those findings.

The Web UIs also lets us derive many other quantitative and qualitative information about our portfolio. For example, in Fig. 4.26, we can see how actually in the portfolio analyzed, only a small percentage of the SKUs are intermittent and flashy, while the majority are stable. In addition, we can also notice how for the ABC segment A there are only stable products, while same flashy and intermittent products fall into the B and C segments, especially in the Z category.

There are multiple options to perform graphical analysis allowing for different levels of filtering and customizations in dashboards. In Fig. 4.27, a comprehensive customized dashboard is displayed, where some individualized filters have been applied. In the top left part, the historical sales are mapped per year and per category "S", "F" and "I"; in the bottom part, we display the same concept but with

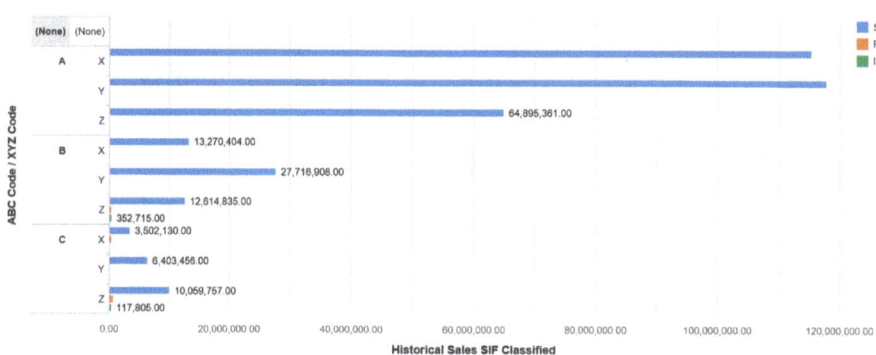

**Fig. 4.26** SAP IBP demand clustering dashboard 1

an additional filtering: year/*ABC* code/*XYZ* code. The focus is only on the flashy products—the blue bar—and the intermittent products—the orange bar. Finally, on the top right, the highest example of granularity where the trend of a specific "*C*" flashy product is displayed throughout the years.

As a conclusion, we reinforce the idea of how the purpose of demand segmentation and classification has been fulfilled: Define suitable process segments, and indicate the most structured way forward!

The concept is illustrated in Fig. 4.28 and largely explained in the second book of the Integrated Business Planning books (Kepczynski et al., 2018).

## 4.2   Identifying Seasonality

For identifying a seasonal pattern within a time series, there might be different methods. Some of those are more suitable to certain type of data distributions while others to certain data patterns. The field of seasonality as it has already been mentioned is quite vast; consequently, we will focus on some suitable methods and tests whose automation in SAP IBP could bring an extra value to the end-to-end process. At the same time, we introduce some graphical techniques that coupled with the more quantitative and automated ones might increase the performance of the process itself.

From Fig. 4.29, we can clearly distinguish between the two main flows:

– Quantitative and automated techniques that allow the system to run smoothly from end to end
– Qualitative and manual techniques that permit the end user to double check manually the outcomes of the quantitative and automated procedures, inspect the most crucial SKUs and investigate some products whose quantitative outputs may go under more thorough investigation.

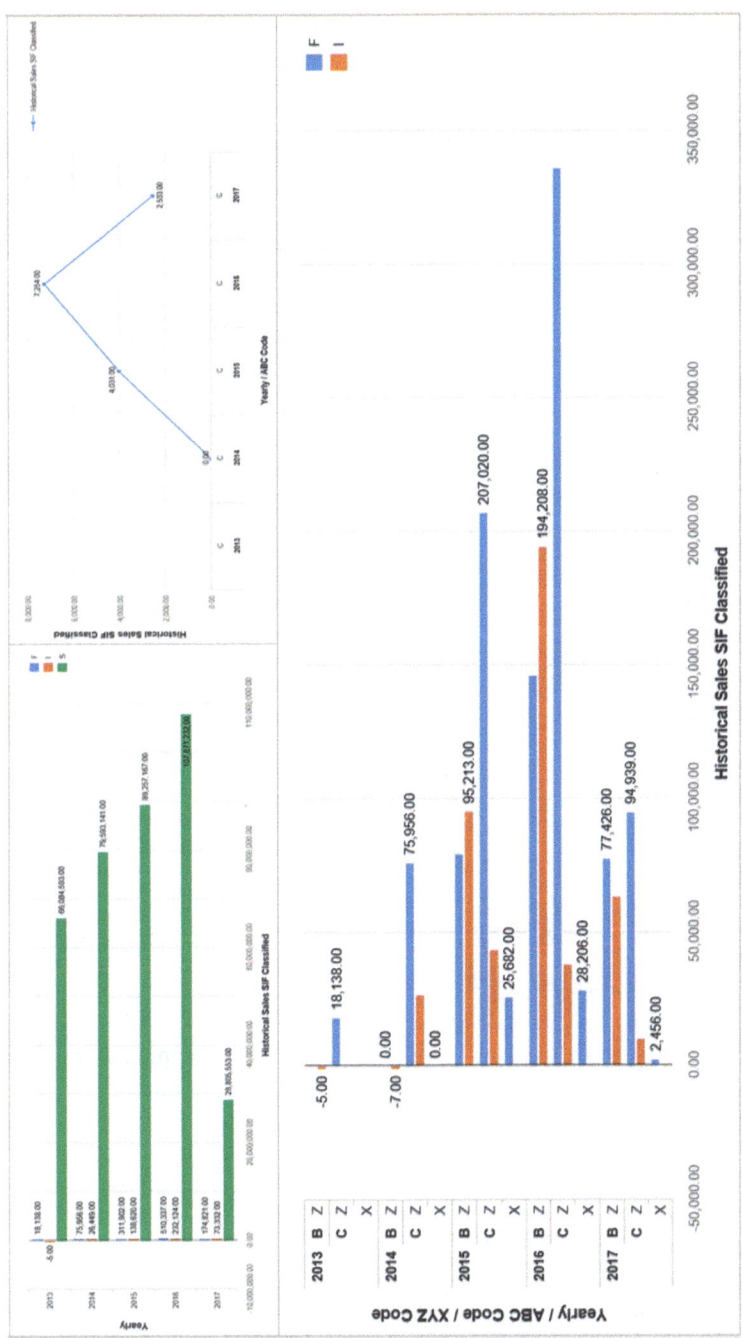

**Fig. 4.27**  SAP IBP example of personalized dashboard

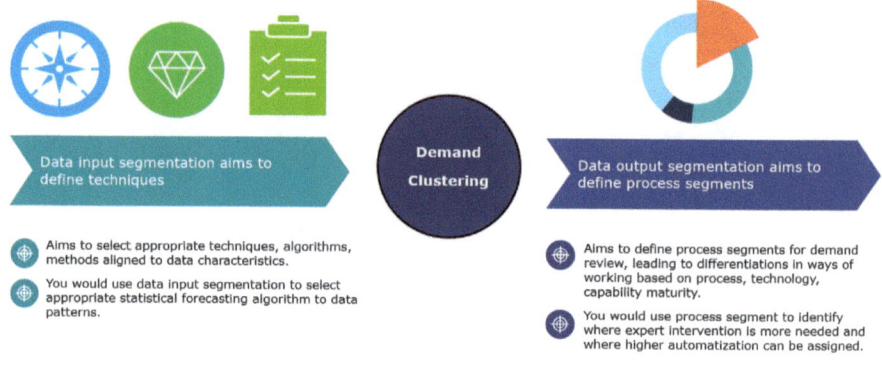

**Fig. 4.28** Demand clustering for process definition

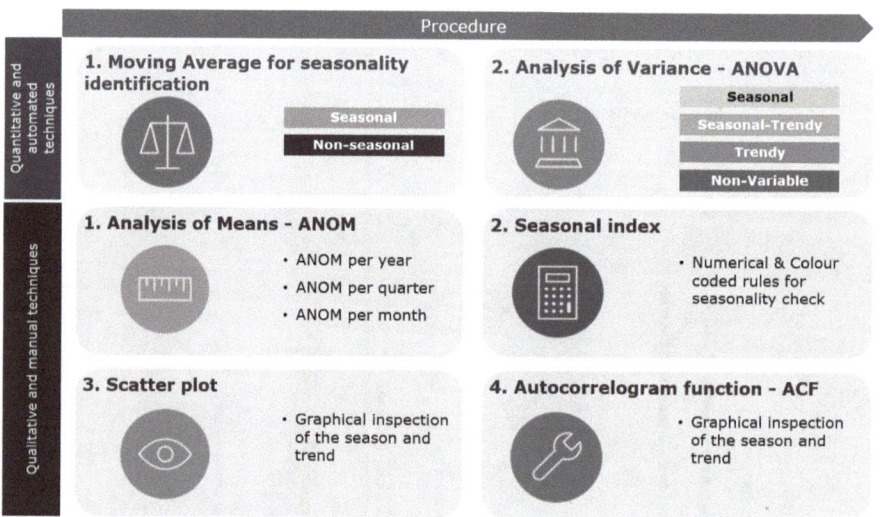

**Fig. 4.29** Analyzing seasonality

All the techniques introduced in Fig. 4.29 will be largely explained further.

*Moving Average for Seasonality Identification*

The first method we selected is the simplest, and it has the purpose of setting a ground knowledge toward seasonality and its key issues. Its outputs can be also displayed graphically, reinforcing the message and the value of the test itself. Let's deal with the Moving Average for Seasonality Identification.

The method consists of disposing of the data in two columns:

1. The first one accounts for the month numbering.
2. The second one accounts for the real sales/demand.

Successively, we need to set the number of periods to be considered for the moving average. As it has already been described, there might be different choices for setting the periods "$k$"; however, in this case and after several tentative to reach the optimal result, we identified as the most suitable indicator the value of four.

As a first step, we calculate the moving average per month. It has to be reminded that for the first month, the MA will equal to the sales/demand itself, for the second month to the average of the first two months and so on, until we reach the end of the data set.

As a next step, we introduce a Boolean index that has the function of identifying the following concept:

- Index equals to 1, if the moving average with "$k$" = 4 is inferior to the average of the historical sales.
- Index equals to 0, if the moving average with "$k$" = 4 is greater than the average of the historical sales

Consequently, based on the Boolean index, we establish the following sequence:

- Length of the sequence above the average. It indicates the sum of the string on values equal to 1. When in the Boolean column, we experience a switch of the Boolean number the counting restarts.
- Length of the sequence below the average. It indicates the sum of the string on values equal to 0. When in the Boolean column, we experience a switch of the Boolean number the counting restarts.

Figure 4.30 is the illustrative explicative model of the method just described.

The final criterion for the selecting and filtering of the SKUs that will result as seasonal and those that will not is the following:

- If the average of the column "length of sequence above the average" is greater than three and the average of the column "length of sequence below the average" is as well greater than 3, then the SKU can be considered seasonal.
- On the contrary, the SKU will not be filtered as seasonal.

By setting the threshold to three, it is believed to detect at least, as the smallest seasonal pattern, an SKU with a seasonal length of three months.

Furthermore, by applying this method, we manage also to assess a possible estimation of the length of the season, which equals the rounded value of the largest average between the two sequences. If, for example, the average of the length of the sequence above the average equals 3 and 8 and the average of the length of the sequence below the average equals 4 and 1, we can deduct the following indications:

| Time periods | Historical sales | Moving Average | Moving Average "k"=4 | Boolean sales | Length of sequence above the average | Length of sequence below the average |
|---|---|---|---|---|---|---|
| Jan | 5'358 | 5'358 | - | | | |
| Feb | 5'999 | 5'679 | - | | | |
| March | 2'802 | 4'720 | - | | | |
| Apr | 6'288 | 5'112 | - | | | |
| May | 12'797 | 6'649 | 5'122 | 1 | | |
| Jun | 11'910 | 7'526 | 6'972 | 1 | 2 | |
| ... | ... | ... | ... | | | |
| Jan | 2'909 | 8'064 | 5'641 | 0 | | 1 |
| Feb | 5'557 | 7'908 | 4'723 | 1 | | |
| March | 11'664 | 8'129 | 4'913 | 1 | | |
| Apr | 6'764 | 8'053 | 6'465 | 1 | 3 | |
| May | 1'900 | 7'729 | 6'724 | 0 | | 1 |
| | | | | Average | 3,8 | 4,1 |
| | | | | Max of the Average | 4,1 | |
| | | | | Length of the season | 4 | |

**Fig. 4.30** Moving Average for Seasonality Identification

- The SKU will be filtered as seasonal.
- The length of the season is estimated at 4.
- The frequency of the season estimated to 8.

As introduced before, a graphical representation is provided as well to reiterate the concept behind the method. See Fig. 4.31. It displays in orange the sales/demand per month, while in green the sequencing of the Boolean index. It is noticeable how the method approximately detects the seasonal patterns throughout the years.

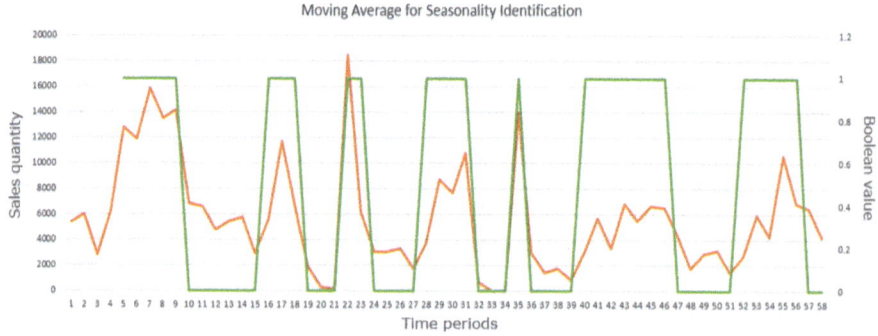

**Fig. 4.31** Graphical representation of MA for seasonality identification

This is the preliminary approach toward seasonality identification. We will now have a look at its specific use case, and then we will move into more mathematical and statistic reliant test.

### 4.2.1   SAP Use Case: Moving Average for Seasonality Identification

Figure 4.32 represents the outcomes of the Moving Average for Seasonality Identification. As it is possible to detect, per SKU there is a specific column called Seasonal Heurisit Results, where the insights out of the calculations described above are displayed:

– NS stands for non-seasonal.
– S stands for seasonal.

The historical sales seasonality heuristic classified accounts for the sales history of the relevant SKU, while the Boolean index is stored in the key figure called "Is Historical Sales GT 4 months MA." In the upper part of the figure, a scatter plot is shown: On the X-axis, there is the time, while on the Y-axis the blue line indicates the sales history and the green line the Boolean series. The green check marks tell us that the SKU considered for this example is seasonal and its proof is demonstrated by the fact that the Boolean series almost matches and detects the seasonal periods.

On the contrary, in a case when the Seasonal Heuristic Results show NS, the expected outcome is something similar to Fig. 4.33, where the check mark is red.

Moving our focus to the Web UI, it is possible, as we have already seen from the previous applications, to go further in the analysis and summarize the insights out of the Moving Average for Seasonality Identification. Figure 4.34 is an example that goes exactly in this direction: Per year, we display the total sales related to seasonal and non-seasonal SKUs. Any type of trend, recurring pattern or changes in the data sales/demand could be analyzed.

A similar dashboard is built to extrapolate even further information in relation to the seasonal products. For example, Fig. 4.35 comprises the historical sales on the Y-axis and the year, ABC code and XYZ code on the X-axis; the focus is on the total sales/demand of the seasonal SKUs per year and within the clusters pre-mentioned. The recurring pattern we are able to detect from the figure below is that the majority of the seasonal sales/demand falls into the AY class for all the years considered!

*Analysis of Variance—ANOVA*

The ANOVA method, which stands for analysis of variance, provides complementary insights for the demand components analysis, and it can be also used as a stand-alone test for seasonality identification.

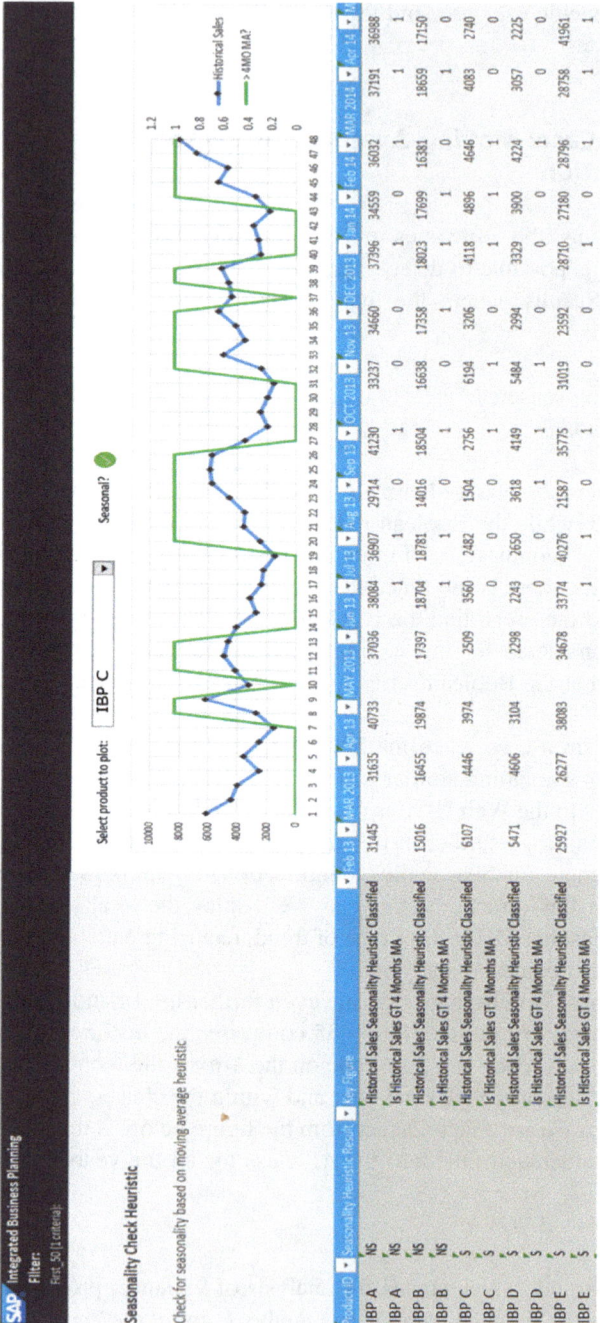

**Fig. 4.32** SAP IBP Moving Average for Seasonality Identification

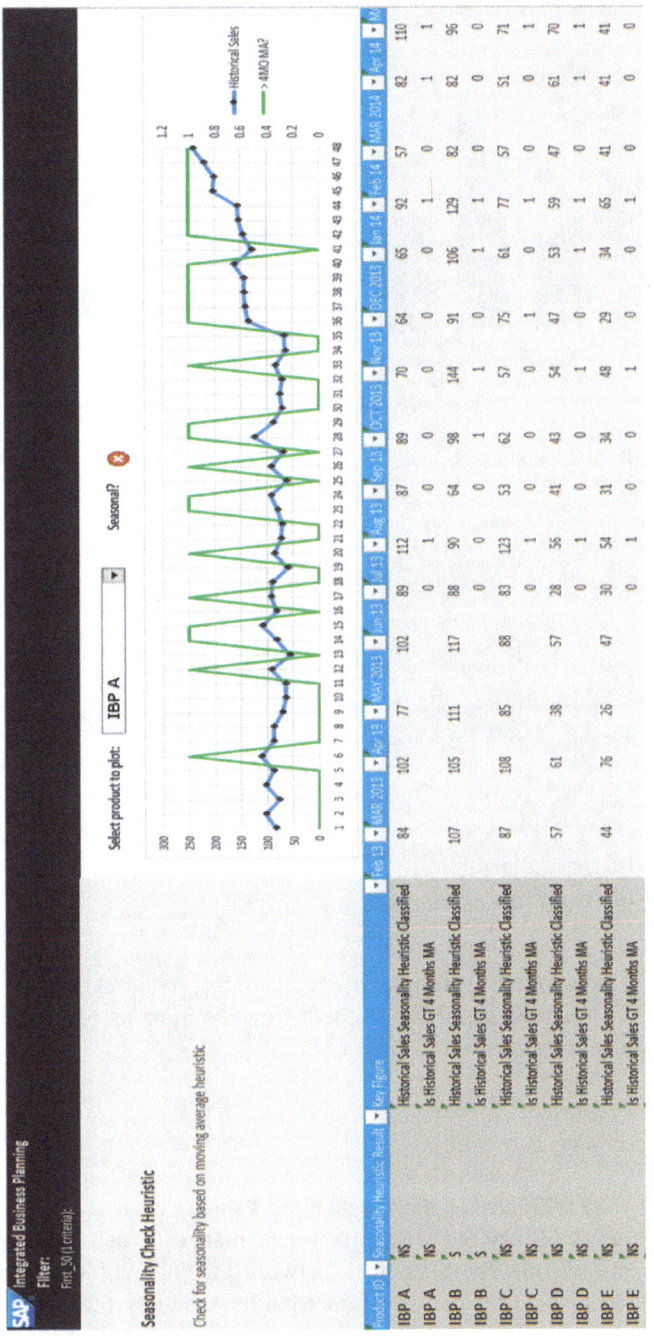

**Fig. 4.33**   SAP IBP MA for SI (non-seasonal)

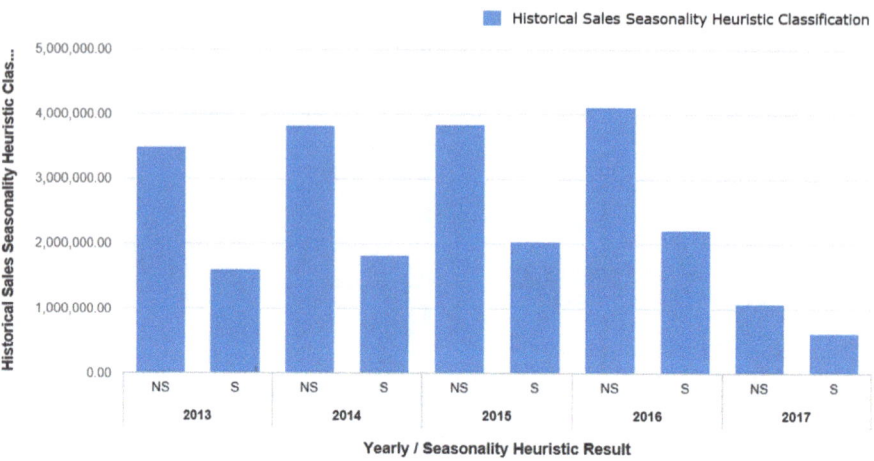

**Fig. 4.34** SAP IBP MA for SI dashboard 1

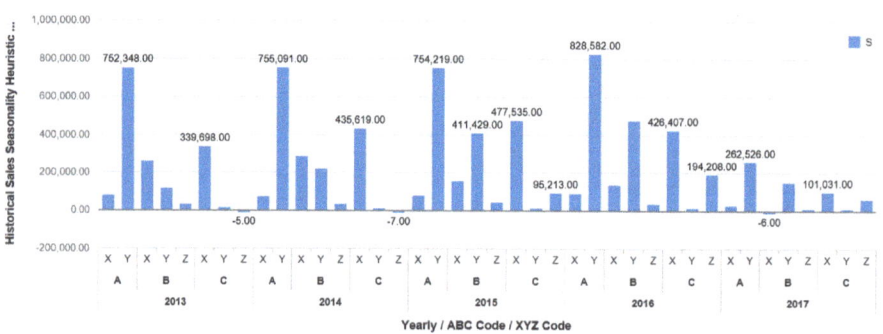

**Fig. 4.35** SAP IBP MA for SI with *ABC XYZ*

The ANOVA method is a simple mechanism that requires a specific data organization and structure in order to benefit directly from its technicalities. Its specific structure is composed of as follows:

- Each column represents a year.
- Each row represents a month.

Consequently, we will have as a first reticulum a matrix of data. For example, if we have four years of history, we will get a 4 * 12 matrix: 48 cells. By setting the data in such a way, we clearly distinguish between the columns 'contributions in terms of sales, which stand for the years' contribution, and the rows' contributions in terms of sales, which stands for the specific month's sales through the years (see Fig. 4.36).

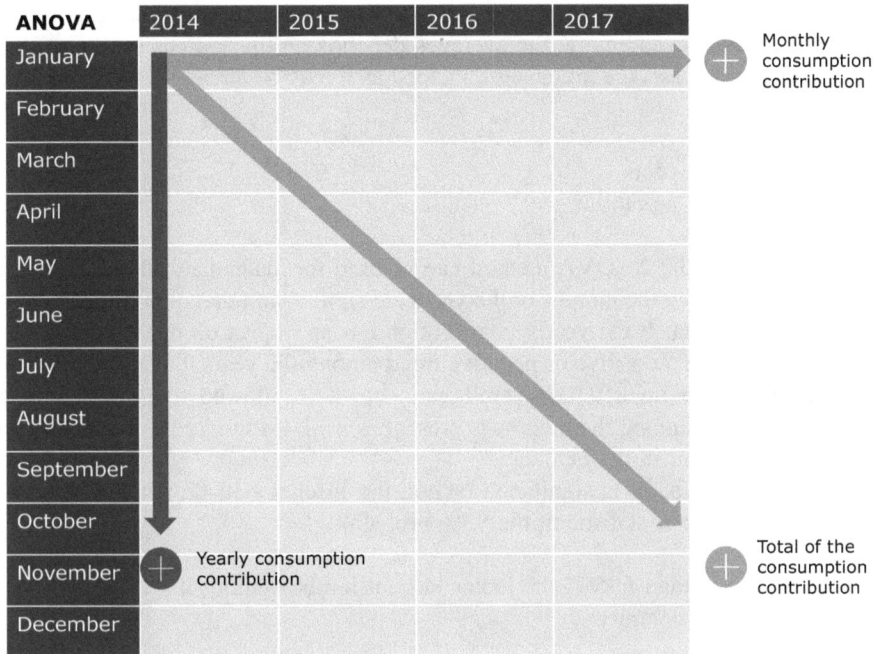

**Fig. 4.36** ANOVA data structure principle

The strength of the ANOVA method is of being capable of quantifying the rows and columns effects in terms of their relative contributions to the total variation in a data table. In relation to our business purposes, it means that the method is able to assess and quantify the weight of the sales/demand among the years (column) and among the months (rows). A too strong contribution of the year's component could lead to a positive or negative trend within the data set, while a too strong contribution of the month's component could suggest a seasonal component in the data.

From a pure statistic point of view, the ANOVA, analysis of variance, is a descriptive procedure that separates or partitions the variation observable in a response variable into two basic components: variation due to assignable cause (in our specific case the seasonal and trendy component) and to uncontrolled or random variation (noise factors that influence the demand sales/demand). The assignable causes refer to known or suspected sources of variation from variates that are controlled or measured while conducting the experiment/analysis. Random variation includes the effects of all other sources not controlled or measured during the experiment/analysis (Gunst, Mason, & Hess, 2003).

The analysis of variance is considered a test omnibus that allows to accept the hypothesis that the different groups of data compared to have the same average. It can be run with a single factor, for example, a machine, a car, a year or with multiple influencer factors. If the factor does not influence the results, it is clear that the data of the groups analyzed are equals; otherwise, it can be demonstrated that the variance calculated among the averages depends on the sources of variances.

In our specific case, the influencing factors, as it may be already grasped, are the following:

– Factor "$a$": the years
– Factor "$b$": the months.

Consequently, the ANOVA method can be used for mathematically detecting if the variations among the months or the years are significant in relation to the overall variance of the data. If the yearly contribution has an impact on the variance, it is possible to assume a positive or negative trend among the years, but if the months' sales/demands also impact the overall variance, it is allowed to assume that a certain variability among the months is present as well, leading to the presence of a seasonal component in the demand.

To decide if a factor is significant or not, the Fischer statistic $F$ must be compared with the Fisher statistic at the 95% probability.

– If $F$ is greater than $F95\%$, the factor in question is significant.
– Otherwise, the contrary.

By mentioning the 95% probability, it means that the results proposed by the test are accurate with a 95% confidence, while leaving 5% of possible errors.

It is also acceptable to have only the years or the months significant, or both of them. At the same time, the inner variability of the data set can also be detected and calculated. Unfortunately, due to the fact that we cannot replicate the data and reasonably enlarge the data set, it is not possible to run ANOVA with more replications. The values of sales/demands stay unique, and the replication test is not available. The usefulness of running a test with a set of replicated values from the same sample lies in the fact that the randomness of the data is treated as a factor, and as a result, it is possible to assess if the noise factors are significant or not, and if they are likely to impact the way in which the SKU or the product is consumed or sold.

Consequently, by missing this opportunity, from a business standpoint, we lose the possibility to verify if the inner variability is intrinsic of the data set or if it is, in a large or small part, due to the interaction of the factors "year" and "months."

## 4.2.2  SAP Use Case: Analysis of Variance—ANOVA

Based on the analysis of variance method, ANOVA, the practitioner has an easy way to filter the portfolio in four additional categories:

– Seasonal
– Seasonal and trendy

- Internal variability
- Trendy.

Figure 4.37 illustrates how the ANOVA categories are listed against each SKU. In addition, the key figure "Historical sales STMN classes" reports for the average of each year averages.

For each of these categories, we can prove graphically the goodness of the test.

For example, Fig. 4.38 shows how the selected SKU has been identified by the method as a seasonal one. The graphical solution, similar to the Moving Average for Seasonality Identification test, proves the presence of the season, while the graph to the right-hand side depicts how actually the monthly averages of the selected product dispose themselves on a typical seasonal pattern.

Similar representations are illustrated also for the other categories. Figure 4.39 indicates the trendy and non-variable example. The top section of the visualization reports the non-variable SKU where neither the seasonality nor the trend component has been detected. The monthly averages are very stables as well as the simple monthly sales/demand. On the bottom part, a trendy SKU is depicted. The monthly averages suggest a slight increase in the sales/demand as well as from the scatter plot. The trendy product is characterized by a constant alternation of months whose moving average is superior to the actual sales/demand and months whose moving average is inferior to the actual sales/demand. Consequently, in the graph we see a frequent turnover of 1 and 0.

A final comment should be addressed to those SKU that face an inner variability. Being variable does not necessarily only mean not having a really flat sales/demand. It may also mean that the types of inner variations of the data do not match the recurring pattern of a season or a decreasing or increasing pattern of a trend. In this case, the only possible way to detect what is really happening for that specific SKU is the scatter plot.

**SAP** Integrated Business Planning
Filter:

| Product ID | STMN Code | Key Figure | 2013 | 2014 | 2015 | 2016 |
|---|---|---|---|---|---|---|
| IBP A | TS | Historical Sales STMN Classified | 0 | 4914 | 8478 | 2137 |
| IBP B | TS | Historical Sales STMN Classified | 0 | 22198 | 21232 | 20578 |
| IBP C | S | Historical Sales STMN Classified | 1300 | 2334 | 2610 | 2455 |
| IBP D | TS | Historical Sales STMN Classified | 0 | 18878 | 24011 | 26455 |
| IBP E | TS | Historical Sales STMN Classified | 80100 | 191163 | 268081 | 292750 |
| IBP F | S | Historical Sales STMN Classified | 128955 | 125907 | 129343 | 120832 |
| IBP G | T | Historical Sales STMN Classified | 51043 | 43241 | 52366 | 54289 |
| IBP H | TS | Historical Sales STMN Classified | 505255 | 495684 | 496493 | 561059 |
| IBP I | IV | Historical Sales STMN Classified | 602 | 714 | 628 | 819 |
| IBP L | IV | Historical Sales STMN Classified | 105956 | 114064 | 99227 | 92295 |
| IBP M | TS | Historical Sales STMN Classified | 9520 | 9284 | 9235 | 15118 |
| IBP N | T | Historical Sales STMN Classified | 5906 | 13454 | 12836 | 13057 |
| IBP O | TS | Historical Sales STMN Classified | 78475 | 83725 | 79283 | 69301 |

**Fig. 4.37**  SAP IBP ANOVA categories

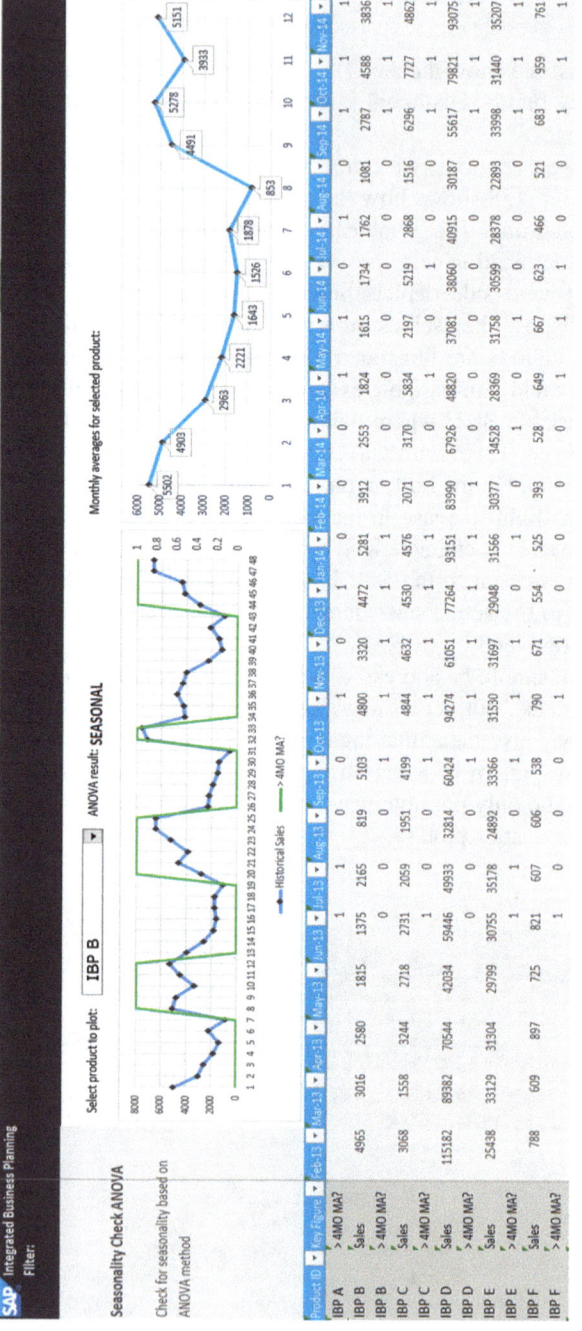

**Fig. 4.38** ANOVA method: seasonal SKU

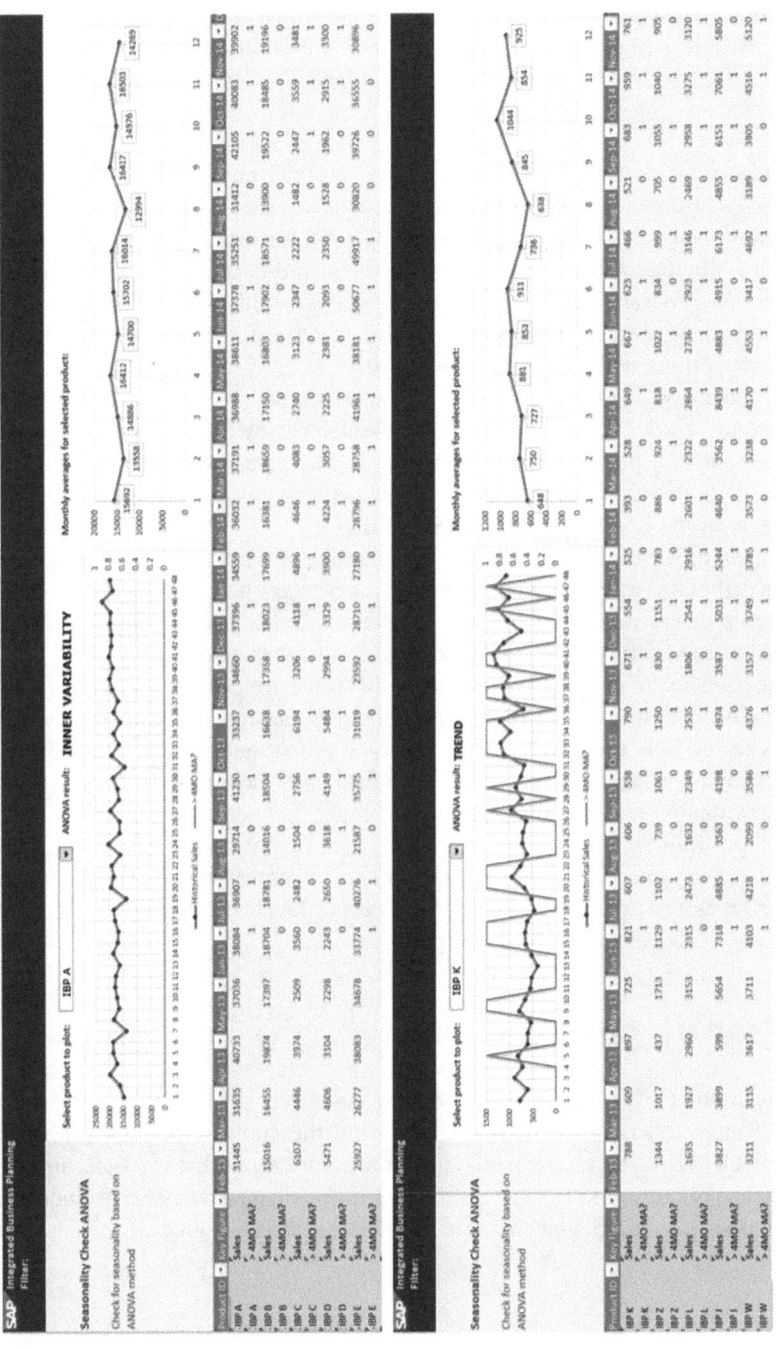

**Fig. 4.39** SAP IBP ANOVA example

Consequently, being variable in sales/demand and volatile does not necessarily mean having a seasonal cycle. This is the reason why a scatter plot is thought to be a good test to continue assessing the causes of variability.

*Scatter plot*

Another possible method for detecting a seasonal component in a data set is characterized by the use of the scatter plot; it is considered to be one of the best graphical tools to start assessing or validating for a seasonal pattern as it will allow to see any fluctuations, deviations or erratic movements. Within the seasonality identification process, the scatter plot is employed with the aim of filtering and double-checking the seasonal SKUs: Those that once plotted do not show any cyclical repetitions will be kept out of scope.

More precisely, a scatter plot reveals the relationships or associations between two variables. Such relationships manifest themselves by any non-random structure in the plot. It is a plot of values of $Y$ versus the corresponding values of $X$; the response variable lies in the $X$-axis while the variable suspected to be related to the response is in the horizontal axis (NIST, 2012).

A scatter plot can help in identifying relationships between variables, correlations, distributions and outliers. However, a scatter plot can never prove and demonstrate cause and effect, but it is on the researcher and, in our case the daily practitioner, to clarify that through a qualitative further analysis.

The drawback of the scatter plot is at the same time its value add: a manual graphical inspection. It is the "plus" of the analysis, because with a greater accuracy it allows to see how the data behave so that the practitioners can understand which types of demand sales/demand they have to deal with; however, on the contrary, its lack of automation makes it really time consuming, not permitting to scatter plotting an entire portfolio!

Consequently, we recommend it only for specific cases such forecasting reviews, tricky or known as "painful" SKUs or at a deeper level of portfolio filtering, when the purpose is to get more and more precise.

## 4.2.3   SAP Use Case: Scatter Plot

As an example, Fig. 4.40 shows how during the winter season the sales/demand of the SKU analyzed is much higher than during the summer periods. The pattern repeats itself for 4 years, and some spikes are present, as for instance during the 2016, 2017 winter, while a trend component in the demand may be excluded since we do not see any particular increase or decrease in the degree of the seasonality among the years.

**Fig. 4.40**   Scatter plot of a seasonal example

*Seasonal index*

The seasonal index is a complementary technique that allows the user to assess the seasonality component of a demand series. The method itself is based on the same year versus month matrix structure of the ANOVA method.

The seasonal index is represented by the ratio of the monthly sales/demand over the yearly average. For example, if in January 2015 the sales/demand accounts for 100 units and the 2015 yearly average accounts for 200 units, the January 2015 seasonal index will account for 0.5.

In simpler terms, each month that has a seasonal index inferior to 1 can be considered as a below average season, while every month with a seasonal index greater than 1 as an above the average season. If it is equal to 1, then the monthly sales/demand is equal to the average of the year.

The overall result will be a second matrix, where instead of the monthly sales/demand, each cell contains its seasonal index. Eventually, all the seasonal indexes of the same month (rows) can be averaged again in order to obtain a final unique 12 record series of seasonal indexes. The same principle applies to those indexes. Color coding this test can lead to more intuitive insights.

Figure 4.41 illustrates graphically the structure of the test and its calculation.

We can notice from the color coding and from the seasonal indexes greater than 1 that the high seasons are expected in autumn and winter (Fig. 4.42).

From the above, we can see immediately the benefits of a graphical analysis based on the seasonal index. For example, the graph on the left not only suggests a higher sales/demand pattern in the fall and winter seasons, but it also highlights the presence of a trend throughout the years since the 2016 sales/demand marked in blue is superior to the one of the 2015 and so on back to the 2013.

On the right-hand side of the template, the averaged seasonal indexes are plotted in a graph whose value add is to recognize and confirm once again the presence of the season and its yearly occurrence.

| Seasonal index | 2014 | 2015 | 2016 | 2017 | Averaged Seasonal Index |
|---|---|---|---|---|---|
| January | =Jan(2014)/AVG(2014) | | | 0.6 | AVG(January) |
| February | | =Feb(2015)/AVG(2015) | | 0.7 | ... |
| March | | | =March(2016)/AVG(2016) | 0.6 | |
| April | | | | 1.4 | |
| May | | | | 1.6 | |
| June | | | | 1.5 | |
| July | | | | 1.4 | |
| August | | | | 1.2 | |
| September | | | | 1.2 | |
| October | | | | 0.7 | |
| November | | | | 0.7 | |
| December | | | | 0.6 | |

**Colour code rule for the seasonal index**

**Fig. 4.41**   Building a seasonal index

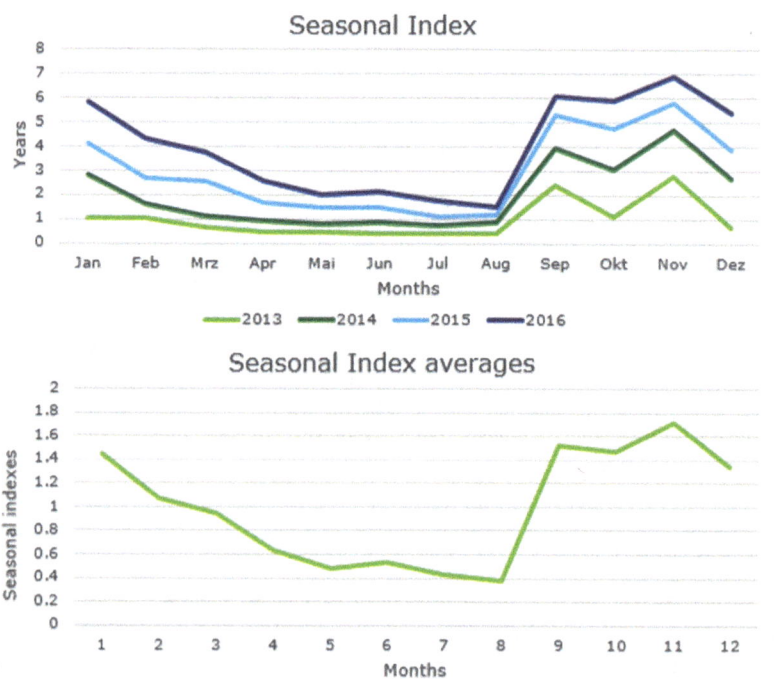

**Fig. 4.42**   Seasonal index

*Autocorrelogram—ACF*

Another possible technique is to generate the autocorrelation function and plot the autocorrelogram to visually identify the seasonal component of the demand.

A correlogram which is also called autocorrelation function ACF plot or autocorrelation plot is a visual way to show serial correlation in data that changes over time, for instance time series (WordPress, 2016).

As it has already been mentioned in the previous chapters, the autocorrelation measures the linear relationship for lagged values. Autocorrelation coefficients constitute the autocorrelation function (ACF) also known as correlogram (Hyndman & Athanasopoulos, 2014).

A correlogram gives a **summary of correlation** at different periods of time. The plot shows the correlation coefficient for the series lagged by one delay at a time. For example, at $x = 1$ you might be comparing January to February or February to March. The horizontal scale is the time lag, and the vertical axis is the autocorrelation coefficient (ACF).

The correlation coefficient measures the strength of a linear relationship. It ranges from $-1$ which means no correlation to 1 which means that all points are correlated.

If dealing with time series, it may be useful to understand the explanatory relationship between variables. Autocorrelation and autocovariance measures are useful for these purposes especially if the observations of the same time series are lagged by one, two or several periods (Makridakis, Wheelwright, & Hyndman, 1998).

Each lag series will be considered independent and comparable with the others. Following mathematical formula below, we obtain a correlation number ($r$) for each lagged period.

$$r_k = \frac{\sum_{i=1}^{N-k} \left(Y_i - \overline{Y}\right)\left(Y_{i+k} - \overline{Y}\right)}{\sum_{i=1}^{N}\left(Y_i - \overline{Y}\right)^2}$$

Combining graphically together all the $r$, we obtain the autocorrelation function ACF. It is a standard tool to detect cycle, trend and seasonality. The use of a graph is crucial as the plot exhibits an alternating sequence of positive and negative spikes. These spikes are not decaying to zero. Such a pattern is the autocorrelation plot signature of a sinusoidal model (NIST, 2012).

Eventually, when experiencing a sinusoidal pattern we might expect to confirm the assumption that a seasonal component is present in the data set.

In Fig. 4.43, an example of correlogram is displayed. In the *X*-axis, the month's periods are set, while on the Y-axis the autocorrelogram function is reported. As we can detect, the alternating pattern of the ACF allows to identify a season throughout the years considered. In the figure, the upper and lower limit is shown as well; hypothetically, when the ACF related to a specific month overcomes, the upper or lower threshold may indicate a potential outlier!

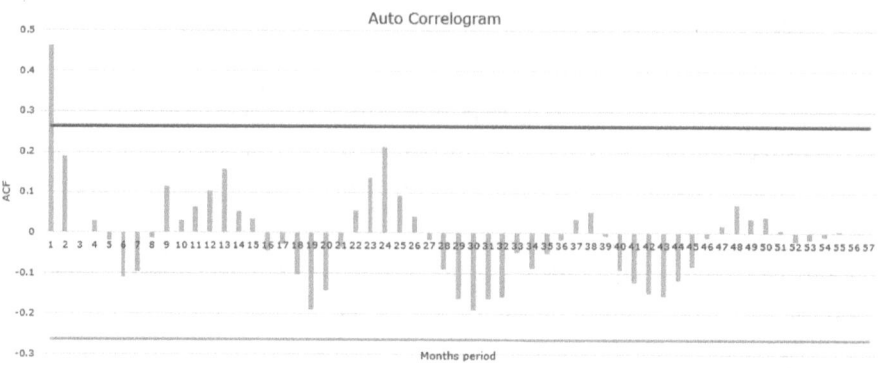

**Fig. 4.43** Autocorrelogram

*Analysis of Means—ANOM*

The analysis of means has different application fields. For our specific purposes, it has been employed in a simplistic way to analyze the progression of the monthly, quarterly and yearly means.

The inputs for the test are quite simple and could be also derived from the previous calculations:

- Average of each specific month throughout the years considered
- Average of the year.

Eventually, based on the chosen aggregations from the possible inputs, different graphical outputs may be gathered. Automating such a method may be counterproductive. Its value add relies on the ease and simplicity of the plotted solutions.

## 4.2.4   SAP Use Case: Analysis of Means—ANOM

In the Excel user interface, we are able to build the different ANOM visualizations based on the key figures calculations configured for other tests. In Fig. 4.44, for instance, we plot on the *Y*-axis the average sales/demand of each quarter throughout the years analyzed and on the *X*-axis the quarters in questions. It is visible how a periodical behavior is spotted by comparing the magnitude of each bar. Consequently, the quarters 4 and 1 are those that experience the highest seasonal peaks, while the quarters 2 and 3 the lowest seasonal peaks.

By increasing the granularity, we may plot on the Y-axis the simple monthly average throughout the years while on the X-axis the months numbering. Figure 4.45 illustrates the findings.

As we were expecting, the months 1, 2, 3 ,10, 11 and 12 represent the length of the highest season (quarters 4 and 1), while the months 4, 5, 6, 7, 8 and 9 indicate

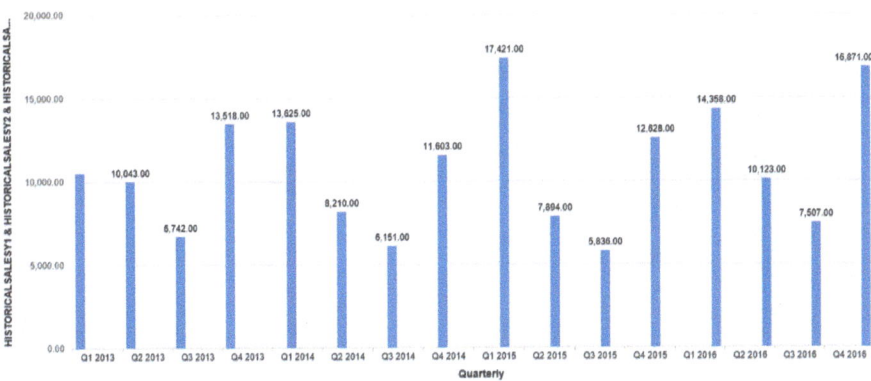

**Fig. 4.44** ANOM by quarters

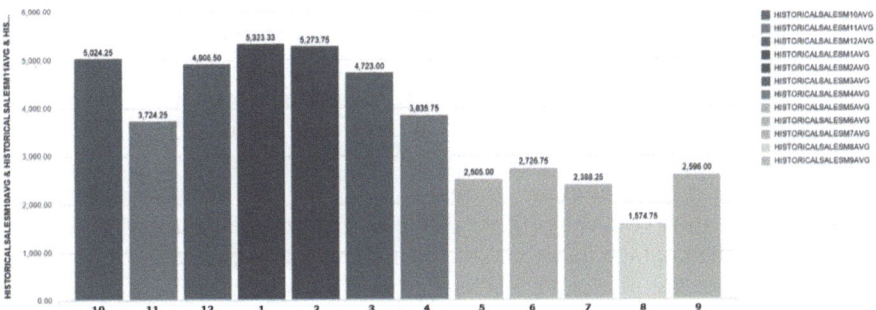

**Fig. 4.45** ANOM by months

the months of the lowest season. Therefore, we were able to unfold the structure of each quarter and inspect the average monthly behavior. For a deeper analysis, a normal scatter plot is the ultimate solution.

On the contrary, as per shown in Fig. 4.46, by increasing the granularity, the practitioner may be able to detect the overall pattern of the selected SKU along the years. The visualization shows the years in the $X$-axis and the yearly average on the $Y$-axis. For example, a decreasing trend is detected among 2013 and 2015, while a consistent growth characterized the year 2016.

Concluding, all those graphical insights may be leveraged by the users and practitioners to evaluate the results out of the standard techniques, but also to complement all types of analysis based on the priority of each SKU or cluster.

*Inputs—Procedure—Outcomes*

Based on the discussed techniques, we were able to configure for this sub-process, a means to proceed with a maximum possible guarantee toward

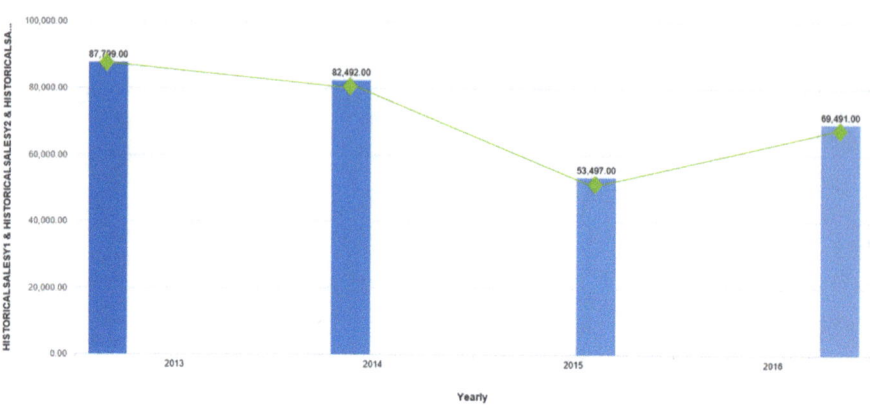

**Fig. 4.46** ANOM by year

accurate results. This does fit into the concept of differentiated forecasting highlighted in (Kepczynski et al., 2018).

The first procedure to be followed is the quantitative one. It is illustrated in Fig. 4.47. The visualization is composed of three main streams:

– Inputs: It consists of selecting the right cluster out of the demand segmentation and classification. Considering we want to analyze the seasonal SKUs, we decided to filter out the flashy and the intermittent categories, while focusing on the stable one. The products considered as stable may contain seasonal patterns, and the purpose of the procedure is to identify exactly those new seasonal clusters.
– Quantitative procedure: It consists of two separate ways of running:

1. Applying the seasonality check via the Moving Average for Seasonal Identification
2. Applying the analysis of variance—ANOVA method.

– Outputs: Based on the procedure, two different matrices are defined as output:

1. The first matrix maps the *ABC* and *XYZ* categories against the clusters "stable and seasonal" and "stable and non-seasonal."
2. The second matrix maps the *ABC* and *XYZ* categories against the clusters "stable and seasonal" and "stable and seasonal trendy," "stable and trendy" and "stable and internal variability."

Besides, as we mentioned during the explanations of each of the techniques, along with the pure quantitative and automated methods we provide a series of qualitative and visual checks that can enhance the effectiveness of the clustering.

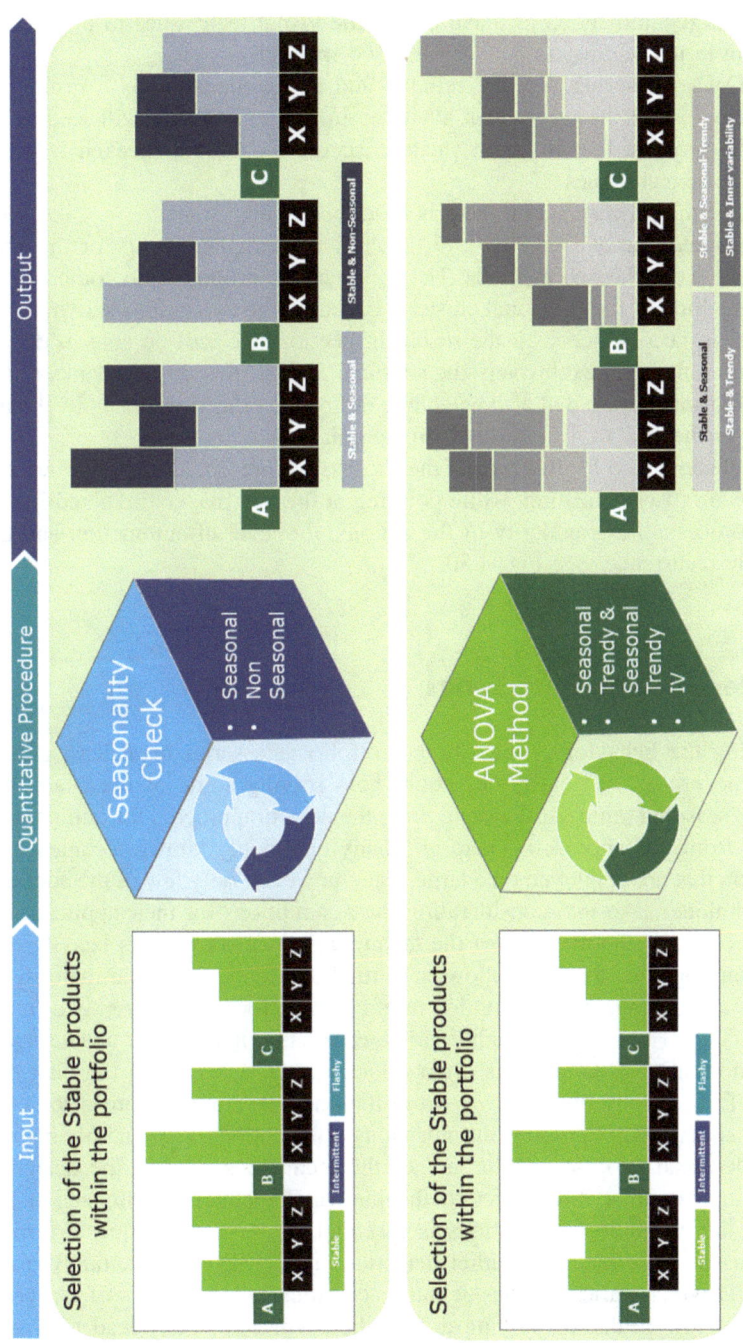

**Fig. 4.47** Analyzing seasonality—quantitative procedure

Furthermore, considering that we have two mathematical methods that we can rely upon, it is recommended to make use of the visual techniques to inspect the differences in terms of clusters between the two methods.

The ANOVA clustering is more reliable and comprehensive; as a result, we suggest to employ all the techniques available in a direction that will lead as an output of this process, four different clusters, accurately double checked with the most appropriate techniques.

This part of the process engineering is described in Fig. 4.48.

The visualization above in Fig. 4.49 displays the template setup for the final comparison between the two methods. The approach we propose is to compare and verify the matching of the "seasonal cluster." Based on the two graphs shown in the template and in accordance with the visual inspection, we will be able to defy a robust cluster containing exclusively the seasonal SKUs. In addition, thanks to the ANOVA performance, we will also be able to define the other clusters and validate, store and save the ANOVA column of this template.

As a conclusion, also for this part of the process we present all the concatenated steps in a waterfall visualization, while pointing at the key players involved in this part of the process, the granularity of the actions, the level of automation and the most suitable recurrence. See Fig. 4.50.

## 4.3 Understanding Data Series

Understanding the behavior of the whole portfolio data series or at least cluster them in some pre-defined categories could help solving some of the headaches linked to the seasonal topic. At the same time, the detection process for outliers will also benefit from this approach. There are many commonly known techniques to detect outliers that are employed on a large scale; however, only few of the adopters of those techniques take into consideration the assumptions for their applications.

More specifically, the majority of the techniques to detect outliers heavily rely on the assumptions that the data follows a normal distribution. For the majority of the SKUs of a company, that assumption might be true, for instance trendy or inner variable products. However, for highly variable, volatile, intermittent and seasonal SKUs, the normality assumption is often difficult to be accepted as the data distributes itself in a totally different way from the ones we are accustomed to.

The consequences of ignoring the normality assumptions without running the checks needed lead to false insights out of the techniques used in the detection processes. For example, if we refer to the known $Z$ method, the impact of not considering the normality assumptions is essential, as those techniques are most commonly used in the realm of outlier detection and correction. Eventually, for a seasonal SKU which varies in sales/demand according to the periods of the years with high and low peaks, employing a $Z$ method will completely lead to wrong results in the detection phase; the correction step will suffer as a consequence, and the overall forecasting process will result poorer in accuracy.

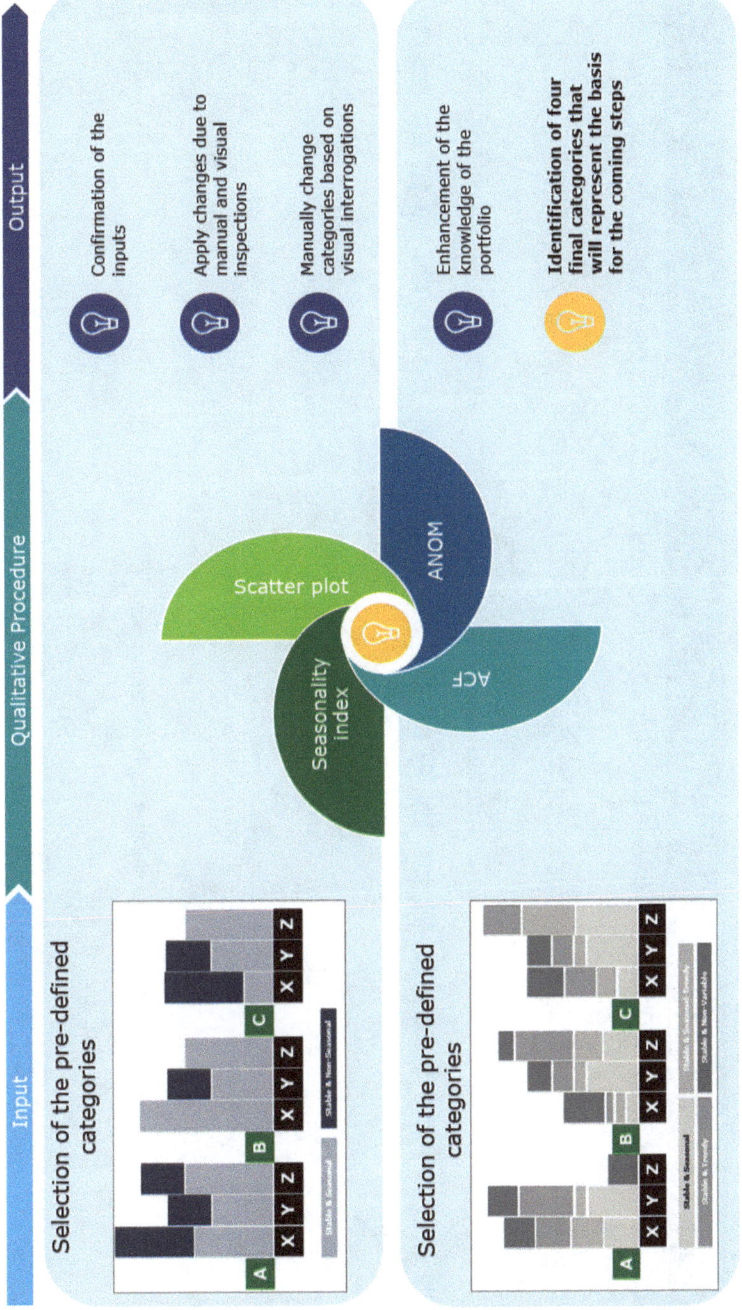

**Fig. 4.48** Analyzing seasonality—qualitative procedure

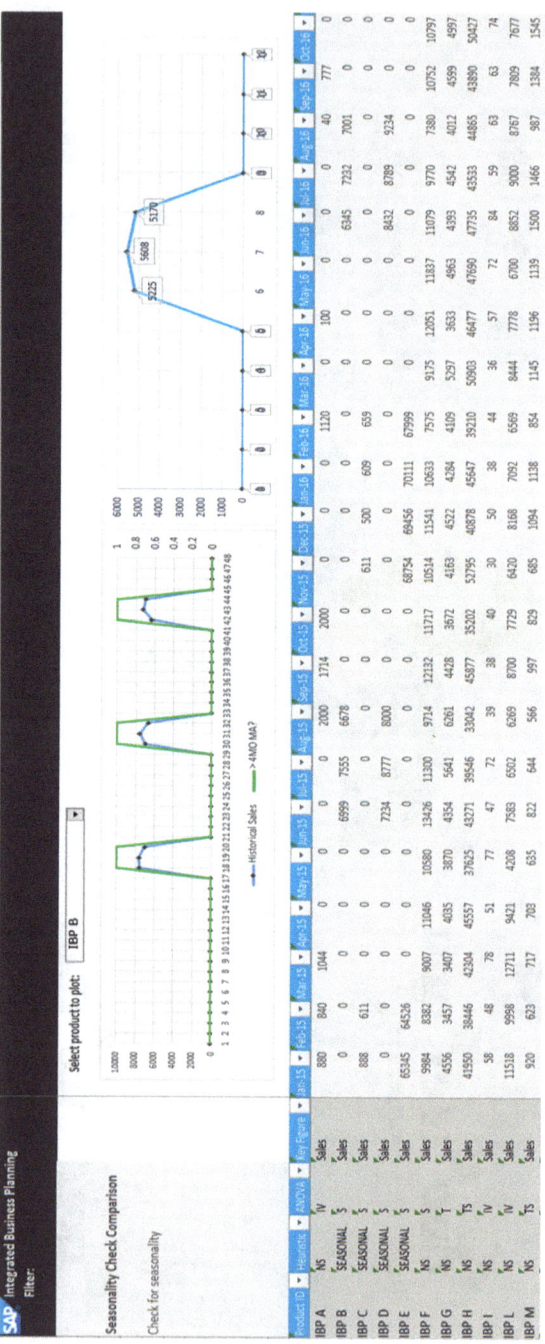

**Fig. 4.49** SAP IBP quantitative methods' comparison

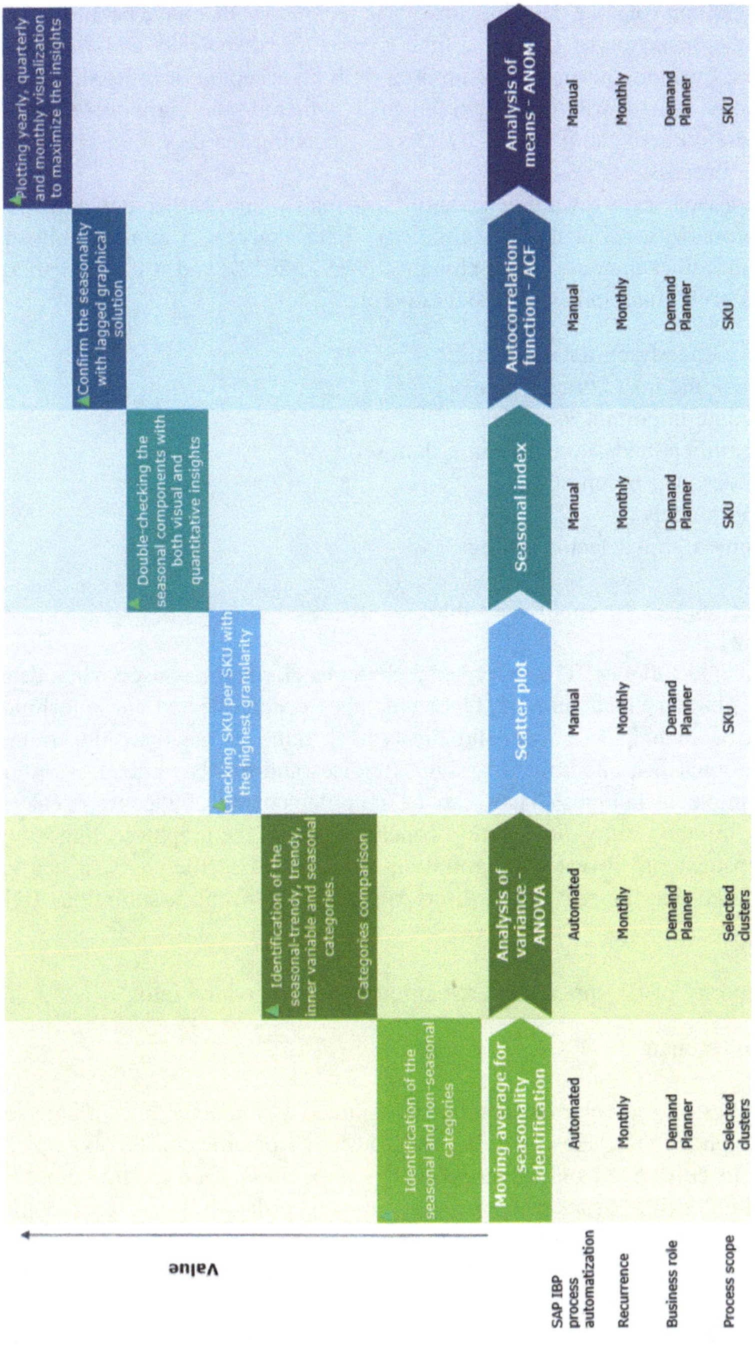

**Fig. 4.50** Analyzing seasonality—waterfall

Having set the basis for understanding why the normality assumption covers such an important role, we describe now some techniques that have been configured to detect the behavior of the data, their symmetry, dispersion and finally their distribution. Once the normality assumption will be accepted or refused, and some insights about the distributions will be also gathered, the right techniques for detecting the outliers can be perfectly chosen, reducing the degree of errors in the forecasting process.

The approach used toward normality, seasonality and outlier detection is the EDA, exploratory data analysis. Exploratory data analysis is more a philosophy toward data, rather than a set of techniques (NIST, 2012), and it uses a variety of techniques both quantitative and qualitative to:

1. Uncover underlying data structures
2. Maximize the insights of a data set
3. Extrapolate important variables
4. Detect outliers and anomalies in a data set
5. Test underlying assumptions
6. Develop models
7. Determine optimal factor settings.

EDA techniques are subdivided into:

- Graphical techniques: The graphical techniques are the most used when dealing with exploratory data analysis. Once data have been collected, these techniques should be of help to understand the typical value of the data, uncertainties, distributional fits, effect factors, signals, noises and finally outliers.
- Quantitative techniques: They can be complementary of the graphical techniques, but they can yield different conclusions than the graphics, suggesting as a consequence to invest some more efforts. In most of the cases, it has to be highlighted that the reasons of discrepancies lie in wrong assumptions (NIST, 2012).

The majority of the quantitative techniques are subdivided into:

1. Interval estimation

In statistics, it is a common practice to estimate a parameter from a data set or from a sample of data. However, the most accurate parameters, for example, the "mean," can be derived only over the entire population. Due to the complexity, unavailability or time issues of considering all the population data, a good common practice is to rely on the sample data by defining what is normally called the "estimation," for our example, of the mean. The interval estimation adds to the uncertainty linked to this estimation by adding an upper and lower limit to the possible values of the parameter approximated. A comparison in the business world appears as follows:

– Let's assume we use a sample data for a specific SKU of 36 periods. This is not the entire population data, but only those available for our estimation of the parameters. Secondly, let's assume we want to extrapolate the "mean" of the data and consequently forecast the next period with a moving average algorithm.
– Due to the fact that both mean and forecast are estimated from the sample, their estimation will be surrounded by upper and lower limits.

2. Hypothesis testing

Hypothesis tests also address the uncertainty of the sample estimate. However, instead of providing an interval, a hypothesis test attempts to refuse a specific claim about a population parameter based on the sample data. For example, the hypothesis might be one of the following:

- The population mean is equal to 100.
- The population standard deviation is equal to 2.5.
- The means from two populations are equal.
- The standard deviations from 10 populations are equal.

In our case, we will focus our attention on population where the data are normally distributed.

To reject a hypothesis means making the conclusion that it is false. However, to accept a hypothesis does not mean that it is true, only that we do not have enough evidence to believe otherwise. Thus, hypothesis tests are usually stated in terms of both a condition that is doubted (null hypothesis) and a condition that is believed (alternative hypothesis).

A common format for a hypothesis test is:

| $H_0$: | A statement of the null hypothesis: for example, a population is normally distributed |
|---|---|
| $H_a$: | A statement of the alternative hypothesis: for example, a population is not normally distributed |
| Test statistic: | The test statistic is based on the specific hypothesis test |
| Significance level: | The significance level, $\alpha$, defines the sensitivity of the test. A value of $\alpha = 0.05$ means that we inadvertently reject the null hypothesis 5% of the time when it is in fact true. This is also called the type I error. The choice of $\alpha$ is arbitrary, although in practice values of 0.1, 0.05 and 0.01 are commonly used<br><br>The probability of rejecting the null hypothesis, when it is in fact false, is called the power of the test and is denoted by $1 - \beta$. Its complement, the probability of accepting the null hypothesis when the alternative hypothesis is, in fact, true (type II error), is called $\beta$ and can only be computed for a specific alternative hypothesis |
| Critical region: | The critical region encompasses those values of the test statistics that lead to a rejection of the null hypothesis. Based on the distribution of the test statistic and the significance level, a cut-off value for the test statistic is computed. Values either above or below or both (depending on the direction of the test) this cut-off define the critical region |

Consequently, we can realize how the analysis of variance method, ANOVA, is actually an hypothesis test!

It is important to distinguish between statistical significance and practical significance. Statistical significance simply means that we reject the null hypothesis. The ability of the test to detect differences that lead to rejection of the null hypothesis depends on the sample size. For example, for a particularly large sample, the test may reject the null hypothesis that the population is normally distributed. However, in practice the difference between normality and non-normality may be relatively small to the point of having no real engineering significance. Similarly, if the sample size is small, a difference that is large in engineering terms may not lead to rejection of the null hypothesis. The practitioner should not just blindly apply the tests, but should combine engineering judgment with statistical analysis (NIST, 2012).

This is the reason why, it is always advisable, to collect as much data as possible; in our case, it could be historical sales data, paying attention at the goodness of the data collected. The engineering judgment can be easily transposed to the "external" or the "market" judgments that a company possess internally. Once again, the combination of first level statistics and qualitative inputs reveals itself as a key success factor!

Before moving in detail to the next step, as a conclusion for this introduction we report in Fig. 4.51 the list of the quantitative automated and qualitative–visual techniques that will help us to understand data distribution and normality assumptions.

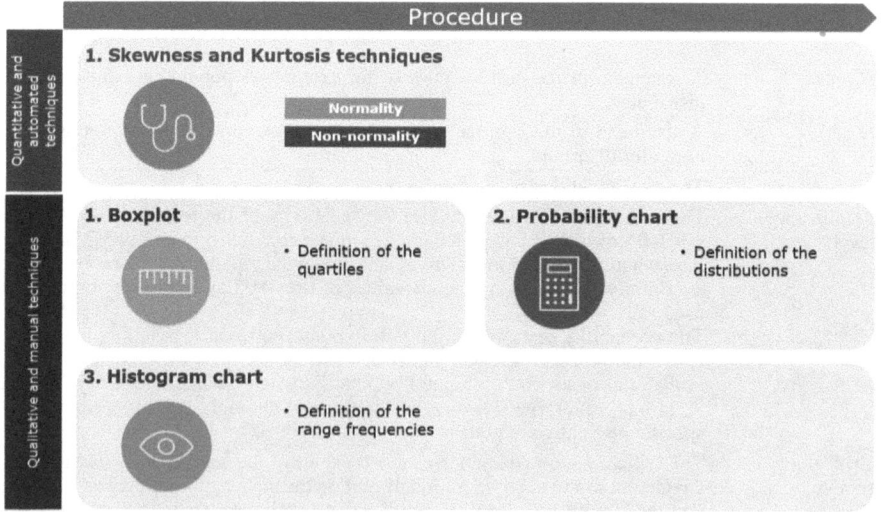

**Fig. 4.51** Understanding data series—steps

*Skewness*

The next step of the process will then go into the matter of understanding the data distributions and the general behavior of each data set in order to assess the most suitable techniques for the future steps of the forecasting process.

The first recommended action for this field of the analysis is the skewness indicator:

– From data standpoint, the skewness is a measure of the asymmetry of the probability distribution of a random variable around its mean.
– From a business point of view, skewness means trying to assess if the data considered are symmetric and consequently assess if half of the data are plotted below the mean and the other half above the mean. Is the sales/demand of our SKU condensed around its mean? Are there many zero points that trigger the fact that the data are focusing in the sector below the mean? Are we having exceptional sales leading the data to be much higher than the mean?

The skewness analysis leads to the calculation of the skew index. It can be positive, negative or zero:

– If it is zero, the distribution is symmetric.
– If it is less than zero, the tail on the left side is longer or fatter than the right side.
– If it is greater than zero, vice versa.

The skew index is calculated as follows, where $n$ is the sample size and $s$ the standard deviation:

$$a = \frac{\sum (X_i - \overline{X})^3}{n * s^3}$$

Figure 4.52 displays how typically we could benefit from a graphical analysis of the kurtosis. In the upper side of the visualization, the graphic shows how the tail on the right side appears longer or fatter than the left side. Consequently, the skew index suggests that it is highly improbable to expect a normal distribution out of this SKU and it highlights how the mass of the data is concentrated on the left part of the figure, with values lower than the mean.

On the contrary, on the lower side of the figure, we have an extreme right-skewed distribution where the majority of the data are higher than the mean. Its skew index will result in being greater than zero.

## 4.3.1  SAP Use Case: Skewness

From Fig. 4.53, we see the typical skewness template where we are able to differentiate the behavior of the data and classify them into specific clusters:

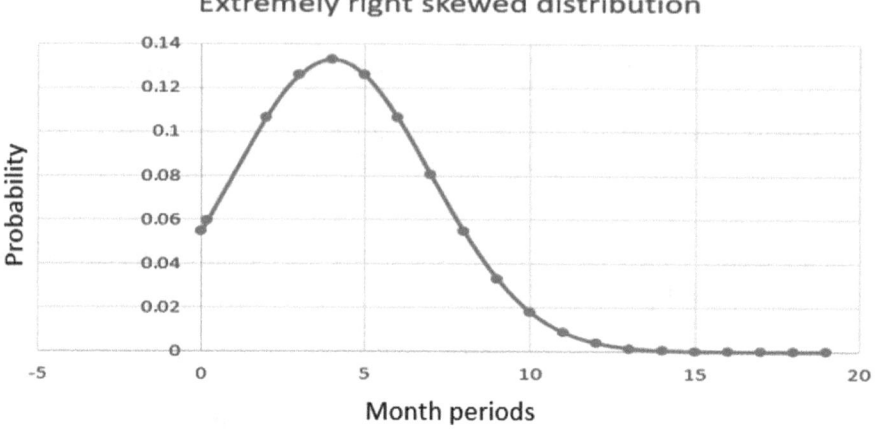

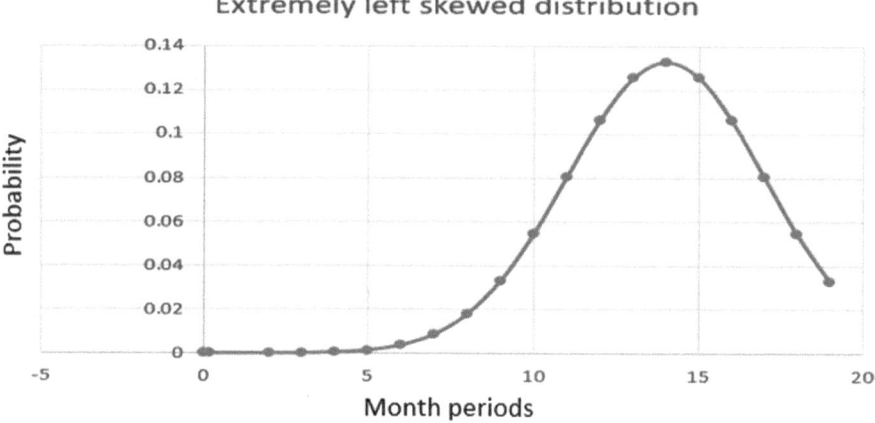

**Fig. 4.52** Left- and right-skewed distribution

- NSH: High Negative Skewness
- NSM: Medium Negative Skewness
- SYM: Symmetric
- PSM: Medium Positive Skewness
- PSH: High Positive Skewness.

For each SKU, the key figure indicates the actual value of the skew index. For example, for the SKU 44005004 the index accounts for 1.0447: maybe a seasonal product?

| Product ID | Skewness | Key Figure | Jan-13 | Feb-13 | Mar-13 | Apr-13 | May-13 |
|---|---|---|---|---|---|---|---|
| IBP A | POSITIVE SKEW HIGH | Skewness (for VIZ) | 2.3381 | 2.3381 | 2.3381 | 2.3381 | 2.3381 |
| IBP B | POSITIVE SKEW HIGH | Skewness (for VIZ) | 1.3453 | 1.3453 | 1.3453 | 1.3453 | 1.3453 |
| IBP C | POSITIVE SKEW HIGH | Skewness (for VIZ) | 1.0409 | 1.0409 | 1.0409 | 1.0409 | 1.0409 |
| IBP D | POSITIVE SKEW HIGH | Skewness (for VIZ) | 1.4291 | 1.4291 | 1.4291 | 1.4291 | 1.4291 |
| IBP E | POSITIVE SKEW HIGH | Skewness (for VIZ) | 1.0954 | 1.0954 | 1.0954 | 1.0954 | 1.0954 |
| IBP F | SYMMETRIC | Skewness (for VIZ) | -0.0938 | -0.0938 | -0.0938 | -0.0938 | -0.0938 |
| IBP G | POSITIVE SKEW MEDIUM | Skewness (for VIZ) | 0.6364 | 0.6364 | 0.6364 | 0.6364 | 0.6364 |
| IBP H | SYMMETRIC | Skewness (for VIZ) | -0.0805 | -0.0805 | -0.0805 | -0.0805 | -0.0805 |
| IBP I | POSITIVE SKEW HIGH | Skewness (for VIZ) | 1.2752 | 1.2752 | 1.2752 | 1.2752 | 1.2752 |
| IBP L | POSITIVE SKEW MEDIUM | Skewness (for VIZ) | 0.7225 | 0.7225 | 0.7225 | 0.7225 | 0.7225 |
| IBP M | POSITIVE SKEW MEDIUM | Skewness (for VIZ) | 0.8971 | 0.8971 | 0.8971 | 0.8971 | 0.8971 |

**Fig. 4.53** SAP IBP skewness table

*Kurtosis*

The second step toward understanding the behavior of the data will be to check for the data kurtosis in order to have a first insight if the data may follow or not a normal distribution.

The kurtosis formula is the following, where $n$ indicates the sample size and $s$ the standard deviation of the sample:

$$k = \frac{\sum (X_i - \overline{X})^4}{n * s^4}$$

– If $k$ is equal to 3, the distribution is similar to a normal one and it is said mesokurtic.
– If $k$ is greater than 3, the distribution is more dispersed than a normal one and it is said leptokurtic.
– If $k$ is lower than 3, the distribution is less dispersed than a normal one and it is called platykurtic.

In Fig. 4.54, it is possible to distinguish more or less dispersed distributions keeping as an indicator the kurtosis index equals to 3. For example, the green bell is less dispersed than a normal distribution suggesting that the great majority of the data are centered on the mean, and consequently, their variations might be very low. On the contrary, for the violet bell, the dispersion of the data is much higher, leading to the consideration that there might be quite a lot of fluctuations in the data points.

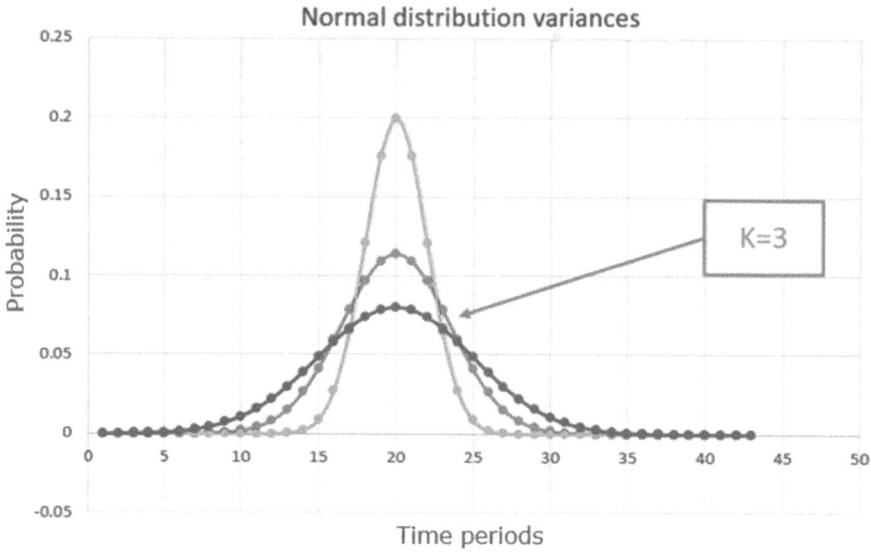

**Fig. 4.54** Normal distribution variances applied to the kurtosis index

From a practical point of view, a practitioner can derive from this index whether the sales/demand of a SKU or of a cluster of SKUs that share a similar kurtosis index is immediately dispersed from its mean or if there are a lot of data whose values make them going far away from the central mean value.

For example, a normal dispersed distribution could indicate a stable sales/demand product with a trend or inner cyclicality. A less than a normal dispersed distribution suggests a stable product where probably the sales/demand throughout the period is so steady that even by applying a simple average forecasting model, an optimal forecast accuracy could be reached.

A bit trickier is the scenario where the data are more dispersed than in a normal distribution. Those type of data could have a high variability, very seasonal or not stable at all. Flashy, lumpy, intermittent or erratic products would definitely fall in this category.

### 4.3.2   SAP Use Case: Kurtosis

Figure 4.55 suggests, as an instance, a first SKU with an index greater than 5 which implies a distribution more dispersed than a normal one. As a result, the majority of the data seems to have completely different sales/demands very distant from the mean.

| Product ID ▼ | Kurtosis ▼ | Key Figure ▼ | Jan-13 ▼ | Feb-13 ▼ | Mar-13 ▼ | Apr-13 ▼ | May-13 ▼ |
|---|---|---|---|---|---|---|---|
| IBP A | LEPTYKURTIC | Kurtosis (for VIZ) | 5.4454 | 5.4454 | 5.4454 | 5.4454 | 5.4454 |
| IBP B | PLATYKURTIC | Kurtosis (for VIZ) | -0.1772 | -0.1772 | -0.1772 | -0.1772 | -0.1772 |
| IBP C | PLATYKURTIC | Kurtosis (for VIZ) | -0.6816 | -0.6816 | -0.6816 | -0.6816 | -0.6816 |
| IBP D | PLATYKURTIC | Kurtosis (for VIZ) | 0.1940 | 0.1940 | 0.1940 | 0.1940 | 0.1940 |
| IBP E | PLATYKURTIC | Kurtosis (for VIZ) | -0.5871 | -0.5871 | -0.5871 | -0.5871 | -0.5871 |
| IBP F | PLATYKURTIC | Kurtosis (for VIZ) | 0.4480 | 0.4480 | 0.4480 | 0.4480 | 0.4480 |
| IBP G | PLATYKURTIC | Kurtosis (for VIZ) | 0.5454 | 0.5454 | 0.5454 | 0.5454 | 0.5454 |
| IBP H | PLATYKURTIC | Kurtosis (for VIZ) | -0.2216 | -0.2216 | -0.2216 | -0.2216 | -0.2216 |
| IBP I | PLATYKURTIC | Kurtosis (for VIZ) | 2.9680 | 2.9680 | 2.9680 | 2.9680 | 2.9680 |
| IBP L | PLATYKURTIC | Kurtosis (for VIZ) | 0.9663 | 0.9663 | 0.9663 | 0.9663 | 0.9663 |
| IBP M | PLATYKURTIC | Kurtosis (for VIZ) | 0.0638 | 0.0638 | 0.0638 | 0.0638 | 0.0638 |

**SAP** Integrated Business Planning
Filter:

**Kurtosis**

Results summary

**Fig. 4.55** SAP IBP kurtosis analysis

## 4.4   Checking Normality Assumption

Figure 4.56 displays how it is possible to leverage skewness and kurtosis to derive
our new outputs for the process. As it is possible to see, for the normality inspection
we need to provide the right inputs: The SKUs that will have to undergo the
inspection are most likely the stable and seasonal and the stable and seasonal
trendy. Up to now, considering the focus of our digression on the seasonal products,
we will only go further for this specific segments; however, with the right
assumptions and logic, the same approach could be conducted for all the portfolio
clusters defined so far.

Once the clusters have been identified, the products will be inspected by the
skewness and kurtosis tests. Based on a specific condition, the outputs will be two
distinguished categories:

- If the skewness index "$a$" is comprised between $-0.5$ and $0.5$ and the kurtosis
  index "$k$" is lower than 3, the SKU can be considered as if it follows a normal
  distribution.
- Otherwise, if the skewness index "$a$" is inferior to $-0.5$ or greater than $0.5$, and
  the kurtosis index "$k$" greater than 3, the SKU can be stated as not following the
  normal distribution.

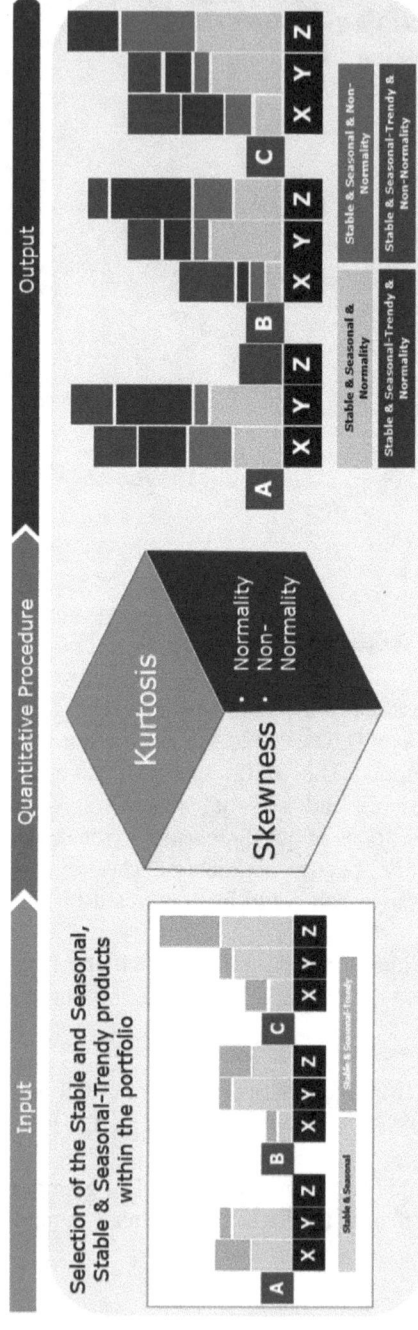

**Fig. 4.56** Checking normality assumptions—quantitative procedure

The reasoning behind it is associated with the meaning of the very techniques. Allowing the data to be comprised near the 0, for the "$a$" index, and around or inferior to the value 3 for the "$k$" may suggest normality, while for all the conditions we will refuse the normality assumption.

### 4.4.1 SAP Use Case: Normality Assumption Conditions

The results of the normality filtering conditions and settings are visualized in Fig. 4.57. Next to the previous categories, we had been able to identify in the previous stages, and we can add the normality assumption key figure where the results of this specific check are stored. As we may see from the visualization not all the seasonal or seasonal trendy SKU are marked as "normal," consequently for those, the detection and correction technique will be adapted considering the normality assumption.

Moving forward and as it happened already for the previous phases of the process, we were able to combine, complement or juxtapose to the more quantitative techniques also a series of visual and qualitative techniques that may come in help to the practitioners to solve issues and diving into the investigation mode.

The input for the qualitative checking is the new matrix defined by the normality and non-normality clusters. The output will be a more solid and robust clustering that will be at the basis of the coming process steps. See Fig. 4.58.

**SAP** Integrated Business Planning
Filter:

| Product ID | ABC Code | XYZ Code | SIF CODE | STMN Code | Normality Assumption |
|------------|----------|----------|----------|-----------|----------------------|
| IBP A | A | Z | INTERMITTENT | SEASONAL | NOT NORMAL |
| IBP B | A | Z | INTERMITTENT | SEASONAL | NOT NORMAL |
| IBP C | A | Z | INTERMITTENT | SEASONAL | NOT NORMAL |
| IBP D | A | Z | INTERMITTENT | TREND-SEASONAL | NOT NORMAL |
| IBP E | A | Z | INTERMITTENT | TREND-SEASONAL | NOT NORMAL |
| IBP F | A | Z | INTERMITTENT | TREND-SEASONAL | NOT NORMAL |
| IBP G | A | X | STABLE | SEASONAL | NORMAL |
| IBP H | A | X | STABLE | SEASONAL | NORMAL |
| IBP I | A | X | STABLE | SEASONAL | NORMAL |
| IBP L | B | X | STABLE | TREND | NOT NORMAL |
| IBP M | B | X | STABLE | TREND | NOT NORMAL |
| IBP N | B | X | STABLE | TREND | NOT NORMAL |
| IBP O | A | X | STABLE | TREND-SEASONAL | NORMAL |
| IBP P | A | X | STABLE | TREND-SEASONAL | NORMAL |
| IBP Q | A | X | STABLE | TREND-SEASONAL | NORMAL |
| IBP R | B | Y | STABLE | INTERNAL VARIABILITY | NOT NORMAL |
| IBP S | B | Y | STABLE | INTERNAL VARIABILITY | NOT NORMAL |

**Fig. 4.57** SAP IBP normal versus not-normal SKUs

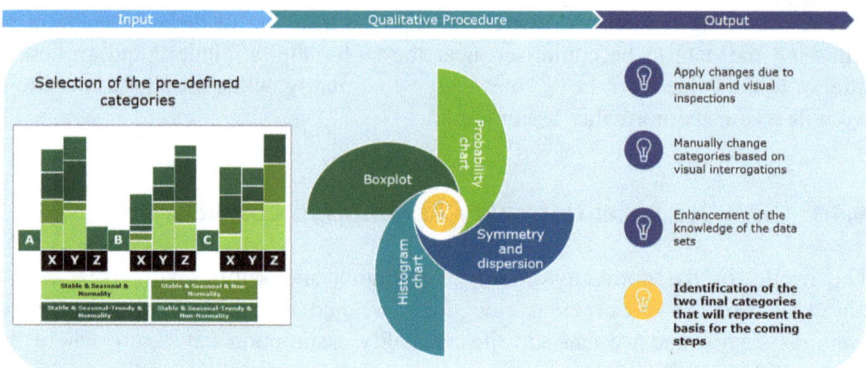

**Fig. 4.58** Checking normality assumption—qualitative procedure

*Box plot*

The visual inspection makes the use of three combined techniques to assess the actual distribution of the data and then take advantage of the results to tailor suite the best clusters and techniques for the further steps of the process.

The first technique is the box plot. Box plots are an excellent tool for conveying positioning and variation information in data sets, particularly for detecting and illustrating positioning and variation changes between different groups of data.

A box plot requires to:

- Calculate the median and the quartiles (the lower quartile is the 25th percentile and the upper quartile is the 75th percentile).
- Plot a symbol at the median and draw a box between the lower and upper quartiles; this box represents the middle 50% of the data which is considered the "body" or the "bulk" of the data.
- Draw a line from the lower quartile to the minimum point and another line from the upper quartile to the maximum point. Typically, a symbol is drawn at these minimum and maximum points, although this is optional.

With the objective of identifying the data distribution, the box plot can help understanding where the majority of the data fits on a schema delimited by an upper limit (MAX) and a lower limit (MIN).

For example, if the majority of the data fall in the middle of the box plot, we could start assuming a normal distribution or an Erlang distribution; if they fall in the lower part of the graph, we could assume instead an exponential distribution.

When we are not certain of where the data exactly fit in the box plot, the lognormal transformation is recommended to double check if the data may be normal or exponential distributed.

It has to be reminded that a box plot is a graphical tool that needs to be coupled with a probability chart in order to suggest with more accuracy the type of distribution.

### 4.4.2 SAP Use Case: Box Plot

Figure 4.59 underlines, on the left, as the majority of the data are distributed on the lower part of the box plot. It gives us the idea of an exponential distribution or at least a distribution where the bulk of the data have values lower than the mean. However, it is certain that the data cannot respect the normality assumption. While, on the right, the normality assumption may be accepted in a first rough analysis.

Consequently, based on this graphical representation the practitioner could confirm or refuse the previous clusters or get a clearer picture.

*Probability chart*

As a second step, a probability chart is run. A probability chart allows to plot experimental points. In the $X$-axis, there are the values of the variable in question, and in the $Y$-axis, the probabilities are plotted. These charts are built in a way in which the cumulative probability is a straight line. For example, if the data lie as a line, it means that the data follow the normal distribution assumed.

Probability charts exist for normal, Weibull, lognormal and exponential distributions.

The data are sorted in ascendant order from 1 to $n$, and every point is associated with a probability. Furthermore, there are many different methods to calculate the probability. Below some examples:

White method for probability definition:

$$F(x_j) = \frac{j - 3/8}{n + 0.25}$$

Medium range for probability definition:

$$F(x_j) = \frac{j - 0.3}{n + 0.4}$$

It is common to run a probability plot as a following step for detecting normality. The data are plotted against a theoretical distribution in such a way that the points should form approximately a straight line. Any departures from the straight line indicate departures from the specific distribution. To come back to our example, the distribution we assume is the normal one.

Figure 4.60 indicates the specific patterns for four different distributions. For example, the normal distribution is expected when a straight line is plotted; the other patterns are reported below.

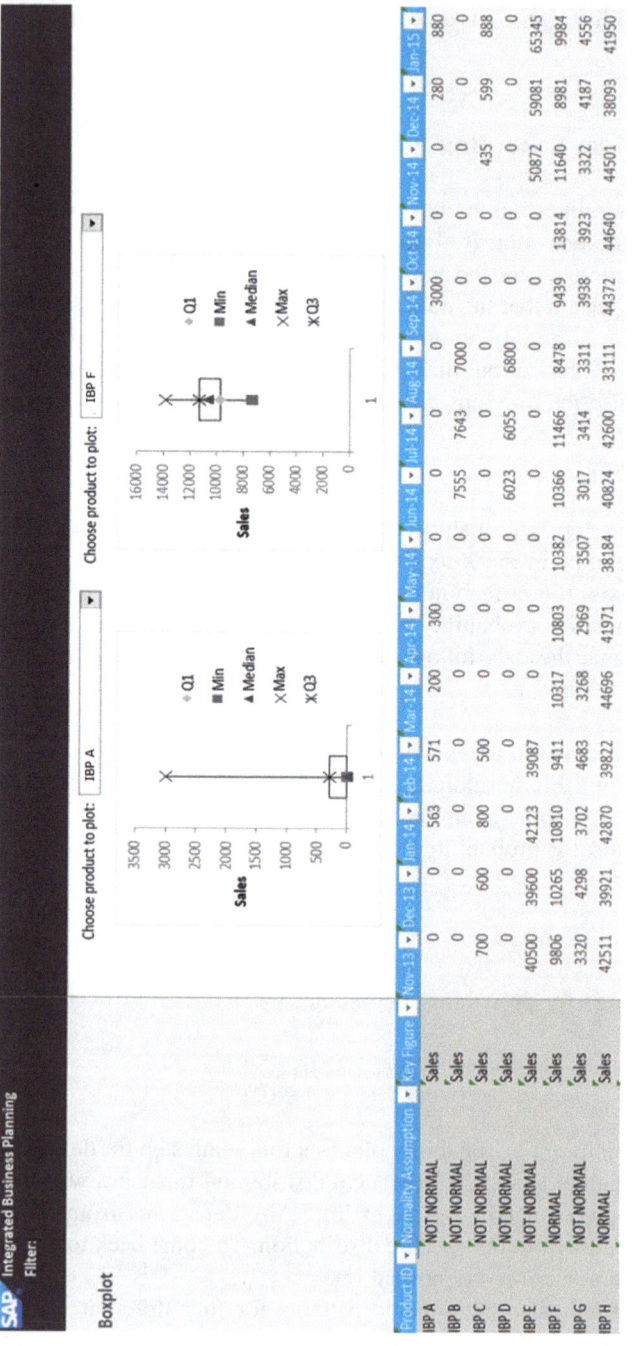

**Fig. 4.59** SAP IBP box plot

**Fig. 4.60**  Probability charts versus types of distributions

### 4.4.3  SAP Use Case: Probability Chart

Figure 4.61 represents the probability chart of two specific SKUs taken from the portfolio of the data available. The first SKU plotted on the left seems to suggest an exponential behavior as the majority of the data concentrates near the value 0. While, the SKU on the right has a much more stable probability chart whose approximation can be considered as straight as the trend line. Consequently, a normal behavior may be assumed by this SKU.

*Histogram analysis*

To complete the assessment of a distribution, the histogram analysis is conducted. A histogram analysis is a graphical representation of the distribution of numerical data. It is composed of the following steps:

- Bin the range of values.
- Divide the entire range of the historical values into a series of intervals.
- Count how many historical data fit into each interval.
- Plot the historical sales frequency for each interval.

Figure 4.62 illustrates in the same visualization the most common frequency histograms per type of distributions.

For example, the normal distribution is expected when the data form a sort of bell shape. The Erlang one slightly deviates from the typical straight line. The exponential distribution is typically represented when the highest bar plot in the left

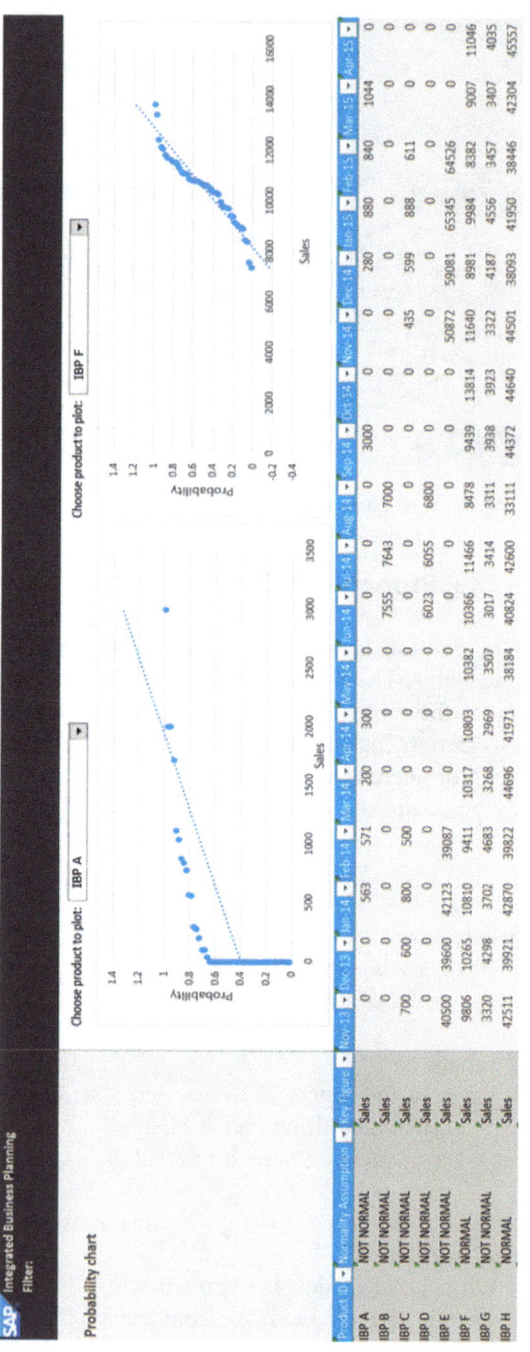

**Fig. 4.61** SAP IBP probability chart

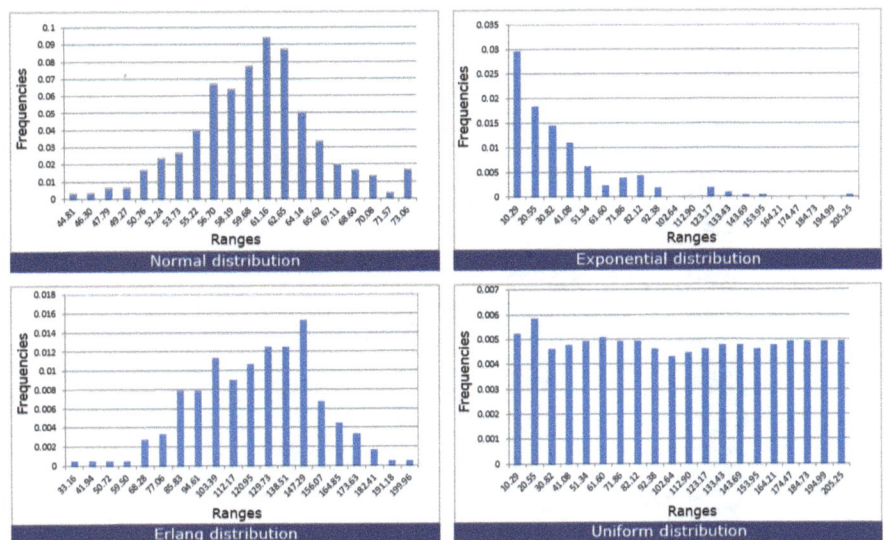

**Fig. 4.62** Frequency histogram versus types of distributions

side of the graph. Eventually, the uniform distribution reveals itself when almost all the bars have the same height throughout all the ranges.

For a planner, it means, for instance, that a uniform distribution can be expected for a stable product with very low variability, and an exponential distribution may be caused by a new product introduction or a flashy one, or intermittent one. The normal distribution as well as the Erlang can lead to very stable product sales/demand where some minor fluctuations may happen.

Eventually, it is crucial to recognize when a data set differs from a normal distribution, for the reasons explained above. This might have a great impact on the coming steps.

### 4.4.4  SAP Use Case: Histogram Analysis

In Fig. 4.63, it is illustrated an example from the SAP IBP system of the frequency histogram. By selecting the chosen SKU, it is then possible to visually analyze the frequency of each sales range. The SKU on the right suggests an exponential distribution, while the one on the right may lead to the normality conclusion.

It is important to remark how, in reality, it is almost impossible to experience an exact behavior of the data as in the theory. Consequently, we should not expect an exact match with the literature graphs, but rather make use of the concepts learnt and develop self-reasoning for interpretation.

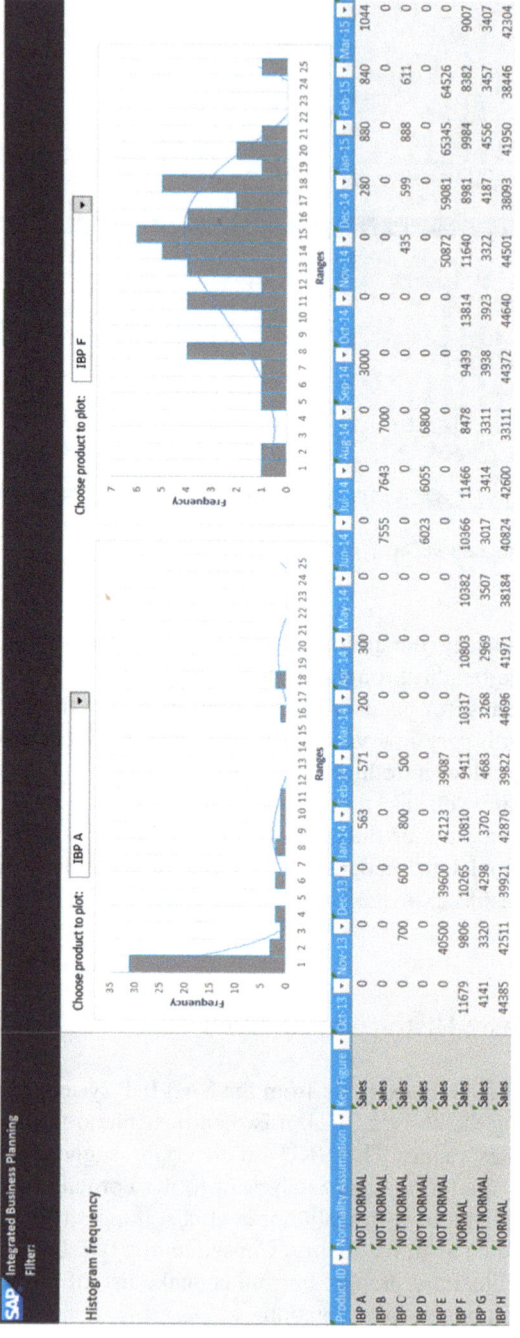

**Fig. 4.63** SAP IBP frequency histogram

*Checking visually the normality assumption*

As a final step, the ideal procedure requires the combination of all the inputs explained so far and makes use of them to take the most effective decisions. In regard to the visual and qualitative techniques, a compound analysis is described below. It should reinforce or validate or even reshuffle the assumptions made on the previous steps, and let the user autonomously proceed with the best knowledge in mind of his/her portfolio.

For example, Fig. 4.64 shows the ideal graphical representations for the normal distribution. When facing a combination of graphs as the ones below, the practitioner can state the validity of the normality assumption based on the theory explained above. The three graphs comply with each other.

Figure 4.65 shows the ideal graphical representations for the exponential distribution. Once again, the user can confirm how the majority of the data analyzed for the specific SKU converge near the value of 0. In all the graphs, the majority of the distribution value points, or the frequency of the points of sales, or the second and third quartile are concentrated on the left.

Figure 4.66 shows the ideal graphical representations for the uniform distribution. This type of distribution suggests an almost constant and low variable frequency of sales data points for all the sorted sales ranges. The three graphs juxtaposed below show how all the data are equally present among the quartiles, ranges or data points.

The final Fig. 4.67 shows the ideal graphical representations for the Erlang distribution. As we can see, it is quite similar to the normal distribution. Considering the demand planning and statistical forecasting purposed, it is reported only for complementary purposes; however, from a user perspective, it does not necessitate a different approach compared to the ones used for the normal distributed data.

Knowing in which quartile the data fits or their frequencies in specific ranges as well as a plotted distribution will help when manual interventions and key decision points will be required in the detection and correction phase of the outliers.

As a conclusion of this phase of the process, we report the typical waterfall chart where we depict the added value steps for understanding the data and checking the normal distribution assumption. As accustomed to, the business role, the recurrence, the automation and the business scope are also indicated (Fig. 4.68).

## 4.4.5 SAP Use Case: Visual Control of Normality Assumption

As we can see from Fig. 4.69, the end user can select in a specified template the particular SKU where he would like to shed some further light. In the example above, by plotting next to each other the three graphical solutions we can agree on the validation and confirmation of the normality assumption.

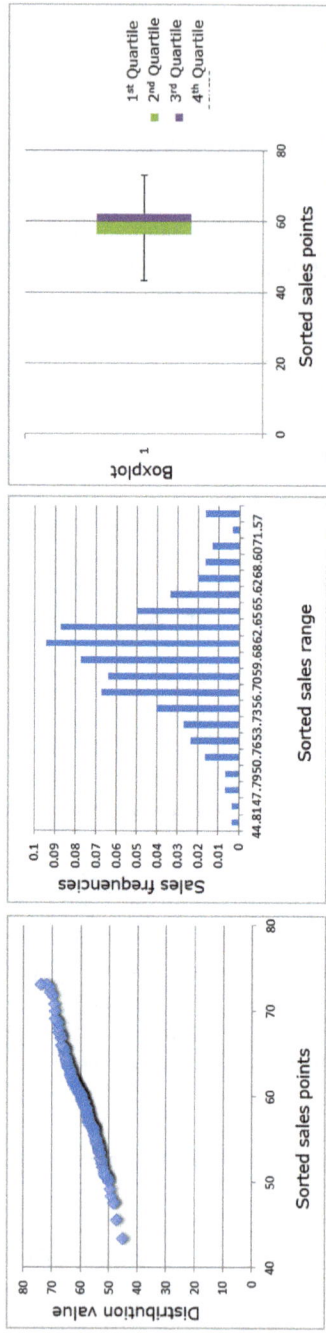

**Fig. 4.64** Normal distribution graphical identification

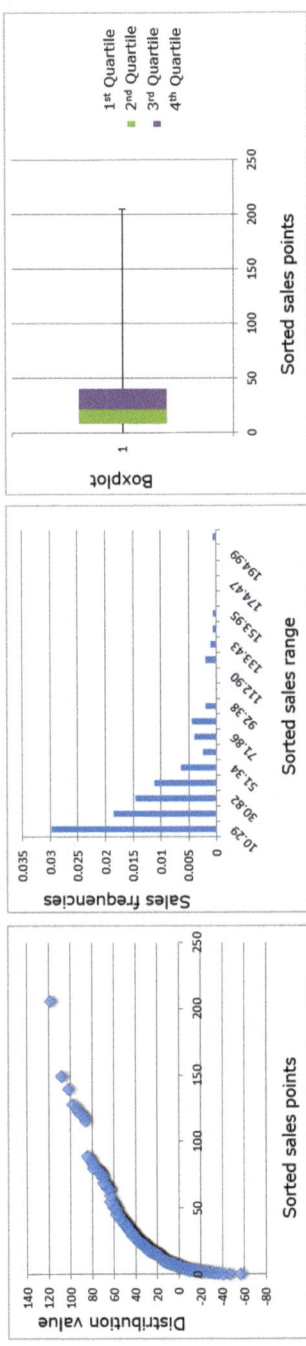

**Fig. 4.65**  Exponential distribution graphical identification

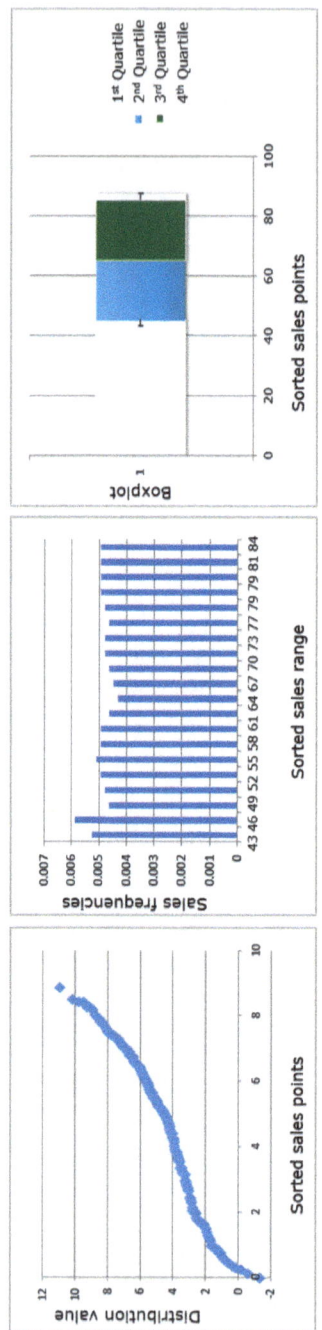

**Fig. 4.66** Uniform distribution graphical identification

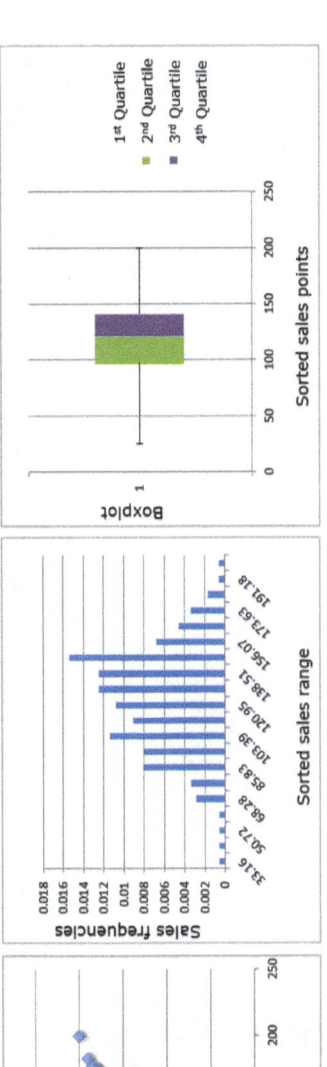

**Fig. 4.67** Erlang distribution graphical identification

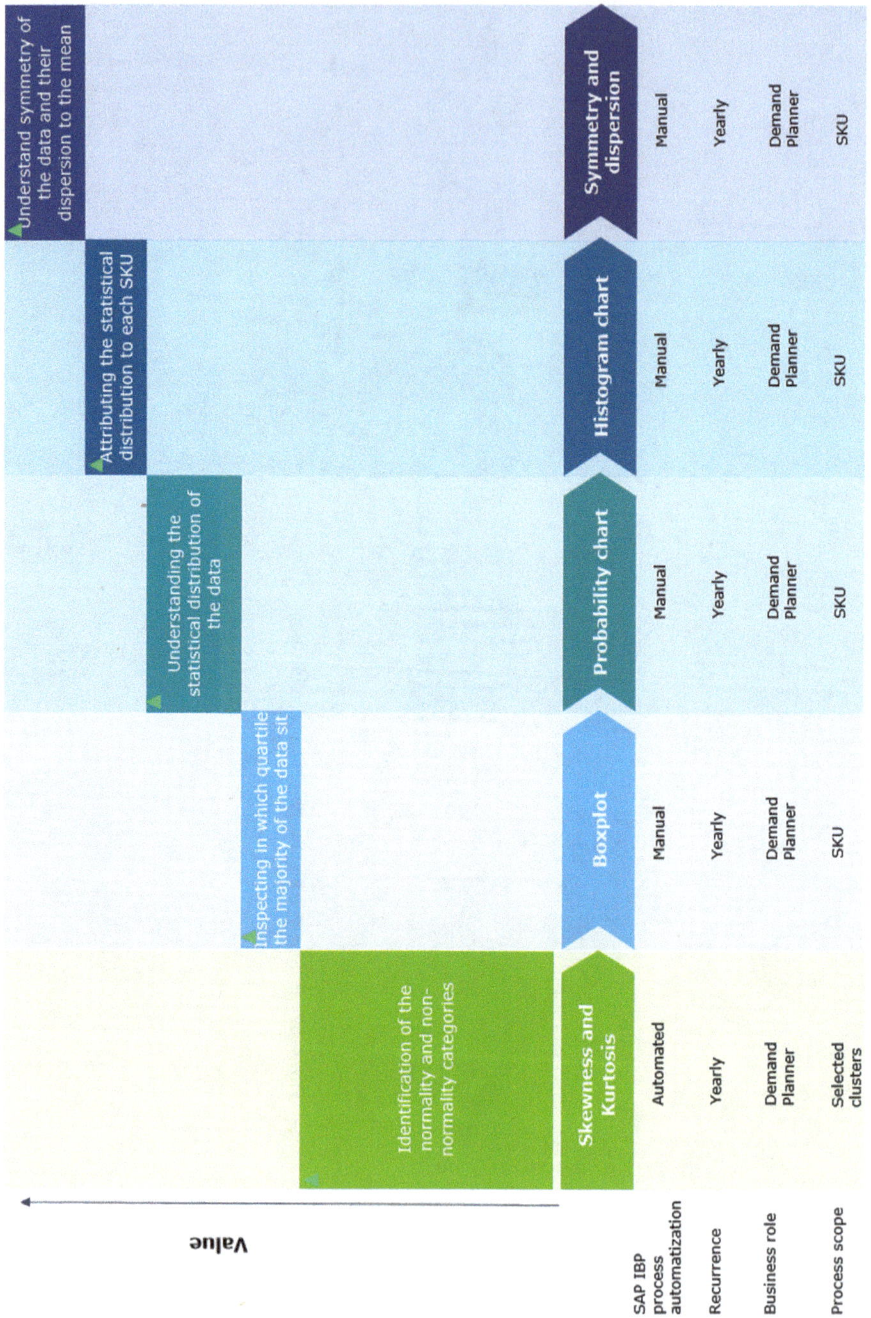

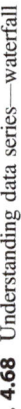

**Fig. 4.68** Understanding data series—waterfall

| | Skewness and Kurtosis | Boxplot | Probability chart | Histogram chart | Symmetry and dispersion |
|---|---|---|---|---|---|
| | Identification of the normality and non-normality categories | Inspecting in which quartile the majority of the data sit | Understanding the statistical distribution of the data | Attributing the statistical distribution to each SKU | Understand symmetry of the data and their dispersion to the mean |
| SAP IBP process automatization | Automated | Manual | Manual | Manual | Manual |
| Recurrence | Yearly | Yearly | Yearly | Yearly | Yearly |
| Business role | Demand Planner | Demand Planner | Demand Planner | Demand Planner | Demand Planner |
| Process scope | Selected clusters | SKU | SKU | SKU | SKU |

Value

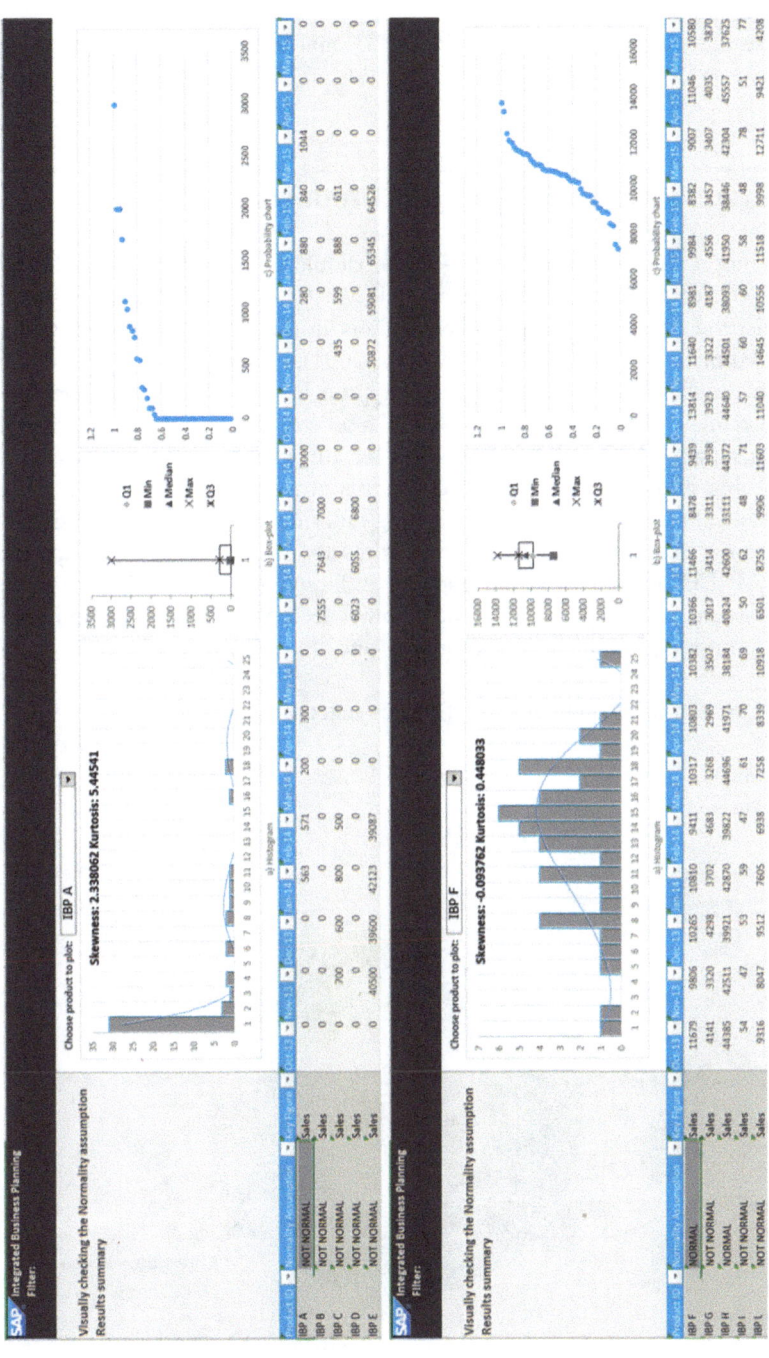

**Fig. 4.69** SAP IBP visual normality assumption check

The upper side of the visualization manifests an exponential distribution, while the lower part a normal one.

As a result, we will proceed with that SKU analyzed clustered as "normally distributed."

## 4.5   Outlier Detection for Seasonal Products

Whether or not a data point in a given sample should be considered as an outlier depends on the underlying distribution model. Most of the samples are assumed normally distributed. Others have studied outliers in the class of exponential distributions (Mittnik, Rachev, & Samorodnitsky, 2001).

In specific, to clarify how the users should approach the field of outlier detection, there will be a set of techniques exclusively reserved for the normal distributed SKUs and a separate group of tests available for all types of distributed data.

Before going into the details and facets of this process step, Fig. 4.70 lists the most suitable techniques available for detecting outlying points. As it is possible to notice from the visualization, the variance test and the interquartile test are marked with the SAP IBP logo; this is the mark to differentiate the current techniques available as standard functionalities and the other techniques that have been configured on purpose to enhance the goodness and the reliability of the detection process.

The new configured techniques are the ones listed below:

– Grubbs' test
– Thompson's test

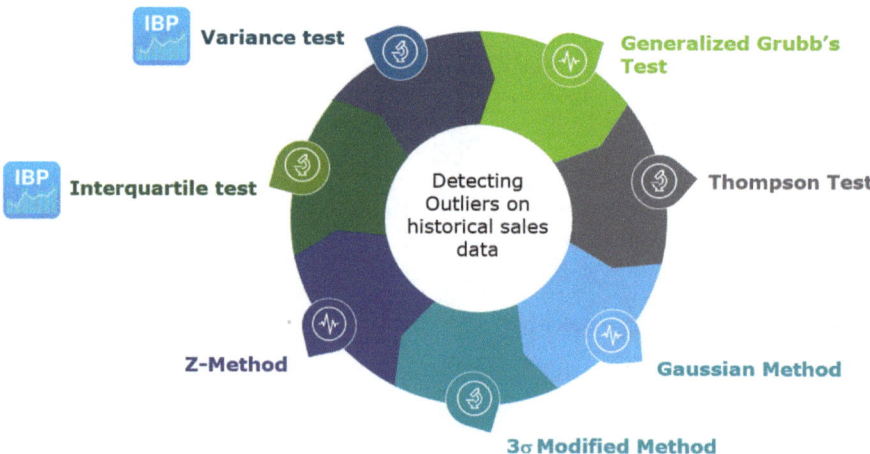

**Fig. 4.70**  Outlier detection techniques

– Gaussian test
– Z method
– 3σ modified method.

Before going in greater detail, let us specify the two clusters defined for the outlier detection techniques. As it has been discussed before, the reliability of the normality assumption has an impact on the outlier technique to be used for a specific product. As a consequence, at this point of time of the custom process, we use two specific categories out of our initial vast portfolio:

1. Non-normal distributed data
2. Normal distributed data.

Based on those two categories, we can assign the most adept outlier techniques:

1. Thompson's test
2. Grubbs' test, $Z$ method, $3\sigma$ modified method, Gaussian method and the other two methods available in the standard functionality.

It is of paramount relevance to assign to each of the two clusters only the viable outlier detection models.

Figure 4.71 illustrates the splitting concept.

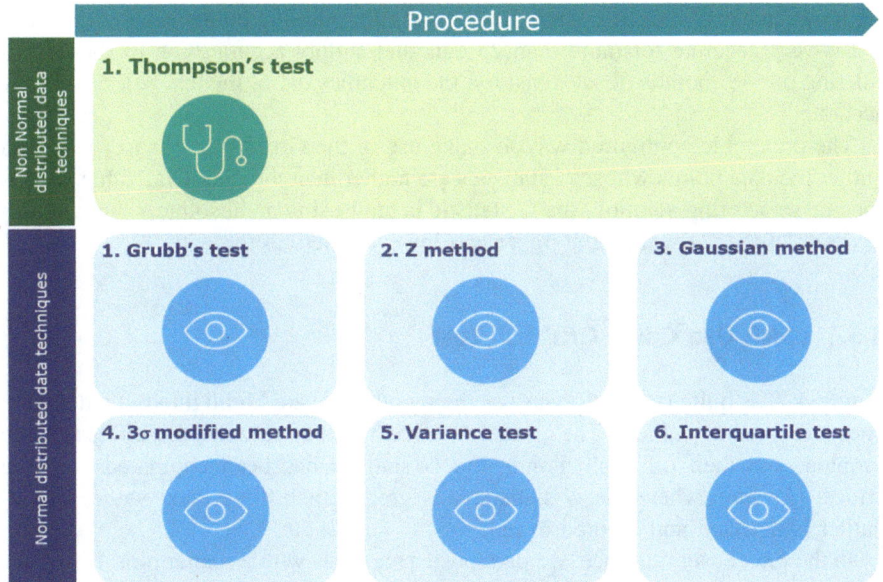

**Fig. 4.71** Outlier detection—normality versus not-normality clusters

Keeping in mind the utilization mode of each the techniques, let's now delve into the detection technicalities and functionalities.

*Grubbs' test*

The Grubbs' test is used to detect a single outlier in a univariate data set that is supposed to follow a normal distribution (NIST, 2012). This test uses rations of two sums of squares (Gunst et al., 2003) (Report of statistics of the statistical engineering division, 2004). Grubbs' test is also known as the maximum normed residual test.

This test allows to identify the maximum or the minimum value as an outlier. Grubbs' test should not be used without a plot of data or a visual inspection. Besides, a small significance level should be used for this test, for example, 0.01.

The way in which the test has been thought and configured is really close to a similar test called generalized extreme studentized deviate (ESD) test. We will not dive into its technicalities, but it is important to ponder over the usefulness of the adjustments applied: The modified Grubbs' technique overcomes the limitations of a simple Grubbs' test, because it is no more required to specify the number of outliers expected, but it is needed only an upper bound for the suspected number of exceptions.

Given an upper bound, "$r$", the modified Grubbs' test essentially performs $r$ separate tests. Essentially, it means that a test is run for one outlier, a second test for two outliers and so on. Considering our data set of 48 periods, the maximum number of testing runs could be, in a really large extend, assigned to 48.

The enhancement in relation to our detecting purposes is quite obvious, as we are now capable of detecting the overall number of outlying points in a data set. The test is very accurate for more than 25 data and simply accurate for 15 data. Considering our 48 months of sales history, the outcomes out of the test will result very accurate.

The preferable configured way to make use of the Grubbs' test is to state as an outlier the data points whose $G$ statistics are higher than the $G$ critical value. In this specific refactoring solution, the $G$ statistic is built using an absolute value in order to detect at the same time the upper and lower outliers in the data.

## 4.5.1 SAP Use Case: Grubbs' Test

Figure 4.72 is quite straightforward as the months that are highlighted in red are the ones identified as outliers. The critical $G$ value has been calculated with its specific formula, and then for each month, the $G$ statistic has been compared with the critical $G$ value, where the $G$ statistic was greater than the critical value, and an outlier is detected and colored in red.

In the Excel user interface, we juxtapose a bar chart with a scatter plot. If we take as an example the SKU that appear in the "select product to plot" field, we immediately see that the sales/demand of the month 19 is considered abnormal from

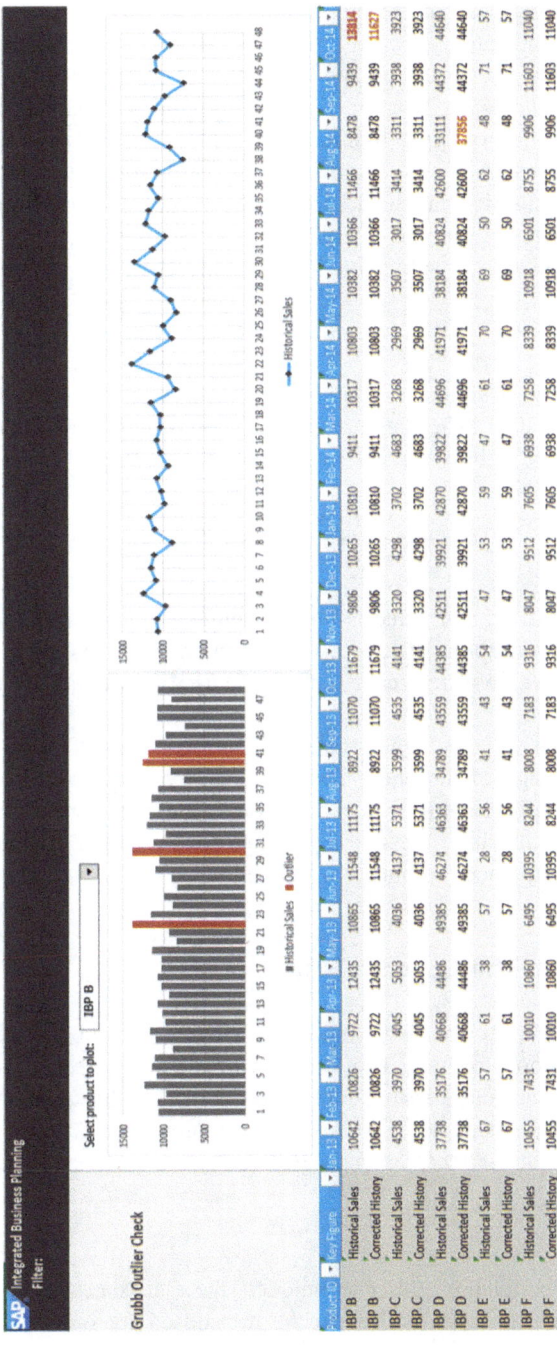

**Fig. 4.72**  SAP IBP Grubbs' method

a data perspective. The scatter plot, employed for its ease in the interpretation, confirms the corresponding peak of the month.

Moreover, Fig. 4.72 indicates per each product the historical sales, whose data are used for the detection of the outliers and the corrected history whose meaning will be discussed later during the chapter. Graphically, and red marked, October 2014 is identified as the first outlying month.

Concluding, the Grubbs' method is thought to be a fundamental mathematical test for detecting outliers as its statistical background combined with its intuitive visualization allow for a practitioner to easily recognize the outlying points without extra manipulation of the data or subjective touches during the run of the test.

*Thompson's test*

Thompson Tau method is similar to Grubbs' test; however, it must be used for non-normally distributed data as it does not rely on the normality assumption.

The Thompson statistic is built on the $\tau$ value:

$$\tau = \frac{t * (n - 1)}{\sqrt{n} * \sqrt{n - 2 + t^2}}$$

The Thompson statistic critical value is built by multiplying the standard deviation with the calculated or tabulated $\tau$; according to the number of data in the set, the $\tau$ assumes a specific value of reference that can be used as the multiplier of the Thompson statistic formula.

The Thompson critical value is then compared to the absolute difference of each data point with the average of the entire data set. The hypothesis for outliers is rejected if each month statistic is lower than the critical value; otherwise if a month statistic overcomes the threshold defined by the test, the outlier hypothesis is accepted, and as a consequence, an outlier is defined.

## 4.5.2  SAP Use Case: Thompson's Test

As per described in the previous test, Fig. 4.73 is the graphical and technical representation of the Thompson test. The structure of the worksheet is the usual one, with a histogram chart and a scatter plot. The red marked bar and record are considered outlying in sales/demand. If we take as an example the product selected in the field "select product the plot," we can graphically see the peak in red.

*The Gaussian method*

Proceeding with the available outlier techniques, the Gaussian method is frequently used in statistical analysis and it can be transposed for outlier detection scopes. The Gaussian method is quite reasonable if the data are symmetric and mound shaped. Some of the tests seen before, such as the skewness and kurtosis,

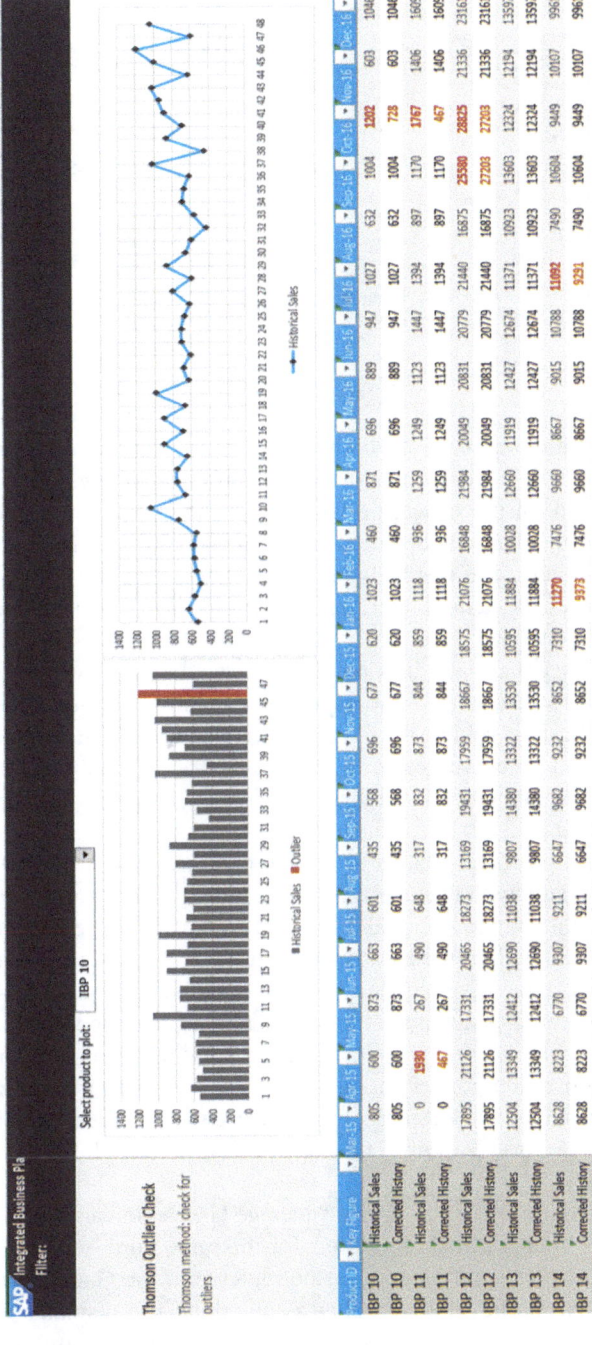

**Fig. 4.73** Thompson method for stable products

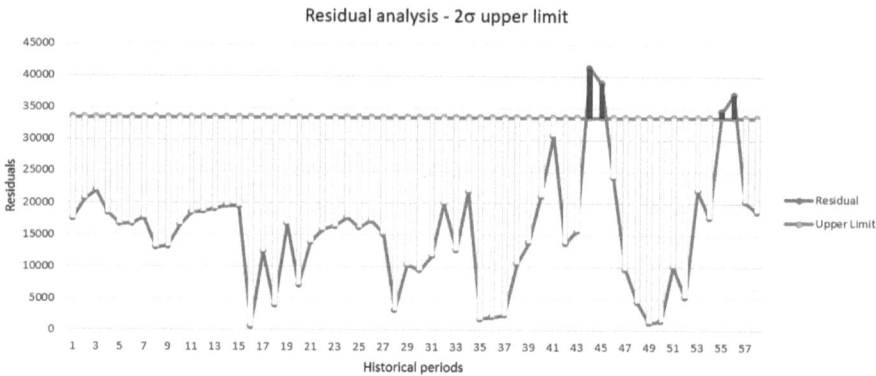

**Fig. 4.74** Residual plot for outlier detection

provide some help with the understanding of the data plotting and mapping, allowing to understand if it is reasonable or not to apply the following method.

The method is based on the concept of residuals. The deduction of each data point to the average of the data set considered represents one of the viable solutions to obtain a list of residuals. The residuals, in simple words and in relation to this case, indicate how much deviations there are from each data point to the fitting model: in this case the average.

Once we have the residual data, it is possible to calculate the average and the standard deviations. As a second step, the upper limit and lower limit are identified by inserting a multiplicative value to the standard deviations of the residuals and adding to this component the average of the residuals. The method will assess as outliers all the residuals points that fall beyond the mentioned upper or lower limits, generally identified as 2 or 3 times the standard deviation.

The example taken from Fig. 4.74 illustrates the historical periods in the $X$-axis and the residuals calculated with the average fitting model on the $Y$-axis. The upper limit is indicated with the orange line, and it is based on the 2 sigma calculation. As it is clear from the visualization, the data points that are above the upper limit are considered as outlying ones. Consequently, if the residual for the period 45 is outlying, it means that the sales/demand of the period 45 has been abnormal as well.

Another possible viable solution to investigate the presence of outliers in a data set is to make use of the regression techniques to acquire the residual list. The logic would be to fit a model of the desired form to the data and then examine the residuals while looking for the points that are poorly predicted by the model (Watson et al., 1991).

Consequently, instead of using the simple "average" model to earn the residuals we can leverage more sophisticated algorithms for the same purpose.

A reminder here is crucial: at the core of the regression, the Gaussian method and of the residual analysis lies the normality assumption! The residuals must be normally distributed, but at the same time the data on which the regressive technique or the Gaussian method is to be applied have to be normal distributed. In addition, the variance within the data set needs to be as stable as possible or, homogenous, as per statistical slang.

A viable way to test if the residuals are normally distributed or not would be to reproduce the normality checks and techniques discussed in the previous sections and get a validation of the assumption.

It is recommended to plot the residuals in a scatter plot versus the corresponding predicted responses. Outliers generally occur as points far above or below the bulk of the plotted residuals. Other possible techniques include plotting the residuals in box plots and normal quantile–quantile plots.

Let us digress on the usefulness and at the same time on the side effects of a regression analysis for outlier detection. A regression model is a technique that aims at defining the best backward or onward model to fit your data. For example, the model can be a linear one, the so-called model to the power of one, meaning that your data set will be approximated on the basis of a straight line. Or, it could be a multiple linear regression model, for example, a model to the power of two, where the data will try to be approximated by a parabola.

The goodness of the fitting model is commonly expressed by the so-called correlation index. The reasoning is very straightforward. The index can assume values from 0 to 1. The closer the correlation index to 1 the better the estimation of the model, the closer to 0 the poorer the accuracy.

As an example, Fig. 4.75 illustrates the working principle of the regression. The black straight line in the graph represents the fitting model. The equation of the model suggested is displayed on the right-hand side. The correlation index is marked in bold, underlying a medium accuracy estimation. The blue dots are the sales points.

It is a common practice to start regressing the data from the simplest regressive model to the higher in power models in order to get the "famous" correlation index closer to 1. However, this practice can be misleading and it is not recommended on a large scale, since increasing to the highest power the fitting regression model

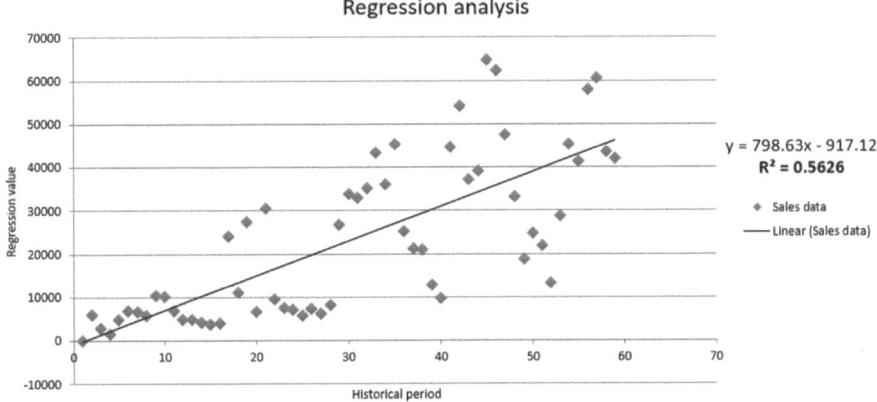

**Fig. 4.75**  Example of regression analysis to the power of one

could simply lead to a model where the estimated curve simply unites all the data dots, without leaving the space for any kind of data approximation! When it comes to these particular situations, one major error is at the basis of the whole exercise: The normality assumption has not been verified!

The second option, as much valid as the previous one, attributes the poor approximation performances to the high degree of variability of the data.

The demonstration of the issue identified above is reported in Fig. 4.76. It is structure as the previous visualization; however, we can detect how the fitting model got more sophisticated: to the power of six. We can notice as well, how we tried to make a 4-month projection in the future with the fitting model: The increasing foreseen trend is displayed by the black curve from periods 58 to 62.

It is essential to notice the following: Due to the highest level of variability in the data, even with an increase in the power of the test, the correlation index stayed almost unvaried (from 0.56 to 0.59). As a conclusion, the regressive effort to expand the power of the model does not justify the enhancements in the outcomes.

Eventually, it has to be stated, how for highly typical seasonal products the behavior of a sine or cosine function could normally approximate with good results the behavior of the data.

Therefore, considering that per year we have 12 periods, we need to translate the number of periods in radians since the sinusoidal functions make use of the radian. Knowing that the round angle is 360°, if we divide the angle by the number of periods, we obtain the value of 30°. We can then calculate the sine or the cosine function of the radian with a frequency of 30° and as many times as per the time periods, remembering that the sine function is more appropriate for the summer seasonality, while the winter peaks are more suitable for the cosine function.

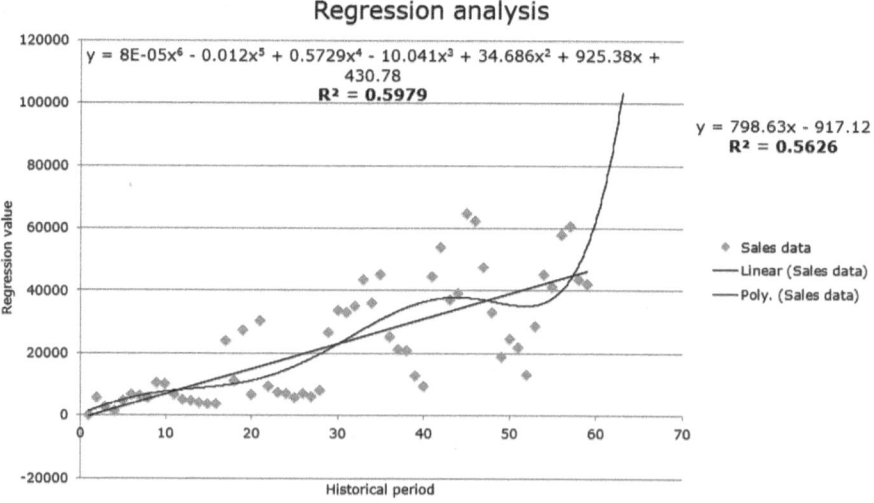

**Fig. 4.76** MLR analysis

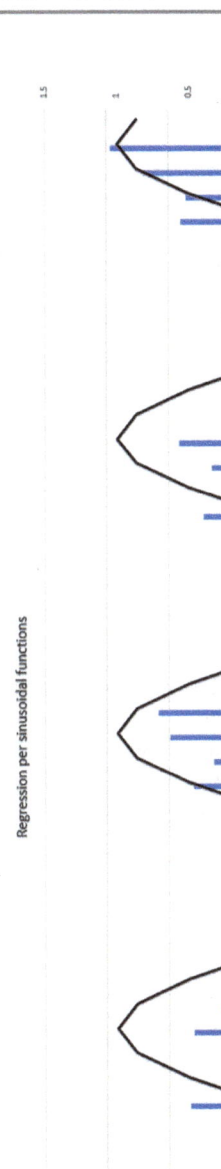
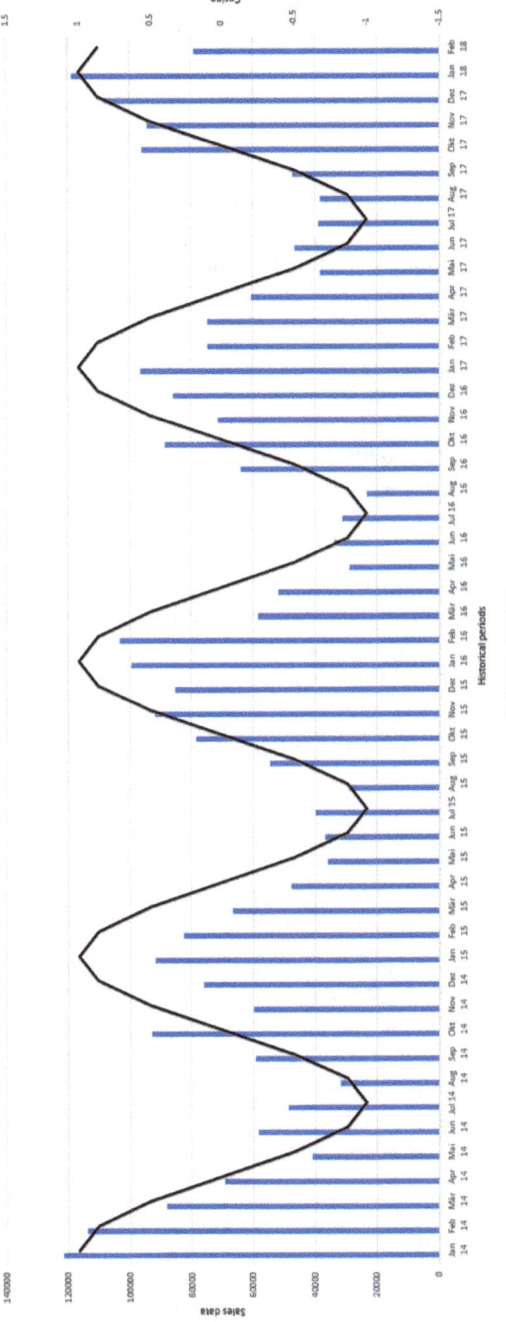

**Fig. 4.77** Example of cosine regression

Figure 4.77 illustrates how the fitting model matches almost exactly, the seasonal behavior of the data. In fact, the blue bars are the historical sales while the black line is the cosine sinusoidal estimating model.

Residuals out of these regressive techniques will have to be tested for normality and then plotted.

### 4.5.3   SAP Use Case: Gaussian Method

In Fig. 4.78, we are able to detect the outlying points based on the residuals calculated. The key figure that stores the absolute difference between the sales point and the overall average of the data set is then displayed in both the histogram and scatter plot. By setting the outlier threshold to a limit of twice the standard deviations of the residuals, we are then able to detect and identify the outliers as the points that overcome the upper limit.

The absolute difference between the sales and the average that relates to the outlying data is marked as well in red in the template.

*Z method*

The *Z* method is a quite simplistic model that can be used for detection purposes. The term "*Z*" stands for the standardized normal distribution. Once again, at the basis of this test lies the assumption that the data have to follow the normality assumption.

To standardize the normal distribution and consequently obtaining the *Z* values, it is necessary the following formula:

$$Z = \frac{ABS\left(X_i - \overline{X}\right)}{\sigma}$$

where $\sigma$ stands for the standard distribution.

Eventually, the user will get as much as *Z* values as the number of time periods considered. Each period will have its own *Z* value. The detection technique relies then on the following principles:

- If we set $Z = 2$ as the highest limit, all the *Z* values superior to 2 will be identified as outlying points.
- If we set $Z = 3$, the same concept applies.

As a concluding note, we must be very careful with the setting of the *Z* threshold since it determines the robustness of the test, but also its restrictions. For example, a *Z* value equal to 2 may lead to a certain number of outliers, while on the same data set a *Z* value equal to 3 may lead to 0 outliers detected. The precision is paramount.

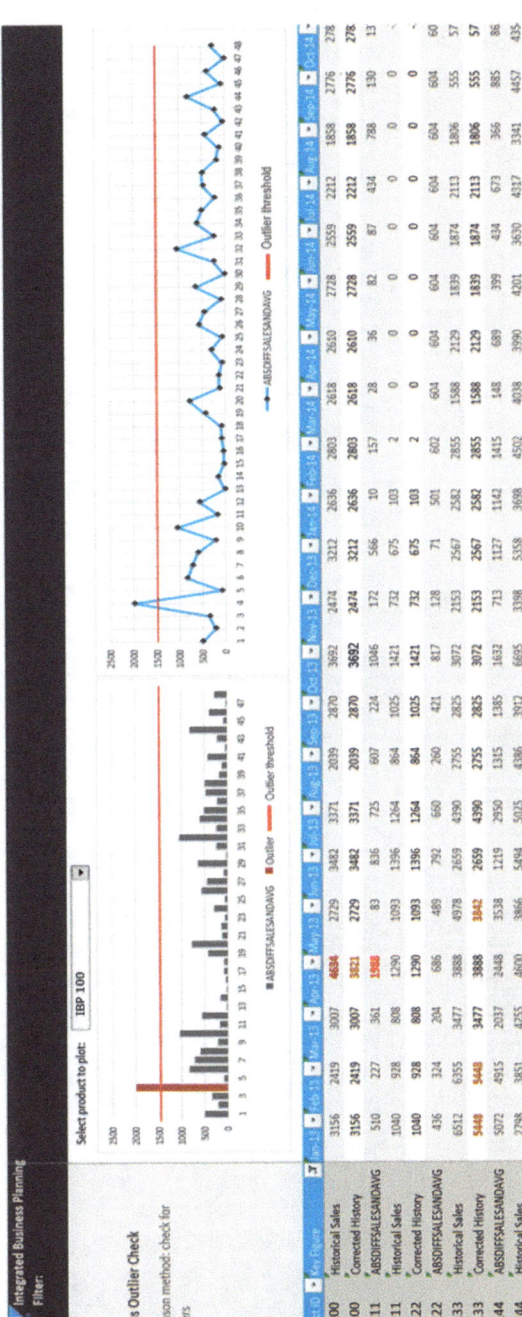

**Fig. 4.78** SAP IBP residual Gaussian model

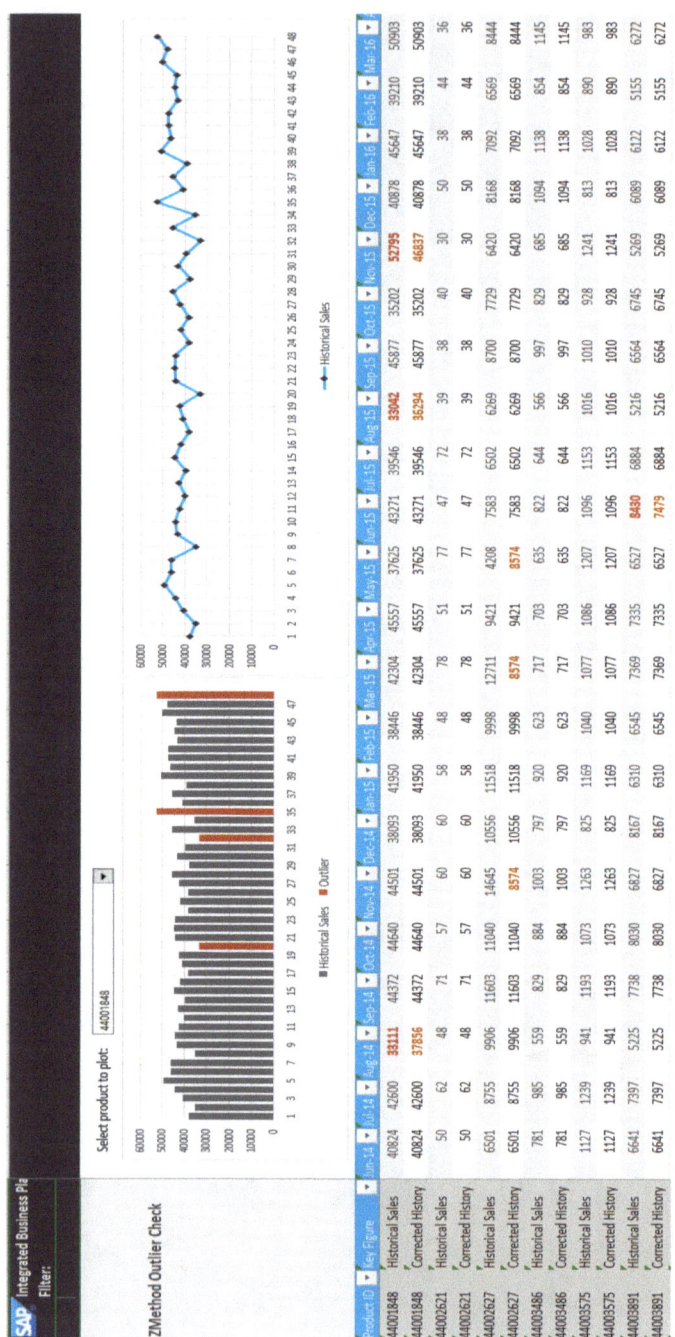

**Fig. 4.79** Z method analysis

### 4.5.4  SAP Use Case: *Z* Method

Also in Fig. 4.79, the outlying points are detected by the red bars. The functioning of the method is as per described above with a *Z* value set to 2. We can spot graphically that two out of the four outliers are due to low peaks, while the other ones represent the highest peaks.

*Modified 3σ method*

Another similar approach only used for normally distributed data is the $3\sigma$ modified method that allows to eliminate or keep the maximum value of a time series. If the maximum value has a statistic lower than 0.1, it is considered an outlier; otherwise, it is a point that has to be kept in the series.

Below the reasoning of the test:

$$y' = \text{absolute value of } \frac{x' - \bar{x}}{s}$$

$$a = 1 - F(y')$$

$$\text{if } n * a \leq 0.1 \text{ an outlier is detected}$$

This test can be used only to detect single outliers, proving useful when a further check is needed for a specific doubtful outlying point.

Besides, the most beneficial use for this test would be to associate it to the stable and low variable SKUs. For such types of data distributions, an interquartile test will only highlight the bulk of the data without letting result the highest point in sales/demand. At the same time, a variance test will perform under its capabilities since the overall inner variance of the data will be quite small.

Eventually, it is recommended for the practitioner to test the outlier presence with the $3\sigma$ modified method for the types of profiles above discussed.

### 4.5.5  SAP Use Case: 3 Sigma Modified

Figure 4.80 displays the results out of the 3 sigma modified method. Similar to the other methods, the bar chart illustration is the same; however, the scatter plot displays, in addition the only possible outlying points that can undergo investigation through the 3 sigma modified method.

Eventually, we must state that this method is much more restricted than the others as it detects fewer outlying points. Consequently, it must be used in conjunction with others.

*Detection mechanism*

As a conclusion for this part, the usual illustration that serves as a vehicle for clarity and understanding is provided. It clearly identifies as an input the two

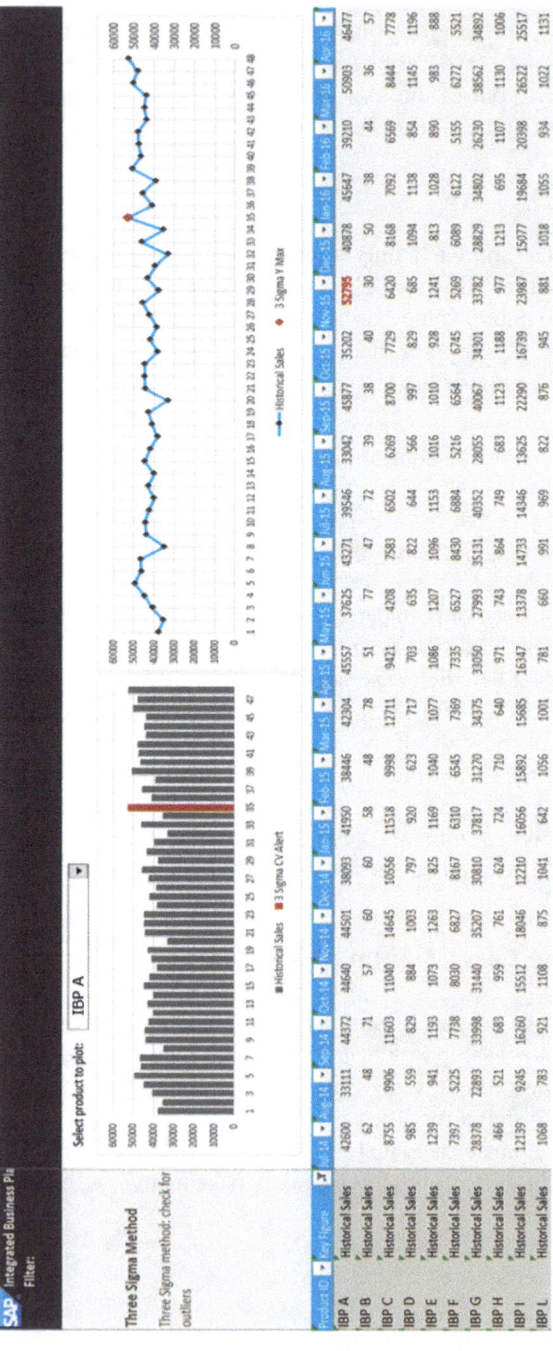

**Fig. 4.80** 3 sigma modified method

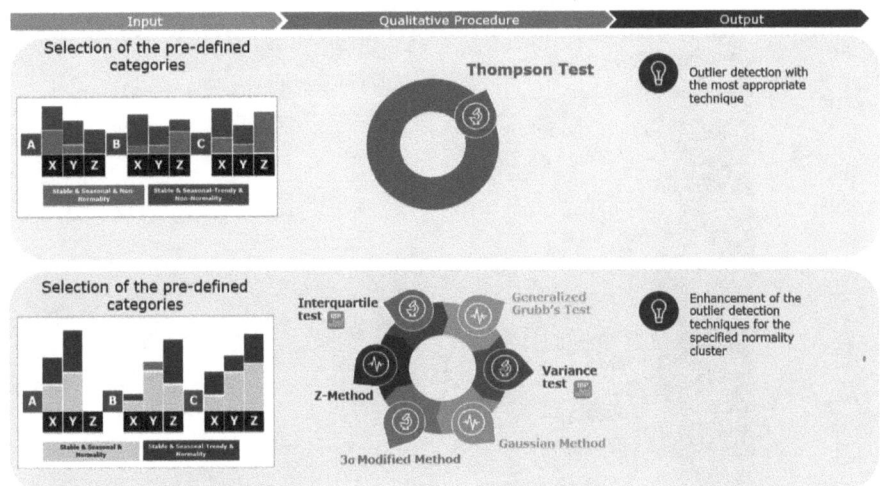

**Fig. 4.81**  Detecting outliers—procedure

relevant matrices and as a procedure the most appropriate detection techniques. Once the outliers will be identified, we will be able to move to the correction phase. See Fig. 4.81.

The group of detection techniques can be benchmarked one with the others or could be checked simultaneously to validate a specific decision.

Each of this technique, independently on the normality assumption, is automated in the end-to-end process. The demand planner should be the key player in the detection technique for an exercise that has to be run monthly. Finally, the process scope can vary from SKU to SKU or from cluster to cluster.

Let's now see how the detection logic works within SAP IBP. The outlier detection template is shown in Fig. 4.82. To simplify, the reasoning three different SKUs are displayed in SAP IBP view. Those SKUs had been submitted to the outlier detection process:

- The first one displayed in the visualization is categorized as "normal," and consequently, all the outlier detection techniques except the Thompson method are available for the checking. As we can see from the picture, the Thompson key figure is on purpose without records as it cannot be considered and leveraged for this particular SKU. On the contrary, all the other techniques will play a key role. For each of the row of each SKU, a specific method is run. For example, the row "ISOUTLIERGRUBB" reports the insights out of the Grubbs' test. If for a specific month, the key figure accounts for 0 it means that none outliers have been detected, while if it accounts for 1, that specific month is considered as outlying. Eventually, for the first SKU analyzed and within the time frame of the visualization none methods detected an outlier.
- Interestingly, the second SKU analyzed accounts for an outlier, but the ground rules for his detection are different. This SKU is marked as non-normal

**SAP** Integrated Business Planning
Filter:

| Product ID | Normality Assumption | STWIN Code | Key Figure | Jan-13 | Feb-13 | Mar-13 | Apr-13 | May-13 | Jun-13 | Jul-13 | Aug-13 | Sep-13 | Oct-13 | Nov-13 |
|---|---|---|---|---|---|---|---|---|---|---|---|---|---|---|
| IBP 4 | NORMAL | SEASONAL | ISOUTLIERGAUSSIAN | 0 | 0 | 0 | 0 | 0 | 0 | 0 | 0 | 0 | 0 | 0 |
| IBP 4 | NORMAL | SEASONAL | ISOUTLIERGRUBB | 0 | 0 | 0 | 0 | 0 | 0 | 0 | 0 | 0 | 0 | 0 |
| IBP 4 | NORMAL | SEASONAL | ISOUTLIERTHOMSON | 0 | 0 | 0 | 0 | 0 | 0 | 0 | 0 | 0 | 0 | 0 |
| IBP 4 | NORMAL | SEASONAL | ISOUTLIERZMETHOD | 0 | 0 | 0 | 0 | 0 | 0 | 0 | 0 | 0 | 0 | 0 |
| IBP 4 | NORMAL | SEASONAL | Is Outlier (Composite Check) | | | | | | | | | | | |
| IBP 4 | NORMAL | SEASONAL | Historical Sales | 10642 | 10826 | 9722 | 12435 | 10865 | 11548 | 11175 | 8922 | 11070 | 11679 | 9806 |
| IBP 5 | NOT NORMAL | TREND-SEASONAL | ISOUTLIERGAUSSIAN | | | | | | | | | | | |
| IBP 5 | NOT NORMAL | TREND-SEASONAL | ISOUTLIERGRUBB | 0 | 0 | 0 | 0 | 0 | 0 | 0 | 0 | 0 | 0 | 0 |
| IBP 5 | NOT NORMAL | TREND-SEASONAL | ISOUTLIERTHOMSON | 0 | 0 | 1 | 0 | 0 | 0 | 0 | 0 | 0 | 0 | 0 |
| IBP 5 | NOT NORMAL | TREND-SEASONAL | ISOUTLIERZMETHOD | | | | | | | | | | | |
| IBP 5 | NOT NORMAL | TREND-SEASONAL | Is Outlier (Composite Check) | | | ⊗1 | | | | | | | | |
| IBP 5 | NOT NORMAL | TREND-SEASONAL | Historical Sales | 798 | 752 | 486 | 902 | 781 | 1082 | 966 | 818 | 760 | 1102 | 758 |
| IBP 6 | NORMAL | TREND-SEASONAL | ISOUTLIERGAUSSIAN | 0 | 0 | 0 | 0 | 0 | 0 | 0 | 0 | 0 | 0 | 0 |
| IBP 6 | NORMAL | TREND-SEASONAL | ISOUTLIERGRUBB | 0 | 0 | 0 | 0 | 1 | 0 | 0 | 0 | 0 | 0 | 0 |
| IBP 6 | NORMAL | TREND-SEASONAL | ISOUTLIERTHOMSON | 0 | 0 | 0 | 0 | 1 | 0 | 0 | 0 | 0 | 0 | 0 |
| IBP 6 | NORMAL | TREND-SEASONAL | ISOUTLIERZMETHOD | 0 | 0 | 0 | 1 | 1 | 0 | 0 | 0 | 0 | 1 | 0 |
| IBP 6 | NORMAL | TREND-SEASONAL | Is Outlier (Composite Check) | | | | ⊗1 | | | | | | ⊗1 | |
| IBP 6 | NORMAL | TREND-SEASONAL | Historical Sales | 3156 | 2419 | 3007 | 4634 | 2729 | 3482 | 3371 | 2039 | 2870 | 3692 | 2474 |

**Fig. 4.82** SAP IBP detection mechanism

distributed; consequently, the only possible outlier technique to be leveraged is the Thompson one, while all the others do not display any record. In addition, on March 13 an outlier is detected and the ISOUTLIERTHOMPSON key figured turned to the value of 1. At the same time, also the historical sales for the month of March 13 got highlighted in red.

– The third and final example comes back to a normal distributed SKU where for the same month all of the different, available for the normality, outlier techniques detected a bizarre sales/demand point. As it is possible to see, all the Gaussian, Grubb and $Z$ method turned to the value of 1 for the month of April 13. In such a situation, the fundamental role of the composite check key figure comes into significance. Basically, for each month, the composite check turns to 0 if none of the available techniques detected an outlier or it turns to 1 if at least one of the detecting solutions highlighted an extra sales/demand data. October 2013 accounted also for an outlier and we can identify how the composite check turned to 1 because the $Z$ method detected one outlying points, resulting in the historical sales month of October 2013 marked in red.

After having analyzed each SKU and detected all the possible outlying points, it is time to move the final correction phase of the process.

### 4.5.6 SAP Use Case: The Benefit of Normality Assumption in Outlier Detection

Figure 4.83 shows a comparison between an outlier detection method appropriate for a normally distributed data (variance or $Z$ method for example) and another one suitable for a non-normally distributed data (Thompson's test). Let's see how they differ.

The selected SKU is a non-normally distributed one, with a strong variability due to a seasonal component in the demand. In the upper part of the visualization, we report what may happen if we apply the wrong outlier detection technique to this profile:

– We detect nine outlying points. Eight of those are marked in red in the bar chart, while the one in period 14 cannot be noticed by the red mark since it has a too small sales/demand.

On the contrary, with the adoption of Thompson's technique, applicable for non-normal data, the outlying points identified are only three:

– January 2013
– February 2014 and
– March 2015.

In at a glance, we perceive how the number of extra sales/demand points hugely differs between the two products, demonstrating how the variance or the $Z$ test

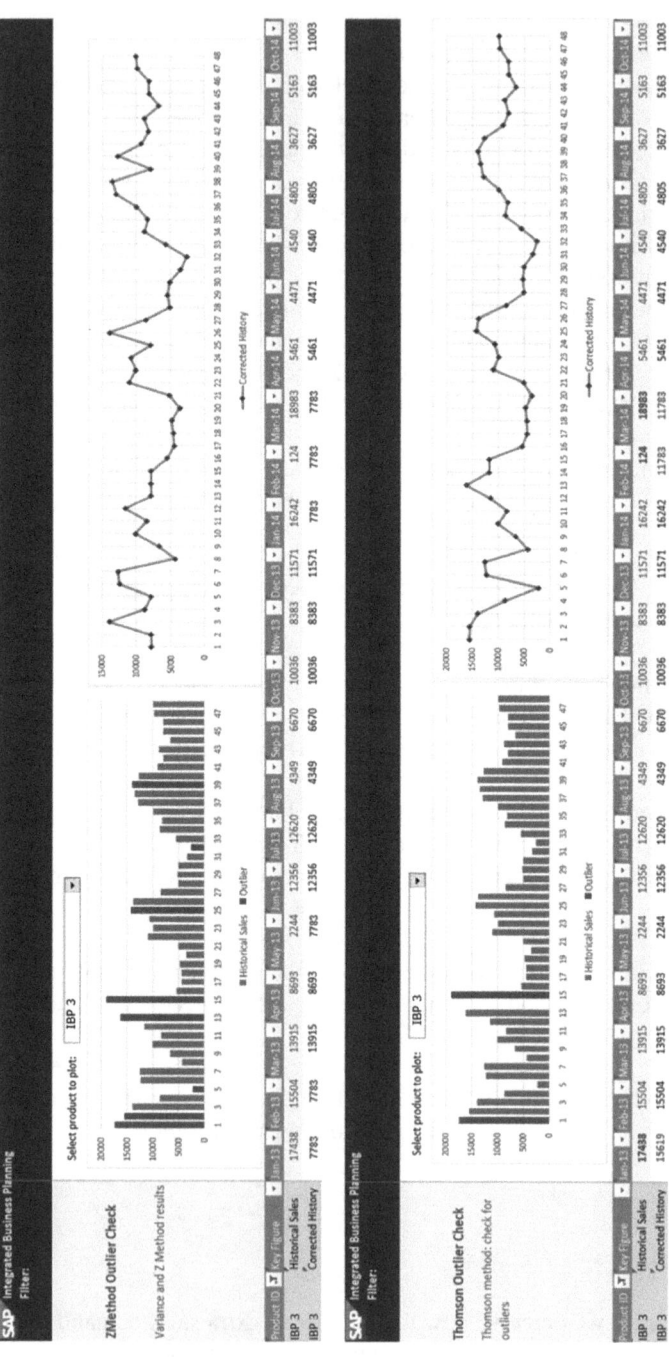

**Fig. 4.83** SAP IBP normality assumption for outlier detection

identifies some points that should not have been identified. Basically, due to the high variance within the data, almost every time we have a low season peak or a high season peak the test returns for a marked sales/demand data. The resulting effect is an outlier test that tends to destroy the inner seasonality of the data itself, while smoothing the highest peaks and lowest drops!

The visual result is illustrated with the right-hand side scatter plot of the corrected history. For our purpose, on the top right scatter plot the correction of the historical sales has been run with the average of the data excluding the outliers. As we can see, the behavior of the data drastically changed.

On the contrary, by applying the correction technique that will be largely explained in the coming chapter, the corrected history results in the scatter plot positioned in the right bottom part. The season schema has not been transformed, and the data schema still respected.

Let's discover now what we think as a good-fitting correction technique.

## 4.6 Outlier Correction for Seasonal Products

The correction phase itself plays as much a crucial role as the detecting phase. Based on our experience, correcting an outlying point has always been considered one of the trickiest actions to undergo since there is no recommended way to do it that could suitably apply to all the products in the portfolio. Consequently, the same constraints, which we had to deal with during the detection process, also apply in this phase where depending on the types of products, demand patterns and sequences of zeros, a chosen solution may result to be more or less beneficial.

The methods available on SAP IBP to correct outliers are the following:

- Correction to mean (with and without outliers included)
- Correction with tolerance (excluding outliers) and
- Correction with median (with and without outliers included).

For example, if a practitioner is dealing with a stable product with a very limited amount of internal variability, the above-listed correction techniques may all be suitably applicable. Since there is no huge variability in that specific type of sales/demand pattern, correcting the outlying points to the mean or the median will allow a sort of stabilization and leveling of all the data set, guaranteeing in well-performing future predictions.

However, when dealing with more variable types of sales/demand as the seasonal ones or even the trendy–seasonal, the impact of a leveling correction technique may denaturalize the sales/demand pattern itself. Let's imagine we use a seasonal SKU where each winter we have three high peaks and each summer we have three low peaks. If we detect those highs and lows as outlying sales/demand data and correct them to the mean, the overall result will be a "new" SKU where almost no season is present anymore. As a consequence, based on this corrected history, none of the forecasting models will be able to foresee the same seasonal schema in the future!

This is the reason why, for the seasonal and seasonal trendy products, we came up with a new available method that allows the practitioners to correct the outlying point with the average sales/demand of its own season.

The detection concept, its configuration in SAP IBP and his graphical template are reported in Fig. 4.84.

Let's analyze in detail the configuration of the solution and the outcomes analyzing two products that serve as an example. The first product is a seasonal one, not normally distributed, while the second one is categorized with an internal variability and also not normally distributed. As a note, for the correcting phase, the normality assumption does not play a crucial role, but it simply states which detection techniques could have been used in the detection phase.

The structure of the SAP IBP configuration for each of the SKU is as follows:

- The period counter: It simply counts the number of periods (months) and reports the numbering.
- Composite check: It reports the results out of the detection phase. Value of 1 for an outlier is identified and 0 for no outliers.
- Periods to average for outlier correction: It states the number of periods that will be used to average the sales/demand of each season.
- Periods per season (Heuristic Estimate): It reports the finding of the Moving Average for Seasonality Identification where the length of the season could be estimated for the first time.
- Markers for season average: It is 0 every time that the amount of the season average amount of sales/demand to be used for the correction changes. It changes to 1 for the periods in which the same average of the season sales/demand has to be used for the detection.
- Season average: It calculates the average of the sales/demand of each season based on the periods per season reported above.
- Average to use for outlier: It is a string that reports the average of the season that has to be used depending on the month period.
- The corrected history reports than the values that have been changed and the ones that stayed identical to the historical sales.

For example, the first SKU analyzed, it is a seasonal one with an outlier in January 15 and another one on March 15. Thanks to the Moving Average for Seasonality Identification, we identify as length of the season the value of 1. Consequently, every 4 periods, the sales/demand is averaged. For example, the average value of 27,593 that has to be used from December 2014 to March 2015 is the average of September, October, November and December 2014. The string with the values of the season averages gets then populated, and according to the month positioning of the outlier, the respective average is picked for the correction.

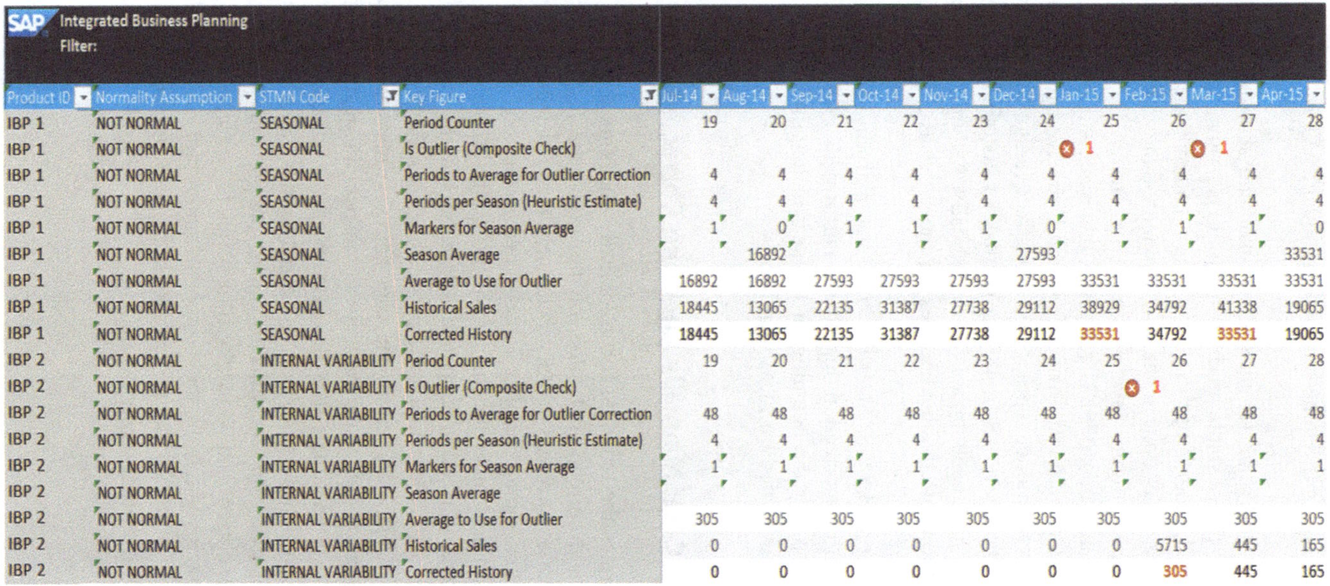

| Product ID | Normality Assumption | STMN Code | Key Figure | Jul-14 | Aug-14 | Sep-14 | Oct-14 | Nov-14 | Dec-14 | Jan-15 | Feb-15 | Mar-15 | Apr-15 |
|---|---|---|---|---|---|---|---|---|---|---|---|---|---|
| IBP 1 | NOT NORMAL | SEASONAL | Period Counter | 19 | 20 | 21 | 22 | 23 | 24 | 25 | 26 | 27 | 28 |
| IBP 1 | NOT NORMAL | SEASONAL | Is Outlier (Composite Check) | | | | | | | ✗ 1 | | ✗ 1 | |
| IBP 1 | NOT NORMAL | SEASONAL | Periods to Average for Outlier Correction | 4 | 4 | 4 | 4 | 4 | 4 | 4 | 4 | 4 | 4 |
| IBP 1 | NOT NORMAL | SEASONAL | Periods per Season (Heuristic Estimate) | 4 | 4 | 4 | 4 | 4 | 4 | 4 | 4 | 4 | 4 |
| IBP 1 | NOT NORMAL | SEASONAL | Markers for Season Average | 1 | 1 | 1 | 1 | 1 | 1 | 1 | 1 | 1 | 1 |
| IBP 1 | NOT NORMAL | SEASONAL | Season Average | | 16892 | | | | 27593 | | | | 33531 |
| IBP 1 | NOT NORMAL | SEASONAL | Average to Use for Outlier | 16892 | 16892 | 27593 | 27593 | 27593 | 27593 | 33531 | 33531 | 33531 | 33531 |
| IBP 1 | NOT NORMAL | SEASONAL | Historical Sales | 18445 | 13065 | 22135 | 31387 | 27738 | 29112 | 38929 | 34792 | 41338 | 19065 |
| IBP 1 | NOT NORMAL | SEASONAL | Corrected History | 18445 | 13065 | 22135 | 31387 | 27738 | 29112 | 33531 | 34792 | 33531 | 19065 |
| IBP 2 | NOT NORMAL | INTERNAL VARIABILITY | Period Counter | 19 | 20 | 21 | 22 | 23 | 24 | 25 | 26 | 27 | 28 |
| IBP 2 | NOT NORMAL | INTERNAL VARIABILITY | Is Outlier (Composite Check) | | | | | | | | ✗ 1 | | |
| IBP 2 | NOT NORMAL | INTERNAL VARIABILITY | Periods to Average for Outlier Correction | 48 | 48 | 48 | 48 | 48 | 48 | 48 | 48 | 48 | 48 |
| IBP 2 | NOT NORMAL | INTERNAL VARIABILITY | Periods per Season (Heuristic Estimate) | 4 | 4 | 4 | 4 | 4 | 4 | 4 | 4 | 4 | 4 |
| IBP 2 | NOT NORMAL | INTERNAL VARIABILITY | Markers for Season Average | 1 | 1 | 1 | 1 | 1 | 1 | 1 | 1 | 1 | 1 |
| IBP 2 | NOT NORMAL | INTERNAL VARIABILITY | Season Average | | | | | | | | | | 305 |
| IBP 2 | NOT NORMAL | INTERNAL VARIABILITY | Average to Use for Outlier | 305 | 305 | 305 | 305 | 305 | 305 | 305 | 305 | 305 | 305 |
| IBP 2 | NOT NORMAL | INTERNAL VARIABILITY | Historical Sales | 0 | 0 | 0 | 0 | 0 | 0 | 0 | 5715 | 445 | 445 |
| IBP 2 | NOT NORMAL | INTERNAL VARIABILITY | Corrected History | 0 | 0 | 0 | 0 | 0 | 0 | 305 | 305 | 305 | 165 |

Filter:

**Fig. 4.84** SAP IBP correction method

In January 2015, the season average to be used accounts for 33,531, and as a result, the corrected value for January 2015 accounts as well for the same value. March 2015 is included in the same season; consequently, it will be replaced by the same average.

The reasoning is the same for all the seasonal and seasonal trendy products, while for the other types of stable products the logic is a bit simplified since there is no more need to track records of the season length and average. For those types of products, the correction is done using the average of the entire data set, conveniently stored in the key figure "average to use for outlier."

As an example, the second SKU falls into this case, since the outlying point in February 2015 matches the value of 305, which is the average of the full data set. Interestingly, for such product types, the periods to average for outlier correction will always automatically be set to 48, the number of historical sales periods.

Once the outliers have been replaced, automatically, without changing the values of the indexes, the forecasted value changes for the better as it approximates closer to the actual values.

As concluding remark, we underline how the majority of the configuration process for the outlier correction had been performed with the standard IBP functionalities, except for the counting of the season lengths and the consequent seasonal averages performed on local members.

### 4.6.1  SAP Use Case: Manually Checking Corrected History

Figure 4.85 illustrates the template for graphically checking the results out of the outlier detection and correction. It plots on the graph the historical sales with a yellow line and the corrected history with the gray histogram bars. We can immediately see that month number 7 accounted for an outlier, and it has been corrected to the average of its season, while the month 42 recorded an outlier as well, but this time the correction happened with a much higher sales/demand record since that specific season was much higher.

Thanks to the visual illustration, the user can also manually apply their own changes when the correction phase seems to not respect the qualitative, graphical or market insights the practitioners may have or may have gained during the process run. This correction phase has to be considered as the moment in which all the information and analysis outputs collected during the previous process steps can be leveraged to better correct and adjust the time series to be forecasted. For example, it could be a data insight from the previous scatter plot, or from the monthly analysis of means (ANOM) or, as an additional and fundamental opinion, an external information coming from the market.

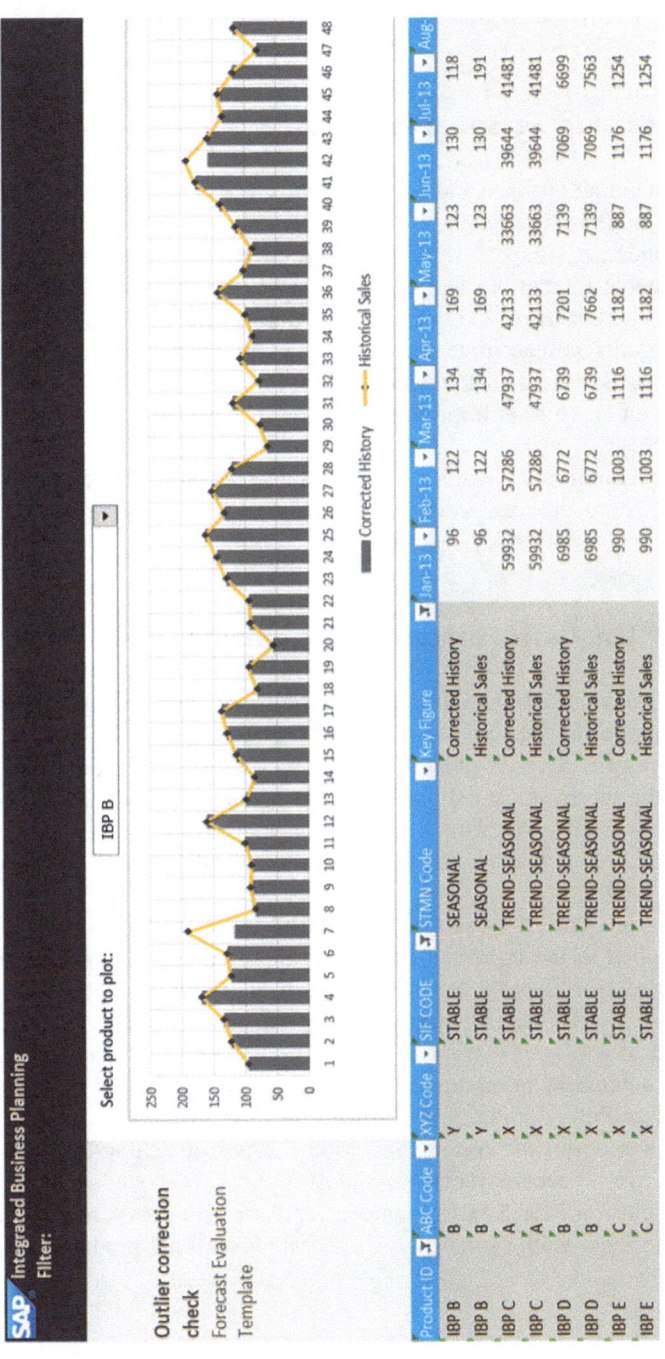

**Fig. 4.85**  SAP IBP checking corrected history

Ideally, the better the correction phase the easier, the more accurate and the less time consuming will be the final forecasting process of the clustering!

## 4.7  Forecasting Seasonal Products

After understanding our data and correcting the outliers, we finally arrive at the last stage of the process: forecasting!

As a reminder, in Chap. 3, we already introduced, explained and recommended, the most suitable forecasting techniques when it comes to the seasonal filed. We saw how the classical triple exponential smoothing or the more advanced SARIMA method represents both accurate and viable solution. Furthermore, we presented the concept of the Solver, a mathematical algorithm for nonlinear optimization that could lead even to a further improvement in the forecast accuracy when forecasting with the TES.

All these techniques are still valid; we will now see how they could fit at best in the overall custom process, leading eventually to forecasts as much accurate as possible.

### 4.7.1  SAP Use Case: Forecasting Seasonality

Figure 4.86 shows a custom illustration of the triple exponential smoothing forecasting technique. In the upper part of the visualization, the sales history of the concerned seasonal SKU is plotted in gray, as well as the ex-post forecasting in yellow and the future statistical forecasting in green. As we might see, on the top right-hand side, we provided also a visual schema for the forecast accuracy: Currently, the MAPE accounts for 41.05% and complementary the accuracy for 54.88%.

On the bottom side of the picture, the statistical forecasting solution of the TES has been applied to the corrected historical sales. We can notice from the scatter plot how some crucial peaks and lows have been modified. The ex-post and the statistical forecasts' patterns changed, showing an accuracy of 59% and an enhancement of 4%.

A further enhancement on the accuracy of the selected SKU is performed by the SARIMA algorithm. As Fig. 4.87 depicts, the SARIMA model expects a quite smoothened season for the coming year, while almost matching the 2016 seasonal pattern. The overall accuracy reaches almost 81%.

As a conclusion, the SARIMA model and the triple exponential smoothing represents the most viable solution for forecasting seasonal products.

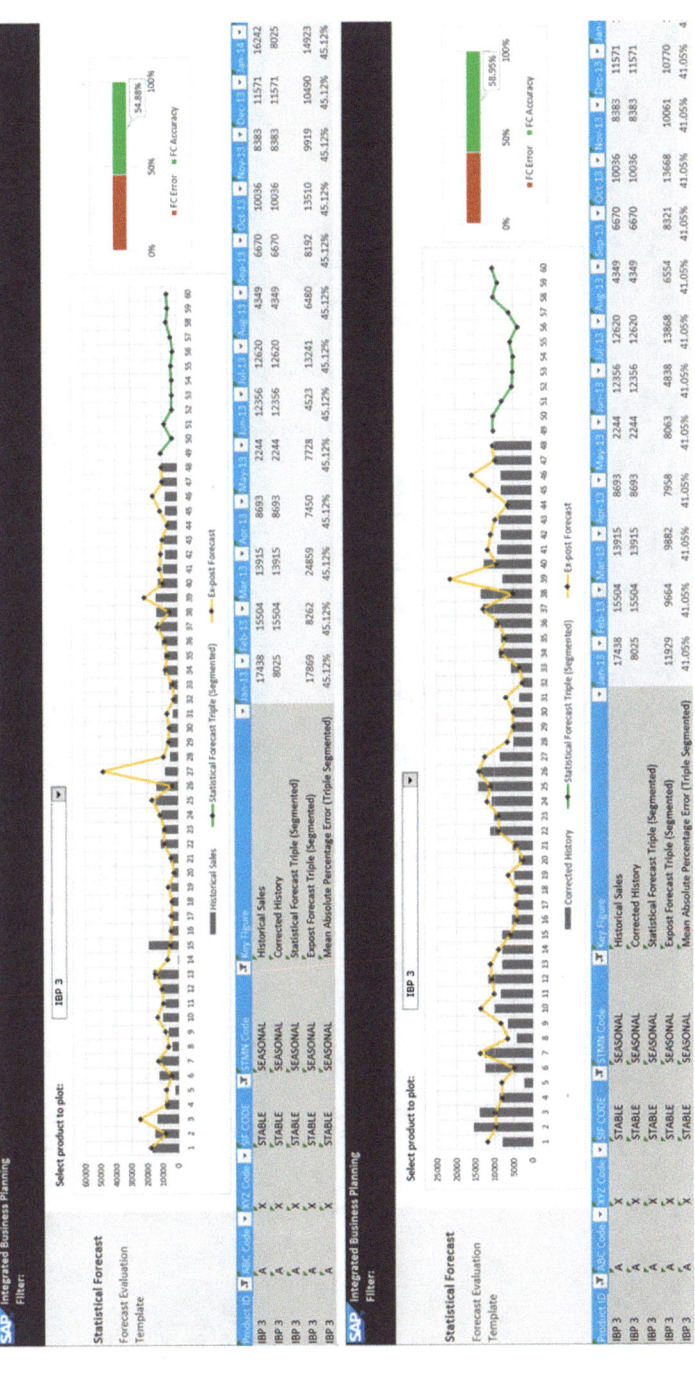

**Fig. 4.86** SAP IBP forecasting seasonality

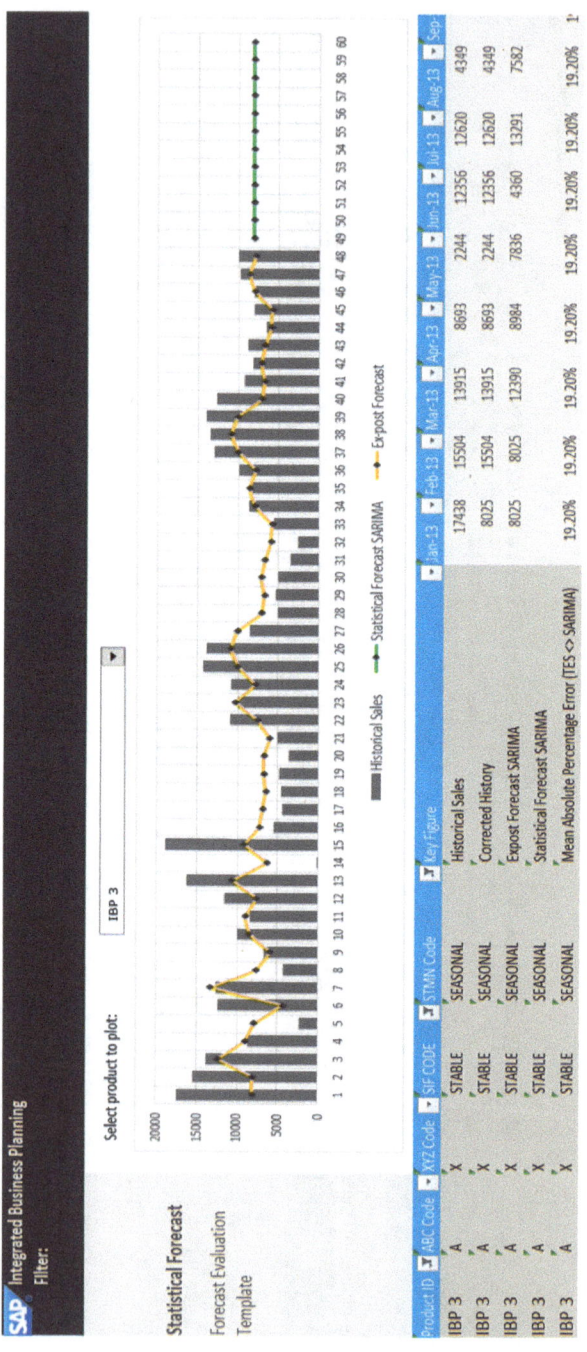

**Fig. 4.87** SAP IBP SARIMA for seasonal products

# References

Demand classification. (2017). Available at: https://frepple.com/blog/demand-classification/.

Gunst, R. F., Mason, R. L., & Hess, J. L. (2003). *Statistical design and analysis of experiment* (2nd ed). Wiley-Interscience.

Hyndman, R. J., & Athanasopoulos, G. (2014). *Forecasting: Principles and practice*. OTexts.

Kepczynski, R., Jandhyala, R., Sankaran, G., & Dimofte, A. (2018). *Integrated business planning—How to integrate planning processes, organizational structures and capabilities, and leverage sap IBP technology*. Switzerland: Springer.

Makridakis, S. G., Wheelwright, S. C., & Hyndman, R. J. (1998). *Forecasting, methods and applications*. New York: Wiley.

Mittnik, S., Rachev, S. T., & Samorodnitsky, G. (2001). The distribution of test statistics for outlier detection in heavy-tailed samples. *Mathematical and Computer Modelling*.

NIST. (2012). Engineering statistical handbook.

Report of statistics of the statistical engineering division. (2004). *NIST*.

Watson, S. M., et al. (1991). *Detection of outliers in time series. Institute of Transport Studies*, University of Leeds.

WordPress. (2016). *Statistics how to*. WordPress. Available at: https://www.statisticshowto.datasciencecentral.com/correlogram/.

# Custom Method to Forecast Intermittent Products

**5**

## 5.1 Custom Method for Intermittent Demand Forecasting and Planning

*A n-state Markovian analysis*

Since intermittent demands are randomly distributed and have a large percentage of zero values, the estimation of the demand distribution is particularly complicated.

As the method proposed by Croston, the suggested approach towards forecasting states is to subdivide the main problem into sub-independent problems:

- Determine the probability of having a non-zero demand over a period of time $t$.
- Make a forecast on the timing of the non-zero demand.
- Determine a demand pattern.

In Fig. 5.1, a typical example of intermittent historical sales is shown. On the top of the figure, we can notice how the intermittency pattern is quite marked, with non-zero sales/demand in the first two months followed by a wait of six months where sales/demand reappears. On the left side, the Boolean sales histogram chart is displayed; every time the monthly sales/demand is greater than 0, and the Boolean index switches to 1, while if the sales/demand accounts for 0, the Boolean index turns to 0 as well. On the right-hand side, the non-zero sales histogram chart is displayed; basically, the zero components have been removed from the data, so that only the months with a real sales/demand are illustrated.

Besides, we can notice how for this example, even by removing the zero points, the variability of the months with a sales/demand stays quite high. In the same graph, the red dots represent the end of non-zero demand sequences.

If we decompose the problem, we might say that the crucial points to be addressed are:

© Springer Nature Switzerland AG 2019
G. Sankaran et al., *Improving Forecasts with Integrated Business Planning*,
Management for Professionals, https://doi.org/10.1007/978-3-030-05381-9_5

**Fig. 5.1**  Example of an intermittent demand series and the respective decomposition

1. Identify the probability that a specific month will incur in a sales in more than 0 units (Markovian analysis).
2. How to size at best the demand for the months that actually experience a demand bigger than 0 units (SES).

The methodology we will describe below proposes to use Markov's theory to answer the first issue and the single exponential smoothing technique to size the demand (Fig. 5.2).

The main goal is to provide the planners with the most effective information to be able to take the right decision.

Let us elaborate on the process steps. Each module aims to determine the parameters that will be used, in an integrated way, in the final module that deals with demand forecasting. The detailed examination of each module and the single partial objectives are listed below.

**Fig. 5.2**  Custom forecasting processes for intermittent demand

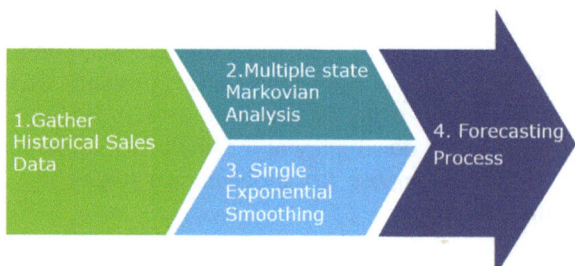

Step 1   Gather the historical data

To collect the right data from a huge portfolio is often a complex task. For our purposes, the ideal data sets will be the intermittent ones, which mean looking for the specific time series containing an alternating schema of zero and non-zero points. To properly filter a portfolio in this direction, we refer to the reading of 4.1 and its related SAP IBP use case.

Step 2   Multiple state Markovian analysis

Taking into account the current data patterns, the Markovian analysis determines two sets of prediction probabilities:

- The first one with the existence of a non-zero demand for the following period to be forecasted, giving also the probability that this specific month will have a sales/demand.
- The second one provides the probability of at least a non-zero demand in the three following periods; it gives the planner the tool to measure the probability of a long overstocking. The idea that lies behind this statement is related to the impact of a non-correct forecast; taking in account the characteristics of intermittent demand, an error in the forecast can lead to two possible alternatives:

  - The prediction is underestimated, and the best case is a zero forecast while the actual value is non-zero.
  - The prediction is overestimated, and the best case is a non-zero forecast while the actual value is zero.

  To smooth the impact of the former case, and also of the variability of non-zero demand, a safety stock is usually adopted while the latter case often leads to carry on inventory unneeded goods with additional cost due to extra throughput time, extra space, etc.

  A high value of the probability of at least a non-zero demand in the three following periods indicates that the goods will not remain for a long time in inventory and a forecast error will not have severe economic impacts.

Step 3   SES analysis

The single exponential smoothing is used to determine the size of the future demand, taking in account the sales history of non-zero demand; it must also be considered that planners could use any forecast method available on SAP. To refer to the theory behind the model, click on Sect. 3.3.2.

Step 4   Forecasting process

The aim of this module is to use all the previous inputs to suggest to the planner the right quantity to be authorized, considering the 1-month and 3-month probabilities of non-zero demand and the volumes of sales predicted by the SES analysis.

Concluding this introduction, Markov chains are powerful tools to model many organizational processes, finding its applications, for example, in manufacturing and inventory management. Applications of Markov chains and higher-order Markov chain techniques are frequently used to make predictions about data sequences; that is why transposing those concepts in the intermittent demand forecasting is useful.

More specifically, predicting data sequences implies making a prediction based on the "conditions" that a particular schema will assume in the future. In this case, when we refer to the word "condition," it mean a particular way data is expected to behave. For example, to make it immediate, if the future month to be forecasted $(t + 1)$ is predicted with a very low probability of having a sales/demand, its "condition" is 0. If the next month $(t + 2)$, on the contrary, it is almost certain to incur in a sales/demand, its "condition" will change and switch to 1.

It should now be clear why the $n$-order Markov chain models are appropriate to guarantee an enhancement of the accuracy and effectiveness of the forecasting procedure: the aptitude of the intermittent products of having two "conditions" the 0 sales/demands and the greater than 0 sales/demands, coupled with the lengths of the respective 0 and higher than 0 sequences!

## 5.2   Predicting Probabilities of Zero/Non-zero Demand with Markov Analysis

A discrete Markov process is a stochastic process, a sequence of events in which the outcome at any stage (discrete time intervals) depends on some probability (Häggström, 2002). Before disclosing the properties of a Markov chain, we will go through a simple example to set the ground rules and knowledge requirements to fully leverage the method itself.

Let's imagine a scheme made up by a gambler who bets on the tossing of a coin. As per shown in Fig. 5.3, there are two possible states assumed by the scheme:

– State 1 "win"
– State 0 "lose."

In addition, within the scheme described, there are also two possible outcomes that are:

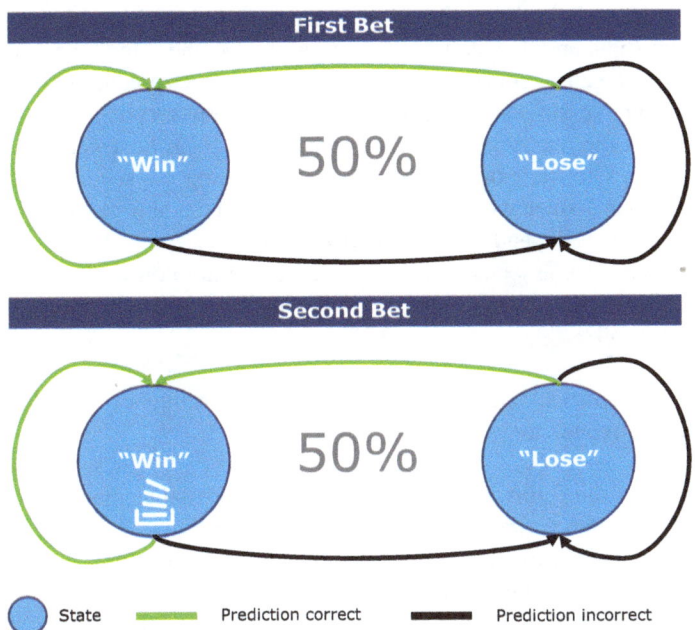

**Fig. 5.3** "Gambler" schema

- Outcome 1 "correct prediction" or
- Outcome 0 "incorrect prediction."

Given the simplicity of the scheme and assuming the coin is not rigged, the probability of occurrence of either outcome is well known before hands. Both outcomes have the same probability of happening:

- Probability of occurrence of Outcome 1 = 50%
- Probability of occurrence of Outcome 0 = 50%.

The meaning of the diagram in Fig. 5.3 is as follows:

- If the gambler has won the first bet ("win" state), he has a 50% probability of winning again ("correct prediction" outcome) and a 50% probability of losing ("incorrect prediction" outcome).
- The same if he has lost the last bet.

Let us describe then the scheme's properties, keeping an eye on the example above:

(a) The number of possible outcomes or states is finite. From our example, the states are finite and they equal to 2, win or lose. At the same time, the outcomes are finite as well, a correct prediction or an incorrect prediction.

(b) The outcome at any stage depends only on the outcome of the previous stage. This means the outcomes depend on the current state in which the schema is. Coming back to the gambler schema, when starting the second bet, we are in the state "win," since we had won the first bet and the new outcome, the one for this second bet, depends on the previous one.

(c) The probabilities associated with each outcome are constant over time. From our example, it is easy to notice and remember that the probability stays constant at 50%.

Going two steps back and relating again to the intermittency topic, the meaning of the outcome relates to:

− The value of the following month's demand: 0 or higher than 0 and also how much higher than 0 (the stochastic value)
− The state relates to the current month's sales situation: 0 or non-zero sales/demand (the actual condition of the schema).

Grouping the different probabilities in a matrix in which the rows describe the initial state and the columns describe the final one—the so-called transition matrix—indicates what is the probability of the gambler, who has won or lost the last bet, to be the winner or loser after the following bet.

The state space diagram, previously illustrated, and the transition matrix fully describe the behavior of the "gambler" schema. See Fig. 5.4.

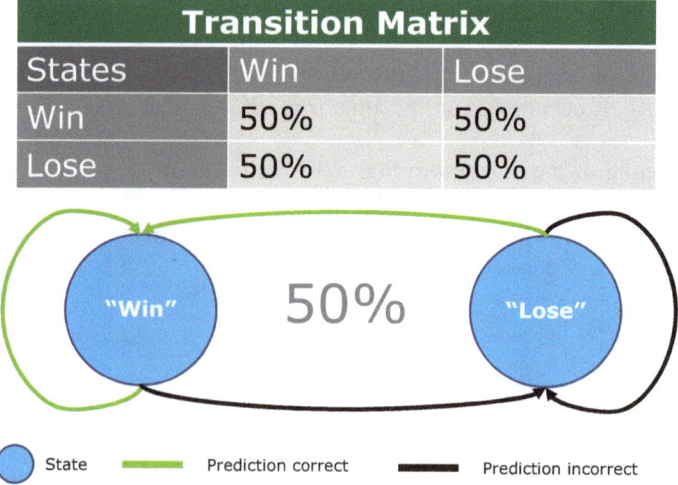

| Transition Matrix | | |
| --- | --- | --- |
| States | Win | Lose |
| Win | 50% | 50% |
| Lose | 50% | 50% |

**Fig. 5.4** "Gambler"—state space diagram and transition matrix

The "gambler" schema is very simple, and most of all in our case, the transition matrix is known before hands; but in a real case, the transition matrix could not be determined "a priori" and would have been calculated theoretically (if the underlying phenomenon could be described using probabilities, for instance in reality the practitioner can use failure rates of simple components to define the probability of failure of a complex schema) or empirically using the behavior of the schema in the past.

To give a simple visual representation of how a Markov analysis works when the transition matrix has to be empirically determined using the past outcomes, let's imagine the following example described in Fig. 5.5.

A man can move between two rooms. In each of those, there is a lottery box containing white and black balls in different proportions. The proportions of the different balls in the two rooms are unknown to the man.

At each interval of time, the man draws a ball from the lottery box of the room where he is located, and he notes the color and puts back the ball in the lottery box. In this way, the condition that the probabilities are consistent over time is respected.

Depending on the color of the drawn ball, the man decides whether to stay in the room (black ball) or move to the other room (white ball).

After a sufficiently long time, by examining the sequence of states assumed by the schema (rooms), it is possible to make an inference on the proportion of black and white balls in both rooms (calculate the conditional probability) and then, knowing in which state (room) the schema in $t$ is, make a forecast about the next state (room) in which the schema will be found in $t + 1$.

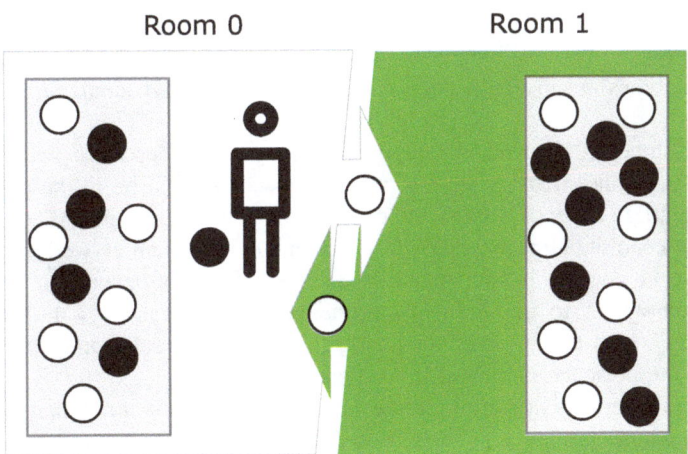

**Fig. 5.5**  A visual representation of a Markov schema

The Markov chain represents the sequence of states assumed by the schema:

– 0100001111000111000001010101111100001110

It can help giving an answer to the question: How many white and black balls are in each raffle box?

Eventually, the typical contradistinctive structure of intermittent demand data, which usually contains a significant proportion of zero values, with non-zero values mixed in randomly, with quantities that may be highly variable, suggests the use of $n$-order Markov chain models to obtain more accurate forecasts!

As it has been explained in the previous example concerning an "empirical" transition matrix, we will gather the historical sales data and use them to calculate the transition matrix of a product characterized by an intermittent demand.

*Markov Process for Intermittent Demand*

Let's define a schema in which, given a specific product, the initial state is the Boolean value of sales in the current month, the final state is the Boolean value of sales in the following month, and the outcome is the existence of a non-zero demand in the following month.

It is a two-state schema:

– We define that the schema is in "state 0" for all the months where the value of sales is zero.
– The schema is in "state 1" for all the months where the value of sales is non-zero.

The outcomes are given by the occurrence of a non-zero demand or of a zero demand.

If we assume the demand of the given product can be described with a Markov process, this implies that the state in which the schema will be in the period $t + 1$ (e.g., April 2018) depends exclusively on the state of the current period $t$ (e.g., March 2018). The conditional probabilities have to remain consistent as well; in other, we deduct that the demand behavior, but the quantity, does not depend on time.

The next step is to transform the sequence of historical sales into a Boolean sequence in which the "0" corresponds to the absence of sales and the "1" corresponds to the presence of a non-zero demand.

So, if the schema is in period $t$ in the "state 0"—no sales—it remains in the same state if in the interval $t \rightarrow t + 1$ no demand occurs; while it is transiting to the "state 1"—non-zero demand—if a non-zero demand occurs in the same time interval.

If the schema is in "state 1," the opposite logic happens. That is, the schema remains in "state 1" if there is a non-zero demand in the next period; otherwise, it goes into "state 0" if no demand occurs (see Fig. 5.6).

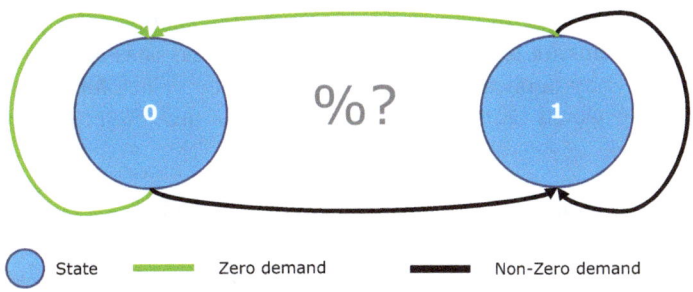

**Fig. 5.6**  A two-state process of demand

Taking up the simple example described in the previous paragraph, the occurrence of a non-zero demand is equivalent to drawing a white ball in room 0 and drawing a black ball into room 1.

By analyzing the sequence of events that have elapsed until the generic period t in the historical Boolean sequence of sales, it is possible to calculate the conditional probabilities of transition from "state 0" and "state 1" to the possible final states; and consequently, make use of these probabilities to make a forecast about which state the schema will assume in future periods.

The algorithm to calculate these conditional probabilities can be explained by the following steps:

Step 1  Counting the number of period in which the initial state is "0" or "1" (the last period in the historical sequence has to be ignored because its final state is unknown), the results are $N(0)$ and $N(1)$.

Step 2  For each initial state "0", counting how many time the final state is "0" or "1", the results are $N(0,0)$ and $N(1,0)$.

Step 3  Repeat step to for initial state "1", and the results are $N(0,1)$ and $N(1,1)$.

Step 4  Calculate the following ratio; $N(0,0)/N(0)$, $N(1,0)/N(0)$, $N(0,1)/N(1)$, $N(1,1)/N(1)$.

Step 5  The transition matrix is given in Fig. 5.7.

Let's assume, as an example, that we use as historical sales data, the numbers displayed in the second row of Fig. 5.8. The demand pattern is clearly intermittent as is deductible from the presence of zero and non-zero points. The Boolean sales

| Transition Matrix | | |
|---|---|---|
| States | 0 – "zero demand" | 1 – "non-zero demand" |
| 0 – "zero demand" | $N(0,0)/N(0)$ | $N(1,0)/N(0)$ |
| 1 – "non-zero demand" | $N(0,1)/N(1)$ | $N(1,1)/N(1)$ |

**Fig. 5.7**  Transition matrix for intermittent patterns

indicator, shown in the row number three, attributes the value 1 when the sales/demand is superior to 0, while the value 0 when the sales/demand matches 0.

Consequently, by duplicating this row, we have the values for the initial state. The further step would be to populate the outcomes row. Here, the reasoning is quite simple:

– If the initial state month ($t$) accounts for 0 and the initial state next month ($t + 1$) accounts also for 0 as, the outcomes will be populated with the value 0. Let's take as an example, April 2016 and May 2016. Since their initial states are both 1, the outcomes for the cell of April 2016 will result in 1.
– On the contrary, if for instance, we analyze May and June 2016, we see how there is a change in the state from 1 to 0: Consequently, the outcomes of May 2016 will account for 0.

Eventually, by copying the outcomes values to the final state row, we are able to reach the end of the processing. As a concluding note, the last two cells in the bottom right side are grayed out, as per suggested by good practices.

To initiate the calculation for the conditional probabilities, we first need to count our sequencing we obtained from Fig. 5.8.

The process is illustrated in the left table of Fig. 5.9. The states $N(0)$ account for 11 wins since if we count the number of zeros in the final state row, we find the number 11. The same reasoning applies for $N(1)$.

| Months | 04.16 | 05.16 | 06.16 | 07.16 | 08.16 | 09.16 | 10.16 | 11.16 | 12.16 | 01.17 | 02.17 | 03.17 | 04.17 | 05.17 | 06.17 | 07.17 | 08.17 | 09.17 | 10.17 | 11.17 | 12.17 | 01.18 | 02.18 | 03.18 |
|---|---|---|---|---|---|---|---|---|---|---|---|---|---|---|---|---|---|---|---|---|---|---|---|---|
| Historical sales | 68 | 404 | 0 | 0 | 0 | 80 | 139 | 25 | 10 | 100 | 270 | 70 | 0 | 110 | 0 | 0 | 0 | 0 | 0 | 0 | 0 | 348 | 100 | 150 |
| Boolean sales | 1 | 1 | 0 | 0 | 0 | 1 | 1 | 1 | 1 | 1 | 1 | 1 | 0 | 1 | 0 | 0 | 0 | 0 | 0 | 0 | 0 | 1 | 1 | 1 |
| Initial states | 1 | 1 | 0 | 0 | 0 | 1 | 1 | 1 | 1 | 1 | 1 | 1 | 0 | 1 | 0 | 0 | 0 | 0 | 0 | 0 | 0 | 1 | 1 | 1 |
| Outcomes | 1 | 0 | 0 | 0 | 1 | 1 | 1 | 1 | 1 | 1 | 1 | 0 | 1 | 0 | 0 | 0 | 0 | 0 | 0 | 0 | 1 | 1 | 1 | |
| Final state | 1 | 0 | 0 | 0 | 1 | 1 | 1 | 1 | 1 | 1 | 1 | 0 | 1 | 0 | 0 | 0 | 0 | 0 | 0 | 0 | 1 | 1 | 1 | |

**Fig. 5.8** Data to compute the conditional probabilities

| States | Win |
|---|---|
| N(0) | 11 |
| N(1) | 12 |
| N(0,0) | 8 |
| N(1,0) | 3 |
| N(0,1) | 9 |
| N(1,1) | 3 |

| Transition Matrix | | |
|---|---|---|
| States | 0 | 1 |
| 0 | 72,7% | 27,3% |
| 1 | 25% | 75% |

**Fig. 5.9** Process to compute the conditional probabilities

Additionally, for $N(0,0)$ we count, in the final state row, how many times a 0 final state is followed by another 0. The same logic is for the other conditional counting.

Finally, we have all the information to populate the transition matrix illustrated in the right-hand side of Fig. 5.8. If we want to calculate the conditional probability for the state (0,0), the logic implies to divide the $N(0,0)$ value, which indicates how many times from an initial state of 0 the times series kept being on a 0 state also on the following month, with the overall number of zeros in the final states' row, $N(0)$.

The conditional probability for the state (0,1) is complementary, while for the second row of the transition matrix the same logic applies.

The transition matrix that has been calculated allows the practitioner to make a forecast about the existence of a non-zero demand in April 2018.

The meaning of Fig. 5.10 is the following: Given that in March 2018 a non-zero sales occurred, meaning that the schema is in "state 1," there is a 75% probability that in April 2018, a non-zero demand occurs and the schema will remain in "state 1."

Using the same method that has been used for the transition matrix and, defining the outcomes as "at least a non-zero demand in the following three months" or "no demand in the following three months," it is also possible to calculate, for each initial state, the probability to have at least a period of non-zero demand in the given time span. The result will be a matrix of probability in which for each initial state is determined the probability to have "at least a non-zero demand in the following three months" or "no demand in the following three months."

This information is significant if the forecast for the following month fails and instead of a zero value, a non-zero sales/demand is predicted; this case will lead the planner to schedule the production of the product, and the final consequence is to carry on too much inventory and unneeded goods that will cause additional costs.

In Fig. 5.11, it is explained how, since in April 2016 the initial state was "1" and, in the following three months, there has been a non-zero demand, recorded in May, followed by no demand in June and July, the outcome 3 months of April will account for "1". The logical path is also illustrated with a color code:

**Fig. 5.10** Non-zero demand forecasting

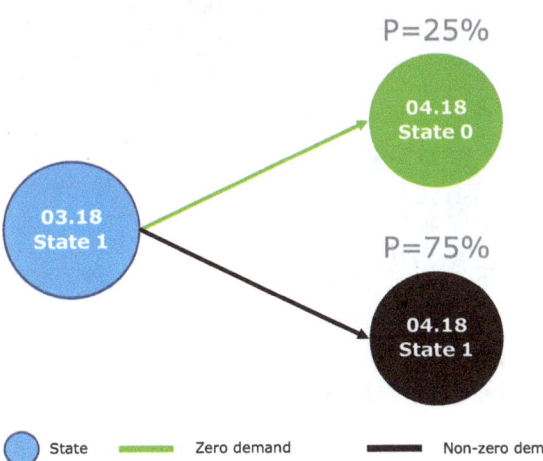

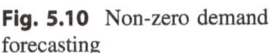

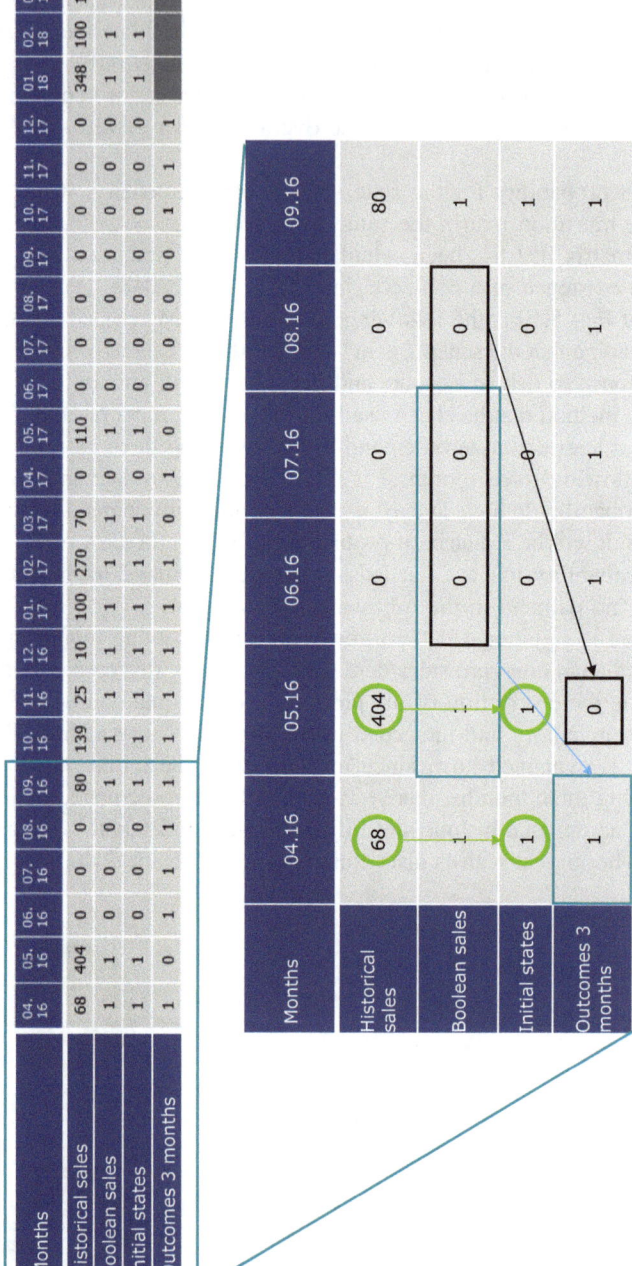

| Months | 04.16 | 05.16 | 06.16 | 07.16 | 08.16 | 09.16 | 10.16 | 11.16 | 12.16 | 01.17 | 02.17 | 03.17 | 04.17 | 05.17 | 06.17 | 07.17 | 08.17 | 09.17 | 10.17 | 11.17 | 12.17 | 01.18 | 02.18 | 03.18 |
|---|---|---|---|---|---|---|---|---|---|---|---|---|---|---|---|---|---|---|---|---|---|---|---|---|
| Historical sales | 68 | 404 | 0 | 0 | 0 | 80 | 139 | 25 | 10 | 100 | 270 | 70 | 0 | 110 | 0 | 0 | 0 | 0 | 0 | 0 | 0 | 348 | 100 | 150 |
| Boolean sales | 1 | 1 | 0 | 0 | 0 | 1 | 1 | 1 | 1 | 1 | 1 | 1 | 0 | 1 | 0 | 0 | 0 | 0 | 0 | 0 | 0 | 1 | 1 | 1 |
| Initial states | 1 | 1 | 0 | 0 | 0 | 1 | 1 | 1 | 1 | 1 | 1 | 1 | 0 | 1 | 0 | 0 | 0 | 0 | 0 | 0 | 0 | 1 | 1 | 1 |
| Outcomes 3 months | 1 | 0 | 1 | 1 | 1 | 1 | 1 | 1 | 1 | 1 | 1 | 0 | 1 | 0 | 0 | 0 | 0 | 0 | 1 | 1 | 1 | | | |

**Fig. 5.11** Determining the 3 months forecast

- The green connections are the basics for the initial state.
- The light blue squares represent the reasoning for the outcomes 3 months value.

In May 2016, the initial state was "1", but no demand occurs in June, July and August, so the outcome 3 month of May was "0". This logic is shown with the black boxes.

The process described in the previous paragraph is based on the assumption that the scheme is completely described only by two states. This implies exclusivity of the occurrence of the demand in the current period and the fact that the trajectory (that corresponds to the sequence of states) that brought the schema to its current state is not considered.

Its advantage lies in simplicity, but its limitation is in the nature itself of the intermittent demand data. Unfortunately, the concluding results are transition matrices in which the probability of transition to "state 0" is overestimated. However, to avoid this lack of accuracy, it is possible to describe the schema using more than two states.

A state is a description, information, about the current condition of the schema; if we need more accurate information, it is needed to record not only the Boolean sales of the current period but also the ones of the previous periods. For instance, May could be described not only by the Boolean sales of itself, but also by the Boolean sales of past April, March, February and so on.

Let's assume we consider the last two months in addition to the current one; in Fig. 5.12, the process is explained.

If we consider June 2016, the initial state is "011" since no demand has occurred in June, while in May and in April, a non-zero demand occurred. The logic to populate the initial state Boolean has been exemplified with a color code in Fig. 5.12:

- The first Boolean number of the month June 2016 is "0": It refers to the sales/demand of June itself, and it is light blue colored.

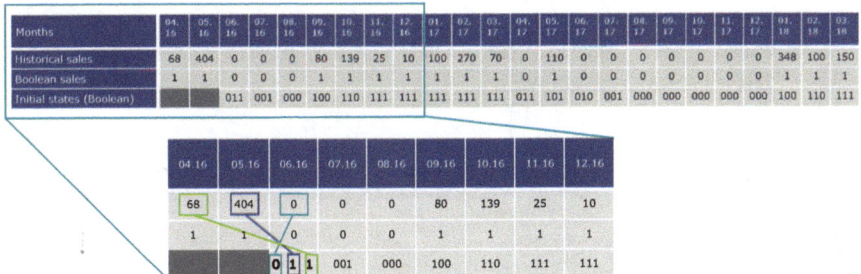

| Months | 04.16 | 05.16 | 06.16 | 07.16 | 08.16 | 09.16 | 10.16 | 11.16 | 12.16 | 01.17 | 02.17 | 03.17 | 04.17 | 05.17 | 06.17 | 07.17 | 08.17 | 09.17 | 10.17 | 11.17 | 12.17 | 01.18 | 02.18 | 03.18 |
|---|---|---|---|---|---|---|---|---|---|---|---|---|---|---|---|---|---|---|---|---|---|---|---|---|
| Historical sales | 68 | 404 | 0 | 0 | 0 | 80 | 139 | 25 | 10 | 100 | 270 | 70 | 0 | 110 | 0 | 0 | 0 | 0 | 0 | 0 | 0 | 348 | 100 | 150 |
| Boolean sales | 1 | 1 | 0 | 0 | 0 | 1 | 1 | 1 | 1 | 1 | 1 | 1 | 0 | 1 | 0 | 0 | 0 | 0 | 0 | 0 | 0 | 1 | 1 | 1 |
| Initial states (Boolean) | | | 011 | 001 | 000 | 100 | 110 | 111 | 111 | 111 | 111 | 111 | 011 | 101 | 010 | 001 | 000 | 000 | 000 | 000 | 000 | 100 | 110 | 111 |

| | 04.16 | 05.16 | 06.16 | 07.16 | 08.16 | 09.16 | 10.16 | 11.16 | 12.16 |
|---|---|---|---|---|---|---|---|---|---|
| | 68 | 404 | 0 | 0 | 0 | 80 | 139 | 25 | 10 |
| | 1 | 1 | 0 | 0 | 0 | 1 | 1 | 1 | 1 |
| | | | 0 1 1 | 001 | 000 | 100 | 110 | 111 | 111 |

**Fig. 5.12** 3-month initial states (binary)

- The second Boolean number of the month June 2016 is "1": It refers to the sales/demand of May 2016, and it is dark blue colored.
- The third Boolean number of the month June 2016 is "1": It refers to the sales/demand of April, and it is green colored.

To populate all the other Boolean states for the following months, the same logic needs to be applied.

To simplify the Boolean number associated with each state, while preserving the information behind it, it is possible to consider the three-digit string made by "0" and "1" as a binary number, and consequently, convert it in a decimal number.

It has to be remembered that a three-digit binary number will generate as a maximum eight different states, defined between 0 and 7.

As shown in Fig. 5.13, the initial states' Boolean row has been converted into the initial states decimal row, by applying the three-digit string transformation. By looking at the bottom of Fig. 5.13, we can see the corresponding digital number for each of the eight Boolean strings.

For example, in September 2016, where the Boolean string was equal to "100", the corresponding decimal number will be "4".

Figure 5.14 aims at describing the subsequent steps to reach the final state decimal output. The upper part of the figure contains the overall overview from the historical sales to the final state, which will then be used for the probability calculations. The first highlight of the process is shown in the middle layer called "initial state calculation":

- Considering the previous three months sales/demand, we assign the Boolean string and its converted decimal number.

Consequently, the final layer can be tackled, understanding the reasoning behind the final outcome calculation:

- To populate the cell of the last row of the table, we need to consider the $t + 1$ sales/demand; for example, if we are aiming at inserting the final state for June 2016, we have to look at what happened in July 2016. In our case, July 2016 experienced a zero sales/demand. This is the first reason why the outcome of June 2016 is set to zero as well.

| Months | 04. 16 | 05. 16 | 06. 16 | 07. 16 | 08. 16 | 09. 16 | 10. 16 | 11. 16 | 12. 16 | 01. 17 | 02. 17 | 03. 17 | 04. 17 | 05. 17 | 06. 17 | 07. 17 | 08. 17 | 09. 17 | 10. 17 | 11. 17 | 12. 17 | 01. 18 | 02. 18 | 03. 18 |
|---|---|---|---|---|---|---|---|---|---|---|---|---|---|---|---|---|---|---|---|---|---|---|---|---|
| Historical sales | 68 | 404 | 0 | 0 | 0 | 80 | 139 | 25 | 10 | 100 | 270 | 70 | 0 | 110 | 0 | 0 | 0 | 0 | 0 | 0 | 0 | 348 | 100 | 150 |
| Boolean sales | 1 | 1 | 0 | 0 | 0 | 1 | 1 | 1 | 1 | 1 | 1 | 1 | 0 | 1 | 0 | 0 | 0 | 0 | 0 | 0 | 0 | 1 | 1 | 1 |
| Initial states (Boolean) | | | 011 | 001 | 000 | 100 | 110 | 111 | 111 | 111 | 111 | 111 | 011 | 101 | 010 | 001 | 000 | 000 | 000 | 000 | 000 | 100 | 110 | 111 |
| Initial states (Decimal) | | | 3 | 1 | 0 | 4 | 6 | 7 | 7 | 7 | 7 | 7 | 3 | 5 | 2 | 1 | 0 | 0 | 0 | 0 | 0 | 4 | 6 | 7 |

| Boolean | 000 | 001 | 010 | 011 | 100 | 101 | 110 | 111 |
|---|---|---|---|---|---|---|---|---|
| Decimal | 0 | 1 | 2 | 3 | 4 | 5 | 6 | 7 |

**Fig. 5.13**  3-month initial states (decimal)

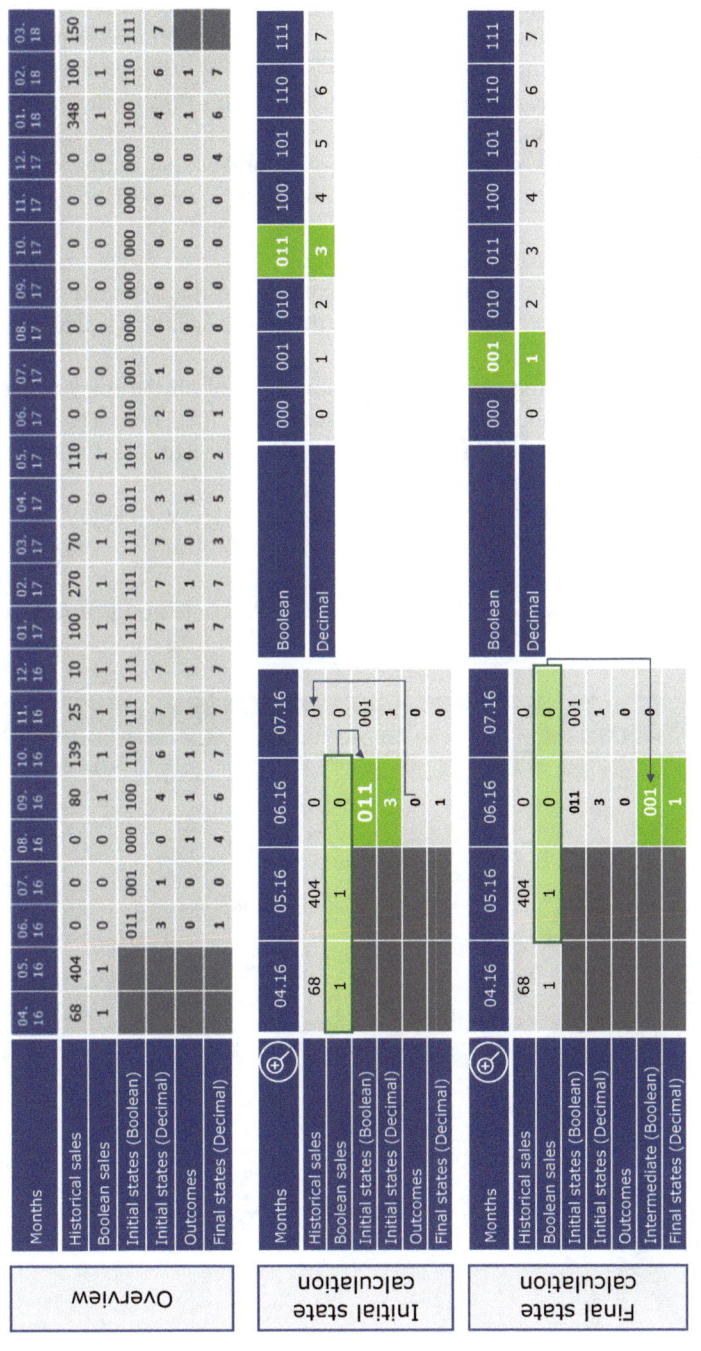

**Fig. 5.14** 3-month final states (decimal)

- Successively, we need to recreate what has been called "intermediate (Boolean)," by considering the $t + 1$ month (July), the $t$ month (June itself) and the $t - 1$ month (May). Since July accounted for a sales/demand equal to zero (Boolean = "0"), June the same (Boolean ="0"), and May for a sales/demand of 404, (Boolean ="1"), the final string will be "001". This result is displayed in the green cell of its specific layer.
- Eventually, we go back checking the decimal number that corresponds to the string "001", and we attribute the decimal number "1" as per shown in green.

The same reasoning is for all the other periods.

Using the same procedure that has been explained in the two-state schema, by considering the states defined by three months, the results will be a square transition matrix 8 × 8.

Figure 5.15 requires some further explanation. First of all the rows of the table describe the initial state and the columns describe the final one. The green area represents an outcome equal "0" (zero demand) while the azure one represents the outcome "1" (non-zero demand).

If we go to analyze the overview panel of Fig. 5.16, we clearly detect this distinction:

- For the decimal numbers equal to 0, 1, 2 and 3, the outcome is always 0.

| Transition Matrix | | | | | | | | |
|---|---|---|---|---|---|---|---|---|
| State | 0 | 1 | 2 | 3 | 4 | 5 | 6 | 7 |
| 0 | P(0,0) | | | | P(4,0) | | | |
| 1 | P(0,1) | | | | P(4,1) | | | |
| 2 | | P(1,2) | | | | P(5,2) | | |
| 3 | | P(1,3) | | | | P(5,1) | | |
| 4 | | | P(2,4) | | | | P(6,4) | |
| 5 | | | P(2,5) | | | | P(6,5) | |
| 6 | | | | P(3,6) | | | | P(7,6) |
| 7 | | | | P(3,7) | | | | P(7,7) |

**Fig. 5.15** 3-month states, determining the transition matrix

Overview

| Months | 04.16 | 05.16 | 06.16 | 07.16 | 08.16 | 09.16 | 10.16 | 11.16 | 12.16 | 01.17 | 02.17 | 03.17 |
|---|---|---|---|---|---|---|---|---|---|---|---|---|
| Historical sales | 68 | 404 | 0 | 0 | 0 | 80 | 139 | 25 | 10 | 100 | 270 | 70 |
| Boolean sales | 1 | 1 | 0 | 0 | 0 | 1 | 1 | 1 | 1 | 1 | 1 | 1 |
| Initial states (Boolean) | | | 011 | 001 | 000 | 100 | 110 | 111 | 111 | 111 | 111 | 111 |
| Initial states (Decimal) | | | 3 | 1 | 0 | 4 | 6 | 7 | 7 | 7 | 7 | 7 |
| Outcomes | | | 0 | 0 | 1 | 1 | 1 | 1 | 1 | 1 | 1 | 0 |
| Final states (Decimal) | | | 1 | 0 | 4 | 6 | 7 | 7 | 7 | 7 | 7 | 3 |

| Months | 04.17 | 05.17 | 06.17 | 07.17 | 08.17 | 09.17 | 10.17 | 11.17 | 12.17 | 01.18 | 02.18 | 03.18 |
|---|---|---|---|---|---|---|---|---|---|---|---|---|
| Historical sales | 0 | 110 | 0 | 0 | 0 | 0 | 0 | 0 | 0 | 348 | 100 | 150 |
| Boolean sales | 0 | 1 | 0 | 0 | 0 | 0 | 0 | 0 | 0 | 1 | 1 | 1 |
| Initial states (Boolean) | 011 | 101 | 010 | 001 | 000 | 000 | 000 | 000 | 000 | 100 | 110 | 111 |
| Initial states (Decimal) | 3 | 5 | 2 | 1 | 0 | 0 | 0 | 0 | 0 | 4 | 6 | 7 |
| Outcomes | 1 | 0 | 0 | 0 | 0 | 0 | 0 | 0 | 0 | 1 | 1 | |
| Final states (Decimal) | 5 | 2 | 1 | 0 | 0 | 0 | 0 | 0 | 0 | 4 | 6 | |

**Fig. 5.16** 3-month states' distinction

– For the decimal numbers equal to 4, 5, 6, and 7, the outcome is always 1.

Furthermore, it has to be underlined that since the transition from one state to another is determined by the presence or absence of a non-zero demand in the following period, not all the transitions between the states are allowed. For example, if the current state is "2" (binary state = 010) the only admissible transitions are to state "5" (binary state = 101) if the following period has a non-zero demand or to state "1" (binary state = 001) if the demand of the following period is zero.

This is the reason why the transition matrix is populated only partially. The probabilities displayed are those that can be numerically identified.

The $P(j, i)$ displayed in the transition matrix are the probabilities that an initial state "$j$" becomes a final state "$i$", so that:

– If the final state "$i$" is in the green area, in the following period the demand will be zero.
– If "$i$" is in the azure area, there will be a non-zero demand in the following month.

Besides, using the same method that has been used for the transition matrix and, defining the outcomes as "at least a non-zero demand in the following three months" or "no demand in the following three months," we can calculate for each initial state the probability to have at least a period of non-zero demand in the given time span.

The result will be a matrix of probability in which for each initial state is determined the probability to have "at least a non-zero demand in the following three months" or "no demand in the following three months."

To face the problem of deciding for how long the information is needed, consequently for how long it must be stored in the definition of the state, it is necessary to consider that an information of length "$n$" gives origin to transition matrices in which the total number of cells is $(2^n)^2$ and the number of cells containing a probability is equal to $2^{(n + 1)}$.

This concept implies that the number of available data must be at least such to guarantee that all the $2^n$ states are adequately represented.

On the other hand, the use of many data implies the fact of relating to periods very distant from the current one. Old periods as well as the most recent ones are equally taken into consideration. Besides, by a mathematical point of view, all data have the same importance, the most recent as the older ones. Consequently, the insights from the older time periods may likely condition the adequate representation of the current demand trend even if they denote a pattern that is too ancient, so no longer valid as a model.

Furthermore, relying on the same principles and using the three-month outcomes, the three-month matrices can be determined; their meaning is to record if at least one non-zero demand period has occurred in the three months that followed the reference period.

For practical purposes, it is advisable to:

- consider periods equal to the lead time of the product
- use a length equals to 3 periods
- have at least 40 data to be able to determine the matrices with a time horizon of 1 period and 3 periods
- periodically update the database following the demand timeline and keeping the sample size constant.

All in all, the results of this procedure are:

- a transition matrix that will allow the planner to make forecast for the following periods
- a probability matrix that gives the planner an estimation of the time that the unsold products will spend in inventory.

## 5.3  Sizing Non-zero Demand Predictions with Single Exponential Smoothing

In defining the amplitude of the forecasted demand, the SES procedure has been used, but the planner could use any other forecasting technique.

Single exponential smoothing (SES) is a technique in which historical periods are weighted progressively higher, in the calculation of the forecast, from older to more recent periods. The relative weights depend on the smoothing constant used—called $\alpha$, alpha.

To adapt this technique to the nature of intermittent demand, characterized by the presence of zero values randomly distributed, the formula previously illustrated in 3.3.2 must be changed in:

If $X_t \neq 0$, then:

$$F_{t+1} = \alpha X_t + (1 - \alpha)F_t$$

If $X_t = 0$, then:

$$F_{t+1} = F_t$$

where:

- $F_{t+1}$ denotes the forecast for the period $t + 1$
- $F_t$ denotes the forecast for the period $t$
- $X_t$ denotes the actual demand observed in the period $t$.

The smoothing constant $\alpha$ takes on a value between 0 and 1. The formula, translated in a more business language, means that the new forecast (at the end of period $t + 1$) equals a certain percentage ($\alpha$) of the forecast error plus the previous forecast. So, the higher the value of $\alpha$, the higher will be the weights assigned to the more recent periods.

As a "rule of thumb," to define the value of the smoothing constant $\alpha$, the planner has to consider if a non-zero demand series is still running or is finished and, in the latter case, how further away was a non-zero demand series in the past.

If the non-zero demand series is still running or it is finished within two periods (including the current period), $\alpha$ assumes a value in the range 0.3–0.4, giving in this way more significance to the recent periods. Otherwise, it is advisable to set $\alpha$ on values closer to 0.1.

It is also suggested to run the preprocessing procedure to correct the outliers in the historical sales sequence.

It is obvious that to take in account the actual behavior of the demand, the whole procedure and specifically the SES analysis must be periodically repeated; the optimal solution would be to run the forecasting procedure every period.

## 5.4  Forecasting Intermittent Demand

The process of non-zero demand forecasting is coupled with the single exponential smoothing in order to make a full prediction about future sales.

The forecasting process is based on the preliminary calculation of the following elements:

- The forecasting matrix 1 month ahead was obtained using the historical series of sales.
- The average length of the zero demand sequences AZDI and average length of non-zero demand sequences ADI were obtained using the historical series of sales.
- The state was taken by the demand in the last recorded month in the historical series.
- The value was taken by the Boolean demand in the last recorded month.
- The current length of the Boolean sequence to which the last Boolean demand belongs, for example, if the last known month had a non-zero demand, with a Boolean value of 1, and the same result had also occurred in the previous 3 months, and then the current length of the Boolean series is equal to 4.
- The future demand sizing was obtained using the single exponential smoothing adapted to an intermittent demand.

The iterative process evolves according to the following steps:

1. Determine the future value of the non-zero demand by applying the single exponential smoothing or any other forecasting technique. However, the forecast could be generated using any model that results in a quantity that appropriately represents the amplitude in case a non-zero demand is predicted for a given forecast period.
2. Determine the current state of the demand.
3. Determine whether the current series corresponds to a zero or a non-zero demand.
4. Compare the current length of the sequence of outcomes with the corresponding average value:

    4.1. AZDI, if it is a zero demand sequence
    4.2. ADI, if it is a non-zero demand sequence.

5. Depending on whether the sequence current length is less than the corresponding average length or greater/equal, two alternative routes will be taken

    5.1. If the previous comparison has determined that the current length is less than the average value of the corresponding series, then the future state is deduced from the combination of the highest value of probability in the forecast matrix 1 month ahead corresponding to the current initial state and the transition matrix for the current initial state and the highest probability.
    5.2. If the previous comparison has determined that the current length is equal to or greater than the average value of the corresponding series (breaking condition), then the future state is deduced from the combination of the lowest value of the forecast matrix 1 month ahead corresponding to the current initial state and the transition matrix for the current initial state and the lowest probability.

6. Based on the state provided in the preceding steps, determine the Boolean outcome of the demand which will correspond to 0 if the forecasted state assumes values 0, 1, 2 and 3 or 1 if the forecasted state assumes values 4, 5, 6 and 7.
7. Determine the value assumed by the demand by calculating the product between the Boolean output calculated in the previous point and the value of the non-zero demand obtained in the previous step (1).
8. The forecasted state becomes the last known state, and the process is repeated starting at step (2) until the forecast has reached the entire time horizon to be analyzed.

The constraint applied in step 5.2 avoids that a zero or non-zero demand sequence has an excessive length given by a closed loop in forecasting matrix.

The results are:

- using the 1-month ahead probabilities, making a forecast which will be the state assumed by the system in the following month, that corresponds to a prediction about the existence of a non-zero demand in the following period
- allowing the practitioner to know which the probability of the proposed forecast is and which the probability to have at least a non-zero demand in the following three periods will be
- based on the SES analysis, sizing a non-zero demand. However, the forecast could be generated using any model that results in a quantity that appropriately represents the amplitude in case a non-zero demand is predicted for a given forecast period.

In layman's terms, the procedure uses the last actual state to determine the state prediction for the following month.

The newly generated forecast will become the reference state based on which to determine the predicted state for the following month. This process will be repeated until all the forecasts are generated in the reference time horizon.

The foregoing implies that the accuracy of the forecast will decrease, moving away from the last period for which the actual values of the demand are known, since the subsequent forecasts will themselves be based on forecasts and not on actual data; therefore, the most accurate forecasts refer to the first months following the last period with actual values of the demand.

Given this effect, it is advisable to periodically repeat the procedure; the frequency suggested for carrying out the analysis is the same with which the demand's data are collected.

### 5.4.1  SAP Use Case: Custom Method to Forecast Intermittent Demand

The aim of the SAP use case is to determine the forecast using the multi-state Markovian analysis and at the same time compare its accuracy with the standard Croston method used to create a sporadic forecast. The process has been applied to the SKUs defined "flashy" or "intermittent," since for "stable" ones the forecasting methods are defined in the following chapter and "unforecastable" SKUs have a few non-zero demand period too small to infer probabilities.

It also gives information on the process that has been used to adapt the theoretical method to the tools given by the SAP system.

The SAP use case process is based on the following steps:

1. Pre-calculation 1: Calculate zero demand and non-zero demand sequence; determine average zero demand sequence.
2. Classification: Stable—Intermittent—Flashy—Unforecastable (if zero demand sequence > threshold (default = 18)).

3. Pre-calculation 2: Generate forecast based on Croston for all products classified as "flashy" or "intermittent."
4. Forecast matrix determination: Calculate forecast matrix based on 3-chain and 2-chain Boolean states.
5. Generate 1-month ahead state forecast: Calculate 1-month ahead state forecast— based on 3-chain forecast matrix if current zero demand sequence < average zero demand sequence; otherwise, switch state and determine next period state.
6. Define demand amplitude for non-zero Boolean forecast: If the forecasted state is 1, use the Croston forecast (profile setting is set to generate non-sporadic forecast); otherwise, set forecast to 0.
7. Calculate accuracy: Use "Forecast Accuracy" app to generate accuracy measures.
8. Results analysis (Excel): Compare accuracy in Excel.
9. Results analysis (Analytics): Compare accuracy in Web dashboard.

Using some figures, the steps are described.

Step 1   Pre-calculation 1

Initially, analyzing the Boolean historical demand, zero demand and non-zero demand sequences are detected to determine average zero demand sequence and average non-zero demand sequence.

The first value is used in the classification, then together with the average non-zero demand sequence will be used as a breaking condition in step 5.

Zero and non-zero demand sequence local members count the consecutive occurrences of zero and non-zero demands, respectively.

The average zero demand sequence ("Zero Demand Sequence" in the screenshot is then used in the classification of SKUs in a later step (if sequence > {threshold} then classification = non-forecastable) (Fig. 5.17).

Step 2   Classification

Using the criteria described in the following section, the whole portfolio is classified to determine "flashy" and "intermittent" SKUs; the forecasting process will include these SKUs.

The classification of SKUs as "stable", "intermittent", "flashy" or "unfore-castable" is done with help of an attribute transformation (Fig 5.18).

Classification rules:

• IF zero demand sequence > threshold (default = 18) for unforecastable THEN "U"
• IF range of zero demand sequence (max—min zero demand sequence) or range of non-zero demand sequence = NULL THEN "S"
• IF range of zero demand sequence AND range of non-zero demand sequence > 2 THEN "F"

| Product ID | Key Figure | Jan-14 | Feb-14 | Mar-14 | Apr-14 | May-14 | Jun-14 | Jul-14 | Aug-14 | Sep-14 | Oct-14 | Nov-14 | Dec-14 | Jan-15 | Feb-15 | Mar-15 | Apr-15 | May-15 | Jun-15 |
|---|---|---|---|---|---|---|---|---|---|---|---|---|---|---|---|---|---|---|---|
| IBP 1 | HKZEROESCOUNTPC | 1 | 1 | 1 | 1 | 1 | 1 | 1 | 1 | 1 | 1 | 1 | 1 | 1 | 1 | 1 | 1 | 1 | 1 |
| IBP 2 | NZDS1 | 1 | | | | | | | | | 9 | | 10 | | | | | | 15 |
| IBP 2 | NZDS2 | 1 | 1 | 1 | 1 | 1 | 1 | 1 | 1 | 9 | 9 | 10 | 10 | 10 | 10 | 10 | 15 | | |
| IBP 2 | NZDS | 1 | | | | | | | | 8 | | 1 | | | | | | | 5 |
| IBP 2 | Historical Sales | 2464 | 0 | 1200 | 3000 | 2000 | 2400 | 1408 | 1335 | 172 | 962 | 0 | 1712 | 0 | 3857 | 2817 | 1000 | 1000 | 3721 |
| IBP 2 | ZDS1 | 1 | | | | | | | | 2 | | 3 | | | | | | | |
| IBP 2 | ZDS2 | 1 | 1 | 1 | 1 | 1 | 1 | 1 | 1 | 1 | 2 | 2 | 3 | 3 | 3 | 3 | 3 | 3 | |
| IBP 2 | ZDS | 1 | | | | | | | | 1 | | 1 | | | | | | | |
| IBP 2 | Zero Demand Sequence | 1 | | | | | | | | 1 | | 1 | | | | | | | |
| IBP 2 | Non-zero Demand Sequence | 1 | | | | | | | | 8 | | 1 | | | | | | | 5 |
| IBP 2 | HKRANGEZDS | 1 | 1 | 1 | 1 | 1 | 1 | 1 | 1 | 1 | 1 | 1 | 1 | 1 | 1 | 1 | 1 | 1 | 1 |
| IBP 2 | HKRANGENZDS | 9 | 9 | 9 | 9 | 9 | 9 | 9 | 9 | 9 | 9 | 9 | 9 | 9 | 9 | 9 | 9 | 9 | 9 |
| IBP 2 | HKCOUNTZEROES | 8 | 8 | 8 | 8 | 8 | 8 | 8 | 8 | 8 | 8 | 8 | 8 | 8 | 8 | 8 | 8 | 8 | 8 |
| IBP 2 | HKZEROESCOUNTPC | 0 | 0 | 0 | 0 | 0 | 0 | 0 | 0 | 0 | 0 | 0 | 0 | 0 | 0 | 0 | 0 | 0 | 0 |
| IBP 3 | NZDS1 | | | | | | | | | | | | | | | | | | |
| IBP 3 | NZDS2 | | | | | | | | | | | | | | | | | | |
| IBP 3 | NZDS | | | | | | | | | | | | | | | | | | |
| IBP 3 | Historical Sales | 0 | 0 | 0 | 0 | 0 | 0 | 0 | 0 | 0 | 0 | 0 | 0 | 0 | 0 | 0 | 0 | 0 | 0 |
| IBP 3 | ZDS1 | | | | | | | | | | | | | | | | | | 18 |
| IBP 3 | ZDS2 | | | | | | | | | | | | | | | | | | 18 |
| IBP 3 | ZDS | | | | | | | | | | | | | | | | | | 18 |
| IBP 3 | Zero Demand Sequence | | | | | | | | | | | | | | | | | | 18 |
| IBP 3 | Non-zero Demand Sequence | | | | | | | | | | | | | | | | | | |
| IBP 3 | HKRANGEZDS | 17 | 17 | 17 | 17 | 17 | 17 | 17 | 17 | 17 | 17 | 17 | 17 | 17 | 17 | 17 | 17 | 17 | 17 |
| IBP 3 | HKRANGENZDS | 3 | 3 | 3 | 3 | 3 | 3 | 3 | 3 | 3 | 3 | 3 | 3 | 3 | 3 | 3 | 3 | 3 | 3 |
| IBP 3 | HKCOUNTZEROES | 26 | 26 | 26 | 26 | 26 | 26 | 26 | 26 | 26 | 26 | 26 | 26 | 26 | 26 | 26 | 26 | 26 | 26 |
| IBP 3 | HKZEROESCOUNTPC | 1 | 1 | 1 | 1 | 1 | 1 | 1 | 1 | 1 | 1 | 1 | 1 | 1 | 1 | 1 | 1 | 1 | 1 |
| IBP 4 | NZDS1 | | | | | | | | | | | | | | | | | | |
| IBP 4 | NZDS2 | | | | | | | | | | | | | | | | | | |
| IBP 4 | NZDS | | | | | | | | | | | | | | | | | | |
| IBP 4 | Historical Sales | 0 | 0 | 0 | 0 | 0 | 0 | 0 | 0 | 0 | 0 | 0 | 0 | 0 | 0 | 0 | 0 | 0 | 0 |
| IBP 4 | ZDS1 | | | | | | | | | | | | | | | | | | 18 |

**Fig. 5.17** Calculation of zero demand and non-zero demand sequence

- ELSE "I".

After the classification process, the portfolio (in this example 100 SKUs) is divided into four SIFU classes, and the amplitude of each class is defined considering the volume of sales. The figure also presents the trend of the portfolio in a reference period of 4 years (Fig. 5.19).

Step 3   Pre-calculation 2

When Markovian model predicts a Boolean 1 state, the Markovian forecast is set to the forecast in the key figure "Statistical Forecast Markovian Input." In our example, Croston model with the sporadic indicator set to false is used. However, the forecast could be generated using any model that results in a quantity that appropriately represents the amplitude in case a non-zero demand is predicted for a given forecast period (Fig. 5.20).

Step 4   Forecast matrix determination

Key figures are created for 3-chain, 2-chain and 1-chain states. These key figures predict the outcome for the next month and over the next 3 months (1M ahead and 3M ahead). The predictions are based on conditional probabilities calculated based on counting occurrences of a Boolean 0 or 1 occurring after a given Boolean sequence defined by the state (e.g., state 4 translates to a 3-chain sequence of 100—decimal to binary conversion) therefore counting what follows this sequence historically enables calculation of conditional probabilities (Fig. 5.21).

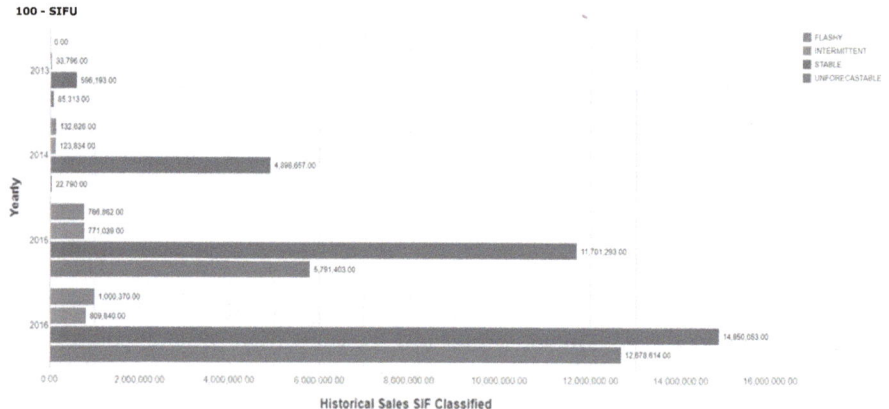

**Fig. 5.18**  Classification: Stable–Intermittent–Flashy–Unforecastable

**Fig. 5.19**  Classification of SKUs portfolio

The system is also calculating the transition matrix defining which is the most probable future state 1 month ahead and which is the future state in the case a breaking condition is encountered; a breaking condition corresponds to the case in which the length of the current sequence of outcomes is greater than AZDI if the sequence value is 0 or the ADI if the sequence value is 1 (Fig. 5.22).

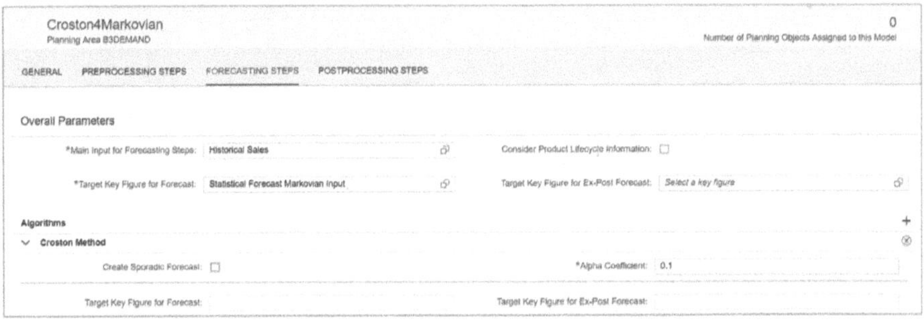

**Fig. 5.20**  Setting the model to predict demand amplitude

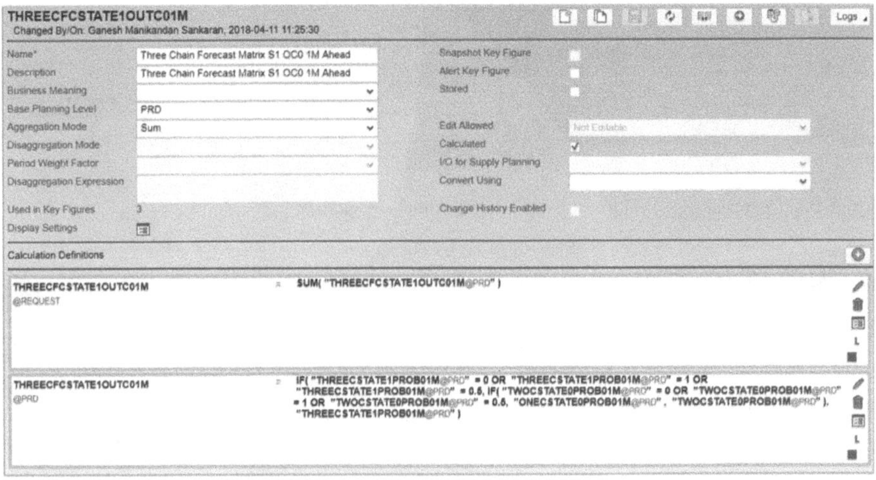

**Fig. 5.21**  Forecast matrix algorithm

Step 5   Generate 1-month ahead state forecast

The forecasted state from the forecast matrix is used unless there is a breaking condition encountered—the breaking condition is when the zero demand sequence is equal or greater than the zero demand sequence average for the SKU in question.

In this example, as the average zero demand sequence is 1.33 (rounded to 1), breaking condition is encountered in December 2016.

The evaluation is done in a local member called "switch Boolean state." Once switched, this is then appended to the previous states to calculate the adjusted forecasted state and the corresponding $N$-month ahead forecast Boolean outcome (Fig. 5.23).

Step 6   Define demand amplitude for non-zero Boolean forecast

Forecasted Boolean states are used to take over forecast from the input key figure for demand amplitude ("Statistical Forecast Markovian Input" in our case).

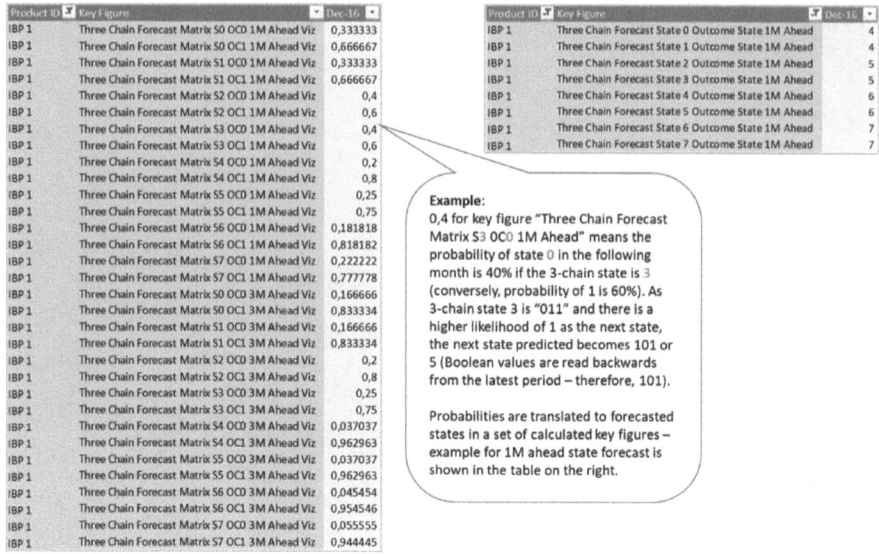

| Product ID | Key Figure | Dec-16 |
|---|---|---|
| IBP 1 | Three Chain Forecast Matrix S0 OC0 1M Ahead Viz | 0,333333 |
| IBP 1 | Three Chain Forecast Matrix S0 OC1 1M Ahead Viz | 0,666667 |
| IBP 1 | Three Chain Forecast Matrix S1 OC0 1M Ahead Viz | 0,333333 |
| IBP 1 | Three Chain Forecast Matrix S1 OC1 1M Ahead Viz | 0,666667 |
| IBP 1 | Three Chain Forecast Matrix S2 OC0 1M Ahead Viz | 0,4 |
| IBP 1 | Three Chain Forecast Matrix S2 OC1 1M Ahead Viz | 0,6 |
| IBP 1 | Three Chain Forecast Matrix S3 OC0 1M Ahead Viz | 0,4 |
| IBP 1 | Three Chain Forecast Matrix S3 OC1 1M Ahead Viz | 0,6 |
| IBP 1 | Three Chain Forecast Matrix S4 OC0 1M Ahead Viz | 0,2 |
| IBP 1 | Three Chain Forecast Matrix S4 OC1 1M Ahead Viz | 0,8 |
| IBP 1 | Three Chain Forecast Matrix S5 OC0 1M Ahead Viz | 0,25 |
| IBP 1 | Three Chain Forecast Matrix S5 OC1 1M Ahead Viz | 0,75 |
| IBP 1 | Three Chain Forecast Matrix S6 OC0 1M Ahead Viz | 0,181818 |
| IBP 1 | Three Chain Forecast Matrix S6 OC1 1M Ahead Viz | 0,818182 |
| IBP 1 | Three Chain Forecast Matrix S7 OC0 1M Ahead Viz | 0,222222 |
| IBP 1 | Three Chain Forecast Matrix S7 OC1 1M Ahead Viz | 0,777778 |
| IBP 1 | Three Chain Forecast Matrix S0 OC0 3M Ahead Viz | 0,166666 |
| IBP 1 | Three Chain Forecast Matrix S0 OC1 3M Ahead Viz | 0,833334 |
| IBP 1 | Three Chain Forecast Matrix S1 OC0 3M Ahead Viz | 0,166666 |
| IBP 1 | Three Chain Forecast Matrix S1 OC1 3M Ahead Viz | 0,833334 |
| IBP 1 | Three Chain Forecast Matrix S2 OC0 3M Ahead Viz | 0,2 |
| IBP 1 | Three Chain Forecast Matrix S2 OC1 3M Ahead Viz | 0,8 |
| IBP 1 | Three Chain Forecast Matrix S3 OC0 3M Ahead Viz | 0,25 |
| IBP 1 | Three Chain Forecast Matrix S3 OC1 3M Ahead Viz | 0,75 |
| IBP 1 | Three Chain Forecast Matrix S4 OC0 3M Ahead Viz | 0,037037 |
| IBP 1 | Three Chain Forecast Matrix S4 OC1 3M Ahead Viz | 0,962963 |
| IBP 1 | Three Chain Forecast Matrix S5 OC0 3M Ahead Viz | 0,037037 |
| IBP 1 | Three Chain Forecast Matrix S5 OC1 3M Ahead Viz | 0,962963 |
| IBP 1 | Three Chain Forecast Matrix S6 OC0 3M Ahead Viz | 0,045454 |
| IBP 1 | Three Chain Forecast Matrix S6 OC1 3M Ahead Viz | 0,954546 |
| IBP 1 | Three Chain Forecast Matrix S7 OC0 3M Ahead Viz | 0,055555 |
| IBP 1 | Three Chain Forecast Matrix S7 OC1 3M Ahead Viz | 0,944445 |

| Product ID | Key Figure | Dec-16 |
|---|---|---|
| IBP 1 | Three Chain Forecast State 0 Outcome State 1M Ahead | 4 |
| IBP 1 | Three Chain Forecast State 1 Outcome State 1M Ahead | 4 |
| IBP 1 | Three Chain Forecast State 2 Outcome State 1M Ahead | 5 |
| IBP 1 | Three Chain Forecast State 3 Outcome State 1M Ahead | 5 |
| IBP 1 | Three Chain Forecast State 4 Outcome State 1M Ahead | 6 |
| IBP 1 | Three Chain Forecast State 5 Outcome State 1M Ahead | 6 |
| IBP 1 | Three Chain Forecast State 6 Outcome State 1M Ahead | 7 |
| IBP 1 | Three Chain Forecast State 7 Outcome State 1M Ahead | 7 |

**Example:**
0,4 for key figure "Three Chain Forecast Matrix S3 OC0 1M Ahead" means the probability of state 0 in the following month is 40% if the 3-chain state is 3 (conversely, probability of 1 is 60%). As 3-chain state 3 is "011" and there is a higher likelihood of 1 as the next state, the next state predicted becomes 101 or 5 (Boolean values are read backwards from the latest period – therefore, 101).

Probabilities are translated to forecasted states in a set of calculated key figures – example for 1M ahead state forecast is shown in the table on the right.

**Fig. 5.22** Forecast matrix 1 month ahead and transition matrix

| Product ID | Key Figure | Aug-16 | Sep-16 | Oct-16 | Nov-16 | Dec-16 | Jan-17 | Feb-17 | Mar-17 | Apr-17 | May-17 | Jun-17 | Jul-17 |
|---|---|---|---|---|---|---|---|---|---|---|---|---|---|
| IBP 1 | Historical Sales | 1694 | 1084 | 1249 | 0 | 0 | 1047 | 2067 | 2161 | | | | |
| IBP 1 | Boolean Sales | 1 | 1 | 1 | 0 | 0 | | | | | | | |
| IBP 1 | Demand Sequence Counter | 2 | 3 | 4 | 5 | 1 | 1 | 2 | 3 | 4 | 5 | 1 | 1 |
| IBP 1 | Switch Boolean State | 0 | 0 | 0 | 0 | 1 | 1 | 0 | 0 | 0 | 0 | 1 | 1 |
| IBP 1 | Three Chain State Current Month | 7 | 7 | 7 | 7 | 5 | 4 | 6 | 7 | 7 | 7 | 7 | 5 |
| IBP 1 | Three Chain State Current Month 2 | 7 | 7 | 7 | 7 | 3 | 5 | 6 | 7 | 7 | 7 | 3 | 5 |
| IBP 1 | Mixed Boolean State | 1 | 1 | 1 | 1 | 0 | 1 | 1 | 1 | 1 | 1 | 0 | 1 |
| IBP 1 | Three Chain State Previous Month | 7 | 7 | 7 | 7 | 7 | 3 | 1 | | | | | |
| IBP 1 | Average Zero Demand Sequence | 1,333333 | 1,333333 | 1,333333 | 1,333333 | 1,333333 | 1,333333 | 1,333333 | 1,333333 | 1,333333 | 1,333333 | 1,333333 | 1,333333 |
| IBP 1 | Average Non-Zero Demand Sequence | 4,666666 | 4,666666 | 4,666666 | 4,666666 | 4,666666 | 4,666666 | 4,666666 | 4,666666 | 4,666666 | 4,666666 | 4,666666 | 4,666666 |
| IBP 1 | Three Chain Forecast State 0 Outcome State 1M Ahead | 4 | 4 | 4 | 4 | 4 | 4 | 4 | 4 | 4 | 4 | 4 | 4 |
| IBP 1 | Three Chain Forecast State 1 Outcome State 1M Ahead | 4 | 4 | 4 | 4 | 4 | 4 | 4 | 4 | 4 | 4 | 4 | 4 |
| IBP 1 | Three Chain Forecast State 2 Outcome State 1M Ahead | 5 | 5 | 5 | 5 | 5 | 5 | 5 | 5 | 5 | 5 | 5 | 5 |
| IBP 1 | Three Chain Forecast State 3 Outcome State 1M Ahead | 5 | 5 | 5 | 5 | 5 | 5 | 5 | 5 | 5 | 5 | 5 | 5 |
| IBP 1 | Three Chain Forecast State 4 Outcome State 1M Ahead | 6 | 6 | 6 | 6 | 6 | 6 | 6 | 6 | 6 | 6 | 6 | 6 |
| IBP 1 | Three Chain Forecast State 5 Outcome State 1M Ahead | 6 | 6 | 6 | 6 | 6 | 6 | 6 | 6 | 6 | 6 | 6 | 6 |
| IBP 1 | Three Chain Forecast State 6 Outcome State 1M Ahead | 7 | 7 | 7 | 7 | 7 | 7 | 7 | 7 | 7 | 7 | 7 | 7 |
| IBP 1 | Three Chain Forecast State 7 Outcome State 1M Ahead | 7 | 7 | 7 | 7 | 7 | 7 | 7 | 7 | 7 | 7 | 7 | 7 |
| IBP 1 | Forecasted Boolean Sales | 1 | 1 | 1 | 1 | 0 | 1 | 1 | 1 | 1 | 1 | 0 | 1 |
| IBP 1 | Statistical Forecast Croston (Segmented) | | | | | | 6690,282488 | 6690,282488 | 6690,282488 | 6690,282488 | 6690,282488 | 6690,282488 | 6690,282488 |
| IBP 1 | Markovian Forecast | 1780,21707 | 1780,21707 | 1780,21707 | 1780,21707 | | 1780,21707 | 1780,21707 | 1780,21707 | 1780,21707 | 1780,21707 | | 1780,21707 |

**Fig. 5.23** 1-month ahead state forecast

Note that key figure "Markovian Forecast" is null in month Jun-17 where forecasted Boolean sales is 0 (Fig. 5.24).

Step 7  Calculate accuracy

Statistical forecast accuracy of Markovian forecast is calculated using the "Manage Forecast Error Calculations" app (Fig. 5.25).

| Product ID | Key Figure | Jan-17 | Feb-17 | Mar-17 | Apr-17 | May-17 | Jun-17 | Jul-17 | Aug-17 | Sep-17 | Oct-17 | Nov-17 | Dec-17 |
|---|---|---|---|---|---|---|---|---|---|---|---|---|---|
| IBP 1 | Historical Sales | 1047 | 2067 | 2161 | | | | | | | | | |
| IBP 1 | Boolean Sales | | | | | | | | | | | | |
| IBP 1 | Three Chain State Previous Month | 1 | | | | | | | | | | | |
| IBP 1 | Average Zero Demand Sequence | 1.333333 | 1.333333 | 1.333333 | 1.333333 | 1.333333 | 1.333333 | 1.333333 | 1.333333 | 1.333333 | 1.333333 | 1.333333 | 1.333333 |
| IBP 1 | Average Non-Zero Demand Sequence | 4.666666 | 4.666666 | 4.666666 | 4.666666 | 4.666666 | 4.666666 | 4.666666 | 4.666666 | 4.666666 | 4.666666 | 4.666666 | 4.666666 |
| IBP 1 | Three Chain Forecast State 0 Outcome State 1M Ahead | 4 | 4 | 4 | 4 | 4 | 4 | 4 | 4 | 4 | 4 | 4 | 4 |
| IBP 1 | Three Chain Forecast State 1 Outcome State 1M Ahead | 4 | 4 | 4 | 4 | 4 | 4 | 4 | 4 | 4 | 4 | 4 | 4 |
| IBP 1 | Three Chain Forecast State 2 Outcome State 1M Ahead | 5 | 5 | 5 | 5 | 5 | 5 | 5 | 5 | 5 | 5 | 5 | 5 |
| IBP 1 | Three Chain Forecast State 3 Outcome State 1M Ahead | 5 | 5 | 5 | 5 | 5 | 5 | 5 | 5 | 5 | 5 | 5 | 5 |
| IBP 1 | Three Chain Forecast State 4 Outcome State 1M Ahead | 6 | 6 | 6 | 6 | 6 | 6 | 6 | 6 | 6 | 6 | 6 | 6 |
| IBP 1 | Three Chain Forecast State 5 Outcome State 1M Ahead | 6 | 6 | 6 | 6 | 6 | 6 | 6 | 6 | 6 | 6 | 6 | 6 |
| IBP 1 | Three Chain Forecast State 6 Outcome State 1M Ahead | 7 | 7 | 7 | 7 | 7 | 7 | 7 | 7 | 7 | 7 | 7 | 7 |
| IBP 1 | Three Chain Forecast State 7 Outcome State 1M Ahead | 7 | 7 | 7 | 7 | 7 | 7 | 7 | 7 | 7 | 7 | 7 | 7 |
| IBP 1 | Forecasted Boolean Sales | 1 | 1 | 1 | 1 | 1 | 0 | 1 | 1 | 1 | 1 | 1 | 0 |
| IBP 1 | Statistical Forecast Croston (Segmented) | 6690.282488 | 6690.282488 | 6690.282488 | 6690.282488 | 6690.282488 | 6690.282488 | 6690.282488 | 6690.282488 | 6690.282488 | 6690.282488 | 6690.282488 | 6690.282488 |
| IBP 1 | Markovian Forecast | 1513.918915 | 1513.918915 | 1513.918915 | 1513.918915 | 1513.918915 | | 1513.918915 | 1513.918915 | 1513.918915 | 1513.918915 | 1513.918915 | |

**Fig. 5.24**  Markov demand forecast

Croston_Markov / Markov

## Markov

### Input Settings

| | | |
|---|---|---|
| Sales History Key Figure: | Historical Sales | |
| Forecast Key Figure: | Markovian Forecast | |
| Lag of Chosen Forecast Key Figure: | | Monthly |
| Time Periods in the Past: | 12 | Monthly |
| Offset Used for Time Periods: | -14 | Monthly |

-36                                                                                          0

## Output Settings

| | |
|---|---|
| Planning Level of Output Key Figures: | Product (PRD) |
| Periodicity of the Output Planning Level: | Time Independent |

☐  Measures to Calculate                            Output Key Figures

**Forecast Error Measures**

☑  Mean Absolute Percentage Error (MAPE)        MAPE Markovian (Segmented)               *Lag 0

**Fig. 5.25**  Setting accuracy calculation

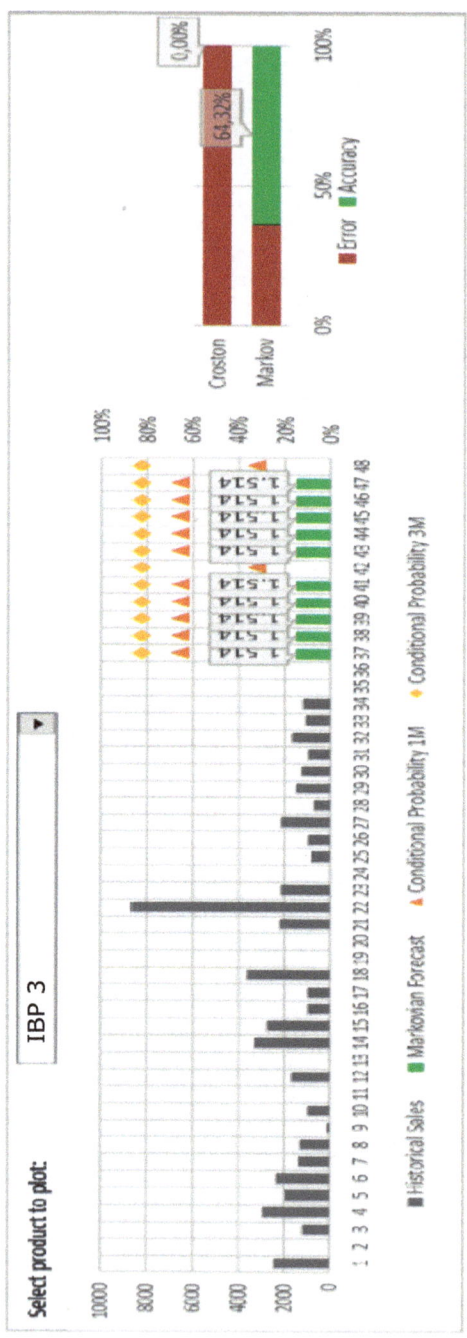

**Fig. 5.26** Markov dashboard

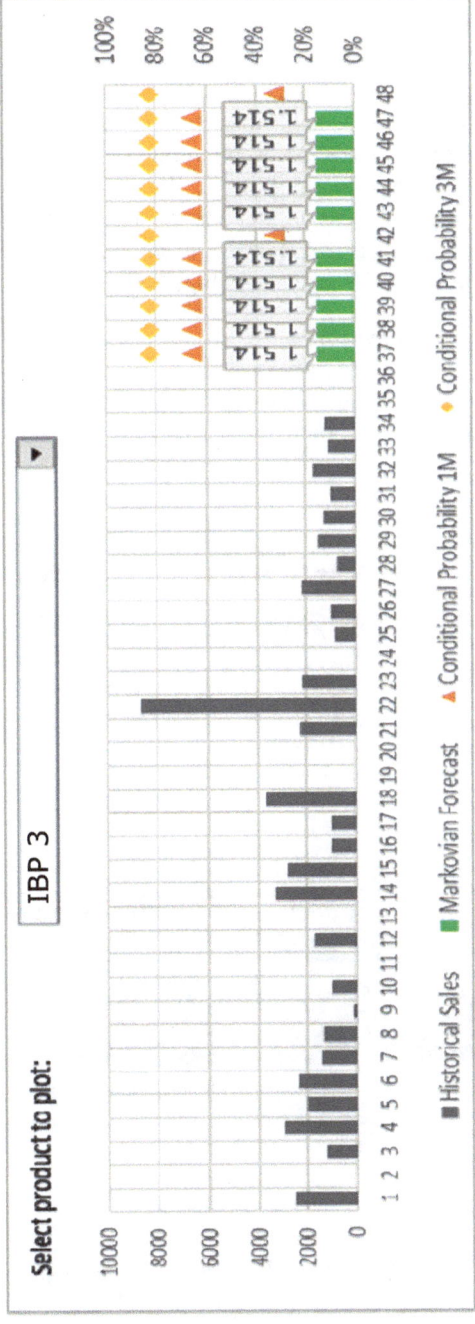

**Fig. 5.27** Markov dashboard, forecasted demand and conditional probabilities

Step 8  Result analysis (Excel)

Historical sales are the gray bars. Markovian forecast, which is equal to the "Statistical Forecast Markovian Input" key figure for forecast periods where forecasted Boolean state is 1, are the green bars (Fig. 5.26).

Conditional probabilities are visualized as orange triangles (1 month ahead) and yellow diamonds (3 month ahead—to be interpreted as probability of a non-zero demand in the next 3 months) (Fig. 5.27).

Forecast accuracy measurement results for the chosen SKU for Croston and Markovian are compared in this chart. For this example, accuracy of Croston is 0% and Markovian results in 64.32% accuracy (Fig. 5.28).

Step 9  Result analysis (Analytics)

Comparison of Markovian and Croston forecast accuracy for a selection of SKUs by ABC classification is shown in Fig. 5.29.

**Fig. 5.28**  Markov dashboard, accuracy comparison

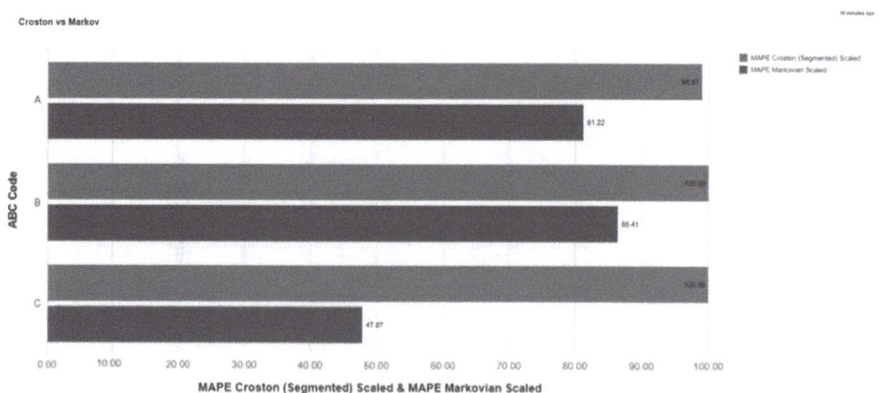

**Fig. 5.29**  Accuracy comparison of the whole portfolio

# Reference

Häggström, O. (2002). *Finite Markov chains and algorithmic applications*. Cambridge: Cambridge University Press.

# Value of Forecasting with Custom Methods

**6**

Measurement and assessment of the value add of statistical forecasting are not only about benchmarking statistical forecasting methods. We believe that in this regard, there are six cross-organization and end-to-end focus dimensions that will allow a firm to reach effective results:

- Mission
- Governance
- Talent
- Process
- Technology
- Analytics.

At the very core of those dimensions, there are the three main company's drivers that represent the links among the dimensions, but at the same time the underlying visions, constraints and objectives.

Figure 6.1 illustrates more in detail the reasoning just explained.

It is important to assign proper ownership and accountability to statistical forecasting solutions. Assigning responsibilities to crucial and periodic activities will ensure process adherence and sustainability. Let's analyze in this chapter how it might be possible to make a difference and unearth value in the demand planning process using a holistic approach.

When a practitioner faces the whole company portfolio, the mountain seems too high to climb. How many seasonal products are there in the portfolio? How many are trendy? What are the products with a low volatility and the ones very volatile?

It often happens that when a company perceives the need for a change toward statistical forecasting, the management looks for the quickest solution to predict the future. Often, a one-size-fits-all solution is put in place and stays forever. No differentiation of efforts, methods and techniques is embedded in the process.

© Springer Nature Switzerland AG 2019
G. Sankaran et al., *Improving Forecasts with Integrated Business Planning*,
Management for Professionals, https://doi.org/10.1007/978-3-030-05381-9_6

**MISSION**
Statistical forecasting should be "how" you run the predictions activities, and it should deliver competitive advantage to your organization

**PROCESS**
A cross-functional set of process steps and activities designed to align the organization to one desired outcome

**GOVERNANCE**
Clear roles, decision rights, and policies and incentives that promote behaviour to drive the organization to achieve its mission

**TECHNOLOGY**
The technologies (software and hardware) and tools required to support the capability

**TALENT**
The competencies, skills and workforce for demand planning that enable an optimal talent base to execute the capability in the context of the "Future of Work"

**ANALYTICS**
The capabilities needed to drive demand scenario planning and real-time, insight-driven decision-making

**Fig. 6.1** Leading statistical forecasting

Because of this thinking, the two most frequent scenarios that we have experienced are the following:

1. The results in terms of forecast accuracy and forecast bias are not satisfactory from the very first time that an assessment is performed.
2. During a pre-demand review meeting, the key participants involved as the demand planners and the key account managers realize that for some products, the statistical projections "make sense", while for others the forecasts look just like nonsense.

Without reiterating the concept of how difficult it is to predict the future and how far a projection can deviate from the actuals, mostly, due to unknown uncertainties, we attribute to the one-fits-for-all approach, a possible cause for the less accurate than expected results.

Applying the same algorithms to the entire portfolio does not lead to optimal results nor does standardizing the algorithm parameters of the statistical models yield improvements. We believe that only an optimized selection of the forecasting algorithms combined with an optimized setting of the parameters of the forecasting models could lead to improvements.

Furthermore, it is also important to remind how an optic of continuous improvement is crucial to bring the baseline of statistical forecasting to the next level: one that is more accurate and mature. We explain that in the 6-sigma methods in Chap. 8.

To better emphasize the concept of optimized selection and configuration, it has been decided to start with a full picture and decompose the approaches used as we progress within this chapter. This is the reason why Fig. 6.2 illustrates the full summary of all the methods that will be compared in the next pages. We depicted here the declining trend of the Weighted MAPE and Bias from the very

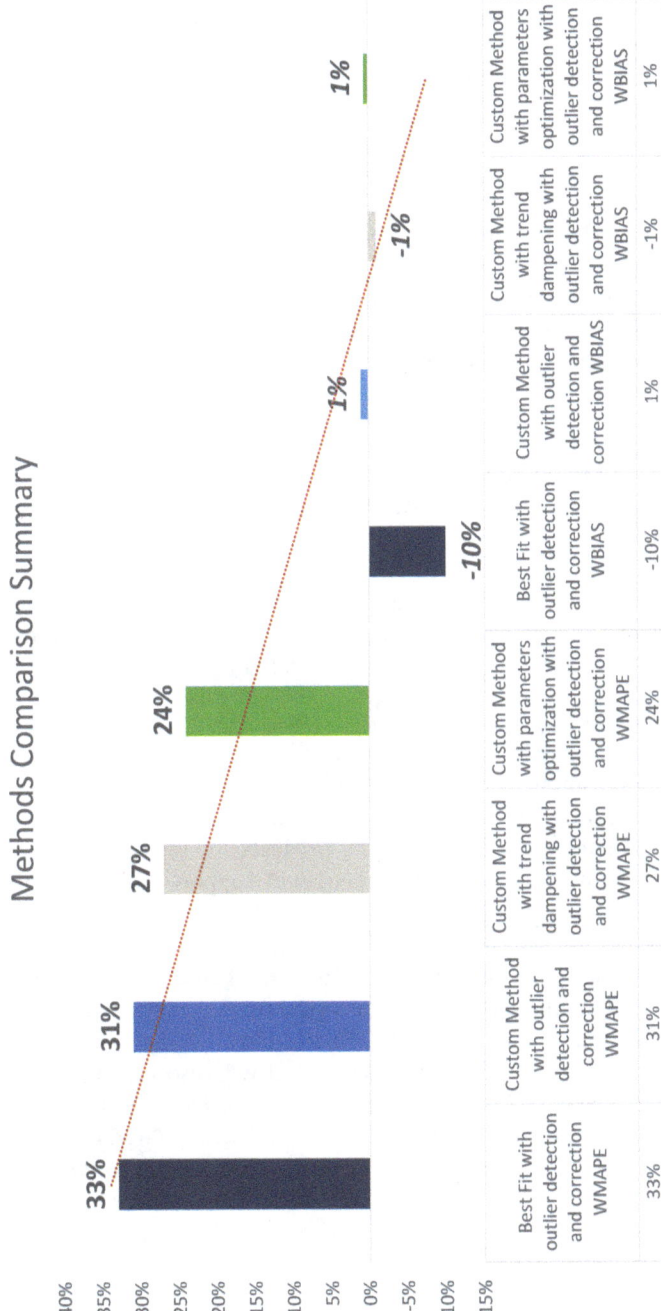

**Fig. 6.2** Methods comparison summary

first technique that was applied leveraging the out-of-the-box best fit functionality of SAP IBP to the last method centered on the parameters optimization of the proposed differentiated statistical forecasting approach.

Results improved and errors decreased; let's disclose now how we managed to get there, focusing on the methods chosen for comparisons along with explanations.

## 6.1  Value of Custom Portfolio Classification

To reach a mature statistical forecasting process, the starting point is formed by a custom portfolio classification that not only allows to have the basis for a proper optimization of the forecasting models selection, but also represents a real value in terms of demand and portfolio understanding.

**Methodology**
We randomly selected 200 products that will represent our sample for the following exercise. We can assume that those 200 products are representative for a sample of a company portfolio.

Successively, we follow the instructions, theories and methods described in the previous chapters to gain the relevant insights that are needed to forecast at best.
The following steps compose the methodology:

1. ABC–XYZ analysis: The prioritization on volume and volatility will be performed, and the results will be displayed in the relevant dashboards.
2. SIFU classification: The stable (S), intermittent (I), flashy (F) and unforecastable (U) classification will allow us to make the distinction within the full portfolio among the stable, intermittent, flashy products and those whose predictability is almost random. A specific dashboard will support this step highlighting the composition of the sample. (We specifically decided to keep unforecastable SKUs out of the sample for benchmarking purposes.)
3. ANOVA analysis: A specific code will be attributed to each product depending on the data patterns shown in the historical periods. They might be seasonal (S), trendy (T), trendy and seasonal (TS) and those products that exhibit a simple inner variability (IV). A specific dashboard will also highlight this analysis.
4. Skewness analysis: Analyzing the symmetry of the data distribution and categorizing the degree of the dispersion in low/medium/high category.
5. Normality versus non-normality analysis: Each product within each of the categories will be examined to see  if it does or doesn't follow a normal distribution.

The results of this classification and analysis will be stored in relevant attributes/characteristics and used in the demand planning process. It is important to highlight the importance of conducting this exercise in the first place, as it will allow to benchmark the same classes of products among different methodologies, where differentiated usage of statistical forecasting will apply. Segmenting and analysis of demand and portfolio in such a way are a custom method of using instruments available in SAP IBP.

## 6.1.1 SAP IBP Use Case: Custom Portfolio Segmentation

Following the steps of the above methodology, we were able to carve out the following insights (Fig. 6.3) from the ABC–XYZ classification:

(For a reminder of the technique in question, please refer to page 203 segmenting and classifying demand)

- The portfolio is composed of 29 A products, 46 B products and 125 C products.
- Among the A (very important) products, 22 are X products (low variability), 3 Y (medium variability) and 4 Z (high variability).
- Among the B (medium important) products, 28 are X products, 5 Y and 13 Z.
- Among the C (lowest importance) products, 28 are X products, 13 Y and 84 Z.

The analysis related to the exact no of the SKUs can be completed by its sales value, as depicted in Fig. 6.4:

- As expected, the segment AX accounts for most of the sales, roughly 44 M.
- The segment BY has an important relative weight for the entire portfolio.
- The 84 products of the CZ segment, which represent 42% of the SKU, account for only 2.5 M in sales.

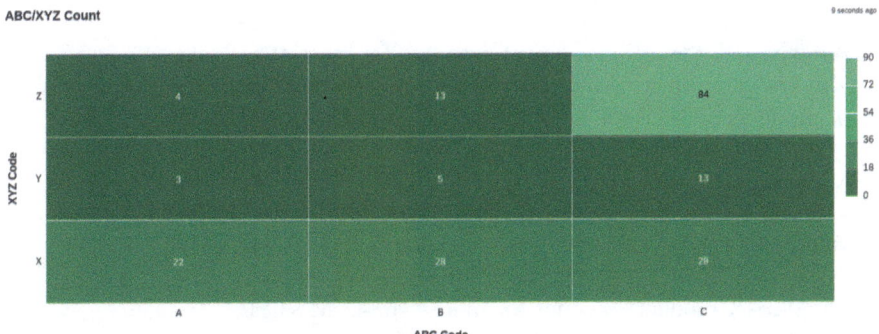

**Fig. 6.3** ABC/XYZ portfolio SKU split

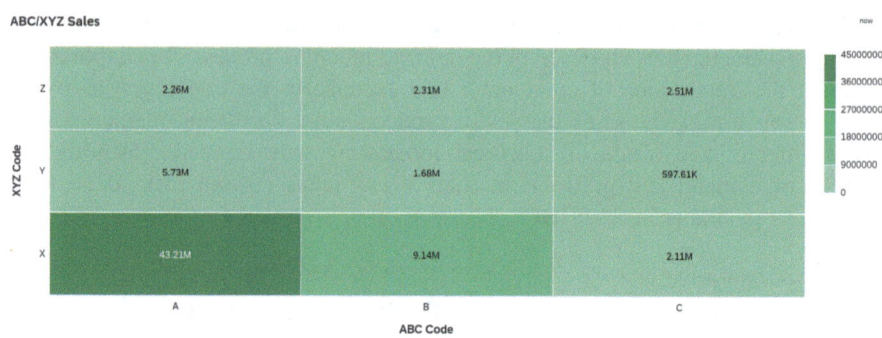

**Fig. 6.4** ABC/XYZ portfolio sales

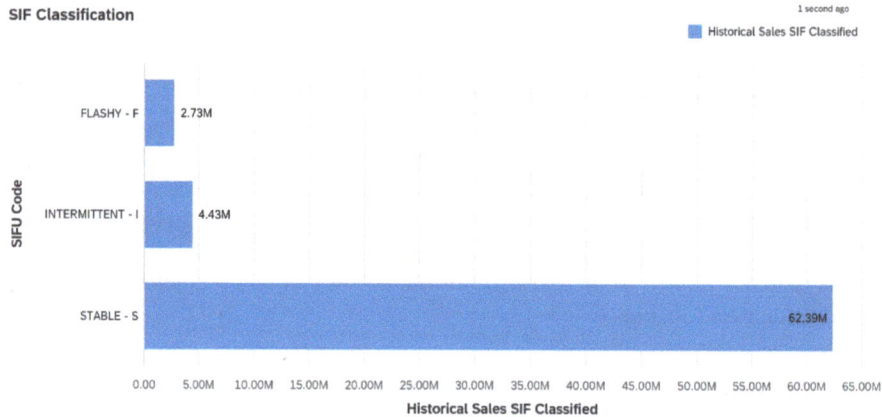

**Fig. 6.5** Portfolio SIF classification

Further, we want to understand the nature of demand and classify it. Considering a portfolio of circa 70 M sales, we can immediately attribute and weight the "contribution" of each of the clusters (Fig. 6.5):

–  As expected, the stable segment accounts for most of the sales.
–  The flashy and the intermittent segment comprised of almost the same amount of products account for  a total contribution of circa 7M in sales.

At the same time, if we try to explore in detail about the composition of the 200 selected SKUs, we can derive the following results out of the SIF (seasonal–intermittent–flashy) classification (Figs. 6.6 and 6.7) versus ABC/XYZ:

–  The 22 AX products account for more than 43 M sales.
–  The 3 AY products account for roughly 6 M sales.

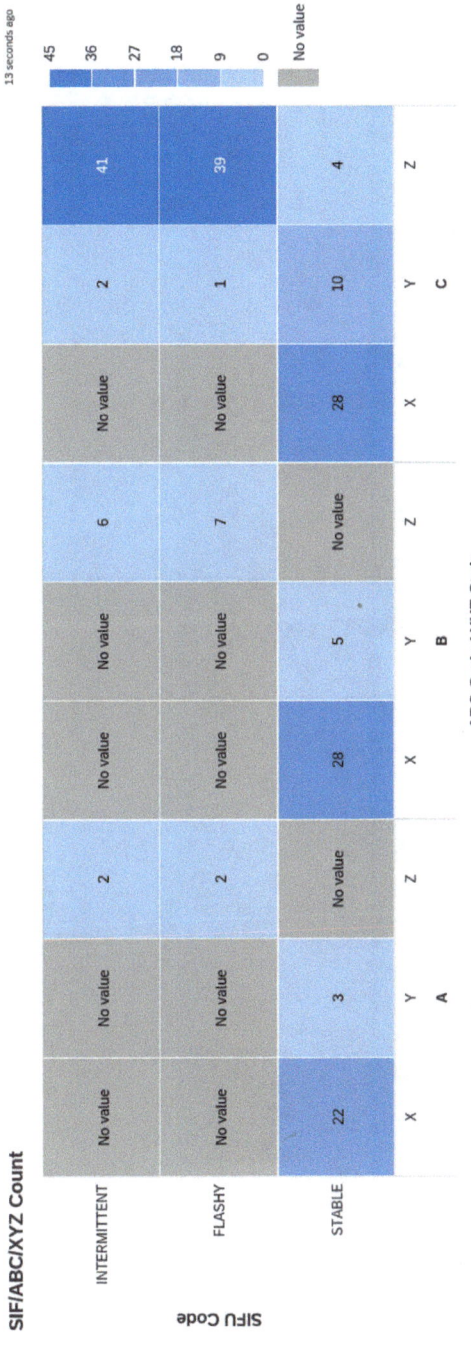

**Fig. 6.6** SIF/ABC/XYZ portfolio split

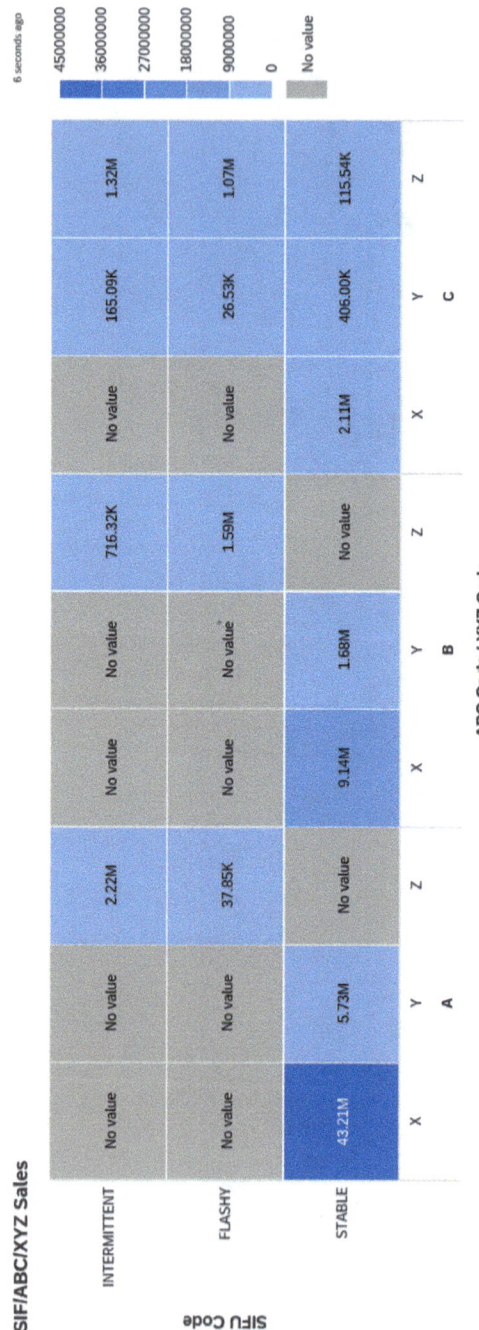

**Fig. 6.7**  SIF/ABC/XYZ portfolio sales

- There are two flashy and two intermittent AZ products which justify the high variability pre-detected by the XYZ classification.
- The BX category composed of stable products accounts for a total of 9 M sales.
- The 2.31 M sales accounted for the BZ category are generated by only flashy and intermittent products.
- The C category is the one that contains the most differentiated sub-portfolio.
- The majority of the intermittent and flashy products are within the CZ category.

Moving to the ANOVA (STMN) analysis, we can add the following information to the products analyzed (Figs. 6.8 and 6.9):

(For a reminder of the analysis in question, refer to page 225 identifying seasonality and SAP Use case: analysis of variance—ANOVA)

- There are 48 trendy and C products. The highest number accounted for this classification.
- There are 47 C products with internal variability.
- There are only 13 seasonal products accounting for 10 M sales.
- There are 49 trendy and seasonal products with a total of 36 M sales.
- There are 61 internal variable products accounting for 6 M sales.
- There are 77 trendy products that account for a total of 19 M sales.

Furthermore, combining the previous analysis with the one just investigated, we can conclude the following results (Figs. 6.10 and 6.11):

- The majority of the internal variable products are Z—intermittent (27) and Z—flashy (18).
- The majority of the seasonal products are also stable (10).
- The majority of the trendy products are also stable (46), with a big contribution of C—intermittent products (12) and C—flashy products (20).
- Almost all of the trendy and seasonal products are also stable.
- The greatest contribution in sales is brought by the A—trendy–seasonal and stable segment with almost 30 M sales.
- The second most important quadrant is represented by the A—trendy–stable segment with almost 9 M sales.

Reaching the last stage of the custom portfolio segmentation, we can define the normally distributed data segments versus the non-normally distributed data. Insights from data distribution analysis will be crucial for the outlier detection and correction phase, since there are differences in approaching outliers for normally and non-normally distributed data.

From Figs. 6.12 and 6.13, we highlight the following:

- There are more not normally distributed (130) rather than normally distributed products (70).

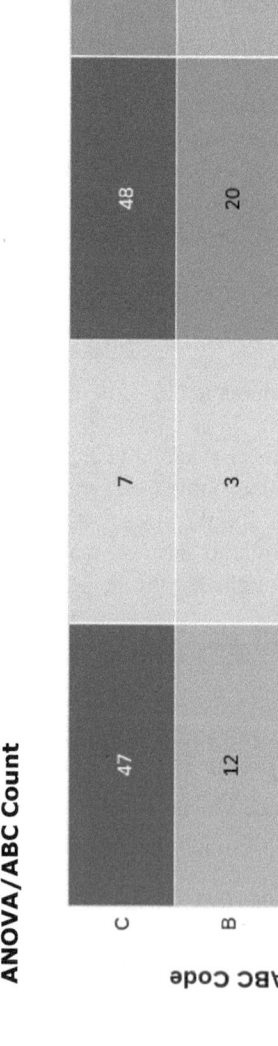

**Fig. 6.8**   ANOVA/ABC portfolio SKU split

*TS – Trendy and Seasonal, T – Trendy, S – Seasonal, IV – Internal Variability*

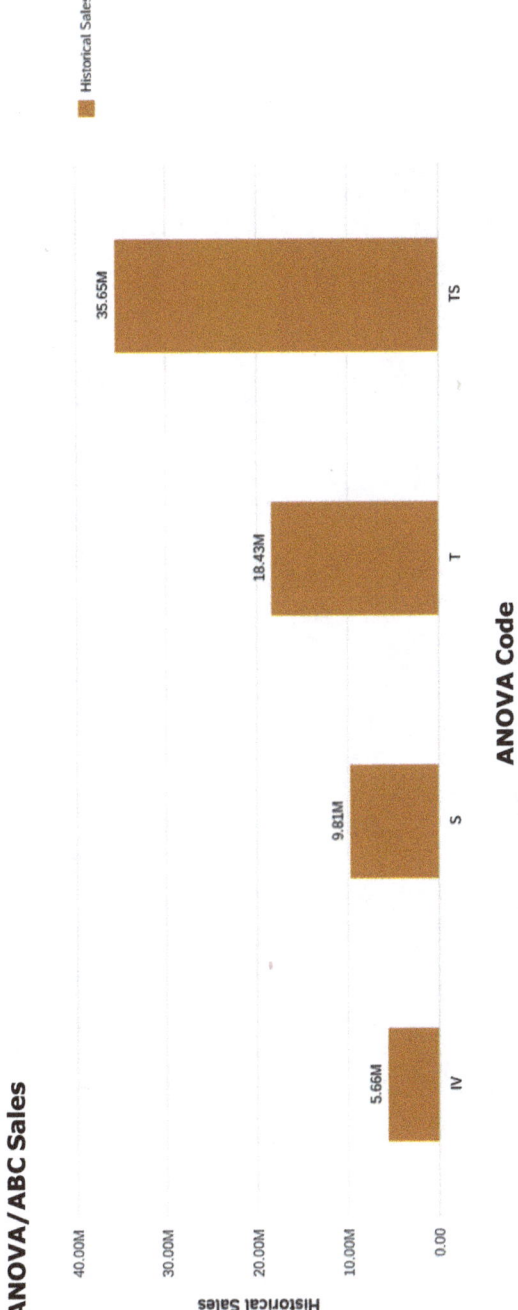

**Fig. 6.9** ANOVA/ABC portfolio sales

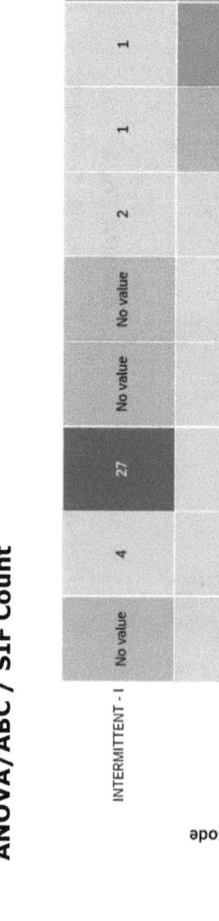

**Fig. 6.10** ANOVA/ABC/SIF portfolio SKU split

*TS – Trendy and Seasonal, T – Trendy, S – Seasonal, IV – Internal Variability*

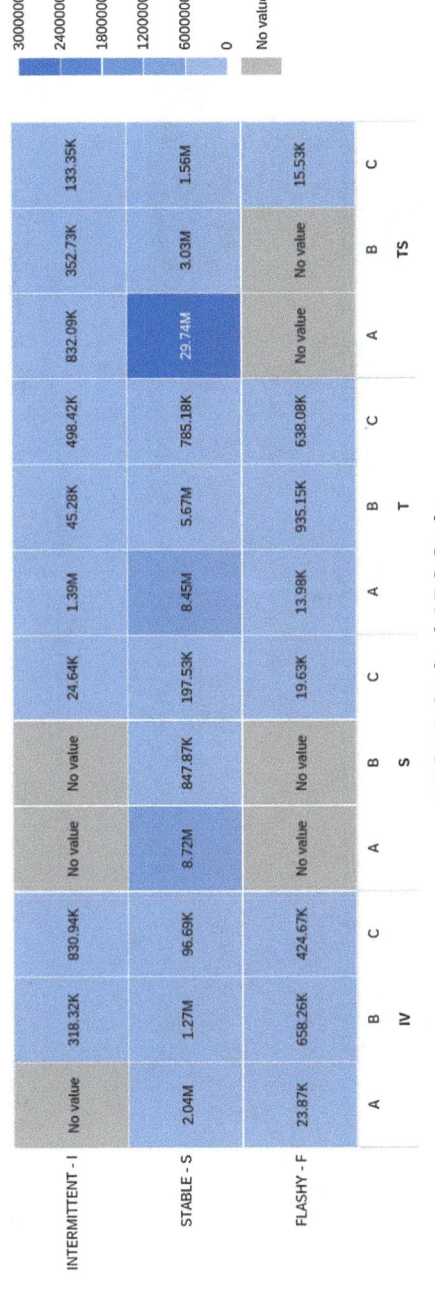

**Fig. 6.11**  ANOVA/ABC/SIF portfolio sales

TS – Trendy and Seasonal, T – Trendy, S – Seasonal, IV – Internal Variability

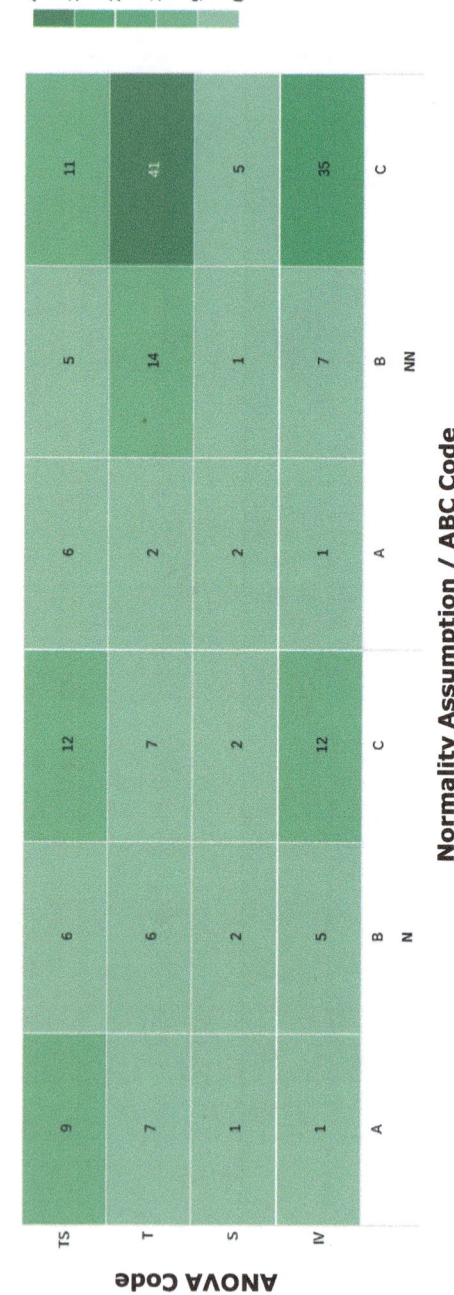

**Fig. 6.12** Normal/not normal ANOVA ABC portfolio count

*TS – Trendy and Seasonal, T – Trendy, S – Seasonal, IV – Internal Variability, N – Normality, NN – Non Normality*

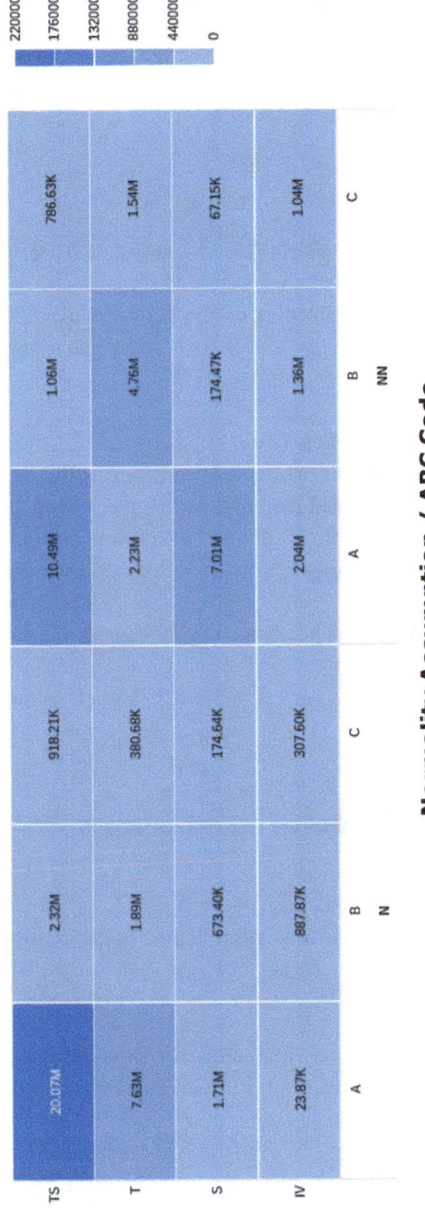

**Fig. 6.13** Normal/not ANOVA ABC Portfolio sales

*TS – Trendy and Seasonal, T – Trendy, S – Seasonal, IV – Internal Variability, N – Normality, NN – Non Normality*

- The trendy products are those that fall, for the majority, in the not normal cluster.
- The normal—A—trendy and seasonal products account for 20 M sales, while the not normal—A—trendy and seasonal products account for 11 M sales. Those two segments together account for almost half of the portfolio sales.

However, they would have to be treated differently to achieve the most accurate results.

## 6.2   Custom Method for Statistical Forecasting

Based on the outcomes of the custom portfolio segmentation, the practitioners' job for the model selection is extremely simplified as for each classification a recommended forecasting model can be proposed:

- The internal variability cluster (IV) is assigned to the single exponential smoothing as it should be able to detect the random fluctuations.
- The trend cluster (T) is assigned to the double exponential smoothing with trend dampening as it should be able to detect a growing or decreasing trend.
- The seasonal cluster (S) is assigned to the triple exponential smoothing as per suggested before.
- The trend and seasonal (TS) clusters are assigned to the triple exponential smoothing.
- The intermittent and flashy clusters (I—F) are assigned to the Markov algorithm.

### 6.2.1   SAP IBP Use Case: Best Fit and Custom W/O Outlier Correction

**Methodology for custom selection of algorithms without outlier detection and correction**

1. Make use of 48 periods of historical sales for the 200 selected SKUs.
2. The calculation horizon period applied goes from April 2016 to March 2017.
3. Run statistical forecast for the optimized selection of algorithms.
4. Store the Weighted MAPE and Weighted Bias for the defined data horizon.

## Best fit versus custom method, both w/o outlier detection and correction

The benchmarking aims at comparing the forecast accuracy and bias of the best fit practice without outlier detection and correction versus the custom selection of algorithms without the outlier detection and correction.

The assessment will be performed on the same levels as that of the previous exercise. The goal for this exercise would be to evaluate the value brought by a tailor-made portfolio classification coupled with an optimized selection and assignment of the statistical forecasting models.

In Assign Forecast Models app of the demand planner panel, the end user is able to access the specific section where a custom selection of the algorithms can be assigned. In order to filter the demand categories where the statistical models need to be applied, we need to customize the filter panel so that the attributes that we want to filter are displayed (Fig. 6.14).

For our purposes, we selected:

- ABC code
- Product ID
- SIFU code—stable (S), intermittent (I), flashy (F) and unforecastable (U)
- ANOVA code—trend (T), seasonal (S), trendy and seasonal (TS) and internal variability (IV)
- Assigned forecast model.

As an example, the procedure to assign the single exponential smoothing algorithm to the "stable" and "internal variability" cluster consists on filtering by those fields and clicking on edit assignment and selecting the single exponential smoothing.

After all the 200 SKUs have their respective clusters and forecast models assigned in the data model, it is possible to run statistical forecasting for all SKUs at once with the pre-assigned customized algorithms.

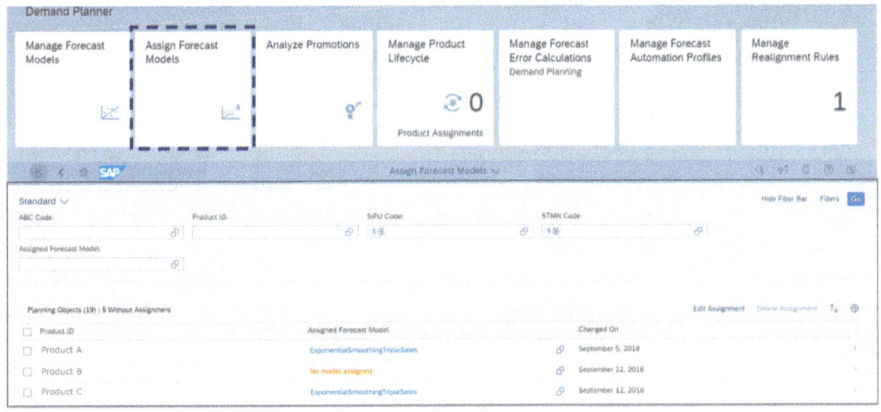

**Fig. 6.14** SAP IBP forecast model assignment

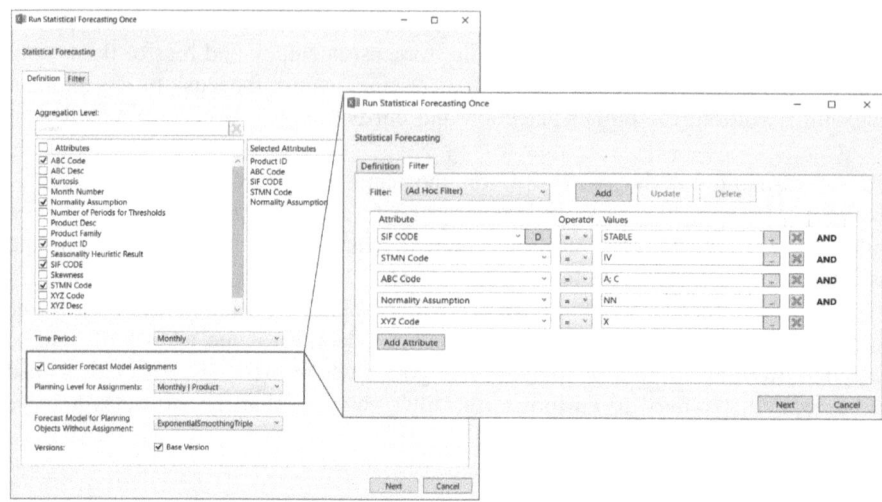

**Fig. 6.15**  Excel UI Assign Forecast Models

In addition, as a second viable option, it is also possible to filter by attribute so that if a specific cluster needs to be forecasted, the selected algorithm will be executed only for the specific filters (Fig. 6.15). To run statistical forecasting only for some selected algorithms and when using the Excel UI filters, the end user will have to untick the "Consider Forecast Model Assignments" box, as the assignment will be performed manually on the filtering screen.

Having explained how to run the custom selection of algorithms, let's analyze the results out of it in Fig. 6.16:

- The custom method without outlier detection and correction registers an overall accuracy of 67.2%, that is, 2% inferior to the best fit without outlier detection and correction.
- The direction of the forecasted error assumes a less marked negative error, almost reaching an equal balance between over- and underforecasting.

Using the same algorithms of the best fit, but restricting their use to only specific clusters of the demand decreased the error to 31%. The more we deviate from this threshold, the less accurate would be the demand classification and the selection and assignment of the algorithms. A deviating percentage of only 2% let us confirm the goodness of the approach.

Nonetheless, having set as a criterion for the best fit optimization the MAPE, it is possible to notice some differences in the Weighted MAPE of each SKU and in the ABC/XYZ quadrants. In addition, the Markovian approach toward the flashy and intermittent products could positively or negatively balance the overall results.

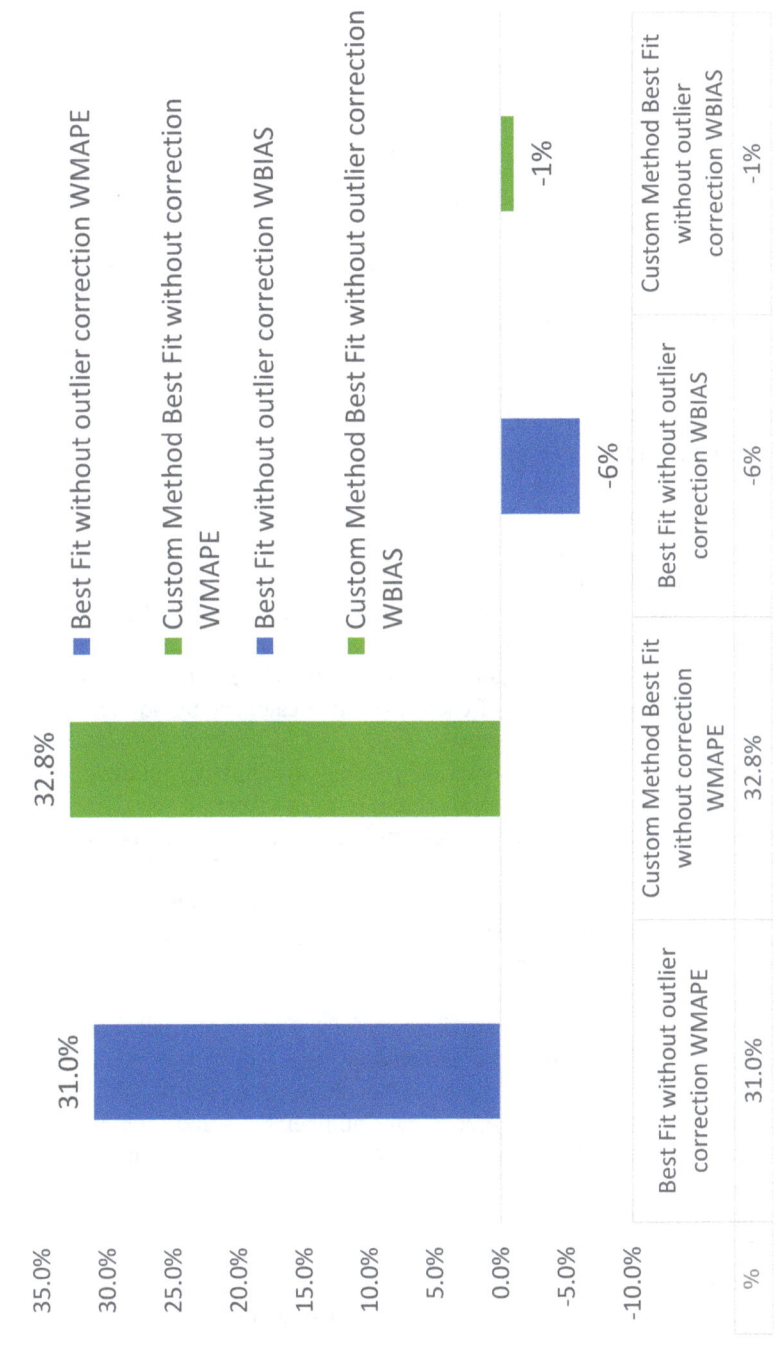

**Fig. 6.16** Custom method w/o OD and OC versus best fit w/o OD and OC

Figure 6.17 displays the allocation of the accuracy improvements and deteriorations:

- 75 products stayed unvaried.
- 58 products worsened.
- 67 products improved.

Such distribution of the classes explains the equilibrium between the two models.

Finally, plotting the results in the ABC/XYZ matrix, we notice the (Fig. 6.18):

- The X classes slightly worsened, keeping an acceptable accuracy threshold.
- AY and CY slightly worsened, while the BY improved by 12%.
- CY and CZ almost did not vary.
- AZ drastically improved by 21%.
- The high tendency of underforecasting the CZ products still persists.

As a comment, the AZ products account for roughly 2.3 M of sales and they are composed of two flashy and two intermittent products. Consequently, for intermittent products, the Markovian run of the Croston model assured the great improvement in the accuracy of those four products. Nonetheless, 37% of accuracy still has to be considered low.

After having proved a statistical difference between the methods, we are also able to investigate the KPIs of each respective category by addressing the positive and negative issues of each cluster (Fig. 6.19).

This type of data evaluation is only viable after having run the custom portfolio segmentation as it allows the practitioners to not treat all the 200 SKUs with the same approach, fostering a ramification logic and a differentiated approach.

In the chart, we opted to display the Weighted MAPE and Weighted Bias considering the stable products as a unique sub-portfolio and the flashy–intermittent as the second unique sub-portfolio. Weighting the two sub-portfolios separately exhibits results that are almost poles apart:

- The flashy category has an accuracy of 8% with a small tendency of under-forecasting. This might be justified by the fact that it is quite probable to statistically forecast some figures when there are no actual sales, but at the same time to not statistically forecast any number for some months where demand would have actually occurred. As a conclusion, demand timing seems to be the key issue.
- The intermittent category reaches an accuracy of 13%, but with a direction of the forecast error pronounced on the negative side (−40%). As a result, it might be assumed that the key issue of the method was not the timing of the statistical forecasts, but rather the quantity forecasted against the real demand.

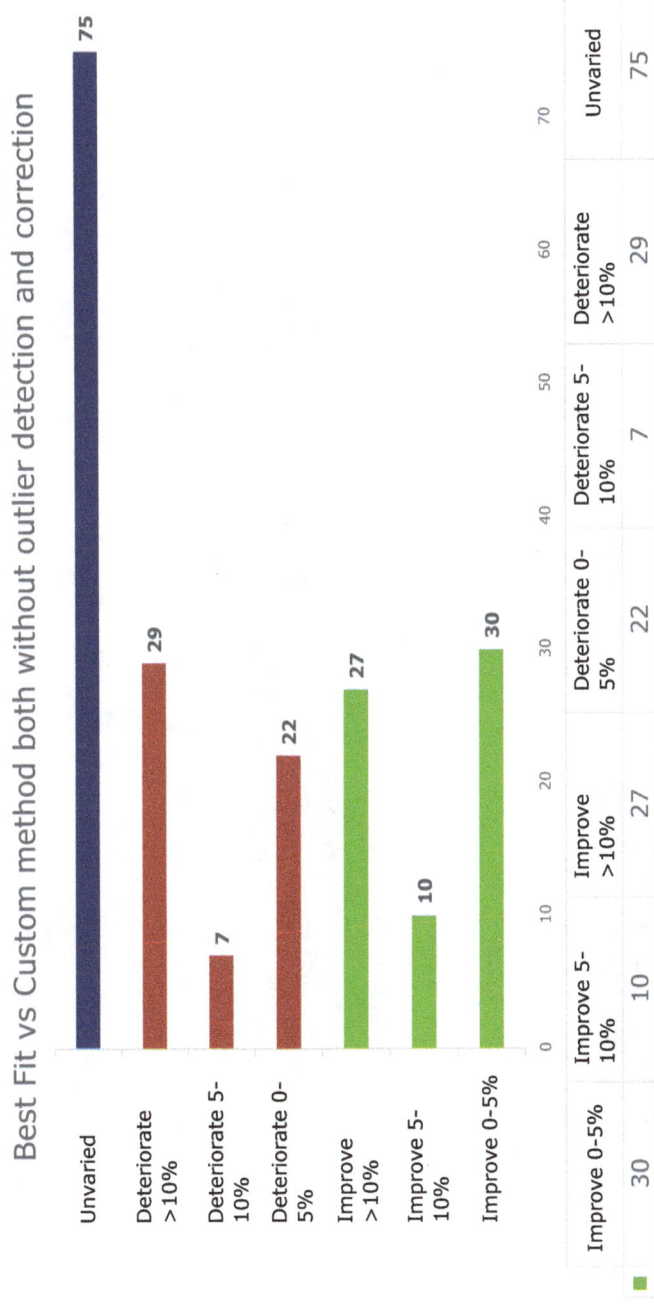

**Fig. 6.17** Custom method benchmarking classes of improvement

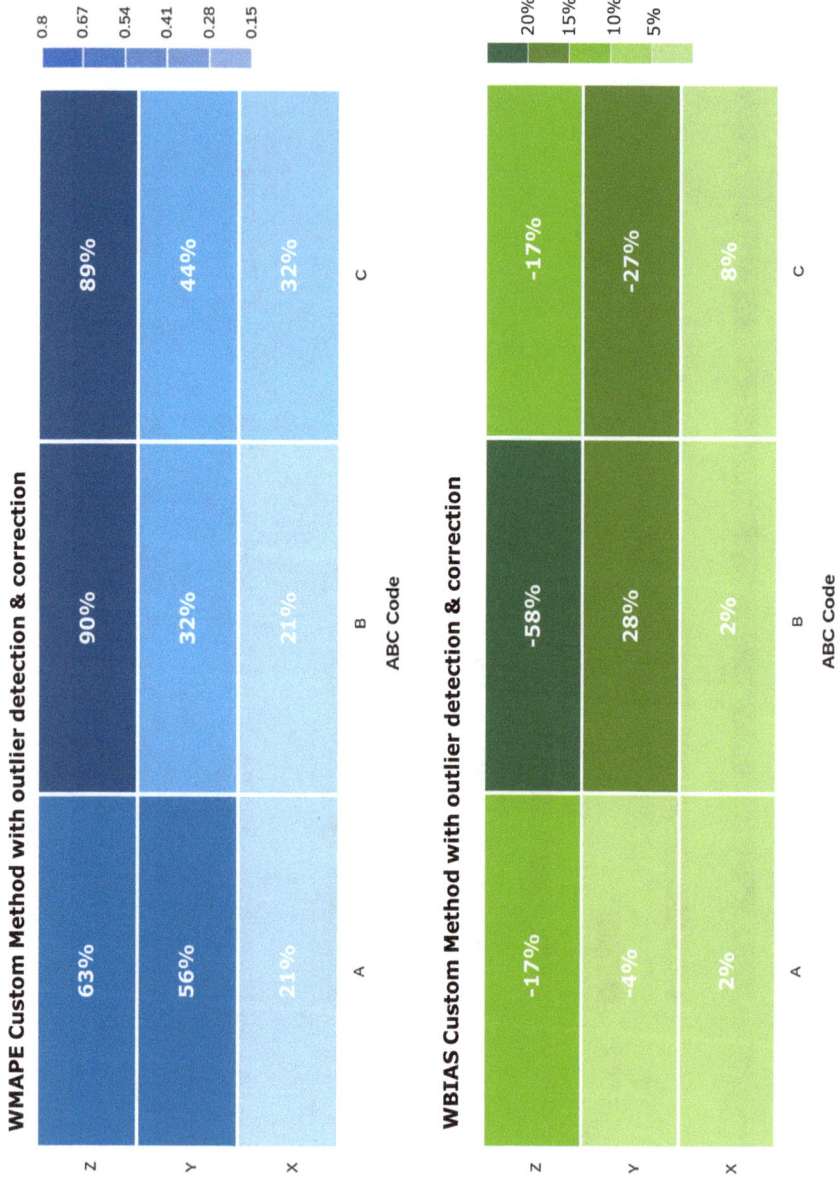

**Fig. 6.18** Weighted MAPE and Weighted Bias custom method w/o OD and OC

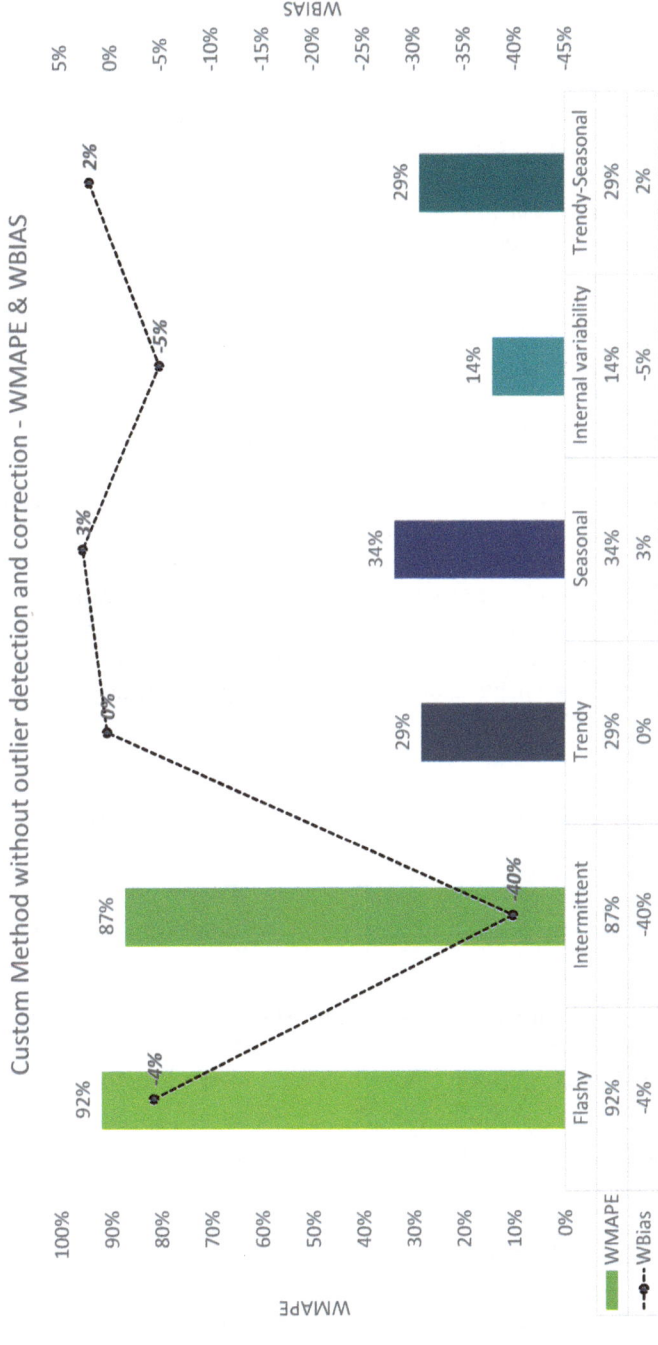

**Fig. 6.19** Custom method w/o OD and OC—KPIs per demand classification

As a conclusion and as expected, the flashy and intermittent sub-portfolios stay the most difficult to predict. Not all of these products fall in the Z category; nonetheless, they account for only 10% of the total sales of the 200 SKUs sample.

It has to be also reminded that a 1:1 comparison with the best fit results is not applicable at this point of time, as such differentiation was not present while running the method. Consequently, the results for the flashy and intermittent products during the running of the best fit model were purely driven by the race toward the highest accuracy, without considering how the data actually behaves.

On the other hand, we can derive the following results out of the other 100 stable SKUs:

- The trendy cluster reaches an accuracy of 71% with a forecast bias of 0%.
- The seasonal cluster accounts for an accuracy of 66%, slightly overforecasted by 3%.
- The internal variability cluster is the most accurate with a 86% and a forecast bias of −5%.
- The trendy and seasonal clusters account for an accuracy of 71% with a positive forecast bias of 2%.

As a conclusion, for a first customized run of the selected algorithms, the results look quite optimistic, especially for the stable sub-portfolio that accounts for 90% of the sales. Let's see in the next stages, how to leverage some of the techniques described in the previous chapters to lower the forecast errors and stand out in accuracy.

## 6.2.2  SAP IBP Use Case: Custom with Versus W/O Outlier Correction

**Methodology for custom selection of algorithms with outlier correction**

1. Custom outlier detection and correction based on the theories explained in the previous chapters
2. Rerun of the statistical forecasting models for optimized selection of algorithms.

**Custom methods w/o versus without outlier correction**
The benchmarking aims at comparing the forecast accuracy and bias of the custom method without outlier detection and correction versus the custom selection of algorithms with outlier detection and correction.

As for the previous benchmarking, the assessment is performed on the same levels. The objective would be to assess and analyze the value add brought by the custom outlier detection and correction versus a process where the correction of the sales history is not implied.

To reach a further step toward a better prediction of the portfolio used, we run the customized solution for outlier detection and correction. Figure 6.20 discloses the results comparison for the KPIs analyzed. At a first glance, we deduct the following:

- The outlier detection and correction have brought an improvement of 2% in terms of forecast accuracy.
- For what relates to the forecast bias, its value is kept under control with a positive direction toward overforecasting of 1%.

After having run the tailored algorithm to correct the history, we noticed the (Fig. 6.21):

- The Weighted MAPE of 60 products stayed unvaried before and after the algorithm run.
- Each class of improvements accounts for a larger number of SKU count compared to the equivalent class of deterioration:

  a. Twenty-two products deteriorated their accuracy for more than 10%, but 26 did the opposite within the same magnitude range.
  b. Seven products decreased their accuracy from 5 to 10%, but nine increased their accuracy within the same limits.
  c. Finally, 29 worsened between 0 and 5%, but 47 registered the same amplitude of the change in the positive class.

To understand better the implications of the custom method for outlier detection and correction, we plot and comment the results on the ABC/XYZ (Fig. 6.22):

- The benefits on the X classes are important as for all A, B and C, the accuracy is higher than 80%, with a huge improvement in the category CX (from 32 to 19%) and a small improvement for AX (from 21 to 19%) and BX (from 21 to 18%).
- The opposite is experienced for the Y classes, where only the CY class managed to improve by 1%, while AY and BY drastically worsened.
- The Z classes maintain high values of forecast errors.
- The forecast bias of the X categories almost did not vary apart from the CX category. In fact, we suppose that reducing the bias from 8 to 2% guaranteed the 13% improvements in the accuracy.
- On the contrary, for the AY and BY classes, there has been an improvement in the forecast bias, generating a higher degree of overforecasting and causing a worsening in the accuracy.

A substantial increase or decrease in the direction of the forecasted quantity may be caused by a too aggressive or unappropriated correction of certain outliers for

**Fig. 6.20** Custom method with or without outlier detection and correction

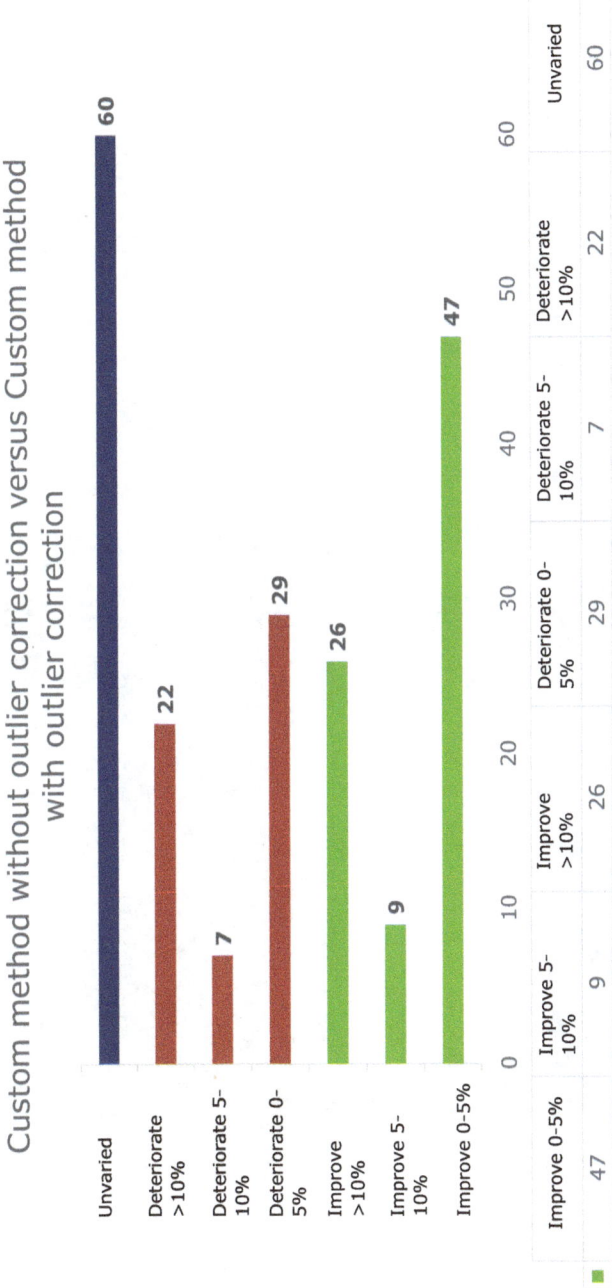

**Fig. 6.21** Custom method with outlier detection and correction versus custom method w/o outlier detection and correction—benchmarking classes of improvements

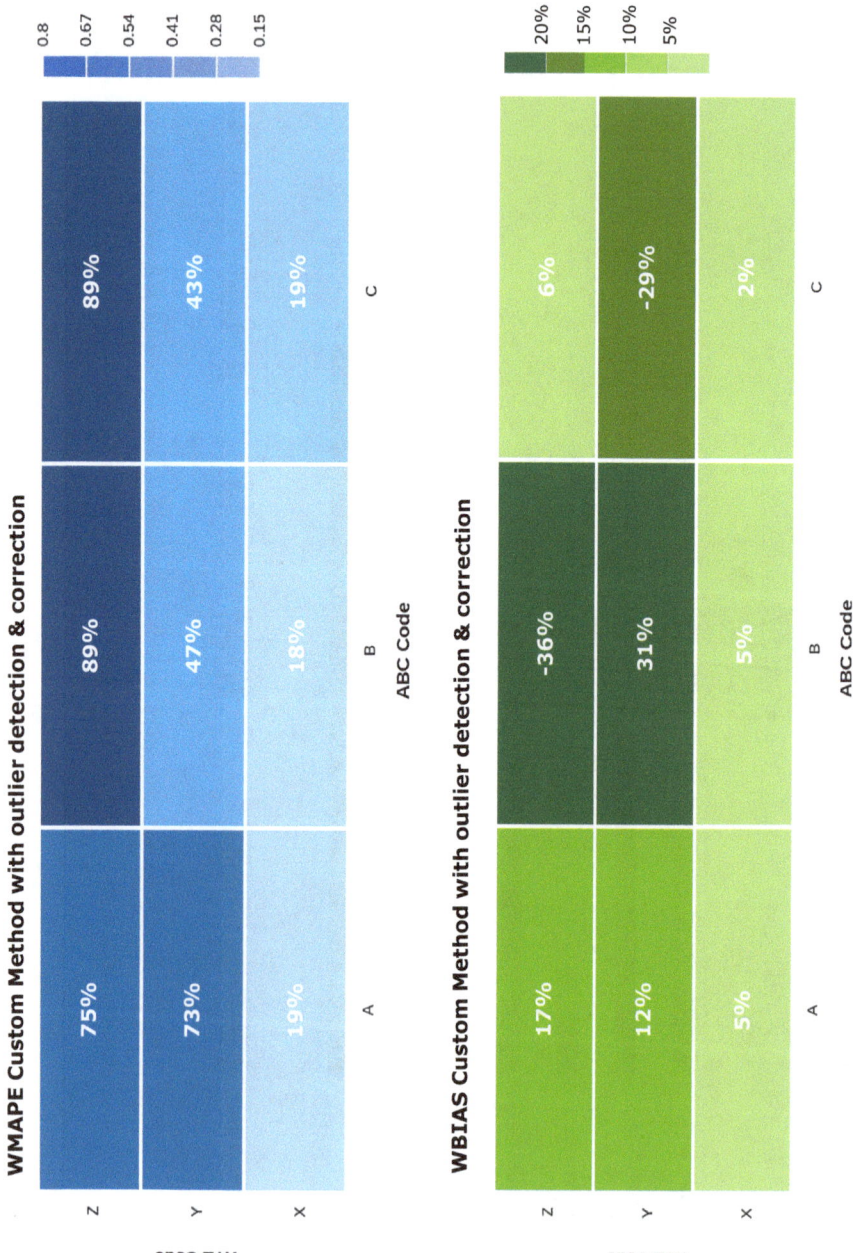

**Fig. 6.22** Weighted MAPE and Weighted Bias custom method with outlier detection and correction

certain specific products. Once again, we have the proof that automation can lead to improvement, but it should be always coupled with human intelligence.

As we displayed for the previous comparison, we report also the accuracy and bias within each of the demand categories of the portfolio in order to identify the respective KPIs (Fig. 6.23):

- If the outlier detection and correction did not bring substantial enhancements or declines in the flashy and intermittent accuracies, it did reduce drastically the forecast bias of the intermittent cluster, from −40% to an acceptable level of −7%.
- For the stable portfolio, the direction of the forecast error slightly changed from positive to negative and vice versa, depending on the cluster, but it did improve the average accuracy of roughly 2% (from a Weighted MAPE of 24% to a Weighted MAPE of 22%).

Finally, Fig. 6.24 illustrates the variations of the KPIs between the two custom methods with and without outlier detection and correction. We derive that:

- The trendy category improved by 10%.
- The seasonal increased the accuracy of 2%.
- The internal variability clusters reduced the Weighted MAPE of 3%.
- The trendy and seasonal clusters suffered from the detection and correction, worsening on average of 1%.

**Custom method versus best fit, both with outlier correction**
The benchmarking aims at comparing the forecast accuracy and bias of the best fit practice without outlier detection and correction versus the custom selection of algorithms with outlier detection and correction.

As for the previous benchmarking, the assessment is performed on the same levels. The objective would be to assess and analyze the value add of a custom outlier detection and correction versus the automated out-of-the-box solution delivered by SAP IBP.

### 6.2.3    SAP IBP Use Case: Best Fit Versus Custom Method, Both with Outlier Correction

To compare the two methods in question, we will leverage the insights from Figs. 6.25 and 6.26. From the charts, the following statements emerge:

- The custom method with outlier detection and correction shows an accuracy of 69% versus an accuracy of 67% of the best fit model with automatic outlier detection and correction.

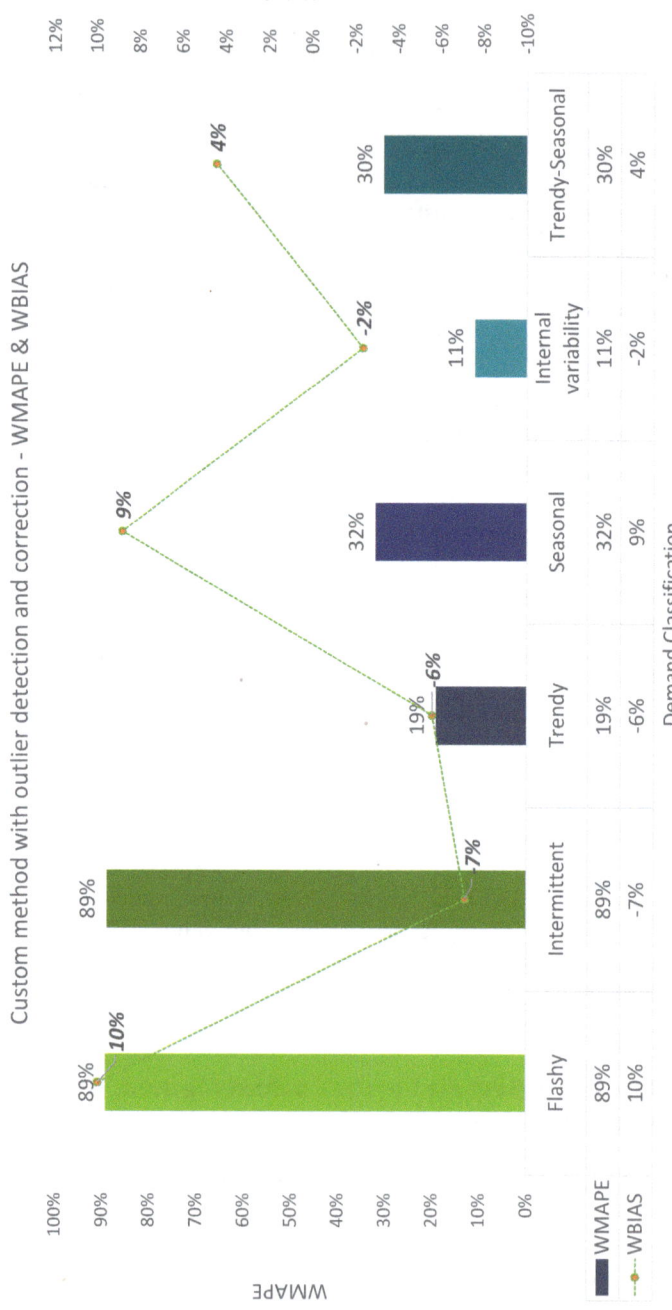

**Fig. 6.23** Custom method with OD and OC—KPIs per demand classification

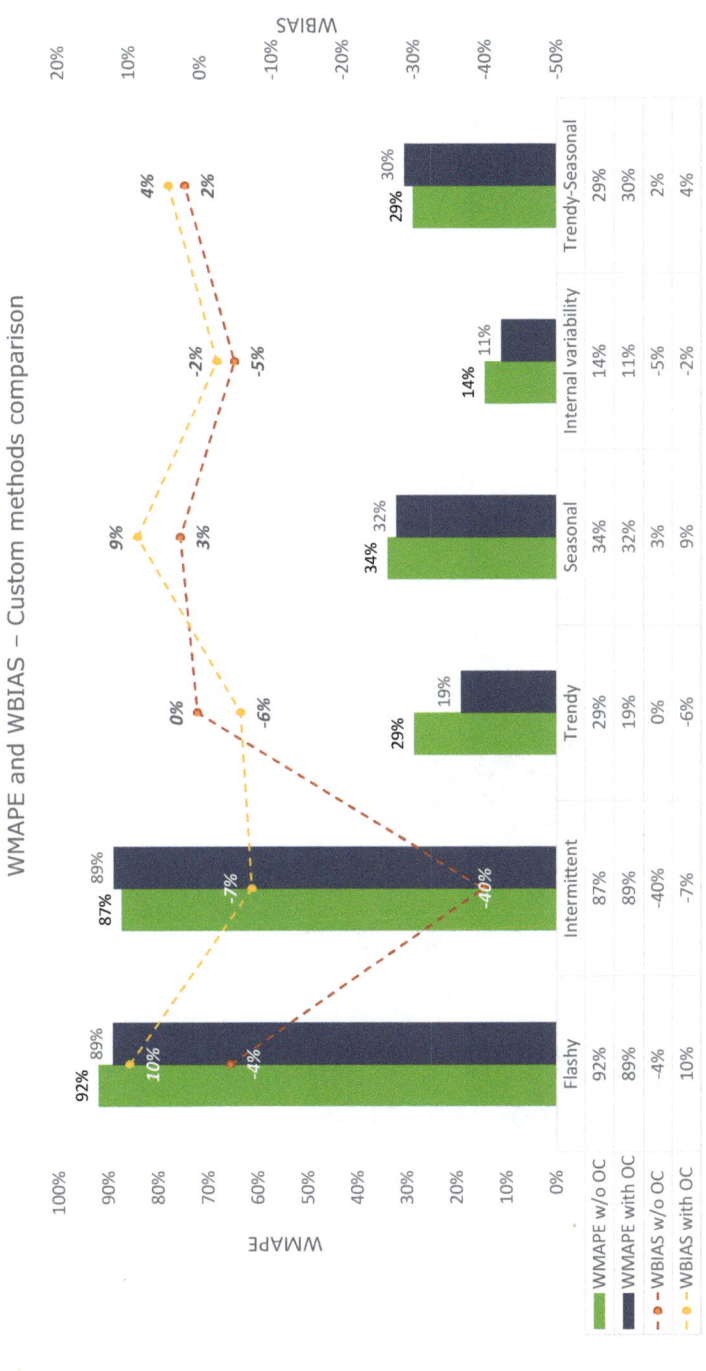

**Fig. 6.24** Custom methods comparison—KPIs per demand classification

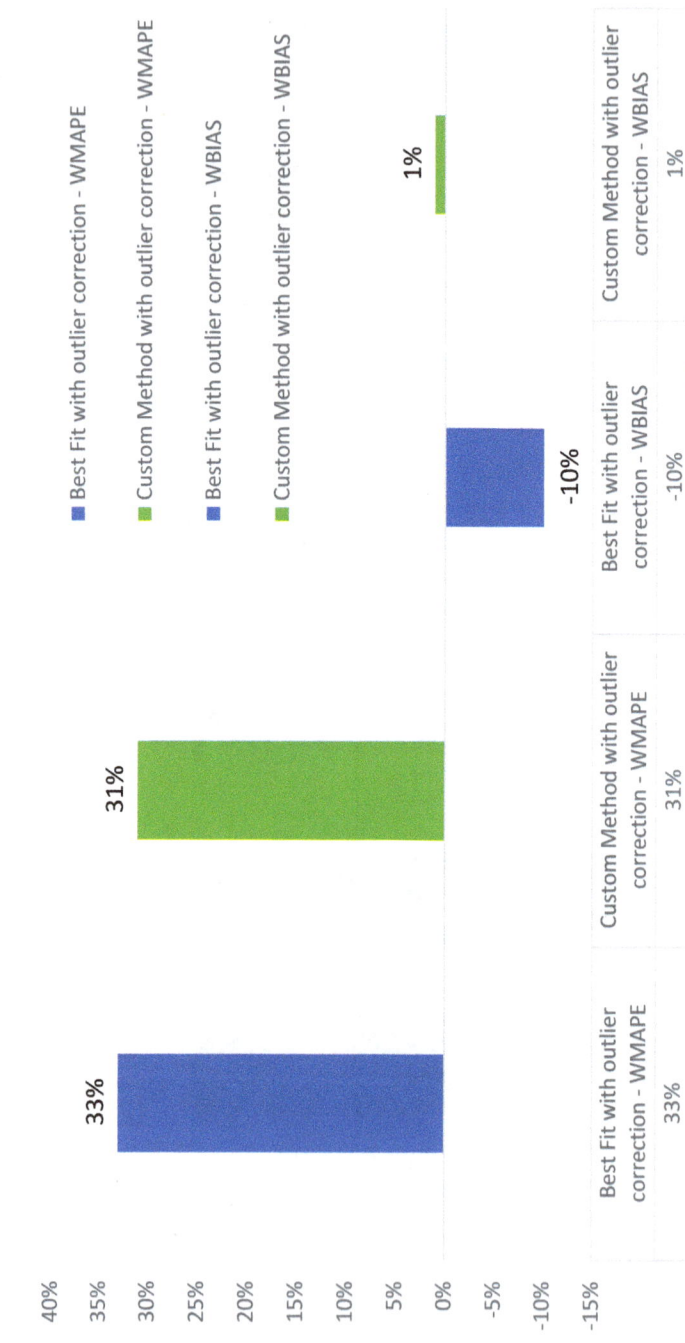

**Fig. 6.25**  Best fit versus custom method, outlier detection and correction

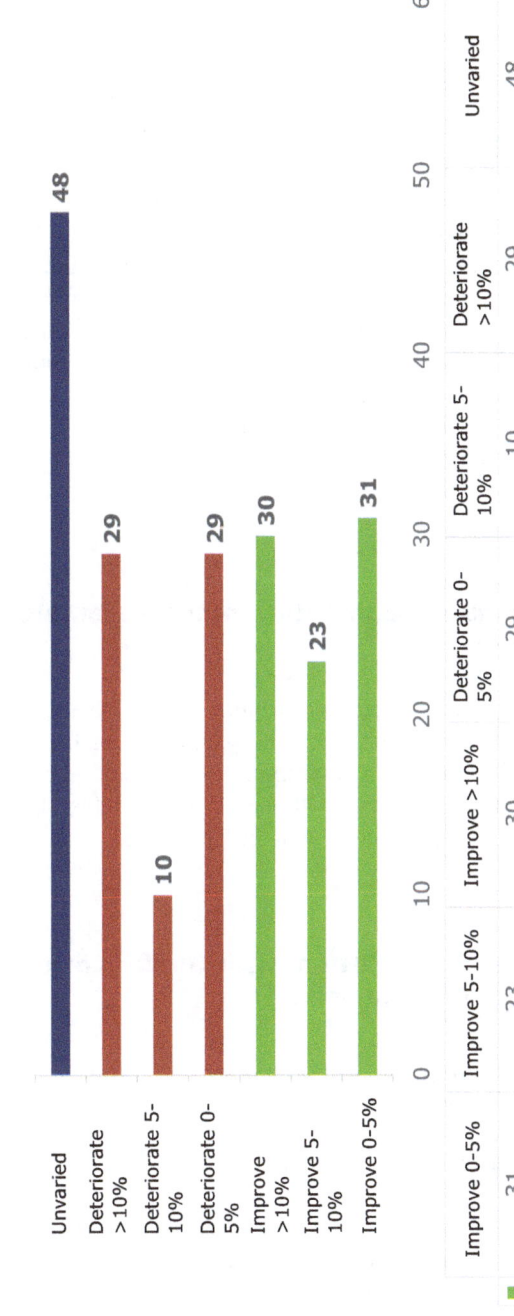

**Fig. 6.26** OD and OC for custom method versus best fit—benchmarking classes of improvements

–  The forecast bias for the custom method appears to have a better equilibrium compared to the one of the automatic best fit model (1% versus −10%).

Consequently, the automatic detection and correction of outliers seem more aggressive compared to the customized approach leading to a high degree of underforecasting.

The two methods prove themselves also quite different as only 48 products saw their accuracy unvaried. For the others, we can almost detect a complementary alternation of positive and negative classes of improvements and deteriorations. However, the class of improvement from 5 to 10% with its 23 products seems leading to the more accurate results of the customized solutions.

As final steps, we will now propose how to complement the custom method with the custom outlier detection and correction, what we could call our baseline, with the other solutions brought to enhance the level of the predictions further by:

–  Dampening the algorithms where appropriate.
–  Optimizing the parameters of the algorithms.

## 6.3   Custom Demand Segmentation and Parameters Optimization

The final run implies the ultimate optimization of the statistical forecasting performance via an optimized selection of the parameters of the smoothing models based on a nonlinear optimization algorithm. As described in the previous chapter, the nonlinear algorithm is performed with the MS Excel Solver. Furthermore, where appropriate, the dampening function will be applied to a specific cluster of the portfolio.

### 6.3.1   SAP IBP Use Case: Custom with Outlier Correction Versus Demand Dampening

**Methodology for custom demand dampening**

1. Custom outlier detection and correction
2. Custom selection of algorithms
3. Apply demand dampening to the trendy–seasonal category
4. Store the Weighted MAPE and Weighted Bias for the defined data horizon, which goes from April 2016 to March 2017.

**Benchmarking Custom method with outlier detection and correction versus Custom method with demand dampening**

The benchmarking aims at comparing the forecast accuracy and bias of the custom method with outlier detection and correction versus the custom method with demand dampening and outlier detection and correction.

The assessment will be run in a manner similar to the previous tests, while the objective of the comparison lies in identifying the value add brought by a more suitable setting of the parameters with appropriate dampening of trend in the demand.

We have seen that enabling the trend dampening on the smoothing parameters can lead to both enhancements and deteriorations of the outcomes depending on the data patterns. Once we have detected the range of products that may have a specific trend coupled with other demand characteristics, such as season, cycle or random fluctuations, ticking the trend dampening function available on the smoothing algorithms is supposed to provide better results.

We also need to mention that the negative or positive trend does not need to be analyzed to apply such a function, as the algorithm automatically adjusts the results based on the past historical sales.

Consequently, analyzing the forecast bias to decide whether or not to apply the dampening is not going to add any value. The best approach would be to let the trendy and seasonal categories undergo through the trend dampening function of the triple exponential smoothing.

Figure 6.27 reminds us how the TS category is composed of 4 intermittent products, 1 flashy and 44 stable products. We will focus on the 44 stable as only for those the customized selection of algorithms foresees to apply the TES. Tackling those products means addressing circa 30 M of the total sales.

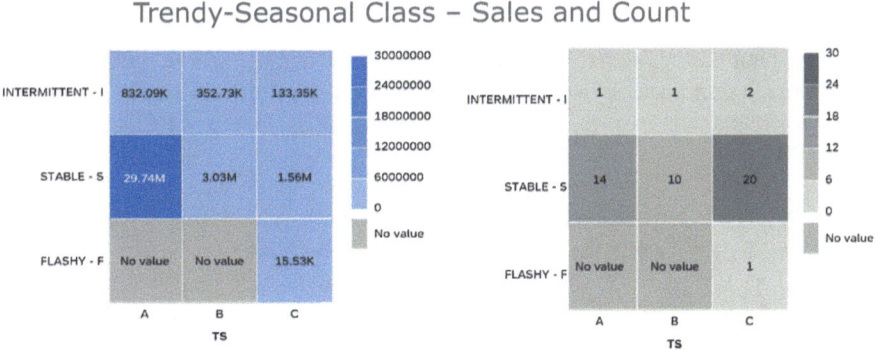

**Fig. 6.27**  Trend–seasonal class—sales and count

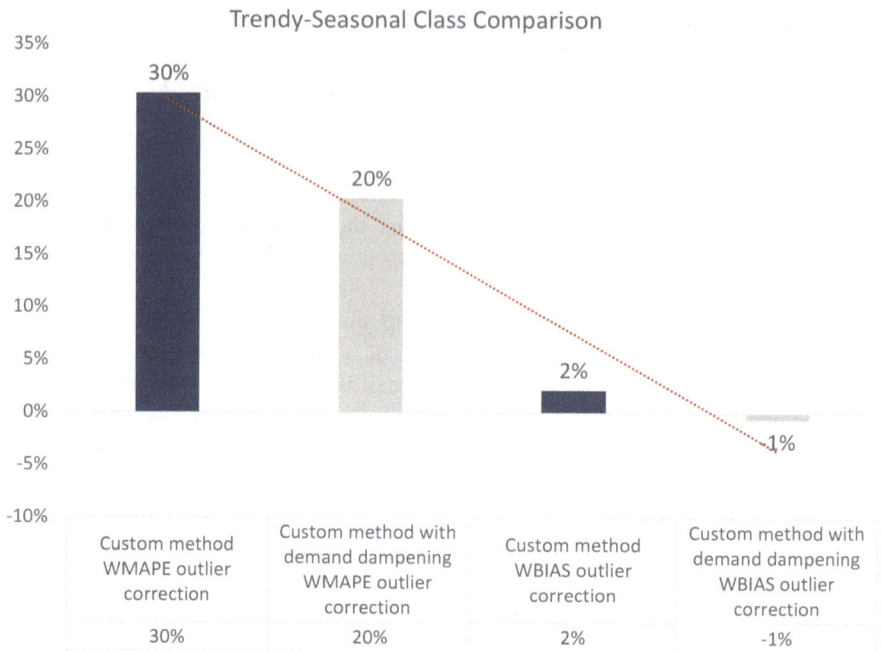

**Fig. 6.28** Trend–seasonal class KPIs

The results after running the new algorithm are very positive as the forecast bias lies on 1% and the accuracy for the category in question improved by 10% reaching a Weighted MAPE of 20% and consequently an accuracy of 80%.

Analyzing the impact of the improvement of this category on the overall portfolio is visible in Fig. 6.28 that shows us how the overall percentage of Weighted MAPE decreased by 4 points, reaching an overall accuracy of the full portfolio of 73%.

Consequently, the overall Weighted MAPE of the stable portfolio got reduced to 18%, meaning an accuracy of 82% for the 90% of the portfolio's sales.

As a conclusion, we can analyze the new KPIs on the ABC/XYZ matrix (Fig. 6.29):

– The X classes experienced a further improvement. The AX and AY class got reduced by 4%, while the AZ class of 2 percentage points.
– The class BY and CY slightly improved by roughly 2%, but it is on the AY class, the most relevant of the Y clusters, that we experience that highest reduction on the forecast error, from 73 to 37%.
– The Z classes stayed approximately unvaried (Fig. 6.30).

The benefits of such improvements are mostly due to a better comprehension of the trend pattern within the data concerned. As a demonstration of the goodness of

**Fig. 6.29** Custom method with trend dampening versus. Custom method with OD and OC

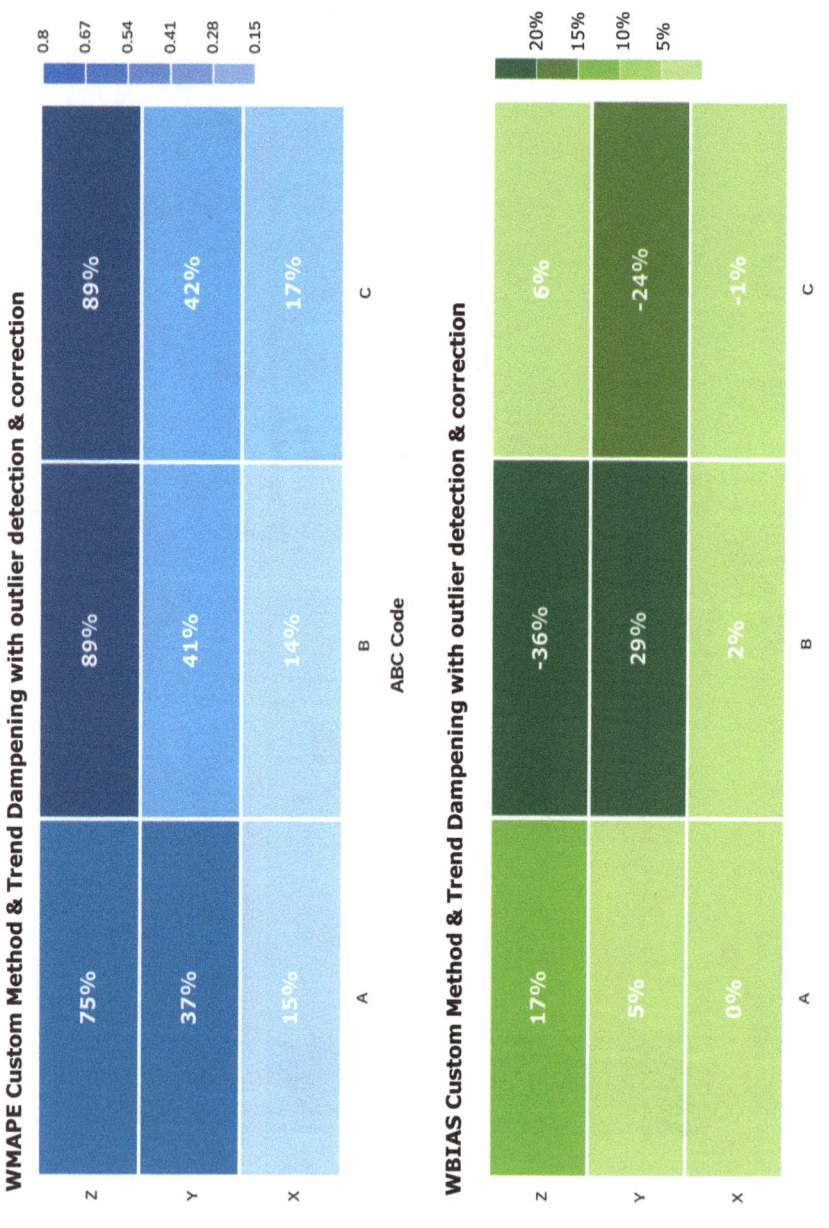

**Fig. 6.30** Weighted MAPE and Weighted Bias custom method with trend dampening and with OD and OC

the enhancement, the forecast bias reduced, guaranteeing for the X class a stabilization over the threshold of 85% of accuracy and leading the AY class through a better prediction by diminishing the tendency of overforecasting from 12% to only 5%.

## 6.3.2  SAP IBP Use Case: Custom Parameters Optimization and Outlier Correction

**Methodology for custom selection of algorithms with parameters optimization**

1. Optimization of the parameters for the smoothing forecasting models
2. Store the Weighted MAPE and Weighted Bias for the defined data horizon, which goes from April 2016 to March 2017.

**Custom methods versus custom parameters optimization with outlier detection and correction**
The benchmarking aims at comparing the forecast accuracy and bias of the custom methods versus the custom parameters optimization with outlier detection and correction.

The assessment will be run similar to the previous tests, while the objective of the comparison lies in identifying the value add brought by an optimization of the parameters of the smoothing forecasting models.

Applying for each of the SKUs their own optimized parameters represents a step that might be time consuming considering that there is no automated way to apply a full optimization of the smoothing algorithms based on the principles of the Excel Solver described in the above chapters.

Consequently, the approach would be to run separately on an Excel file the Solver optimization for each of the SKUs, store the results and create a specific forecasting model for each of the SKUs. To make the approach realistic and less time consuming, we have decided to split the optimization of the parameters into two separate ramifications:

- Flashy and intermittent
- Stable.

For the former, we opted to run a best fit model composed by the following algorithms:

- Markovian model based on the exponential smoothing single with alpha equal to 0.1

– Markovian model based on the exponential smoothing single with alpha equal
  0.5
– Markovian model based on the exponential smoothing single with alpha equal
  0.9.

The outcome will result in the method with the lowest Weighted MAPE. The
motivation for such a choice has been based on the logic that for the majority of the
products falling within the flashy and intermittent categories, the difficulties for the
predictions did not only come from the timing of the foreseen consumption, but also
on the quantity forecasted. As a result, by switching the alpha parameters from 0.1
to 0.9, for each of the SKUs, we tried to simulate different scenarios where the most
the parameters had the most influence (0.1), the least influence (0.9) and where the
influence was moderate (0.5).

For the latter, the stable portfolio, we decided to prioritize the products falling
into A and B categories that still accounted for high level of Weighted MAPE. Only
for those, we identified the optimized parameters of the respective exponential
smoothing models and successively we run the new models and collected the new
results.

Figure 6.31 represents the ultimate results in terms of Weighted MAPE and
Weighted Bias that we managed to derive from the 200 SKUs sample:

– Flashy products: 14% accuracy
– Intermittent products: 18% accuracy
– Trendy products: 83% accuracy
– Seasonal products 83% accuracy
– Internal variable products: 89% accuracy
– Trendy and seasonal 81% accuracy.

The weighted forecast bias maintains itself in equilibrium for the stable products,
while it still indicates a tendency toward under- and overforecasting for the intermittent and flashy products.

To sum up the results and weighting all together the 200 products of the portfolio, we managed to reach the following:

– A forecast accuracy of 76%
– A forecast bias of 0.53%.

Considering the sub-portfolios, we can also state the following insights:

– A forecast accuracy of 82% and a forecast bias of −3% for the stable portfolio
  (100 products accounting for 90% of the sales)
– A forecast accuracy of 16% and a forecast bias of 1% for the flashy and
  intermittent portfolios (100 products accounting for 10% of the sales).

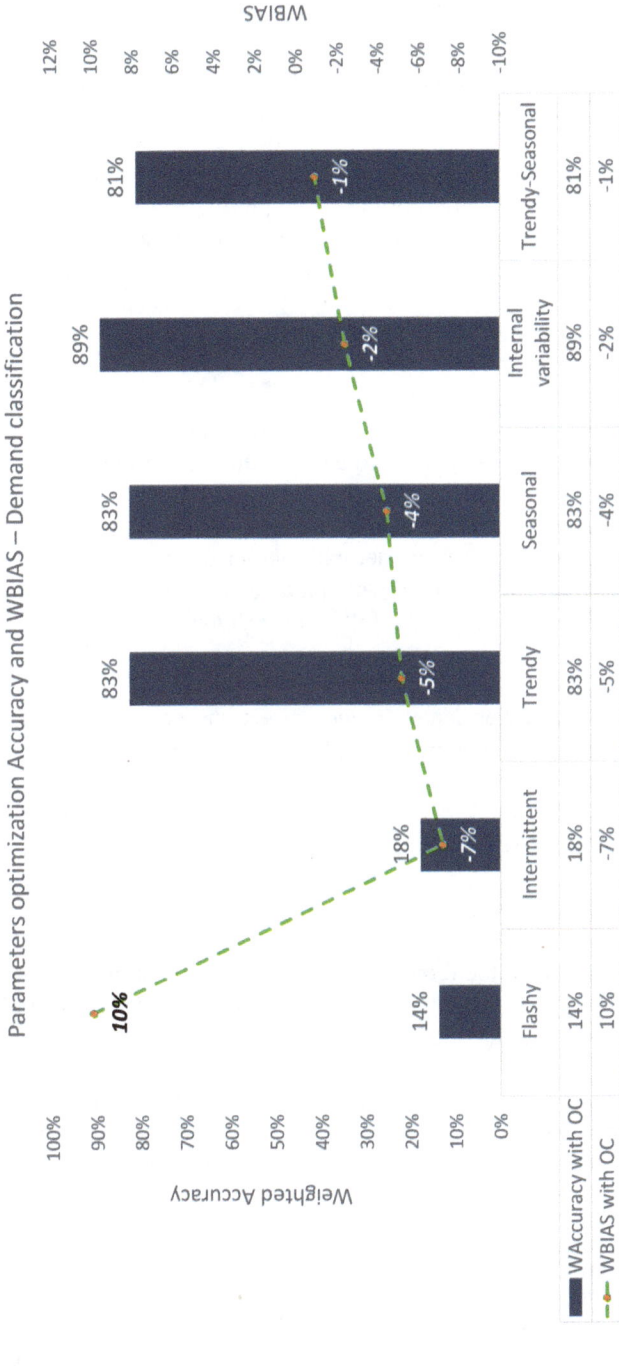

**Fig. 6.31** Custom method with parameters optimization—KPIs per demand classification

Figure 6.32 illustrates the ranges of improvements led by the parameters optimization of both the stable and flashy–intermittent sub-portfolios. It has to be underlined that only 25 stable products have been submitted for the parameters optimization, and all scored more accurate results. At the same time, all the flashy and intermittent products did go through the "best fit" run of the Markovian solution.

Having a total of 52 products that show an enhancement, and knowing that 25 products come from the optimization of the stable products, we can derive that the other 27 products have been optimized by the Markovian best fit solution.

## 6.3.3   Concluding Remarks

The circle has now been closed.

We started from the end, with an illustrative description of all the methods already compared, and then, we dived into each of them from the very first to the last.

Let's then go back to Fig. 6.2 and analyze more in detail our way backward, from the first running of the best fit model with outlier detection and correction to the latest run of the custom method with parameters optimization and outlier detection and correction. We derive the following results:

- Best fit with outlier detection and correction Weighted MAPE: 33%
- Custom method with outlier detection and correction Weighted MAPE: 31%
- Custom method with trend dampening and with outlier detection and correction Weighted MAPE: 27%
- Custom method with parameters optimization and with outlier detection and correction Weighted MAPE: 24%.

Finally, it results that from the beginning to the end we nibbled away 9% of accuracy.

Considering the aspects of the forecast bias, we can state that only the automatic detection and correction of the outliers led to a marked tendency of underforecasting (−10%), while for all the methods where the custom solution toward outlier detection and correction was applied, the bias varied over a range of −1 to 1%.

The same reasoning can be applied to the specific demand categories of our portfolio, but the comparison cannot include the best fit model as at that time, and applying only that model, the practitioner had not and could not have any view on the demand categories of its portfolio.

Figures 6.33 and 6.34 display the following results:

- The flashy category managed to reduce its forecast error by only 3%, maintaining a tendency of overforecasting around 10%.
- The intermittent category reduced its forecast error by 7%, with a negative direction of the error.

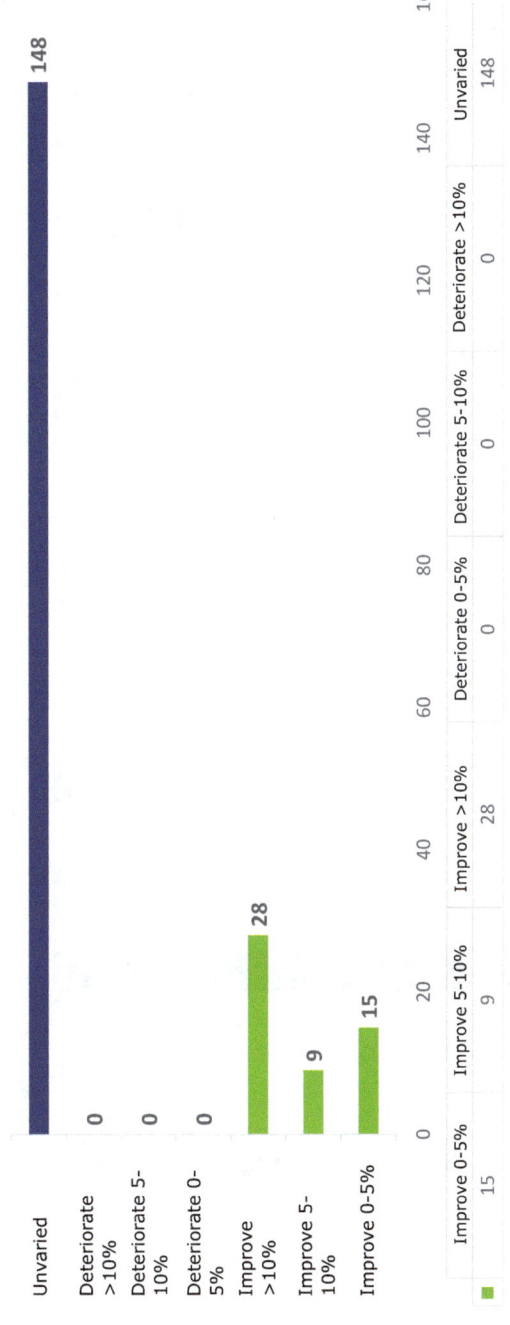

**Fig. 6.32** Custom method with parameters optimization—benchmarking classes of improvements

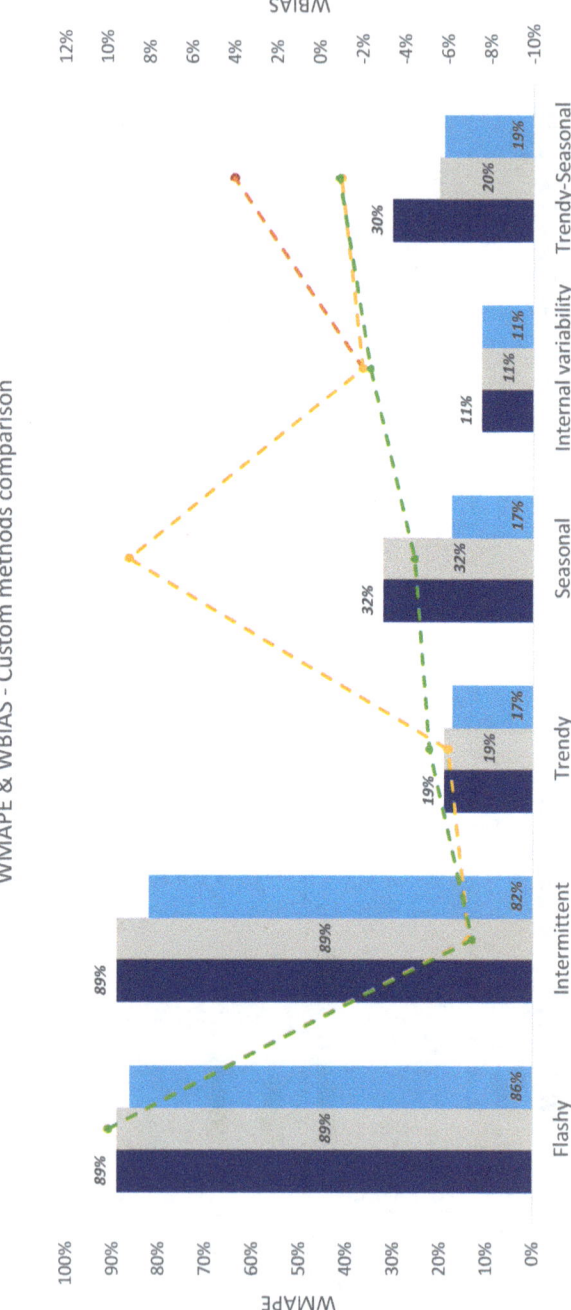

**Fig. 6.33** Weighted MAPE and Weighted Bias—custom methods comparison per demand classification (1)

| Methods / Classification | Flashy | Intermittent | Trendy | Seasonal | Internal Variability | Trendy Seasonal |
|---|---|---|---|---|---|---|
| Custom method with outlier detection and correction WMAPE | 89% | 89% | 19% | 32% | 11% | 30% |
| Custom method with trend dampening with outlier detection and correction WMAPE | 89% | 89% | 19% | 32% | 11% | 20% |
| Custom method with parameters optimization with outlier detection and correction WMAPE | 86% | 82% | 17% | 17% | 11% | 19% |
| Custom method with outlier detection and correction WBIAS | 10% | -7% | -6% | 9% | -2% | 4% |
| Custom method with trend dampening with outlier detection and correction WBIAS | 10% | -7% | -6% | 9% | -2% | -1% |
| Custom method with parameters optimization with outlier detection and correction BIAS | 10% | -7% | -5% | -4% | -2% | -1% |

**Fig. 6.34** Weighted MAPE and Weighted Bias—custom methods comparison per demand classification (2)

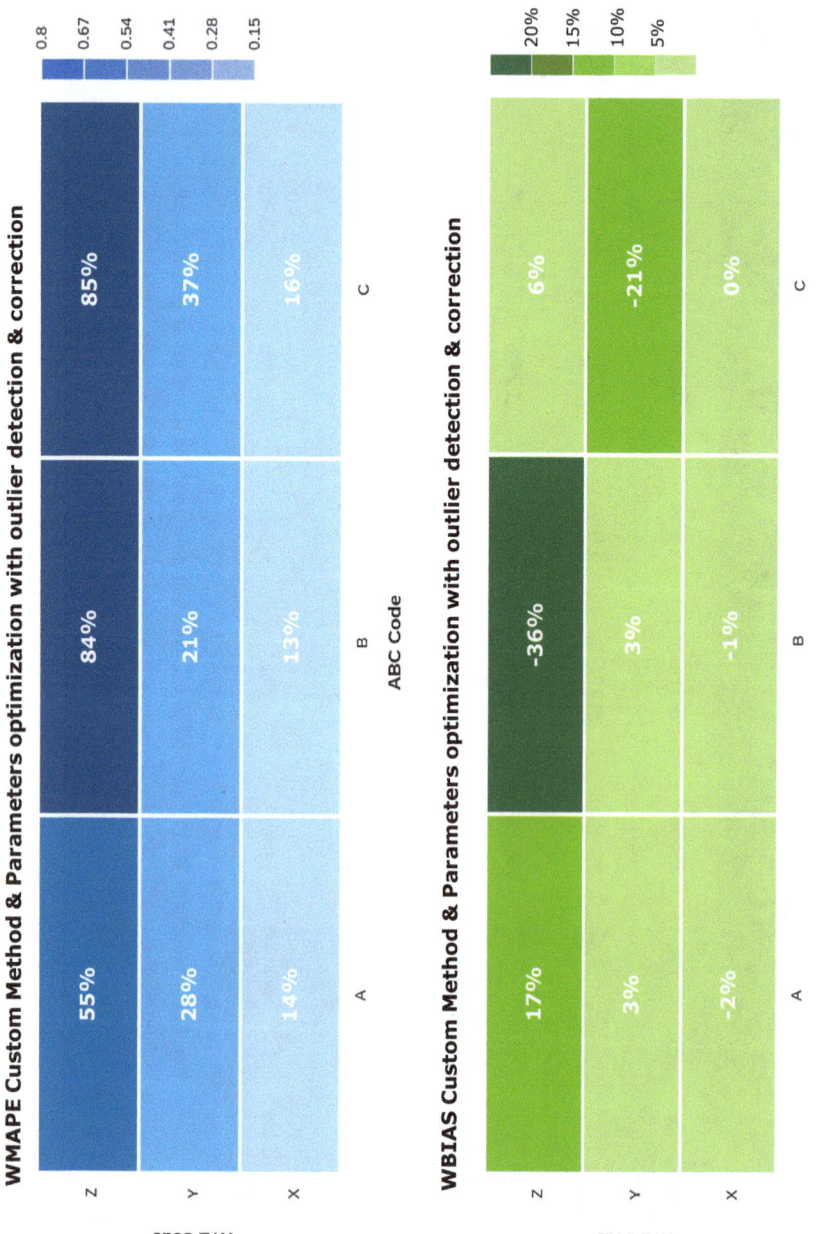

**Fig. 6.35** Weighted MAPE and Weighted Bias custom method with parameters optimization and with OD and OC

- The trendy category gained 2% from the smoothing settings optimization.
- The seasonal category gained 15% of accuracy from the smoothing settings optimization.
- The trendy and seasonal categories gained 10% from the demand dampening and another 1% from the parameters optimization.

As a last point, we also notice how the green-dotted line, indicating the forecast bias of the latest run of the custom method with parameters optimization, reaches an equilibrium around the values of −1% down to −5% for all the categories of the stable demand. Therefore, the high and low peaks of the forecast bias have been almost eliminated.

The last but not least comes the final matrix of the ABC/XYZ with the Weighted MAPE and Bias plotted (Fig. 6.35). This is a summary of custom method with optimized parameters and with outlier correction. From the matrix, we can notice that:

- The AX quadrant reaches its lowest level of MAPE (14%) with a forecast bias of −2%. Consequently, the class that accounts for 43.21 M sales, that is, 61% of the total sales, is forecasted with an accuracy of 86%.
- The BX quadrant reaches also its lowest MAPE of 13% and a forecast bias of −1%. This class accounts for 9.14 M of the overall sales (13% of the overall sales) and is forecasted with an accuracy of 87%.
- The CZ class performs in the same direction with a null forecast bias and a MAPE of 16%.
- The AY class reaches its minimum in terms of forecast error with an overall accuracy of 72% and a forecast bias of 2%. It has improved by 9% because of the parameters optimization.
- The same trend, but even stronger, is registered for the BY category that shows an accuracy of 79%, a bias of 3% and an enhancement of 20% thanks to the parameters optimization.
- The class CY improved by 5%.
- The class AZ improved by 20%, resulting in a forecast accuracy of 45%.
- The rest of the Z classes slightly improved by few percentage points.

If we average the X quadrants and the AY and BY quadrants, we can state that, on average, we are predicting with a forecast accuracy of 82%, 61.9 M of sales representing 88% of the overall sales.

# Improving Short-Term Forecast with Demand Sensing

**7**

Demand planning is a keystone process that is relevant across all three levels of the planning hierarchy—be it long term, tactical or operational. True demand planning excellence requires excellent performance along all three planning levels (and the corresponding horizons of long, medium and short).

Now, this begs the question "what constitutes excellent performance?". Performance can be measured based on the quality of decision support provided by demand planning across the levels of planning. A sampling of key decisions along these levels is illustrated in Fig. 7.1.

Traditionally, there has been good support from a tool perspective for demand forecasting in the long and medium term (think planning granularity of years or months). The same cannot really be said about short-term forecasting (think weeks or days). Short-term forecasting has for a long time been devoid of solid algorithmic support. Demand sensing is an effort to address this. It is designed with the particular needs of short-term forecasting in mind. As one gets closer to execution, the level of detail increases (increase in planning granularity), but the degrees of freedom become narrow. That is, one is bound by decisions that are taken at higher levels. So, forecasting in the short term is less about optimization as in most cases resources have already been committed to a certain anticipated outcome and more about gaining clarity on or predicting more accurately the most likely outcome in order to come up with as profitable a response as possible. Also, from the perspective of Gartner's CORE (Configure, Optimize, Respond, and Execute) framework for categorizing supply chain processes, demand sensing is clearly a respond process which is defined as "helping to create an intelligent response to execution events that keep the short-term plan as close as possible to the company goals."

© Springer Nature Switzerland AG 2019
G. Sankaran et al., *Improving Forecasts with Integrated Business Planning*,
Management for Professionals, https://doi.org/10.1007/978-3-030-05381-9_7

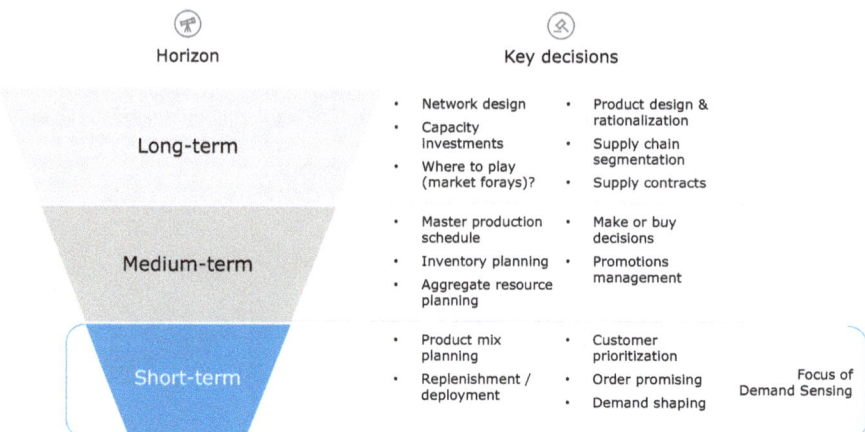

**Fig. 7.1** Key decisions based on forecast across supply chain decision phases

## 7.1    Demand Sensing Trends in Modern Supply Chains

Recent years have seen an unprecedented growth in data generated and collected by organizations. This does not automatically translate to benefits or improvements in performance. Just accumulating humongous data amounts to nothing if insights cannot be operationalized. This is particularly relevant for short-term forecasting as proper analytical support can help unwrap the shroud of uncertainty around customer orders, thereby improving accuracy.

In "Leading Digital," the author talks about how digitalization is breaking down paradoxes of the past, between standardization and empowerment, controlling and innovating or orchestrating and unleashing. The equation to characterize such trade-offs is shifting from "either-or" to "both-and" (McAfee & Didier Bonnet, 2014). It is also true of the age-old trade-off between efficiency and responsiveness. Supply chains of today have to become, as Gartner calls it "bimodal," which is to mean the ability to seamlessly integrate elements driven by cost efficiency and responsiveness considerations. With shortening of lead times, customer centricity and mass customization becoming trends du jour and with the "locus shifting to the customer," a quicker cadence is crucial to planning processes, particularly that fall into the "respond" realm like demand sensing (Subramaniam & Bala Iyer, 2016). Figure 7.2 illustrates how quicker cadence/shorter lags, supported by algorithms, can help reduce latency in processing events that are likely to influence demand. Also, the volumes of data involved means algorithmic support is inevitable. The approach of APS (e.g., SAP APO) of adjusting what is essentially a 30-day lag forecast based on exceptions is a thing of the past. This is where demand sensing comes in.

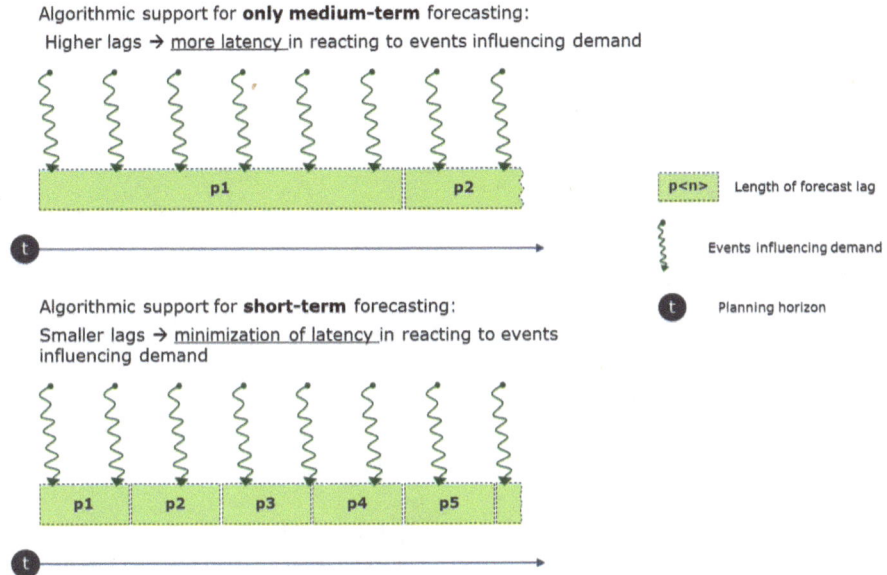

Algorithmic support for **only medium-term** forecasting:
Higher lags → more latency in reacting to events influencing demand

Algorithmic support for **short-term** forecasting:
Smaller lags → minimization of latency in reacting to events influencing demand

p<n>   Length of forecast lag

Events influencing demand

t   Planning horizon

**Fig. 7.2** Quicker cadence enhances the ability to react to demand relevant events

## 7.2 Benefits of Demand Sensing

### 7.2.1 Variability Dampening

Proliferation of SKUs and deep supply chain networks necessitated by customer proximity are key contributing factors to variability amplification as one gets closer to the customer: From a product structure standpoint, this could mean variability increase as one moves from raw materials to finished products. The increase is particularly pronounced in the case of different product flows (a lot more finished SKUs than input materials). From a distribution network perspective, this could mean as one moves from suppliers to retailers. From a time granularity perspective, this could be as one switches from months to days. This variability amplification is further sharpened by the infamous bullwhip effect. This is illustrated in Fig. 7.3.

We have seen in the earlier section how demand sensing implies increasing the cadence—that is, systematically reacting to events influencing demand with minimal latency. This approach of using analytical support to process demand signals—both historical and forward-looking—to make predictions in the near term leads to lowering of uncertainty "felt" by the supply chain. The dampening effect of increasing the number of demand observations on uncertainty (or variability) can be proved quantitatively.

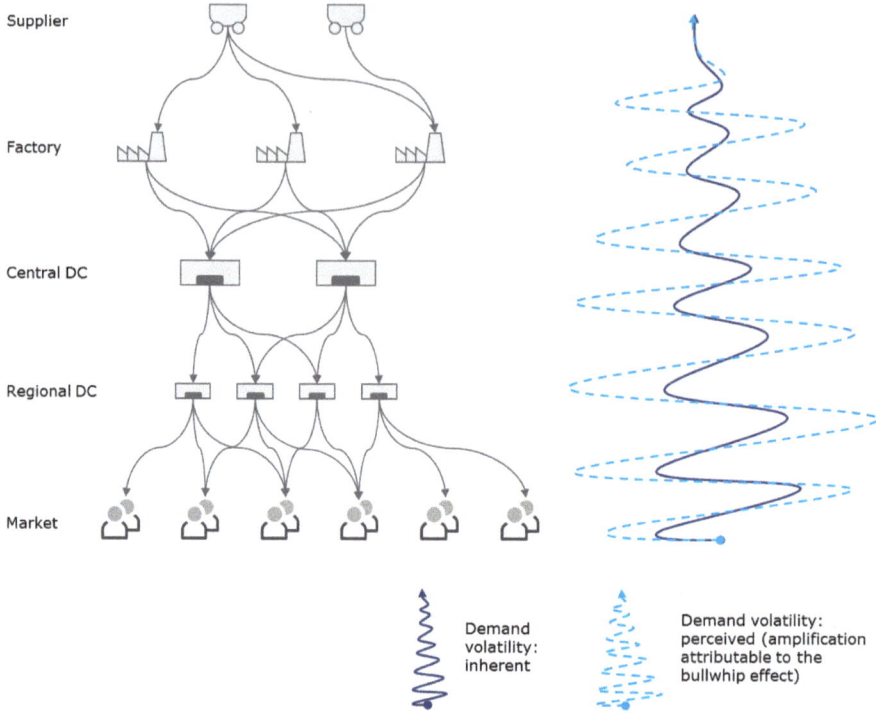

Supplier

Factory

Central DC

Regional DC

Market

Demand
volatility:
inherent

Demand volatility:
perceived (amplification
attributable to the
bullwhip effect)

**Fig. 7.3** Illustration of variability amplification as one moves closer to customer

Technical note: It can be proved that (Simchi, 1999)

$$\frac{\text{Variance of orders placed by the retailer at the manufacturer/}}{\text{Variance of demand as seen by the retailer}} \geq 1 + \frac{2L}{p} + \frac{2L^3}{p^3}$$

where $L$ = lead time and $p$ = number of demand observations.

Many companies follow market trends to become demand driven. Demand-driven principles have been gaining traction with agility becoming more and more important to building "respond" capabilities. One of the core principles of demand driven is enshrined in the phrase "position and pull instead of push and promote" (Debra Smith, 2016). This means positioning the decoupling point further downstream, which could potentially lead to grabbing more market share by becoming more attractive (response time-wise) versus competition. The idea is illustrated in Fig. 7.4.

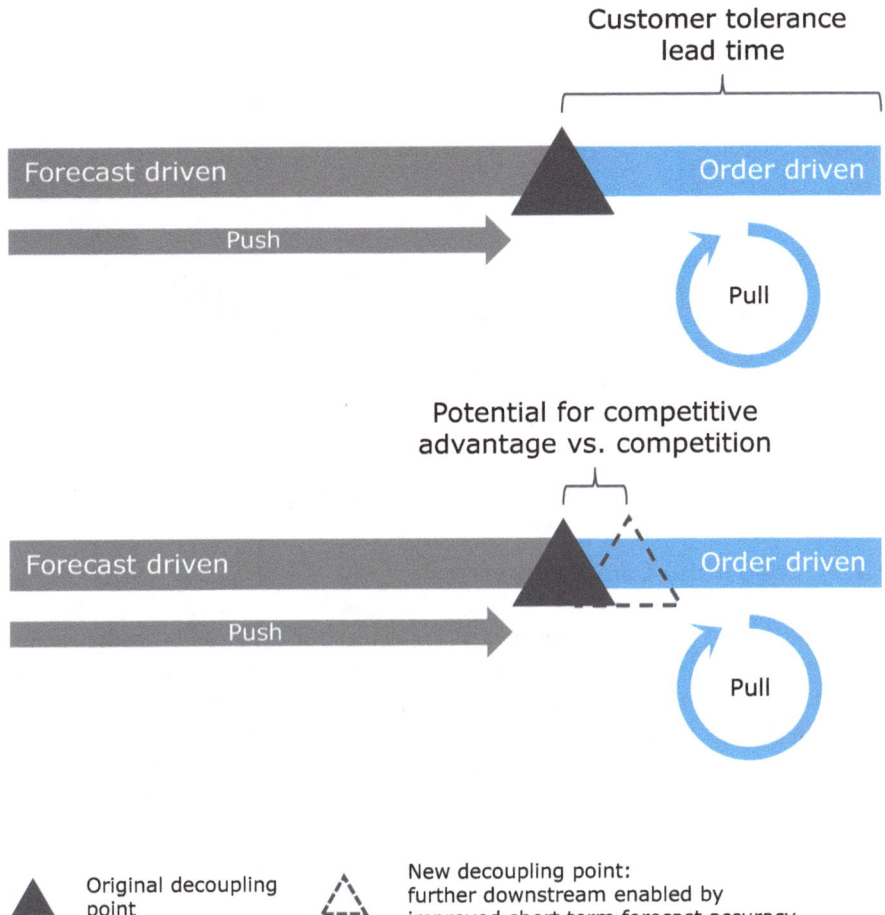

**Fig. 7.4**  Repositioning of decoupling point further downstream

## 7.2.2  Working Capital Rationalization

There is also a clear correlation between forecast variability and inventory. Greater the variability, higher is the required level of stocks to ensure a certain desired service level. As can be seen from Fig. 7.5, this relationship is nonlinear, and this represents a significant opportunity. Improvements in accuracy or reduction in variability can have a positive impact on working capital. One could either offer the same level of service at a reduced inventory or improve the service level keeping inventory investments the same.

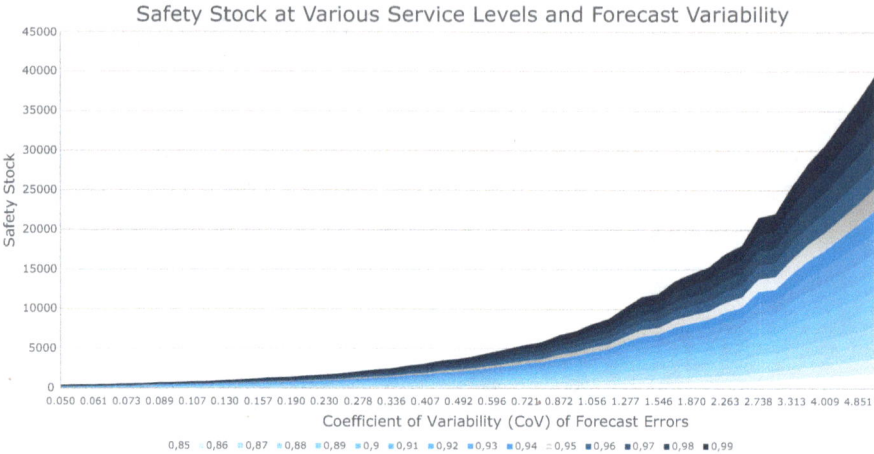

**Fig. 7.5** Forecast variability, customer service level and safety inventory

## 7.2.3   Lead Time Compression

Reduction of lead times is another area where demand sensing can bring in benefits. This is explained well using a numerical example: We have a bill of material (BOM) that consists of parts that are all made to order (say, because of high demand variability like in the case of a highly customizable product). Demands for these parts cannot be reliably predicted at higher lags (for instance, 30 days or more). However, let's say, by increasing the cadence and leveraging analytical support, forecast variability could be reduced for some of these parts to a level that makes a switch from make-to-order to make-to-stock viable. Let's analyze the impact of this. We'll do so by focusing on the critical path of the BOM, which is the longest path that represents the lead time experienced by the customer. The critical path changes as we progressively switch the strategy for parts where the variability decrease is significant enough to make this a viable option.

As we can see from the illustration in Fig. 7.6, over four iterations, the lead time is progressively reduced from 55 to 27 days. The progression is as follows:

Iteration 1 (1–2 in graphic)—original state where the critical path is [j → f b → a] for a lead time of 55 days. Part j, which is on the critical path, is a candidate for switching to MTS as there is a forecast variability for this part that is significant enough to enable it to be treated as a stock item. This switch shifts the critical path to [k → h → c → a] for a lead time of 47 days.

Iteration 2 (2–3 in graphic)—The process is repeated, and part k is similarly switched to MTS, which leads to a further reduction to get to a lead time of 45 days with the new critical path being [i → f → b → a].

Iteration 3 (3–4 in graphic)—In the final iteration, "i" is switched, which gives us the final lead time of 27 days. The process stops once we've exhausted all

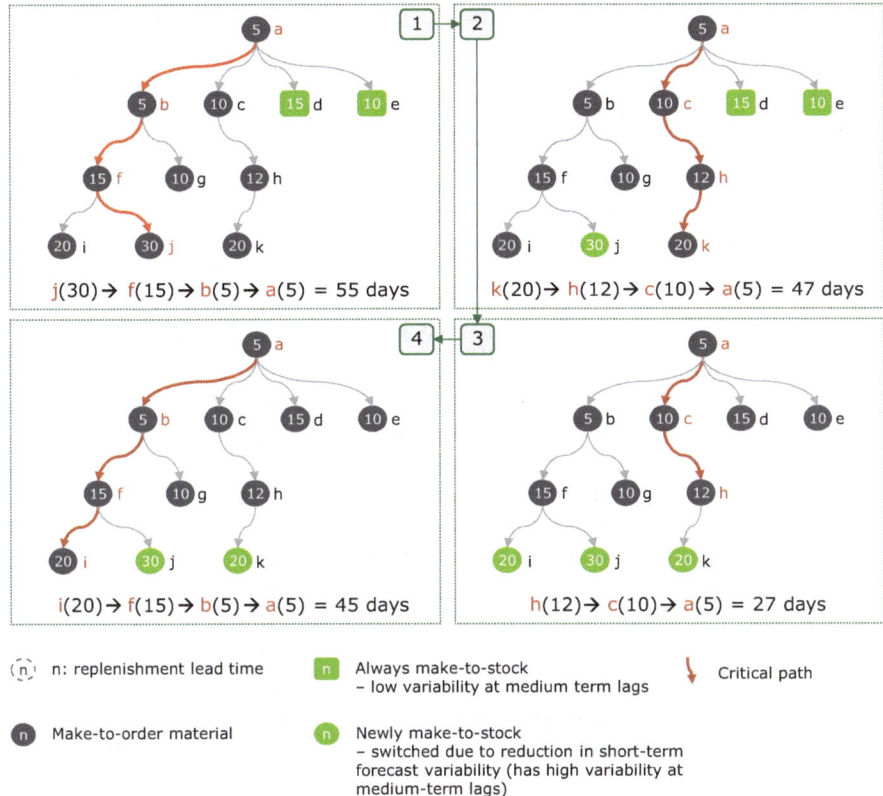

**Fig. 7.6** Lead time compression by switching certain parts from MTO to MTS

candidates for switching to MTS owing to forecast variability reduction afforded by demand sensing.

**Note**: On the other hand, materials that are not on the critical path do not have a direct influence on lead time and could be potential candidates for a make-to-order approach, thereby reducing overall inventory.

Earlier, we talked about how new trends such as digitalization and IoT have necessitated breaking traditional paradoxes between efficiency and responsiveness. Toward this end, demand sensing is an important tool in a digital supply chain's toolbox. By improving near-term accuracy, it provides the requisite analytical support to improve capacity utilization, increase production scheduling efficiency and accuracy, increase accuracy of replenishment planning, rationalize inventory, increase transportation planning efficiency and accuracy, etc., all contributing toward cost efficiency while at the same time not compromising on responsiveness.

## 7.2.4   Demand Sensing Overview

Let's start with a general definition of demand sensing provided by Gartner: It is defined as the "translation of demand information with minimal latency to detect who is buying the product, what attributes are selling and what impact demand shaping programs are having" (Tohamy, Scott, & Steutermann, 2012). The operative phrase is "minimal latency." If we are able to use the power of analytics to interpret demand signals with minimal latency and turn them into insights, for instance, in the form of more accurate short-term forecasts, we are then able to drive better decisions. The key is leveraging multiple streams of data that help predict future demands at speed and at scale. Clearly, the traditional principle of management by exception alone won't do. IBP's demand sensing algorithms provide the necessary tool support that allows interpretation of demand signals *at speed and at scale*. The illustration in Fig. 7.7 provides a conceptual illustration of the key principles at work. There are various inputs such as historical orders, historical consensus forecast (also known as consensus revisions—more on this later), future orders that are captured at multiple lags, meaning at different points in time prior to the actual business event (say, customer order shipment) occurring, which are systematically processed by the demand sensing algorithm to provide a "sensed demand" that encapsulates the insights of the various input streams. With this, one is able to transit from a descriptive/diagnostic (a la alerts) approach that tends to be reactive in nature to a prescriptive/predictive one that is proactive. Of course, real benefits will depend on a supply chain's ability to operationalize the insights gained. However, in some cases, just being able to identify potential issues early enough, so that remedial actions can be analyzed, is in itself an invaluable benefit.

If we talk about SAP IBP support for demand sensing, although the algorithm itself is proprietary and details of the inner workings are not in the public domain, the main steps can be deduced based on experimental results. The process described below is based on numerous runs of the algorithm for a number of deliberately created data sets to examine its behavior.

The algorithm can be said to consist of four key steps.[1] This is depicted in Fig. 7.8.

---

[1]This excludes any preprocessing steps. For example, cleansing the consensus demand of promotions is a typical preprocessing step. The assumption made is that the consensus key figure input is one without promotions.

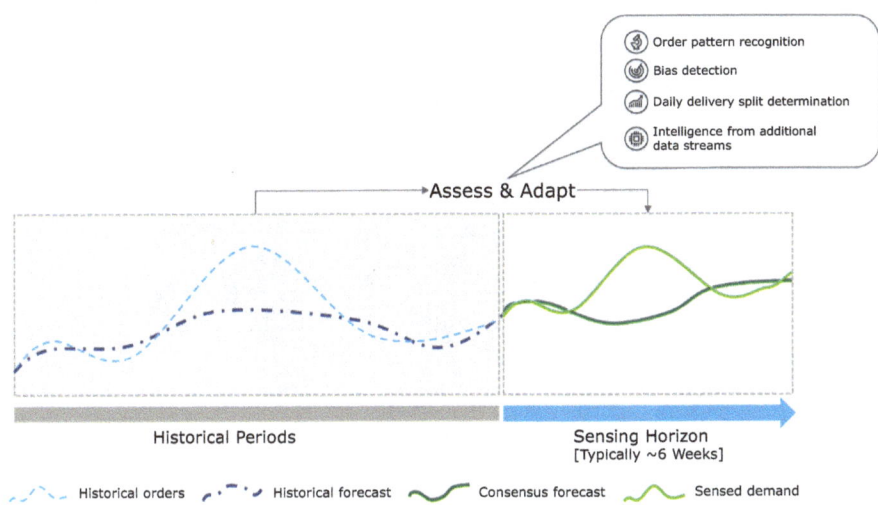

**Fig. 7.7**  Illustration of principles behind SAP IBP's demand sensing algorithm

| | Historical data for forecasting | Future order quantity | Sensed demand | Delivery quantity |
|---|---|---|---|---|
| **Key figures** | Consensus revisions / snapshots | Historical order quantity | Adjusted sensed demand | Adjusted delivery quantity |

| | 1 Detect Bias | 2 Recognize Order Patterns | 3 Calculate Weekly Sensed Demand | 4 Determine Daily Distribution Factors |
|---|---|---|---|---|

| | Bias horizons | Order quantity ratio calculation horizon | Min/max forecast adjustment bandwidth | Daily average calculation horizon |
|---|---|---|---|---|
| **Settings** | Lags | | Minimum accuracy improvement threshold | Working days |

**Fig. 7.8**  Peek under the hood: IBP's demand sensing algorithm

## 7.2.5   SAP Use Case: Bias Detection

For detecting bias, besides the historical demand data itself (actual orders), consensus forecast revisions in the form of snapshots are a prerequisite. Consensus revisions will have to be available ideally for the length of the historical data horizon (say, 52 weeks). Based on this input, historical forecast bias at multiple lags is calculated by the algorithm.

The concept of calculation of historical consensus bias, using revisions, at multiple lags will be explained with the help of Fig. 7.9. A consensus revision consists of a revision date (date on which the consensus "snapshot" is taken) and

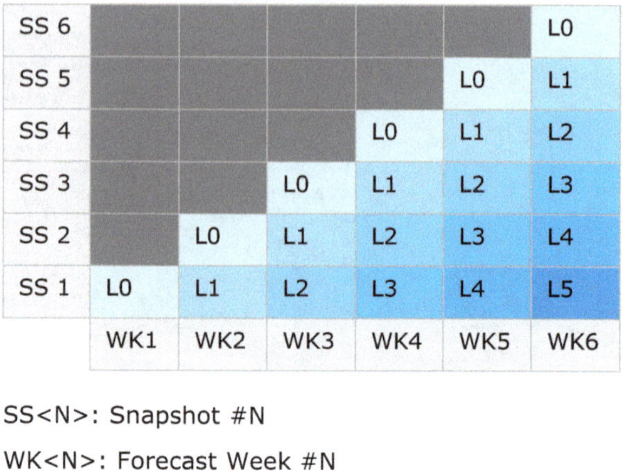

| SS 6 |     |     |     |     |     | L0 |
|------|-----|-----|-----|-----|-----|-----|
| SS 5 |     |     |     |     | L0  | L1 |
| SS 4 |     |     |     | L0  | L1  | L2 |
| SS 3 |     |     | L0  | L1  | L2  | L3 |
| SS 2 |     | L0  | L1  | L2  | L3  | L4 |
| SS 1 | L0  | L1  | L2  | L3  | L4  | L5 |
|      | WK1 | WK2 | WK3 | WK4 | WK5 | WK6 |

SS<N>: Snapshot #N

WK<N>: Forecast Week #N

**Fig. 7.9** Snapshots and lags explained

quantities along the forecast horizon qualified by key figure dates. For a given snapshot, lag refers to the difference in periods (weeks in our case) between the period when the snapshot is taken and the forecasted week. In the example below, for the first snapshot SS1 which is taken in week 1 (WK1), lag 0 is WK1, lag 1 is WK2 and so on. Therefore, lag X bias can be calculated by comparing the snapshot taken X periods before with the actual demands. To calculate one bias metric for a given lag, the bias for this lag is calculated over all historical snapshots and summarized.

In the demand sensing forecast profile (accessed through the manage forecast models app), the key figure where forecast revisions are stored is specified. It is determined by the algorithm by concatenating the consensus forecast key figure and the snapshot suffix (see 1b in Fig. 7.10).

To determine bias correction to be applied, historical periods that are evaluated for calculating bias coefficients that inform the calculation of correction factors are specified in the field bias horizons (see 1c in Fig. 7.10). These need to be seen relative to the current period. For example, bias horizon of 2 refers to the second historical period for which lag-based bias will be calculated. A total of six bias horizons can be specified. If periods in the recent past are specified, the sensing algorithm is more sensitive to recent changes than when the periods specified are older.

Lag-based accuracy can either converge on the actual demand (accuracy improves as lags get shorter) or diverge or be some combination of the two. Demand sensing uses an analysis of this aspect to apply corrections to the future consensus forecast. For example, systematic positive or negative biases can be corrected by increasing or decreasing the consensus forecast commensurate to the magnitude of the bias detected.

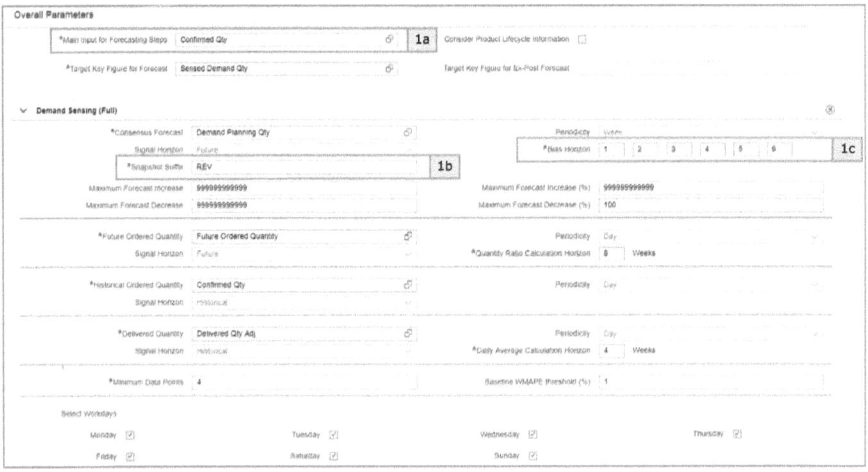

**Fig. 7.10** Settings relevant for detecting bias

**Note**: The number of lags that are analyzed is a function of the forecast horizon. In the example provided, there are six lags being analyzed as the forecast horizon is six weeks long.

## 7.2.6 SAP Use Case: Sales Order Pattern Recognition

The underlying concept is quite intuitive. Based on the material availability date (expected date of warehouse shipment) and order creation date, one could determine order quantities at multiple lags and trace the evolution of orders for a given planning combination (say, product–location–customer). This concept is illustrated in Fig. 7.11. The illustration shows the evolution of order quantities starting from eight weeks (lag 8) in the past with respect to the material availability date until lag 0 (week of the material availability date). The cumulative % is the cumulated order quantities vis-à-vis the final order quantity (requested or confirmed as the case may be).

An analysis of the evolution of order quantities across multiple lags is then used by the algorithm as one of the ways to predict future orders. Simplistically, if analysis of the entire historical horizon for a given combination should reveal that the lag-based evolution of quantities over four lags (3-2-1-0) is always 25% each, an order quantity for 25 units for this combination with material availability three weeks out can be used to predict that the eventual demand will be 100. Although this is an oversimplification, as order pattern recognition is only one among the signals used to calculate sensed demand, it nevertheless helps underscore the key underlying principle.

In the forecast profile, the key figures that hold future order quantity and historical order quantity relevant for order pattern recognition are specified (see 2a and

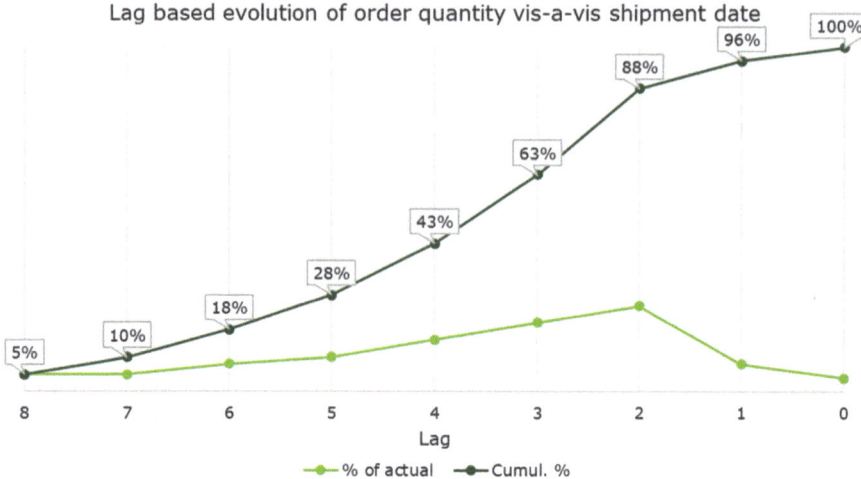

**Fig. 7.11** Evolution of order quantities across multiple lags

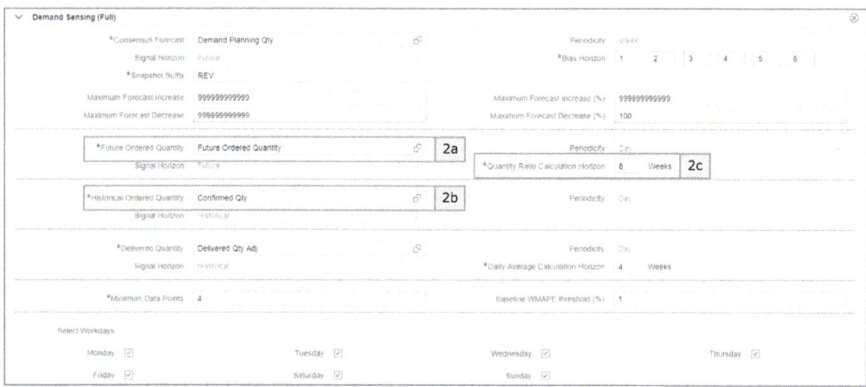

**Fig. 7.12** Settings relevant for order pattern recognition

2b in Fig. 7.12). Quantity ration calculation horizon in the profile specifies the horizon over which lag-based analysis for order pattern recognition should happen.

Bias and order patterns are two key considerations for the algorithm to deriving sensed demand. As one can imagine, there is considerable quantitative heft involved in determining appropriate weights for each of these considerations for calculating the final sensed demand.

### 7.2.7  SAP Use Case: Calculation of Weekly Sensed Demand

The main output of the sensing algorithm is weekly sensed demand. To prevent drastic automatic adjustments to consensus forecast, thresholds can be established that cap the magnitude of change in absolute or percentage terms. Also, an accuracy improvement threshold can be provided that prevents sensed demand from being different from consensus demand unless the MAPE of consensus demand is less than or equal to the threshold provided (see 3a and 3b in Fig. 7.13).

In addition, the planner can review and override her/his input into the adjusted sensed demand key figure. If this is a non-null value, it flows into the final sensed demand key figure; otherwise, the main output of the algorithm which is the sensed demand quantity is used.

### 7.2.8  SAP Use Case: Determination of Daily Distribution Factors

The final step of the process is to break down weekly sensed demand into daily buckets. There are two factors to be considered: historical daily split, which is calculated based on an average calculated over a given horizon (specified in the profile, see 4a in Fig. 7.14) and definition of working days (see 4b in Fig. 7.14).

### 7.2.9  SAP Use Case: Forecasting Sensed Demand

The following system scenarios show the algorithm in action and should help demonstrate the four key steps described in the earlier section.

We have seen that one of the key input data streams to the demand sensing algorithm is consensus revisions. Let's analyze this more closely in the first

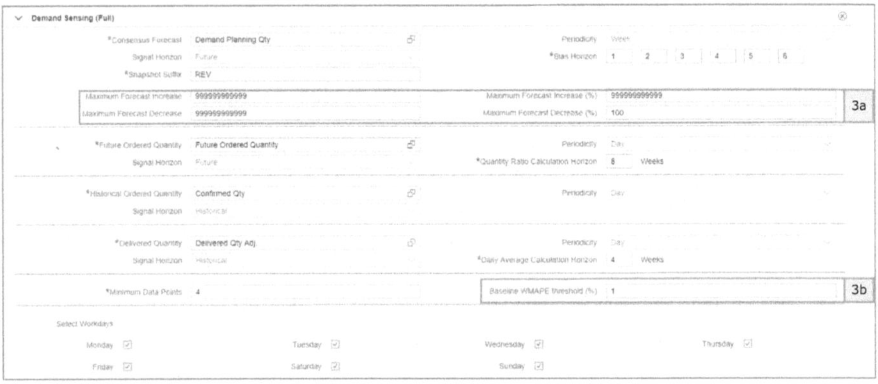

**Fig. 7.13** Thresholds to cap magnitude

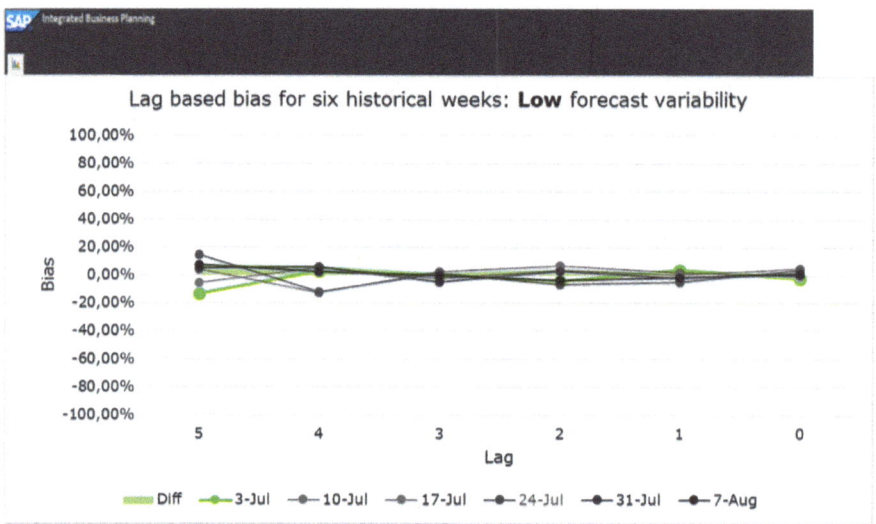

**Fig. 7.14** Settings for determining daily split

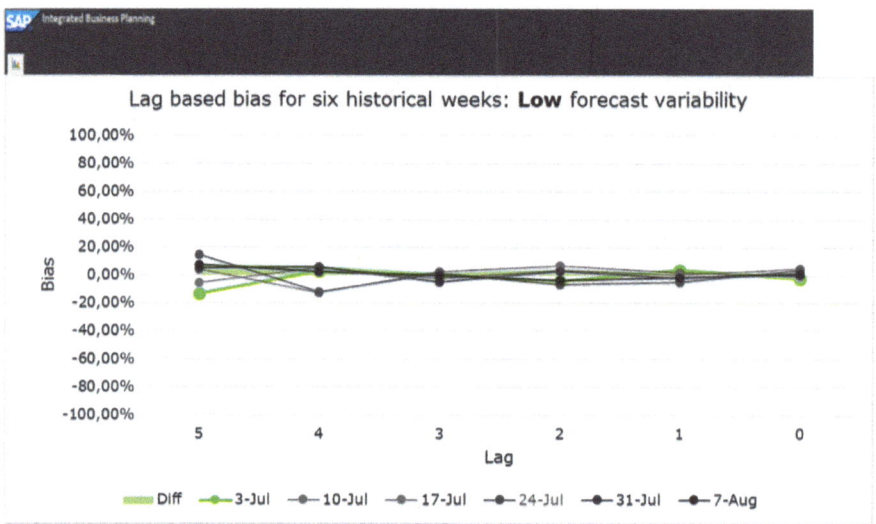

**Fig. 7.15** Lag-based bias for DC1—low variability scenario

example. For this example, a data set (for location "DC1") has been simulated to produce a lag-based bias that looks like shown in Fig. 7.15.

As can be seen, the lag-based accuracy increases or bias decreases as one gets closer to execution—that is, move toward lag 0. In Fig. 7.15, lag-based bias is shown for six historical periods. The data series "diff" in the figure denotes the average bias across these historical periods over the lags. This can be seen to be decreasing as one gets closer to lag 0.

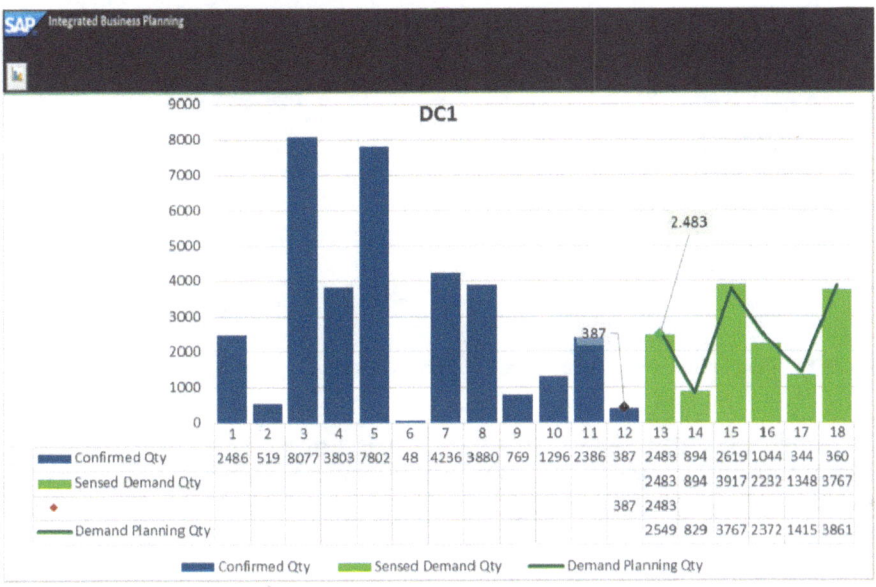

**Fig. 7.16**  Result of demand sensing run—low bias scenario (DC1)

The results of the algorithm for this data set are discussed next. Intuitively, one can expect that in this case, greater lags will undergo larger adjustments compared to smaller lags. This is confirmed by the result of the demand sensing run summarized in Fig. 7.16.

From the data table provided, we can see that the adjustments to the demand planning quantity (specified as the consensus key figure) as evidenced in sensed demand quantity key figure are relatively small. What can also be seen is that the magnitude of changes at higher lags is greater than for smaller lags. As explained in the process description in the earlier section, the algorithm calculates bias at different lags and comes up with adjustment factors (more on this later) that are applied to the consensus forecast. The correlation between lag and forecasted periods is depicted in Fig. 7.17. Therefore, a bias adjustment based on lag 0 is applied to week 0 (relative to the current period), based on lag 1 is applied to week 1 and so on.

As bias increases, or in other words a read on consensus forecast becomes more unreliable, more weight starts to be assigned to adjustments attributable to detection of order patterns. To understand this, let's consider a second scenario (DC2) where the input consensus forecast bias is as shown in Fig. 7.18.

Focusing on the data series for average bias over periods analyzed ("diff"), it is clear that the bias is higher than the scenario earlier (for instance, absolute bias at lag 5 is less than 20% for DC1, but is around 40% for DC2). The result of demand sensing run for this scenario is shown in Fig. 7.19.

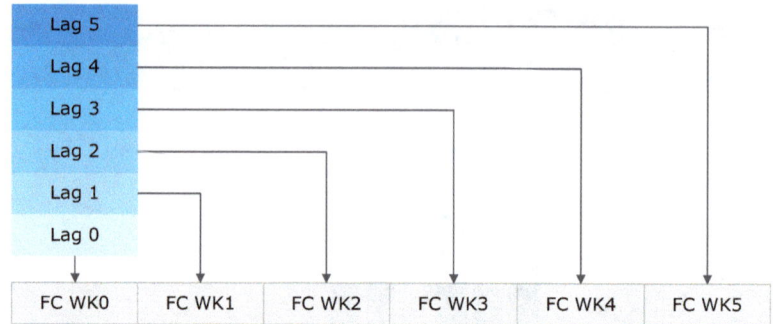

**Fig. 7.17** Relation between lag and forecast periods

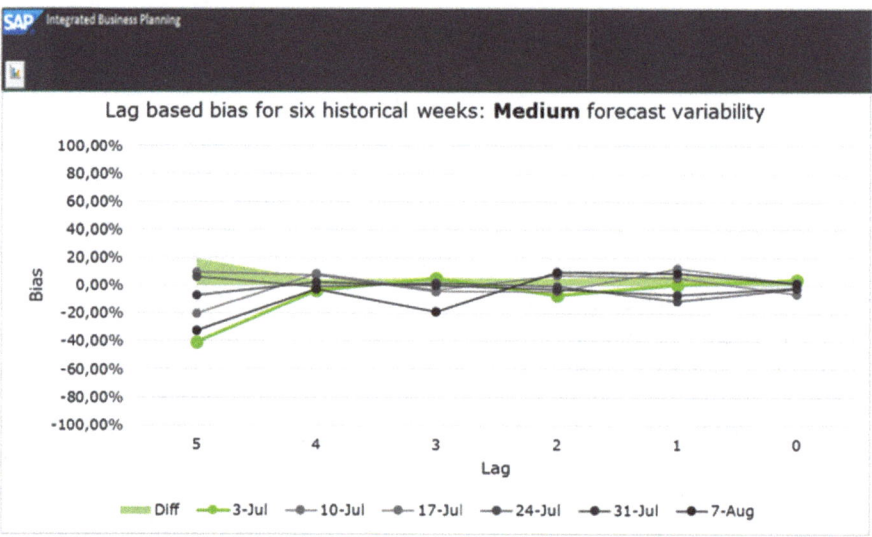

**Fig. 7.18** Lag-based bias for DC2—medium variability scenario

As opposed to the previous case, we see that the magnitude of adjustments for DC2 (difference between demand planning and sensed demand quantity) is higher. As in both cases, accuracy improves progressively as one moves toward lag 0; adjustments are lower for smaller lags compared to higher lags.

We have talked about how there are multiple signals or streams that are weighted to then calculate adjustment factors that are applied to the consensus forecast key figure. Let's dwell on this a little more closely by analyzing the internal mechanism at play. To do this, a brief introduction to the internally calculated key figures is in order.

These key figures are shown in Fig. 7.20. We have discussed the main input key figures and the ultimate output key figure. Turning our attention to key figures

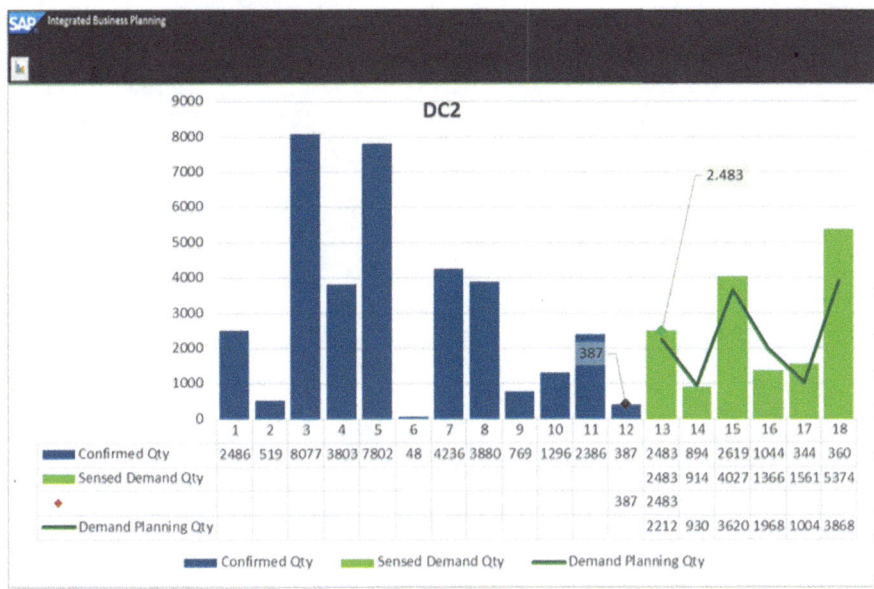

**Fig. 7.19**  Result of demand sensing run—medium bias scenario (DC2)

internally calculated by the algorithm, there are four categories of key figures (marked A through D in Fig. 7.20; their technical names and a brief description informing their use are provided):

A. Weights for chosen bias horizons: For each of the bias horizons that are specified in the forecast profile (see section on the process for a description) that need to be analyzed to detect bias in order to determine adjustments to future forecast required, bias coefficient key figures are used. There is one for each of the six horizons that can be specified in the profile.
B. To assess the impact of sensed demand due to bias correction and correction attributable to order pattern detection, equivalent accuracy measures are calculated and stored in corresponding key figures.
C. This category belongs to weights assigned to bias correction and correction based on order pattern recognition.
D. Finally, this category belongs to the calculated adjustment factors that are then applied to the consensus demand key figure to calculate the sensed demand quantity.

Let's compare these key figures for the two scenarios we have discussed. They are visualized in Figs. 7.21 and 7.22, respectively.

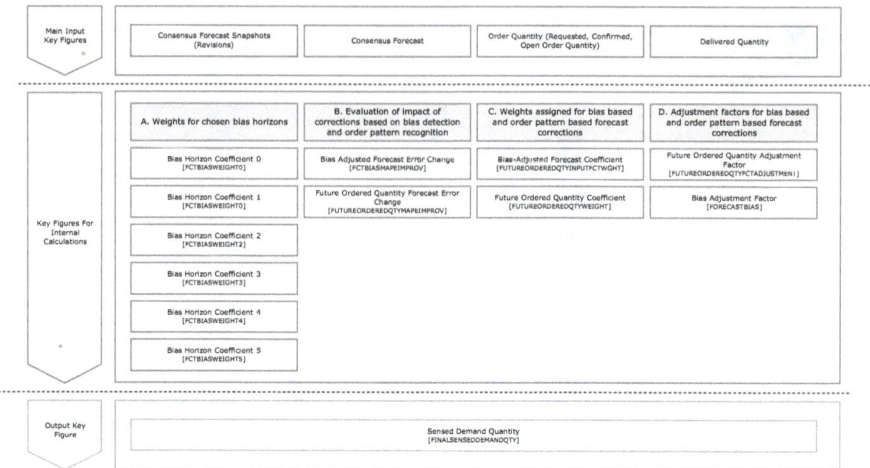

**Fig. 7.20**  Key figures for internal use calculated by the demand sensing algorithm

| Location | Lag | Time | BAF | BHC0 | BHC1 | BHC2 | BHC3 | BHC4 | BHC5 | BAFCC | BAFCEC | FOQAF | FOQFCEC |
|----------|-----|------|-----|------|------|------|------|------|------|-------|--------|-------|---------|
| DC1 | 0 | W36 2017 | 0,0008 | 0,1393 | -0,6283 | 0,0012 | 0,9016 | 1,5989 | -0,3792 | 0,0000 | 0,2266 | 0,9748 | 0,2467 |
| DC1 | 1 | W36 2017 | 0,0703 | -0,3055 | -0,0224 | -0,3174 | 0,5453 | -2,6308 | 3,8034 | 0,9759 | 0,2006 | 1,0495 | 0,0022 |
| DC1 | 2 | W36 2017 | -0,0727 | -0,1142 | -0,1249 | 1,1439 | -1,9332 | 1,2577 | 0,7444 | 0,9750 | 0,1023 | 0,9903 | 0,0023 |
| DC1 | 3 | W36 2017 | 0,0632 | -0,0752 | 0,1583 | -0,2881 | -1,6879 | 3,9441 | -1,4112 | 0,9503 | 0,0808 | 1,0044 | 0,0092 |
| DC1 | 4 | W36 2017 | 0,0704 | 0,1518 | -0,2910 | 0,5576 | -0,2765 | 2,5117 | -2,1703 | 0,9745 | 0,0778 | 1,0251 | 0,0020 |
| DC1 | 5 | W36 2017 | 0,0212 | -0,0406 | -0,3784 | 1,6461 | 0,0317 | 2,0200 | -2,5415 | 0,9904 | 0,1723 | 0,9969 | 0,0034 |

**Fig. 7.21**  Internally calculated key figures for scenario 1 (DC1)

| Location | Lag | Time | BAF | BHC0 | BHC1 | BHC2 | BHC3 | BHC4 | BHC5 | BAFCC | BAFCEC | FOQAF | FOQFCEC |
|----------|-----|------|-----|------|------|------|------|------|------|-------|--------|-------|---------|
| DC2 | 0 | W36 2017 | -0,4024 | 0,7450 | -1,0841 | -0,6003 | 2,2033 | -1,0498 | 0,9837 | 0,0000 | 0,2104 | 0,8004 | 0,2972 |
| DC2 | 1 | W36 2017 | 0,0886 | -0,0902 | -0,7833 | 0,9699 | 0,2220 | -0,9739 | 1,5087 | 0,9659 | 0,1556 | 1,0784 | 0,0086 |
| DC2 | 2 | W36 2017 | -0,1278 | 0,0803 | 0,0531 | 0,7169 | -0,5332 | 0,0845 | 0,3278 | 0,9549 | 0,1110 | 0,9863 | 0,0068 |
| DC2 | 3 | W36 2017 | 0,3206 | 0,3445 | -0,3182 | -0,7492 | 3,0617 | -2,0465 | 0,1605 | 0,9776 | 0,1767 | 1,0218 | 0,0004 |
| DC2 | 4 | W36 2017 | -0,4376 | -0,1557 | 0,4100 | -1,6047 | 2,7705 | -1,0309 | -1,1714 | 0,8834 | 0,1195 | 1,0814 | 0,0169 |
| DC2 | 5 | W36 2017 | -0,4412 | -0,5491 | 0,5307 | -1,7033 | 0,0231 | -0,3826 | 1,2399 | 0,9323 | 0,0590 | 0,9641 | 0,0084 |

**Fig. 7.22**  Internally calculated key figures for scenario 2 (DC2)

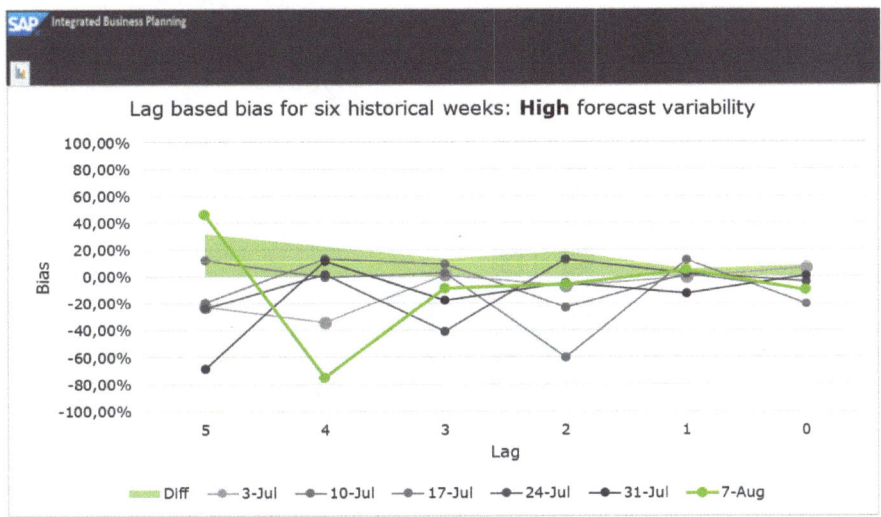

**Fig. 7.23**  Lag-based bias for DC3—high variability scenario

We'll only focus on a couple of salient aspects of the results that we see. Firstly, all the key figures are calculated at multiple lags and the number of lags equals the forecast horizon (six weeks in this case). We also see that the bias adjustment factor (column BAF) for scenario 1 is smaller than for scenario 2, which we intuitively surmised based on the simulated input biases used. We can also see that the key figures that denote importance given to adjustments based on order pattern recognition (mainly future order quantity adjustment factor) have higher values for scenario 2 than for scenario 1. That is to say that when consensus revisions become unreliable and as their inaccuracy increases, adjustments based on order patterns start to become more relevant—also something that makes intuitive sense. This statement can be further supported by scenario 3 where the input bias variability is even higher than scenario 2 (see Fig. 7.23).

From the results of the demand sensing run (visualized in Fig. 7.24), we are able to see that the magnitude of changes is by far the highest.

Turning to the internally calculated key figures, we see that the future order quantity-based adjustment factors receive greater focus confirming our earlier statement (see Fig. 7.25).

In Fig. 7.26, all three scenarios are visualized side by side for comparison. We see differences in delta between consensus demand and sensed demand per distribution center.

The final step is the distribution of weekly sensed demand down to days. In Fig. 7.27, we see the simulated split of the key figure denoting deliveries that is then used by the algorithm as input.

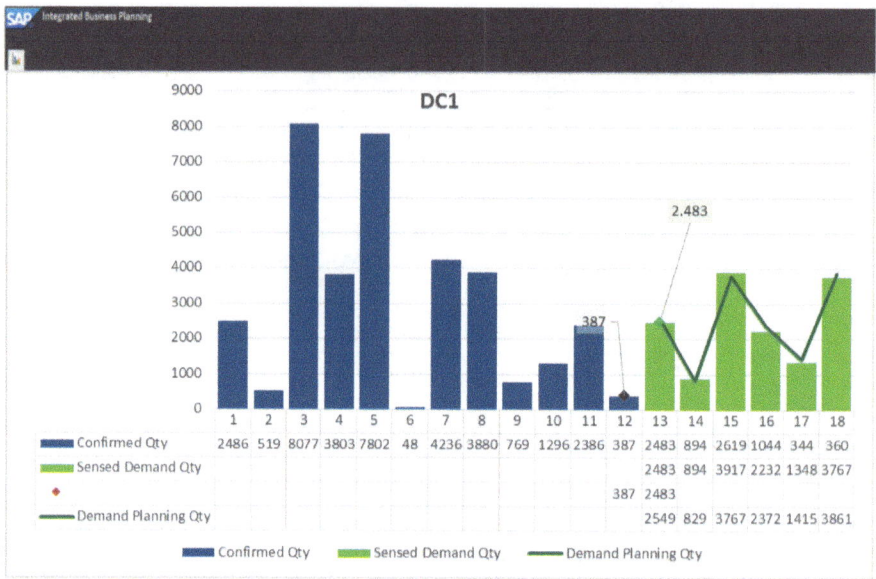

**Fig. 7.24**  Result of demand sensing run—high variability scenario

| Location | Lag | Time | BAF | BHC0 | BHC1 | BHC2 | BHC3 | BHC4 | BHC5 | BAFCC | BAFCEC | FOQAF | FOQFCEC |
|---|---|---|---|---|---|---|---|---|---|---|---|---|---|
| DC3 | 0 | W36 2017 | 0,0051 | -0,0764 | 0,2915 | -5,4997 | 0,6923 | 0,3068 | -0,5111 | 0,0000 | 0,1871 | 0,8860 | 0,4543 |
| DC3 | 1 | W36 2017 | -0,1551 | -0,0184 | -0,1056 | -0,0287 | 0,9971 | -0,1307 | 0,0350 | 1,0000 | 0,1795 | 1,0000 | 0,0000 |
| DC3 | 2 | W36 2017 | -0,1238 | -0,2387 | 0,3558 | -5,5607 | 1,1294 | -2,3271 | 2,4299 | 0,9760 | 0,1419 | 0,9853 | 0,0063 |
| DC3 | 3 | W36 2017 | -0,5207 | 0,5581 | -0,8354 | 1,1971 | -1,7448 | 1,9535 | -0,4761 | 1,0000 | 0,2980 | 1,0000 | 0,0000 |
| DC3 | 4 | W36 2017 | -1,0686 | 0,1686 | -0,4596 | 0,5685 | 0,6595 | -0,2589 | -0,3968 | 0,8372 | 0,1566 | 1,1504 | 0,0772 |
| DC3 | 5 | W36 2017 | -2,6961 | 0,1088 | 0,0309 | 0,2407 | -1,0643 | 2,4600 | -5,2283 | 0,8659 | 0,1150 | 0,8943 | 0,0457 |

**Fig. 7.25**  Internally calculated key figures for scenario 3 (DC3)

The result can be seen in Fig. 7.28. There are seven internal shipment profile key figures (each representing a day of the week). As can be seen, the % values of these key figures closely mirror the input split. These key figures are then used to disaggregate the weekly sensed demand down to days.

**Fig. 7.26**  Graphical comparison of all three scenarios side by side

**Delivery Split**

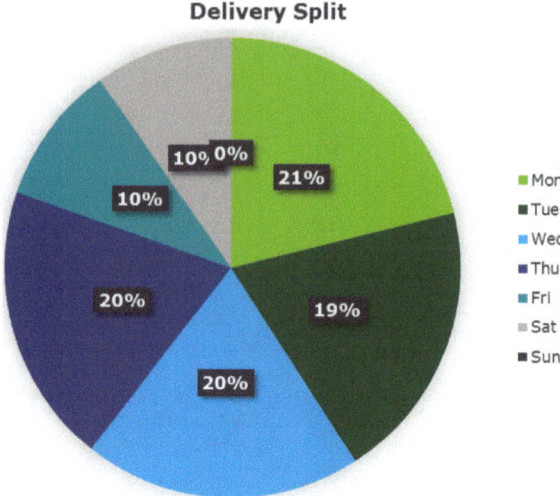

Fig. 7.27  Simulated input delivery split by working day

| Product ID | Lag | Time | SHP0 | SHP1 | SHP2 | SHP3 | SHP4 | SHP5 | SHP6 |
|---|---|---|---|---|---|---|---|---|---|
| IBP_L001 | IBP_P001 | 0 | W36 2017 | 1,0000 | 0,0000 | 0,0000 | 0,0000 | 0,0000 | 0,0000 0,0000 |
| IBP_L001 | IBP_P001 | 1 | W36 2017 | 1,0000 | 0,0000 | 0,0000 | 0,0000 | 0,0000 | 0,0000 0,0000 |
| IBP_L001 | IBP_P001 | 2 | W36 2017 | 1,0000 | 0,0000 | 0,0000 | 0,0000 | 0,0000 | 0,0000 0,0000 |
| IBP_L001 | IBP_P001 | 3 | W36 2017 | 1,0000 | 0,0000 | 0,0000 | 0,0000 | 0,0000 | 0,0000 0,0000 |
| IBP_L001 | IBP_P001 | 4 | W36 2017 | 1,0000 | 0,0000 | 0,0000 | 0,0000 | 0,0000 | 0,0000 0,0000 |
| IBP_L001 | IBP_P001 | 5 | W36 2017 | 1,0000 | 0,0000 | 0,0000 | 0,0000 | 0,0000 | 0,0000 0,0000 |
| IBP_L002 | IBP_P001 | 0 | W36 2017 | 1,0000 | 0,0000 | 0,0000 | 0,0000 | 0,0000 | 0,0000 0,0000 |
| IBP_L002 | IBP_P001 | 1 | W36 2017 | 1,0000 | 0,0000 | 0,0000 | 0,0000 | 0,0000 | 0,0000 0,0000 |
| IBP_L002 | IBP_P001 | 2 | W36 2017 | 1,0000 | 0,0000 | 0,0000 | 0,0000 | 0,0000 | 0,0000 0,0000 |
| IBP_L002 | IBP_P001 | 3 | W36 2017 | 1,0000 | 0,0000 | 0,0000 | 0,0000 | 0,0000 | 0,0000 0,0000 |
| IBP_L002 | IBP_P001 | 4 | W36 2017 | 1,0000 | 0,0000 | 0,0000 | 0,0000 | 0,0000 | 0,0000 0,0000 |
| IBP_L002 | IBP_P001 | 5 | W36 2017 | 1,0000 | 0,0000 | 0,0000 | 0,0000 | 0,0000 | 0,0000 0,0000 |
| IBP_L003 | IBP_P001 | 0 | W36 2017 | 0,1999 | 0,1999 | 0,1999 | 0,1999 | 0,1002 | 0,1002 0,0000 |
| IBP_L003 | IBP_P001 | 1 | W36 2017 | 0,1999 | 0,1999 | 0,1999 | 0,1999 | 0,1002 | 0,1002 0,0000 |
| IBP_L003 | IBP_P001 | 2 | W36 2017 | 0,1999 | 0,1999 | 0,1999 | 0,1999 | 0,1002 | 0,1002 0,0000 |
| IBP_L003 | IBP_P001 | 3 | W36 2017 | 0,1999 | 0,1999 | 0,1999 | 0,1999 | 0,1002 | 0,1002 0,0000 |
| IBP_L003 | IBP_P001 | 4 | W36 2017 | 0,1999 | 0,1999 | 0,1999 | 0,1999 | 0,1002 | 0,1002 0,0000 |
| IBP_L003 | IBP_P001 | 5 | W36 2017 | 0,1999 | 0,1999 | 0,1999 | 0,1999 | 0,1002 | 0,1002 0,0000 |

Fig. 7.28  Calculated results—shipment profile (0–6 for each day of the week)

## 7.2.10   Concluding Remarks

Demand sensing in no way diminishes the importance of medium-term forecasting.
A good consensus forecast is a prerequisite for an effective demand sensing process.
For instance, demand patterns such as seasonality and trend are not detected by

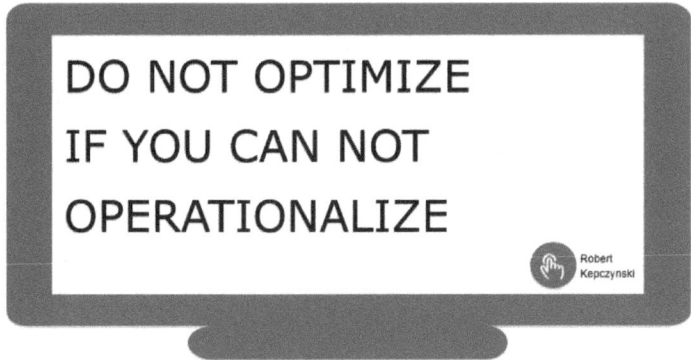

**Fig. 7.29** Do not optimize if you cannot operationalize

sensing. It assumes that these are incorporated in the consensus forecast and relies on insights gained by processing short-term demand signals and analysis of historical forecast performance to adjust consensus forecast (and derive sensed demand).

The true power of demand sensing cannot be realized unless insights gained cannot be operationalized (Fig 7.29). Therefore, agile execution processes are important to turn insights into a profitable response. In some cases, even if lead times are too long to adapt to demand shifts predicted by demand sensing, early detection of potential issues can itself provide benefits. For example, being able to predict potential shortage might provide an opportunity to explore alternative scenarios, one of which could be switching to a supplier closer to home with a shorter lead time.

## References

Debra Smith, C. S. (2016). *Demand Driven Performance Using Smart Metrics*. New York: McGraw-Hill.

McAfee, A., & Didier Bonnet, G. W. (2014). 'Leading Digital', *Sogeti Executive Summit Munich*.

Simchi, L. (1999). *Designing and managing the supply chain: Concepts, strategies, and case studies*. McGraw-Hill: McGraw-Hill.

Subramaniam, M., & Bala Iyer, G. C. K. (2016). Mass Customization and the Do-It-Yourself Supply Chain, *MIT Sloan Management Review*.

Tohamy, N., Scott, F., & Steutermann, S. (2012). *How to build an effective Demand Planning organization*. USA: Gartner.

# How to Measure and Improve Forecasting

8

## 8.1 Measure Value Add

There are several effectiveness measures, and they can help you to understand goodness of fit of the forecast model for the given data inputs. A short overview of typical metrics and some guidelines for choosing among them are presented here. Once you understand your process effectiveness measures you will be able to understand value add of specific process step, adjustments, stat. forecast technique. Here are some of the typical effectiveness measures:

**Mean Error.** It is calculated as Actual $t$—Forecast $t$ for a given time period $t$. It gives the average distance between forecast and actual values. As positive and negative errors offset each other, this measure is used to determine if there is a systematic bias in the model. An example is provided in below. If the spate of progressively lower values in this example is simply a temporary effect, an algorithm such as pick the best method could conceivably misinterpret this as a declining trend and assign a double exponential smoothing algorithm with trend dampening turned on leading to forecast as indicated by the dark blue line.

However, as shown in Fig. 8.1, a single exponential smoothing model may well be the more appropriate choice (light blue line) that gives due consideration to the relatively stable time series overall. If the trend model was in fact chosen, mean error will show a positive bias and it will continue to increase.

**Mean Absolute Deviation** (MAD). This measure expresses the scale of error. As the term absolute indicated, positive and negative values are treated the same. This measure is quite easy to understand as it is in the same units as the original data. If the quantities are quite small, MAD is a suitable choice.

**Mean Squared Error** (MSE). This metric as well neutralizes the sign, but by squaring the error, which leads to large errors being overrepresented. This is desirable if the model needs to be sensitive to large errors—for example, if there are buffers in place to deal with small deviations, but large errors would result in disruptions that are not easily handled, MSE is a good measure to keep an eye on.

© Springer Nature Switzerland AG 2019

387

G. Sankaran et al., *Improving Forecasts with Integrated Business Planning*,
Management for Professionals, https://doi.org/10.1007/978-3-030-05381-9_8

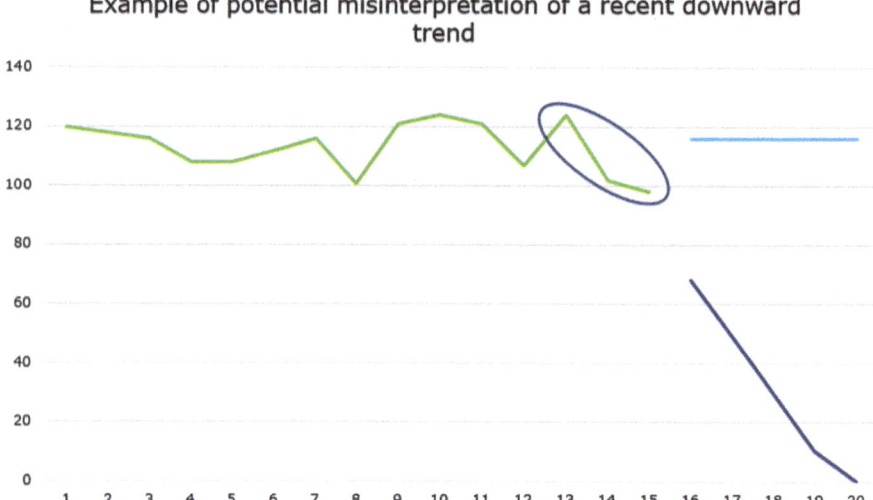

**Fig. 8.1**   Potential misinterpretation of a recent downward trend

It is also a measure that is typically used by model optimization algorithms to find appropriate parameters (by trying to minimize it over an initialization data set).

**Mean Absolute Percentage Error** (MAPE). With the measures discussed so far, comparisons are difficult as they does not take into consideration the scale of demand. MAPE addresses that by expressing the (absolute) error in percentage terms. It is particularly useful for seasonal products where the scale of demand should be a factor in assessing the severity of the error.

**Mean Absolute Scaled Error** (MASE). Please see the technical note on MLR for a description of how it is calculated. MASE comes in very handy as it has in its denominator the accuracy measure for naïve forecast (NF1), which is the same as saying forecast equals last-demand observation. This means that, with MASE, the accuracy of the model in use is expressed in terms of the improvement it offers over NF1. Concretely:

If MASE = 1: the model is only as good as NF1. You could just as well spare additional costs potentially incurred by using anything more advanced.
If MASE > 1: model in use is worse. This definitely calls for deeper investigation. It can also be that the planning cluster (owing to its importance) demands an advanced model, but it has not been setup properly and is grossly underperforming.
If MASE < 1: model is better than NF1. How close it is to 0 than to 1 is a measure of how good the model in use is.

Bottom line—MASE can be used to establish a barrier for entry for a model that is more advanced than NF1 (visualized in Fig. 8.2).

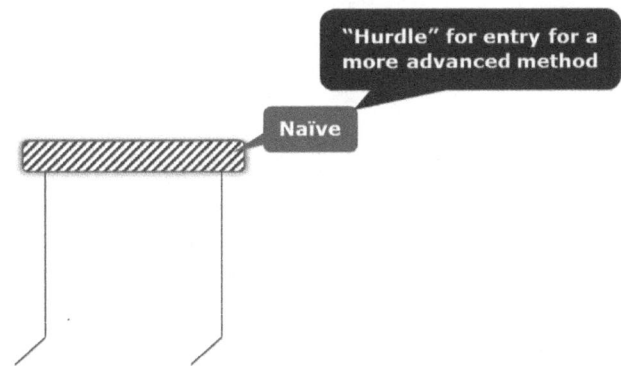

**Fig. 8.2** Barrier to entry for a model

Rich forecasting process not always delivers the expected results. We have seen too many times that huge efforts are being invested in collecting inputs from many functions but the results were not meeting management expectations. It was often perceived that the inputs from sales and marketing have to come from all the people in this stakeholder group and by doing so, forecast will become better. Let us talk about measuring value add in forecasting process.

**Forecast value-add analysis** (FVA) helps to assess performance of all inputs and expose value-adding steps and non-value-adding steps, it does expose waste. Waste could be understood as time, e.g., lack of adherence to process and need for extra reconciliations resulting in too long processing time. Waste can be understood as making accuracy worse between process steps. Waste can be as mismatch between product importance and variability versus forecasting methods, granularity of forecasting. You may consider to run a Six Sigma improvement project focused on forecasting as extensive way of running FVA. Common ground for FVA and Six Sigma would be focus on removing waste and use of data.

FVA can be understood as an instrument to:

– Assess also forecast analysts performances and deciding for rewards (positive FVA) or a recall (negative FVA)
– Analyze which of the forecasting/demand-planning process steps adds value or is "beating" the naïve models (Gilliland, 2015).

The example illustrated in Fig. 8.3 would perfectly fit as a use case for FVA in qualitative forecasting based on sales team inputs. The questions raised above have to be answered. If we assume initial process design to follow "bottom-up" forecasting input may be adjusted based on the FVA findings. Bottom-up input has a lot of "qualitative value" but maybe not all the steps mirroring organizational structure of sales team would make sense to be captured in the forecasting process. It is important to understand which steps are really needed and which ones are nice to

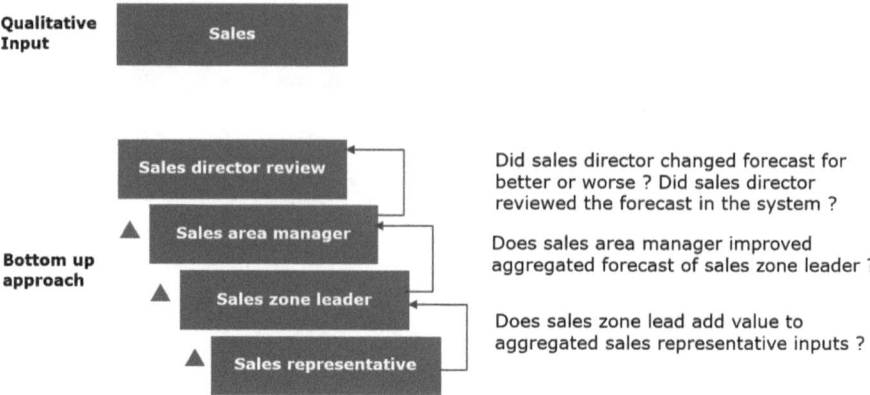

**Fig. 8.3** FVA for qualitative inputs

have. It was proven in many cases that too many stakeholders adjusting forecast can introduce as well many errors.

A very obvious step to be assessed is the sales director review; do you need to have represented in the process as data or just aggregation of inputs from sales areas? Is your sales director reviewing and updating data in the system or he/she expects report analysis to be provided to them, before the demand review meeting?

If we ask ourselves a question: "How to assess if a process step is value or non-value adding", the answers are in statistics. At first, you need to have data. Each of the process steps has to be stored in the system separately, then each of it has to be measured, for example, with mean absolute scaled error (MASE) and then each of them has to be compared to each other.

MASE was proposed by Hyndman and Koehler as an alternative to using percentage errors, especially in the case of comparing forecast error (Hyndman & Koehler, 2005). FVA in its nature does compare forecast errors, therefore, we recommend this measure for this purpose. It was proposed to use a naïve forecast as reference. If MASE is above, it means the forecast is worse than naïve forecasts (e.g., Fig. 8.4).

Many companies instead of comparing inputs to reference Naïve method (like through use of mean absolute scaled error), compare qualitative inputs versus statistical forecast. We see this way of comparison "not clean" since statistical forecast is as the way a process which has its own maturity and can bring its own error.

Once the inputs are being measured and compared its clearer where investigation should go further. On above example, we would recommend to:

– Investigate error trends in sales zone leader versus sales representative inputs, evaluate inputs attributed to a specific person
– Conduct interviews with sales zone leaders who provide forecast reviews and forecast inputs

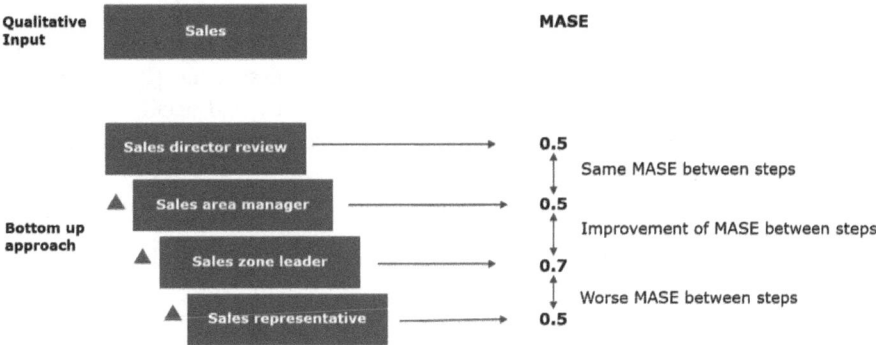

**Fig. 8.4** MASE as value-add measurement

- Investigate the logic of how sales area managers have improved sales leaders' input
- Investigate if sales director step is really captured in the system as change in data. As comment please prepare for such discussions with data, e.g., check logs before you conduct interview with sales director.

Once having quantitative and qualitative views on the process steps, we would recommend to agree which process steps can be removed.

There are researches which say:
FVA is a leading practice as shown on examples from various industries:

- Pharmaceuticals: FVA demonstrated that depending on products forecasting performances were hugely different
- Retail: FVA demonstrated that 75% of the time the forecast baseline coming out from the software was enough accurate and did not require changes
- Technology manufacturing: FVA demonstrated that half of the time naïve forecasting performed better or as well as override adjustments
- Home furnishings: FVA demonstrated that the best way to improve performance was to challenge the analysts and let emerge their competitive nature
- Automotive: FVA demonstrated that management adjustments were too small and did not bring enough benefits compared with the costs of maintaining that service
- Food and Beverage: FVA demonstrated that forecasting at a higher granularity did not bring added value and the company let the analysts focusing on another most value-adding tasks (Gilliland, 2015).

Forecasting gurus say:

Focus on value add is there in forecasting. Forecast value-added analysis has to be conducted to check if manual overrides bring value to the process and to the whole organizational profits. You should aim to assess the performance and also the length of a normal forecasting process identifying the phases adding values, and the ones that are purely waste. Wastes can be produced because of lack of forecasting skills, tools, experience, or even motivation. Few companies assess the performance of each step of the forecasting process; generally, efficiency and accuracy are measured only at the aggregated level, but if measured it should be visualized in *y* scorecard manner (Chase, 2009).

To conclude: "There is a huge value in doing Forecast Value-add Analysis".

## 8.2   Measure Inventory, Service Level Impact for Intermittent Demand

The performance of any forecasting method needs to be evaluated by some metric, to measure how closely the forecasted value matches the true value. Intermittent demand series turn out to be unusually tricky to evaluate; typical forecasting accuracy metrics are often either inappropriate or even impossible to apply.

These tools for measuring accuracy are mathematical techniques based on the evaluation of precision, i.e., the bias between the actual demand and the expected value. But if precision can be a target in the research field, it is difficult to adapt it to manufacturing companies whose targets are rather:

- customer satisfaction,
- profit maximization,
- cost minimization,
- etc.

and, therefore, in addition to precision, the evaluation tool has to deal with costs related to stock keeping, obsolescence, stock-out and all the aspects related to them.

Concluding, we believe that, instead of measuring only mathematical accuracy, it is more important to evaluate the ability of the forecasting tool to maximize customer satisfaction and at the same time minimize the use of financial, human, instrumental resources, etc. To achieve that we suggest using the inventory-related measures, forecast error measures relating to inventory performance include:

I.   Service level $\alpha$—measures the probability that demand will be below stock level if we replenish stock based on our forecasts (can be thought of as the probability an arbitrary customer is served straightaway).

II.   Service level $\beta$—measures the quantity of demand met immediately over the total demand (or the probability an arbitrary unit of demand is satisfied straightaway).

III.   Periods In Stock (PIS)—the formula for this is defined as

$$\text{PIS}_n = -\sum_{i=1}^{n}\sum_{j=1}^{i}\left(A_j - F_j\right)$$

The idea is that we assume the existence of a "fictitious stock" to which the number in our forecast at each time period is delivered, and then the number of units demanded in that time period is removed.

## 8.3   Improve Forecasting with Six Sigma

Integrated Business Planning process framework and its connected processes generate huge amount of data which can be used for process improvement. SAP IBP is based on a unified planning area which runs on HANA; this architecture enables to capture data from various process steps (e.g., product, demand, supply review, integrated reconciliation, and management business review) and planning types (e.g., operational planning, tactical S&OP, long-term planning). The data being captured in HANA through SAP IBP processes can be then used in improvement initiatives (Fig. 8.5). In this chapter, we share with you how you could leverage data from SAP IBP within the Six Sigma process improvement initiative.

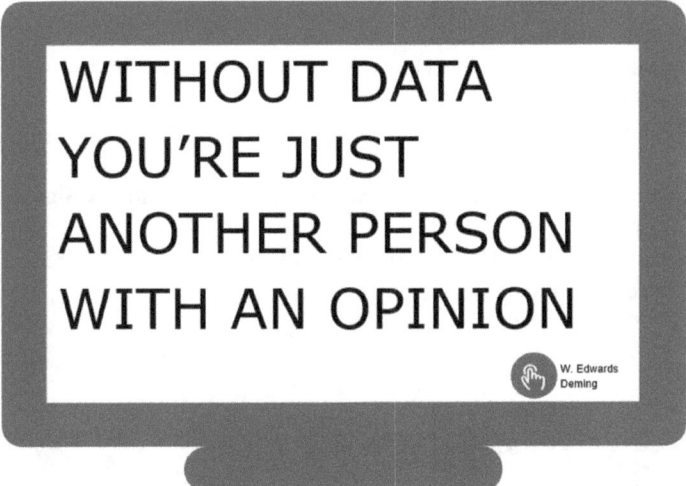

**Fig. 8.5** Without data you have only opinion

The seven points below represent seven good starting reasons to consider when defining your forecasting improvement initiative:

- Improve the consensus demand-planning process
- Build accountability for the forecast
- Understand the sources of error in the forecast
- Establish a baseline and promoted volume forecast
- Measure your demand planners for their value contribution
- Shift from sell-in to sell-through
- Build a make-to-order capability to manage inventory (Steutermann, 2015).

Process design followed by technical on SAP IBP should aim to cope with process improvement requirements. Let me explain it on one example: if you want to design qualitative forecasting inputs for the sales department which starts from sales representative, sales leader to sales manager and sales director, you may consider to store their inputs on separate key figures in SAP IBP. You could measure their performance separately to identify value add and avoid problems of data ownership in the specific case in which you allow inputs overwriting. When forecasting inputs will be stored on separate key figures, you would be able to recognize patterns in the error even linked to specific individual.

Six Sigma is a data-driven process improvement methodology. Once you will execute one project following Six Sigma methodology, it will make a mark in your behavior. It did it on me and my colleagues. Below some relevant marks:

- Start from the problem definition
- Perform data analysis
- Perform business expert interviews and solution brainstormings
- Pilot solution first
- Assess pilot before scale-up.

Sounds familiar? Then you were already using some of the Six Sigma principles outlined in Fig. 8.6.

In next subchapters, we have extracted key information from real Six Sigma project focused on forecasting.

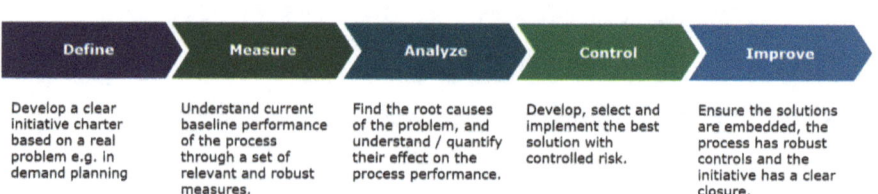

**Fig. 8.6** Six Sigma process steps

## 8.3.1   Define—What the Problem Is

Define phase should help you to:

- Define the problem
- Organize a project or small initiative
- Structure your thoughts about what you and other stakeholders think about it
- Define objective and timelines
- Define possible costs and benefits
- Define team who will work with you
- Identify people you will affect with the improvement.

Let us go through some typical deliverables of "Define" phase in the context of demand planning and demand management in IBP.

**Problem statement**: Formulate in one or two sentences what the problem and not the solution is! An example could be as "Forecasting process takes too much efforts compared to quality of the outcome. Process efficiency and error does not meet company expectations." Problem statement should be confirmed with a broader stakeholder group.

**Project objectives**: Formulate what you want to achieve "Reduce time spends on forecasting at least by 20% and decrease forecast error by at least 5%". Make your objective very tangible.

**Planned deliverables**: Formulate what you will consider to do

- Improve efficiency of forecast input and demand review processes
- Adjust process accountabilities if needed
- Validate if differentiated ways of working will bring benefits
- Improve process effectiveness measured with forecast error measures
- Document change in the process and prepare training documents
- Define measures to make the improvements sustainable.

This is not a final list of activities, and you will learn much more when you start analyzing your data and error root causes. This list is rather an instrument to capture your initial view on the improvement scope.

**Scope**: Define what is in scope and what is not in scope

Specify process, product, geographical scope, e.g., demand planning for business line A was defined by the S&OP stakeholders as the most representative for the problem statement in European countries. The change of software or upgrade of functionality was considered in the scope. Specify what is not in scope, e.g., adjustments and changes in legacy systems.

**Metrics**: Define how you will measure outcome of the project

Here you need to identify metrics and impact of the improvement. You need to specify, e.g., process effectiveness measures (MASE, Weighted MAPE), process efficiency measures (number of forecasting combinations available in sales input) and process adherence measures (working day 3 as deadline to achieve consensus forecast).

**Key milestones**: Agree realistic timelines. Divide your initiatives into phases and set the timelines for it.

**Team:** Define a cross-functional team. Organize a team who will work with you. Do not list all of stakeholders here, just those who work on the project to ensure you give credit for it to relevant ones.

**Voice of Customer (VoC)**: Collect from your "internal customers" (if possible from external as well) their expectation toward the improvement.

Define a short questionnaire or run a workshop targeted on capturing VoC from your stakeholders converted to needs. An example of VoC converted to need is in Fig. 8.7.

As you see from the table, key element of VoC is conversion to the need. Need is the element you need to act upon.

**Best practice reference for the forecast error reduction**: Consider external information to benchmark objectives for your improvement project.

If you want your project "to fly," you should consider referencing industry or at least overall external performance in forecasting. When referencing external sources versus your internal performance try to understand the context of the parameters

| Who | Voice of the internal customer | Need |
|---|---|---|
| Sales lead | I spend too much time on forecasting | Reduce time being spend on forecasting |
| Sales director | In the current forecasting process, sales team treats all products the same way, same focus. | Introduce way of working which will increase process efficiency without losing on forecast error. |
| Sales director | We should be more accurate in forecasting. | Reduce forecast error by 5% |
| Demand manager | Statistical forecasting seems to be generating low value | Assess and improve data inputs, outlier detection and correction, algorithms being used. |

**Fig. 8.7** Voice of customer

being used in measurement like level, time lag, and aggregation window but as well maturity level for process, system and capabilities.

Look on Fig. 8.8 where performance figures are positioned against process context. It does bring more meaning, do not you think?

**Preliminary business case**: One of the key deliverables in the define phase is the preparation of a preliminary business case and assumptions associated with it. We say preliminary since you should revise it once you learn more insights in Analyze or Control phase.

Inventory is an ultimate result of demand- and supply-planning processes; therefore, we would recommend to build your business case on impact which will be created on inventory. You may consider to capture upside sales and logistic cost reduction as well.

Over- and underforecasting affect business in different ways (see Fig. 8.9). In our project example, we will focus on how to address overforecasting and its effects on inventory levels.

Forecasting demand is not the only process which can influence inventory. We have seen and experienced that only part of the excess inventory problems come from forecasting and demand-planning errors. You should consider certain degree of correlation between forecast error and inventory optimization when defining your business case.

In Fig. 8.10, we visualize that inventory level depends on the correlation of the forecasting error, which is measured with appropriate time lag, appropriate level and aggregation window to match the process characteristics.

In preparation of preliminary business case, it would make sense to take into account:

- inventory exposed (correlated) to forecasting error impact
- agreed forecast error improvement linked to correlated inventory.

How to address the calculation of the inventory exposed/correlated to the forecasting error improvement? You may consider the following steps:

- Measure as-is inventory (see Fig. 8.11 column avg. monthly inventory)
- Measure as-is forecast error
- Correlate the forecast error to the inventory and calculate the correlation factor, e.g., per country (see Fig. 8.11 column forecast error correlation to inventory). Note: forecast error should be correlated to inventory, e.g., by using adequate time lag and aggregation
- Calculate the maximum potential forecast error improvement and its impact on inventory based on the correlation between forecasting error and inventory (see Fig. 8.11 column monthly avg. correlated inventory).

**Fig. 8.8** Example of contextualized forecast performance benchmark

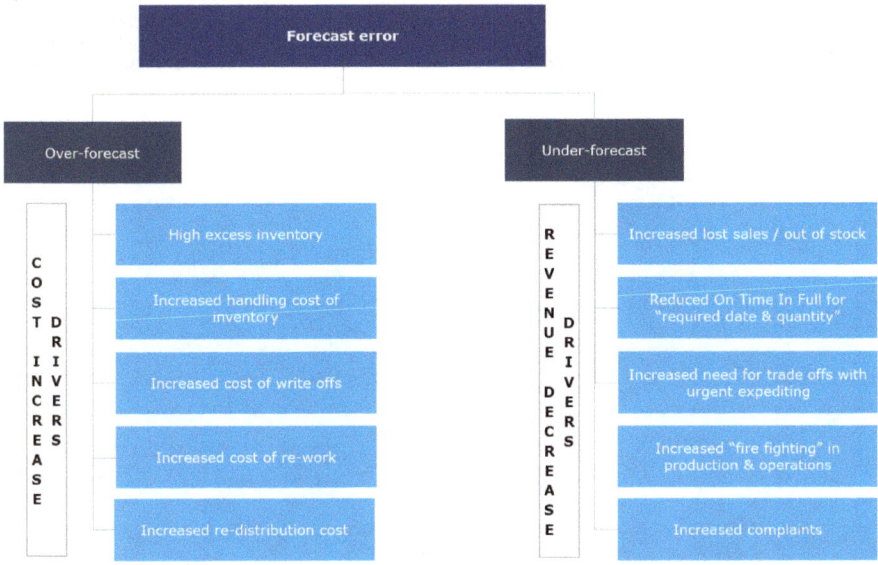

**Fig. 8.9**  Over- and underforecasting based on (Journal of Business Forecasting)

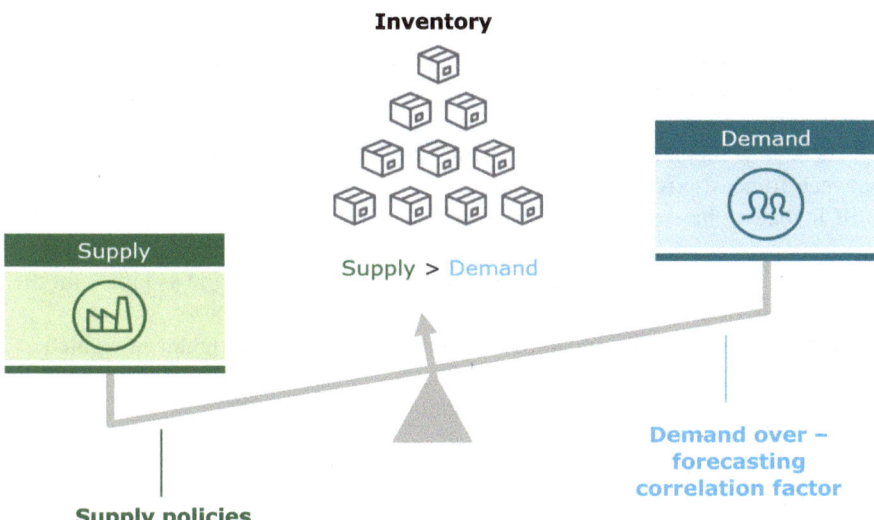

**Fig. 8.10**  Forecast error correlation between demand- and supply-planning processes

Once you have calculated the inventory which can be correlated to forecast error improvement (Fig. 8.11, column monthly avg. correlated inventory), you would need to establish how much of this total maximum improvement pool can be really realized via forecast error improvement. In other words, how much of 100%

| Country | Avg. monthly inventory [vol] | Avg. monthly inventory [$] | Forecast error correlation to inventory (over and under forecast) | Monthly avg. correlated inventory [VOL], only over forecasting | Monthly avg. correlated inventory [VAL], only over forecasting |
|---|---|---|---|---|---|
| Country 1 | 3'561'445.0 | 30'635'228.0 | 15.1 | 122'813.0 | 905'403.0 |
| Country 4 | 27'397'125.0 | 213'353'737.0 | 56.5 | 9'954'269.0 | 76'324'485.0 |
| Country 5 | 6'012'268.0 | 47'079'025.0 | 35.8 | 588'433.0 | 4'742'443.0 |
| Country 6 | 2'628'388.0 | 27'797'178.0 | 28.5 | 241'002.0 | 2'944'854.0 |
| Country 7 | 7'771'641.0 | 66'140'264.0 | 53.4 | 1'383'777.0 | 12'530'376.0 |
| Country 8 | 6'701'530.0 | 65'545'569.0 | 28.3 | 652'790.0 | 7'083'479.0 |
| Country 10 | 5'442'904.0 | 32'948'464.0 | 85.2 | 2'180'726.0 | 8'947'110.0 |
| Country 11 | 5'130'197.0 | 45'010'456.0 | 61.9 | 1'956'172.0 | 15'180'893.0 |
| Country 12 | 1'952'065.0 | 13'928'395.0 | 46.8 | 494'545.0 | 3'321'092.0 |
| Country 13 | 3'436'872.0 | 21'935'606.0 | 27.7 | 529'140.0 | 3'956'457.0 |
| Country 14 | 6'725'479.0 | 48'844'932.0 | 23.5 | 654'494.0 | 4'235'382.0 |
| Country 15 | 9'598'696.0 | 78'153'376.0 | 90.0 | 5'581'779.0 | 38'905'299.0 |
| .... | .... | .... | .... | .... | .... |
| Total | 491'821'676.0 | 3'243'421'428.0 | 46.1 | 33'645'590.0 | 240'499'325.0 |

**Fig. 8.11** Forecast error correlation to inventory

reduction in overforecasting bias you can expect and how much inventory optimization you may gain for agreed and expected improvement level. Improvement level you may take from voice of customer and/or additional data analysis you need to perform.

There is a fundamental learning from the calculation of the correlation factor between forecast error and inventory:

If inventory has relatively high correlation to forecast error,

- we could assume supply processes use forecast in large extend as inputs for their planning.
- In this case, demand- and supply-planning processes are tighter integrated.

If inventory has relatively low correlation to forecast error,

- we could assume supply processes do not use forecast in large extend as input to planning.
- In this case, demand- and supply-planning processes are not well integrated, which may be caused by work in silos.

How you may use the above insights? We think you may use them to spot the biggest areas of improvement expressed in forecast error and high correlation to inventory. In the countries/regions following highest correlation between forecast error and inventory, you may expect biggest and fastest impact on the "bottom line", fastest return on investment since inventory level is highly to forecast error. You may use this as an instrument to prioritize your pilot and rollouts.

**High-level process map**: map as-is process steps and stakeholders. Mapping your as-is process can be done as combination of swim lane process map and Supplier, Input, Process, Output, Customer (SIPOC). In establishing the roles in the process, you may use Responsible, Accountable, Consulted, and Informed (RACI) model.

Example of swim lane process map (Fig. 8.12):

Swim lane could be used to layout accountable people, process steps, timelines but details most probably will be better to capture with SIPOC method.

Example of SIPOC (Fig. 8.13). SIPOC stands for Supplier, Input, Process, Output, Customer. SIPOC process mapping method can be enriched with RACI.

SIPOC could be extended with some key process parameters like granularity, measurement formula, and sample document.

**Stakeholder map**: map your stakeholders (Fig. 8.14). Think of how you should approach them to influence their perception to and get required support or engagement. When picking up the right tactics to approach stakeholder put yourself into the perspective "what is in it for him/her". Define where they are, where there should be and what impact can they make. Think of the tactics for how to communicate and engage stakeholders when preparing this analysis.

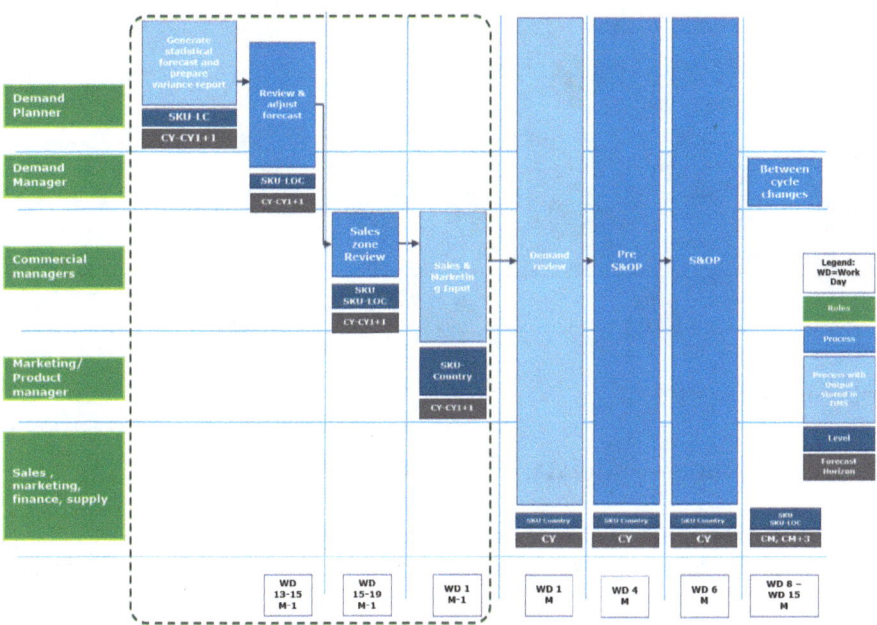

**Fig. 8.12** As-is swim lane process example (to be updated)

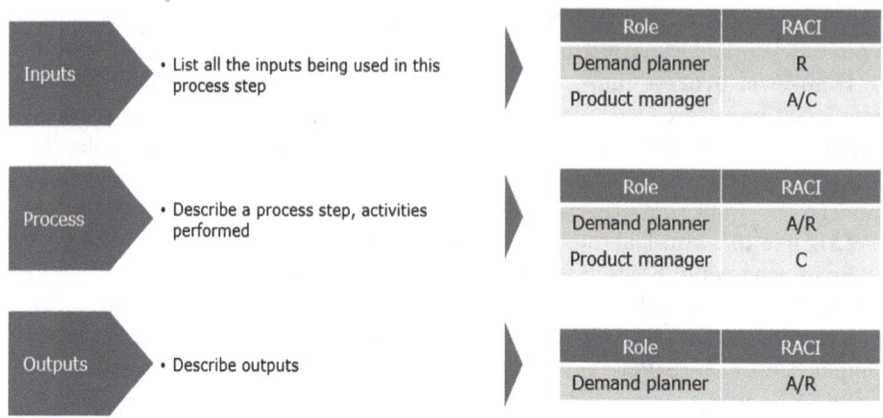

**Fig. 8.13**  SIPOC/RACI model

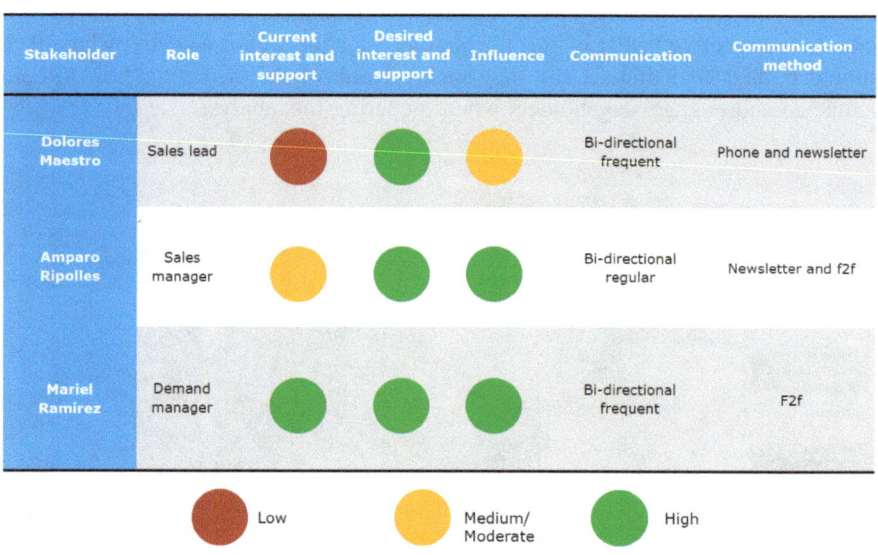

**Fig. 8.14**  Stakeholder map

## 8.3.2  Measure—Understand Your Current Performance

In measure phase, you will focus on collecting data for data analysis. Let us go through typical deliverables of "Measure" phase in the context of demand planning and demand management in IBP.

**Data collection plan**: this is a must do exercise for initiative which aims to collect a lot of data on various levels. SAP IBP HANA unified planning area will be definitely your main source of data but you use data from other sources, especially

| No | What data | Key figures | Time horizon | Level | Who will collect | Remarks | Source system |
|---|---|---|---|---|---|---|---|
| 1 | Shipment | Shipment Qty | Last 5 years | Product-customer-plant | Amparo | | Business warehouse |
| 2 | Sales forecast input | Sales Represent. forecast qty | Last 5 years | Product-customer-plant | Dolores | | IBP |

**Fig. 8.15** Data collection plan

when validating your measurement "system". Data collection plan (Fig. 8.15) should be as detail as possible.

**Data preparation**: in case your process design has not established required system support for measurement (every forecast input being measured separately), you may need to calculate performance by yourself. It is important to use measurement parameters like time lag, aggregation window, and level aligned to process outputs.

**Data quality**: if Weighted MAPE/Bias is calculated directly in your IBP system, you would need to validate data which is used in Weighted MAPE/Bias error calculation. You need to have evidence that "actuals" being used in IBP are the same as "actuals" beings stored in source system. This exercise is called validation of measurement system. This exercise provides an answer to question "Does data represent what you think it does?".

**Process behavior and baseline process capability**: Each of the forecast inputs like sales representative, sales leader, sales manager, sales director, product manager, demand planner, and statistical forecast would have its own forecast error data which you need to analyze. We assume that your process design will enable those inputs stored separately in the key figures and that you will have them backed up for analytical and process improvement purposes.

Process capability would be expressed in parts per million (PPM) or defects per million opportunities (DPMO). What does it actually mean? Process capability helps you to understand how your forecast errors are being distributed per forecast input, by various stakeholders. In data analysis, outliers will play an important role. Process capability provides understanding of how variable your process is, is it predictable and stable but has certain deviations from expectations (limits) or it is highly unstable, once good once very bad. You may get some insights, including comparison of performance between forecast inputs from your stakeholder group. In process capability analysis, you would need to define lower and upper control limits (UCL, LCL) and understand how to interpret $C_p$ and $C_{pk}$ values (see Fig. 8.17).

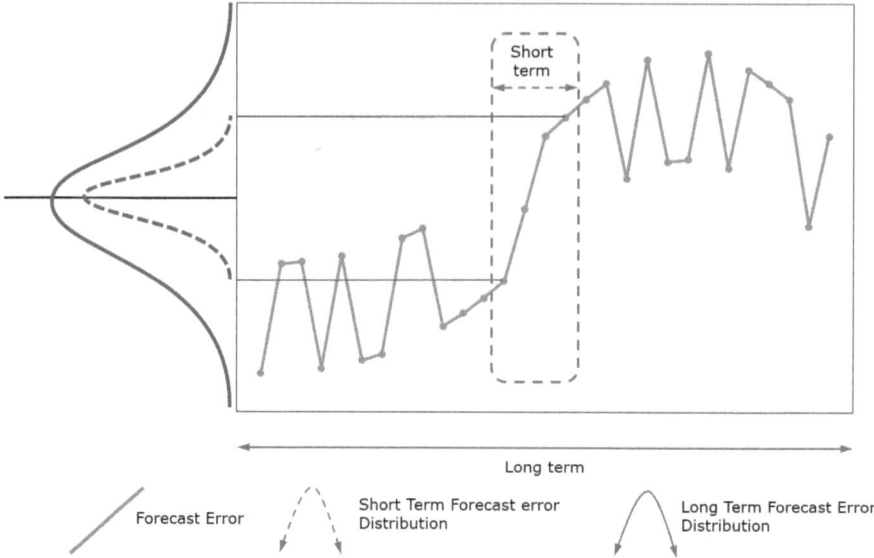

**Fig. 8.16** How to understand histogram

In your Six Sigma project, you will learn what normal and not normal distribution is. I have found below figure as very useful explanation to understand how time series plot on the right can be mapped into histogram on the left (Fig. 8.16).

Figure 8.16 shows on right side (green line) typical time series plot of forecast error and on left side how this is translated to histogram (gray curve). Histogram shows forecast error data distribution. Forecast error data distribution is extremely important.

In figure below, you can see some examples how to interpret histogram and process capability statistics $C_p$ and $C_{pk}$ (Fig. 8.17).

You may not fully understand how to interpret forecast error histogram from process variability perspective. Below you will find explanation of histograms (Fig. 8.18). As you see variability of the process captured in variability of forecast error can give you some insights about process improvement challenge. It is normally easier to center variability around expected values compared to challenge linked to make variability in the process much lower.

There is more of basic statistics which you can learn from Six Sigma. Have you ever thought about difference between median and average, and when to use which one.

Graphical presentation of difference between median and average is shown in Fig. 8.19.

Median you may consider to use when you have a lot of outliers and most often when data distribution is not normal or skewed. Mean (average) you may consider to use if you do not have many outliers and most often when data distribution is normal or centric around specific value.

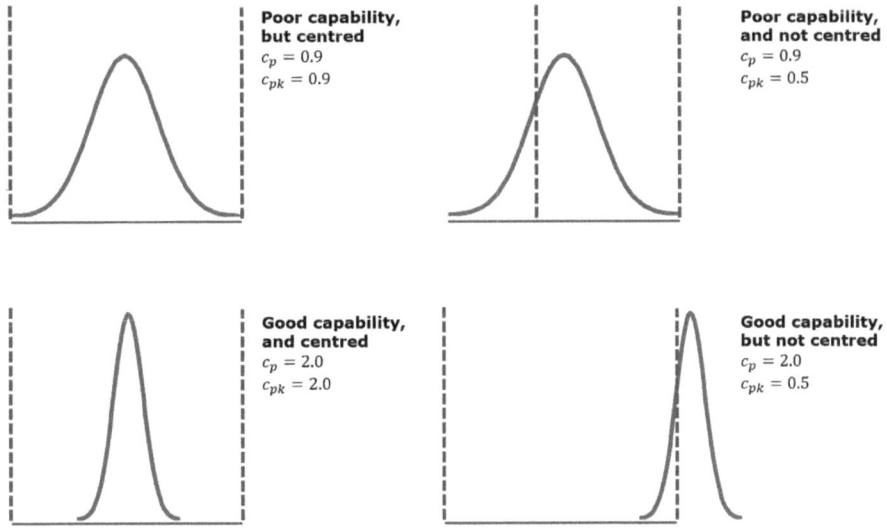

**Fig. 8.17** How to understand capability charts

In process capability assessment, we should understand impact of outliers. Let us have a look on outliers so events which do not fit to the pattern. Some call it "black swans", see Fig. 8.20.

Outliers in your process behavior may be detected with various methods above you see standard deviation method (where +/− 3 sigma is a tolerance limit). The other methods are described in other chapters of this book.

Why would you need to run outlier tests? One of the reasons is the fact that in Analyze phase, you would need to select specific hypothesis testing methods and results of test may be influenced by number of outliers.

## 8.3.3   Analyze—Find Root Causes of the Problem

You are correct to assume to be surprised and the end of this phase. You may find correlations, error patterns related to specific people, product lines, geographies which you would not expect (Fig. 8.21).

In the beginning of Analyze phase, you should focus on getting understanding about:

- What types of trends in error we see?
- Where we sell and what/how we sell?
- How big the errors are and where, do we find any pattern in specific product segment, product line, person providing input?
- Do we have different error patterns in sales peak season than in normal season?
- Does the error look different Year over Year and per months?

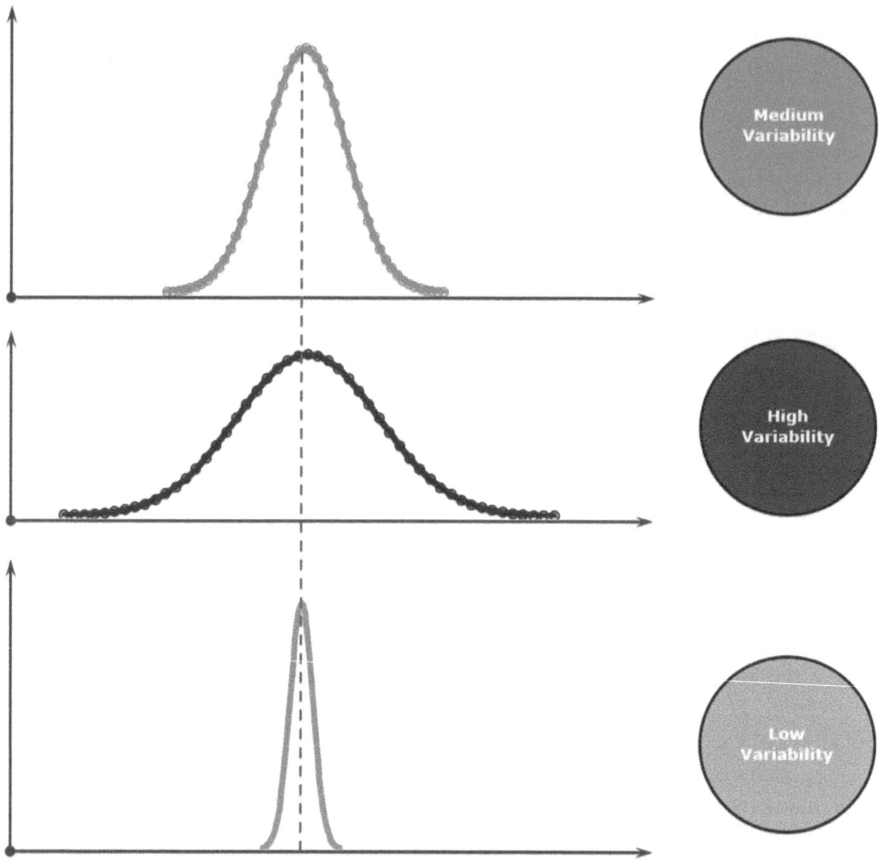

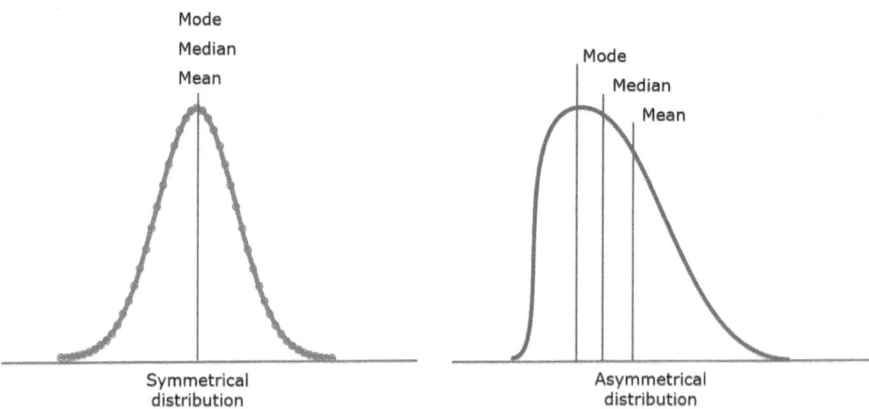

**Fig. 8.18** How to understand forecast error distribution

**Fig. 8.19** Types of distribution and basic statistics

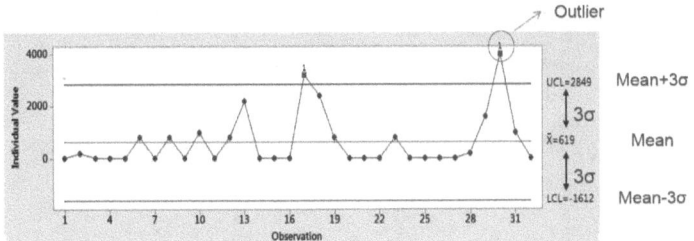

**Fig. 8.20** Run chart sigma errors (Minitab chart)

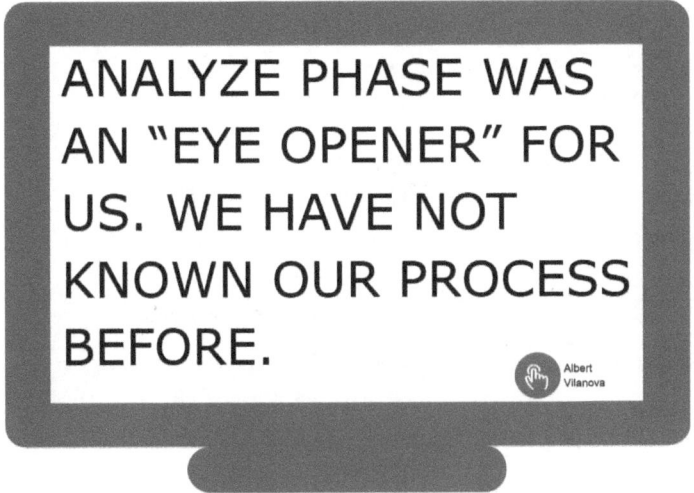

**Fig. 8.21** Analyze phase is an "eye opener"

- Do we have trends in over/underforecasting in product lines, people, and locations?
- Does forecast error differ when we have dominant customer behind the SKU?

In other words, you need to understand where errors are, if there are any trends, seasonality or correlations.

Trend in forecast error (forecast—actuals) may look like on Fig. 8.22. You may understand how big the errors are and when they happen. You can observe seasonality in forecast error pattern.

It may be important to understand spread of your portfolio versus geographies versus average volumetric sales. Example below (Fig. 8.23) is to visualize big differences between Germany and Spain and average vol./SKU ratio. In Spain, we sell in average bigger lots, and it could be correlated with fact that big sales can generate big forecast errors.

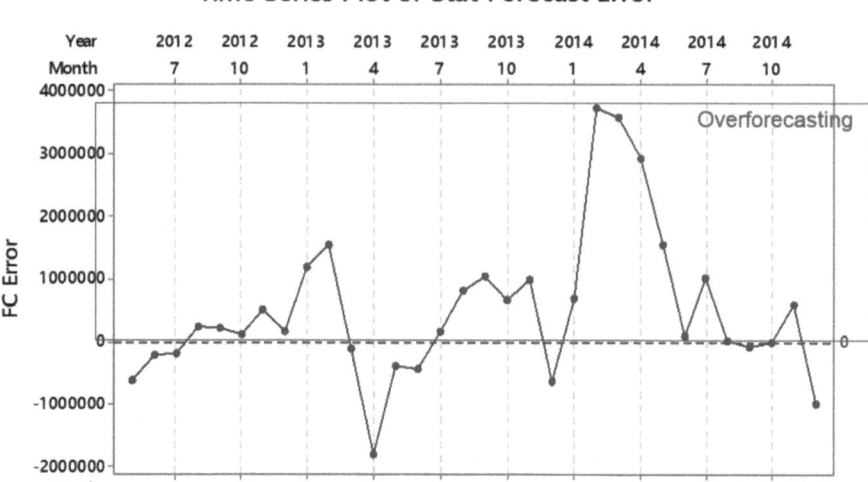

**Fig. 8.22** Run chart over/underforecasting (Minitab chart)

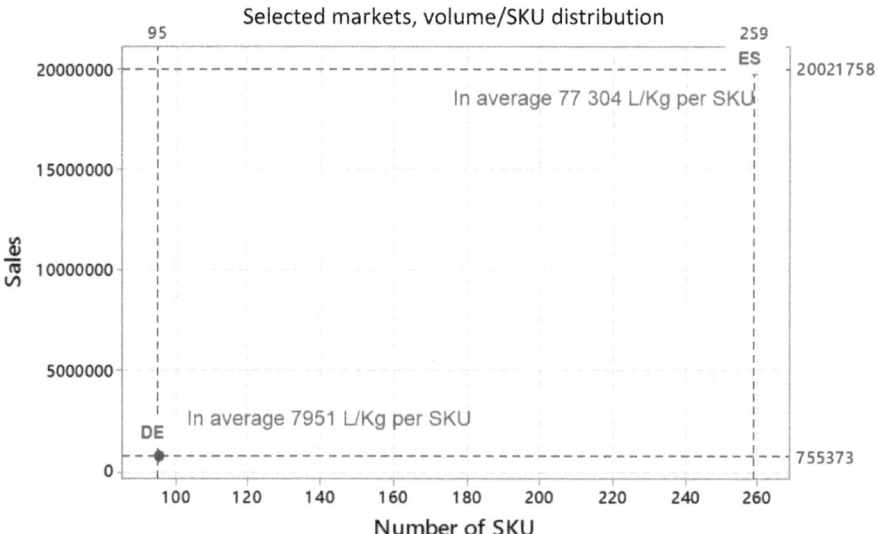

**Fig. 8.23** Product/country sales positioning (Minitab chart)

You may want to understand how your specific country Weighted MAPE distribution looks like against product segmentation (see Fig. 8.24). Product segmentation could have two dimensions—ABCD which could be based on volume, revenue, cost or profit contribution, and XYZ which could be based on coefficient

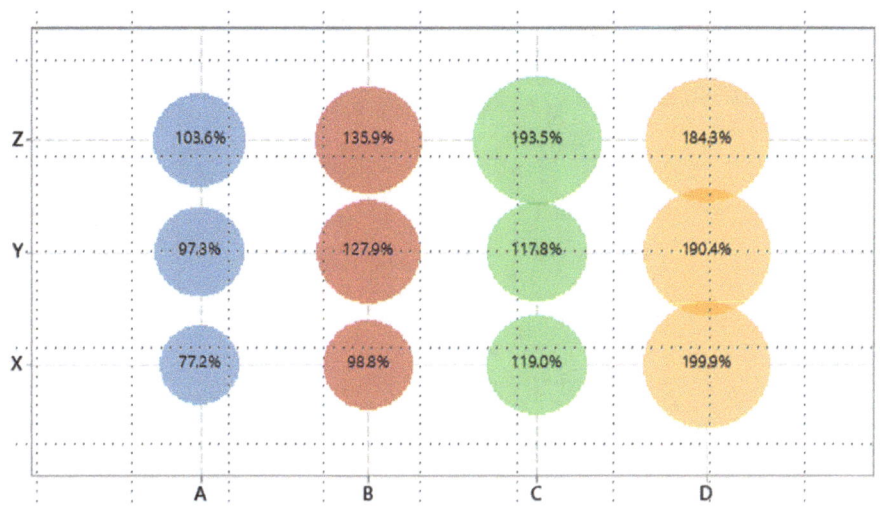

**Fig. 8.24** Portfolio segmentation forecast error (Minitab chart)

of variation (for selected measure, e.g., forecast error). Product segmentation can be calculated (if not existing as integral part of the process yet) in data collection/preparation phase.

Above diagram shows where significance of errors is linked to.

You may need to understand how intermittent or seasonal your demand is. How many zero-demand SKU/location data points you have over time? You may understand through this analysis that many product location combinations are not active anymore (Fig. 8.25).

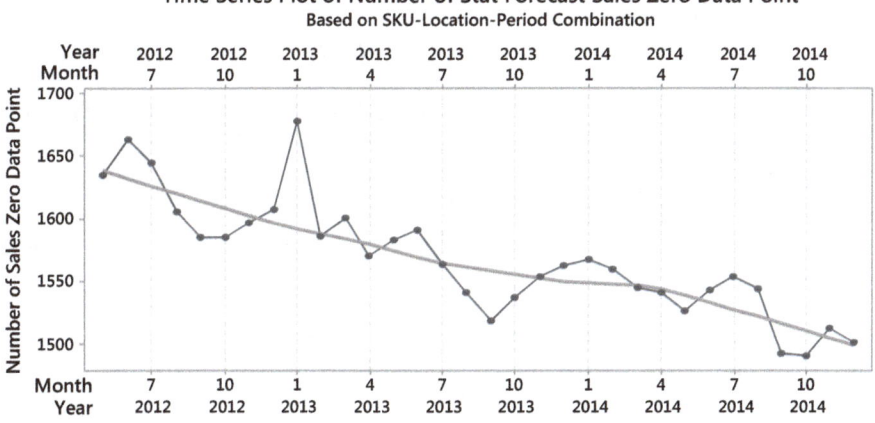

**Fig. 8.25** Time series plot—zero data points (Minitab chart)

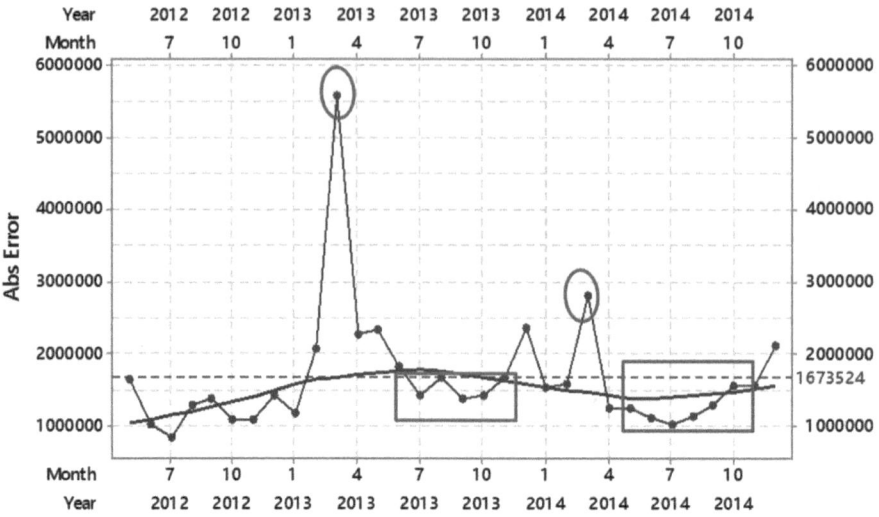

**Fig. 8.26** Absolute error per month—seasonality of errors (Minitab chart)

There may be various reasons why you have decline trend in zero data points, e.g., you expose your data-cleansing activity paying off.

You may deep dive into trends for absolute errors. You may notice certain patterns in summer–autumn periods and high peaks in Q1 like in Fig. 8.26.

This first set of analysis should aim to build your understanding about potential options for correlations of measures (analysis) and help you to prepare hypothesis list of root causes.

Then based on some initial findings, you would need to explore correlations. Below you will find some examples, where term statistically significant will pop up. Statistically significant error or trend means that it was observed in the past and it had significant value and can be repeated in the future if "environment/conditions" will not change.

Many times, we would ensure that we understand correlation between certain data. Let us start with how to interpret basic statistics, see Fig. 8.27. Correlation may have a direction which can be explained like with growth of one measure absolute forecast error inventory level grows as well.

In the example below, we wanted to test if there is correlation between absolute forecast error (expressed in volume) and average inventory volume (Fig. 8.28).

As part of the test, we had statistical evidence that correlation is statistically significant (Fig. 8.29).

In the test result, we observe a high correlation ($R^2$ is almost 63%) which is statistically significant ($p$ value less than 0.001) between average absolute forecast error and average inventory volume. This data show in more simple words higher forecasting absolute error higher inventory level.

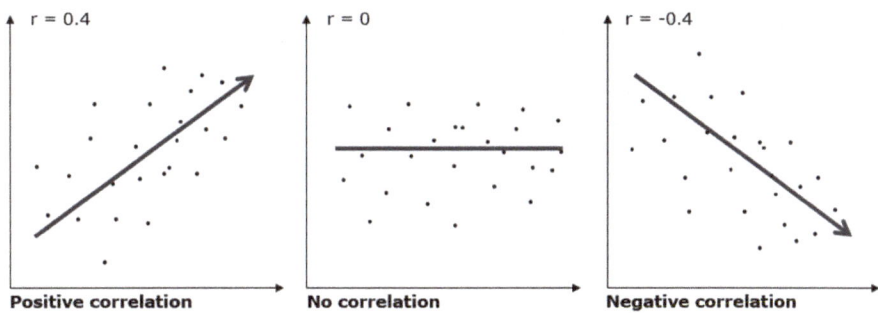

**Fig. 8.27** How to understand correlations

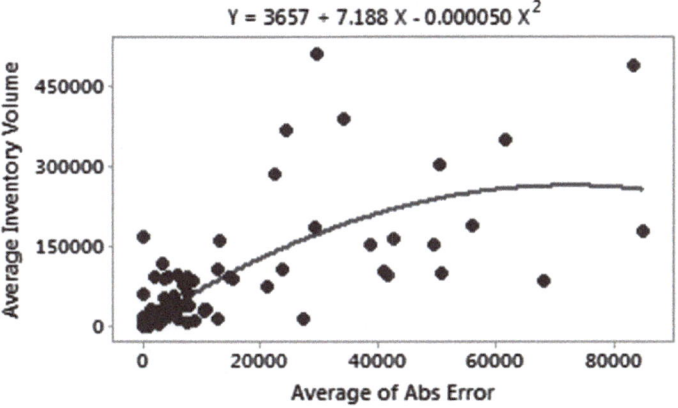

**Fig. 8.28** Correlation between inventory and absolute error (Minitab chart)

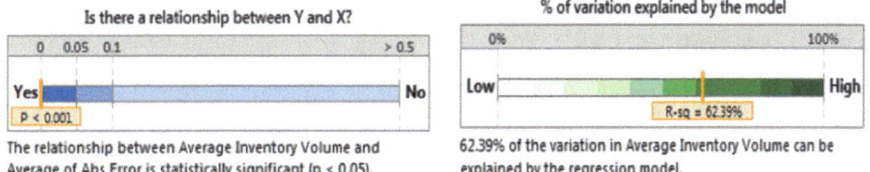

## Correlation: Average of Abs Error; Average Inventory Volume

Pearson correlation of Average of Abs Error and Average Inventory Volume = 0.764
P-Value = 0.000

**Fig. 8.29** Statistics for correlation between inventory and absolute error (Minitab chart)

We wanted to understand if same absolute forecasting error is correlated with warehousing costs (see Fig. 8.30).

We have understood that cost correlation is even stronger, expressed in $R^2$ 74.06% (see Fig. 8.31).

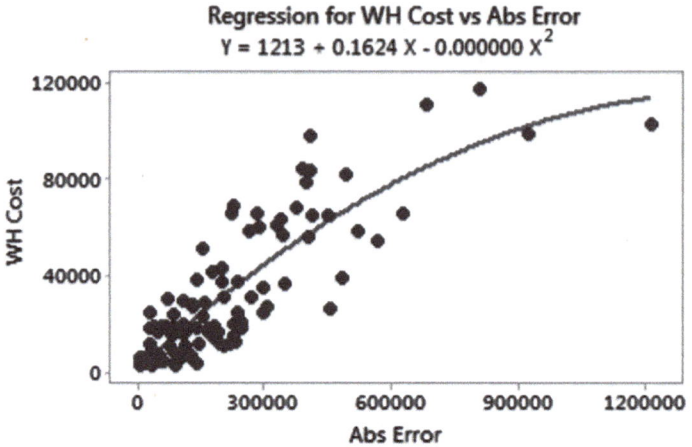

**Fig. 8.30** Regression between warehousing costs and forecasting errors (Minitab chart)

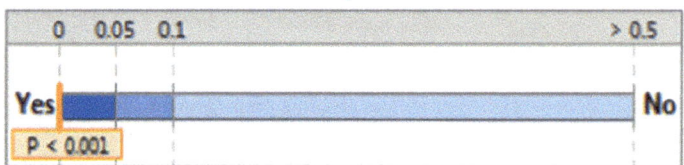

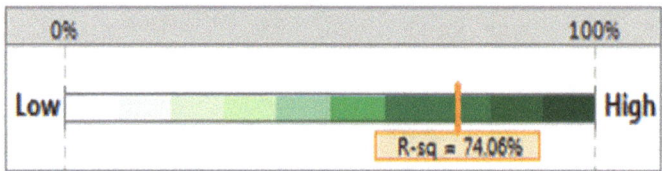

**Fig. 8.31** Statistics for warehousing costs and forecasting errors (Minitab chart)

As shown, there is a very high correlation between absolute forecast error and warehouse cost. It means there is a very strong case that if absolute error is growing, warehouse cost is also growing. This test did help us to be convinced that inventory and warehousing cost can be used as improvement measure and business case driver.

Your data may show other correlation, and above examples may not fit to what you will find in your data. Based on initial analysis and findings where errors are really positioned, we came up with some ideas to formulate hypothesis about what caused an error. We will talk about Hypothesis testing! Below you will find few examples of hypothesis which were formed based on data analysis and review with business stakeholders.

**Hypothesis testing**

Hypothesis 1: We wanted to validate if using product segmentation in forecasting process may bring us some insights to differentiate ways of working, to align ways of working with portfolio segments. We gathered relevant forecast performance data and calculated portfolio segmentation upfront.

We defined hypothesis as follows:

$H_o$: No difference in process performance for different product segments
$H_a$: Significant difference in process performance for different product categories.

We did run tests and analyzed results of it (Fig. 8.34).

Test for ABC (we see spread of MAPE per category which is statistically significant because $p$ is less than 0.05) (Fig. 8.32).

Test for XYZ (we see spread of MAPE per category which is statistically significant because $p$ is less than 0.05) (Fig. 8.33).

Test for ABC/XYZ (we see spread of MAPE per segment which is statistically significant because $p$ is less than 0.05) (Fig. 8.34).

**Statistical Conclusion**: 0.05. $P$ is smaller than 0.05 → *reject* $H_o$. It means that we have rejected hypothesis that there is no difference in performance cross-portfolio segments.

**Practical Conclusion**: There is a significant difference between the MAPE of different product segments. We were very happy to see that performance is so much different.

This test has helped us to make decision that we should introduce portfolio segmentation in the forecasting process.

Then, we formed another hypothesis. Hypothesis 2: We wanted to validate if specific stakeholder (their knowledge of portfolio) would affect forecast error.

$H_o$: No difference in process performance for different product managers
$H_a$: Significant difference in process performance for different product managers.

## Results for: Product Categories

## Mood Median Test: MAPE versus Product Category

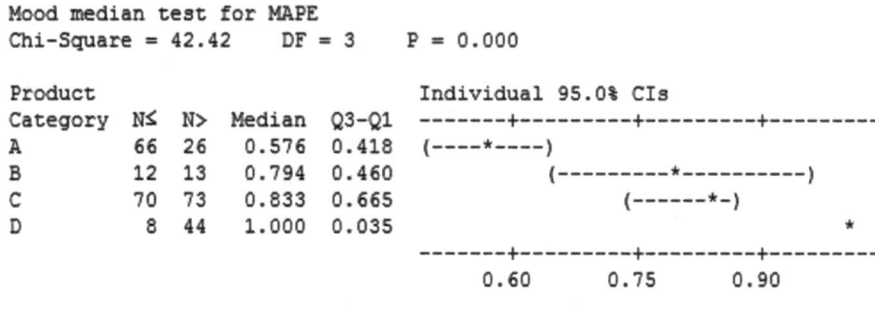

```
Mood median test for MAPE
Chi-Square = 42.42      DF = 3      P = 0.000

Product                                      Individual 95.0% CIs
Category  N≤  N>  Median  Q3-Q1   -------+---------+---------+---------
A         66  26   0.576  0.418   (----*----)
B         12  13   0.794  0.460               (---------*----------)
C         70  73   0.833  0.665                       (------*-)
D          8  44   1.000  0.035                                            *
                                   -------+---------+---------+---------
                                       0.60      0.75      0.90
```

Overall median = 0.793

**Fig. 8.32** Median test for data set with large number of outliers—Significant differences in ABCD categories

## Mood Median Test: MAPE XYZ versus Product Category XYZ

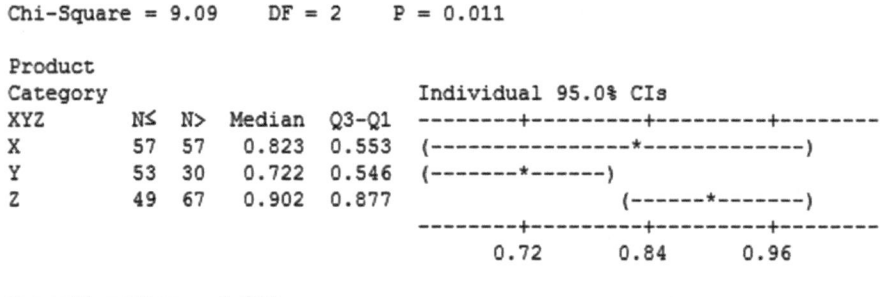

```
Mood median test for MAPE XYZ
Chi-Square = 9.09      DF = 2      P = 0.011

Product
Category                                     Individual 95.0% CIs
XYZ       N≤  N>  Median  Q3-Q1   -------+---------+---------+--------
X         57  57   0.823  0.553   (----------------*-------------)
Y         53  30   0.722  0.546   (-------*------)
Z         49  67   0.902  0.877                   (------*-------)
                                   -------+---------+---------+--------
                                       0.72      0.84      0.96
```

Overall median = 0.833

**Fig. 8.33** XYZ hypothesis testing (Minitab)

There is a significant difference between the forecast MAPE provided by different product managers (portfolio manager). Spread and magnitude of error was visualized against the portfolio manager (1–10). There were substantial differences (see Fig. 8.35).

**Practical Conclusion**: There is a significant difference between the forecast error between product managers even correlated to their years of experience.

We formed another hypothesis. Hypothesis 3: We wanted to validate if forecasting level has an impact on forecasting error.

```
Mood median test for MAPE ABCD_XYZ
Chi-Square = 88.06    DF = 11    P = 0.000


Product
Category                              Individual 95.0% CIs
ABCD_XYZ  N≤   N>  Median  Q3-Q1  ---+---------+---------+---------+---
AX        25    3    0.43   0.19  (-*
AY        12    3    0.64   0.36    (---*--)
AZ        16    8    0.77   0.44      (--*--)
BX        18    7    0.61   0.49   (--*--)
BY        16    8    0.66   0.83     (*-------)
BZ        13    8    0.67   0.49   (-*----)
CX        13   13    0.82   0.65    (---*----)
CY        23   13    0.75   0.70    (--*--)
CZ        18   31    0.91   0.88      (*-----)
DX         1   34    1.00   0.00          *
DY         2    6    1.00   0.73  (---------*----------------)
DZ         2   20    1.30   1.05          (-----*----------)
```

**Fig. 8.34** ABC/XYZ hypothesis testing (Minitab)

## Mood Median Test: MAPE versus Portfolio Manager

```
Mood median test for MAPE
Chi-Square = 32.47    DF = 9    P = 0.000

Portfolio                            Individual 95.0% CIs
Manager  N≤   N>  Median  Q3-Q1  ----+---------+---------+---------+--
1         2   11    1.00   1.28              (--*-------------------)
2        15    3    0.60   0.30   (---*)
3        11    2    0.52   0.33  (---*--)
4        14   21    0.84   0.57        (--*--)
5        11   16    0.87   0.85        (-*-----)
6        17   19    0.82   0.76     (----*---)
7        22    8    0.61   0.36   (-*--)
8        37   35    0.74   0.53    (--*-)
9        13   20    0.89   1.22     (----*---------)
10        9   15    1.00   0.44       (-----*
                                 ----+---------+---------+---------+--
                                   0.50      1.00      1.50      2.00
```

**Fig. 8.35** Forecast error driven by personal bias hypothesis testing (Minitab)

$H_o$: No difference in process performance due to forecasting on different levels
$H_a$: Significant difference in process performance due to forecasting on different levels.

**Statistical Conclusion**: 0.05. *P* is less than 0.05 → *reject $H_o$*. We proved that level (1–2–3) on which you do statistical forecasting brings differences which are significant (see Fig. 8.36).

**Results for: Forecasting Level**

**Mood Median Test: MAPE versus Forecasting Level**

```
Mood median test for MAPE
Chi-Square = 135.27    DF = 2     P = 0.000

Forecasting                              Individual 95.0% CIs
Level       N≤   N>   Median  Q3-Q1   --+---------+---------+---------+----
1           82  236   1.355   0.817                               (--*---)
2          167  151   1.000   0.853                        *--)
3          228   90   0.833   0.597   (---*--)
                                      --+---------+---------+---------+----
                                      0.80      1.00      1.20      1.40

Overall median = 1.003
```

**Fig. 8.36** Forecast error driven by forecasting level hypothesis testing (Minitab)

**Practical Conclusion**: There is a significant difference between the MAPE in the different forecasting levels.

One of the tests was focused on number of outliers and their impact on forecast error. Hypothesis 4: We wanted to validate if product groups/segments with or without outlier have different behaviors.

$H_o$: No difference in process performance due to number of data outliers
$H_a$: Significant difference in process performance due to number of data outliers.

**Statistical Conclusion**: 0.05. *P* is less than 0.05 → *reject $H_o$*. It means that there was a significant difference in forecast performance depending if input data had outliers or not (see Fig. 8.37).

**Mood Median Test: MAPE versus With or No Outliers**

```
Mood median test for MAPE
Chi-Square = 5.46     DF = 1     P = 0.020

With or No                               Individual 95.0% CIs
Outliers    N≤   N>   Median  Q3-Q1   ---+---------+---------+---------+---
0           13   23   0.897   0.401            (--------------*-----------)
1           28   17   0.725   0.469   (----*------------)
                                      ---+---------+---------+---------+---
                                      0.70      0.80      0.90      1.00

Overall median = 0.845


A 95.0% CI for median(0) - median(1): (0.001;0.349)
```

**Fig. 8.37** Forecast error versus no. of outliers hypothesis testing (Minitab)

**Practical Conclusion**: There is a significant difference between the MAPE for the group of SKUs with or without outliers. The outlier is referred to the historical sales data which were being used as input to generate statistical forecast.

Based on all hypothesis testing results, we have formulated with business stakeholders' proposed solutions. Above tests were only few out of which we have done, we wanted to share with you that:

– Segmentation
– People experience
– Forecasting level
– Outliers were one of the drivers which led design solution toward specific direction. This solution we have used to call **differentiated forecasting**.


## 8.3.4  Improve—Propose and Pilot Solution

Based on full set of analysis, hypothesis tests and interviews with business stake-holders' project team have decided to pilot differentiated ways of working enabled by:

• Product segmentation
• Process measurement
• Combination of improved statistical forecasting and qualitative inputs
• Support provided by demand planning
• Demand review preparation facilitated by use of ABC/XYZ.

On the workshop, we have brainstormed which solution is more important to us, which will have bigger impact (Fig. 8.38).

Based on this matrix, decision was taken to pilot improvement.

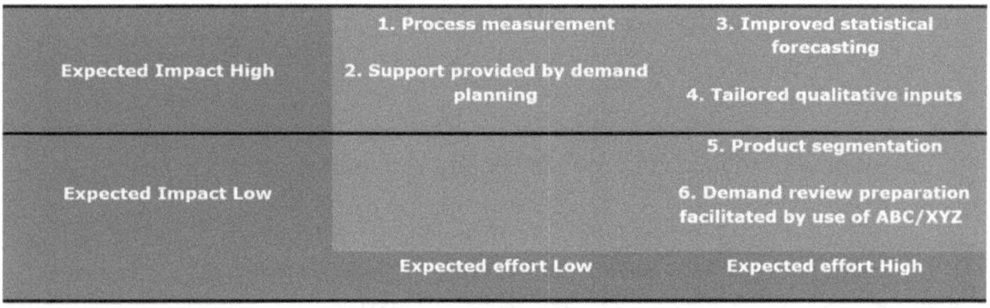

| | | |
|---|---|---|
| **Expected Impact High** | 1. Process measurement<br><br>2. Support provided by demand planning | 3. Improved statistical forecasting<br><br>4. Tailored qualitative inputs |
| **Expected Impact Low** | | 5. Product segmentation<br><br>6. Demand review preparation facilitated by use of ABC/XYZ |
| | **Expected effort Low** | **Expected effort High** |

**Fig. 8.38** Impact versus effort

Scope of piloted improvement:

- Introduction of data-cleansing step (correction of outliers) proceeding statistical forecasting
- Regular adjustments and review of stat. forecast algorithms' parameters
- Introduction of market product segmentation based on

  - XYZ forecast performance score where measure would be MASE
  - ABCD forecasted profit contribution based on consensus forecast and forecasted margin

- Demand planning additional trainings and preparation of demand review
- Demand planning responsible for forecast preparation (mainly statistical forecast driven) for CX, CY, BX category, coupled with removal of sales and marketing input for product and product customer combinations where predictability score was high
- Focus qualitative input provided by sales and marketing on AZ, AY, AX, BZ
- Special focus on CZ and D segments provided by marketing. We wanted to use product segmentation as instrument to inform product rationalization activities and definition of replenishment strategies (like reorder point)
- Demand planner would prepare consensus demand forecast based on weighted combined forecast formula.

New process was documented and approved. Training materials were prepared. Solution was tested and measured for few months.

Results of pilot were very promising:

- Sales and marketing gained more time for sales and marketing activities
- Demand planning were more involved and were accountable for forecast preparation for specific segments
- Demand planners led detection and correction of outliers for statistical forecasting
- Demand planning were entitled to prepare demand review consensus proposal often based on weighted combined forecast
- Portfolio managers have reviewed "D" class, many of SKUs were identified for rationalizations
- Supply chain planning team used product segmentation to introduce market-specific replenishment strategy, e.g., reorder point.

It was time to scale up and realize full benefits.

### 8.3.5   Control—Scale-up in Sustainable Way

In this phase, we have focused to scale up whole solution and to put in place measures which should show us if were deviating from desired performance and solution. In this phase, we focused our efforts on change management, trainings and deployment. We designed and built forecast performance dashboard with new set of KPIs. Dashboard was used in demand review meeting as one of key instruments to check if we deviate from expected improvement and performance targets.

## 8.4   Concluding Remarks

- Forecasting process becomes consensus-driven. Many inputs are being considered and need to be evaluated, therefore measurement of value add becomes more important than ever.
- Measurement of intermittent demand is proposed to be done with service level, inventory levels and not standard forecasting measures.
- Six Sigma project was exceeding our expectation in terms of insights and deliverables:

  - In total process efficiency measured by sales representative forecasting combination was reduced by 66%
  - In average forecast error was reduced by almost 15%.

As part of scale-up, initiative was deployed globally. A key to successful deployment was to find right way to communicate initiative and Six Sigma. Here are some key learnings and their explanations:

1. Cross-regional and cross-functional stakeholder onboarding
2. Success formula
3. Monetization of the impact
4. Clear definition of process measurement parameters
5. Visualization of performance, correlation of measures
6. Enabling FVA
7. Easy to access documentation and support.

Ad. 1.

We have prepared road show posters to as instrument to get familiar and onboard x-functional and x-regional teams.

- Prepare 1 single poster which does explain project rationale, phases and deliverables—this would be for management
- Prepare 1 poster per phase to describe deliverables and approach in each phase—this would be for experts.

**Fig. 8.39** Process improvement success formula

Ad. 2.

Project team has acknowledged and confirmed that process improvement depends on functional quality of the improvement but as well to acceptance/change management (Fig. 8.39).

Ad. 3.

We acknowledged that monetization of improvement provided by independent finance person was well received in the organization.

Ad. 4.

We have faced some problems when defining parameters for forecast measurement. Sales and marketing were pushing for measurement parameters which gave good "fake" performance since they were not aligned to process and business characteristics. Example of it was aggregation window for Weighted MAPE. Aggregation window should be aligned to cycle in which you produce forecast, in which you run S&OP and see impact on your inventory position, financial situation. We have seen impact on monthly basis, so we used aggregation window 1.

Ad. 5.

We have found that enriching demand review with data visualizations did help a lot to focus on facts not opinions.

Ad. 6.

We have found out that we should regularly asses value of the forecast adjustments provided in the consensus and differentiated forecasting process. It was decided to enable in the system separation of inputs which enabled introduction of forecast value-add analysis.

Ad. 7 and 8.

Last but not least, sustainability of the change was based on regular trainings which were provided, on easy to access documentation and frequent discussions/exchange of information about process adherence and potential improvements. We have understood that forming Center of Expertise would be a key to sustainability of improvements.

## References

Chase, C. W. (2009). *Demand-driven forecasting: A structured approach to forecasting*. New York: Wiley & Sons.
Gilliland, M. (2015). *Forecast value added analysis*. Wiley Online Library. Available at: www.sas.com/office.
Hyndman, R. J., & Koehler, A. B. (2005). Another look at measures of forecast accuracy another look at measures of forecast accuracy. *International Journal of Forecasting, 22*(4), 679–688.
Steutermann, S. (2015). *Take seven actions to improve demand management capability in consumer products*. Stamford: Gartner.

FSC
www.fsc.org
MIX
Papier | Fördert
gute Waldnutzung
FSC® C083411

Zeitfracht Medien GmbH
Ferdinand-Jühlke-Straße 7
99095 Erfurt, Deutschland
produktsicherheit@kolibri360.de